THE GENERAL AVIATION HANDBOOK

Rod Simpson

MIDLAND
An imprint of
Ian Allan Publishing

The General Aviation Handbook
© 2005 Rod Simpson

ISBN (10) 1 85780 222 5
ISBN (13) 978 1 85780 222 1

Published by Midland Publishing
4 Watling Drive, Hinckley, LE10 3EY, England
Tel: 01455 254 490 Fax: 01455 254 495
E-mail: midlandbooks@compuserve.com

Midland Publishing is an imprint of
Ian Allan Publishing Ltd

Worldwide distribution (except North America):
Midland Counties Publications
4 Watling Drive, Hinckley, LE10 3EY, England
Telephone: 01455 254 450 Fax: 01455 233 737
E-mail: midlandbooks@compuserve.com
www.midlandcountiessuperstore.com

North American trade distribution:
Specialty Press Publishers & Wholesalers Inc.
39966 Grand Avenue, North Branch, MN 55056
Tel: 651 277 1400 Fax: 651 277 1203
Toll free telephone: 800 895 4585
www.specialtypress.com

Design and concept
© 2005 Midland Publishing
Layout by Sue Bushell

Printed in England
by Ian Allan Printing Ltd
Riverdene Business Park, Molesey Road,
Hersham, Surrey, KT12 4RG

Visit the Ian Allan Publishing website at:
www.ianallanpublishing.com

Title page:
Learjet 31A N31LR. Bombardier

Contents

Introduction

The General Aviation Handbook is intended to provide a quick reference to all manufacturers who have built fixed-wing powered aircraft in production quantities since 1945. At the outset, it is necessary to explain clearly what is meant by 'General Aviation' – but it is not a simple task. The title 'General Aviation' is a catch-all term to embrace everything that cannot be categorised under commercial air carrier (airline) or military operations. As a result, the variety of aircraft types is enormous and General Aviation embraces many roles including personal private flying, business travel, non-scheduled air taxi operations, flying training, carriage of freight, banner towing, bush operations, air racing, exhibition flying, experimental testing and agricultural and fire-fighting activities. In practice, the range of tasks is fulfilled by a huge worldwide fleet. Just in the United States, there are 356,000 registered aircraft – of which at least 90% fall into the General Aviation category. Cessna, alone has built 167,000 aircraft since World War Two.

In The General Aviation Handbook, there are a number of aspects of civil aviation which are not covered, and these are detailed later, but it is important that one particular sector must be mentioned, namely, amateur-built aircraft (either from kits or plans) which are not included unless they are also available in factory-complete flyable form. Unfortunately, to have included this particular slice of aviation would have doubled the size of the book! In the decade since the last edition of this book was published (as *Airlife's General Aviation*), there have been profound changes for the manufacturers of General Aviation aircraft. For most of the sixty years since the end of World War Two the General Aviation industry was dominated by the American 'Big Three' – Beech, Cessna and Piper. Until the early 1980s, these three companies produced a comprehensive offering of private aircraft ranging from entry-level trainers such as the Cessna 150/152 and Piper Cherokee to turbine business aircraft in the Beech King Air and Cessna Citation class. Other manufacturers such as Gulfstream, Maule, Mooney, Rockwell and SOCATA occupied niche positions but the output of the three market leaders was overwhelming with over 15,000 aircraft (87% of total sales) being delivered by them in the peak year of 1978. Particularly among the smaller manufacturers, there have been numerous name changes and aircraft designs have altered hands regularly. We hope that The General Aviation Handbook will highlight these changes and, by way of the index, readers will be able to uncover the detailed background history to almost any light aircraft built since World War Two.

Light Aviation after the Product Liability Crisis

General Aviation has, inevitably, been American-led with the main market and the main manufacturers located there. The 1980s brought the Product Liability crisis led by predatory American tort lawyers and this led to Beech, Cessna and Piper abandoning manufacture of low profit margin single-engined light aircraft. They did return to this market in August 1994 when the Statute of Repose legislation put limits on legal product liability claims, but the choice of models never returned to pre-1980 levels. In any case, business aviation was booming and Cessna, particularly, concentrated on expanding its business jet range, which, today, embraces eight different models. Other business aircraft manufacturers emerged and the terrorist attack of 11th September 2001 encouraged more and more corporate users to turn to the security and flexibility of business aircraft. This trend was further encouraged with the emergence of fractional ownership schemes that allowed owners to purchase shares in a business aircraft. The attractions of turbine power spread in the wake of the Millennium celebrations with the launch of numerous projects for very light jets such as the Eclipse 500, Adam A700 and Citation Mustang. These aircraft will provide a much-needed replacement for ageing cabin-class piston twins such as the Navajo, Queen Air and Cessna 421 at prices which are affordable for small companies and individuals. Confidence in the reliability of turbine engines grew during the late 1990s and single-engined turboprops such as the Pilatus PC-12, SOCATA TBM700 and Cessna Caravan have become well established.

These trends found the single-engined private aircraft market becoming neglected. The sophisticated dealer/distributor marketing networks, which had been established in the 1960s and 1970s by Beech, Cessna and Piper and had driven huge sales volume, were dismantled during the Product Liability years and this infrastructure has never been fully restored. With the existing light aircraft fleet becoming increasingly elderly and fewer aircraft dealers to encourage demand, conventional light aviation remained in the doldrums during the 1990s. However, this opened up an enormous opportunity for a new route into low-cost private flying.

Eastern Europe and the Soviet Union

Major changes have, of course, taken place in the former Soviet Union and its Warsaw Pact allies. The Aviation Design Bureaux (OKBs) and Aircraft Production Plants of the Soviet Union produced a large range of light aircraft designs following World War Two and, in many cases, these types (particularly the Yak-18, Yak-12 and An-2) were manufactured in huge numbers and production responsibility allocated to Poland and Czechoslovakia. With the collapse of the Soviet Union, many of these designs have taken on a new life under independent Russian companies that have risen from the ashes of the previous State organisations. New companies have been established on the western model with design and production in the same entity and numerous new aircraft projects have been proposed although the most successful have generally been in the ultralight and heavy ultralight categories. Unless carried out by a principal manufacturer, these projects are outside the scope of this book and have not been included.

The historical division between aircraft design and aircraft production has persisted insofar as designs such as the Yak-18T have been manufactured by several different organisations. Accurate calculation of the number of aircraft built by the emergent Russian general aviation industry is often impossible due to the incompleteness of official information. Serial number allocations in the Soviet bloc followed a fairly strict system and Yakovlev, Sukhoi and other Russian manufacturers' models have been built in batches. This means that it is necessary to know the number of aircraft in each batch in order to make sense of their manufacturing output. The c/n structure varies from factory to factory and is sometimes so complex as to be indecipherable. Frequently, serial numbers consist of the year of construction, a two or three digit batch number and a two-digit individual aircraft number within the batch. Most batches have been fairly small (ie, between five and fifteen aircraft). In the post-Soviet era, new manufacturers have tended to use simple numbering systems but the traditional structures do persist in the existing factories.

The Ultralight Revolution

In 1995, ultralights (known as microlights in the UK and ULMs – Ultra-Léger Motorisé – in France) were regarded as a quaint option for cheap flying – but scarcely a viable alternative to the all-metal products from Wichita or Vero Beach. At that time, ultralights were mainly weight-shift trikes (unkindly described by some as 'powered umbrellas') – but things were about to change. In many respects, aviation has always been driven by availability of powerplants. For most of the postwar period the piston engine market has been dominated by two companies – Lycoming and Continental – and their excellent engines have determined light aircraft design. The 1990s saw the growth of Rotax, owned by Bombardier, who developed a range of lightweight aero engines in the 40hp to 100hp category. Furthermore, the liberation of Eastern Europe became a catalyst for newly designed conventional light aircraft that technically fell into the ultralight weight category but had all the normal characteristics of conventional two-seat Cessnas and Pipers. For some years, the definition of ultralights varied from country to country but an explosion in output and usage across Europe brought the airworthiness authorities to the realisation that they could not hope to control ultralights under the same airworthiness and certification regulations that applied to larger production light aircraft.

The solution to the ultralight dilemma was to set decentralised standards for airworthiness control (which would be less onerous and less expensive for owners) and to establish a maximum gross weight limit and associated technical specifications for this new category. This maximum weight commonly set was 992.2 lb (450kg) – although some countries persisted with limits that varied from this – and related specifications were also set for the new JAR-VLA aircraft (Very Light Aircraft certificated under the Joint Airworthiness Regulations) with a 1,650 lb (750kg) maximum weight. In the United States, similar moves were afoot which established the new Sport Pilot category. This provides a layer of regulation covering two-seat aircraft that are too heavy to be FAR Part.103 ultralights but have a gross weight under 1,232 lb (558.7kg). Certification, airworthiness validation and regulation of the Sport Pilot/Sport Aircraft category is substantially simpler than that for fully certificated light aircraft and a number of existing production types (such as the Piper J-3 Cub and Taylorcraft BC) will be eligible for this deregulated status. These regulations also extended to simplified pilot qualifications that will undoubtedly encourage the spread of leisure flying.

Not surprisingly, the changes in Europe brought a flood of light aircraft with 450kg gross weights. More significantly, however, many of these, originating in Poland, the Czech Republic, Ukraine and Russia, are built from composites. These materials are a combination of glassfibre, carbon fibre and other plastic materials. Such construction was far from new in aviation. Sailplanes had been built with plastics for several decades and the first successful production glassfibre/plastic light aircraft (the Wassmer Wa.52) first flew in 1966.

This revolution in light aviation has meant that this edition of 'General Aviation' is greatly expanded. Clearly, it has been essential to include all the new 'heavy' ultralights but the line has been drawn at the 450kg weight level and these types are only included if they are available as factory-complete ready-to-fly aircraft. Weight-shift ultralights are excluded, as are various other small aircraft of substantially less than 450kg. We believe that we have included the majority of the significant types – but please accept our apologies if any qualifying types have been omitted!

Some Definitions

- The General Aviation Handbook is presented in alphabetical order by manufacturer.
- Manufacturers are included if they have built powered aircraft in production quantities.
- Only manufacturers and aircraft since 1st January 1946 are included
- Powered aircraft of less than 992.25 lb (450kg) are not included unless they are mentioned as part of the overall history of the manufacturer
- Where aircraft have been produced by several manufacturers they are normally collected under the entry for the company that originally designed and built the type
- In certain cases aircraft design bureaux have initiated designs but not built them in quantity (for example, Stelio Frati). Individual entries are included for these designers.
- The main piston engine manufacturers have changed ownership and corporate names several times. Continental Motors is now Teledyne Continental and Lycoming has been known as Avco-Lycoming and Textron Lycoming. For the purposes of this volume, they are referred to simply as Continental and Lycoming (sometimes abbreviated to Cont and Lyc).
- Details of gross weights and other relevant measurements are all given in Imperial units. While aircraft designed in Europe and some other countries have been conceived in metric units the vast majority of General Aviation aircraft have been designed in the USA (or, sometimes, Britain) where Imperial is the accepted measure. For guidance, data can be converted as follows:
  0.454 kilograms = 1 lb 0.3048 metres = 1 imperial foot 0.7456 kilowatts = 1 horsepower
- So far as possible, the serial number systems are described for all manufacturers, but details of these are sometimes unavailable and where assumptions have been made, this is explained in the text.
- Numbers of aircraft built are given for all aircraft types and these are based on assessments following detailed examination of production lists and information from manufacturers. It should be noted that industry-published figures (for example, annual reports form the General Aviation Manufacturer's Association) are based on sales deliveries and may not be exactly the same as the production totals.
- Since many aircraft in the '450kg ultralight' category may be sold as factory-complete or in kit form, the production data is often based on best estimates or information supplied by the manufacturers

Not included, and outside the scope of the book, are:

- Detailed specifications of aircraft dimensions, weights and performance
- Sailplanes and gliders (even though many modern sailplanes are fitted with low-powered auxiliary engines)
- Balloons and Airships
- Helicopters and other rotary-wing aircraft
- Ultralights (microlights) below 992.25 lb (450kg)
- Amateur-built aircraft, either from kits, plans or original design unless the type is also available as a factory-complete machine.

Acknowledgments

I would like to thank the many historians and enthusiasts, particularly the members of Air-Britain, who have contributed their expertise to refining the content and accuracy of this volume. I am especially indebted to Barry Collman, John Blake, John Davis, Peter Funk, Pierre Gaillard, Peter-Michael Gerhardt, Mike Hooks, Paul Jackson, Alex Kvassay, Vaclav Kudela, Michael Magnusson, Bernard Martin, Tony Morris, Bob Parmerter, Roger Peperell, Steinar Savdal, Bob Rongé, Willem Rongé, Dave Richardson, Peter Simmonds, Peter Vercruisse, Hendrik van der Veen, Jimmy Wadia and Dave Wise. In addition, I would acknowledge Xavier Massé whose books on Jodel, Robin, Piel and Mudry have been invaluable and the editors and authors of 'Janes All The World's Aircraft' and other specialist reference books that have been searched for vital missing details. Finally, my thanks to Paul Turnbull and the contributors to Aerodata whose Quantum Plus database has been of immense value

Manufacturers A-Z

Adam Aircraft
United States

Adam Aircraft Industries was formed in 1998 to develop a push-pull piston-engined executive twin. To initiate the design Adam used Scaled Composites to design and build a proof of concept prototype, the Adam M-309 (Rutan's 309th design, registered N309A), which first flew at Mojave on 21st March 2000. It had a twin-boom layout, was of all carbon-composite construction with a pair of 350hp Teledyne Continental TSIO-550 piston engines mounted in the nose and rear fuselage and had a six-seat pressurized cabin. This led to the definitive A500 which had repositioned cabin windows to allow a new full-depth airstair entry door to be inserted between the cockpit and wing leading edge, changes to the wing to straighten out the gull-wing centre section, modified flaps and ailerons, removal of the cowl flaps, a larger tail elevator and higher-powered TSIO-550E engines flat-rated at 350hp with three-bladed scimitar propellers. The A500 prototype (N500AX, c/n 001) was flown on 11th July 2002 and three further aircraft (N501AX, N502AX and N504AX, c/n 0002 to 0004) had been completed by the end of 2004 and final stages of certification were being completed with first deliveries in the summer of 2005. In October 2002, Adam announced the A700 twin-jet version and the prototype (N700JJ, c/n 0001 – later re-registered N700AJ) first flew on 27th July 2003. Developed from the A500, A700 has a fuselage plug between the wing leading edge and the entry door with two additional cabin windows fitted on each side. Behind the rear pressure bulkhead, the A700 tailcone mounts twin Williams FJ33 turbofans. A definitive production prototype A700 was due to be flown in mid-2005.

Adam A700 N700JJ. Adam Aircraft

Adam A500 N501AX

Aermacchi   Italy

Aeronautica Macchi SpA first entered the light aircraft field in 1947 following wartime fighter production. Their first design was the wood and fabric MB.308, an advanced design with a cantilever wing and fixed tricycle undercarriage. An order for 80 aircraft came from the Italian Air Force who leased MB.308s to the national flying clubs. Macchi also granted a license to the Argentine glider manufacturer, German Bianco. Between September 1958 and June 1967, 46 MB.308Gs were built in Argentina (c/n 501 to 546) equipped with either the 90hp or 100hp Continental engine. Production techniques employed on the MB.308 were also used on their next design, the light twin MB.320. This was first flown in 1949 and eight were produced (c/n 5874, 5875 and 5907 to 5912), most of which ended up in East Africa. Macchi made a fruitless production agreement with SFCA in France whereby the MB.320 would be built there as the VEMA-51.

In the 1960s, Aermacchi took on licence production of the Lockheed LASA-60 utility aircraft and became principal manufacturer of the type. Created as the CL-402 by Lockheed Georgia Company under the direction of Al Mooney, prototype, N601L (later XB-GUZ) first flew at Marietta, Georgia on 15th September 1959. It was manufactured by Lockheed-Azcarate SA in Mexico at a newly established plant at San Luis Potosi. The first aircraft, XB-KIL, was rolled out in October 1960 and it is believed that 36 aircraft (c/n 1001 to 1036) were built, including ten for the Mexican Air Force- although some sources suggest a total of up to 44. Some were the CL.402-2 with a 250hp Continental IO-470-R but the majority were fitted with a 260hp TSIO-470-B. Lockheed-Kaizer in Argentina were intended to build LASA-60s but, apparently, this plan failed to get off the ground although some sources reported 12 built.

The Aermacchi version was virtually identical to the Mexican aircraft and was sold around the world including Canada, where it was marketed by Northwest Industries as the Ranger. As production advanced, a number of different models were introduced with a steady increase in power and gross weight. A large number of AL-60s reached military customers – including the Rhodesian Air Force, which was having difficulty at that time in procuring aircraft from abroad. The design of the AL-60 also formed the basis for the Atlas AL-60-C4M Kudu, which was built in South Africa, and for the AM.3C observation aircraft. The first of three Kudu prototypes (c/n 001 to 003) flew in February 1974 and

38 were built for the South African Air Force (c/n 11 to 29 and 30/21 to 48/39) of which many have been released onto the civil register. 40 AM.3Cs were also built by Atlas (c/n 2001 to 2040) and, again, a number are now privately owned in South Africa and the USA.

Aermacchi has used a dual serial system consisting of an allocation from the main company consecutive numbering sequence and a serial number allocated to the individual type: eg, MB.308 I-SIDI carries c/n 82/5855, which shows it is the 82nd MB.308 and the 5,855th aircraft built by the company. Initial postwar production covered MB.308s and MB.320s, serialled from c/n 5774 to 5914. AL-60s fell into batches from c/n 6143 to 6150, c/n 6154 to 6170, c/n 6206 to 6279 and c/n 6406 to 6408. Details of Aermacchi's light aircraft production are as follows:

Model	Built	Notes
MB.308	137	High-wing side-by-side two-seat cabin monoplane powered by one 85hp or 90hp Continental. Prototype I-PABR
MB.308G		Three-seat MB.308 with extra cabin windows and 90hp Cont C.90
MB.308-100	46	MB.308G built by German Bianco with 100hp Cont O-200-A
MB.320	8	Six-seat low-wing cabin monoplane with retractable tricycle u/c, powered by two 184hp Continental E-185 engines. Prototype I-RAIA (c/n 5874) FF 20 May 1949
AL60-B1	4	High-wing all-metal six-seat cabin monoplane with fixed tricycle u/c and one 250hp Cont IO-470-R engine. Named Santa Maria. First aircraft I-MACO (c/n 6143/1) FF 15 Sep 1959
AL60-B2	81	AL60 with turbocharged Continental TSIO-470-B engine
AL60-C4	1	AL60 with 340hp Lyc GSO-480-B1, tailwheel u/c, separate pilot's door and enlarged vertical tail. Prototype I-MACP (c/n 6231/51)
AL60-C5	13	AL60-C4 with further airframe strengthening and 400hp Lycoming IO-720-A1A engine. Named Conestoga
AL60-D3	1	AL60-B2 with Continental GIO-470-R. I-RAIR (c/n 6233/53)
AL60-F5	1	Conestoga with tricycle u/c. I-MABD (c/n 6271/91)
Atlas C4M Kudu	40	Atlas-built 8-seat utility aircraft with AL-60 wing, new square-section fuselage, fixed t/w u/c and 340hp Lyc GSO-480-B1B3 engine. Prototype ZS-IZF (c/n 01) FF 16 Feb 1974
AM.3	2	High-wing 3-seat observation aircraft with fixed tailwheel u/c, powered by one 340hp Continental GTSIO-520-C. Originally designated MB.335. Prototype I-AEAM FF 12 May 1967
AM.3C		AM.3 refitted with 340hp Lycoming GSO-480-B1B6 engine
Atlas AM.3C	43	Licence-built Aermacchi AM.3C military observation aircraft

German Bianco/Macchi MB.308 LV-GLR

Macchi MB.320 ZS-CBA. Ken Smy

Aermacchi AL-60-F5 N96038

Avia L-60SF Brigadyr N71GC

Aero   Czech Republic

Before the war, Czechoslovakia could boast of a strong aircraft industry composed of six major companies – Aero, Avia, Benes-Mraz, Letov, Praga and Zlinska Letecka. Under German wartime control, these companies were all absorbed into larger armament manufacturing groups. The move of Czechoslovakia into the Soviet sphere gave rise to a reorganisation, in 1949, which brought all the country's motor vehicle and aircraft manufacturing under a state holding company known as the Ceskoslovenske Zavody Automobilove a Letecke (CZAL). Under the CZAL umbrella, light aircraft were designed and constructed by the original factories of Letov, Praga, Zlin, Aero and Mraz and a wide variety of gliders and powered aircraft, including some 138 examples of the Fieseler Storch (named Mraz Cap), were produced. In 1950, this situation was formalised by the establishment of three new companies – Moravan, LET and Aero – which absorbed the activities of all the five original businesses. All marketing of their aircraft was handled by a national Foreign Trade Corporation (Omnipol). Moravan and LET were, broadly, dedicated to civil aircraft and Aero, which had been a major light aircraft producer, specialised in military types such as the L-29 Delfin and L-39 Albatross jet trainers.

During the war, Aero had been building the Bücker Jungmann (see section on Bücker) but the first post-war light aircraft to come out of their factory at Prague-Vysocany was the Aero 45 (so named because it was a 4/5 seater). This was an all-metal low-wing light twin with a retractable tailwheel undercarriage and a pair of 105hp Walter Minor 4-III in-line engines. It was characterised by its smoothly swept cabin and nose profile and the prototype (OK-BCA) made its first flight on 21st July 1947. Aero put it into production and built a total of 200 examples during the period 1949 to 1951, many of which were exported to western European countries. Serial numbers of these were c/n 4901 to 51-200 with the first two digits indicating the year built. At this stage, it was decided that Aero should concentrate on military aircraft and further production of the Aero 45 was passed to LET at Kunovice (see section on LET).

The Aero design office developed several new projects in the early 1950s. One of these was the Aero 50 – a two-seat high-wing utility and military observation aircraft with a pod-and-boom fuselage and a Walter Minor 4-III engine. Only a single prototype was completed and this first flew on 14th April 1949. The Aero 50 was succeeded by a larger three-seat design of more conventional layout. The XL-60 was, again, a high-wing aircraft bearing more than a passing resemblance to the Mraz Cap. It featured integrated strut bracing for undercarriage and wings and a fully glazed 360° vision cabin and was equipped with leading edge slats and large double-slotted flaps for good low-speed handling.

The XL-60 prototype, built at Chocen, was powered initially by an Argus 10C engine. It was first flown on 24th December 1953 and subsequently fitted with a 240hp M-208B engine. This was followed by a further much-modified prototype, OK-JEA. The production model was named Brigadyr and had a 220hp Praga Doris B (which was derived from the M-208B), an enlarged cabin to provide an optional fourth seat, a modified rear fuselage and an extended dorsal fin.

A batch of around 50 L-60As (K-60) was delivered to the Czech Air Force. Others went to flying clubs for general use and for glider towing as the L-60F and L-60D. An L-60B specialised crop spraying model was produced with a hopper in the rear cabin and a large duster unit under the fuselage or underwing spray bars and an ambulance version was designated L-60E. Problems with the Doris B engine resulted in many Brigadyrs being modified subsequently by Aerotechnik to L-60S standard with a Polish-built 260hp Ivchenko AI-14RA radial engine or as the L-60SF with the M-462RF radial engine.

A total of 273 Brigadyrs were completed between 1958 and 1968 with a significant number being exported, particularly to East Germany. Brigadyr serial numbers started at c/n 150001 and consisted of '15' as a prefix followed by a two-digit batch number and a two-digit individual number. Initial batches consisted of up to 15 aircraft but these were increased to 30 units from Batch 7 (ie, c/n 150701). The final production aircraft was c/n 151330.

Aero subsequently moved into design and production of the L-29 Delfin and the L-39 and L-59 Albatros military jet trainers but, in 1990, they announced a new project – the L-270. This was a cantilever high-wing utility aircraft similar to the Cessna Caravan with a fixed tricycle undercarriage and a 750shp Walter M-601E turboprop engine driving a five-bladed propeller. This project was abandoned by Aero Vodochody (as the business is now named) in favour of the Ae-270 that was announced in June 1991. This is detailed under the section on Ibis Aerospace.

Aero   Poland

Aero SP.zo.o. of Warsaw is manufacturing the Aero AT-3 all-metal two-seater as either a factory-complete or kit aircraft. Built in their factory at Krosnow, this is one of several derivations of the Pottier P.220S Koala homebuilt and it has a low wing, fixed tricycle undercarriage and a side-by-side cockpit enclosed by a forward-hinged blister canopy. The prototype AT-2 (SP-PUL c/n 001), powered by a 75hp Limbach engine, was based on a P.220S kit from Aerotechnik-Evektor and first flew on 12th December 1995. The definitive AT-3 L100 (SP-PUH c/n 003), which was fitted with the more powerful 90hp Limbach L-2400 and had a modified tail, an altered undercarriage and a streamlined cockpit canopy, flew on 18th January 1998. In the event, the Limbach engine was dropped for production aircraft and the standard model is the AT-3 R100 with a 100hp Rotax 912S engine with a two-bladed fixed pitch propeller. Plans to sell the AT-3 in the USA as the AveoTech AveoX (kit built), Aveo Sport (Light Sport Aircraft category) and AveoXTC (certificated day-VFR version) appear to have foundered. 14 AT-3s had been built by early 2005.

Aero AT-3 SP-TPG

Aero Boero   Argentina

The leading Argentine constructor of light aircraft was Aero Boero SA and it was established in 1952 as Aero Tallares Boero S.R.L. by Hector and Caesar Boero. Operating from Cordoba, its initial model was the Aero Boero 95, which was a conventional strut-braced high-wing monoplane of steel tube and fabric construction with a rear bench seat for one passenger and two front seats for the pilots. The prototype flew on 12th March 1959 and the production version, which was built from 1961 onwards, was fitted with a 95hp Continental C-90-12F engine. Subsequently, the company also built the Aero Boero 95A which was uprated to a 100hp Continental O-200-A powerplant and was used for glider towing and in a flying club role. Both models were also built in agricultural configuration as the 'Fumigador' with spray bars and a 55-imp gallon chemical hopper fitted in the rear cabin.

Although Aero Boero also built a prototype of the 150hp Model 95B they decided to re-engine the Model 95 with a 115hp Lycoming O-235 engine as the AB.95-115, 12 of which were finally built. The Model 95-115 was further developed into the AB.115, first flown in March 1969, which introduced a number of refinements including metal ailerons and flaps and a modified undercarriage. In 1972 the AB.115 (initially designated AB.115BS) was fitted with a modified wing of greater span and a swept vertical tail. The company had also built a prototype of the enlarged four-seat Aero Boero 180 Condor with a larger tail and a 180hp Lycoming O-360-A1A engine but no production ensued. However the basic airframe was modified to take the 150hp Lycoming O-320-A2B and five AB.115/150AG agricultural aircraft were completed and the airframe was further upgraded to AB.180 standard with a 180hp Lycoming O-360.

The final main change to the Aero Boero airframe was the introduction of an optional version with a cut-down rear fuselage and rear vision window – identified by the suffix 'RV' in the designation. In this configuration it was the basis for a range of models with various powerplants and special equipment for crop spraying and glider towing. The company gained a very large order for the Model 115 for the Brazilian Government and also delivered some Model 180s for Brazilian flying clubs. Aero Boero is believed to have built 542 aircraft but is no longer in production. The main models were:

Model	Notes
AB.115	High-wing trainer powered by one 115hp Lycoming O-235-C2A engine, with tandem seating and dual controls but rear bench seat available for two people if required and ability to carry stretcher in ambulance role
AB.115/150RV	AB.115 powered by 150hp Lycoming O-320-A2B with cut-down fuselage and rear vision window for training and club use
AB.115/150AG	Agricultural variant of AB.115/150 with 60 gallon external belly spray tank
AB.180RV	AB.115/150RV with a 180hp O-360-A1A engine
AB.180AG	Agricultural AB.180RV fitted with belly tank, single seat and spray bars
AB.180SP	Experimental AB.180AG with additional lower sesquiplane wing containing spray tanks. Prototype LV-LPY FF 1982
AB.180RVR	AB.180RV fitted with glider towing equipment

Aero Boero built the prototype of a low-wing crop sprayer – the AB.260AG (LV-X-48). This used the standard Aero Boero tail section and wings with strut bracing married to a new fuselage. The powerplant was a 260hp Lycoming O-540-H2-B5D. The prototype flew on 23rd December 1972 but production plans were shelved in favour of the AB.180AG. The company also built a prototype of the Aero Boero 210 (LV-X-46), which was a three-seat tourer with a swept tail and tricycle undercarriage. It was intended that this should be followed by a four-seat version, but, in the end, neither model went into production. An experimental improved version of the Piper PA-38 Tomahawk was also flown (LV-OHJ) with a larger engine and enlarged vertical tail, but this was not developed.

Aero Boero production was in two blocks – the Model 95 and 115 in one sequence (c/n 001 to 389) and the Model 180 and 150AG in another sequence (c/n 001 to 153). Within the first batch, 32 of the Model 95 were built (c/n 110 to 025, 030, 132 to 036 and 058) and the remaining 357 were Model 115 (although it is not clear whether c/n 053 to 055 and 061 were built). Aircraft for Brazil had the c/n suffixed -B (eg, 145-B). The second sequence was primarily the 180RVR (129 aircraft) but included 19 of the 180AG and five Model 150AG (c/n 030, 031, 037, 039). Again, Brazilian aircraft had -B suffixed c/ns (c/n 085-B to 091-B and 100-B to 153-B).

Aero Boero 115, PP-GLK

Aero Commander — United States

Ted R Smith, a former project engineer with Douglas, founded The Aero Design and Engineering Company in 1945. With a group of associates, he designed and built the prototype L.3805 – a five/six-seat all-metal light business twin with a high wing, retractable tricycle undercarriage and a pair of 190hp Lycoming O-435-A piston engines. The L.3805 prototype made its first flight in April 1948 and its performance was promising enough for the company to obtain financial backing for a production version to be known as the Aero Commander 520. The 520 was built in a new factory at Bethany, near Oklahoma City, and the first production machine (N4001B c/n 520-1) was rolled out on 25th August 1951. Compared with the L.3805, the Model 520 had 260hp engines, the cabin size was increased and the tail was considerably modified.

The Model 520 was the basis for a long and varied line of piston twins with generally similar characteristics but embodying a variety of powerplant and airframe modifications. These aircraft were exported widely and were used by the US Army and United States Air Force as the L-26 (U-4). From the Model 560 onwards, they all had the familiar Aero Commander swept tail – and they generally had the appearance of much larger aircraft than the equivalent types produced by other manufacturers.

In an attempt to penetrate the lighter twin market, hitherto dominated by the Cessna 310 and Piper Apache, Aero Commander developed the Model 360 which was a stripped down Model 560E with 180hp engines, but this was not a success. The first pressurized Commander was the Model 720. This type, named the Alti Cruiser, first flew in February 1957 and joined the Models 500, 560E and 680E in production at Bethany. Shortly afterwards, in 1958, Aero Commander became part of the growing empire of Col Willard F Rockwell.

In October 1960, the Company's name was changed to Aero Commander Inc. Eventually, the company became the Aero Commander Division of the Rockwell-Standard Corporation, still based at Bethany, OK and it was later renamed Aero Commander – Bethany Division. The four Aero Commander models were considerably improved with fuel-injected engines and slimmer, pointed engine nacelles which necessitated a new main undercarriage unit which turned the wheels during the retraction process to lie flat in the rear of the nacelle. The most important development, though, was the 680FL which first flew in late 1962. By stretching the fuselage of the 680F the designers were able to increase seating from seven to eleven. The Grand Commander, as it was known, had two 380hp Lycoming engines and a redesigned undercarriage and tailplane. This proved to be an ideal vehicle for further expansion of the model range and the company next modified it with a pressurized cabin under the designation 680FL(P) Pressurized Grand Commander. In turn, this led to the turboprop Model 680T Turbo Commander, which made its first flight in December 1964. All of these models continued under the aegis of North American Rockwell (Aero Commander Division) until 1969 when the 680FL (latterly named 'Courser') and the 680FL(P) were dropped from the line.

Aero Commander had moved into the business jet market during the early 1960s. The prototype Model 1121 Jet Commander was first flown in January 1963 and a substantial number of production aircraft were sold. However, when Rockwell Standard acquired North American in September 1967 it was decided that having two competing business jets (the Jet Commander and the Sabreliner) brought them in conflict with American anti-trust legislation. Accordingly, Rockwell sold the Jet Commander rights to Israel Aircraft Industries who continued to build it as the IAI Commodore.

By 1964, Aero Commander had decided that there was little advantage in having the four standard piston-engined Commanders in parallel production and they decided to replace them by a single model. This was the 500U, which eventually became known as the Shrike and was powered by two 290hp Lycoming IO-540s. The 500U was later replaced by the 500S. By the start of the 1970s, North American Rockwell found itself building just two types – the 500S and the turboprop Model 681 Hawk Commander that had succeeded the earlier 680T, 680V and 680W.

The Shrike was finally terminated in 1979 and, apart from being offered, latterly, in an optional deluxe 'Esquire' version, it had contin-

ued unchanged for 13 years. The Model 681 did see further development, the first change being an economy model – the 681B with a reduced trim standard. This was followed by the 690 which featured an extension of the wings inboard of the engine nacelles together with higher-powered TPE331 turboprops. It was probably the most popular of the Turbo Commander series and some have been upgraded as 'Dash-10 Supreme Commanders' with new 1,000shp TPE331-10T turboprops. An equivalent piston-powered version, the Model 685, was also built until 1975. In France, the Société Turboméca experimented with an upgraded Turbo Commander which had the turboprops removed and replaced by a pair of Astafan engines in underslung nacelles. These were, essentially, Astazou turboprops fitted within a circular casing and the prototype Astafan Commander (F-WSTM, c/n 15406) flew on 8th April 1971. A second aircraft (F-BXAS c/n 11240) was converted but no further development took place.

In February 1981, Rockwell International moved out of General Aviation and sold all rights to the Commander twins to Gulfstream American Corporation (late Gulfstream Aerospace). This deal covered four turboprop models – the Commander 840, Commander 980, Commander 900 and Commander 1000. Gulfstream continued to build these and also flew the prototype of a further development, the Commander 1200, which was the fastest of all the Commander turboprops. In January 1985 Gulfstream ceased production and, in late 1989, sold the Aero Commander type certificates and all rights to Precision Airmotive of Everett, Washington (now Twin Commander Aircraft Corporation – TCAC) but they have not resumed production. However, many ageing Commander twins are receiving upgrades from TCAC including the 'Renaissance Commander' program, which includes replacement of virtually all critical parts, an engine upgrade and interior and exterior refurbishment and paint. Other upgrades have been the Century Turbo model with TPE331-1-151K engines and the addition of winglets by Command-Aero.

The system used by Aero Commander for allocating type numbers to the various aircraft was quite complex. Initially, they related the model number of each aircraft to the combined flat-rated horsepower of the two engines. The initial Model 520 received this number because of its two 260hp Lycoming O-435-As – and the 560 had two 280hp engines, the 680 had two 340hp Lycomings and the experimental 360 had 180 horsepower on each side. This method continued up to the Model 500 (250hp) but, thereafter, the numbers 680 and 500 lost this significance and were generally used with a suffix letter. Suffix letters were also used on the 690 series. Interestingly, the marketing names for the Jetprop 840 and Jetprop 980 again incorporated the shaft horsepower of the engines.

Suffix letters were used in two contexts. Sometimes a suffix letter was routinely applied to a new model to signify a sub-type; for example, the 560A that was developed from the 560. On other occasions the suffix had a special descriptive significance, for instance:

E Used on the 560E to identify the 'Extended' wing on this model
P Used to denote certain pressurized models: eg, the 680FL(P)
L Used to identify the 'Long' fuselage of the 680FL Grand Commander
T Used to identify the 'Turboprop' Turbo Commander 680T. Subsequent Turbo Commanders were given the chronological letters 'V' and 'W'

Aero Commander 520

Aero Commander gave each aircraft a simple chronological serial number, which commenced at c/n 1 in 1952 and continued until c/n 1876 issued in 1970. All models were included in these 'factory line numbers' but the full serial number also included the model type number and the number of the individual aircraft of that type. For example, N6190X was an Aero Commander 560F and its full serial number was c/n 560F-1007-9 made up of the Model Number (560F), the Overall Aero Commander sequence number (1007) and the individual c/n in the Model 560F sequence (9).

In 1970, each major model was given its own separate sequence of serial numbers. The Model 500S was already in production at this time and, therefore, some of this type have numbers in the old sequence and some in the new. Certain prototypes had their own individual numbers (for example, the Model 360 had the number 360-1). The allocated blocks for various production models have been as follows:

Model 500S	c/n 3050 to c/n 3319	Model 690C	c/n 11600 to c/n 11735†
Model 681	c/n 6001 to c/n 6072	Model 690D	c/n 15001 to c/n 15042
Model 685	c/n 12000 to c/n 12064	Model 695	c/n 95000 to c/n 95084
Model 690 to 690B	c/n 11000 to c/n 11079*	Model 695A	c/n 96000 to c/n 96100‡
Model 690A	c/n 11100 to c/n 11344	Model 695B	c/n 96201 to c/n 96208
Model 690B	c/n 11350 to c/n 11566	Model 1121	c/n 1 to 150

* Excluding c/n 11070; † Excluding c/n 11704 to 11718, c/n 11709 allocated to converted c/n 95064; ‡ Excluding c/n 96090.

In total 2,067 piston-engined Aero Commanders were built and 1,110 of the turboprops. The following table details all of the Aero Commander models:

Model	Name	Built	Notes
L.3805	-	1	Prototype 5/6-seat high-wing cabin monoplane with retractable tricycle u/c. Two 190hp Lycoming GO-435-C engines. Prototype NX1946 (c/n 1) FF 23 Apr 1948
520	Commander 520	150	Developed L.3805 with taller fin, larger cabin and two 290hp Lycoming GO-435-C engines
560	Commander 560	80	Model 520 with swept tail, 500 lb TOGW increase, strengthened structure, seven seats and Lycoming GO-480-B engines
560A	Commander 560A	99	Model 560 with new engine nacelles and increased fuel. Prototype N2731B (c/n 231)
560	Commander 560E	93	Replacement for Model 560A. Increased wingspan, revised u/c and fuel system
560F	Commander 560F	73	680F with unsupercharged IGO-540 engines and 500 lb TOGW reduction
360	-	1	560E with four seats, u/c retracting into the fuselage, and two 180hp engines. Prototype N8444C (c/n 360-1)
500	Commander 500	101	560E with 250hp Lycoming GO-540-A engines. Prototype N6217B (c/n 618)
500A	Commander 500	99	500 with fuel-injected Continental IO-470-M engines in redesigned engine nacelles. Prototype N9362R (c/n 875) FF 26 Mar 1960
500B	Commander 500B	217	560E with fuel-injected Lyc IO-540 -B1A5 (later -B1C5 and E1A5) engines
500U	Shrike Commander	56	500B with pointed nose and squared-off fin. Two 290hp Lycoming IO-540 engines. Replaced Models 500A, 500B, 560F, 680F. Utility category certification
500S	Shrike Commander	316	500U certificated in Standard category
680	Super	254	560A with 340hp Lycoming GSO-480-A engines, increased fuel. Prototype N2742B FF 14 May 1960. US military L-26C (U-4B)
680	Commander 680E	100	560E with 500 lb lower gross weight and 560A type undercarriage
680F	Commander 680F	126	680E with new u/c and fuel-injected Lycoming IGSO-540 engines in new nacelles
680FP	Commander 680FP	26	Pressurized 680F. FF 14 Jul 1961
720	Alti Cruiser	13	680 with pressurized cabin, extended wing and increased gross weight. Prot N7200 (c/n 501)
680FL	Grand Commander	157	680F with stretched fuselage to give max 11-place seating with 4 square cabin windows. Later named Courser Commander. Prototype N78386 (c/n 1261) FF 24 Apr 1962
680FL(P)	Pressurized Grand Commander	37	680FL with pressurized cabin. Model 680 prototype converted as prototype 680FL(P) and FF as such on 30 Jul 1964
680T	Turbo Commander	66	680FL(P) with two AiResearch TPE331-43 turboprops. 8,950 lb TOGW. Prototype N6381U (c/n 1473) FF 31 Dec 1964. Turbo II deluxe equipment version. 48 aircraft upgraded to 680T/V standard with 9,400 lb TOGW
680V	Turbo Commander	29	680T with 9,400 lb TOGW. Modified brakes, engine mountings etc. First a/c N5413 (c/n 1609-45)
680W	Turbo II Commander	46	680V with pointed nose, squared-off fin, one panoramic and two small cabin windows and new engine nacelles
681	Hawk Commander	45	680W with improved pressurization, air conditioning system and nose design
681B	Turbo Commander	27	Marketing designation for economy version of Model 681
685	Commander 685	66	690 powered by two 435hp Continental GTSIO-520-K piston engines
690	Commander 690	79	681 with new wing centre section and engines moved outwards. Powered by two AiResearch TPE331-5-251 turboprops. Prototype N9100N (c/n 6031 – later 11001)
690A	Commander 690A	245	690 with changed cockpit layout and pressurization increased to 5.2psi
690B	Commander 690B	217	690A with improved soundproofing, internal lavatory, 126 lb increase in useful load and higher cruise speed
690C	Jetprop 840	121	690B with increased wingspan, wet wing fuel tanks and wingtip winglets. Two 840shp TPE331-5-254K turboprops. Introduced with Jetprop 980 in Nov 1979
690D	Jetprop 900	42	Similar to 690C with internal rear cabin extension, five square cabin windows, 35,000ft service ceiling and improved pressurization. Four converted to Model 695A
695	Jetprop 980	85	Similar to 690C with higher-powered 735shp TPE331-10-501K engines
695A	Jetprop 1000	99	690D with 11,200 lb TOGW and higher power TPE331-10-501K engines. 6 conv to 695B
695A	Commander 1200	1	695A with larger engines and enlarged fin fairing. Prot N120GA (c/n 96062) FF Aug 1983
695B	Jetprop 1000B	8	695A with minor modifications
800	Commander 800	2	Proposed replacement for 500S with circular section fuselage, higher-set wing, two GTSIO-520-D piston engines, 680W nose, eight-place interior with toilet. Prototypes N9030N (c/n 800-1724-1, later revised to 800-8001) and N8800 (c/n 800-8000)
	Total Production	*3,177*	*Aero Commander props/turboprops*
1121	Jet Commander	119	8/10-seat mid-wing business jet with two 2,850 lbst General Electric CJ610-1 turbojets, 17,500 lb TOGW. Prototype N610J (c/n 1). FF 27 Jan 1963
1121A	Jet Commander	9	Unofficial designation for improved 1121 with better wheels and brakes, modified fuel system and upgraded interior
1121B	Jet Commander	27	1121A with 2,950 lbst CJ610-5 engines, 18,500 lb TOGW, stronger u/c. 3 completed as IAI-1121C by Israel Aircraft Industries
1122	Jet Commander		Proposed 1121 with system changes. No production
	GRAND TOTAL	*3,332*	*Aero Commander propeller and jet models*

Aero Commander 560E N6215B

Aero Commander 500S N59088

North American Rockwell 680W Turbo II Commander N2755B

Aero Kuhlmann Scub 75-MH

Aero Kuhlmann — France

Aero Kuhlmann designed and built the Scub ultralight aircraft. It made its debut at the Paris Air Show in 1997 following a first flight on 5th May 1996. A tandem two-seater, it has a high strut-braced wing, and a fixed tailwheel undercarriage. The wings can be folded for ground transportation or storage and the cabin has large transparencies that give excellent all-round vision. Construction is of steel tube, wood and fabric. It has been supplied as a factory-complete aircraft with JAR-VLA certification and was built by Aero Kuhlmann at La Ferté Alais near Paris. A total of 27 Scubs had been completed by the middle of 1999. The Scub is used in some numbers for crop spraying in Madagascar and several examples have been delivered with twin floats. The powerplant is a four-cylinder JPX engine of 75hp driving a two-bladed ground-adjustable propeller.

Aeromere — Italy

Trento-based Aeromere took over licence production of the Stelio Frati-designed F.8L Falco following earlier production by Aviamilano and started delivering the F.8L Falco III in 1959. The Falco was a wooden low-wing two-seater with a sliding bubble canopy and retractable tricycle undercarriage. The Aeromere version was virtually the same as the Aviamilano Falco II but was certificated to FAA CAR Part 3 regulations and known as the 'America'. 36 aircraft were built (c/n 201 to 236). Aeromere subsequently passed manufacture of the Falco to Laverda who built a further 20 aircraft.

Aeromot — Brazil

As described in the section on Fournier, the design and tooling of the Fournier/Aerostructure RF-10 were taken over by Aeromot of Porto Alegre in Brazil who started building the AMT-100 Ximango in 1986. The first aircraft was PP-RAN (c/n 100-001) and 45 aircraft were completed (up to c/n 100-045) including some AMT-100P and AMT-100R police and surveillance aircraft. In standard form the Ximango has an 80hp Limbach L.2000-EO1 engine but the AMT-200 Super Ximango, now the principal production version, has an 80hp Rotax 912A and first flew in July 1992. The AMT-200S, which has winglets and a Rotax 912S4 engine, is designed for dual training and gliding/soaring The AMT-300 Turbo Ximango Shark, fitted with winglets and a turbocharged Rotax 914 engine, has also been developed, the prototype (PT-ZAM) flying in July 1997 and Aeromot has produced a military surveillance version with an external sensor pod and a glider tug variant (AMT-300R Reboque). Production of the AMT-200 totalled 118 by early 2004, including four of the AMT-300 and these two models are in a common serial sequence which started at c/n 200046 and has reached c/n 200163. The AMT-300s have c/ns prefixed 300 (eg, 300107). The Ximango has been ordered by the US Air Force as a primary flight screener with the designation TG-14. A low-cost club trainer development is the AMT-600 Guri which has a modified shorter-span wing, a fixed tricycle undercarriage and a 115hp Lycoming O-235-NBR engine. The prototype (PP-XBS c/n 600-001) first flew on 13th July 1999 and one further example has been built (PR-LCB c/n 600-002).

Aeromere Falco F8L D-EKMK

Aeromot AMT-200 Super Ximango D-KFBW

Aeropract   Russia

The Aeropract design bureau has been formed as the Russian offshoot of the former Aeroprakt OKB which had been in operation since the mid-1970s. The original organisation's primary focus was on gliders but the newly constituted Russian company developed a new range of composite light aircraft which have been sold largely in Russia to individuals and flying clubs. To avoid confusion with the Ukrainian Aeroprakt company, odd model numbers have been allocated and the models produced to date include:

Model	Built*	Notes
A-21M Solo	2	Low wing single-seater with fixed tricycle u/c and one 65hp Hirth 2706 engine. Prototype FLARF-02135 (?) FF 14 Aug 1991
A-23M Dragon	2	Pod-and-boom tandem two-seater with fixed tricycle u/c, strut-braced high wing and pusher 64hp Rotax 582UL engine. Prototype FF 1997
A-25 Breeze	1	Side-by-side two-seat amphibian with cantilever mid wing, cruciform tail, retractable tricycle u/c and one pusher 207hp LOM M337 engine mounted above centre section. Prototype FLARF-02495 FF 9 Nov 1994
A-27	1	High-wing side-by-side two-seat cabin monoplane with fixed tricycle u/c and one 98hp Rotax 912ULS engine. Prototype FLARF-02647 FF 22 June 1998

* Estimated number of aircraft built.

Aeroprakt A-20 Vista LY-3002

Aeroprakt   Ukraine

This company was re-formed at Kiev in 1991 by former Antonov staff as the Ukrainian part of the former Aeroprakt OKB. It is partially backed by finances from the UAE. Aeroprakt Ltd (not to be confused with the Russian Aeropract offshoot) started with the T-8 ultralight and then developed the A-20 pod-and-boom two-seater that was developed into the twin-engined A-26. The most popular model to date has been the A-22, known as the Foxbat in Britain and the Valor in the USA and this has been sold both as a factory-complete aircraft and as a kit. The other aircraft in this range are factory-built and ready to fly. Aeroprakt allocates simple construction numbers starting at c/n 001 for each model but UK kit-built examples all carry PFA (Popular Flying Association) serial numbers. To avoid confusion with the Russian Aeropract company, even model numbers have been allocated and the models produced to date, which are shown with their US marketing names, are as follows:

Model	Built*	Notes
A-20 Vista	40	Tandem two-seat pod-and-boom light aircraft with strut-braced high-wing, fixed tailwheel u/c, T-tail. Powered by one pusher 50hp Rotax 503. Prototype FF 5 Aug 1991. A-20 V-Cruiser and Super Cruiser have 98hp Rotax 912 ULS engine and A-20 Varlet has 100hp Rotax 912S

Aeroprakt A-22 Foxbat G-TADC

A-22 Valor	80	Side-by-side two-seater with high-wing, fixed tricycle u/c, extensively glazed cabin and one nose-mounted 98hp Rotax 912ULS engine. Also known as the Talon and as Foxbat in UK and Vision in Europe. Prototype FF 21 Oct 1996. Produced as complete aircraft or kit
A-24 Viking	1	Three-seat amphibian with strut-braced parasol wing, pod-and-boom fuselage and T-tail. Powered by one tractor 64hp Rotax 582UL engine mounted on beam above cockpit
A-26 Twin Vista	2	Modified A-20 with slightly swept wings. Powered by two pusher 64hp Rotax 582UL engines mounted on wings. Formerly named Vulcan
A-28 Victor	1	Four-seat cabin twin with low wing mounting two 98hp Rotax 912ULS engines, T-tail and fixed tailwheel undercarriage. Prototype N61450 (c/n SA-28-001)
A-36 Vulcan	1	Developed A-26 for police, forestry, border patrol and other special uses with metal wing and composite fuselage. 1,660 lb TOGW. Powered by two 100hp Rotax 912S engines

* Estimated number of aircraft built.

Aeroprakt A-28 Victor N61450

Aeropro   Slovakia

The Kitfox, designed by Don Denney, has been produced commercially by a number of manufacturers in Europe, notably by Aeropro of Nitra in Slovakia who sell the 450kg Eurofox in factory-complete or kit form. The original Kitfox, which was first flown on 7th May 1984, has strut-braced foldable wings with full-span flaperons, an enclosed side-by-side two-seat cockpit, a tailwheel undercarriage and a circular-section cowling enclosing the Rotax engine. It is built from steel tube, fabric and aluminium and the original Kitfox I had a 52hp Rotax 503 or 64hp Rotax 532 engine but this was later changed on the Kitfox III, introduced in 1990, to the 80hp Rotax 912. The later Kitfox IV (and Kitfox Speedster) had shorter wings with a new aerofoil section and other speed-enhancing features and this has been marketed by Skystar Aircraft Corp as the Classic IV with optional Rotax 503, 618 or 912 engines, long or short wings and an optional float undercarriage. The Series 5 is a higher-performance touring aircraft with a strengthened structure and a wider cabin and rear baggage hold which can be fitted with the Rotax 912 or 914 or with a Continental O-200 or O-240. The Safari (also named Outback) is the Series 5 equipped with a 125hp Continental IO-540B engine and spring steel rough field gear and the Vixen (later named Voyager) is the Series 5 with a tricycle undercarriage and swept vertical tail.

The Eurofox is, essentially, a Kitfox IV with the 80hp Rotax 912 engine (or optional 100hp Rotax 912S). Aeropro Ltd, which was established in 1992, started delivering the Eurofox in 1995 and had built 171 examples (to c/n 17104) by mid-2004. Since 1999, two versions have been available – the Eurofox Basic with a tailwheel undercarriage and tri-gear Eurofox Pro and the JAR-VLA certificated Eurofox-Space with tricycle gear. Serial numbers consist of the individual aircraft number followed by the year of construction (eg, c/n 14803 – aircraft number 148, built in 2003). In addition to Aeropro, several other companies have sold kits for the Kitfox, including Apollo Ultralight Aircraft in Hungary, who have built nine examples of the Apollo Fox to date (c/n 01 to 09), and Philippine Aircraft Company Inc who launched the PACI Skyfox (prototype RP-X44) in 1988. In Australia, the Kitfox was the basis for the Skyfox (see separate entry).

Aeropro Eurofox PH-3N5

Aeroprogress T-101 Grach FLARF-01466

Aeroprogress   Russia

The T-101 Grach was designed in 1991 by the Roks-Aero design bureau as a replacement for the An-2 utility aircraft. It is a single-turboprop design with a strut-braced high-wing, a square section fuselage capable of accommodating passengers or freight in remote area operations and a fixed tailwheel undercarriage. The Grach is powered by a 1,230shp Pratt & Whitney PT6A turboprop engine and the T-101 prototype (FLARF-01466) first flew on 7th December 1994. Production of the aircraft is the responsibility of MAPO at Lukhovitsy and at least one production example has been completed although production of up to ten further examples appears to have been started.

Aerospace Technologies of Australia

Aerospace Technologies of Australia (ASTA) was created from the reconstruction and public flotation of The Government Aircraft Factory (GAF) on 1st July 1987. The ASTA Group also includes Pacific Aerospace Corporation (described in the separate chapter on Pacific Aerospace). GAF was originally established on 1st July 1939 as a department of the Australian Government to build the Bristol Beaufort light bomber. During the war, 700 Beauforts and 365 Beaufighters were completed and this was followed by production of Avro Lincolns, Jindivik targets, Canberras and Mirage III fighters.

GAF Nomad N.22B VH-SNX

During the 1960s, a slowdown in military procurement had prompted the design of a twin-turboprop utility aircraft aimed primarily at Australian Army needs but also at commercial operators. The N2 Nomad was a strut-braced high-wing monoplane with twin 400shp Allison 250-B17 turboprops, a boxy 12-passenger fuselage with an upswept rear section and a cruciform tail. It had a retractable tricycle undercarriage, the main units of which were housed in external sponsons attached to the lower fuselage.

The Nomad prototype (VH-SUP c/n N2-01) was first flown on 23rd July 1971 followed by a second aircraft (VH-SUR c/n N2-02) in the following December. The initial production models were the Australian Army N.22 and the N.22B, which was for civil customers and export military users including the Indonesian Navy, Thai Navy and Air Force and the Philippines Air Force. Civil deliveries of the N.22B started in 1975 with a number of aircraft going to the Royal Flying Doctor Service and sales to commercial operators in the south Pacific. GAF further developed the Nomad into the stretched N.24, which could accommodate up to 17 passengers.

The Nomad suffered from various problems including a number of premature prop reduction gearbox failures and sales of the aircraft were slow with the result that GAF closed the Nomad line in 1984. Nomads were given serial numbers from c/n 1 to 170 in an integrated series covering all models. These serials were prefixed by the identity of the model concerned (eg, N22SB-103; N24A-44). Details of the Nomad models are as follows:

Model	Built	Notes
N.22	14	Basic short fuselage aircraft with strut-braced high-wing, retractable tricycle u/c with main units housed in external sponsons. Max seating for 2 crew and 13 passengers. Powered by two 400shp Allison 250-B17B turboprops. Largely Australian Army deliveries
N.22B	95	N.22 configured for civil use
N.22C	1	All-cargo version of N.22
N.22SB	6	Coastal patrol Search Master B model with nose radome containing Bendix RDR1400 search radar. 3 additional conversions from N.22B
N.22SL	10	Improved Search Master L with uprated navigation systems, external radome beneath nose and Litton APS.504 radar. 6 additional conversions from N.22B
N.24	7	N.22 with fuselage plugs ahead of and behind wings totalling 5ft 9in, two extra windows each side, four extra seats. Prototype VH-DHF (c/n 10) FF 17 Dec 1975
N.24A	36	N.24 with minor performance improvements
N.24SB	1	N.24A equipped to Search Master B standard
N.24BF		Conversions of N.24A with twin amphibious Wipline floats

Aérospatiale   France

Aérospatiale was formed on 1st January 1970 through amalgamation of Nord Aviation, Sud-Aviation and SEREB. One of their first designs was the SN-600 light business jet which had been a joint venture project of Nord and Sud prior to the merger. The SN-600 was a low-wing aircraft with a cruciform tail and two Turboméca Larzac engines in rear fuselage pods. The prototype (F-WRSN c/n 01) first flew on 16th July 1970 at Melun-Villaroche. It was equipped with Pratt & Whitney JT15D engines, due to the unavailability of the Larzacs, and JT15Ds were fitted to all subsequent aircraft.

Unfortunately, the prototype SN-600 crashed on 23rd March 1971 and the resulting redesign produced the SN-601, which had a lengthened rear fuselage and a taller fin. The SN-601 prototype (F-WUAS c/n 1) made its maiden flight on 20th December 1972. Production started at St Nazaire in 1973 with the aircraft named 'Corvette 100' and several examples were equipped with optional 77-gallon wingtip fuel tanks. Aérospatiale intended to build a Corvette 200 with a lengthened fuselage and 18 seats and a three-engined Corvette 300. However, the operating economics of the SN-601 were unattractive and many of the 40 units built (c/n 1 to 40) were leased to various operators on short-term arrangements by the manufacturers. In 1978, the Corvette line

Aérospatiale SN-601 Corvette EC-DQG

Morane-Saulnier MS.760 Paris II N207MJ

Morane-Saulnier MS.571 F-BEJM

was closed and all further General Aviation production was handled by Aérospatiale's subsidiary company, SOCATA, which had been formed by Sud-Aviation to take over the activities of the bankrupt Morane-Saulnier company.

Morane-Saulnier

The Société Morane-Saulnier was one of the oldest-established French aviation manufacturers. Formed on 10th October 1911, it was famous for its military aircraft including the parasol-wing MS.230 and the MS.405 fighter. At the end of World War Two, Morane created a series of light civil aircraft. These included the MS.560 low-wing all-metal monoplane aimed at the civil club and touring market, which was the start of a family of single and two-seat prototypes that achieved very limited production. Morane also unsuccessfully entered examples of the MS.601 and MS.602 for the SALS competition for an 'aeronef de grand vulgarisation'. The later MS.660 was a most ungainly high-wing single-seater with a 40hp Train engine and the company also built three examples of the MS.700 four-seat light twin. This was intended to appeal to the French colonies as an air ambulance, light transport and trainer – but its payload was too small to be commercially attractive and it was eventually abandoned. Details of these various designs are:

Model	Built	Notes
MS.560	1	Single-seat all-metal low-wing trainer with retractable tricycle u/c, bubble canopy and 75hp Train 6D-01 engine. Prototype F-WBBB FF 1 Sep 1945
MS.561	1	MS.560 with 100hp Mathis G-4Z engine
MS.563	1	MS.560 with 105hp Walter Minor. F-WBGC FF 6 Apr 1949
MS.570	1	Two-seat MS.560 with 140hp Renault 5PEI engine. F-WBBC FF 19 Dec 1945
MS.571	7	3/4-seat version of MS.570. Prototype F-WBGB FF 18 Jul 1946
MS.572	2	MS.571 with 140hp Potez 4D-01. Prototype F-WCDZ FF 28 May 1947
MS.600	1	Two-seat low-wing aircraft with one 75hp Mathis G-4F engine. Prototype F-WCZT FF 4 Jun 1947
MS.601	1	MS.600 with 75hp Regnier 4JO engine
MS.602	1	MS.601 with 75hp Minie 4DA engine. Prototype F-WCZU FF 24 Jun 1947
MS.603		F-WCZT with Hirth 504A-2 engine and tricycle u/c. Reregd F-PHJC
MS.660	1	Single-seat strut-braced high-wing monoplane with fixed tricycle u/c and 40hp Train 4E-01 engine. Prototype F-WBGA FF 17 Feb 1946
MS.700	2	Four-seat low-wing light twin with retractable tricycle u/c and two 160hp Potez 4d-33 engines. Prototype F-WFDC FF 8 Jan 1949. Second aircraft became MS.701 with 180hp Mathis 8G-20 engines
MS.703	1	Stretched six-seat MS.700 with 240hp Salmson 8.AS.00 engines. Prototype F-WFDD FF 3 Jan 1951

Following these disappointments in civil aviation, Morane designed the MS.730 Alcyon all-metal military trainer, 142 of which were delivered to the French military forces and Cambodia from 1951 onwards.

Several appeared on the civil register, and, in particular, were used by the training school at St Yan. Also aimed at the military market was the MS.755 Fleuret, which was a side-by-side two-seat jet trainer with a T-tail and a pair of Marboré turbojets buried in the wing roots. This was succeeded by the Fleuret II, which was enlarged to provide four seats. With some further development, the aircraft became the MS.760 Paris that was ordered by the Armée de l'Air, the Aéronavale and the air forces of Brazil and Argentina. The company built 27 MS.760s for civil customers around the world and, in 1955, Morane entered into a short-lived deal with Beech Aircraft Corporation under which Beech would market the Paris in North America. The Paris was also built under licence in Argentina with some 36 being built to supplement the original twelve delivered direct from France. In total, 156 aircraft were completed (excluding the two prototypes) with c/n 001 to 119 for the French aircraft and c/n A-1 to A-136 for the Argentine-produced machines. The different Paris variants were, in detail:

Model	Built	Notes
MS.755 Fleuret	1	Two-seat trainer with two 800 lbst Marboré II jets. Prototype F-ZWRS FF 29 Jan 1953
MS.760 Paris	1	Four-seat development of Fleuret. Prototype F-WGVO (c/n 01) FF 29 Jul 1954
MS.760A Paris	109	Production Paris with detail changes for military and civil customers
MS.760A Paris	36	Argentine production by FMA
MS.760B Paris II	10	MS.760A with increased fuel and 1,058 lbst Marboré VI jets. F-WGVO flown as Paris II, 12 Dec 1960
MS.760C Paris III	1	5/6-seat development of MS.760 with fully integral cabin, enlarged wing, increased fuel, no tip tanks and Marboré VI engines. F-WLKL (c/n III-01) FF 28 Feb 1964
Total Built	*158*	

On 10th June 1959, Morane-Saulnier flew the prototype of a completely new all-metal light aircraft – the MS.880 Rallye. This all-metal side-by-side two-seater was built in response to a light aircraft competition sponsored by SFATAT. The first aircraft, powered by a 90hp Continental engine, had a fixed tailwheel undercarriage and advanced automatic leading edge slats that had been developed on the experimental MS.1500 Epervier ground-attack prototypes and gave excellent safety at low speed. A tricycle undercarriage was soon fitted and the definitive prototype had a longer three-seat cockpit with a lower canopy profile, swept tail surfaces and numerous detail design changes to facilitate economic production. As the MS.880B it entered full-scale production and was soon joined by the higher-powered MS.885 Super Rallye. However, by the end of 1962, the pressure of expansion into high volume had stretched the company's working capital. Morane filed a bankruptcy petition on 19th November 1962 and, on 6th January 1963, by order of the Tribunal de Commerce de la Seine, management control passed into the hands of the Établissements Henri Potez.

SOCATA MS.894 Minerva 220 OE-KTH

Sud-Aviation and SOCATA

The reorganised company became the Société d'Exploitation des Établissements Morane-Saulnier (SEEMS). Three years later, on 20th May 1965, the role of Potez was taken over by Sud-Aviation who set up a new subsidiary – Gérance des Établissements Morane-Saulnier (GEMS) to manage the business. In 1966, the company became a full subsidiary of Sud-Aviation with the new title Société de Construction d'Avions de Tourisme et d'Affaires (SOCATA).

Sud-Aviation had already been much involved in light aviation through its production of the GY-80 Horizon. This all-metal four-seat light tourer with a retractable tricycle undercarriage had been designed in 1960 by Yves Gardan (creator of the Minicab and Supercab) and the prototype (F-WJDU) made its maiden flight on 21st July 1960. A respectable 265 examples of the Horizon emerged from the Sud factories at Nantes and Rochefort with either a 150hp Lycoming O-320-A, 160hp Lycoming O-320-B or 180hp Lycoming O-360-A3A engine.

The GY-80 design was developed into the ST-10 Super Horizon 200. This aircraft had a larger 200hp Lycoming IO-360-C1B engine, redesigned cabin area and a new tail unit. The prototype was F-WOFN (first flown on 7th November 1967) and 55 were built by SOCATA

between 1970 and 1972 as the 'Provence' or the 'Diplomate'. SOCATA also tested a larger aircraft – the ST.60 Rallye 7. The first of two aircraft (F-WPXN) first flew on 3rd January 1969 and resembled a Piper Cherokee Lance. It had a seven-seat cabin and a retractable tricycle undercarriage and was powered by a 300hp Lycoming IO-540-K engine. The second Rallye 7 (F-ZWRR) was similar but had a fixed undercarriage. In the end, SOCATA could not see a sufficiently large market for this model and abandoned further development.

In taking over the Rallye design, SOCATA inherited an enhancement programme that concentrated on the four-seat MS.890 Rallye Commodore with a heavier airframe. The light airframe MS.880 series continued in parallel production with the Commodore and numerous versions of both types were built by SOCATA with a variety of different engines. With the 115-horsepower MS.883 variant, it was found necessary to enlarge the tail unit and a large dorsal fin was adopted, but later MS.880 models with higher power used the larger Commodore tail instead. This tail was also fitted to the spinnable Rallye 100S and 100ST models.

The MS.890 designs were given a more streamlined image in 1967 when a contoured dorsal fin fairing was introduced, the cockpit

Aérospatiale GY-80 Horizon F-BNQL

Aérospatiale ST-10 Diplomate D-EOPE

canopy was given a more rounded shape and new undercarriage fairings were adopted. Shortly afterwards, SOCATA started to drop the MS.880 and MS.890 type numbers and used the marketing names as designations (eg, Rallye 235E). They also produced a specialised agricultural Rallye (the 235CA Gaucho) with a tailwheel undercarriage and rear cockpit hopper, and a military close-support version named Guerrier. The Rallye production line at Tarbes-Ossun finally closed in 1983 to give way to expanding output of SOCATA's TB series of aircraft although a small additional batch of the Rallye 235F was built in 1992. Production of the Rallye continued under PZL in Poland and is covered in the chapter on Polish Aviation. Details of the Rallye line are:

Model	Built	Notes
Lightweight Airframes		
MS.880	1	Two-seat metal low-wing monoplane with fixed tailwheel u/c, sliding cockpit canopy and one 90hp Cont C90-14F engine. Prot F-WJDM FF 10 Jun 1959
MS.880A	1	MS.880 with swept fin, three seats and larger cockpit. Prototype F-WJSE FF 12 Feb 1961
MS.880B Rallye Club	1,100	Production version of MS.880 with 100hp Cont O-200-A engine. Prototype F-WJSF FF 24 May 1961
MS.881 Rallye 105	17	MS.880 with 105hp. Potez 4E-20A engine
MS.880 Rallye 100S Sport	55	Two-seat spinnable trainer version of Rallye 100T with larger tail and 100hp Cont O-200-A engine. FF 30 Mar 1973
Rallye 100T	3	MS.880B trainer with minor changes. Non-spinnable
Rallye 100ST	92	3/4-seat 100S with 45 lb TOGW increase
Rallye 110ST Galopin	76	Rallye 100ST with 155hp Lycoming O-320-L2A
Rallye 150T	25	Rallye 100T with enlarged tail, four seats, higher TOGW and 150hp Lycoming O-320-E2A
Rallye 150ST	66	Rallye 150T stressed for spinning
Rallye 150SV Garnement	5	Rallye 150ST with 155hp Lycoming O-320-D2A
Rallye 180T Galerien	102	Rallye 150T with 180hp Lycoming O-360-A3A
MS.882 Rallye Club	1	Four-seat MS.880B with 115hp Potez 4E-20 engine. Prototype F-BKZP FF 1 Aug 1963
MS.883 Rallye 115	70	MS.880B with large dorsal fin and 115hp Lycoming O-235-C2A engine
MS.884 Rallye Minerva 125	1	MS.880B for US market with 125hp Franklin 4A-235 engine. N991WA (c/n 888)
MS.885 Super Rallye	215	MS.880B with 110 lb TOGW increase and 145hp Continental O-300-A engine. Prototype F-WJSG (c/n 04) FF 20 Apr 1961
MS.885S Super Rallye	1	MS.885 with tailwheel u/c and skis. F-WKUN
MS.886 Super Rallye	2	MS.880B with 150hp Lycoming O-320-E2A engine. Prototype F-WKKU FF 19 May 1964
MS.887 Rallye 125	25	Four-seat MS.880B with 70 lb TOGW increase and 125hp Lycoming O-235-F2A engine. Prototype F-WTRB (c/n 2040) FF 10 Feb 1972
Total Production	1,857	
Heavier Rallye Commodore Airframes		
MS.890A Commodore	5	Heavier airframe with enlarged tail, improved trim and equipment and 145hp Cont O-300-B engine. Prototype F-WJSG (c/n 01)
MS.890B Commodore	2	MS.890A with Continental O-300D-2A engine
MS.892 Commodore	4	MS.890 with 150hp Lycoming O-320 engine
MS.892A Commodore 150	281	Production MS.892. Contoured tail and streamlined canopy introduced in 1967
MS.892B Commodore 150	1	MS.892A with increased fuel. F-WLBA
MS.892E Rallye 150GT	21	MS.892A with minor 'GT' changes including electric flaps, new control wheel and improved trim
MS.893 Commodore	1	MS.890 with 180hp Lycoming O-360-A2A engine. Prototype F-WLSQ (c/n 10454) FF 7 Dec 1964
MS.893A Commodore 180	459	Production MS.893. Contoured tail and streamlined canopy introduced in 1967
MS.893E 180GT Gaillard	318	MS.893 with 'GT' detail changes
MS.894A Minerva 220	211	MS.893 with 220hp Franklin 6A-350-C1 engine and detail changes. Sold by Waco in the USA
MS.894C Minerva 220	1	MS.894A with tailwheel u/c and skis. F-WPXP
MS.894E Minerva 220GT	35	MS.894A with 'GT' detail changes
Rallye 235E & 235GT	132	Gabier. MS.893 with 235hp Lycoming O-540-B4B5 engine. Prototype F-WXDT

SOCATA TB10 Tobago GT N167GT. SOCATA

SOCATA TB20 Trinidad F-GDNE

Rallye 235F	10	Rallye 235E with basic instrumentation and glider towing equipment – built from spares from 1992/93
Rallye 235G Guerrier	1	Military Rallye 235E with strengthened airframe and underwing hardpoints. F-ZWRT (c/n 12105)
Rallye 235CA Gaucho	9	Crop spraying version of 235E with tailwheel u/c and hopper in rear cabin
Total Production	*1,360*	
GRAND TOTAL	*3,217*	

Note: All Commodore names are prefixed 'Rallye' (eg, MS.892A Rallye Commodore 150).

The TB series was designed in 1975 to give a more modern image and to be more economical to build than the Rallye. A new two-seater (the X-270) had been proposed but it was abandoned in favour of a universal four-seat airframe that could be fitted with various engines to create a range of light aircraft. Designated TB10, the prototype made its first flight in February 1977 and was followed by three development aircraft with a considerable number of detailed changes.

The very streamlined TB10 with its fixed tricycle undercarriage was largely of metal construction with some GRP components and featured a sports car style of interior trim and seating. The initial production version, with a 180hp engine, started to reach customers in 1979 and, in 1980 was supplemented by the 160hp Tampico. The theme of airframe flexibility was reinforced later that year when the TB20 Trinidad flew with a 250hp Lycoming and a retractable undercarriage and SOCATA later added the Trinidad TC with a turbocharged engine. During 1991-1993, 21 TB9s and 3 TB10s were assembled by PZL-Mielec in Poland but these all appear to have been passed over to SOCATA for onward sale. The TB line was given a major facelift in 1999 with the NG (Nouvelle Generation) models, all of which were given designations suffixed 'GT'. The main changes were a higher cabin roofline, reshaped rear windows, a fin fairing, larger baggage door and internal trim alterations. By the end of 2004, TB production had slowed to a trickle and was on a minimum batch order basis. Only three TB10s and two TB20s were delivered in 2004. The various TB models have been as follows:

Model	Built	Notes
TB9 Tampico	387	TB10 with 160hp Lycoming O-320-D2A engine. TB9 Sprint has new trailing link main u/c
TB9C Club	70	TB9 with reduced specification for club training
TB9 Tampico GT	1	TB9 with GT mods including higher cabin roof, faired fin, reshaped windows etc
TB10 Tobago	657	All-metal low-wing cabin four-seater with fixed tricycle u/c and one 180hp Lycoming O-360-A1AD engine. Prototype F-WZJP FF 23 Feb 1977
TB10 Tobago GT	17	TB10 with GT mods as on TB9GT
TB200 Tobago XL	93	TB10 with 200hp Lycoming IO-360-A1B6 engine. Prototype F-WJXL (c/n 1214)
TB200 Tobago GT	21	TB200 with GT mods
MS.180		TB10 powered by one 180hp MR180 engine. Not built
TB11		Original designation for 180hp TB10
TB15		Tobago with Porsche PFM.3200 engine. Not built
TB16		Trinidad with 212hp Porsche PFM.3200N engine. Prototype F-GBLL c/n 490 (not flown)
TB20 Trinidad	628	TB10 with retractable u/c and 250hp Lyc IO-540-C4D5 engine. Prototype F-WDBA FF 14 Nov 1980
TB20C Trinidad		TB20 with large rear port-side cargo door
TB20 Trinidad GT	118	TB20 with GT mods
MS.250	1	Experimental TB20 with 250hp MR250 engine. F-WWRS FF 3 Mar 1998
TB20 Colibri		Experimental TB20 F-WHGQ (c/n 1227) modified by Rene Hirsch with T-tail and adjustable nose-mounted 'moustaches' for improved control in turbulent weather. FF 13 Mar 1995
TB21 Trinidad TC	81	TB20 with turbocharged Lyc TIO-540-AB1AD engine
TB21 Trinidad Turbo	36	TB21 with GT mods

Aérospatiale's General Aviation Division (now part of EADS and named EADS-SOCATA) is in production with the TBM700 eight-seat pressurized single-engined business turboprop. This was inspired by the Mooney M.301 project and started as a cooperative venture between

Aérospatiale and Mooney. The prototype TBM700 (F-WTBM) first flew at Tarbes on 14th July 1988 with the second aircraft (F-WKPG) following on 3rd August 1989. The first prototype used a 700shp Pratt & Whitney PT6A-40/1 turboprop engine but production aircraft, which were first delivered in the third quarter of 1990, had an improved PT6A-64 with a four-bladed Hartzell propeller. French type certification was awarded in January 1990 and in May 1991 Mooney pulled out of the venture and production became the responsibility of Aerospatiale at Tarbes. Mooney finally sold its stake back to Aérospatiale in 1995. In 1999, the initial TBM700A was replaced by the TBM700B (from c/n 126), which is equipped with a large port-side cargo door and supplementary crew entry hatch. The latest versions, announced in November 2002, with a strengthened structure are the TBM700C-1 for non-US sale and the TBM700C-2 for the American market that has a 7,394 lb gross weight compared with 6,578 lb for the 700B. SOCATA have also considered a stretched version, the TBM700-S, with a maximum of nine passenger seats and a high-altitude surveillance model (the 'HALE') with a high aspect ratio wing and enlarged tail, but neither has been built. 311 TBM700s had been built by the end of 2004 and 31 aircraft were delivered in that year.

In May 1995, SOCATA signed an agreement with American General Aircraft Corporation for the rights to manufacture the GA-7 Cougar (see American Aviation). This was renamed the TB.320 Tangara and SOCATA carried out development testing with Grumman-built N738G/F-WWRS (c/n GA7-0106). Two further development aircraft (F-WWRT and WWRU) were acquired and fitted with two 180hp Lycoming O-360-A1G6 engines in which form they were designated TB.360. No production has taken place to date.

SOCATA has generally used a simple serial number system under which each primary model has its own series starting at c/n 1. Prototypes and pre-production units are usually prefixed '0'. Horizon pre-production units were c/n 01 to 07 and production aircraft ran from c/n 1 to 260 (but probably excluding c/n 124 and 125, not built). The ST-10 started at c/n 101 and ran to c/n 154 before production ceased in August 1972. The TB10 prototypes were c/n 01 to 04 and production TB aircraft (all models) started at c/n 5 and had reached c/n 1928 when the GT series was introduced from c/n 2001. Production had reached c/n 2226 by the middle of 2004. Polish aircraft had dual c/ns including PZL numbers P-006 to P-021 or a dual number believed to be from BKA00-07/P-007 to BKA001-021/P-021. The prototypes of the TB700 were c/n 01 to 03 and production started at c/n 1 and had reached c/n 328 by the end of 2004 although 20 c/ns were not used (c/n 36, 37, 40 to 45, 47,48, 51, 54, 55, 56, 64, 65, 66, 79 and 81).

With the Rallye series, the company identified the aircraft with heavy (Commodore) airframes by prefixing the serial numbers with '1' (eg, c/n 12199). In fact, this started in the c/n 900 batch of numbers and the first aircraft to be so designated was c/n 10923. Early in the production cycle of the Rallye it was decided that certain exports should be specifically identified and, after c/n 080, these machines had '5' as a prefix – with this arrangement continuing until approximately c/n 5426. The range of numbers allocated to Rallyes ran from 01 to 04 (prototypes) and from c/n 1 to c/n 3387. The 1992/93 additional production Rallye 235F aircraft commenced at c/n 3388.

SOCATA TBM-700. SOCATA

Aerospool   Slovak Republic

Based at Prievidza, Aerospool manufactures the all-composite WT9 Dynamic. This 450kg aircraft is externally very similar to the Lancair 320 with a low wing, side-by-side two-seat cockpit enclosed by a bubble canopy and tricycle undercarriage. The undercarriage can be fixed (on the Club and Tow versions) or retractable according to customer requirements although the retractable (Speed Dynamic) version has a higher gross weight. The Dynamic is sold factory-complete, powered by an 80hp Rotax 912UL engine. The prototype, D-MXWT, first flew in 2001 and 81 had been completed at the end of 2004 with serial numbers from DY003/01 to DY01/04. The serial numbers include the individual aircraft serial followed by the year of construction.

Aerospool WT9 Dynamic Club N62DY

Aerostar   Romania

Aerostar SA was formed as an aircraft repair centre in 1953 under the name URA and this was later retitled IRAv. It subsequently became Intreprinderea de Avioane Bacau (I Av Bacau) before renaming as Aerostar following the collapse of the Ceaucescu regime. In February 2000 the private consortium that had acquired 30% of Aerostar acquired the Romanian Government's 70% share to fully privatise the company.

In the mid-1970s it was decided that future production of the Russian Yakovlev Yak-52 trainer would be carried out in Romania and I Av Bacau was selected for the task. The Yak-52 was developed from the Yak-50 with the cockpit extended forward to provide a second seat. It also had a tricycle undercarriage incorporating forward-retracting main legs and wheels that remained slightly exposed when retracted (to ease wheels-up landings) and a 360hp Vedeneyev M-14P nine-cylinder radial engine. The Russian prototype, built at Arsen'yev flew in 1978 and Romanian production started in 1979 with the 1,500th example (now designated Iak-52) being delivered in 1990. In 1999, the Iak-52W was made available with a new cockpit with western instrumentation, additional wing fuel tanks, a rear baggage compartment, metal-covered control surfaces and new wheels and brakes. A tailwheel version, the Iak-52TW, made its first flight on 2nd July 2001 and is now part of the range, fitted with the 400hp M14P-XDK engine. One further development of the Yak-52 is the Yak-52M, which has been pro-

Aerostar 1 N1062M

posed as an upgrade to existing Russian Air Force aircraft. A test aircraft has been flown by the Ivanovo Overhaul Facility and it features a new blister canopy, SKS-94 ejector seats, improved avionics and strengthened wings. The Ukrainian Air Force also intends to upgrade Yak-52s with ZMKB-Progress AI-450 turboprop engines.

Serial numbers for the Iak-52 consist of two digits to indicate the year of construction, a two- or three-digit batch number and an indi-

Aerostar Iak-52 ZK-ZAY

vidual two-digit aircraft number. Up to 15 aircraft are built in each batch and Aerostar had reached Batch 125 (eg, c/n 0312506) by late-2003, including the first Yak-52TWs in batches 124 and 125. It appears that total production to date is approximately 1,850 aircraft. Aerostar has also developed and built the AirLight Wild Thing ultralight (referred to separately) and the new Aerostar 1 ultralight. The prototype Aerostar 1 (YR-6138) first flew on 31st May 2001. Renamed Festival R40S for American sale as a Sport category aircraft, it is a low-wing side-by-side two-seater with a fixed tricycle undercarriage, powered by a 100hp Rotax 912ULS (or Jabiru 2200) engine and it shares many components with the Wild Thing. Limited production has taken place in ready-to-fly and kit form and at least two aircraft (the first and second production machines, c/n 010101 and 010102) have been sold in the USA.

Aerostyle   Germany

Aerostyle's Breezer is an all-metal low-wing light aircraft with side-by-side seating for two and a fixed tricycle undercarriage. It is manufactured by Aerostyle of Bordelum as a kit but is available in factory-complete form from Ikarus-Comco. It can be powered by either an 80hp Rotax 912 or 100hp Rotax 912S and a 100hp BMW 1100 Take Off engine option is also available. The prototype, D-MOOV (c/n 001) first flew in December 1999 and 45 aircraft sets had been completed by the end of 2004 (c/n 001 to 045), of which 12 were ready-to-fly.

Aerostyle Breezer D-MEAA

Aerotec   Brazil

This small company was started at Sao Jose dos Campos near Sao Paulo in 1962 by Amir Mederos, Vladimir Carneiro and Carlos Goncalvez. Under the direction of Goncalvez, they designed a small low-wing side-by-side two-seat trainer, the A-122 Uirapuru, for use by the Brazilian Air Force and civilian flying clubs. The prototype of the all-metal Uirapuru (PP-ZTF) was powered by a 108hp Lycoming O-235-C1 engine and it first flew on 2nd June 1965. It was followed by a second aircraft (PP-ZTT) with a 112hp Lycoming O-320-A engine and two pre-production A-122A military aircraft (designated T-23 in FAB service) with 150hp O-320A engines. The production T-23 had the 160hp O-320-B2B.

Aerotec also produced 24 examples of the civil A-122B that had a full sliding canopy (whereas on the military aircraft only the centre section of the canopy moved), control wheels instead of sticks and fully adjustable seats. Production ended in 1977 after completion of the 99 military aircraft, 24 civil aircraft and two prototypes. The company also flew a prototype (s/n 1000) of the YT-17 Tangara, based on the Uirapuru but powered by a 160hp Lycoming O-320-B2B engine, but this did not go into production. Serial numbers of the Uirapuru were c/n 001 and 002 for the prototypes, c/n 004 to 100 and c/n 104 and 105 for military production and c/n 101 to 126 (except 104 and 105) for the civil aircraft.

Aerotechnik/Evektor   Czech Republic

Aerotechnik was established in 1970 and, initially, produced the A-70 light single- or two-seat autogyro. Their first fixed-wing aircraft was the L-13E Vivat, an all-metal motor glider derived from the L-13 Blanik sailplane. Aerotechnik had experimented with Blaniks with a Walter engine (the XL-13M), Jawa M-150 (XL-13J) and, in 1970, a Trabant engine (XL-13T) mounted on a pylon above the centre section. However, the L-13B had the wing, rear fuselage and tail unit of the Blanik married to a new forward fuselage containing a side-by-side two-seat cockpit and the engine bay. The prototype XL-13B (OK-064) had a shoulder-set wing but the XL-113, fitted with a tricycle undercarriage and the definitive L-13SW, had the wing lowered to a centre fuselage position. The L-13SW with a retractable monowheel undercarriage first flew in September 1989 powered by a Rotax 503 engine. The later L-13SE used an Aerotechnik-built 65hp Walter Mikron IIIAE in-line engine and was later offered as the L-13SDM with a conventional tailwheel undercarriage. A further version with a Limbach L-2000-EO1 engine is designated L-13SDL. The first production Vivat appeared in 1983 and production ceased in 1998 after 621 had been built (c/n 830001 to 980621). The serial numbers include the year of construction followed by a four-digit individual identity.

In 1996 Aerotechnik and the Evektor design bureau merged and shortly after launched a version of the French-designed Pottier P.220UL Koala. 35 complete aircraft and 7 kits were sold before the aircraft was modified to 450kg ultralight standards and designated EV-97

Aerotec A-122 Uirapuru PP-KBM

Aerotechnik L-13E Vivat OM-5107

Team Eurostar EV-97 F-JGEM

Evektor VUT-100 Cobra, OK-EVE

Eurostar. It is marketed under the business title 'team Eurostar'. The prototype EV-97 (OK-CUR-97) first flew in May 1997. The aircraft is an all-metal side-by-side low-wing two-seater with a fixed tricycle undercarriage and an 80hp Rotax 912UL engine. The most recent development is the Eurostar 2000, which has a steerable nosewheel, wider fuselage and upturned wingtips. A JAR-VLA version, the Harmony, has also been launched with a 550kg gross weight and a turbocharged 100hp Rotax 912ULS engine together with the SportStar, which complies with American Light Sport Aircraft standards.

The Eurostar is sold either as a kit or in factory-complete form and is also being built in China under a joint venture with Shenyang Aircraft. It is thought that the standard eastern European system of serial numbers is used, consisting of a 4-digit year, a two-digit batch number and an individual aircraft number within the batch. Batches are thought to be 15 aircraft and had reached c/n 20031716 by late 2003. It appears that kits are included in the system (although the manufacturer's c/n is often not quoted), so, while over 250 airframe sets have probably been completed, there were around 150 flying examples of the Eurostar flying as at mid-2004. On 11th November 2004, the company flew the prototype VUT-100 Cobra (OK-EVE c/n 0001). This is a five-seat all-metal low-wing design and will be built as the VUT-100-120i with a 200hp Lycoming IO-360-A1B6 engine and the VUT-100-131i with a 315hp Continental IO-580-B. Evektor is also planning the EV-55 twin-turboprop business and utility aircraft.

Air Light/ULBI   Germany

The Air Light (ULBI) Wild Thing is a strut-braced high-wing 450kg aircraft of all-metal construction and with a side-by-side two-seat cabin based on the Murphy Rebel. The wings are foldable for storage and the Wild Thing WT.01 (also known as the WT.01 Serengeti for utility purposes) has a fixed tailwheel undercarriage as standard, but the WT.02 version can be fitted with tricycle gear. It is also fitted with an emergency parachute system. The standard powerplant is the 80hp Jabiru 2200 but the Rotax 912 can also be specified and the WT.02 has a 100hp Jabiru 3300 or Rotax 912S. It is marketed by Ultraleicht Bau International (ULBI), formerly known as Air Light and built by Aerostar in Romania, although production is expected to be moved to Germany. The prototype, YR-6107, was flown in Romania in mid-1995 and the aircraft is available in factory-complete or kit form. The standard engine is the 80hp Jabiru but the Wild Thing can also be supplied with a Hirth F.30 engine. By the end of 2004, 74 complete aircraft and 24 kits had been sold. ULBI is also marketing the Corvus Corone, which is an all-composite side-by-side low-wing two-seater with a fixed tricy-

cle undercarriage and a Jabiru 2200 engine. The Corone, which meets German ultralight rules and is built in Hungary, first flew in 2004 and five development examples had been built by the spring of 2005.

Air Light Wild Thing D-MHAU

Air Tractor   United States

After selling the rights to his S-2 agricultural aircraft line to Rockwell International, Leland Snow established a new company at Wichita Falls, Texas and embarked on design of a new low-wing agricultural aircraft – the AT-300 Air Tractor. This was considerably larger than the S-2 and Snow flew the first prototype in September 1973. It received its type certificate (A9SW) on 30th November 1973. The Air Tractor followed the standard layout for low-wing agricultural types, having a fixed tailwheel undercarriage and a hopper located between the pilot's cockpit and the engine firewall.

The Air Tractor AT-300 went into production at Olney, Texas in 1974 and, subsequently, Air Tractor introduced further models in the AT-400, AT-500 and AT-800 series with progressively larger and stronger airframes and higher gross weights. Engines fitted to the various models

have included the traditional R985 piston engine and several versions of the PT6A and LTP101 turboprop with different power outputs. Later examples with turboprops have been titled Turbo Air Tractor. Air Tractor's type designation system can be detailed as follows:

Series	Hopper Size (US gal)	Piston engine version	Turboprop version
AT300	320	AT301	AT302
AT400	400	AT401	AT402
AT500	500	AT501	AT502
AT600	630	None	AT602
AT800	800	None	AT802

The Air Tractors have become used widely as fire bombers both on wheels and floats. All these types are detailed in the following table:

Air Tractor AT-301 N7311X

Model	Notes
AT-300	Low-wing single-seat all-metal agricultural aircraft with spring steel fixed tailwheel u/c and one 450hp Pratt & Whitney R985-AN1 radial piston engine. 5,000 lb TOGW. 320 US gallon hopper. Prototype N44200 (c/n 300-0001) FF Sept 1973
AT-301	AT-300 with 600hp Pratt & Whitney Wasp R1340-AN1. Some converted from AT-300. 7,300 lb TOGW
AT-301B	AT-301 with 350 US gal hopper
AT-302	AT-301 with 600shp Lycoming LTP101-A1A turboprop engine. Prototype N4441S (c/n 302-0101) FF Jun 1977. Certificated 2nd December 1977
AT-302A	AT-302 with 385 US gal Hopper and 7,700 lb TOGW
AT-250	AT-300 with reduced (41ft 6in) wingspan and 260 US gal hopper. Prototype only, N31634 FF Jul 1982
AT-400	AT-301 with 680shp P&W PT6A-15AG turboprop, squared-off fin, 400 US gallon hopper and 7,800 lb TOGW. Prototype N36493 (c/n 400-0244) FF Dec 1979. Certificated 11 Apr 1980
AT-400A	AT-400 with 550shp P&W PT6A-20 turboprop. 320 US gal hopper
AT-401	AT-301 with 4ft longer span wings and 400 US gallon hopper. 600hp Pratt & Whitney Wasp R-1340 engine. Prototype N8888S (c/n 401-0001) FF 1986
AT-401A	AT-400 with 592hp PZL-3S radial engine. One aircraft only N1014L (c/n 401A-0733) FF Oct 1989
AT-401B	AT-401 with 24-inch longer wingspan and cambered Hoerner wingtips
AT-402	AT-400 with long-span AT-401 wings and 680hp PT6A-15AG, PT6A-27 or PT6A-28 turboprop. 7,800 lb TOGW. Prototype N1005V FF Dec 1988
AT-402A	AT-402 with 550shp PT6A-11AG turboprop. Prototype N10189 (c/n 402A-0738) FF Jan 1990
AT-402B	AT-402 with same wing improvements as AT-401B and crew seat buried in rear fuselage
AT-501	AT-503 with one 600hp Pratt & Whitney R-1340-S3H1G piston engine and 2ft longer fuselage. Prototype N7314C (c/n 501-0002)
AT-502	AT-503 with 2ft longer wing 750shp P&W PT6A-34 or 680shp PT6A-15AG engine, 1500 litre hopper and single-seat cockpit. Prototype N7314D (c/n 502-0003) FF Apr 1987
AT-502A	AT-502 with same wing improvements as AT-401B, enlarged rudder and 1,100shp Pratt & Whitney PT6A-45R turboprop
AT-502B	AT502 with same wing improvements as AT-401B
AT-503	AT-401 with 22-inch fuselage stretch, increased wingspan, two-seat cockpit, 502 US gallon hopper and one 1,100shp P&W PT6A-45R turboprop. 8,500 lb TOGW. Prototype N7309X (c/n AT503-0001) FF 25 Apr 1986
AT-503A	AT-503 equipped as dual control trainer with short-span AT-502 wings and 750shp PT6A-34AG turboprop
AT-602	AT-502A with lengthened 56-ft. wingspan, taller fin, larger tailplane, strengthened u/c, 630 gal hopper and 12,500 lb TOGW. Powered by one 1,050shp PT6-60AG or 1,295shp PT6A-65AG turboprop. Prototype N6084K (c/n 602-0337) FF 1 Dec 1995
AT-802	AT-503 tandem two-seater with belly-mounted hopper of 830 US gallon capacity fitted with computer-controlled doors, 8ft wingspan increase, 16,000 lb TOGW, increased fuel and 1,173shp PT6A-45R, -65AG or -67AG turboprop. Prototype N802LS (c/n 802-0001) FF 30 Oct 1990
AT-802A	Single-seat version of AT-802 with PT6A-45. Prototype N1558W (c/n 802A-0004) FF Jun 1992
AT-802F	AT-802 configured for firefighting

Nearly 2,500 Air Tractors of all models had been complete by the end of 2004. Serial numbers for the base model started at c/n 300-0001 (the prototype) and ran to c/n 300-0243 at which point 400- series aircraft (eg, c/n 400-0244) started to be included. The last 300 series aircraft was c/n 301-0688. Serials had reached c/n 402A-1159 by the end of 2004. These serials are in a common series but the prefix indicates which model is concerned (eg, 401A-0733, 402-0840). The AT-500 series started a new sequence of serials at c/n 503-0001 and the same c/n sequence is also used for the AT-602. By the end of 2003 production had reached approximately 502B-0702 and 602-1129. The AT-802 started another new sequence at c/n 802-001 and production had reached 802A-0200 by the end of 2004.

Air Tractor AT-802A N6159F

AISA   Spain

Iberavia SA was a well-established Spanish manufacturer of training gliders for the military forces. In 1950, the company built the prototype of the I-11 Peque civil training aircraft. This was a side-by-side low-wing all-wood two-seater, powered by an 85hp Continental C.85 engine, with a fixed tricycle undercarriage and a cabin enclosed by a large clear sliding canopy. While the single I-11 prototype was still under development, Iberavia was taken over by Aeronautica Industrial SA (AISA) who completed development work.

AISA decided to give the I-11B a tailwheel undercarriage, and the canopy was reduced in size. The powerplant was also changed to a 90hp Continental C90-12F. The prototype I-11B Peque (EC-WIV) made its maiden flight on 16th October 1953 and AISA subsequently built 206 production aircraft (c/n 002 to 207) of which 136 were fitted with full blind-flying equipment. 125 of the I-11Bs produced were delivered to the Spanish Air Force as the L.8C for use in general liaison and training and many of these were later sold to civil users.

AISA built 200 examples of the I-115 tandem two-seat military trainer as the E-6 for the Spanish Air Force (c/n 1 to 200) and many of these were also subsequently civilianised. The I-115 was a wooden aircraft with a low wing, fixed tailwheel undercarriage and a sliding multi-

AISA I-11B Peque EC-BKB

section canopy. It was powered by a 150hp ENMA Tigre G-IVB in-line engine and the prototype first flew on 16th July 1952. Production started in mid-1954 at the AISA plant at Carabanchel-Alto near to the Madrid airfield of Cuatro Vientos. Between 1967 and 1970, the company also assembled a batch of 10 SIAI-Marchetti S.205s under licence.

Alaparma   Italy

During World War Two, Adriano Mantelli built a single-seat light aircraft designated the AM-6. It was a twin-boomed machine derived from a number of previous glider designs with a single fin and rudder, bubble canopy and pusher Volkswagen engine. The designation was an indicator of the area of the aircraft's wings in square metres. The AM-6 was followed, in 1946, by the slightly larger AM-8 (I-DONB c/n 1), which used various engines including a 38hp ABC Scorpion and a 38hp CNAC2. In turn, this led to the larger two-seat AM-9 (I-DONC c/n 1) and the AM-10 (prototype I-RAIA/I-DONA c/n 1) of which four are believed to have been built. Mantelli formed the Alaparma SpA and a developed version of the AM-10, designated AM-65 Baldo went into production, powered by a 65hp Walter Mikron engine. This had a monowheel main undercarriage with outrigger wheels at the wingtips and just one was completed (I-DOND c/n 31) because the main production variant was the AM-75, which used a 75hp Praga D engine. It seems that 13 AM-75 aircraft were completed (c/n 30 to 42) between 1950 and 1953, the majority being under an Italian Aviation Ministry contract for use by approved national flying clubs. It appears that Ala-

Alaparma Baldo AM-75 I-DONP

parma also built two examples of the AM-12 Argentina (serialled MM100035 and MM100036) which were tested by the Italian military test centre between 1955 and 1964 and each of these was fitted with Turboméca Palas jet engine – but no further details are known.

Ali Viberti   Italy

Ali Viberti was set up in 1947 by Dr Angelo Viberti to build a range of light aircraft designed by Ing Franco Muscareillo. The first model to be built was the Viberti Musca I – a low-wing side-by-side tailwheel two-seater built of wood and fabric with plywood covering. The Musca I (I-RAIA c/n 1bis) had a 60hp C.N.A. D.4 powerplant and some of the 12 units built were fitted with dual controls and served with Italian flying clubs during the 1940s and 1950s. Several aircraft were fitted with other engines in the 65hp to 85hp range, including the 65hp Walter Mikron and Continental C.85. These production aircraft were given serial numbers in the range c/n 1-1 to 1-8 and c/n 9 to 12.

Further derivatives of the Musca were planned, but the Officine Viberti ceased operations in 1952. However, Ing Muscareillo continued further development of the Musca with the Musca 1-ter that had a new single-strut undercarriage mounted on the forward wing spar and a modified clearview cockpit canopy. This variant was powered by a 75hp Walter Mikron III.

Ali Viberti Musca I I-VIBE

Alpla   Austria

The Alpla Samburo originated as the AVo.60 designed by Dipl Ing Wernher Vogel and built by the Alpla-Werke Alwin Lehner OHG. It was a low-wing wood and fabric motor glider with a monowheel undercarriage and side-by-side seating for two. The powerplant was a 60hp Limbach and the prototype (OE-9094) first flew on 4th July 1974. Production of the AVo.68-V, which had foldable outer wings and a 68hp Limbach SL.1700E1 engine started at Wiener Neustadt in 1977 and variants of the basic design included the AVo.68-S-2000 with a Limbach L-2000EC engine and the AVo.68-V-2000 with a Limbach L.2000E-01. Some Samburos have been built with standard tailwheel undercarriages. 28 production Samburos were completed (c/n 2 to 29) of which 14 were the AVo.68-S. Production ceased in 1979 but recommenced in 1999 in Germany with Nitsche Flugzeugbau whose new version had a wider cabin, sliding canopy and other refinements. Versions include the AVo.68-R-80 (80hp Rotax 912A3), AVo.68-R-100 (100hp Rotax 912FS3) and AVo.68-R-115 (115hp Rotax 14F3). The prototype was D-KFGN (c/n 024R), converted from an Alpla aircraft and production

Alpla Samburo AVo.68 D-KYSS

of the definitive version with a lengthened fuselage commenced with D-KSAM (c/n 001) with five further examples (c/n 002 to 006) being built by mid-2004.

Ambrosini   Italy

The Societa Aeronautica Italiana (SAI) dates from the 1930s and was based at Passignano, near to Trasimeno, becoming part of the Ambrosini group in 1934. In the mid-1930s they built the SAI-2 and SAI-2S four-seat tourers. After World War Two, in addition to building several gliders, including the Canguru, Allievo Cantu and Asiago 2, they produced a small production run of 13 S.1001 Grifo private touring aircraft (c/n 1 to 13). This was, essentially, an improved version of the SAI-2S and was a low-wing wooden four-seat machine with a fixed tailwheel undercarriage, powered by a 130hp Alfa 110 in-line engine, the prototype being I-RANA (c/n 1). A seaplane version with twin floats was also tested. Using the S.1001 airframe, they produced a two-seat training version known as the S.1002 Trasimenus (and modified S.1002R Girfalco) although it appears that only around six examples were completed.

Ambrosini then produced a large batch of around 112 S-7 (single-seat) and 26 S-7B (tandem two-seat) trainers for the Italian Air Force. The S-7 was a high-performance low-wing aircraft with a retractable tailwheel undercarriage and a 225hp Alfa Romeo 115-Iter in-line engine. It was followed by a small series of ten S-7 Supersettes with the 340hp DH Gipsy Queen 70-3 engine. Many of the S-7 series were subsequently civilianised and handed over to Italian flying clubs. Ambrosini's next light aircraft project was the F.4 Rondone I, which had been designed by Stelio Frati. This was a wooden side-by-side two-seat low-wing cabin monoplane with a retractable tricycle undercarriage and powered by an 85hp Continental. The prototype (I-RAID) was built by CVV and nine production Rondones (c/n 013 to 021) with 90hp Continental C.90 engines were built by Ambrosini (with Aeronautica Lombardi). The later F.7 Rondone II, which had three seats in an extended rear cabin with extra side windows, flew in prototype form (as I-ADRJ c/n 2-01, built by Pasotti) on 10 February 1954. Nine further examples were built by Pasotti (c/n 02 to 010) and one F.4 was

Ambrosini F.4 Rondone I F-PGTU

Ambrosini S.1001 Grifo I-RANG

converted to F.7 standard. Among other Ambrosini projects was the P.18 basic side-by-side two-seat jet trainer which reached an advanced stage in 1957 but was abandoned without the prototype flying.

American Aviation   United States

American Aviation was formed in 1964 to build the BD-1 light trainer which had been created by Jim Bede. Bede, a prolific designer, had flown his prototype BD-1 (N624BD, c/n 2) on 11th July 1963 but had been unable to get production started through his own resources.

The BD-1 was a conventional all-metal side-by-side two-seater with a fixed tricycle undercarriage and a 65hp Continental A65-8 engine. American Aviation's production version – the AA-1 Yankee differed in having greater wingspan, a lengthened fuselage, narrower chord fin, fibreglass undercarriage legs and a 115hp Lycoming O-235-C2A engine. It employed metal-to-metal bonding of components which was

a technique not hitherto used to any great degree in general aviation aircraft and it also used a large amount of high strength aluminium honeycomb material within the fuselage structure. The aircraft went into production at Cuyahoga County Airport near Cleveland, Ohio with the first production unit flying on 16th July 1968 and the Type Certificate, A11EA, being awarded on 16th July 1968 and Over 300 units were delivered by the end of 1969.

The AA-1 formed the basis for a series of two- and four-seat models which included the AA-5 series, certificated on 12th November 1971, and these found a ready market in the United States and abroad. Details of individual single-engined aircraft built by the company are as follows:

American Aviation AA-1A Trainer N9246L

American General AG-5B Tiger D-EAGT

Model	Name	Built	Notes
AA-1	Yankee	461	Basic two-seat model developed from BD-1 with one 115hp Lyc O-235-C2C engine. Prototype N888M (c/n 6)
AA-1A	Trainer	470	Dual control trainer version of AA-1 with wing using NACA642-415 aerofoil. Prototype N9301L (c/n AA1A-0001) FF 25 Mar 1970
AA-1B	Trainer	680	AA-1A development with 60 lb useful load increase. Also built as Tr-2 touring and sports model from 1972
AA-1C	T-Cat/Lynx	211	AA-1B fitted with 115hp Lycoming O-235-L2C engine, AA-5 tailplane and new engine installation. T-Cat replaced the Trainer and Lynx replaced Tr-2. Prototype N1551R (c/n AA1B-0601)
AA-2	Patriot	2	Four-seater developed from AA-1, with one 180hp Lycoming O-360-A1H. Prototype N484AA (c/n 301) FF Feb 1970. Development dropped in favour of AA-5
AA-5	Traveler	834	Four-seat AA-1 with 150hp Lycoming O-320-A2G. Prototype N342AA (c/n P-102) FF 21 Aug 1970
AA-5A	Cheetah	900	Traveler with cleaned-up airframe including larger fin fillet and no ventral fin fairing, redesigned engine cowling, longer rear windows. Introduced in 1976
AA-5B	Tiger	1,323	AA-5A with 180hp Lycoming O-360-A4K and 200 lb TOGW increase. Introduced 1974
AG-5B	Tiger	180	American General model with new nosebowl, carbon fibre cowling, relocated landing lights and 24-volt electrical system. Prototype N7978A (c/n AG5B 99997) FF 21 Apr 1990
AG-5B	Tiger	52	Tiger Aircraft model built from 2001. Minor cosmetic changes only
AA-5C	-	1	Prototype only, N7755B (c/n AA5-0129). No further details known

In 1972, Grumman Corporation had purchased 80% of the issued stock of American Aviation and changed the name of the company to Grumman American Aviation Corporation. The 2,000th aircraft was rolled out in October 1974 from the Cleveland plant, but Grumman

Grumman American GA-7 Cougar N797GA

American moved all production of its light aircraft range to Savannah, Georgia in 1976.

The next development from Grumman American was a light twin that was viewed as a logical extension of the full product range. The prototype GA-7 Cougar (N777GA c/n GA70001) first flew on 20th December 1974. It had a similar wing to that of the AA-5 and featured a sliding canopy and twin 160hp Lycoming O-320 engines. Accommodation was for four people and the aircraft had a retractable tricycle undercarriage. During testing of the prototype it became clear that the sliding canopy was unsatisfactory for this type of aircraft and the production prototype (N877X c/n 0001) adopted an integral cabin with a starboard side door, a third window on either side and construction based on the bonded methods of the single-engined Grummans. The Cougar gained its type certificate (A17SO) on 22nd September 1977 and 115 examples were built. In February 1991, American General signed an agreement with Tbilisi Aircraft Manufacturing Association in the Republic of Georgia to build the GA-7 Cougar in a factory which hitherto built Sukhoi SU-25 fighters but the project was abandoned. Rights to the Cougar were granted to Aérospatiale in May 1995 and SOCATA intended to put the aircraft back in production as the TB.320 Tangara with 180hp Lycoming engines, increased electrical supply and a redesigned cockpit and standard avionics. Plans for Tangara production were abandoned following development work using an existing Cougar (N738G c/n GA7-0106).

Grumman's interest in Grumman American was bought by American Jet Industries on 1st September 1978, and they again changed the company name to Gulfstream American Corporation. They continued to manufacture the AA-1, the larger four-seat AA-5 series and the Cougar under this name until production was suspended in late-1979. In June 1989, it was announced that Gulfstream had sold all rights to the AA-1 Lynx, AA-5A Cheetah, AA-5B Tiger and GA-7 Cougar to American General Aircraft Co of Greenville, Mississippi. The first new model introduced by them in 1990 was the AG-5B Tiger which featured a number of improvements. American General was acquired by Teleflex Inc of Limerick, Pa. in early 1992, aiming to build the Tiger and Cheetah at Oklahoma City but declared Chapter 11 bankruptcy in January 1994 and suspended production at that time. The Tiger was returned to production by Tiger Aircraft LLC of Martinsburg, West Virginia with first deliveries taking place in December 2001 and in the calendar year 2004 the company delivered 19 AG-5Bs.

Each model had its own series of construction numbers, starting at 0001 and prefixed by the model number. Prototypes were generally serialled 0001 but others had numbers prefixed P- (eg, P-102). New serial batches were established by American General (starting at AG5B9997) and Tiger Aircraft (starting at 10201). The batches of production serial numbers allocated were:

Model	Serials	Model	Serials
AA-1	AA1-0001 to 0461	AA-5A	AA5A-0001 to 0900
AA-1	A AA1A-0001 to 0470	AA-5B	AA5B-0001 to 1323
AA-1B	AA1B-0001 to 0680	AG-5B	AG5B 9997 to 10176
AA-1C	AA1C-0001 to 0211	Tiger AG-5B	10201 to 10252+
AA-5	AA5-0001 to 0834	GA-7	0001 to 0115

AMF Microflight   United Kingdom

One of the earliest 'heavy microlights' was the AMF Chevvron, designed by Angus Fleming and Peter Wright and built at Membury Airfield, Wiltshire. The original Chevvron (G-MNPW, c/n CH.001) was a motorised glider constructed of carbon fibre/composite sandwich panels with lightweight polyester film covering and it had an enclosed side-by-side two-seat cockpit, mid-set laminar-flow wings and a fixed tricycle undercarriage. The first aircraft had a V-tail but the definitive prototype G-MNFL, c/n CH.002, which flew in October 1986, had a conventional tail and was powered by a 32hp König SD570 two-stroke radial engine. A seaplane version used a higher-powered 48hp König. The Chevvron 2-32 (indicating that it was a two-seater with a 32hp engine) received BCAR Part S type approval and went into production in 1987 with manufacture continuing until 1998 when the project ceased. In total, 38 Chevvrons were built, including the two prototypes (c/n CH.001 to CH.006, 008 to 012, 014 to 029, 031 to 040 and 054).

The successor company to AMF was Aviation Enterprises, who took over rights to the Chevvron but have not built any further examples.

AMF Chevvron 2-32 59-NL

Aviation Enterprises are developing the Magnum VLA, which is a low-wing all-composite two-seater with a retractable tricycle undercarriage and a 100hp Rotax 914S engine. The prototype, G-61-2, first flew on 5th June 2003.

Anahuac   Mexico

The Fabrica de Aviones Anahuac was established in 1967 to produce a single-seat agricultural aircraft for Mexican conditions. The Anahuac Tauro 300 was a strut-braced constant-chord low-wing aircraft with a fixed tailwheel undercarriage. Spray bars were fitted along the length of the wing trailing edge. The prototype Tauro (XB-TAX) first flew on 3rd December 1968 powered by a 300hp Jacobs R.755-A2M1 uncowled radial engine and this powerplant was used on the seven production Tauro 300s. A subsequent batch of four examples of the Tauro 350 was built and these featured improved systems and used the 350hp Jacobs R-755-SM engine. Tauro serial numbers were c/n TA-001 to TA-012.

Anahuac Tauro 300 XB-AUL. H B Adams

Antonov   Ukraine

The An-2 utility biplane was designed by Oleg K Antonov as an agricultural and general utility aircraft intended as a replacement for the Polikarpov Po-2. It is an all-metal single-engined biplane with a fixed tailwheel undercarriage and a capacious fuselage that is able to accommodate 14 passengers or freight or a large hopper for crop spraying. It was first flown on 31st August 1947, initially with an ASh-21 radial engine but the production version used an upgraded ASh-621R. It went into production at Kiev in 1948 and 5,450 examples had been

Antonov An-2PF HA-YHD

built by 1960. Production responsibility for the An-2 was passed to Poland (PZL) in 1959 and full details of the An-2 models are shown under PZL. It was built in China as the Y-5. On 13th May 1980 Antonov flew the prototype of the An-3. This aircraft (CCCP-37901, c/n 1G163-21), which was based on a Polish-built An-2 airframe, had an Omsk TV2-117S turboprop. A further prototype (marked 9801 and designated An-3T) with a reshaped rudder and a TVD-20M engine has been built in Russia by Polyot and flew on 19th February 1998. No new production appears to have taken place but at least 21 PZL-built An-2Rs have been converted to An-3T standard (conv nos 20-01 to 22-21).

Aquila — Germany

Aquila Technische Entwicklungen GmbH of Schönhagen developed the Aquila A210 two-seat trainer/tourer as a JAR-VLA certificated aircraft, and the prototype (D-EQUI c/n AT.001) first flew on 5th March 2000. The Aquila was built from composites with an advanced computer-designed wing featuring a curved outboard leading edge and straight trailing edge. It was fitted with a fixed tricycle undercarriage and powered by a 99hp Rotax 912ULS engine with a variable-pitch propeller. 27 production aircraft had been completed by the end of 2004 (c/n AT01-101 to AT01-127) but output ceased with the company becoming insolvent on 19th January 2005.

Aquila A210 D-EQUI

Arctic Aircraft — United States

The Interstate S-1A Cadet was designed by Interstate Engineering Corporation as a basic trainer for the pre-war Civilian Pilot Training Program. It was a classic high-wing strut-braced monoplane with side-by-side seating and a fixed tailwheel undercarriage. The prototype first flew on 20th April 1940 and, powered by a 65hp Continental A-65-8 engine, 321 examples were built (c/n 1 to 321) before the company changed to the military specification version that had more extensive cabin glazing and a 113hp Franklin O-200-5 engine. This was the Interstate XO-63 (later the L-6) of which 253 were built. After the war, many L-6s were converted for civil use as the S-1B1. Design rights for the S-1B1 were sold to Callair, who are believed to have built two examples (N2923V and N2922V, c/n 1001 and 1002), but the rights subsequently passed to Bill Diehl of Anchorage, Alaska who revived the design in 1975 and established the Arctic Aircraft Company. The S-1B1 was redesigned as the S-1B2 Arctic Tern. The aircraft's construction was converted to modern materials and the Tern used a 150hp Lycoming O-320 engine and could be fitted with floats or skis. Following the prototype (N50AA c/n 1001 – which was probably created from the first Callair aircraft) Arctic built 31 production Terns (c/n 1002 to 1032) at its factory in Anchorage, Alaska. The majority of Terns remained in service in Alaska where it was well accepted as a bush aircraft as it was equipped with very large cargo compartment to allow the loading of long and bulky items. All tooling and assets of Arctic Aircraft were acquired by Interstate Aircraft Co who set up a factory in Lebanon, New Hampshire to build a new S-1B2 with an aluminium mainspar and wing struts, constant-speed propeller and a higher gross weight. The first new production aircraft (c/n 2001 to 2003) were under construction in mid-2004. The company has also developed a four-seat version of the Tern with a longer cabin and a large rear cargo hatch, and five development aircraft have been built (c/n 001 to 005). These were initially named the Arctic Privateer but production aircraft will probably be titled Arctic Peregrine.

Arctic Aircraft S-1B2 Tern N74AT

ARV — United Kingdom

ARV Aviation Ltd was established in December 1983 by Richard Noble to design and build the ARV Super2 low cost two-seater. The company was based at Sandown, Isle of Wight and it made the first flight of the prototype Super2 (G-OARV c/n 001) on 11th March 1985 followed by a further two aircraft (c/n 002 and 003). The Super2 was a 'shoulder-wing' side-by-side two-seater of conventional appearance with a fixed tricycle undercarriage. It was built from Supral light alloy that permitted low-cost pressing of multi-curvature panels – but the most unusual feature was its 77hp three-cylinder two-stroke Hewland AE.75 engine.

The Super2 was to be built both as a factory-complete aircraft and as a kit for homebuilders and the initial five production aircraft were issued in kit form (c/n K004 to K009). Thereafter, the majority of sales were made to flying clubs, but technical problems with the Hewland engine led to the grounding of the Super2 between October 1987 and January 1988. Some aircraft were converted to an 80hp Rotax 912 flat-four engine. ARV went into administration on 17th June 1988 by which time production had reached approximately c/n 028. The company was sold to Taurus Aviation Ltd which later became Island Aviation Ltd but the Super2 programme was taken over by Aviation (Scotland) Ltd (ASL) of Hamilton, West Lothian and aircraft c/n 029 to 034 were completed and flown with further airframes up to c/n 041 in progress. ASL

ARV Super2 G-BWBZ

intended to deliver new Super2s as either the Series 100 with the Hewland engine or as the Series 200 equipped with a twin rotor 100hp Mid-West Aero Engines AE.100R engine. In 1993, ASL set up a joint venture company with Uvan Invest AB, named ASL Hagfors Aero AB to build the Super2 at Hagfors, Sweden. The aircraft was retitled Opus 280 and equipped with a Rotax 912A engine and minor changes to cabin ventilation and fuel capacity. Three development aircraft (SE-KYP, c/n 033 and c/n 40 and 41) were used to achieve JAR-VLA certification but ASL

Hagfors went into liquidation in mid-1995. Airframes c/n 035 to 039 were not completed. The Super2 then passed to the American company, SkyCraft International Inc of Homeworth, Ohio who marketed kits to amateur builders for completion with Rotax 912 engines. In the latest development, a new company, Opus Aircraft, has been formed to produce the Super2 under the new American LSA rules. Including kit-built aircraft, 36 ARV Super2s have been built to date.

ATEC   Czech Republic

ATEC vos was formed in the Czech Republic in 1992 and designed the Zephyr composite 450kg ultralight. The prototype (OK-CUA 01) first flew in 1997 powered by an 80hp Rotax 912UL engine. It has a laminar-flow low wing built of wood, fabric and composite with complex aerodynamic features for maximum performance, a T-tail and a fixed tricycle undercarriage. ATEC sells the aircraft as a kit or as a factory-complete aircraft and had built 90 aircraft-sets by mid-2004. The original version is known as the Zephyr Standard but this was modified to become the Zephyr 2000 (now the Zephyr 2004C) with a 99hp Rotax 912ULS engine and shorter wingspan. The ATEC Faeta 321 is a redesigned Zephyr of all-carbon fibre sandwich construction with a redesigned wing and a 473kg maximum weight. The prototype, OK-IUG-15, flew in 2003. A single-seat version, the Zephyr Solo was first flown on 29th October 2000 (prototype OK-FUH 01) and this was followed by the definitive ATEC-212 Solo (OK-KUG 32) which has a low wing, fixed tailwheel undercarriage and conventional tail. It is powered by a 65hp Rotax 582DCDI engine. The ATEC system of construction numbers is unclear.

ATEC Zephyr 08-EB

Auster   United Kingdom

Auster Aircraft Ltd was formed on 8th March 1946 as a successor to Taylorcraft Aeroplanes (England) Ltd, which had been established in 1938 to build the American Taylorcraft high-wing light aircraft under licence. This led to wartime production of the military observation Austers at Rearsby, Leicestershire supported by manufacturing of com-

ponents at Thurmaston and other 'shadow factories'. Each of these types, beginning with the Model Plus C, had a separate letter designation, and at the end of the war the company had reached the type letter 'J' which identified the Auster AOP.5 air observation post that was in production at that time.

With postwar civil sales in view, Auster took the Model J airframe and fitted it with a Cirrus Minor engine – in which form it became the J/1

Auster Mk 5 G-APBE

Auster J/5G Cirrus Autocar G-ARUG

Autocrat three-seater. They produced further Auster 5s, powered by American Lycoming engines, together with the two-seat J/2 Arrow and J/4 Archer which, respectively, used Continental A.65 and Cirrus Minor engines. Because Auster was the best-known British producer of light aircraft they were under great pressure to keep pace with demand for the J/1, particularly as they had also moved into building specific models for the overseas markets which opened up. These included the J/5 Adventurer, which had a sloping engine bulkhead and optional ventral fuel tank and was shipped in some numbers to Australia where it was fitted with a 120hp Gipsy Major 1 engine.

By 1948, the light aircraft market was contracting rapidly and the company's production slowed to a trickle. However, the J/1B Aiglet and the almost identical J/1N Alpha were brought into the product line and, in a parallel development, the J/5 fuselage was modified with a higher and wider rear cabin to become the four-seat J/5B Autocar. All subsequent civil Austers had either the narrow J/1 airframe or the larger J/5B airframe. A large range of Autocar variants was built with many different engines for both domestic and export sale, but commercial business continued to be slow and Auster was largely kept afloat during this period by military orders. The AOP.6 was built for the British Army and a significant number of Aiglet Trainers were ordered by overseas military forces. In 1954, Auster flew the prototype of a new air observation post, the Model B.5 (AOP.9), which moved the company from its traditional tube-and-fabric construction to an all-metal airframe. It was derived from the experimental Model S and powered by a Blackburn Cirrus Bombardier engine. In addition to British orders

for the AOP.9 the company managed to sell 35 examples to India and two to South Africa.

Several other new Austers appeared in the early 1950s, including a single example of the B.4 Ambulance/Freighter, which had a pod-and-boom layout with a rear-fuselage-loading door and the fin and tailplane set on a high tail boom. Departing from their traditional high-wing layout, Auster produced the low-wing B.8 Agricola agricultural type, which had a 1,680 lb hopper capacity and was aimed at the top dressing market in New Zealand. A small (and wholly uneconomic) production batch was produced at Rearsby during 1956. The Agricola was fitted with a modern Continental horizontally-opposed engine and this trend away from the British in-line engines was also applied to the standard high-wing Auster models.

The first of the new Austers was the J/1U Workmaster, which was primarily produced for agricultural use, fitted with Micronair rotary atomisers under the wings. Auster was also fortunate in obtaining a large order for training aircraft for Portugal. This requirement was satisfied by a combination of manufacture by Auster and by the Oficinas Gerais de Matereal Aeronautico (OGMA) and the aircraft concerned were the new 100hp Auster D.4 and the three-seat, 160hp Auster D.5. A few D.4s were sold in the United Kingdom and the company built a handful of Autocar-based D.6s for sale in Britain and Europe.

By this time, however, the traditional light aircraft scene was being invaded by Piper Tri-Pacers and Cessna 172s from the United States. With minimal military orders, Auster was quite unable to remain commercially sound and compete with these comfortable, well-equipped four-seat designs. They did build a prototype of the C.6 Atlantic which was similar to the Tri-Pacer, but it was not put into production and, in 1960, Auster became a part of the new British Executive and General Aviation Company – BEAGLE.

Serial numbers used by Auster and the predecessor Taylorcraft company are shown in the following table. It should be noted that some 90 AOP.6s and all of the T.7s and most of the AOP.9s followed common late-war practice and were given no serial number at all.

Model	C/n Blocks	Model	C/n Blocks
Model C	100 - 123	Auster 6	2815 - 2870
Model D	124 - 132	Auster J/5	2871 - 2906
Auster 1	133 - 232	Auster J/5B, J/5G, J/5H	2908 - 2989
Auster 3	233 - 722*	Auster J/5	3000 - 3050
Auster 4	732 - 991*	Auster J/5B, J/5G, J/8F prot	3152 - 3200
Auster 5	992 - 1821*	Auster J/5Q	3201 - 3250

Auster J/5F Aiglet Trainer G-AMZU

Auster 5 & J/1	1822 - 1900*	Auster J/5B, J/5G, J/5P	3251 - 3300
Auster 6	1901 - 1950	Auster J/5R	3301 - 3350
Auster 5 & J/1	1951 - 2065	Auster J/1N, J/5T	3401 - 3421
Auster J/4	2066 - 2090	AOP.9	3422 - 3446
Auster J/5	2093 - 2099	C6	3447
Auster J/1, J/3 prot	2100 - 2250	Auster J/1U	3497 - 3507
Auster 6	2251 - 2300	Auster J/5L	3547 - 3559
Auster J/1	2301 - 2350	Auster J/1W, D.4	3600 - 3606
Auster J/2	2351 - 2400	Auster D.4	3651 - 3676
Auster J/2	2401 - 2415	Auster D.5	3677 - 3691
Auster J/5	2416 - 2450	Auster B.8	B101 - B118†
Auster 6	2451 - 2600	OGMA D.5	1 - 33
Auster J/1, J/1B, J/5F	2601 - 2800	OGMA D.4	34 - 42
Auster J/5	2801 - 2814	OGMA D.5	43 - 129

* Some not used; † B109 to B118 not completed.

The serial numbers of a number of the one-off types are included in the following table of models:

Model	Built	Notes
C Taylorcraft Plus C	24	High-wing two-seater based on US Taylorcraft Model B. Powered by one 55hp Lycoming O-145-A2. Prototype G-AFNW (c/n 100) FF 3 May 1939. Some conv to C/2 with 90hp Cirrus Minor 1
D Taylorcraft Plus D	9	Plus C with 90hp Cirrus Minor 1 engine
D/1 Auster Mk 1	99	Plus D with enlarged windows for AOP work
E Auster Mk 3	483	Auster 1 powered by 130hp Gipsy Major 1 and fitted with split flaps
F Auster Mk 2	2	Auster 1 with 130hp Lycoming O-290
G Auster Mk 4	260	New airframe with enlarged cockpit glazing. 130hp Lycoming O-290-3 engine
H	-	Experimental tandem two-seat training glider converted from Taylorcraft B
J Auster Mk 5	860	Auster Mk 4 with blind flying panel and improved trimming system
J Auster Mk 5D		Mk 5 converted with 130hp Gipsy Major 1 engine and enlarged fin. Prototype G-AJYU (c/n 2666)
J Auster Mk 5 Alpha		Postwar civil production Mk 5
J/1 Autocrat	363	Three-seat civil model based on Mk 5 with single-piece windscreen, 100hp Cirrus Minor 2 engine. Prototype G-AFWN (c/n 124)
J/1B Aiglet	86	J/1 with enlarged tail and 130hp Gipsy Major 1 engine
J/1N Alpha	100	J/1B without oil cooler
J/1S Autocrat	-	J/1 G-AMVM (c/n 3102) fitted with 145hp Gipsy Major 10-2/2 engine
J/1U Workmaster	11	J/1 with strengthened airframe, larger tail, heavy duty u/c, 180hp Lycoming O-360-A1A. 7 aircraft built as crop sprayers. Prototype G-APKP (c/n 3497) FF 22 Feb 1958
J/1W Autocrat	1	J/1 fitted with 160hp Lycoming O-320 engine. One aircraft, G-25-6 (c/n 3600)
J/2 Arrow	41	Two-seat J/1 with covered-in rear and upper cabin. 75hp Continental C-75-12 engine. Prototype G-AGPS (c/n 1660)
J/3 Atom	3	J/2 with 65hp Continental C-65-12 engine. Prototype G-AHSY (c/n 2250) FF 6 Sep 1946
J/4 Archer	29	J/2 with 90hp Cirrus Minor 1 engine
J/5 Adventurer	59	J/1 with sloping engine firewall mounting the starter and 130hp Gipsy Major 1 engine
J/5B Autocar	80	Four-seat J/5 with enlarged rear cabin with raised decking and bigger fin/rudder. Prototype G-AJYK (c/n 2908)
J/5E Autocar	1	J/5B with shortened wings, modified u/c, 155hp Cirrus Minor 3. G-AJYS (c/n 2917)
J/5F Aiglet Trainer	92	Four-seat J/5 with aerobatic stressing and short span wings. Prototype G-AMKF (c/n 2709)
J/5G Autocar	94	J/5B for crop spraying with 155hp Cirrus Major 3 engine
J/5H Autocar		J/5G with 145hp Cirrus Major 2 Engine
J/5K Aiglet Trainer	2	J/5F with 155hp Cirrus Major 3. Prototype G-AMMS (c/n 2745)
J/5L Aiglet Trainer	27	J/5F with 145hp Gipsy Major 10-2/1
J/5P Autocar	25	J/5B with 145hp Gipsy Major 10-2
J/5Q Alpine	4	J/5R with 130hp Gipsy Major 1
J/5R Alpine	7	Three-seat J/5L with J/5B wings and Gipsy Major 10-1 engine. Prototype G-ANXC (c/n 3153)
J/5T Autocar	1	J/5B with 108hp Lycoming O-235 engine. One aircraft G-25-4 (c/n 3421)
J/5V Autocar	1	J/5B with 160hp Lycoming O-320-B2B. G-APUW (c/n 3273)
J/6	-	Three-seater based on J/1 with 145hp Gipsy Major X. Prototype c/n 2837 not completed
J/7	-	Proposed two-seater similar to J/2 with 100hp Cirrus Minor. Not built
J/8F Aiglet Trainer	-	J/5K with central flap lever and Gipsy Major 1 engine. Prototype G-ANVJ (c/n 3152) not completed
J/8K Aiglet Trainer	-	Proposed J/8F with Cirrus Major 3
J/8L Aiglet Trainer	-	J/5K (G-AMYI) refitted with 145hp Gipsy Major 10-1/3 engine
K Auster AOP.6	379	Auster AOP.5 with strengthened rear fuselage, external flaps, 253 lb TOGW increase and 145hp Gipsy Major 7. Prototype TJ707 (c/n 1592) FF 1 May 1945
L	-	Proposed 2/3-seat strut-braced low-wing monoplane with Model G airframe and 130hp Lycoming O-290-3. Not built
M A2/45	1	2/3-seat high-wing AOP aircraft with 160hp Gipsy Major 31. Prototype VL522
N A2/45	1	Model M with 250hp Gipsy Queen 32. Prototype VL523
P Avis	2	Four-seater based on J/1 with slimmer circular section rear fuselage, new u/c, four doors, external flaps and 145hp Gipsy Major 10. Prototype G-AJXW (c/n 2838)
Q Auster T.7	83	Two-seat trainer version of AOP.6. Prototype VF665. Six aircraft converted to T.10
S	1	AOP aircraft based on AOP.6 with enlarged tail, Bombardier engine and new u/c. Prototype WJ316
A2		See Model M and Model N
A7		Light twin project. Not built
B1		Mid-wing AOP project. Not built
B3	149	Radio-controlled target drone
B4 Ambulance/ Freighter	1	Light freighter with rear loading door, high-set tail boom and 180hp Bombardier 702 engine. Prototype G-AMKL (c/n 2983) FF 7 Sep 1951

Beagle D.5/180 Husky G-AXBF

Auster B8 Agricola G-APFZ

B5 Auster AOP.9	182	2/3-seat AOP aircraft with all-metal wing and 185hp Bombardier 203 engine. Prototype WZ662 FF 19 Mar 1954
B6		Projected low-wing agricultural type
B8 Agricola	8	Low-wing single-seat agricultural aircraft with fixed tailwheel u/c, and 240hp Continental O-470-B engine. Prototype G-ANYG (c/n B101) FF 8 Dec 1955
B9		Ramjet helicopter project
C4 Antarctic	2	Auster T7 modified for Antarctic support
C6 Atlantic	1	Four-seat high-wing touring monoplane with fixed tricycle u/c and 185hp Continental E-185-10. Prototype G-APHT (c/n 3447)
D4	40	Two-seat development of J/2 with 108hp Lycoming O-235-C1. Prototype G-25-8 (c/n 3601)
D5 Husky	155	J/1N Alpha with modified tail and 160hp Lycoming O-320-A or 180hp O-360-A1A
D6	4	J/5B with 180hp Lycoming O-360-A1A. Prototype G-25-10 (c/n 3701)
D8	-	Initial designation for Beagle Airedale
E3	1	AOP.9 with Cont IO-470-D engine. Also designated A.115 (AOP.11). Prototype G-ASCC (c/n B701) FF 18 Aug 1961

Australian Lightwing — Australia

A part of the Hughes Group of Companies, based at Ballina on Australia's east coast, Australian Lightwing produced its first prototype ultralight two-seater in 1985. This aircraft, known as the Babe, had a strut-braced high wing, tailwheel undercarriage and a Rotax 503 engine. It formed the basis for the production Lightwing, which is built as a factory-complete aircraft or in kit form. The initial production-standard Lightwing GR-532 (c/n 001 and registered 25-0032) flew in 1986 and was designed in accordance with the Australian ultralight standard CAO.95.25. The company produces aircraft at the rate of 10 per annum and 160 had been built by mid-2004. The two principal models are the Lightwing GR-912 with tailwheel (or float) gear and a 100hp Rotax 912 engine and the Sport 2000, which has tricycle gear.

Australian Light Wing GR-532 25-3

AVIA-Lombardi — Italy

In 1936, Francis Lombardi flew the prototype of the low-wing side-by-side two-seat L.3 monoplane (I-ABJR c/n 1). It was a wood and fabric aircraft with a fixed tailwheel undercarriage and an enclosed cockpit and was powered by a 40hp CNA engine. Lombardi formed the Anonima poi Azionara Vercellese Industrie Aeronautiche (AVIA) and, following an Air Ministry competition, the company gained a production contract for an L.3 derivative using the rather more powerful CNA D.IV engine.

The civil L.3 had an enclosed cockpit, but the main production order was for 338 of an open-cockpit model for the Regia Aeronautica.

These were built between 1940 and 1942 together with 10 units for the Croatian Air Force. Output of the L.3 was shared with Agusta who built 165 machines. After the war, many of the surviving L.3s were civilianised for use by flying clubs. AVIA also built a light twin version – the L.4, powered by a pair of C.N.A. D.IV engines – but this did not progress beyond the prototype stage.

AVIA resumed production of the L.3 Aviastarlet in 1947 and was then reorganised as the Francis Lombardi Co, following which the aircraft were referred to as the FL.3. Some 53 aircraft had been built when the line was finally closed in 1949. Lombardi also built the larger LM.5 Aviastar, designed by Pieraldo Mortara (which explains the 'M' in the designation and the prototype registration, I-PIER). It was a two-seat cabin

Lombardi FL.3 I-NUMA

Meteor FL.54 OE-ABA. J Blake

3-I Sky Arrow 1450L N450JH

aircraft with a low wing and retractable tailwheel undercarriage powered by a 90hp Continental C90-12F engine. Seven examples were built, including the prototype (c/n 1 to 7) together with two of the three-seat LM.7s (I-TTEN c/n 1 and I-PACK c/n 2).

In 1949, Francis Lombardi ceased production and in 1953, its aircraft production assets and designs were sold to the glider manufacturer Meteor SpA of Trieste, which had originally been established in April 1947. They redesigned the FL.3 as the Meteor FL.53 with tubular steel construction, a cut-down rear fuselage and bubble canopy. A total of 37 Meteors of various kinds were built during the period up to 1959 (c/n 1101 to 1137) and several of these aircraft were sold as crop sprayers and with ski or float undercarriages. The different Meteor models were:

Model	Built	Notes
FL.53	8	Meteor-built FL.3 with steel tube fuselage and cut-down rear decking. Powered by 65hp Continental A65 engine
FL.53BM	4	FL.53 fitted with 90hp Continental C90-12F engine
FL.54	10	Three-seat FL.53 with 85hp or 90hp Continental
FL.55	4	Four-seat FL.54 with strengthened airframe and 135hp Lycoming O-290-3 engine
FL.55BM	10	FL.55 with modified fin and rudder and 150hp Lyc O-320-A1A engine
FL.55CM	1	FL.55 with 180hp Lycoming O-360-A1A engine
Super	1	FL.55 with enlarged vertical tail and 220hp Meteor Alpha engine
Bis	1	Two-seat Super with 110hp Meteor Alpha 2 engine

Meteor SpA was reconstituted as Initiative Industriale Italiane SpA (known as 3-I) and in the early 1990s designed and established manufacture of the popular Sky Arrow tandem two-seat light aircraft. The Sky Arrow is of carbon fibre construction with a pod-and-boom fuselage, pusher engine, strut-braced high wing, fixed tricycle undercarriage and a T-tail. The aircraft, which first flew in March 1993, has been produced in numerous different versions to meet different country certification requirements and can be fitted with several different pusher Rotax engines. Output by the spring of 2005 totalled 307 aircraft according to the manufacturer. 3-I is also developing the F200TSJ (Twin Seater Jewel) and F300FSJ (Four Seater Jewel), which are low-wing all-composite designs from Stelio Frati with retractable gear and (in the case of the F300) a 310hp Continental IO-550 engine. The serial number system for the Sky Arrow is not clear but the variants are as follows:

Model	Notes
450T	Factory or kit built. 450kg TOGW with 80hp Rotax 912UL engine
450TS	Factory built. 450kg TOGW with 99hp Rotax 912ULS engine
480T	Factory built. 480kg TOGW with 80hp Rotax 912UL engine
480TS	Factory built. 480kg TOGW with 99hp Rotax 912ULS engine
500T	Factory built. 500kg TOGW with 80hp Rotax 912 engine. 500A is amphibian
500TF	Kit built. 450kg TOGW with 80hp Rotax 912 engine
1200LC	Factory built. 545kg TOGW with 80hp Rotax 912 engine. TP10141 certification
1310SP	Factory built. 595kg TOGW with 80hp Rotax 912 engine TP10141 certification
650TC	Factory built. 650kg TOGW with 80hp Rotax 912 engine. JAR22 certification
650TCS	Factory built. 650kg TOGW with 99hp Rotax 912-S2 engine. JAR22 certification
650TCN	Factory built. 650kg TOGW with 80hp Rotax 912A engine. JAR/VLA certification
650TCNS	Factory built. 650kg TOGW with 99hp Rotax 912-S2 engine. JAR/VLA certification
650A	Factory built floatplane. 650kg TOGW. 80hp Rotax 912 engine or 100hp Rotax 914. JAR/VLA certification
650ERA	Factory built. 650kg TOGW environmental research aircraft. Retractable nosewheel and folding main wheels. Prototype I-RAWE
650T	Kit built. 650kg TOGW with 80hp Rotax 912 engine. Also designated 1450L
650SP	Kit built. 650kg TOGW with 80hp Rotax 912 engine
650T/914	Kit built. 650kg TOGW with 115hp Rotax 914 engine
710RG	Retractable undercarriage version of Sky Arrow, certificated April 2005
710 Plus	Fixed gear Sky Arrow with 710kg TOGW, certificated July 2005
750T	Factory built. 750kg TOGW with 116hp Lycoming O-235. FAR23 certification. Known as the Rondine
750TCI	Factory built. 750kg TOGW with 113hp Rotax 914 engine, cantilever wing, retracting undercarriage with main gear sponsons

Aviakit (PJB)   France

The French company, Aviakit (also known as Kitair), founded by Roland Prevôt, designed the Hermès as an ultralight kit-only two-seater. The Hermès, which had a side-by-side cabin with a bubble canopy and a cruciform tail, was constructed of wood and composite materials and was fitted with various engines in the 60 to 80 horsepower range including the Rotax 582, Rotax 912 and the Jabiru. Aviakit was acquired by PJB Aerocomposites and re-established at Troyes-Barberey as Aviakit Flight-Concept and the Hermès was relaunched as the Véga 2000. There are two basic versions, one (the Véga 2000 TR series) with all-composite construction with fabric underside wing covering and the other (the Véga 3000 CR series) of all carbon fibre construction. It is available with tricycle or tailwheel gear and there are alternative versions with a T-tail or conventional cruci-

Aviakit Vega 67-PL

form tail unit. Variants are the Vega 2000 TJ80 and Vega 3000 CJ80 with a Jabiru 2200, the Vega 2000 TR80 and Vega 3000 CR80 with a Rotax 912UL and the Vega 2000 TR100 and Vega 3000 CR100 with a 100hp Rotax 912ULS engine. It is available as a kit (sometimes referred to as the Kit Vega CTK) or factory-complete (approximately 50% being sold in this form) and, according to Aviakit, 38 examples of the Véga 2000 and 20 of the Véga 3000 have been completed.

Aviamilano   Italy

Aviamilano Costruzioni Aeronautiche was established by Ing Mario Vetri in Milan in 1955 to develop and build the F.8 Falco, designed by Ing Stelio Frati. The Falco was a beautifully proportioned and streamlined wooden low-wing two-seater with a sliding bubble canopy and retractable tricycle undercarriage. The prototype was I-RAID (c/n 101) and it first flew on 15th June 1955 powered by a 90hp Continental C.90 engine. Aviamilano launched production of the F.8L Falco I which had a larger wing than the prototype, a redesigned cockpit canopy and a higher-powered 135hp Lycoming O-290-D2B engine. The company built a series of ten aircraft (c/n 102 to 111). They then produced a further ten examples of the F.8L Falco II (c/n 112 to 121) powered by the 150hp Lycoming O-320-A2A engine and fitted with wing fuel tanks and a metal propeller. The last Aviamilano-built Falco was produced in 1958 and later production of the Falco was undertaken by Aeromere and by Laverda.

Aviamilano then moved on to another Frati design, the F.14 Nibbio. This was a scaled-up Falco with an integral four-seat cabin and a retractable tricycle undercarriage. It was powered by a 180hp Lycoming O-360-A1A engine and the prototype, I-GIAR (c/n 201), first flew on 16th January 1958. Ten production aircraft (c/n 202 to 211) were completed by Aviamilano. In 1960, Aviamilano won the Aero Club d'Italia light trainer competition with its P.19 Scricciolo designed by Luigi Pascale. This side-by-side two-seat light aircraft was of wood, tube-and-fabric construction with a fixed tailwheel undercarriage. The prototype (I-MAGY c/n 301) first flew on 13th December 1959 powered by a 95hp Continental C90-12F engine, but the production model was fitted with a 100hp Continental O-200-A and the P.19R glider-towing version, which was built from 1964 onwards, had a 150hp Lycoming O-320-A1A engine. Two batches of 25 production aircraft were built with serial numbers from c/n 302 to 351. Ten aircraft, designated P.19Tr, were fitted with tricycle undercarriages.

Aviamilano F.14 Nibbio G-OWYN

Aviamilano P-19 Scricciolo I-NEGR. M J Hooks

Aviat-Pitts   United States

The Pitts Special is one of the best-known aerobatic sports biplanes in the world and well over 2,000 have been built by amateur builders and by the Pitts factory. Constructed of tube and fabric, it was originally designed, built and flown in 1943 at Jacksonville, Florida by Curtis Pitts, specifically to meet the needs of competition aerobatic pilots, replacing designs such as the Great Lakes and Waco biplanes. This first Pitts, with a 55 horsepower engine, was followed by a succession of machines all known as S-1 Pitts Specials but differing in detail and the powerplant employed. By 1962 the standard powerplant was the 180hp Lycoming and Curtis Pitts established Pitts Enterprises, making plans available to homebuilders for the single-seat Model S-1C. Its wings had a conventional aerofoil section with a flat underside but certain Pitts models have been designed with a symmetrical 'round' aerofoil section. The cockpits of all Pitts Specials are normally fitted with sliding bubble canopies – although the aircraft are often flown without these.

In the summer of 1971, the first factory-built Pitts Specials started to come from the premises of Aerotek. Aerotek had been established by Herb Anderson, who formerly worked for Callair, as a repair and maintenance business in the old Callair plant at Afton, Wyoming. The initial model was the S-2A two-seat Pitts, which had started life as the 'Big Stinker' – created by Curtis Pitts as an aerobatic trainer. Aerotek subsequently also built the S-1S single-seater which had the round wing section and four ailerons and gained its type certificate on 13th February 1973. For many years the Aerotek factory produced annually around 12 examples of the S-1 and 24 of the S-2 but the S-1 was eventually discontinued.

In 1977, Curtis Pitts sold out all his interests in the Pitts Special to Doyle Child and in 1981 the Pitts business was acquired by Frank Christensen. Christensen had originally tried unsuccessfully to buy the Pitts designs so he went ahead with the very similar two-seat Eagle, which was sold as a fully comprehensive kit to homebuilders by Christen Industries from a plant at Hollister, California. After acquiring Pitts, Christensen ran the two businesses separately for some while, calling the Pitts activity 'Pitts Aerobatics' but, eventually, he consolidated all operations at Afton.

By 1982, there had been a marked slowdown in demand for Eagle kits – although the Pitts Special continued to take in a steady stream of

Pitts S-1 Special LV-ZZU

Aviat A-1B Husky N987P

orders. Christensen tried to buy the Piper PA-18, the Champion and the Arctic Tern high-wing designs and also developed a project to revive the Aero Commander Lark. However, Herb Anderson was pressed into creating a new original design. This tandem two-seat Christen A-1 Husky closely resembled the Piper Super Cub. It was of tube-and-fabric construction and powered by a 180hp Lycoming O-360-C1G engine with a Hartzell constant-speed propeller. Christen Industries flew the first prototype (N6070H) in 1986 and the aircraft went into production at Afton in the following year.

The company was renamed Aviat Aircraft Inc in 1988 and in March 1991 it was sold to Malcolm White of White International Ltd The ownership later passed to Stuart Horn. Since then, the Husky line has been developed into the A-1A and A-1B and a lower-powered version, the Husky Pup, has been introduced. Aviat has replaced the Pitts S-2B with the S-2C, which incorporates many features of Curtis Pitts's later S-11 Super Stinker design. They also sell plans for the S-1S and plans and components for the S-1-11B Super Stinker, three of which were completed as factory-built aircraft. In addition, they will factory-build the S-1T to customer order and still supply Eagle kits. The company has pursued a plan to put the Globe Swift back into production as the Millennium Swift with a new engine, redesigned wing and improved undercarriage design. They also acquired rights to the Monocoupe 110, which was to have been built as the Aviat 110 Special. Despite testing a reconfigured Monocoupe 110 prototype, Aviat have now shelved both these projects. Details of the models produced by Pitts and Aviat are as follows:

Aviat-Pitts S-2C N95PS

Model	Built	Notes
S-1	*	Basic single-seat Pitts Special with flat M6 aerofoil section and ailerons on lower wings only. Custom built with various engines
S-1C	*	Amateur-built S-1 from Pitts plans with various engines of 85hp to 150hp
S-1D	*	Amateur-built S-1C with ailerons on all four wings
S-1E	*	Amateur-built S-1C built from factory-produced kit
S-1S	61	Aerotek-built S-1C for competition aerobatics with round aerofoil section, four ailerons, spring steel u/c, 180hp Lycoming IO-360-B4A engine
S-1T	64	Aerotek-built S-1S with 200hp Lycoming AEIO-360-A1E engine in pressure cowling and detail alterations
S-1-11B	3	Pitts S-11 Super Stinker with reshaped tail surfaces, spring steel u/c and 300hp Lyc IO-540 engine with c/s prop. Prototype N11PU
S-2		Scaled-up S-1 with tandem two-seat fuselage and 180hp Lycoming IO-360-B4A engine
S-2A	259	Aerotek-built S-2 with 200hp Lycoming AEIO-360-A1A engine, and constant-speed prop. From c/n 2206 aircraft fitted with longer u/c and 2-inch wider front cockpit
S-2B	292	Aerotek-built S-2A with 260hp Lycoming AEIO-540-D4A5 engine, upper wing auxiliary tank and u/c and upper wings moved forward 6 inches
S-2C	69	S-2B with wings from S-1-11B, stronger airframe, reshaped tail surfaces, new cockpit and spring steel u/c. 260hp Lycoming AEIO-540 with c/s prop
S-2E	*	Amateur-built S-2A from factory-produced kit
S-2S	18	Aerotek-built S-2B without front cockpit and with twin tank fuel system
S-2SE	*	Amateur-built S-2S from factory-produced kit
A-1 Husky	399	Tandem 2-seat strut-braced high-wing light aircraft with fixed tailwheel u/c, flaps, 180hp Lycoming O-360-C1G engine. Prototype N6070H FF 1986
A-1A Husky	68	A-1 with 90 lb inc in TOGW (to 1,890 lb) and useful load, improved seating, strengthened u/c. Prototype N15LF (c/n 1395)
A-1B Husky	290	A1A with 110 lb inc in TOGW (to 2,000 lb) and useful load, new baggage hatch and rear loading extension
A-1B Husky MD	1	A-1B fitted with 200hp Lycoming IO-360 engine, fuel injection and composite propeller. Prototype N6070H (c/n 1000)
A-1B Husky Pup	9	A-1B with a 160hp Lycoming O-320 in a new cowling and fixed pitch prop, no flaps, modified wingtips. Prototype N180HY (c/n NF0001)

| 110 Special | 1 | Monocoupe 110 side-by-side two-seat high-wing tube & fabric strut-braced monoplane with fixed tailwheel u/c, powered by one 200hp Lycoming IO-360-A1B6. Prototype N110XZ FF 25 Jul 1999 |
| Millennium Swift GC-1B | | Upgraded Temco/Globe GC-1B Swift with improved wings, recontoured fuselage, 210hp Cont IO-360-ES engine. Not built |

* More than 1,200 amateur-built Pitts Specials have been completed.

During the calendar year 2004, Aviat delivered 30 A-1B Huskys, three Husky Pups and nine Pitts S-2Cs. Each of the major Pitts models has been allocated a different serial number block and, up until the end of 2004, these blocks were: S-1 c/n 1-0001 to 1-0064; S-1T c/n 1000 to 1063; S-2/S-2A c/n 2001 to 2272; S-2S c/n 3000 to 3017; S-2B c/n 5000 to 5357; S-1-11B c/n 4001 to 4003; S-2C c/n 6001 to 6071. Serial numbers for the Husky are: A-1 c/n 1001 to 1399, A-1A c/n 1400 to 1467, A-1B c/n 2001 to 2299 and Husky Pup c/n NF0001 to NF0009.

Avro   United Kingdom

A V Roe & Co Ltd (Avro) had a distinguished record going back to before the First World War. In 1935, Avro built the first example of the Avro 652 low-wing twin-engined monoplane, which was fitted with a retractable undercarriage and powered by a pair of 290hp Cheetah engines. This became the Model 652A Anson that was built in large quantities for wartime use. When the war ended the company was still building the Anson 12 with its deeper fuselage and 425hp Cheetah 15 engines. Avro modified the aircraft with oval windows and a nine-passenger cabin, and in this form it was known as the Avro 19. The majority of Avro 19s were delivered to the RAF, but 40 Avro 19 Srs 1 commercial aircraft were built (with serials in the range c/n 1204 to 1360). Early examples were diverted from RAF orders and many military aircraft (which did not have c/ns) were subsequently civilianised. A very similar version, the Model 18, was built for the Indian Government (12 aircraft c/n 1477 to 1488) and the Afghanistan Air Force (12 aircraft, c/n 1465 to 1476), and Avro built 12 examples of the Avro 19

Avro XIX G-AHKX

Srs 2 which had longer span metal wings, the prototype being G-AHKX (c/n 1333) which first flew on 13th November 1946. In total, Avro built 8,138 Ansons of all models and 2,882 were built in Canada.

Ayres   United States

Ayres Corporation took over the agricultural aircraft designs originated by Leland Snow. The Snow Aeronautical Company was formed in May 1951 as a crop spraying company. Subsequently, while Leland Snow was studying aeronautical engineering at Texas A & M in 1953 he constructed the prototype of a low-wing single-seat crop duster known as the Model S-1 and this aircraft was extensively tested in Nicaragua. Its successor, the improved Model S-2, first flew in August 1956 and it differed in many minor respects from the S-1 but followed Snow's philosophy of keeping the airframe as simple as possible. The S-2 had an open cockpit protected by a substantial rollover cage, a fixed tailwheel undercarriage and, in its initially certificated version, a variety of engines in the 240 horsepower range. The first production aircraft was rolled out from the Snow Aeronautical Corporation's plant at Olney, Texas at the end of December 1958.

Snow had also brought out a higher-powered variant with the debut, in February 1958, of the 450hp S-2B. This was followed by the S-2C, which was an S-2B with a 600hp engine in a new fuselage with the cockpit situated further forward and with a greater gross weight and hopper capacity. The load was even further enhanced with the S-2D, which made its first flight in January 1965. The S-2R, which was first

Ayres S2R N4005L

flown in December 1966, had an enclosed cockpit for the first time and featured flaps, a 400-gallon fibreglass hopper and a new undercarriage. The S-2R was the main model built by Rockwell after Snow was acquired in November 1965. The S-2R became the Thrush Commander and joined the Callair designs to give Rockwell the most comprehensive range of sprayers and dusters on offer anywhere.

In March 1970 production was relocated at Albany, Georgia and this prompted Leland Snow to leave the organisation. He went on to design the Air Tractor. On 23rd November 1977, Rockwell sold Snow to the Ayres Corporation who continued production at Albany. Ayres had been converting Snows to turboprop power for some while and it was logical for them to start manufacturing the 600hp and 700hp models of the S-2R from scratch. In the hands of Ayres, the Thrush was sold with a number of different engine options – with gross weights and useful loads relative to those powerplants. The aircraft were categorised, depending on the size of hopper fitted, into the Thrush 400 (400 US gallon/53ft³ hopper) and Thrush 510 (510 US gallon/68ft³ hopper). All the Ayres-built S2Rs (other than two specific HG models and the new T660) had a standard 6,000 lb gross weight and those with the larger hopper capacity have a reduced fuel load. In October 1979, the company also gained certification for an optional tandem two-seat cockpit that was required to provide for a training role and for transport of a ground crew member to the spraying site.

Many conversions of Thrush models have been carried out, including turboprop versions from Marsh Aviation and Page Industries. Ayres developed several quasi-military Thrushes for US State Department anti-drug missions. Based on this, they also built a prototype of the Vigilante ground-attack aircraft. Using a 1,376shp PT6A-65AG turboprop, the two-seat Vigilante, only one of which was built, was fitted with underwing hardpoints and a variety of defensive and offensive sensors.

In October 1995, Ayres announced plans for development of a specialised turboprop freighter. This became the Model LM.200 Loadmaster, which earned orders for up to 250 examples for Federal Express. It was intended that the Loadmaster, which had a high wing and fixed tricycle undercarriage, would be powered by two LHTEC CTP800 turboshaft engines driving a single nose-mounted propeller and the main fuselage compartment would carry 34 passengers in transport configuration or four LD3 cargo containers. It was intended to fly the proto-

Ayres S2R-T45DC Turbo Thrush N3298M

type in the third quarter of 1998. In August 1998, Ayres acquired a large majority (93%) holding in the Czech company, LET and started to market the L.420 (Turbolet) in the USA and intended to sell the L.610G regional turboprop to the American market (as the Ayres 7000 and military 7000M) once FAA certification was obtained. In the event, LET was forced into bankruptcy in October 2000 and the financial burden of supporting the Czech company and the startup costs on the Loadmaster resulted in Ayres going into Chapter 11 bankruptcy in November 2000. The Loadmaster prototype was under construction at this time, but Ayres ceased further work and closed down in the following year.

On 30th June 2003 the Ayres assets were acquired by Thrush Aircraft Inc. They returned to production with the Thrush 660 and embarked on a redesign of the Thrush 400 and 510 models. The different models produced to date are:

Model	Built	Notes
S-1	1	Original strut-braced low-wing open-cockpit prototype N5385N (c/n 1001) FF 17 Aug 1953
S-2	3	Pre-production version of S-1 with wing and fuselage modifications. Prototype N75882 c/n 1002
S-2A	73	S-2 built by Snow with Continental or Gulf Coast Dusting W-670-240 radial engine. 3,460 lb TOGW and 1,000 lb hopper
S-2B	19	S-2 powered by 450hp Pratt & Whitney R-985-AN1
S-2C-450	214	S-2B with increased hopper capacity and 4,400 lb TOGW
600-S-2C		S-2C with 600hp P & W R-1340-AN1 engine and 4,800 lb TOGW
600-S-2D	105	600-S-2C with 6,000 lb TOGW and 3,336 lb hopper
S-2R	1,147	Rockwell-built S-2D with enclosed cockpit etc
S2R-1340/400	219	Ayres-built S-2R with standard 53ft³ (Type A) hopper. Also known as S2R-600
S2R-R1820/510	36	Ayres Bull Thrush. Fitted with 1,200hp Wright R-1820 and enlarged 68ft³ (Type B) hopper
S2R-T11/400	20	Turbo Thrush with 500shp PT6A-11AG turboprop
S2R-T15/400	27	Turbo Thrush with 680shp PT6A-15AG turboprop
S2R-T15/510		S2R-T15/400 with Type B hopper
S2R-T34/400	224	Ayres Turbo Thrush with 750shp PT6A-34AG turboprop and Type A hopper
S2R-T34/510		S2R-T34/400 with Type B hopper
S2R-T34HG		S2R-T34/510 with 9,500 lb TOGW
S2R-T41	2	S2R-T34 with PT6A-41AG turboprop
S2R-T45		S2R-T34 with PT6A-45AG turboprop
S2R-T65/400	14	Turbo Thrush with 1,376shp PT6A-65R turboprop and Type A hopper
S2R-T65/400 NEDS	9	Special narcotics eradication herbicide spraying version of S2R-T65 for US State Dept with enlarged tandem two-seat armour-plated cockpit and extensive avionics
S2R-T65/510		S2R-T65/400 with Type B hopper
S2RHG-T65	6	S2R-T65 with increased 10,500 lb TOGW
S2R-G1		Turbo Thrush with 665shp Honeywell TPE331-1 turboprop and Type A hopper
S2R-G6		Turbo Thrush with 750shp Honeywell TPE331-6 turboprop and optional Type B hopper and dual cockpits
S2R-G10		Turbo Thrush with 940shp Honeywell TPE331-10 turboprop
S2R-R3S	11	Turbo Thrush with 600hp PZL-3S engine
V-1A Vigilante		Close support military ground-attack aircraft based on S2R-T65/400NEDS with 4 hardpoints under each wing and military electronic surveillance systems. Prototype N3100A (c/n T65-001DC) FF 15 Apr 1989
T660	10	Turbo Thrush airframe with new spring steel u/c, longer wings with separate centre section, longer fuselage, enlarged vertical fin, enlarged 660US gal split hopper and one 1,300shp PT6A-67 turboprop. Prototype N29A

Note: all Ayres-built turboprop models are named Turbo-Thrush

Serial numbers for Snows commenced at c/n 1001 for the S-1 prototype. The three S-2s were c/n 1002 to 1004. Production from c/n 1005 to 1130 was initially the S-2A but S-2Bs started to be introduced from c/n 1080. From c/n 1050 serial numbers were suffixed with a letter identifying the model concerned (eg, 1050A). From c/n 1131C to 1310C production was exclusively the S-2C. The S-2D was built from c/n 1311D to 1415D and was followed by the S-2R commencing at c/n 1416R with production by Rockwell ceasing at c/n 2393R.

Ayres have used a separate serial number series for each model:

Model	C/n Batch	Model	C/n Batch
S2R-600	2394R - 3002R	T34HG	T34HG-101 - T34HG-106
S2R-600	5001R - 5100R	S2R-G1	G1-101 - G1-115*
S2R-600	R1340-001 - R1340-035*	S2R-T65	T65-001 - T65-014*
S2R-600	D78-001 - D78-004	S2R-T65NEDS	T65-1X - T65-9X
S2R-T11	T11-001 - T11-020	S2R-G5	G5-101 - G5-104
S2R-T15	T15-001 - T15-044*	S2R-G6	G6-101 - G6-155*
S2R-T34	6000R - 6049R*	S2R-G10	G10-101 - G10-168*
S2R-T27, T34,		S2R-R3S	R3S-001 - R3S-011
T36, T41, T42	T34-001 - T34-275†*	S2R-R1820	R1820-001 - R1820-036*
S2R-T45	T45-001 - T45-010*	T660	T660-101 - T660-110

* Where appropriate, the letters 'DC' are placed after the serial number to indicate that the aircraft is the two-seat 'Dual Cockpit' model.

† The T27, T34, T36, T41 and T42 are in a common sequence and the prefix depends on the individual type – eg, T41-175DC, T36-191)

BAE Systems
United Kingdom

British Aerospace was formed on 29th April 1977 by the amalgamation of British Aircraft Corporation (Holdings) Ltd, Hawker Siddeley Aviation Ltd, Hawker Siddeley Dynamics Ltd and Scottish Aviation Ltd. Subsequently, on 30th November 1999, it was renamed BAE Systems plc.

One of the principal constituent Hawker Siddeley companies was the de Havilland Aircraft Co Ltd, which had a leading place in pre-war aviation design and production of light aircraft – including the famous series of Moths and the Dragon, Dragonfly and Dragon Rapide light transports. 1946 saw the company in full production with the Vampire fighter for the RAF, but in September of that year they flew the prototype of the DH.104 Dove all-metal twin-engined transport, which was intended to replace the obsolete Rapide. Initial Doves were built to an 8/10-seat feeder liner specification but the company soon provided a six-seat business version that was designated Dove 2. They also gained a substantial RAF order for the Devon C.1 communications transport. The following individual Dove models were built:

De Havilland DH-104 Dove 8 G-DHDV

Model	Built	Notes
DH.104 Dove 1	207	Low-wing 8/11-passenger transport with retractable tricycle u/c and two DH Gipsy Queen 70 engines. Prototype G-AGPG (c/n 04000/P1) FF 25 Sep 1945
DH.104 Dove 1B	15	Dove 1 with 340hp Gipsy Queen 70-4 engines
DH.104 Dove 2	35	Six-seat executive version of Dove 1
DH.104 Dove 2A	84	Dove 2 for North American sale
DH.104 Dove 2B	7	Six-seat executive version of Dove 1B
DH.104 Dove 3	-	Proposed high-altitude survey model. Not built
DH.104 Dove 4	95	Military Devon C.1 derivative of Dove 1
DH.104 Dove 5	33	Dove 1 with 380hp Gipsy Queen 70-2 engines. Military Sea Devon C.20
DH.104 Dove 6	25	Six-seat executive version of Dove 5
DH.104 Dove 6A	16	Dove 6 for North American sale
DH.104 Dove 7	9	Dove 5 with enlarged cockpit and raised cockpit roof with 400hp Gipsy Queen Mk 3 engines
DH.104 Dove 8	15	Dove 7 for executive use
DH.104 Dove 8A	3	Dove 8 for North American sale
Total Production	*544*	

The Dove airframe offered scope for enlargement and de Havilland stretched the fuselage, lengthened the wings and fitted four engines to produce the DH.114 Heron. The early Heron 1 had a fixed tricycle undercarriage but the majority were built with retractable gear as used on the Dove. 149 Herons were delivered between 1952 and 1964 and

the type became well known for its service with the Queen's Flight and with the Highlands and Islands air ambulance service operated by British European Airways. A number of Herons reached the United States and many were re-engined with 290hp Lycoming IO-540 engines by Riley Aeronautics Corporation. Riley also carried out a similar re-engining process on the Dove and some Riley conversions were carried out in England by McAlpine Aviation. Other more radical conversions included the stretched twin-turboprop Saunders ST-27 and Carstedt CJ600A.

Model	Built	Notes
DH.114 Heron 1	1	Enlarged 17-passenger version of DH.104 with fixed tricycle u/c, 12,500 lb TOGW and four 250hp Gipsy Queen 30 engines. Prototype G-ALZL (c/n 10903) FF 10 May 1950
DH.114 Heron 1B	50	Production version of DH.114 with 13,000 lb TOGW
DH.114 Heron 2	31	Heron 1 with retractable u/c. and 12,500 lb TOGW. Prototype G-AMTS (c/n 14007) FF 14 Dec 1952
DH.114 Heron 2A		Designation for North American deliveries
DH.114 Heron 2B	20	Heron 2 with 13,000 lb TOGW
DH.114 Heron 2C	4	Heron 2B with fully feathering propellers and 13,150 lb TOGW
DH.114 Heron 2D	37	Executive Heron 2C with 13,500 lb TOGW
DH.114 Heron 2DA		Heron 2D for North America
DH.114 Heron 2E	3	Heron 2D with dual executive/high-density cabin
DH.114 Heron 2X		Heron 2A with compressed rubber u/c dampers

De Havilland DH-114 Heron 2B G-AORG

British Aerospace BAe.125-700-II N104JG

DH.114 Heron 3	3	Heron 2D for Queen's Flight. Designated Heron C(VVIP)3
DH.114 Heron 4	1	Heron 2D for RAF. Heron C.4
Saunders ST-27		23-pax version of Heron 2 with 8ft 6in fuselage stretch, forward starboard airstair door and two 715shp PT6A-27 turboprops. Prototype CF-YBM-X FF 18 May 1969. 13 aircraft converted
Saunders ST-27A		Aerodynamic prototype for ST-27B. One aircraft only converted, C-FYBM-X, FF 18 Jul 1974
Saunders ST-27B		Redesigned low-cost version of ST-27 with PT6A-34 engines, larger vertical fin, larger windows. 1 aircraft
Saunders ST-28		Revised designation for ST-27B. One aircraft only converted, C-GYAP FF 12 Dec 1975. Fitted with enlarged cockpit and 4-bladed propellers
Carstedt CJ-600A		Heron 2 with 7ft 3in fuselage stretch and two Garrett TPE-331 turboprops

Total Production   150

In 1961, with an established reputation for building business aircraft, de Havilland embarked on design of the DH.125 business jet. Initially known as the 'Jet Dragon' (a name which was soon dropped), the DH.125 was also intended to meet a 20-aircraft RAF requirement and the military specification airframe permitted considerable later development of new models for civil customers. De Havilland became part of the Hawker Siddeley Group in January 1960. The new aircraft became the HS.125 and went into production at Chester in 1963 with CAA certification being awarded on 28th July 1964 and the first delivery to Chartag on 10th October 1964. Hawker Siddeley was clearly anxious to gain maximum penetration of the United States market and the '125 received its FAA Type Certificate on 24th October 1964.

Hawker Siddeley appointed Atlantic Aviation at Wilmington, Delaware and AiResearch in Los Angeles as American distributors and they completed the 'green' 'A'-model aircraft delivered from Chester, which were initially marketed under the old DH.125 identity. Good sales were achieved but in December 1969, a joint company was set up in cooperation with Beech Aircraft Corporation to promote the aircraft as the Beechcraft-Hawker BH.125. Within a year, however, it was

decided to let this arrangement lapse and Hawker Siddeley set up its own US marketing company.

The most significant change to the HS.125 design came in June 1976 with the first flight of the prototype HS.125-700 powered by two Garrett TFE731 turbofans in place of the Viper turbojets on the initial models. Many earlier HS.125s were subsequently re-engined. The company, which became British Aerospace (Bae) in 1977, built over 200 HS.125-700s. They were followed by the BAe.125-800 which offered a number of further improvements including increased range, a redesigned wing, rear fuselage and vertical tail and a new 'glass' cockpit with a single-piece streamlined windshield. The last major development, which was built alongside the Model 800, was the BAe.1000 with a stretched fuselage, increased range and payload and a pair of Pratt & Whitney PW305 turbofans. Details of all individual '125 models built are as follows:

Model	Built	Notes
DH.125	2	8/10-seat low-wing executive jet powered by two 2,500 lbst Bristol Siddeley Viper 502 (later 511) turbojets. Prototype G-ARYA (c/n 25001) FF 13 Aug 1962
HS.125 Srs 1	7	Production DH.125 with length increased 12in and wingspan increased 3in, larger entry door, 5 windows each side, 21,000 lb TOGW and 3,000 lbst Viper 520 engines
HS.125 Srs 1-521	1	HS.125 with 3,100 lbst Viper 521 engines and 21,200 lb TOGW
HS.125 Srs 1A	35	Production HS.125-1-521 for North American sale
HS.125 Srs 1A-522	28	Srs 1A with 3,360 lbst Viper 522 engines
HS.125 Srs 1A-S522		Srs 1A-522 converted to 21,700 lb TOGW
HS.125 Srs 1B	7	Srs 1A for non-US sale
HS.125 Srs 1B-522	7	Srs 1A-522 for non-US sale
HS.125 Srs 1B-R522	1	G-ATWH (c/n 25094) fitted with 112-gal ventral long-range tank. 22,200 lb TOGW
HS.125 Srs 1B-S522	-	Srs 1A-S522 for non-US sale
HS.125 Srs 2	20	Dominie T.1 crew trainer for RAF with extended centre section ventral fairing and 3,000 lbst Viper 301s. Prototype XS709 (c/n 25011) FF 30 Dec 1964

Raytheon Hawker 1000 N548QS

HS.125 Srs 3	2	Srs 1-522 with improved air conditioning and electrical systems and 21,700 lb TOGW
HS.125 Srs 3A	13	Srs 3 with Viper 522 engines and 21,700 lb TOGW for North American sale
HS.125 Srs 3B	15	Srs 3A for non-US sale
HS.125 Srs 3A/RA	20	Srs 3A with 112-imp gal ventral long-range tank and 22,800 lb TOGW
HS.125 Srs 3B/RA	14	Srs 3A/RA for non-US sale. 22,800 lb TOGW
HS.125 Srs 400A	69	Srs 3A with narrower airstair door, flush radio aerials, improved flightdeck and 23,300 lb TOGW. Aircraft sold by Beechcraft-Hawker designated BH.125
HS.125 Srs 400B	48	Srs 400A for non-US sale
HS.125 Srs 500		Proposed turbofan-powered Srs 400. Not built
HS.125 Srs 600A	40	Srs 400A with 24-inch fuselage stretch, 14-seat capacity, flush cockpit roof, taller fin, lengthened nose, sixth window each side and 3,750 lbst Viper 601 engines. 25,500 lb TOGW. Prototype G-AYBH (c/n 25256). Also BH.125-600
HS.125 Srs 600B	31	Srs 600A for non-US sale
HS.125 Srs 700A	151	Srs 600A with 25,500 lb TOGW, 3,700 lbst Garrett TFE731-3 turbofans, new flight control hydraulics and refuelling systems and internal improvements. Prototype G-BFAN (c/n 25258) FF 28 Jun 1976
HS.125 Srs 700B	64	Srs 700A for non-US sale. RAF CC.3
HS.125-731		Srs 400A retrofitted with TFE731-3 turbofans and Collins avionics by AiResearch
HS.125-F600B		Srs 600A retrofitted with TFE731-3 turbofans by Hawker Siddeley. Also available for earlier models
BAe.700-II		Factory-refurbished HS.125-700
BAe.125 Srs 800	276	Srs 700 with 54-inch wingspan increase, streamlined windscreen, enlarged fin, deeper rear fuselage with optional long-range tank, 5-tube EFIS, 25,500 lb TOGW and 4,300 lbst Garrett TFE731-5 turbofans. Model 800A for American and 800B for non-American sale. Prototype G-BKTF (c/n 258001) FF 26 May 1983. USAF version is C-29A. JASDF model U-125A
Hawker 800XP	471	Srs 800 with 4,460 lbst TFE731-5BR engines and 600 lb TOGW increase (to 28,000 lb), improved air conditioning, thrust reversers. First a/c, G-BVYW (c/n 258277) FF 5 Apr 1995
Hawker 800 XPi	1	Hawker 800XP with Rockwell-Collins IFIS-5000 flight information system, ProLine 21 avionics, increased baggage space and redesigned interior
BAe.1000	52	Developed long-range 125-800 with 33-inch fuselage stretch, max. 15-passenger capacity, 7 cabin windows each side, increased fuel and two 5,200 lbst P&W PW305 turbofans. Prototype G-EXLR (c/n 259001, ex 258151) FF 16 Jun 1990
Total Production	*1,285*	

In April 1992, British Aerospace announced that it was seeking a buyer for its corporate jet business in view of the high development costs involved in the next generation of the 125 line. It formed Corporate Jets Ltd as the operating company for its business jet interests and on 1st June 1993, it was announced that this company would be sold to Raytheon for £250m. The sale was completed on 6th August 1993 and the two 125 models were marketed by Raytheon Corporate Jets as the Hawker 800 and Hawker 1000. Following the renaming of Beech as Raytheon Aircraft, final assembly was transferred to Wichita in 1995 (progressively from c/n 258297 and completely from c/n 258338) but manufacture of the fuselage and wings continues at the Chester factory. The Hawker 1000 was discontinued after 52 had been built but the 800 continues as the Hawker 800XP and had reached c/n 258747 by the end of 2004.

Each model produced by the company has been given a separate series of serial numbers prefixed with a two-digit identity related to the type number. Thus, Doves carried serials c/n 04001 to 04542 and Herons were c/n 14001 to 14148. In addition, the Dove prototypes had special numbers c/n 04000/P1 and 04000/P2 and the prototype Heron was c/n 10903. Each main 125 model has had its own separate block of serial numbers as follows:

DH.125/HS.125	c/n 25001 to 25290	HS.125-700	c/n 257001 to 257215
HS.125-600	c/n 256001 to 256071	BAe.125-800	c/n 258001 to 258276
BAe.1000	c/n 259001 to 259052	Hawker 800XP	c/n 258277 to 258747+

For a period of time, Hawker Siddeley allocated an additional serial number for aircraft for North American delivery. These numbers (NA700 to NA780) applied to aircraft within the range c/n 25134 to 25287.

Beagle   United Kingdom

British Executive and General Aviation (trading as Beagle) was formed on 7th October 1960 as a subsidiary of the Pressed Steel Company under the chairmanship of Peter G Masefield. The company combined the activities of Auster Aircraft Co Ltd and F G Miles Ltd and operations were carried out both at Shoreham (Miles) and at Rearsby (Auster) with the Auster 'D' series designs giving the initial production impetus while a new series of original Beagle designs was created.

Auster had also started to develop a civil conversion of the AOP.6 known as the Auster 6A and, when Beagle took over the company, the glider tug model became the Beagle Tugmaster and a club model with improved trim was sold as the A.61 Terrier 1. The first Terrier 1 was flown in April 1961 and was followed by 17 further conversions before the Terrier 2 was introduced with enlarged tail surfaces, improved flaps and a redesigned undercarriage. Auster also built the Model D5, which was a development of the J/1U Workmaster, and this continued in production as the Beagle Husky. In addition, there were existing contracts for the Auster D.4 for Portugal that Beagle fulfilled and they built four Beagle-Auster D.6s, which were Autocars with the 180hp Lycoming O-360 engine.

The C.6 Atlantic prototype had been flown by Auster in 1967 and this resulted in the B.8 design study for a modern four-seat high-wing tourer. In turn, this led to the A.109 Airedale, which was first flown in April 1961. It was a traditional Auster tube-and-fabric aircraft fitted with a 180hp Lycoming O-360 engine. Following several weight reduction programmes, first deliveries of the Airedale were made in early 1962. Unfortunately, the Airedale's performance was lacklustre and the Piper and Cessna light aircraft that had started to be imported offered such competition that only 36 Airedales were completed.

The Auster-inspired designs were only a stopgap measure because Beagle's Shoreham design office was busy with a range of new types, which included almost everything from a single-engined trainer up to a medium twin. The first design was the Beagle 206 cabin-class twin that was an outgrowth of the Bristol 220 initiated by Masefield when he was Managing Director of Bristol Aircraft. This development was encouraged by the RAF who were in need of an Anson replacement. The prototype (G-ARRM) was a streamlined, low-wing five/seven-seater and was first flown at Shoreham in August 1961. The second prototype, the Model 206Y, which flew a year later was a larger, higher-powered version which was representative of the production civil B.206C and the military B.206R Basset. Beagle had expected a contract for up to 90 Bassets for the RAF but the Beagle 206 entered produc-

Beagle A.109 Airedale G-ARNP

tion in 1964 with only 22 military aircraft on order. The civil B.206C was built alongside the Bassets but this was rapidly upgraded with turbocharged engines to become the B.206S. Beagle also flew an aerodynamic prototype of the ten-seat Series 3 (G-25-38 c/n B074) and followed this with a single pre-production example, but development was then abandoned.

The main Miles contribution to Beagle included the designs of the Model 114 single-engined trainer and the low-wing Model 115 twin. The Miles 115 was redesigned with new flaps and two 145hp Continental engines as the Beagle M.218. It used large amounts of glass-reinforced plastic for non-structural areas and the prototype was enthusiastically received after its first flight in 1962. Because of certification problems it was extensively redesigned, as the B.242, with metal parts replacing many of the GRP components. However, financial pressures led to the B.242 programme being abandoned in early 1966 and the prototype was withdrawn from use.

Miles' single-engined M.114 design was the basis for the M.117 two/three-seat training and touring machine, which was to use similar GRP construction to that of the M.218. When the M.218 was re-engineered in metal the M.117 was similarly changed and became the B.121 Pup. A series of single- and twin-engined Pups were planned but the first prototype, which flew in April 1967, was a two-seat B.121C version with a 100hp Continental O-200A engine. This was followed by a static test unit (c/n B.002) and a four-seat second prototype with a 150hp engine (G-AVLM).

Beagle 206 Srs 1 N181WW

Beagle B.121 Pup 150 G-AZEY

Following award of the certificate of airworthiness on 28th March 1968, the company built 174 Pup airframes, including nine of a 160hp model that was largely sold in Iran. The Pup airframe involved complex multi-curvature metal construction and was, as a consequence, plagued by teething problems that were expensive for Beagle. The aircraft was also grossly underpriced and cost far more to build than had been anticipated. Nevertheless, Beagle pressed on with the next project, the B.125 Bulldog military trainer, which made its first flight in May 1969. They also spent fruitless time and funds on the Wa.116 light autogyro, which had been designed by Wing Commander Ken Wallis and was seen as having an army application.

The original owners of Beagle, Pressed Steel Fisher, were taken over by British Motor Corporation in July 1965 and a major asset was the investment in the aviation development. B.M.C. was unwilling to continue to finance Beagle with little prospect of early profit and so a deal was struck with the British Government under which Beagle became state-owned from December 1966. However, Beagle had failed to achieve adequate production volume at viable commercial prices and was losing money on every aircraft it sold. As a result, the necessary long-term financial support was denied by the Labour government of the day and the company went into receivership in December 1969. A new company, Beagle Aircraft (1969) Ltd was formed to sell off the assets and the only model to survive was the B.125 Bulldog, which was bought by Scottish Aviation and went on to gain large military orders.

In the initial stages of production of Auster designs, Beagle used the existing Auster system of serial numbers. Where AOP.6 aircraft taken in for conversion had an existing number, this was retained when it became a Tugmaster or Terrier. AOP.6s which had no serial received new allocations in the block c/n 3720 to 3744. Eventually, a new system was adopted with a completely new Beagle serial number in the following blocks:

A.61 Terrier	c/n B.601 to B.647	A.109 Airedale	c/n B.501 to B.543
Wa.116	c/n B.201 to B.205	B.218 and B.242	c/n B.051
B.206	c/n B.001 to B.080	B.121 Pup	c/n B.001 to B.177

Full details of Beagle models that reached flying status are:

Model	Built	Notes
A.61 Tugmaster	17	Glider tug conversion of AOP.6 airframes (Auster 6A). Prototype G-ARDX (c/n 1905) FF 5 Jul 1960
A.61 Terrier 1	18	AOP.6 conversion with rear bench seat, electric starter, new exhaust system and civil trim. Prototype G-ARLH (c/n 3720) FF 7 Apr 1961
A.61 Terrier 2	46	Terrier 1 with new u/c and flaps, larger tail and differential ailerons
A.61 Terrier 3	1	Terrier 2 with 160hp Lycoming O-320-B2B engine. G-AVYK (c/n B.642)
A.109 Airedale	43	Four-seat high-wing light tourer with fixed tricycle u/c and 180hp Lycoming O-360-A1A engine. Prototype G-ARKE (c/n B.501) FF 16 Apr 1961
A.111 Airedale		G-ARKE with 175hp Continental GO-300 engine
B.121 Pup 100	70	Two-seat all-metal low-wing trainer with fixed tricycle u/c and 100hp Cont O-200-A engine. Later designated B.121 Srs 1. Prototype G-AVDF (c/n B.001) FF 8 Apr 1967
B.121C Pup 150	97	B.121 with four seats and 150hp Lycoming O-320-A2B engine. Prot G-AVLM (c/n B.003) FF 4 Oct 1967. Also known as Pup 2
B.121 Pup 160	9	B.121 with 160hp Lycoming O-360-A engine
B.125 Bulldog	1	Two-seat military trainer version of B.121 with larger wing, sliding bubble canopy and 200hp Lycoming IO-360 engine. Prototype G-AXEH (c/n 001) FF 19 May 1969
B.206X	1	5/7-seat light twin with retractable tricycle u/c and two 260hp Continental IO-470-A engines. Prototype G-ARRM (c/n B.001) FF 15 Aug 1961
B.206Y	1	Enlarged B.206X with longer cabin and 310hp Cont GIO-470-A engines. Prototype G-ARXM (c/n B.002) FF 12 Aug 1962
B.206C	11	Civil production B.206 based on B.206Y. Known as Beagle 206 Srs 1
B.206R	20	Bassett CC.1 for RAF with airstair rear entry door
B.206S	44	B.206C with longer span wings and turbocharged Continental GTSIO-520-C engines
B.206Z	2	RAF evaluation aircraft for Basset programme
B.206 Srs 3	2	Ten-seat B.206 with deeper fuselage and longer cabin. Prototype G-35-28 (c/n B.074)
B.242	1	M.218 rebuilt with metal components instead of GRP parts. Prototype G-ASTX (c/n B.053) FF 27 Aug 1964
M.218	1	Four-seat light twin of metal and GRP construction powered by two 145hp Continental O-300 engines. Prototype G-ASCK (c/n B.051) FF 19 Aug 1962
Wa.116	5	Single-seat open gyrocopter powered by a 72hp McCulloch 4318A piston engine. Prototype XR942 (c/n B.201) FF 10 May 1962

Beech/Raytheon Aircraft   United States

Following his earlier successful aviation ventures with the Swallow Airplane Corporation and Travel Air Manufacturing Company, Walter H Beech founded Beech Aircraft Company on 1st April 1932. The new company, which became Beech Aircraft Corporation in 1936, acquired land and premises on Central Street to the east of Wichita, Kansas. Raytheon's main production plant and offices still occupy the same site.

Until 1981, Beech Aircraft was firmly under the control of the family – with Walter Beech in charge until his death in 1950 and then with his wife and co-founder, Olive Ann Beech, firmly at the helm. The first product of the Beech Aircraft Corporation was the Model 17 – a high-quality, high-performance five-seat cabin biplane with a retractable undercarriage which first flew on 4th November 1932. With the American economy recovering from the Depression and air racing triumphs under its belt the Model 17 sold very well and appeared in a large number of variants with a wide range of powerplants.

The aircraft that really set Beech on the path to success was the Model 18 'Twin Beech'. The first example (NC15810 c/n 62) first flew on 15th January 1937 – just as World War Two was becoming a possibility. The Model 18 was intended as a flexible light transport that would appeal to both civil and military users, but the pressures of wartime expansion meant that Beech had to move quickly to borrow the necessary funds for a much greater enlargement of the Wichita factory than had been envisaged. The war years were occupied with production of some 5,230 Expeditors, Navigators, Kansans and other variants of the Model 18 for the USA and its allies together with 412 Model 17s and 1,771 wooden AT-10 Wichita. Beech's employment level rose to a high point of 13,387 workers in 1944.

On 14th August 1945, with the end of the war, all military production came to an abrupt halt. Beech had built a strong manufacturing base but it quickly had to change its products to meet the needs of peacetime America. The Model D18S entered production as a business transport and a few Model G17s were also built with the last example (NC80321 c/n B-20) being delivered in late 1946. The war had created a large group of air-minded ex-servicemen and the company joined the rush to meet the need for 'family airplanes'.

This all-metal low-wing monoplane with its V-tail was significant for three reasons. Firstly, because it established Beech's postwar reputation for high quality, secondly because it embodied all of the new technology created during the war years and, most significantly, because the design of the Bonanza has been the basis for many of the single- and light twin-engined aircraft built by Beech since then.

The Beechcraft Bonanza 35 was certificated on 25th March 1947 (certificate A-777) and was in production from 1947 until 1981 with progressive improvement as the years went by. The 'Beechcraft' title was used on all models for many years as a marketing name, even though there was no company branded as Beechcraft Inc, but it was gradually dropped in the 1980s. In line with the policy at Cessna and Piper, Beech became accustomed to announcing a 'new model' every year – even if the change consisted of little more than a new colour scheme. The Model 33 was a version of the Bonanza, with a single fin and rudder and was used as a basis for the military Pave Eagle electronic surveillance aircraft that Beech sold to the United States Air Force in the late 1970s. On 1st May 1968 the Model 36 was certificated with an extended fuselage to give genuine six-seat capacity – and once again this was developed for the US Air Force as the QU-22B quiet reconnaissance aircraft. The Model 36 also formed the basis for the later Model 58 Baron.

The immediate post-war boom in light aircraft was short-lived, but Beech was more fortunate than most companies because it had been able to gain military orders for its new T-34 Mentor trainer. Additionally, it was building components for other manufacturers including generators for Boeing B-47s, ailerons for the Republic F-84F and wings for the Lockheed Starfire. The company also built the prototype of the 12-seat T-36A military crew trainer but this project was cancelled just prior to the prototype's first flight in June 1953. Other prototypes included the Model 34 Twin Quad transport and the Model 73 Jet Mentor, which was based on the airframe of the T-34 piston-engined trainer.

Beech had developed the Twin Bonanza which gained its approval on 25th May 1951 (5A4) and was ordered by the US Army as the L-23 Seminole, in addition to being sold on the civil market. As with the T-34, this aircraft used much of the design work provided by the Bonanza. The company was still building the Model D18S at this time, but it was becoming somewhat dated with its high-drag Pratt & Whitney R-985 radial engines. As a result, the Twin Bonanza was given an enlarged fuselage and developed into the Model 65 Queen Air, which was certificated on 4th February 1959 under type certificate 3A20. This

Beech Super 18 E18S N5609D

Beech B19 Sport 150 N2232L

led to the venerable Model 18 being discontinued in 1969 with the last Model H.18 delivery to Japan.

In its turn, the Queen Air was developed in many ways, first receiving a swept tail unit and then, later, being given a pressurized fuselage. Turboprop engines married to the pressurized Queen Air 88 resulted in the King Air 90, which was approved under the Queen Air type certificate on 19th May 1964. It is still an important model in the Raytheon range and, as with most other Beech types, it has been marketed with various engine options.

With the fuselage stretched, the King Air 90 went on to become the Model 100 and this was then given a T-tail to become the Model 200 and the later Model 300 and 350. A further stretch created the Model 1900 airliner (and with a deeper fuselage, the 1900D), which is used by many of the United States commuter airlines. All the while, Beech was selling variants of the King Air and Queen Air to the United States military forces. The unpressurized military King Air (the U-21) was sold in large numbers for service in Vietnam. Standard U-21s were used as light transports, but a plethora of special missions variants were delivered. Invariably, these had no cabin windows and were fitted with numerous blade aerials attached to wings and tail units.

Another design influence from the Bonanza was the four-seat Model 95-55 Travel Air and Baron series. The initial Travel Air was little more than a Bonanza with a Mentor tail fin and the nose-mounted engine replaced by two 180hp Lycoming engines mounted on the wings. In due course, the engine power was increased and the tail was swept to create the Baron. The six-seat Baron 58 resulted from the combination of a Model 36 stretched fuselage with existing Baron wings and tail and Beech then developed this with a pressurized cabin and with turbocharged engines. One unusual development of the Model 95 was the Marquis, which was built by SFERMA in France from Beech-supplied airframes with a pair of Turboméca Astazou turboprop engines – and this resulted in a very fast light executive aircraft. In another development, a Model 36 airframe was used to create the experimental turboprop Model 38P Lightning that Beech intended as a low-cost high-speed business aircraft and tested extensively from 1982 to 1985. This was eventually abandoned as a production model.

The company has made several attempts to build aircraft at the lighter end of the scale. On 20th February 1962 they were granted a type certificate for the Model 23 Musketeer, which was intended as a challenger for the Cessna 172 and Piper Cherokee. This was progres-

sively developed to give a series of light single-engined aircraft ranging from the two-seat Musketeer Sport to the 200hp Sierra, which was fitted with a retractable undercarriage and up to six seats.

The Beech Skipper was a completely new design with a low wing and fixed undercarriage which was sold from 1979 onwards as an alternative to the Piper Tomahawk and Cessna 150 in the light two-seat trainer market. None of the small single-engined models was really profitable but Beech felt that it was necessary to build training and entry-level aircraft in order to encourage new pilots to select a Beechcraft when they became buyers of new corporate aircraft. These types were the first to be eliminated when the 'Product Liability Crisis' emerged.

The company broadened its manufacturing base with subcontract fabrication, including a contract with Bell Helicopter to build over 1,000 Jet Ranger fuselages. Production of missile target drones, which commenced in 1956 with the KDB-1, was a very profitable activity and the Boulder division became a major supplier of hardware, including LOX storage tanks and valves, for the space programme. Beech also established manufacturing plants at Liberal, Kansas (to handle Model 23 production) and at Salina, Kansas. Many of the smaller models were axed during the product liability crisis but Beech models still in production are the A36, B36TC, 58, C90B, B200, 350, 1900D and 400A.

Diversification moves took Beech into an arrangement to sell the Morane-Saulnier Paris light business jet and, subsequently, a deal was struck for Beech to market the Hawker Siddeley HS.125 in North America. These particular entries into the business jet market resulted in few sales and both were abandoned. Beech reopened its interest in having a business jet in 1985 when it acquired all rights to the Mitsubishi Diamond light jet and put it into production with minor modifications as the Beechjet 400. In addition to corporate sales 43 T-1A Jayhawk versions of the Beechjet were sold to the US Air Force for crew training.

On 8th February 1981, Beech completed the formalities of a share exchange that turned it into a subsidiary of the Raytheon Company. Raytheon was a major supplier of equipment to the United States military forces and Beech was able to provide a valuable balance of civil and military business. Beech pushed forward with modern technology programmes including the Model 2000 Starship, which pioneered large-scale composite airframe design. The canard layout of the Starship, created by Burt Rutan, was a major design innovation for any manufacturer. Despite complications over the certification of the Starship, including a substantial increase in structural strength resulting in a gross weight increase, Beech persevered with this model but completed production in 1994 and subsequently, in 2003, bought back all the Starships for destruction in order to eliminate product liability and spares support problems, breaking up the majority after donating four to museums.

It was also evident that the Beechjet was not suitable to compete in the medium business jet market and, in July 1993, Raytheon acquired the British Aerospace subsidiary, Corporate Jets Ltd for a price of £250m. As Raytheon Corporate Jets this business built the BAe-800 and BAe-1000 derivatives of the HS.125 (renamed Hawker 800 and Hawker 1000) as the top of the Beech product line. In September 1994, Raytheon merged Beech and Corporate Jets under the new title Raytheon Aircraft and progressively moved Hawker 800 final assembly to Wichita – although wings and fuselages continue to be built at the UK factory at Chester.

Acquisition of the British Aerospace programme set Raytheon on a new course to develop a new generation of business jets. The Starship, despite its limited production success, gave Raytheon the technological base to develop the first of a completely new business jet family. The Premier I was announced in October 1995 and received its Type Certificate on 23rd March 2001. Raytheon then announced the mid-sized Hawker Horizon business jet in November 1996. This has a standard eight-seat passenger cabin and was developed by the former British Aerospace team but uses the same composite fuselage and metal wing design concept developed for the Premier I. Raytheon also announced the Model 450 which was intended to fit between the Beechjet 400A and the Hawker 800XP, but this was shelved in 2002. In 2004, Raytheon Aircraft delivered a total of 310 aircraft comprising the following: Bonanza A36 (62), Baron 58 (31), King Air C90B (27), King Air B200 (39), King Air 350 (36), Premier I (37), Hawker 400XP (28), Hawker 800XP (50).

Raytheon/Beech gives each major model a simple type number and identifies changes to the model with a prefix letter. For example, the Bonanza is the Model 35. Its 1955 version was the F35 – and the 1956 model was the G35. In general, the annual changes have consisted of increases in gross weight to allow extra seating fuel or other payload, stretches in the fuselage, additional windows, higher-powered engines and regular revisions to colour schemes. In the 1950s and 1960s detail changes to models in the Beech line-up resulted in an annual designation change, but after the mid-1960s only significant modifications warranted an alteration. The letters 'TC' were added to certain models (eg, A36-TC) to indicate the optional installation of a turbocharged engine. In some cases, a numerical or letter suffix has identified more minor changes to the type (eg, A100-1 or B200CT).

Under the Beech-designed system, where a major new type is created from an existing model, the designation is normally related to the basic type number. For instance, the Model 55 Baron was a derivative of the Model 95 Travel Air – and therefore the Baron should be correctly referred to as the Model 95-55. In practice, the full type number is seldom used. However, it is relevant to the Type Certificate documentation because, like all General Aviation companies, Beech has tried, wherever possible, to minimise the huge cost of certification by attaching new models to an existing Type Certificate. Of course, this is only practicable where a substantial proportion of the structure comes from an existing design. Otherwise a brand new Type Certificate is required. Details of all post-war Beech aircraft are as follows:

Model	Name	Built	Notes
16	-	1	Experimental all-metal low-wing light trainer. Prototype N9716Q (c/n MD-1) FF 12 Jun 1970
G17S	-	20	Postwar production D17S 'Staggerwing' with longer close-fitting engine cowling, single-piece u/c doors, new windshield, 4,250 lb TOGW and 450hp P&W R-985-AN-4 engine
D18CT	-	32	D18 'Twin Beech' equipped as nine-passenger feeder liner with 9,450 lb TOGW and two 525hp Continental R-9A engines. Corporate version – D18C
D18S	-	1,003	Model 18S for postwar business use with streamlined engine nacelles, deluxe interior, 8,750 lb TOGW and two 450hp P&W R-985 engines. First aircraft N44592 (c/n A-1)
E18S	Super 18	460	D18S with higher and longer cabin, new u/c, enlarged wings with square cambered tips, airstair door, four enlarged windows, new windshield, pointed nose and 9,300 lb TOGW. E18S-9700 has 9,700 lb TOGW
G18S	Super 18	149	E18S with new nose, cockpit and windshield, panoramic cabin centre window and 9,700 lb TOGW
H18	Super 18	149	G18S with new fully enclosed u/c, electric cowl flaps, 3-bladed props and optional Volpar tricycle u/c
23	Musketeer	553	All-metal low-wing four-seat cabin monoplane with fixed tricycle u/c, 2,300 lb TOGW, one 160hp Lycoming O-320-B engine. Prototype N948B (c/n M-1) FF 23 Oct 1961

Beech P35 Bonanza N9665Y

Beech F33A Bonanza N53LF

A23	Musketeer II	346	Model 23 with 165hp Cont IO-346-A fuel-injected engine, improved instrument panel, third window each side, 2,350 lb TOGW
A23A	Musketeer Custom III	194	A23 with 2,400 lb TOGW, and minor changes to systems and interior
A23-19	Musketeer Sport III	288	A23 with 150hp Lycoming O-320-E2C engine, two-seat standard interior with optional two rear seats, two windows each side and 2,200 lb TOGW. Club Trainer version. Prototype N2319W (c/n MB-1)
19A	Musketeer Sport	192	A23-19 with minor detail changes. Optional aerobatic version. M19A for Mexico (20 aircraft)
B19	Sport 150	424	19A with new windshield, squared-off side windows, streamlined engine cowling and spinner, 2,250 lb TOGW
B23	Custom	190	A23A with 180hp Lycoming O-360-A2G engine, 2,450 lb TOGW, two-seat aerobatic option, and redesigned engine cowling
C23	Sundowner 180	1,107	B23 with deeper side windows, streamlined windshield, improved instrument panel, standard port and starboard doors and aerobatic option
A23-24	Musketeer Super III	363	A23 with 200hp Lycoming IO-360-A2B fuel injected engine, 2,550 lb TOGW, higher useful load and improved trim. Prototype N2324W (c/n MA-1)
A24	Super	5	A23-24 with optional fifth and sixth seats, constant-speed prop and detail changes
A24R	Musketeer Super R	149	A23-24 with retractable u/c, optional fifth and sixth seats, fourth window each side, 2,750 lb TOGW. Prototype N6071N (c/n MC-1)
B24R	Sierra 200	299	A24R with 200hp Lycoming IO-360-A1B6 engine. New electric trim system, port side extra entry door, enlarged cabin windows
C24R	Sierra	345	B24R with increased fuel capacity, larger propeller, new u/c doors
26	Wichita		Beech designation of wartime AT-10
28	Grizzly	1	Beech designation for XA-38 Grizzly twin-engined attack bomber. FF 7 May 1944
33	Debonair	233	M35 Bonanza with conventional fin and tailplane, utility interior and no rear side windows. Powered by one 225hp Continental IO-470-J. 2,900 lb TOGW. Prototype N829R (c/n CD-1) FF 14 Sep 1959
A33	Debonair	154	Model 33 with rear side windows, improved interior trim, 3,000 lb TOGW
B33	Debonair	426	A33 with contoured fin leading edge, N35 fuel tank mods, P35 instrument panel and minor trim improvements
C33	Debonair	304	B33 with 'teardrop' rear side windows, enlarged fin fairing, improved seats and 3,050 lb TOGW
C33A	Debonair	179	C33 with one 285hp Cont IO-520-B, 3,300 lb TOGW. Optional fifth seat
D33	Debonair	1	S35 modified as military close support prototype with Model 33 tail, 6 under-wing hardpoints and starboard rear door. Prototype N5847K (c/n D-7859). Later Model PD249 powered by one 350hp Cont GIO-520 engine
E33	Bonanza	116	225hp C33 with improved Bonanza trim
E33A	Bonanza	85	E33 with 285hp Continental IO-520-B engine
E33B	Bonanza		E33 with strengthened airframe, full harness etc certificated for aerobatics at 2,800 lb TOGW
E33C	Bonanza	25	E33B with 285hp Continental IO-520-B engine
F33	Bonanza	20	E33 with deeper rear side windows and minor detail improvements
F33A	Bonanza	1,502	F33 with 285hp Cont IO-520-B. Later versions have longer S35/V35 cabin, extra seats and 3,400 lb TOGW
F33C	Bonanza	154	F33A certificated for aerobatics
G33	Bonanza	50	F33 with 260hp Cont IO-470-N engine 3,300 lb TOGW and V35B trim
34	Twin Quad	1	High-wing all-metal 20-passenger transport with V-tail, retractable tricycle u/c and four 375hp Lycoming GSO-580 piston engines driving two propellers. Prototype NX90521 (c/n C-1) FF 1 Oct 1947. Crashed 17 Jan 1949
35	Bonanza	1,500	All-metal four-seat low-wing cabin monoplane with retractable tricycle u/c, V-tail, 2,550 lb TOGW, powered by one 165hp Continental E-185-1. Prototype NX80040 (c/n D-1) FF 22 Dec 1945
35R	Bonanza		14 Model 35s remanufactured to B35/C35 standard with 196hp Continental E-185-11
A35	Bonanza	701	Model 35 with 2,650 lb TOGW, higher useful load and minor internal changes
B35	Bonanza	480	A35 with 165hp Continental E-185-8 engine and minor changes to flaps etc

C35	Bonanza	719	B35 with 185hp Continental E-185-11 engine, metal propeller, larger tail surfaces and 2,700 lb TOGW
D35	Bonanza	298	C35 with 2,725 lb TOGW & detail changes
E35	Bonanza	301	D35 with optional E-225-B engine, strengthened wingspar and minor detail changes
F35	Bonanza	392	E35 with extra rear window each side, strengthened wing and tail, optional auxiliary fuel tanks and 2750 lb TOGW
G35	Bonanza	476	F35 with Continental E-225-8 engine, 2,775 lb TOGW, better soundproofing and trim
H35	Bonanza	464	G35 with 240hp Continental O-470-G engine, 2,900 lb TOGW, new propeller, major structural strengthening and changes to internal trim
J35	Bonanza	396	H35 with 250hp fuel-injected Cont IO-470-C engine, optional autopilot and improved instrumentation
K35	Bonanza	436	J35 with 10 gal fuel increase, optional fifth seat and 2,950 lb TOGW
M35	Bonanza	400	K35 with cambered wingtips and detail changes
N35	Bonanza	280	M35 with 260hp Continental IO-470-N engine, 3,125 lb TOGW, teardrop rear side windows, increased fuel capacity
O35	Bonanza		N35 fitted with experimental laminar-flow wing with integral leading edge fuel tanks. Prototype N388Z (c/n AD-1)
P35	Bonanza	467	N35 with new instrument panel, improved seating etc
S35	Bonanza	668	P35 with 285hp Cont IO-520-B engine, 3,300 lb TOGW, longer cabin interior with optional fifth and sixth seats deeper rear windows, sharper tailcone
V35	Bonanza	555	S35 with 3,400 lb TOGW, external cabin air intake, single-piece windshield
V35TC	Bonanza	79	Model V35 with turbocharged TSIO-520-D engine
V35A	Bonanza	413	V35 with streamlined windshield and minor changes
V35A-TC	Bonanza	46	V35A with turbocharged TSIO-520-D engine
V35B	Bonanza	1,325	V35A with minor improvements to systems and trim
V35B-TC	Bonanza	7	V35B with turbocharged TSIO-520-D engine
36	Bonanza 36	184	E33A with 10-inch fuselage stretch, four cabin windows each side, starboard rear double doors, full six-seat interior, 285hp Continental IO-520-B engine, 3,600 lb TOGW. Prot N6235V (c/n E-1) FF 4 Jan 1968
A36	Bonanza 36	3,392	Model 36 with improved deluxe interior, new fuel system, optional club seating, 3,650 lb TOGW. 1985 model has 300hp Continental IO-550-BB engine and redesigned instrument panel and controls
A36AT	Bonanza		36 Model A36s equipped as dedicated airline trainers with 290hp Cont IO-550-B engine, 3,600 lb TOGW, 3-blade propeller, dual control columns and wing leading-edge vortex generators
A36TC	Bonanza	271	Model 36 with 3-blade propeller & 300hp turbocharged Continental TSIO-520-UB engine
B36TC	Bonanza	423	A36TC with longer span wing, increased range, redesigned instrument panel and controls, 3,850 lb TOGW
T36TC	Bonanza	1	A36 fitted with T-tail and 325hp Cont TSIO-520 engine. Prototype N2065T (c/n EC-1) FF 16 Feb 1979
G36	Bonanza		A36 fitted with Garmin G1000 integrated avionics system. Introduced 2005
38P	Lightning	1	Model PD.336 single-engined turboprop aircraft based on Model 58P airframe with modified tail and Garrett TPE331-9 turboprop engine (later P&W PT6A-40) in the nose. 5,800 lb TOGW. Prototype N336BA (c/n EJ-1) FF 14 June 1982
40	Bonanza	1	Experimental Model 35 with two 180hp Franklin engines mounted in nose driving one propeller. Prototype NX3749N (c/n E-1)
1074	Pave Eagle I	6	E33A with wingtip tanks, turbocharged Continental TSIO-520-D engine, no third rear windows and provision to be flown as a pilotless drone for military electronic surveillance as YQU-22A. Prototype 68-10531 (c/n CED-1)

Beech A36 Bonanza N56MJ

1079	Pave Eagle II	27	Military QU-22B for electronic surveillance based on Bonanza 36 with tip tanks, no rear cabin windows, powered by one 375hp GTSIO-520 engine with dorsal nose fairing housing reduction gear. Prototype 69-7693 (c/n EB-1)
45	Mentor	7	Tandem two-seat low-wing military trainer with Model 35 wings and u/c, conventional fin/rudder, 2,750 lb TOGW. Powered by one 205hp Cont E-185-8 engine. Prototype N8591A (c/n G-1) FF 2 Dec 1948. USAF YT-34 Prototype 50-735 FF May 1950 with 225hp Continental O-470-13 engine
A45	Mentor	350	Production Model 45 built as T-34A for USAF at 2,950 lb TOGW
B45	Mentor	170	Export version of A45
D45	Mentor	423	US Navy T-34B with 225hp Cont O-470-4 engine, 2,985 lb TOGW and increased fuel capacity
45	Turbo Mentor	272	T-34B modified to take a P&W PT6A-25 turboprop. Fitted with enlarged rudder and sold as T-34C to US Navy and export. Also T-34C-1 armaments trainer
46	-	1	T-36A low-wing all-metal crew trainer for USAF powered by two P&W R-2800-52 engines. Prototype c/n J-1 built but cancelled on 10 Jun 1953 before first flight
50	Twin Bonanza	11	All-metal low-wing, six-seat cabin twin with retractable tricycle u/c and 5,500 lb TOGW. Powered by two 260hp Lycoming GO-435-C2 engines. Military L-23A. Prototype N3992N (c/n H-1) FF 11 Nov 1949
B50	Twin Bonanza	99	Model 50 with 6,000 lb TOGW, higher useful load, new metal propellers, extra cabin window each side, improved cabin heating. US Army L-23B
C50	Twin Bonanza	250	B50 fitted with 275hp Lycoming GO-480-F1A6 engines. Military L-23D and RL-23D with ventral SLAR APQ-86 pod (later U-8D Seminole)
D50	Twin Bonanza	11	C50 fitted with 295hp Lyc GO-480-G2C6 engines
D50A	Twin Bonanza	44	D50 fitted with GO-480-G2D6 engines. Military L-23E (U-8E Seminole)
D50B	Twin Bonanza	38	D50A with new passenger steps, improved baggage area etc
D50C	Twin Bonanza	64	D50B with starboard rear airstair entry door, three rows of seats, improved air conditioning, larger baggage area
D50E	Twin Bonanza	47	D50C with extra port side window, squared-off rear starboard window, pointed nose and two 295hp GO-480-G2F6 engines
E50	Twin Bonanza	70	D50 with 7,000 lb TOGW and 340hp supercharged GSO-480-B1B6 engines
F50	Twin Bonanza	25	D50A with GSO-480-B1B6 engines
G50	Twin Bonanza	24	D50B with 340hp IGSO-480-A1A6 engines, increased fuel capacity and 7,150 lb TOGW
H50	Twin Bonanza	30	D50C with 7,300 lb TOGW and IGSO-480-A1A6 engines

Beech E50 Twin Bonanza N29Y

J50	Twin Bonanza	27	D50E with 340hp IGSO-480-A1B6 engines and 7,300 lb TOGW
95-55	Baron	190	B95 Travel Air with swept vertical tail, longer rear side windows, flat-profile engine nacelles, 4,880 lb TOGW and two 260hp Continental IO-470-L engines. Prototype N9695R (c/n TC-1) FF 29 Feb 1960
95-A55	Baron	309	Model 55 with optional sixth seat, narrower fin/rudder and detail changes
95-B55	Baron	1,951	A55 with full six-seat cabin, longer nose with baggage compartment, 5,000 lb TOGW. Later models fitted with single-piece windshield and progressive minor improvements
95-B55B	Cochise	70	B55 for US Army as T-42A with 5,100 lb TOGW, military interior etc
95-C55	Baron	451	B55 with 285hp injected Continental IO-520-C engines, 3-blade props, 5,300 lb TOGW and single-piece windshield
95-D55	Baron	316	C55 with minor system and trim changes
E55	Baron	434	D55 with minor system and trim changes
56TC	Turbo Baron	82	C55 with two Lycoming TIO-541-E1B4 turbocharged engines in enlarged nacelles. 5,990 lb TOGW, improved systems and trim. Prototype N2051W (c/n TG-1) FF 25 May 1966
A56TC	Turbo Baron	12	56TC with minor system and trim changes
SFERMA60	Marquis	19	Model 95 airframe with swept tail and fitted with two 450shp Turboméca Astazou IIJ turboprops. Originally named Turbo Travel Air. Prototype F-WJHC (c/n 01) FF 12 Jul 1960
58	Baron	2,096	E55 with 30-inch longer cabin, dual starboard rear entry doors, extra rear windows, 5,400 lb TOGW and two 285hp Continental IO-520-C engines. Prototype N7953R (c/n TH-1). From 1984 has 5,500 lb TOGW and 300hp Continental IO-550-C engines
58P	Pressurized Baron	497	Model 58 with pressurized cabin, 6,200 lb TOGW, 310hp turbocharged Continental TSIO-520-LB1C engines (later 325hp Continental TSIO-520-WB engines), 3-blade props and strengthened u/c.
			Prototype N3058W (c/n TJ-1) FF 16 Aug 1973
58TC	Baron	151	Unpressurized version of 58P. Prototype N158TC (c/n TK-1) FF 31 Oct 1975
G58	Baron		Model 58 fitted with Garmin G1000 integrated avionics system. Introduced 2005
60	Duke	125	Low-wing all-metal six-seat pressurized twin with retractable tricycle u/c, port side rear entry door, club seating, 6,725 lb TOGW and two 380hp Lycoming TIO-541-E1C4 turbocharged engines. Prototype N8827B (c/n P-1) FF 29 Dec 1966
A60	Duke	121	Model 60 with improved turbocharger, 6,775 lb TOGW and other minor changes
B60	Duke	350	A60 with larger cabin, increased fuel, minor trim and system changes and King Air C.90 pressurization system
65	Queen Air	315	7/9-seat low-wing all-metal cabin monoplane developed from Model 50 with new fuselage and tail, 7,700 lb TOGW and two 340hp Lyc IGSO-480-A1A6 engines. Prototype N821B (c/n L-1) FF 28 Aug 1958. Inc 72 US Army L-23F Seminole (later U-8F/U-8G)
A65	Queen Air	44	Model 65 with swept vertical tail, fourth starboard cabin window etc
A65-8200	Queen Air	52	A65 certificated at 8,200 lb TOGW
70	Queen Air	35	A65 with longer B80 wings and up to 11 seats. Prototype N7458N (c/n LB-1)
73	Jet Mentor	1	Tandem two-seat low-wing jet trainer derived from Model 45, powered by one 920 lbst Cont YJ69-T9 turbojet. Prototype N134B (c/n F-1) FF 18 Dec 1955
76	Duchess	437	Low-wing all-metal four-seat light twin with T-tail, retractable tricycle u/c, 3,900 lb TOGW and two 180hp Lyc O-360-A1G6D engines. Prototype N289BA (c/n 289-1) FF 24 May 1977
77	Skipper	312	Low-wing side-by-side two-seat trainer with fixed tricycle u/c, bubble cabin roof with forward-opening doors, T-tail and one 115hp Lyc O-235-L2C engine. Prototype N285BA (c/n 285-1) FF 6 Feb 1975
79	Queen Airliner		A65 for third-level airlines at 8,200 lb TOGW

65-80	Queen Air	148	Model 65 with swept tail, 8,000 lb TOGW and two 380hp IGSO-540-A1A engines. Prototype N841Q (c/n LD-1) FF 22 Jun 1961
65-A80	Queen Air	121	Model 80 with longer span wing, 11 seats and 8,500 lb TOGW
65-B80	Queen Air	242	A80 with extra starboard cabin window, 380hp IGSO-540-A1D engines, 8,800 lb TOGW and max 13 seats
81		1	Rutan-designed composite low-wing 5-seater with T-tail. Proof-of-Concept prototype N197RA
85D	Queen Air		Initial designation for Model 88
87	NU-8F/L-23G	1	Model A80 fitted with two 500shp P&W PT6A-6 turboprops for military use. Also designated 65-90T. Prototype 61-2902 (c/n LG-1) FF 15 May 1963
65-88	Queen Air	47	A80 with 10-seat pressurized cabin, round porthole windows and modified cockpit glazing, 8,800 lb TOGW. Powered by two 380hp IGSO-540-A1D engines. Prototype N8808B (c/n LP-1) FF 2 Jul 1965. Two conversions to Model 65-90
89	Queen Airliner		A80 for third-level airlines at 8,800 lb TOGW. Later designated Model 65-A80-8800
65-90	King Air	112	Model 88 with 9,000 lb TOGW and two 500shp P&W PT6A-6 turboprops. Prototype N5690K (c/n LJ-1) FF 21 Nov 1963. USAF version VC-6A
65-A90	King Air	206	Model 90 with 9,300 lb TOGW, redesigned cockpit, new engine de-ice system, powered by two 550shp PT6A-20 engines
65-A90-1	Ute	141	Unpressurized military Model 90 derived from Model 87 with square windows and 550shp PT6A-20 engines. Designated U-21A Ute in standard 10/12-seat 9,650 lb TOGW utility version. Variants: EU-21A for electronic surveillance; JU-21A; RU-21A reconnaissance aircraft; RU-21D – as RU-21A with upgraded electronics; U-21G upgraded for USAF from U-21A; RU-21H with higher TOGW upgraded from U-21A. All now wfu and/or civilianised
65-A90-2	Ute	3	Five-seat specialised electronic surveillance version of A90-1 designated RU-21B with PT6A-29 turboprops. First a/c 67-18077 (c/n LS-1)

Beech 77 Skipper N66301

65-A90-3	Ute	2	65-A90-2 developed as RU-21C with improved electronic equipment. First a/c 67-18085 (c/n LT-1)
65-A90-4	Ute	16	Project Guardrail V, RU-21H and RU-21E developments of RU-21D with strengthened airframes, higher gross weight and vertical blade aerials on wings and tailplane
B90	King Air	184	A90 with 9,650 lb TOGW, increased wingspan, improved aileron system, flight instruments and pressurization, new tailcone, extra (4th) side window
B90SE	King Air		Reduced specification B90 introduced 1994
C90	King Air	506	B90 with Model 100 pressurization and cabin environmental systems and 550shp PT6A-21 engines. USAF VC-6B
C90-1	King Air	54	C90 with E90 tailplane, 16% improved power output giving better cruise speed, higher pressurization level
C90A	King Air	237	C90-1 with redesigned 'pitot' engine cowlings, improved u/c retraction and electrical systems, F90-1 pressurization and heating system
C90B	King Air	410	C90A with improved soundproofing, 4-blade propellers, single-tube EFIS and Model 350-style interior. Intro Nov 1991. Japanese JASDF trainer version titled TC-90

Beech 76 Duchess D-GIGY

C90SE	King Air	6	C90B with special Jaguar colour scheme and interior
D90	King Air		Not built. Prototype c/n LK-1 abandoned
E90	King Air	347	C90 with 680shp PT6A-28 engines and 10,100 lb TOGW. Prototype N934K (c/n LW-1) FF 18 Jan 1972
F90	King Air	203	C90 with T-tail, King Air 200 wings, two 750shp PT6A-135 engines, 4-blade props, twin wheel main u/c units. Prototype N9079S (c/n LA-1) FF 16 Jun 1978
F90-1	King Air	33	F90 with PT6A-135A engines in C90A-style cowlings
H90	-	61	C90 modified as T-44A advanced pilot trainer for US Navy with special avionics and 750shp PT6A-34B engines. First aircraft Bu.160839 (c/n LL-1)
95	Travel Air	302	4/5-seat light twin based on G35 Bonanza with Mentor-style tail, faired-in nose, 4,000 lb TOGW and two 180hp Lyc O-360-A1A engines. Initially named Badger. Prototype N395B (c/n TD-1) FF 6 Aug 1956
B95	Travel Air	150	Model 95 with rounded fin leading edge, larger full five-seat cabin, 4,100 lb TOGW and minor system and trim changes
B95A	Travel Air	81	B95 with 180hp injected IO-360-B1A engines, increased baggage, N35-type rear windows and 4,200 lb TOGW
C95A	Baron		Initial designation for Model 95-55
D95A	Travel Air	174	B95A with lengthened nose, IO-360-B1B engines and minor detail changes
E95	Travel Air	14	D95A with streamlined C55 windshield and nose and minor changes
99	-	101	17-seat low-wing unpressurized all-metal third-level airliner based on Model 65-80 with lengthened fuselage, baggage-carrying nose, twin-wheel main u/c, 10,400 lb TOGW and two 550shp P&W PT6A-20 turboprops. Concept Prototype (Model PD.208) N599AT (c/n LR-1) FF Dec 1965. Prototype Model 99 (U-1) FF Jul 1966
99A	-	43	99 with 680shp P&W PT6A-28 engines
A99	-		99 with 10,650 lb TOGW and reduced fuel capacity due to elimination of nacelle tanks
A99A	Airliner	1	A99 with 10,900 lb TOGW and 680shp PT6A-27 turboprops
B99	Airliner	18	A99A with additional 115-US gal fuel capacity in nacelle tanks
C99	Airliner	77	B99 with 11,300 lb TOGW and two 715shp P&W PT6A-36 engines, improved u/c etc
100	King Air	89	B90 with 50-inch fuselage stretch (max 15-seat capacity), larger vertical tail, 2 extra windows each side, twin wheel main u/c, 10,600 lb TOGW and two 680shp P&W PT6A-28 turboprops. Prototype N3100K (c/n B-1) FF 17 Mar 1969
A100	King Air	157	Model 100 with 96 US gal additional fuel, 4-blade props, 11,500 lb TOGW, and minor changes. US Army U-21F
A100-1	King Air	3	Model 200 with PT6A-41 engines for Cefly Lancer programme as RU-21J. Later mod as C-12L
A100A	King Air		A100 with PT6A-28A engines and 11,800 lb TOGW
A100C	King Air		A100A with 750shp PT6A-36 engines
B100	King Air	137	A100A with two 715shp Garrett-AiResearch TPE331-6-252B turboprops. Prototype N41KA (c/n BE-1) FF 20 Mar 1975
C100	King Air		B100 with 750shp PT6A-135 turboprop engines
112	-		1957 twin-turboprop business aircraft project with two Lycoming T-53 engines. Not built
115	-	1	85% scale conceptual prototype for Model 2000 built by Scaled Composites Inc N2000S (c/n 1)
120	-		1962 twin-turboprop pressurized business aircraft project with two Turboméca Bastan engines. Not built
200	Super King Air	809	Model 100 with T-tail, increased wingspan, extra fuel, improved pressurization system, two 850shp P&W PT6A-41 turboprops, 12,500 lb TOGW and detailed systems and trim changes. Prototype N38B (c/n BB-1) FF 27 Oct 1972
200C	Super King Air	92	Model 200 with large rear cargo door
200T	Super King Air	23	Model 200 for aerial survey or maritime patrol with wingtip fuel tanks, 14,000 lb TOGW, under-fuselage fairing housing vertical cameras or electronic equipment
200CT	Super King Air	1	200T with rear cargo door
A200	Super King Air	105	Model 200 with 750shp PT6A-38 engines. C-12A transport for USAF/Army and C-12C with PT6A-41 engines for US Army
A200C	Super King Air	66	A200 for US Navy/Marines as UC-12B with PT6A-41 engines, rear cargo door. UC-12F with upgraded avionics and u/c and PT6A-42 engines. TC-12B pilot trainer. UC-12M is UC-12B/UC-12F with improved cockpit and communications. NC-12B is UC-12B with sonobuoy launchers. RC-12F is UC-12F with surface search radar. Reconnaissance RC-12M has new wings, surface search radar
A200CT	Super King Air	100	A200C for US Army as C-12D with large cargo door, strengthened u/c and wing. Some with tip tanks. Also RC-12D with Guard Rail advanced electronic surveillance mods and no cabin windows, RC-12H Guard Rail V, RC-12K for special electronic missions with 19ft cargo door, enlarged u/c and PT6A-67 engines. RC-12G tactical field support model. RC-12N is RC-12K with -67 engines and increased payload. RC-12P is RC-12N with increased weights and improved electronic systems. RC-12Q is RC-12P with PME (Professional Military Education) improvements and roof-mounted radome
B200	Super King Air	994	200 with 850shp PT6A-42 engines. 4-blade McCauley props, improved interior and systems. Introduced 1992
B200SE	Super King Air	7	Reduced-cost B200 with 3-blade props and pre-specified avionics. Introduced 1994
B200C	Super King Air	116	B200 with 52 x 52-inch cargo door. PT6A-42 engines. USAF C-12F, C-12T with updated cockpit, C-12U with new hydraulic u/c system. C-12R with Bendix EFIS for US Army as personnel/cargo transport
B200CT	Super King Air	8	B200C with supplementary wingtip tanks
B200T	Super King Air	23	B200CT without rear cargo door
300	Super King Air	249	B200 with two 1050shp PT6A-60A engines with 4-blade props in longer cowlings with larger air intakes, extended wing leading edges, 14,000 lb TOGW, trim and system changes. Prototype N4679M (c/n BB-343) FF 6 Oct 1981
300LW	Super King Air		Model 300 certificated to 12,500 lb TOGW for European tax reasons
B300	King Air 350	399	11/13-seat Model 300 with 34-inch fuselage stretch, two extra windows each side, 41-inch wingspan increase and wingtip winglets. PT6A-60A engines. 15,000 lb TOGW. Prototype N6642K (c/n FA-1). USAF C-12S with quick cargo modification

Beech King Air 100 N122U

B300C	King Air 350C	12	Model 350 with cargo door. Prototype N1564D (c/n FM-1)
390	Premier I	116	Model PD-374, 6-seat business jet of all-composite construction powered by two 2,300 lbst Williams/RR FJ44-2A turbofans
400	Beechjet 400	65	Mitsubishi MU-300 Diamond I acquired by Beech, fitted with modified internal trim and systems
400A	Beechjet 400A	363	Model 400 with 13ft³ larger cabin, double club seating, EFIS cockpit and 45,000ft operational ceiling. Prototype N1551B (c/n RJ-51)
400XP	Hawker 400XP	30	Model 400A with 200 lb TOGW increase, TCAS, thrust reversers and new air conditioning. Introduced 2003 from c/n RK-344
400T	Jayhawk	193	Military 400A for USAF TTTS program with strengthened u/c, revised fuel system and extra fuselage tank and fewer cabin windows. Designated T-1A. Prototype N2886B (c/n RK-12 – later c/n TT-1) FF 5 Jul 1991. Also for Japan (1st a/c 41-5051 c/n TX-1)
390	Premier I	105	Light business jet with 6-pax cabin, composite fuselage, metal wing, powered by two 2,300 lbst Willams FJ44-2A turbofans. 12,500 lb TOGW. Prototype N390RA (c/n RB-1) FF 22 Dec 1998
390	Premier IA	1	Premier I with redesigned interior with increased headroom, IFIS-5000 flight information system, ProLine 21 avionics
800XP	Hawker 800XP		Detailed under BAE Systems section
1300		14	13-seat commuter version of Model 200 with belly cargo pod and ventral fins
1900	Airliner	3	21-seat third-level airliner or business aircraft based on Model 200 with fuselage stretch, dual airstair doors, two 850shp PT6A-65B turboprops, extra horizontal tail surfaces on lower rear fuselage, tailplane finlets. Prototype N1900A (c/n UA-1) FF 3 Sep 1982. Military C-12J
1900C	Airliner	74	1900 with starboard rear cargo door in place of airstair
1900C-1	Airliner	180	1900C with 'wet' wings increased fuel and redesigned fuel system. Includes 6 C-12J for US Army/ANG

Raytheon King Air C90B YV-1074CP

1900D	Airliner	439	1900 with 14-inch deeper fuselage, new pressurization, larger entry door, larger windows, wingtip winglets and two PT6A-67 turboprops. Prototype N5584B (c/n UE-1) FF 1 Mar 1990. Replaced 1900C, Oct 1991
2000	Starship I	43	10-seat business aircraft of all-composite construction and canard design with two P&W PT6A-67 turboprops mounted on wings in pusher configuration. Prototype N2000S (c/n NC-1) FF 15 Feb 1986. All grounded, 2003
2000A	Starship I	10	Model 2000 with 8-seat capacity, higher TOGW, longer cabin, stronger u/c and centre section and increased range
-	UTT	1	Medium-size utility transport test aircraft with two tandem high wings and twin turboprop engines. Designed by Scaled Aircraft Composites. Prototype N133SC FF 29 Dec 1987
3000	Beech Mk III	100	PD.373. Modified Pilatus PC-9 built under licence by Beech as the Beech Mk III. Re-titled T-6A Texan II for US and other military deliveries. Prototype N26BA (c/n PT-1). Production Prototype N8284M (c/n PT-2). FF Dec 1992

Raytheon Premier I N380RC

Raytheon Hawker 4000 Horizon N803HH

4000	Hawker Horizon	3	Super-midsize low-wing business jet with T-tail, composite fuselage, metal wings, 8-pax cabin, 36,000 lb TOGW. Powered by two 6,500 lbst P&WC PW308A turbofans. Prototype N4000R (c/n RC-1) FF 11 Aug 2001
PD.290	King Air 400	1	Experimental conversion of King Air 200 N38B (c/n BB-1) with two P&W JT15D-4 turbojets. FF 15 Mar 1975

The Beech serial system clearly defines the individual aircraft model and separates sub-models of the basic type. Before the war, Beech had used a simple numerical basis for its construction numbers; aircraft Number 1 was the Beech 17, NC499R, and the system continued chronologically from there. However, the large volume of Beech 18 production placed stress on this method of numbering and Beech established a new and more flexible formula for its post-war production.

The post-war system consists of an alphabetical prefix denoting the aircraft model and a chronological number for the individual aircraft. Each design is given a basic letter prefix and variants of the primary model are identified by an additional subsidiary letter. For instance, the King Air 100 has numbers prefixed B- (eg, B-67) but the later B100 has BE- construction numbers (eg, BE-3). Models based on the Model 65 Queen Air, such as the Model 70, Model 88 and Model 90, have numbers in the L- series and Travel Air and Baron variants are in the T-series. Quite often the primary letters have been re-used – for instance, where only a prototype was built. Thus, the Beech Jet Mentor prototype used the number F-1, but this block was subsequently applied to production King Air 300s (eg, FF-1). The system shows numerous anomalies that have materialised as the number of models has grown, but the primary prefixes used have been as follows:

Prefix	Model	Prefix	Model	Prefix	Model
A	18	G	Mentor	M	23 Musketeer srs
B	King Air 100/200	H	Twin Bonanza	P	Duke
C	Starship	K	Unmanned	R	Beechjet
D	Bonanza 33/35		target drones	T	Travel Air & Baron
E	Bonanza 36	L	Queen Air/	U	Model 99 & 1900
F	King Air 300		King Air 90	W	Skipper

At one time, it was normal for the subsidiary letter to be placed in front of the basic prefix, but Beech now tends to put this second letter after the primary letter (eg, EA- for the Model A36TC). This feature is clear from the detailed table of serial numbers.

Having allocated the prefix letters to a new model, Beech normally gives numbers to individual aircraft in strict sequence (for instance, King Air 100 production was B-1, B-2, B-3, B-4 etc). Civil, military and export aircraft of the same model are included, so there are normally no gaps in the sequence. There have, however, been variations to this arrangement. Sometimes an existing type forms the basis for a new variant and existing airframes are converted on the production line and given new serial numbers in a different series. For example, the Super King Air 200s ordered by the French IGN organisation were fitted with extensive modifications for survey and mapping operations. They were originally allocated serial numbers in the BB- series used by standard Super King Airs, but later received the designation Model 200T and new serials starting at BT-1. The old serials were not reallocated and appeared as gaps in the numbering sequence. In a similar way, the first 51 aerobatic Bonanza E33Cs and F33Cs were converted from E33A and G33 aircraft, which exchanged their CE- and CD- numbers for CJ- prefixed serials.

Certain non-standard construction numbers have been used from time to time – particularly for rebuilt aircraft. The 1951 remanufacture of Bonanzas to C35 standard resulted in these aircraft having the letter 'R' with a rebuild number added to the end of the existing serial (eg, D-535R6). A number of L-23 Seminoles have been modified at the factory to meet a variety of Army tasks. These L-23s had their serial numbers revised with the letter 'R' in front of the existing serial and a suffix letter after the basic letters 'LH-'. One reworked Seminole, converted with APW radar, was given the new identity RLHE-2. In a similar way, the 'R' prefix was also used for a rework programme on the Musketeer, which resulted in serials in the RM- series.

Special situations where non-standard numbers had to be applied included a King Air 90 that was given the serial LJ-178A as a result of a production line complication. Beech has also used different serial prefixes to identify batches of aircraft delivered to export customers. The Model 45 Mentors built for Japan, Canada and the Argentine used JG-, CG- and AG- prefixes. The T-34 aircraft built under licence by Canadian Car & Foundry carried special numbers prefixed CCF34- (eg, CCF34-26).

Beech has always undertaken a large amount of subcontract work for other manufacturers. A separate numbering system is used for such components – normally based on the primary manufacturer's serial system. Such serial number examples include BC-JH-2 for a Bell 206A fuselage assembly, LBT-G-1 for a Lockheed F-104 fuel tank and MR-301-1 for an F-101 rudder assembly. The company also gives some of its prototypes serial numbers that reflect their Project Design Number. The Beech Duchess is a good example; it was given the Project Number PD-289 by the Beech design office and its prototype carried the serial number 289-1. The other exception to the 'standard' system is the Hawker 800XP, which continues to use the c/n sequence started by British Aerospace. This had reached c/n 258680 by mid-2004. Production of the Hawker 125-1000 was completed at c/n 259052.

Full details of Beech Aircraft serial number batches are shown in this summary table:

Model	Serial Batch	Notes
D18S	A-1 to A-1828	From A-1036 reallocated as MD- and BA-
D18CT	AA-1 to AA-32	A- serials reallocated
C-45G/H	AF-1 to AF-900	US Air Force rebuilds
3N, 3NM, 3TM	CA-1 to CA-281	For Canadian AF (ex A- serials)
E18S, G18S, H18	BA-1 to BA-460	Excluding BA-434, plus BA-497
G18S	BA-461 to BA-617	Excluding BA-497, BA-580. Plus BA-434
H18	BA-618 to BA-765	Plus BA-580

Raytheon King Air B200 LV-WEW

Raytheon Beech 1900C N151YV

G17S	B-1 to B-20	Postwar production
100	B-1 to B-89	Plus B-93
A100	B-90 to B-247	Excluding B-93. B-205 became BE-1
200, A100-1	BB-1 to BB-912	Some changed to BL-,BT- c/ns
B200	BB-913 to BB1866+	Some changed to BL-,BT- c/ns. Inc Model 1300. Current
A200	BC-1 to BC-75	US Army C-12C
A200	BD-1 to BD-30	US Air Force C-12A
B100	BE-1 to BE-137	
C100	BF-	
A200C	BJ-1 to BJ-66	US Navy UC-12B
200C	BL-1 to BL-146	Excluding BL-24,58,59,60 & BL-113 to 117. C-12F, C-12T, C-12U
B200C	BL-37 to BL-148	Excluding BL-114 to 117. Ex BB- c/ns. C-12F
200CT, B200CT	BN-1 to BN-9	Converted from BL-24, 58, 59 & 60 etc
A200CT	BP-1 to BP-71	US Army C-12D, C-12F, C-12T. Some converted to FC- & GR-
200T, B200T	BT-1 to BT-46	Current. Converted from BB- numbers
A200C	BU-1 to BU-12	US Navy UC-12F, RC-12F
A200C	BV-1 to BV-12	US Navy UC-12M
B200C	BW-1 to BW-29	US Army C-12R
34	C-1	
2000	NC-1 to NC-53	
35	D-1 to D-10403	
O-35	AD-1	
33, A33	CD-1 to CD-387	
B33	CD-388 to CD-813	
C33	CD-814 to CD-1118	
E33	CD-1119 to CD-1234	
F33	CD-1235 to CD-1254	
G33	CD-1255 to CD-1325	CD-1305 to 1325 became CJ-31 to 51
C33A	CE-1 to CE-179	
E33A	CE-180 to CE-289	CE236 to 248 became CJ-1 to 13; CE-251 to 255, CE-257 to 259, CE-261 to 263, CE-269 became CJ-14 to 25
F33A	CE-290 to CE-1791	
1074	CED-1 to CED-6	US Air Force YQU-22A
E33C, F33C	CJ-1 to CJ-179	Incl Conversions from CE- and CD- s/ns
2000	NC-1 to NC-53	
36, A36	E-1 to E-3576+	Currently in production

A36TC, B36TC	EA-1 to EA-694+	
1079	EB-1 to EB-27	US Air Force QU-22B
T36TC	EC-1	
38P	EJ-1	
300	FA-1 to FA-230	
A200CT	FC-1 to FC-3	US Army C-12D, RC-12D. Some ex BP- c/ns
A200CT	FE-1 to FE-36	US Army RC-12K, RC-12N, RC-12P
300	FF-1 to FF-19	Federal Aviation Administration
A200CT	FG-1 to FG-2	RC-12K Huron for Israel
B300	FL-1 to FL-370+	Model 350. In production
B300C	FM-1 to FM-11+	In production
B300C	FN-1	Model 350C
45, A45	G-1 to G-1098	Some to BG-, CG- numbers. USAF T-34
45	AG-1 to AG-75	Argentine-built T-34
45	BG-1 to BG-423	US Navy T-34B
B45	CG-1 to CG-319	Some converted to AG- and JG- numbers
45	DG-	T-34B
45	JG-1 to JG-50	Japanese T-34. Some ex CG- numbers
45	GL-1 to GL-353	US Navy T-34C
45	GM-1 to GM-98	T-34C-1 for Morocco, Indonesia etc
45	GP-1 to GP-51	T-34C-1 for Algeria. Some ex GM- c/ns
A200CT	GR-1 to GR-18	US Army RC-12K. Some ex BP- c/ns
50	H-1 to H-1021	Overall sequence. H-12 onwards reallocated as DH, EH etc
50	H-1 to H-11	Initial production
B50	CH-12 to CH-110	H-12 up reallocated
C50	CH-111 to CH-360	H- series reallocated
D50	DH-1 to DH-347	H- series reallocated
E50	EH-1 to EH-70	H- series reallocated
F50	FH-71 to FH-96	H- series reallocated. Excluding FH-94
G50	GH-97 to GH-119	H- series reallocated
H50	HH-120 to HH-149	H- series reallocated
J50	JH-150 to JH-176	H- series reallocated
E50	LH-96 to LH-195	US Army L-23 (U-8D)
E50	LHC-3 to LHC-10	Ex LH- numbers. SLAR and CYFLY mod
E50	LHD-	Project Michigan mod L-23
E50	LHE-6 to LHE-16	Ex LH- numbers. APW-radar mod RU-8D
E50	RLH-1 to RLH-93	
Missile Targets	K-	Various prefixes BK to GK, KA to KT
65	L-1 to L-6	Basic Queen Air prefix. L-23F

Raytheon BeechJet 400A N32AA

F90, F90-1	LA-1 to LA-236		T-6A	PG-1 up	T-6A for Greece
70	LB-1 to LB-35		T-6A	PF-1 up	T-6A for NATO, Canada
65	LC-1 to LC-239		35R	R-1 to R-14	Excluding R-8. Model 35 remanufactured to C35
A65	LC-240 to LC-335		Premier I	RB-1 to RB-116+	Current production
80	LD-1 to LD-150	Excluding LD-34, LD-46	4000 Horizon	RC-1 up	
A80	LD-151 to LD-269	Plus LD-34, LD-36	A200CT	GR-1 to GR-19	US Army RC-12D, RC-12H
B80	LD-270 to LD-511		400	RJ-1 to RJ-65	Built from Mitsubishi components
90	LE-0	Experimental F90 King Air ex c/n LA-1	400A	RK-1 to RK-394+	Current production
65	LF-7 to LF-76	US Army L-23F (U-8F)	55	TC-1 to TC-190	
87	LG-1	NU-8F/YU-21 prototype	A55	TC-191 to TC-501	Excluding TC-350, 371
90, A90, B90, C90	LJ-1 to LJ-1062	Plus LJ-178A	B55	TC-502 to TC-2456	Plus TC-350, 371. TC-1393 to 1396 and TC-1402 became TF-66 to 70
C90A	LJ-1063 to LJ-1299	Excluding LJ-1288, 1295			
C90B	LJ-1299 to 1715+	Plus LJ-1288, 1295. Current production	SFERMA.60	STC-1 to STC-19	Marquis conversion of Model 95
D90	LK-1	Not completed	95	TD-1 to TD-302	
H90	LL-1 to LL-61	US Navy T-44A	B95	TD-303 to TD-452	
A90-1	LM-1 to LM-141	U-21A, RU-21A, RU-21D, U-21G	B95A	TD-453 to TD-533	
85	LN-1	Became Model 88 prototype	D95A	TD-534 to TD-707	
65-88	LP-1 to LP-47	LP-27, 29 to LJ-178A, LJ-116	E95	TD-708 to TD-721	
PD.208	LR-1	Model 99 development prototype	C55	TE-1 to TE-451	Excluding TE-50
A90-2	LS-1 to LS-3	RU-21B	D55	TE-452 to TE-767	
A90-3	LT-1 to LT-2	RU-21C for Civil Air Patrol	E55	TE-768 to TE-1201	
A90-4	LU-1 to LU-16	RU-21H	B55B (T-42A)	TF-1 to TF-70	US Army. TF-66 to 70 for Turkish Army
E90	LW-1 to LW-347		56TC	TG-1 to TG-83	
SNB-4, -5	M-1 to M-88	US Navy Model 18 rebuilds	A56TC	TG-84 to TG-94	
JRB-4	M-144 to M-168	US Navy upgrade programme	58	TH-1 to TH-2096+	Current production
23 to C23	M-1 to M-2392		58P	TJ-1 to TJ-497	
24	MA-1 to MA-368		58TC	TK-1 to TK-151	
19A, B19	MB-1 to MB-905		400T	TT-1 to TT-180	USAF T-1A Jayhawk
24R	MC-1 to MC-795	Excluding MC-151	400T	TX-1 to TX-13	Japanese T400 military trainer
16	MD-1		99 & 99A	U-1 to U-147	Excluding U-146
18MD	MD-1 to MD-26	New SNB-5 for MDAP (ex A-1036 to A-1061)	B99	U-148 to U-164	Plus U-146
76	ME-1 to ME-437		C99	U-165 to U-239	
45	FM-	Fuji built T-34	1900	UA-1 to UA-3	1900 prototypes
18	N-1 to N-1144	US Navy Model 18 rebuilds	1900C	UB-1 to UB-74	
60	P-1 to P-126	Excluding P-123	1900C-1	UC-1 to UC-174	
A60	P-127 to P-246	Plus P-123	1900C-1	UD-1 to UD-6	C-12J for US Army/ANG
B60	P-247 to P-596		1900D	UE-1 to UE-439	
T-6A	PT-1 up	Beech Mk III version of Pilatus PC9	77	WA-1 to WA-312	

Beech / Raytheon Annual Model Designations 1946 to 2005

Model	1946	1947	1948	1949	1950	1951	1952	1953	1954	1955	1956	1957
18 'Twin Beech'	D18S	D18S	D18S	D18S	D18S	D18S	D18S	D18S	D18S	D18S	D18S	D18S
18S Super 18										E18S	E18S	E18S
35 Bonanza		35	35	A35	B35	C35	C35	D35	E35	F35	G35	H35
50 Twin Bonanza							50	B50	C50	C50	D50	D50
50 Twin Bonanza												E50

Model	1958	1959	1960	1961	1962	1963	1964	1965	1966	1967	1968	1969
18S Super 18	E18S	E18S	G18S	G18S	G18S	H18	H18	H18	H18	H18	H18	H18
19 Musketeer Sport									A23-19	A23-19	19A	19A
23 Musketeer						23	A23	A23	A23A	A23A	B23	B23
24 Musketeer Super									A23-24	A23-24	A23-24	A23-24
33 Debonair			33	A33	B33	B33	B33	C33	C33	C33	E33	E33
33C Bonanza											E33C	E33C
35 Bonanza	J35	K35	M35	N35	P35	S35	S35	S35	S35	V35	V35	V35A
35TC Bonanza TC										V35-TC	V35-TC	V35A-TC
36 Bonanza											36	36
50 Twin Bonanza	D50A	D50B	D50C	D50E	D50E	D50E						
50 Twin Bonanza	F50	G50	H50	J50	J50	J50						
55 Baron				55	A55	A55	B55	B55	B55	B55	B55	B55
55 Baron									C55	C55	D55	D55
56 Turbo Baron										56TC	56TC	56TC
60 Duke											60	60
65 Queen Air			65	65	65	65	65	65	65	A65	A65	A65
70 Queen Air												70
80 Queen Air					80	80	A80	A80	B80	B80	B80	B80
88 Queen Air								88	88	88	88	88
90 King Air							90	90	A90	A90	B90	B90
95 Travel Air	95	95	B95	B95A	B95A	D95A	D95A	D95A	D95A	D95A	E95	
99 Airliner											99	99
100 King Air												100

Model	1970	1971	1972	1973	1974	1975	1976	1977	1978	1979	1980	1981
19 Sport	B19	B19	B19	B19	B19	B19	B19	B19	B19			
23 Sundowner	C23	C23	C23	C23	C23	C23	C23	C23	C23	C23	C23	C23
24 Super	A24											
24R Super R					B24R	B24R	B24R	C24R	C24R	C24R	C24R	C24R
33 Bonanza	F33		G33	G33								
33A Bonanza	F33A	F33A	F33A	F33A	F33A	F33A	F33A	F33A	F33A	F33A	F33A	F33A
33C Bonanza				F33C	F33C	F33C	F33C	F33C	F33C	F33C		
35 Bonanza	V35A	V35B	V35B	V35B	V35B	V35B	V35B	V35B	V35B	V35B	V35B	V35B
35 Bonanza TC	V35A-TC	V35B-TC	V35B-TC	V35B-TC								
36 Bonanza	A36	A36	A36	A36	A36	A36	A36	A36	A36	A36	A36	A36
36 Bonanza TC										A36TC	A36TC	A36TC
55 Baron	B55	B55	B55	B55	B55	B55	B55	B55	B55	B55	B55	B55
55 Baron	E55	E55	E55	E55	E55	E55	E55	E55	E55	E55	E55	E55
56 Turbo Baron	A56TC	A56TC										
58 Baron	58	58	58	58	58	58	58	58	58	58	58	58
58P Baron							58P	58P	58P	58P	58P	58P
58TC Baron							58TC	58TC	58TC	58TC	58TC	58TC
60 Duke	A60	A60	A60	A60	B60	B60	B60	B60	B60	B60	B60	B60
65 Queen Air	A65											
70 Queen Air	70	70										
76 Duchess									76	76	76	76
77 Skipper										77	77	77
80 Queen Air	B80	B80	B80	B80	B80	B80	B80					
88 Queen Air												
90 King Air	B90	C90	C90	C90	C90	C90	C90	C90	C90	C90	C90	C90
90 King Air					E90	E90	E90	E90	E90	E90	E90	
90 King Air										F90	F90	F90
95 Travel Air												
99 Airliner	99A	99A	B99	B99	B99	B99	B99					C99
100 King Air	100	100	A100	A100	A100	A100	A100	A100	A100	A100		
100 King Air								B100	B100	B100	B100	B100
200 Super King Air					200	200	200	200	200	200	200	200
200 Super King Air											200C	200C
1900												1900

Model	1982	1983	1984	1985	1986	1987	1988	1989	1990	1991	1992	1993
23 Sundowner	C23	C23	C23									
24R Sierra	C24R											
33 Bonanza	F33A	F33A	F33A	F33A	F33A	F33A	F33A	F33A	F33A	F33A	F33A	F33A
33 Bonanza					F33C	F33C	F33C					
36 Bonanza	A36	A36	A36	A36	A36	A36	A36	A36	A36	A36	A36	A36
36 Bonanza											A36AT	
36 Bonanza TC	A36TC	B36TC	B36TC	B36TC	B36TC	B36TC	B36TC	B36TC	B36TC	B36TC	B36TC	B36TC
55 Baron	B55	B55	B55									
55 Baron	E55		E55	E55								
58 Baron	58	58	58	58	58	58	58	58	58	58	58	58
58P Baron	58P	58P	58P	58P	58P	58P	58P					
58TC Baron	58TC	58TC										
60 Duke	B60											
76 Duchess	76	76	76	76	76							
77 Skipper	77	77										
90 King Air	C90	C90-1	C90A	C90A	C90A	C90A	C90A	C90A	C90A	C90A	C90A	C90A
90 King Air	F90	F90-1	F90-1	F90-1	F90-1	F90-1						
99 Airliner	C99	C99	C99	C99	C99							
100 King Air	B100	B100	B100									
200 Super King Air	B200	B200	B200	B200	B200	B200	B200	B200	B200	B200	B200	B200
200 Super King Air	B200C	B200C	B200C	B200C	B200C	B200C	B200C	B200C	B200C	B200C		
200 Super King Air		B200T	B200T	B200T	B200T	B200T						
300 Super King Air			300	300	300	300	300	300	300	300/LW	300/LW	
300 Super King Air									B300	B300	B300	B300
300 Super King Air												B300C
Model 1300							1300	1300	1300			
Model 1900	1900C	1900C	1900C	1900C	1900C	1900C	1900C	1900C	1900C	1900C	1900D	1900D
400 Beechjet					400	400	400	400A	400A	400A	400A	400A
400 Beechjet										400T	400T	
2000 Starship									2000	2000	2000A	2000A

Model	1994	1995	1996	1997	1998	1999	2000	2001	2002	2003	2004	2005
33A Bonanza	F33A	F33A	F33A									
36 Bonanza	A36	A36	A36	A36	A36	A36	A36	A36	A36	A36	A36	A36
36 Bonanza TC	B36TC	B36TC	B36TC	B36TC	B36TC	B36TC	B36TC	B36TC	B36TC			
58 Baron	58	58	58	58	58	58	58	58	58	58	58	58
90 King Air	C90B	C90B	C90B	C90B	C90B	C90B	C90B	C90B	C90B	C90B	C90B	C90B
200 Super King Air	B200	B200	B200	B200	B200	B200	B200	B200	B200	B200	B200	B200
350 Super King Air	300SE											
350 Super King Air	B300C	B300C	B300C	B300C	B300C	B300C	B300C	B300C	B300C	B300C	B300C	B300C
Model 1900	1900D	1900D	1900D	1900D	1900D	1900D	1900D	1900D	1900D	1900D		
400 Beechjet	400A	400A	400A	400A	400A	400A	400A	400A	400A	400XP	400XP	400XP
Hawker 800	800	800XP	800XP	800XP	800XP	800XP	800XP	800XP	800XP	800XP	800XP	800XP
Hawker 1000	1000	1000	1000	1000								
2000 Starship	2000A	2000A	2000A									
390 Premier I										390	390	390
4000 Horizon												4000

**Beech 2000 Starship I
N26RA**

Beech B60 Duke N430BD

Beech 55 Baron HB-GCG

Raytheon King Air 350 N5149F

Bellanca   United States

In 1937, the Bellanca Aircraft Corporation flew the prototype Model 14-7 Junior from its base at New Castle, Delaware. The Junior was a single-engined low-wing cabin monoplane and the prototype (NX19195 c/n 1001) made its first flight in December 1937. The designation 14-7 was derived from the wing area (140ft²) together with the rating of its 70hp Le Blond 5E engine. The fuselage was designed to give aerofoil lift – a feature that had been introduced on a number of other prototypes of the period. It was soon apparent that its 70hp powerplant was inadequate, so a 90hp Le Blond engine was installed and the aircraft, redesignated Model 14-9, received its type certificate on 24th August 1939.

The 14-9 was designed to carry three people and was distinctive in having a retractable tailwheel undercarriage. It was also notable for the small endplate fins fitted to the tips of the tailplane – and these continued to be a feature throughout the Bellanca 14 series. The company put the 14-9 into production as the Cruisair and built aircraft powered by a variety of different types of small radial engine. These engines were low-powered and tended to create considerable drag so the Cruisair could only just class itself as a three-seater. As a result, in 1941, the 120hp Franklin 6AC-264-A3 horizontally-opposed engine was fitted and a few of these 14-12-F3 aircraft were built before the war forced suspension of production.

In 1945, Bellanca was well positioned to get the Model 14 into the booming light aircraft marketplace. Again, an engine change to 130hp was mooted (resulting in the model 14-13) but the definitive Model 14-13 Cruisair Senior was powered by a 150hp Franklin 6A4-150-B3 engine. The market downturn in 1947 seriously affected Bellanca but they went on building aircraft until 1951 and, in 1949, even produced the updated Model 14-19 with a 190hp Lycoming. Minor internal changes had been introduced progressively in the 14-13 and 14-19, and these were identified by sub-variant numbers (eg, 14-19-2).

Aircraft production was abandoned by Bellanca in 1951, and the Cruisair languished until 1956 when the plans, tools, dies and type certificate for the Model 14-19 passed to Northern Aircraft Inc of Alexandria, Minnesota. Bellanca continued to manufacture target drones and other subcontracted airframe assemblies, but Northern went into production with the four-seat Model 14-19-2 'Northern Cruisemaster' powered by a 230hp Continental O-470-K engine. In 1957, the first production year, a total of 44 aircraft were produced.

Northern Aircraft Inc merged with American Aviation Corporation of Freeland, Michigan in 1957 and subsequently, on 1st January 1959, the company changed its name to Downer Aircraft Industries under the leadership of its chairman, Jay K Downer. It proceeded to develop the 14-19-3 with yet more power (the 260hp Continental IO-470-F). This was approved on 20th February 1959 and marketed as the Bellanca 260 and, in addition to the bigger engine and associated nose redesign, it had a retractable tricycle undercarriage, an enlarged cabin and revised roof contour with fibreglass covering on all external surfaces.

In 1960, a further redesign resulted in larger cabin side windows – thereby eliminating the familiar semi-square Bellanca rear window. The vertical tail was changed to a slightly swept broad-chord unit and the endplate fins were dropped. With a few alterations to the nose cowl this was sold as the Model 260A (14-19-3A) but relatively few examples were produced before Downer ceased production in 1962.

The next chapter opened in 1964 when Downer reorganised as International Aircraft Manufacturing Inc to build the 'Inter-Air Bellanca 260A'. An injection of capital was provided by Miller Flying Service of Alexandria, Minn. and the name was again changed – to Bellanca Sales Manufacturing Inc. Some minor changes were made to the aircraft, which was now sold as the Bellanca 260B and later '260C. The Model 260C was eventually replaced, in late 1967, by the Model 17-30 Viking 300 which was certificated on 23rd September 1966. It is unclear why the model number '17' was adopted – because for some time the wing area had been 161ft², so the original designation system had fallen by the wayside. The -30 part of the designation identified the 300hp Continental IO-520-D engine fitted to the Viking. The Viking airframe remained essentially the same but various engine changes were brought in during the 1970s and there was a repositioning of the fuel tanks when the Super Viking series was introduced.

Bellanca had been successful with the Viking so it set its sights on expansion outside its single product line. In September 1970 the Champion Aircraft Corporation was acquired and the name of the holding company was changed to Bellanca Aircraft Corporation. In October 1976 it entered into a joint venture arrangement with Anderson Greenwood & Co, which involved that company having voting control of Bellanca. Bellanca was to manufacture the high-performance single-engined Model T-250 Aries with investment from Anderson Greenwood that eventually amounted to $ 4.9 million. The Aries had been designed and brought to the stage of type certificate approval

Bellanca 14-19-2 Cruisair N7682B

Bellanca 17-30 Viking 300 N91CE

by Anderson Greenwood and the first production example was completed in late 1979.

At this time, however, Bellanca was facing falling sales of both the Viking and the Champions and, in April 1980 all production of these two lines was halted and the Champion line was sold. Bellanca continued to build the Eagle DW-1 agricultural biplane under a subcontract arrangement and carried out some further work on the Aries T-250. On 25th July 1980, Bellanca's bankers foreclosed and they were forced into Chapter 11 bankruptcy. The type certificate to the Model 17 together with the Bellanca factory and all tooling and other rights were sold to Miller Aviation. In 1981 a new company named Bellanca Aircraft Corporation was formed by Mike Pinckney to buy out James Miller's interest and the Model Super Viking was returned to production. It was marketed as the 17-30B (but still certificated as the 17-30A), the first aircraft being N2XS (c/n 88-301000). 30 aircraft were built but, following the bankruptcy of Bellanca Aircraft in 2000, the Type certificates for the 14-19 and 17-30/31 series were sold, in May 2002, to Alexandria Aircraft LLC with the last completed Bellanca aircraft being c/n 99-301030. Alexandria Aircraft are concentrating on parts support for the existing Bellanca fleet but have recommended limited production at c/n 05-301031 (N283SV, a 2005 model 17-30A). Full details of all Bellanca models are:

Model	Built	Notes
14-7 Junior	1	Low-wing two-seat cabin monoplane with one 70hp Le Blond engine. Re-engined with 90hp Ken Royce 5F. Prototype NX19195 (c/n 1001)
14-9 Junior	40	Similar to Model 14-7 with 90hp Ken Royce 5F or 5G engine. Oval endplate fins
14-9L Junior	3	14-9 with 90hp Lenape LM-5 engine
14-10 Junior	1	Experimental installation of 100hp Lycoming engine in NX25307 (c/n 1039)
14-12 Junior	1	Experimental installation of 120hp Ken Royce engine in OB-22 (c/n 1012)
14-12-F3 Cruisair	13	Similar to 14-9 with 120hp Franklin 6AC-264-F3 engine. Prototype NX28972 (c/n 1042)
14-13 Cruisair Senior	589	14-12-F3 with 150hp Franklin 6A4-150-B3 engine, four-seat interior, improved trim and window shape. Circular endplate fins. Prototype NX41878 (c/n 1060). 1947 model 14-13-2, 1948 model 14-13-3, 1949 model 14-13-4 all with minor changes
14-15	-	Aircraft c/n 1011 re-engined
14-19 Cruisemaster	97	Cruisair with 190hp Lycoming O-435-A engine. Prototype N74142 (c/n 2000). Enlarged endplate fins, deeper rear windows and larger side windows, deeper engine cowl
14-19-2 Cruisemaster	105	Northern Aircraft version with 230hp Cont O-470-K. First aircraft N7650B (c/n 4001) FF 25 Jul 1956
14-19-3 Bellanca 260	123	Updated Cruisemaster with fibreglass covering, tricycle u/c, 260hp Cont IO-470-F and enlarged cabin. Modified engine cowl. Built by Downer and FF 5 Dec 1958
14-19-3A Bellanca 260A	114	14-19-3 with swept fin/rudder, no endplate fins, squared-off side windows, deeper engine cowl with oil cooler intake, modified entry door and windshield
14-19-3B Bellanca 260B		14-19-3A with minor changes
14-19-3C Bellanca 260C		14-19-3B with new fibreglass covering
17-30 Viking 300	263	Similar to Model 260C with 300hp Continental IO-520-D engine. Prototype N6650V (c/n 30001)
17-30A Super Viking	725	New 'A' series airframe with enlarged wing tanks in place of fuselage tank and 300hp Cont IO-520-K1A engine. New engine cowl and u/c fairings introduced in 1971
17-30B Super Viking	22	17-30A with minor internal changes. Unofficial designation
17-31 Viking 300	34	17-30 with 290hp Lycoming IO-540-G1B5 engine
17-31A Super Viking	138	17-30A with Lycoming IO-540-K1E5 engine
17-31TC Turbo Viking	10	17-30 with Rayjay-supercharged 290hp Lycoming IO-540-G1E5. Prototype N7358V (c/n 31001)
17-31-ATC Turbo Super Viking	145	17-30A with Rayjay-supercharged Lycoming IO-540-K1E5 engine
19-25 Skyrocket II	1	
T-250 Aries 250	6	Five-seat low-wing all-metal cabin monoplane with retractable tricycle u/c and one 250hp Lycoming O-540-A4D5 engine. Prot N51AG (c/n 1) FF 10 Jul 1973

Each of the companies building the Bellanca models has used its own serial number system. In general, all Model 14s have a simple four-digit number, but the Model 17 has incorporated a type number (ie, 30 for the 17-30, 31 for the 31TC and 32 for the Model 31). In 1973, the company introduced a prefix indicating the year of construction. The first Turbo Super Viking to use this system had the c/n 73-31043. Serial number blocks used over the years are as follows:

Model	Manufacturer	C/n from-to
14-9	Bellanca Aircraft Corp	1001
14-12-F3	Bellanca Aircraft Corp	1002 - 1059
14-13	Bellanca Aircraft Corp	1060 - 1648
14-19	Bellanca Aircraft Corp	2000 - 2096
14-19-2	Northern Aircraft	4001 - 4105
14-19-3	Downer Aircraft Ind	4106 - 4228
14-19-3	Int Aircraft Mfg	4229 - 4342
17-30	Bellanca Sales	30000 - 30262
17-30A	Bellanca Aircraft Corp	30263 - 30486
17-30A	Bellanca Aircraft Corp	73-30487 - 80-30987
17-30A	Bellanca Aircraft	88-301000 - 99-301030
17-30A	Alexandria Aircraft	05-301031
17-31	Bellanca Sales	32-1 - 3-34
17-31A	Bellanca Aircraft Corp	32-35 - 32-93
17-31A	Bellanca Aircraft Corp	73-32-94 - 78-32-172
17-31TC	Bellanca Sales	31001 - 31010
17-31ATC	Bellanca Aircraft Corp	31011 - 31042
17-31ATC	Bellanca Aircraft Corp	73-31043 - 79-31155
T-250	Bellanca Aircraft Corp	0001-80 - 0005-80

Bellanca T-250 Aries N250DJ

Beriev Be-103 N29KL

Beriev   Russia

Beriev first flew its Be-103 amphibian prototype (RA-37019) on 15th July 1997. Designed as a light passenger/cargo aircraft for operation in remote locations, it has a low wing giving an air cushion effect, a retractable tricycle undercarriage and a six-seat cabin accessed through upward-opening doors in the forward cabin. The prototype was powered by two 175hp VOKBM M-17F piston engines mounted on pylons on the rear fuselage but production aircraft (primarily for the export market) can be fitted with 210hp Continental IO-360-ES4 engines. Both prototypes (RA-37019 and RA-03002) were written-off in accidents. The first three production aircraft have been delivered to the USA (c/n 3301 to 3303). The much larger Be-200 is a utility flying boat powered by a pair of turbofan engines. It is intended, primarily, for fire fighting but also has cargo and search and rescue roles. The prototype (RA-21511, c/n 00.2) first flew on 24th September 1998 and at least a further three aircraft have flown (c/n 00.3, 101.01 and 101.02).

B&F Technik   Germany

The popular range of Funk light aircraft is built by B&F Technik based at Speyer. The company has its origins in the work done in the late 1950s by Otto Funk, an engineer at the Heinkel factory. In 1959, he designed and built a series of one-off gliders starting with the all-metal Greif 1a glider (the FK1), which was later fitted with a small jet engine, and then, in 1962, the Greif 2 (FK2) glider and then the HS203 and FK3. The Sirius 1 of 1970 was based on the FK3, but it had a centre-fuselage-mounted propeller and this concept led to the Rhein Flugzeugbau Fantrainer. In 1970, the FK4 (built as the AK1 by the Akaflieg Karlsruhe) was flown and this was a high-performance sailplane with a pop-up auxiliary engine. The FK5 was an upgraded FK3 (which was not completed) and the FK6 was Otto Funk's first ultralight - a strut-braced high-wing machine with a pod-and-boom layout, V-tail, pusher engine and fixed tailwheel undercarriage. Three were built in 1985 and in 1994 a two-seater (the FK10, D-MTDD c/n 001) was built as a prototype by trainees of MBB at Speyer. Otto Funk also built the low-wing FK11 which had a centre-fuselage car engine driving two propellers mounted on the wings – but this aircraft (D-MSPK c/n 11912), flown in June 1997, remained a prototype only. The FK7 and FK8 were design studies for ultralights but the FK9 was the first design that would be produced commercially.

The tube-and-fabric FK9 was a joint project by Otto Funk and his son, Peter – and the prototype FK9 Mk 1 (D-MXFK c/n 001) was built in 1989 by Peter in his garage, making its first flight on 16th November 1989. It was a conventional strut-braced high-wing monoplane with a fully enclosed two-seat cabin, fixed tailwheel undercarriage and nose-mounted Rotax engine. Peter Funk and Dirk Breitkreuz formed B&F Technik and built a small run of some 40 FK9-503s powered by the 46hp Rotax 503. These were available as factory-complete or kit aircraft. The FK9 Mk 2 was introduced in 1994 and this was redesigned to use larger Rotax engines of up to 80hp. In 1997, Peter Funk redesigned the FK9 as an all-composite aircraft, which substantially changed the appearance of its fuselage. This FK9 Mk 3 was built in parallel with the Mk 2 and the company also offered the FK9 Mk 3 Utility which had a higher gross weight, larger windows, modified flaps, a lager tailplane

B&F Funk FK9 Mk 3 69-PK

B&F FK12 Comet A63A3A

and redesigned wings to allow it to tow gliders and to facilitate its flight training role. The current FK9 Mk4, introduced in 2003, is an improved Mk3 Utility with detail changes and all the FK9s can be fitted with tailwheel or tricycle undercarriages. They are all available as factory-complete or in kit form. The standard Rotax 912 engine can be replaced by a 53hp Suprex engine from the Daimler-Chrysler Smart car (FK9 Smart). Components for the Funk aircraft are produced at Krosno in Poland with final assembly taking place at Speyer and the aircraft is also built under licence in Brazil (Mk3B).

In 1997, two new models were introduced, again in the 450kg category. The first was the FK12 Comet – a tandem two-seat ultralight biplane with a fixed tailwheel undercarriage and a Rotax 912 or 912S engine. The prototype (D-MPLI) first flew in March 1997 and it has a fabric-covered tubular steel fuselage and folding composite wings with either open cockpits or a blister canopy. The second model was the FK14 Polaris which is a low-wing two-seater of all-composite construction (but with an internal steel tube safety structure) with either tricycle or tailwheel gear and, again, powered by the 80hp Rotax 912UL or 99hp Rotax 912ULS. The prototype (D-MVFK c/n 001) first flew in the summer of 1999 and the aircraft is now in production as a factory-complete model. The current version, which replaced it in 2003, is the FK14B, which has a modified wing with slotted flaps. By the end of

B&F Funk FK-14 Polaris D-MABH

2004, B&F had completed approximately 35 FK9 Mk1s and 57 Mk2s, 108 FK9 Mk3 and 55 Mk4s, 64 FK12s and 49 FK14s (including 14 F14Bs). Serial numbers for the FK9 started at 001 but appear to have been expanded from around c/n 130 to show the model, the sub-type and overall serial number (eg, 09-03-130). The Mk4 commenced at approximately c/n 09-04-216. The FK12 and FK14 both have simple c/ns commencing at c/n 001. Since some of these are kits, some will not have been completed and flown.

BHEL   India

In the late 1980s, the Indian Directorate of Civil Aviation's Technical Centre designed a two-seat trainer to meet the requirements of Indian flying clubs. The LT-I was a low-wing aircraft of mixed construction with a fixed tailwheel undercarriage, an enclosed cabin with side-by-side seating and a sliding canopy and powered by a 130hp Continental O-240-A engine. The prototype (VT-XIV) first flew on 17th November 1990 and production was undertaken by BHEL (Bharat Heavy Electricals Ltd), commencing in 1993. The production standard aircraft had tricycle gear and a 116hp Lycoming O-235-N2C engine. The first of these, VT-XSR, first flew on 22nd November 1992 and four aircraft were built to this standard (c/n 60201-U-853-01 to 60201-U-853-04). The second of these (VT-STB) was modified to become the LT-IIM Swati Trainer with a 108hp O-235-N2C engine and 15 examples were completed (c/n 60201-U-853-05 to 60201-U-853-15, 60202-

BHEL Swati Trainer. J Wadia

U-853-01 and 60204-U-853-01 to 60207-U-853-01). As a result of several accidents, the Swati Trainer was grounded by the DCA and is believed now to be out of service.

Boisavia — France

In 1946, Lucien Tiélès built the prototype of a two-seat high-wing tail-wheel monoplane – the B.50 Muscadet, powered by a 100hp Renault engine. Registered F-WBBG (later F-WCZE) it first flew on 13th October 1946. It was redesigned as the four-seat B-60 Mercurey with a higher rear decking and a 140hp Renault 4 Pei engine, making its first flight on 3rd April 1949.

Tiélès established the Société Boisavia to build the aircraft commercially and most production units were the B.601L with a 190hp Lycoming flat-four engine. With the same airframe the company was able to produce small numbers of other versions with different engines and Mercurey production continued until the middle of 1962 with serial numbers from c/n 1 to 5, c/n 18 to 29, c/n 51 to 55 and c/n 100 to 116. In addition, the various prototypes had unique serial numbers.

Boisavia also built the B.80 Chablis parasol-wing two-seater, which was intended for kit production by amateur builders. A more ambitious venture was the B.260 Anjou light twin, which was intended as a competitor for the Piper Apache. Only a single prototype was built and the design passed to SIPA. Boisavia models built between 1954 and 1962 were as follows:

Boisavia B.601L Mercurey F-PIAN

Model	Built	Notes
B.50 Muscadet	1	Three-seat strut-braced high-wing cabin monoplane with fixed tailwheel u/c, and one 100hp Renault 4 Pei engine. Prototype F-WBBG FF 13 Oct 1946
B.60 Mercurey	3	Four-seat development of B.50 with wider rear cabin and built up rear fuselage decking. Prototype F-WFDV (c/n 01) FF 3 Apr 1949
B.601 Mercurey	3	B.60 with 190hp Lycoming O-435-A engine. Prototype F-BFON
B.601L Mercurey	27	B.60 with 190hp Lycoming O-360-C engine
B.602 Mercurey	2	B.60 with 165hp Cont E-165-4. Prototype F-BAIM
B.603R-II Mercurey Special	5	B.60 with 240hp Argus AS.10-C3B. Prototype F-BFRJ, FF 11 Apr 1951
B.604 Mercurey II	1	B.60 with lengthened fuselage for glider towing, powered by 230hp Salmson 9ABC. F-WGVE FF 6 Jan 1954
B.605 Mercurey	4	B.60 with 170hp Regnier 4L-02. Prototype F-BGVF
B.606 Mercurey	1	B.60 with Regnier 4L-00 engine
B.80 Chablis	2	Tandem two-seat open-cockpit parasol-wing monoplane with 65hp Continental A-65 engine. Prototype F-WBGO FF 16 Jul 1950
B.260 Anjou	1	Low-wing four-seat cabin monoplane with retractable tricycle u/c and two 170hp SNECMA Regnier 4L engines. Prototype F-WHHN FF 2 Jun 1956

Bölkow — Germany

The Ingenieurbau Bölkow was formed by Ludwig Bölkow in 1947 and became the Bölkow Entwicklungen KG in 1957. It developed the two-seat Kl.107 trainer/tourer through a joint venture company formed with Hans Klemm Flugzeugbau and named Apparatebau Nabern GmbH. Derived from the pre-war Kl.35 and Kl.105, the prototype of this all-wood light aircraft (D-EXKL) originally flew in 1940 and was followed by five further prototypes. The company flew its definitive postwar aircraft (D-ECAD c/n 101) on 4th September 1956 and a small production run of 25 units of the Kl.107B (c/n 102 to 126) was built before Bölkow took over complete responsibility for the programme.

The next model was the Kl.107C and it had numerous detail improvements to wings, engine cowling and tail unit together with a new undercarriage with streamlined fairings attached to the inner wings rather than the wing roots. 30 Bölkow-built KL.107Cs were delivered (c/n 125 to 154) before the company introduced the improved Model F.207. This had four seats, wing fuel tanks, a modified cockpit canopy and a larger 180hp Lycoming O-360-A1A engine. The F.207 prototype (D-EGSA c/n 201 – converted from Kl.107 c/n 145) made its first flight on 10th December 1960 and Bölkow went on to build 91 production examples (c/n 202 to 292). One of these (c/n 284) had the standard tailwheel gear replaced with a tricycle undercarriage and was known as the Bo.214.

In 1962, when F.207 was in full swing, Bölkow took a licence to build the MFI-9 Junior two-seater, which had been developed by Malmo Flygindustri in Sweden from the designs of Björn Andreasson. Bölkow used a Malmo-built aircraft (D-EBVA c/n 501) as its prototype and found that few changes were needed in order to set up the design for full production. The first Bo.208 Juniors left the newly-established production line at Laupheim in 1962. A fair number of aircraft were imported into the United Kingdom and nine early examples went to the United States. Excluding the prototype and a pair of static test airframes, a total of 186 Juniors were completed with the serial numbers

c/n 503 to 505, c/n 507 to 547, c/n 549 to 550, c/n 555, c/n 560 to 564 and c/n 567 to 709. In addition, in 1997, a Bo.208, designated L-11, was built in the Czech Republic by Letov AS from MFI-9HB plans and the prototype (OK-AYA c/n 960001) was flown on 22nd May 1997 powered by a Continental O-200. This was followed by a 450kg ultralight version known as the MFI-9UL1, produced by LD Aviation Prague sro. The prototype, OK-JUU 55, first flew in the spring of 2005 and is powered by a 100hp Rotax 912ULS engine.

Production of the Junior was terminated in 1971, but by this time Bölkow's Dipl Ing Hermann Mylius had come up with a new model – the MHK-101 – which was based on the Junior but had a low wing, substantially enlarged cockpit and a retractable nosewheel. The MHK-101 prototype (D-EMHK c/n V-0), which was flown on 22nd December 1967, also featured folding wings to allow easy storage. Bölkow produced their own definitive version of the MHK-101 designated Bo.209 (D-EEBC c/n V-1) with modifications to the cockpit canopy and this first flew on 25th September 1970.

Bölkow Bo.208C Junior D-EMUH

Bölkow F207 D-EFQE

Bölkow, which had become a part of the Messerschmitt-Bölkow-Blohm group, built 102 examples of the production Bo.209 Monsun (c/n 101 to 119, 105A, 121 to 201 and c/n 301). Purchasers had a choice of engines, a fixed or retractable nosewheel and a variable or fixed pitch propeller. The Bo.209A did not become a production model (the only example being the re-engined prototype D-EEBC), although there were plans for it to be sold in the USA, and a low-powered Bo.209S was also offered with dual controls, but only one was built (D-EBPJ c/n 119). The Monsun variants were as follows:

Model	Name	hp	Engine	Nosewheel	Propeller
Bo.209A	Monsun 125FF	125	Lyc O-235F	Fixed	Fixed
Bo.209B	Monsun 150FV	150	Lyc O-320-E1C	Fixed	Variable
Bo.209B	Monsun 150RV	150	Lyc O-320-E1C	Retractable	Variable
Bo.209B	Monsun 150FF	150	Lyc O-320-E1C	Fixed	Fixed
Bo.209C	Monsun 160FV	160	Lyc O-320-E1F	Fixed	Variable
Bo.209C	Monsun 160RV	160	Lyc O-320-E1F	Retractable	Variable
Bo.209S	Monsun 130FF	130	RR Cont O-240-A	Fixed	Fixed

After Bo.209 production was complete, Bölkow abandoned light air-craft (and also disposed of their successful Bölkow Phoebus sailplane) to concentrate on helicopter production.

Herr Mylius had built two prototypes of a single-seat aerobatic machine known as the Mylius My.102 Tornado, the first of which was D-EMYS (c/n V-1), which first flew on 7th July 1973 (the second being D-EMYM, c/n V-2). This was not adopted by Bölkow but the Mylius Flugzeugwerk GmbH, formed by Albert Mylius in 1996, updated the My.102 as a side-by-side two-seater with a tricycle undercarriage (incorporating a retractable nosewheel) and 180hp Lycoming IO-360 engine. They flew the prototype My-103 Mistral (D-ETMY c/n V-1) on 23rd May 1998 and it was intended to produce this in quantity as the My-103/180 or My-103/200 (with a 200hp Lycoming AEIO-360 engine). A four-seat version, the My-104/200 with retractable gear and a longer-span wing was also proposed, but, although Mylius built one further prototype (D-ENMY, c/n 01), they have not progressed further with production plans.

Bölkow Bo.209C Monsun 160FV D-EFJM

Mylius My-103 D-ENMY

Canadair CL.415 C-GQBA

Bombardier/Canadair   Canada

Canadair has its origins in the aircraft division of Canadian Vickers Ltd, which was established in 1922. The name was changed to Canadair in 1944, eventually coming under Canadian Government ownership in January 1976 but in August 1986 the Government decided to sell the company to its present owners, Bombardier Inc Bombardier also owns de Havilland Canada, Learjet and Short Brothers. Following its wartime production of some 369 Canso amphibians Canadair had built 71 examples of the Canadair 4 (derivative of the Douglas DC-4) and substantial batches of the T-33 Silver Star, F-86 Sabre, F-5, F-104G and the indigenous CL-41 Tutor jet trainer. They also produced 33 CL-28 Argus maritime reconnaissance aircraft and 39 CL-44s – both derived from the Bristol Britannia.

These types were, essentially, not original Canadair designs but, in February 1966, the company initiated the CL215 utility amphibian, intended as a water bomber for the Canadian provincial governments. The CL215 was a high-wing aircraft with a tricycle undercarriage, the main units of which retracted into open recesses on the slab-sided fuselage. The single-step planing hull was fitted with a large ventral hatch for dumping the water load, which totalled 1,176 imperial gallons and was contained in two fuselage tanks. The CL215 used two 2,100hp Pratt & Whitney CA-3 Double Wasp piston engines mounted above the wings. The prototype (CF-FEU-X c/n 1001) made its first flight at Cartierville on 23rd October 1967 and initial deliveries were made in June 1969. Many of the production CL215s (sometimes referred to as the CL215A and technically designated CL215-1A10) were sold to foreign governments as fire fighters and customers included France (Protection Civile), Greece, Spain, Italy and Yugoslavia in addition to six Canadian provinces. Canadair also sold two examples of the CL215C in a 26-passenger configuration to the Venezuelan Corporacion Ferromineroa de Orinoco and two to the Thai Navy for maritime patrol (designated CL215B).

In early 1990, with 125 aircraft having been built (c/n 1001 to 1125), production moved on to the CL215T, which had a pair of 2,380shp Pratt & Whitney PW123AF turboprops, large wingtip endplates, and auxiliary fins mounted on the tailplane. The prototype (C-FASE c/n 1114) was converted from an existing CL215 and flew on 8th June

1989 with utility category certification being achieved on 24th December 1991. Initially, Canadair converted existing piston-engined aircraft which are designated CL215T (still as the CL215-1A10). The first of two CL215Ts for The Province of Quebec was delivered in January 1992 and the Spanish Air Force received 20 conversions. New-build aircraft were designated CL415 (certificated designation CL215-6B11) with fully powered flight controls, cockpit air conditioning, a new electrical system, four-door water drop system, increased gross weight and useful load and a new EFIS cockpit. Later improvements to the CL415 included tail anti-icing and a larger rear cargo door.

The first CL415 (C-GSCT c/n 2001) made its maiden flight on 6th December 1993, followed in 1995 by the first deliveries to the French Sécurité Civile. Other governmental CL415 customers include Italy, Croatia and the Province of Quebec. A batch of nine aircraft for Greece was designated CL415GR with an increased gross weight and provision for cargo handling and the Greek Government also received one CL415MP maritime patrol and SAR variant. Latterly, the aircraft was marketed as the Canadair 415 SuperScooper and 66 CL415s have been built to date (c/n 2001 to 2066) although manufacture of the aircraft was suspended in late 2002 with c/n 2067 to 2071 in various stages of completion.

Bombardier Challenger CL-601-3R C-FUND

Bombardier Challenger 300 C-GIPZ

In the mid-1970s, Canadair became involved in the Learstar 600 business jet that was being designed by Bill Lear. The aircraft was a wide-bodied business jet with 14 executive passenger seats although it could accommodate 30 passengers in high-density configuration. It was a classic design with a pair of rear-mounted Lycoming ALF502D turbofans and a supercritical wing. Canadair obtained rights to the Learstar in early 1976 but they did some extensive redesign, including a change to T-tail configuration, before the prototype was built and flown two years later.

The CL-600, which was named Challenger, received its Canadian Type Certificate on 11th August 1980 with first deliveries of green aircraft following shortly afterwards. In addition to the standard executive models Challengers have been sold for specialist missions such as aeromedical and to government users including Germany, Malaysia, China and Canada. Production of all the CL-600 variants has been carried out at Montreal-Dorval and, up until 2003, completions were carried out at Tucson, Arizona. The Tucson plant is to be closed by the end of 2005 and all work will be concentrated at Dorval. Several developments of the basic airframe have taken place, as described in the table of models. They have each been given the 'marketing' designation shown, but are certificated as sub-variants of the CL-600, and these designations are also referred to.

Model	Notes
CL-600	Intercontinental business jet with wide-body fuselage, T-tail, supercritical wing and two 7,500 lbst Avco Lycoming ALF502L turbofans. 40,400 lb TOGW. Prototype C-GCGR-X (c/n 1001) FF 8 Nov 1978. Certificated as CL-600-1A10.
CL-600S	CL-600 fitted with winglets and increased TOGW. Certificated as CL-600-1A11
CL-601	CL-600 with 9,140 lbst General Electric CF34-1A turbofans, wingtip winglets, 41,650 lb TOGW. Prototype C-GCGT-X (c/n 3991) FF 10 Apr 1982. Certificated as CL-600-2A12
CL-601-1A	CL-601 with fuel increase from 2,190 gal to 2,451 gal. FF 17 Sept 1982
CL-601-3A	CL-601 with CF34-3A engines, 43,100 lb TOGW, digital avionics and flight management system. FF 28 Sep 1986. Certificated as CL-600-2B16
CL-601-3A-ER	Extended range version of -3A with 44,600 lb TOGW, 184 gal tailcone fuel tank and stronger u/c. FF 8 Nov 1988
CL-601S	CL-601-3A with reduced interior and avionics specification and lower fuel capacity
CL-601-3R	CL-601-3A with CF34-3A1 engines, enlarged fuel capacity, new environmental control system, new cabin windows etc. CL-600-2B16
CL-604	Development of CL-601-3R with new rear tanks and increased range, revised u/c, new underbelly fairing, larger cabin, new Collins avionics suite and CF34-3B engines. Prototype C-FTBZ (c/n 5991) FF 18 Sep 1994. CL-600-2B16

Canadair had designed the Challenger to facilitate further development and their first study was the Challenger 'E' with a stretched fuselage. This was subsequently abandoned but the definitive enlarged variant is the Canadair Regional Jet (CL-600-2B19), which is based on the CL-601-3A with a 20-ft fuselage stretch and 48/50 passengers. The prototype Canadair RJ (C-FCRJ c/n 7001) was first flown on 10th May 1991. The basic production version was the 50-passenger RJ100ER and RJ100LR with CF34-3A1 engines and these were replaced by the essentially similar RJ200LR and RJ200ER with CF34-3B1 engines and by the 44-passenger CRJ440. Bombardier subsequently developed the stretched CRJ700 (CL-600-2C10) that first flew on 27th May 1999 (C-FRJX, c/n 10001) and the further stretched 86-seat CRJ900 (CL-600-2D24) that flew in prototype form on 21st February 2001 (modified from the CRJ700 prototype, C-FRJX). 1,018 examples of the Regional Jet Srs 100/200, 198 of the RJ700 and 28 of the RJ900 had been built by the end of 2004. A corporate version with a 30-passenger interior was launched in November 1991 as the Canadair Corporate Jetliner. This later became the Challenger-SE (CL-600-2B19) and in 2003 was, again, renamed Bombardier Challenger 800. In the spring of 2005, Bombardier further changed its corporate shuttle offering, replacing the Challenger 800 with the Challenger 850 (based on the commercial CRJ200LR), Challenger 870 (CRJ700LR) and Challenger 890 (CRJ900LR).

Bombardier officially launched the Bombardier Global Express (BD-700-1A10) in December 1993. It is a very-long-range corporate

Bombardier Global 5000 C-GERS. Bombardier

transport with a crew of four, 91,000 lb gross weight and up to 19-passenger capacity. While outwardly it appears to have some commonality with the 'RJ' it is a completely new design with a new wing and tail together with two BMW/Rolls-Royce BR710-48-C2 turbofans. The prototype (C-FBGX c/n 9001) first flew on 13th October 1996 and production had reached 140 by the end of 2003. This included the first of five ASTOR (Airborne Stand-Off Radar) aircraft for the Royal Air Force, the concept for this variant having been flight tested on C-FBGX in August 2001. In October 2003 the Global XRS was announced and this replaces the original model and features an extra belly tank giving increased range, enhanced cockpit vision system, improved take-off performance and two extra cabin windows. The prototype, C-FCOI (c/n 9159) first flew on 16th January 2005.

Using the design base of the Global Express, Bombardier have gone on to produce the Global 5000 (BD-700-1A1) which is intended as a smaller capacity (and less expensive) version of the flagship aircraft. Externally very similar and with the same engines as the Global Express, it has a 48-inch reduction in fuselage length and was targeted to compete with the Gulfstream IV-SP and Falcon 900EX. Following

Bombardier Global Express A7-AAM

project launch in October 2001, the prototype (C-GERS c/n 9127) first flew at Downsview on 7th March 2003. Bombardier's other major development was the BD-100 Challenger 300 (BD-100-1A10) which was originally titled Bombardier Continental and announced in October 1998. It is a mid-sized executive jet with the now-familiar low-wing, T-tail configuration and is slightly smaller than the Challenger 604. It is powered by two Honeywell AS907 turbofans and has an 8-passenger main cabin. The prototype, C-GJCJ (c/n 20001) first flew on 14th August 2001 and the type is now in production.

In the calendar year 2004, Bombardier delivered 81 aircraft (excluding Learjets) comprising 28 Challenger 300s, 29 Challenger 604s, 4 Global 5000s and 20 Global Expresses. Production of individual Bombardier aircraft types can be deduced from the following serial number batches allocated as at the end of 2004:

Model	No	C/n Batch	Model	No	C/n Batch
CL-600	85	1001 to 1085	CRJ100/200	1,018	7001 to 8018+
CL-601	66	3001 to 3066	CRJ700	185	10001 to 10185+
CL-601-3A	134	5001 to 5134	CRJ900	26	15001 to 15026+
CL-601-3R	60	5135 to 5194	Global Express/5000	155	9001 to 9155+
CL-604	306	5301 to 5606+	Challenger 300	38	20001 to 20038+

Britten Norman   United Kingdom

Britten Norman Ltd was established in 1955 by John Britten and Desmond Norman to convert and operate agricultural aircraft and to sell their Micronair liquid fertiliser rotary atomiser system. The company built the BN Cushioncraft hovercraft in the mid-1960s and then designed the BN-2 Islander which first flew in June 1965. This 9/10-seat all-metal twin-engined utility aircraft had a minimum of refinements and was fitted with a fixed undercarriage and simple systems to allow maintenance away from normal aircraft workshops. It was certificated on 10th August 1967 and went into production at Bembridge, Isle of Wight shortly afterwards.

By 1968, demand for Islanders had outstripped the capacity of the Bembridge factory and of British Hovercraft Corporation which was doing subassembly work. A contract was signed with IRMA in Romania whereby they would build 'green' Islanders and ship them to Bembridge for finishing. Initially, kits of parts were sent from Britain for local assembly (starting with aircraft c/n 85 – later c/n R.601) but IRMA soon reached the stage of full production of the aircraft. Islanders were also assembled in the Philippines under an agreement struck with PADC in September 1974. Production of 100 aircraft was envisaged but, in the event, only 15 were completed and the remaining stocks of parts and structures were sold back to Wessex Aerospace in the UK during 2001.

Looking to expansion of the product range, the company used the second BN-2 (G-ATWU) to test the stretched Super Islander concept. While this variant was not adopted, it did allow G-ATWU to be converted to the prototype BN-2A Mk III Trislander with an enlarged strengthened vertical tail and a third Lycoming engine mounted on the fin and this model went into production in 1971. In August 1982, the production rights for the Trislander were sold to International Aviation Corporation of Miami who intended to sell the aircraft as the Tri-Commutair. This did not materialise and a deal was struck for the sale of the final batch of 11 Trislanders (plus one other) to Lance Watson in Australia. This deal foundered and eventually two airframes were sold for completion to Anglo Normandy Aero Engineering and the remainder languished in Florida. In 1999, Britten Norman announced the limited reopening of the Trislander line with an order for three aircraft from China but this deal evaporated with the 1999 collapse of the company. The Islander was also developed for military purposes as the Defender with underwing armament points and other equipment to fit the aircraft for light troop transport and ground support roles.

Britten Norman's corporate history has been a succession of crises. The original company was highly financially geared with considerable Government and other loans and at the end of 1970 it was in grave financial difficulty with debts of over £3 million. On 22nd October 1971 a receiver was appointed by the company's bankers who set up a new company – Britten Norman (Bembridge) Ltd In August 1972 this company was sold to the Fairey Group for £4.1 million and a new holding company, Fairey Britten Norman Ltd was formed to control operations of the existing Fairey factory at Gosselies in Belgium and the newly acquired Britten Norman business. Desmond Norman left the company at the time of the financial collapse and established a new business to develop light aircraft. This is fully described under the section on Norman Aircraft. Desmond Norman passed away on 13th November 2002.

Islander and Trislander production was moved to Gosselies with finishing being carried out at Bembridge. By this time, however, Fairey had run into severe financial problems as a result of their involvement in production of the F-16 fighter for the Belgian Air Force. The financial crisis resulted in Fairey calling in a receiver on 3rd August 1977 and the Britten Norman operation continued on a modest scale (with abortive negotiations for takeover being carried out with Short Bros), until July 1978 when Pilatus Flugzeugewerke acquired the business and formed Pilatus-Britten Norman Ltd

Pilatus-Britten Norman launched the Turbine Islander, which first flew on 2nd August 1980 and was a development of the abortive LTP-101 powered Turbo Islander tested by the company in April 1977. The BN-2T Turbine Islander used a pair of Allison 250 turboprops and Islanders and Turbine Islanders continued to be produced at a steady rate with primary production at IRMA and completion at Bembridge. Several specialised variants were developed, including the CASTOR Turbine Islander with a nose-mounted Ferranti surveillance radar and the AEW Defender with a bulbous nose radome housing a Thorn-EMI Searchwater radar. The basic BN-2A and BN-2B piston-engined models were built in a wide variety of combinations of gross weight, engine power (260hp and 300hp), wing configuration and fuel capacity.

In July 1998, Pilatus sold its interest in the company to Biofarm Inc and it was renamed Britten-Norman Ltd In early 1999, Britten Norman announced it had acquired Romaero SA which continues to be the main manufacturing plant for Islanders and Defenders. However, financial pressures re-emerged and under a reorganisation on 5th May 2000 the assets were acquired by B-N Group Ltd (owned by the Zawawi family) and Britten-Norman Ltd went into liquidation. Current models

B-N Islander BN-2A-8 PT-KQS

B-N Defender 4000 G-SURV

offered by the company are the BN-2B-20 and BN-2B-26 Islanders, the BN-2T-4S Defender, which is also offered as the National Defender for homeland security roles, and the BN-2A Mk III Trislander. The principal Islander and Trislander models are:

BN-2	High-wing all-metal 10-seat cabin monoplane with fixed tricycle u/c and two 260hp Lycoming O-540-E4B5 piston engines. 5,700 lb TOGW. Prototype G-ATCT (c/n 1) FF 13 June 1965
BN-2A	BN-2 with minor modifications and TOGW increased to 6,300 lb. 260hp or 300hp Lycoming O-540/IO-540 engines
BN-2A-10	BN-2A-8 with 5,070 lb TOGW and 270hp turbocharged Lycoming TIO-540-H1A engines
BN-2A-41	Turbo Islander with lengthened nose, droop flaps and two Lycoming LTP-101 turboprops. Prototype G-BDPR (c/n 504) FF 6 Apr 1977
BN-2B	New variant based on Defender with 300hp IO-540-K1B5 engines, four underwing hardpoints, optional nose radar and military hardened interior

B-N Trislander BN-2A-III G-BEPH

Norman NAC.1 Freelance G-NACI

BN-2S	Islander Super. BN-2A with 33-inch fuselage stretch
BN-2T	Turbine Islander. BN-2A-26 with two 320shp Allison 250-B17C turboprops and 7,000 lb TOGW
BN-2T-4R	Turbine Islander with nose-mounted Westinghouse radar and other multi-sensor equipment for military surveillance duties. Prototype G-BVHX (c/n 4003) FF 29 Jul 1994
BN-2T-4S	Military Defender 4000 with modified nose, longer strengthened wing, 40% increase in fuel capacity, enlarged fin and tailplane, 30-inch fuselage stretch ahead of wing, 8,500 lb TOGW and 400shp RR-Allison 250-B17F turboprops. Prototype G-SURV FF 17 Aug 1994
BN-2A-III-1	Trislander. 18-seat BN-2A stretched by 7ft 6in with three 260hp Lycoming O-540-E4C5 piston engines, one positioned on middle of fin with tailplane, extended wing and 9,350 lb TOGW. Prototype G-ATWU FF 11 Sep 1970
BN-2A-III-2	Trislander with lengthened nose and 10,000 lb TOGW
BN-2A-III-3	Trislander certificated for US operation
BN-2A-III-4	BN-2A-III-2 fitted with rocket-assisted take-off equipment

The detailed sub variants of the BN-2A and BN-2B with their respective gross weights are detailed as follows:

260hp models*	300hp models†	Features
BN-2 (5,700 lb)		Prototype
BN-2A (6,300 lb)		Early production
BN-2A-1 (6,300 lb)		Increased wingspan with tip tanks
BN-2A-6 (6,300 lb)		Drooped wing leading edge
BN-2A-7 (6,300 lb)		Drooped wing leading edge & tip tanks
BN-2A-8 (6,300 lb)	BN-2A-2 (6,300 lb)	Drooped flaps and wing leading edge
BN-2A-9 (6,300 lb)	BN-2A-3 (6,300 lb)	Drooped flaps, wing leading edge & tip tanks
BN-2A-24 (6,600 lb)		Drooped flaps, wing leading edge, long nose
BN-2A-25 (6,600 lb)	BN-2A-23 (6,600 lb)	Drooped flaps, leading edge, tip tanks, long nose
BN-2A-26 (6,600 lb)	BN-2A-20 (6,600 lb)	Drooped flaps and wing leading edge
BN-2B-26 (6,600 lb)	BN-2B-20 (6,600 lb)	Drooped flaps and wing leading edge
BN-2A-27 (6,600 lb)	BN-2A-21 (6,600 lb)	Drooped flaps, wing leading edge & tip tanks
BN-2B-27 (6,600 lb)	BN-2B-21 (6,600 lb)	Drooped flaps, wing leading edge & tip tanks

* Powered by two Lycoming O-540-E4C5 engines.
† Powered by two Lycoming IO-540-K1B5 engines.

Serial number batches for the 1,192 Islanders and 61 Trislanders built to date were as follows:

Model	C/n Batch	Notes	Model	C/n Batch	Notes
BN-2A	1-599		BN-2A, B	2001-2043	
BN-2A, B	601-915	Romanian built	BN-2A, B	2101-2308	Current Romanian built
BN-2A, B	916,918,919		BN-2A, T	3001-3015	Philippine, PADC
BN-2A-III	1001-1072*		BN-2T-4	4003-4014	Current

* 1062 to 1072 not completed – see text.
C/n 1100 to 1102 allocated to Chinese BN-2A-III but not built

Brochet   France

Maurice Brochet, an active member of the postwar homebuilt aircraft movement, had designed the MB.30 parasol light aircraft and the MB.40 cabin two-seater before the war. After the war he produced the prototype MB.50 open-cockpit single-seat monoplane that flew during 1947 and was sold as plans for amateur construction. He formed Constructions Aéronautiques Maurice Brochet, based at Neauphle-le-Chateau and in June 1949, made the first flight of his new tandem two-seater – the MB.60 Barbastelle. This was of mixed construction and formed the basis for the higher-powered MB.70 series of light aircraft, which entered production in 1950 following a SALS requirement for a new two-seat club aircraft.

The MB.70 was followed by the MB.80, which gained an order for 10 machines from the French Government. Brochet later extended the series to the three-seat MB.100 and MB.101 that were also built in small numbers. The final design from the Brochet factory was the MB.110, which was a substantially heavier variant of the basic theme with a large angular fin and rudder that did not progress beyond the prototype stage.

A separate serial sequence was set up for each different Brochet type. The main MB.80 production batch ran from c/n 01 to 09 and the MB.100 and MB.101 had numbers from c/n 01 to 17. Details of the different models are:

Model	Built	Notes
MB.40	1	High-wing light aircraft powered by one 65hp Continental A.65 engine. Prototype F-WFOH FF 6 Aug 1949
MB.50	12	Pipistrelle. Single-seat open-cockpit pylon-mounted high-wing monoplane with fixed tailwheel u/c and 45hp Salmson 9 Adb radial engine. Prototype F-WEAD FF May 1947. Amateur built with various engines (Train, Sarolea Vautour, Praga etc)
MB.60	1	Barbastelle. Tandem two-seat high-wing cabin monoplane developed from MB.50 with one 83hp Salmson 9 Adb. Prototype F-WFKT FF 24 Jun 1949
MB.70	1	Developed MB.60 with 45hp Salmson engine. Prototype F-WCZF FF 28 Jan 1950
MB.71	1	MB.70 with 75hp Minie 4DC-32 engine. Prototype F-WCZG
MB.72	5	MB.70 with 65hp Continental A.65 engine. Prototype F-PHZA
MB.73	1	MB.70 with 85hp Continental A.65-85 engine. Prototype F-BCZF
MB.74		MB.70 with 75hp Minie 4DA-28 engine
MB.75		MB.70 with Hirth 504-A2 engine
MB.76	1	MB.70 with 90hp Continental C.90-14F engine
MB.80	10	MB.70 with wider fuselage, spring steel u/c and revised rudder, and a 75hp Minie 4DC.32B engine. Prototype F-BGLA FF 15 Nov 1951
MB.81	1	MB.80 with Hirth 500-B2 engine
MB.83	-	MB.80 converted with 90hp Continental C.90-14F engine
MB.84	-	MB.70 converted with 65hp Continental A.65 engine
MB.100	6	Three-seat MB.80 with modified tail and cabin and 100hp Hirth HM504-A2 engine. Prototype F-WBGH FF 3 Jan 1951
MB.101	15	MB.100 with tropical flying modifications

Brochet MB.83 F-PGLF

Brochet MB.50 F-PEBZ

| MB.110 | 2 | Enlarged 4-seat MB.100 with large dorsal fin, modified wings and u/c and 170hp Regnier 4L-02 engine. Prototype F-WDKE FF 12 Mar 1956 |
| MB.120 | 2 | MB.100 with lighter MB.80 wings, modified flaps and Continental C.90 engine. Prototype F-WGVI FF 5 Apr 1954 |

Bücker   Germany

The Bücker Flugzeugbau was established in October 1933 at Johannisthal near Berlin by Carl Clemens Bücker, who had previously set up Svenska Aero AB in Sweden. On his return to Germany, Bücker, with his chief design engineer, Anders J Andersson, designed the Type 131 training and sporting biplane. The prototype Bü-131V-1 (registered D-3150), powered by an 80hp Hirth HM.60R engine, made its first flight on 27th April 1934 and was quickly placed in production as the Bü-131A Jungmann with the first production example being sold to Uruguay. The Jungmann later became the Bü-131B with a more powerful 105hp Hirth HM.504A-2 engine and then the Bü-131D, which incorporated a number of minor structural modifications. The Bü-133 Jungmeister was a single-seat advanced training aerobatic derivative of the Jungmann with a shorter fuselage and a 160hp Siemens Sh.14A-4 radial engine in a helmeted cowling. It has been reported that German production at Berlin-Rangsdorf before and during the war totalled 1,910 aircraft although this may be an under-estimate and some sources claim up to 3,000 were completed. This included batches of Jungmanns exported to 23 countries including South Africa, Hungary (probably 270 aircraft), Czechoslovakia, Yugoslavia (400), Brazil, Finland and Bulgaria.

Bücker delivered 95 Bü-131s to Spain for the Spanish Air Force and this led to licence manufacture by CASA of the C-1131 (sometimes referred to as I-131), commencing in 1941. CASA built three batches of 50 C-1131 aircraft (c/n 101 to 300) between 1941 and 1947, all powered by Hirth engines. In 1950 a new batch of 100 C-1131Bs (c/n 1001 to 1100) was initiated powered by the ENMA Tigre engine and further batches totalling 230 aircraft (c/n 2001 to 2230) were produced between 1953 and 1963. Some Hirth-engined aircraft were refitted with Tigre engines and given new c/ns commencing at 1101. Most of these military aircraft were civilianised in the 1970s, the majority being exported. CASA also built approximately 50 Bü.133 Jungmeisters (as the C-1133). The Bü.131 was built in large numbers in Japan, initially

by Watanabe and then by Kyushu Hikaki, commencing in 1938 and continuing into World War Two. They were produced as the Ki-86A basic trainer for the Imperial Army (1,037 built) and as the K9W-1 Momoji (339 built) for the Imperial Navy. In 1936 the Swiss company, Dornier at Altenrhein started building the Bü.131B and approximately 130 were completed (c/n 1 to 130), including 84 for the Swiss Air Force, together with 52 Bü-133C Jungmeisters. Bücker also licensed Tatra in Czechoslovakia to build Jungmanns and a batch of ten was completed before the war (designated Tatra T-131) and during the German occupation a further 300 were constructed by Aero in Prague. After the war, the Aero production line was re-established and a further 260 Aero C.104s (Jungmanns powered by the 105hp Walter Minor 4.III engine) were completed.

Bücker's other main light aircraft design was the Bü-181 Bestmann. This was another design by Anders Andersson (which inspired the later SAAB Safir). It was a wood and fabric low-wing design with side-by-side

SSH T-131.PA Jungmann SP-YHS

CASA C-1133 Jungmeister G-BVXJ

seating for two and a fixed tailwheel undercarriage. It was procured in substantial numbers for wartime Luftwaffe use and after the war was built in considerable numbers in Egypt, as detailed in the section on Heliopolis. It was also produced as the Z.281 and Z.381 in Czechoslovakia. The different production batches by Bücker and under licence are best shown in the following table. It should be noted that production totals are provisional (largely due to inadequacy of information on wartime production).

Type	Built	Notes
Bü-131 Jungmann	1	Bücker-built two-seat training biplane with fixed u/c and one 80hp Hirth HM.60R engine. Prototype Bü.131V-1 D-3150 FF 27 Apr 1934
Bü-131B Jungmann	1,910	Bü-131 powered by a 105hp Hirth HM.504A-2 engine
Bü-131C Jungmann	1	Bü-131 powered by a 90hp Cirrus Minor. Prototype only
Bü-131D Jungmann		Bü-131B with modified u/c and various refinements
Bü.131	130	Bü-131B built by Dornier in Switzerland
T-131	10	Bü-131B built in Czechoslovakia pre-war by Tatra
Z.131	300	Bü-131B built in Czechoslovakia by Aero for Luftwaffe
C.104	260	Postwar Z.131 built in Czechoslovakia by Aero with 105hp Walter Minor 4.III engine
C-1131	330	Bü-131B built in Spain by CASA
C-1131B	200	C-1131 powered by one ENMA Tigre G.IV A/B engine. Designated E3B in Spanish AF service
K9W-1 Momoji	339	Bü-131B built by Watanabe in Japan for Japanese Navy
Ki-86A	1,037	Bü-131B built for Japanese Army
Bü-133 Jungmeister	2	Development of Bü-131 with shorter single-seat fuselage and 140hp Hirth HM.506 in-line engine. Prototype Bu.133V-1 D-EVEO FF 1935
Bü-133B Jungmeister	2	Bü-133 with 160hp Siemens Bramo Sh.14A-4 radial engine, shorter fuselage and shorter wings
Bü-133C Jungmeister	61	Bü-133B with further shortened fuselage, inverted fuel system, and increased payload
Bü-133D-1	9	Postwar Jungmeisters built by Joseph Bitz
Bü-133	49	Bü-133 built by Dornier in Switzerland (c/n 1 to 49)
Bü-133L		Unofficial designation for various Bü-133 re-engined with Lycoming IO-320 and other model engines
Bü-181 Bestmann	2,730	Low-wing side-by-side cabin two-seat trainer of tube and plywood construction with fixed tailwheel u/c and one 105hp Hirth HM.504 engine. Prototype D-ERBV FF Feb 1939
Bü-181 Bestmann	708	Bestmann built in Holland by Fokker, 1942/44
Bü-181 SK-25	145	Swedish licence-built Bestmann
Zlin Z.281		Czech Bestmann built by Moravan with 100hp Toma-4 engine
Zlin Z.381	465	Czech Bestmann with 105hp Walter Minor. Designated C-106 in Czech military service
Z.481	1	Z.381 with 160hp Walter Minor 6.III engine. Prototype only, OK-YVA

Following World War Two, the Jungmann and Jungmeister maintained their popularity. Out of the Swiss batches of Jungmanns built by Dornier, many aircraft were re-engined with 150hp Lycoming IO-320s by the A P Morand company (now designated APM.131-150). Datwyler at Bleinbach in Switzerland was also responsible for rebuilding four aircraft as Bü.131/R Lerches with the 180hp Lycoming IO-360-B1B and a modified wing section. There have been several post-war initiatives to build new production Jungmanns and Jungmeisters in addition to those manufactured by CASA. In the mid-1960s, Joseph Bitz Flugzeugbau of Haunstetten in Germany built a small series of three Bü.133D-1 aircraft to the order of Jack Canary (c/n 2001 to 2003). These followed the pre-war specification but had glassfibre engine cowlings and modern brakes. Bitz also produced airframes for a further nine aircraft (c/n 2004 to 2012), the first of which was assembled by Wolf Hirth and four others (c/n 2005, 2006, 2008 and 2009) were completed in Switzerland and France.

In Spain, the CASA jigs, spares and production rights are believed to have been acquired by Büker Prado SL based at Albacete. They are believed to have produced at least one new aircraft. In Poland, the Jungmann has been returned to production by SSH (Serwis Samolotow Historycznych) who took over premises at Bielsko-Biala vacated by the bankrupt glider manufacturer, SZD. They have been building the T-131P, based on the Tatra/Aero version and powered by a 105hp Walter Minor 4-III, and the current T-131.PA with a 138hp. LOM M-332AK. The prototype (SP-FPF c/n 01) first flew on 8th July 1994, followed by three pre-production aircraft (c/n 02 to 04). 21 production

aircraft are known to have been built by mid-2004 (c/n 101 to 121), some being sold as kits. SSH have also launched the T-133.PA, a new version of the Jungmeister with a 160hp Siemens-Halske SH-14a radial engine. The Bestmann was also relaunched as the Aeropony and this is covered in the section on Heliopolis.

Bulgarian State Aircraft Works   Bulgaria

Under the Comecon system of allocating particular industrial roles to individual countries, Bulgaria concentrated on agriculture and was not designated to develop an aircraft manufacturing industry. However, in 1946 a specification from the Yugoslav Air Force for a basic trainer prompted Eng Cwietan Lazarov to design and build the prototype LAZ-7. This aircraft won the Yugoslav requirement in the face of competition from the indigenous Aero 2 – but in the end the Aero 2 was built in quantity for the Yugoslav Air Force while the Bulgarian flying club movement acquired a number of examples of the LAZ-7 and its derivatives.

The prototype LAZ-7.1 was a conventional low-wing tandem two-seat cabin monoplane with a fixed tailwheel undercarriage and a 160hp Walter Minor 6-III engine. The third prototype, the LAZ-7.3, together with the production examples had a cut-down rear fuselage decking to give full all-round vision to the occupants plus a rearwards-retracting main undercarriage.

In due course, Lazarov made a number of changes to the LAZ-7 and installed the M-11FR radial engine with a helmeted cowling in which form the aircraft closely resembled the Yak-18 and was designated LAZ-7M. It went into production with the Znamenalo Zavodski Avia-

Lazarov LAZ-7M LZ-M52. J Blake

cionen Kolektiv as the ZAK-1 and was delivered in some numbers to the Bulgarian Air Force where it became the standard primary trainer. Lazarov also designed a derivative of the LAZ-7 designated LAZ-8, which had a four-seat cabin but only flew in prototype form.

CAB   France

The Constructions Aéronautique de Béarn (CAB) was set up in 1948 by Max Laporte with Yves Gardan as Technical Director. Operations started at Pau where Gardan designed a new two-seat low-wing light aircraft – the GY-20 Minicab. Gardan had already produced the design of the similar SIPA 90 – but the Minicab was considerably lighter and mounted a 65hp Continental A65-8 engine compared with the 90hp Continental used in the SIPA 90. The prototype Minicab (F-WFDT c/n 01), built of wood and fabric, first flew at Pau-Idron on 1st February 1949. It had a fixed tailwheel undercarriage and featured a single-piece cockpit canopy that hinged forward for access. In total, CAB manufactured only 22 Minicabs (c/n 1 to 22) but the design was available to amateur builders and at least 27 were completed with serial numbers in the range c/n A101 to A127.

Whilst the GY-20 was in production, Yves Gardan moved on to the GY-30 Supercab. Using the same mixed construction, the Supercab had a manually-operated retractable tailwheel undercarriage with inward-retracting main units. To add to the performance, a 90hp Continental was fitted and this gave a maximum speed of 170mph compared with the 123mph of the Minicab. The prototype was F-WEPO

CAB GY-20 Minicab G-AVRW

(c/n 01) which flew on 5th February 1954 and this was followed by a further two prototypes (c/n 02 and 03) and four production aircraft (c/n 1 to 4) before CAB abandoned further aircraft manufacture. Later aircraft designs by Yves Gardan are detailed in the section on Gardan.

Callair   United States

The Call brothers designed the Model A just before the war and the prototype first flew in 1940, powered by an 80hp Continental engine. This aircraft was a side-by-side two-seat cabin monoplane with a strut-braced low wing and fixed tailwheel undercarriage. In its initial form, the Model A was underpowered and the definitive version certificated on 26th July 1944 was upgraded to a 100hp Lycoming O-235 engine which gave it much better performance when operating from the high altitude of Callair's Afton, Wyoming base. Four of the basic A-1 version were built by the company between 1944 and 1945, the first production aircraft being N26500 (c/n 2).

The Models A-2, A-3 and A-4 followed and these all shared a similar airframe to the A-1 but with a smaller vertical tail and a variety of engines. The A-2 and A-3 were two-seaters and Call Aircraft built a total of 34 examples between 1946 and 1952. The similar A-4, introduced in 1954, was able to carry three people on its main bench seat and this aircraft marked the expansion of the company's activities. The company became Callair Inc and, by 1956, production had risen to almost two aircraft per month. At this time Callair also took over the high-wing Interstate S-1B trainer but that design passed on to Arctic Aircraft (see section on Arctic).

Several of the early Callairs were subsequently re-engined as it was an easy matter to upgrade, say, an A-2 to A-4 standard. In addition, a

Callair A-2 N34841. G Dobson

number of A-4s were extensively modified for agricultural use and these can be identified by the 'A' suffix to their serial numbers. This development led to Callair producing a definitive agricultural machine based on the A-4 but lacking the cabin rear decking. It had reduced-span wings and a tandem open two-seat cockpit offset to the port side with the chemical hopper buried in the starboard side of the fuselage. This Model A-5 was followed by the A-5T, A-6, A-7 and A-7T – all of which were very similar but had different powerplants and progressive minor improvements.

In January 1962 the assets of Callair Inc were acquired at a public sale by the Intermountain Manufacturing Company (IMCO) who used the basic structure of the A-7 to produce the substantially new A-9. This prototype first flew in early 1962 and received its type certificate on 9th November of that year. With a fabric-covered steel tube fuselage and wooden wings it was the first of the Callair crop sprayers to have an enclosed cockpit. This was located above and behind the hopper in the fashion established by the Piper Pawnee. IMCO built the A-9 at a high rate and, in 1965, improved it by introducing a full-span flap system, droop ailerons and a new wing leading edge – all of which improved the take-off performance by over 30% and allowed a higher useful load.

In 1966 IMCO flew the Callair B-1 and then put this model into production alongside the A-9. It was a scaled-up A-9 with metal wings and a hopper capacity of 300 US gallons – almost double that of the smaller aircraft. Later that year, they sold the type certificate, rights, tooling and operations to Rockwell Standard Corporation who continued to build both models at the Afton, Wyoming factory.

In line with their policy of naming aircraft in the Rockwell stable they called the A-9 Sparrow Commander and the A-9B Quail Commander. The B-1 was later re-engined with a Pratt & Whitney R-985 radial engine to become the Snipe Commander. Few of these were built and the B-1 type certificate was subsequently sold to SL Industries of Oklahoma City. Rockwell concentrated on the A-9 variants from 1969 onwards and relocated to a new plant at Albany, Georgia where the Lark Commander was also being produced.

Rockwell's involvement with the Callair line was fairly brief because, in 1971, the A-series type certificate and all stocks, components and production tooling were sold to Aeronautica Agricola Mexicana SA (AAMSA) and all Quail production was transferred to Pasteje, Mexico. The A9B was also built from Mexican components by the AAMSA subsidiary, Aircraft Parts and Development Corporation of Laredo, Texas but most of these aircraft were sold in Mexico. AAMSA also built a small number of the improved A9B-M version. Callair serial number allocations have been as follows:

Callair A9 N8246H

Model	Built	Serials	Model	Built	Serials
A-1	4	2-5	AAMSA A-9B	101	1616-1717
A-2, A-3	31	6-8, 109-136	AAMSA A-9B	36	3001-3036
A-4	66	137, 141-206	A/c Parts A-9B	17	5001-5017
Not used		138-140	B-1	36	10000-10035
A-5, A-6	116	207-322	*Total Built*	*1,024*	

Details of Callair models are:

Model	Notes
A	Two-seat low-wing cabin monoplane powered by one 80hp Cont A-80. Prototype NX27251 (c/n 1) built 1940
A-1	Similar to Model A with 100hp Lycoming O-235 engine
A-2	Similar to A-1 with Lycoming O-290-A engine
A-3	Similar to A-2 with 125hp Continental C-125-2 engine
A-4	Three-seat A-3 with 140hp Lycoming O-290-D2 engine
A-5	Open-cockpit two-seat agricultural aircraft based on A-4 with reduced wingspan. Powered by one 150hp Lycoming O-320-A2A engine. Prot N9953C (c/n 207)
A-5T	A-5 with revised fuselage structure. Named Texan
A-6	A-5 powered by 180hp Lycoming O-360-A1A engine
A-7	Projected A-5 development powered by a Gulf Coast Dusting W670-240 engine. Also A-7T with higher gross weight. Prototype N2944G (c/n 299) converted from an A-6
A-9	Developed A-6 with narrower fuselage frame and enclosed single-seat cockpit situated above and behind hopper. Powered by a 235hp Lycoming O-540-B2B5 engine. Normal category 1,900 lb TOGW. Built by Rockwell as Sparrow Commander. Prototype N3600G (c/n 1000)
A-9A	A-9 with minor modifications and normal cat. 3,000 lb TOGW – possibly for Australian certification
A-9B	A-9A with 260hp Lycoming IO-540-G1C5 engine. Rockwell 'Quail'. AAMSA version fitted with 300hp Lycoming IO-540-K1A5 engine
A-9B-M	AAMSA A-9B with cut-down rear fuselage, increased dihedral, larger ailerons, larger fin
B-1	Scaled-up development of A-9 developed by IMCO and powered by one 400hp Lycoming IO-720-A1A engine. Prototype N7200V (c/n 10000) FF 15 Jan 1966

Caproni   Italy

The company, founded by Gianni Caproni, dates back to 1912 and a wide range of civil and military types were built up to the 1930s and through the World War Two period. On 13th May 1949 they flew the prototype Ca.193 (I-POLO) – a five-seat all-metal aircraft with twin 160hp pusher Walter Minor engines, a twin tail and retractable tricycle undercarriage. This did not reach production. Two years later they built the prototype Caproni F.5 Trento, which was the first of a series of Frati-designed two-seat jet trainers. This all-wood low-wing tandem two-seater had a retractable tricycle undercarriage and was powered by a 330 lbst Turboméca Palas turbojet buried in the lower fuselage. The prototype (I-RAIA, later I-FACT and MM553) first flew on 20th May 1952 but, again, there were no production aircraft. Caproni-Vizzola (as it had become) then acquired rights to the Aviamilano A-2 and A-3 sailplanes, which they put in production and developed into the side-by-side two-seat A-21 (and A-21S) Calif. Three examples of the A-21SJ were built with a Sermel (Microturbo) turbojet fitted in the centre fuselage (prototype I-JETT, c/n 220). Caproni then proceeded with the new C-22J very-light jet trainer, which had a pod-and-boom fuselage with side-by-side seating for two, a T-tail, retractable tricycle undercarriage and two Microturbo TRS.18-01 turbojets buried behind the cabin. The prototype (I-CAVJ) first flew on 21st July 1980 and was followed by two further aircraft (I-GIAC, c/n 002 and I-CAVT, c/n 003). The second two aircraft had shortened wings and wingtip tanks. No further production took place.

Caproni C-22J I-GIAC. M J Hooks

Cessna Aircraft   United States

By a good margin, Cessna Aircraft Co Inc is the largest post-war volume producer of general aviation aircraft. Since the end of World War Two, Cessna has delivered over 168,000 individual civil aircraft and, prior to the product liability crisis of the mid-1980s, had the largest and most comprehensive model range of any manufacturer. It was started as the Cessna-Roos Aircraft Company on 8th September 1927 by Clyde Cessna who had been one of the founders of Travel Air together with Walter Beech and Lloyd Stearman. Under the direction of Clyde Cessna's nephew, Dwane Wallace, Cessna produced a series of high-wing monoplanes during the pre-war years and these grew in sophistication, culminating in the four-seat C-145 and C-165 Airmasters.

After a wartime period in which they produced some 5,400 T-50 Bobcats and 750 Waco CG-4A troop-carrying gliders, Cessna had a manufacturing organisation geared to large-scale production. They launched a new two-seat all-metal light aircraft for the postwar market, the Cessna 120, which was certificated on 21st March 1946. With its Model 140 derivative (equipped with flaps, extra side windows, an electric starter and the distinctive spring steel undercarriage designed by Steve Wittman) it was built in large numbers during the period from 1946 to 1948. For customers needing a larger aircraft, the company built the Model 190 and 195, which were all-metal aircraft owing much to the design of the Airmaster. A number of Cessna 195s were sold to the US Air Force as the LC-126.

Cessna had always been a firm proponent of the high-wing layout for all its single-engined aircraft and they used the basic Model 120 design as the basis of the four-seat Model 170, which gained its type certificate (A-799) on 1st June 1948. This design was progressively re-engined, modified and enlarged to give a range of models including the Model 172, 175, 180, 182 and 185. Each of these models then took on an individual programme of development that made them into quite different aircraft despite their common origins.

Cessna soon adopted very sophisticated marketing techniques – often following the product marketing ideas of the American automobile industry, introducing a new model every year to persuade customers that they would get the latest design features by buying a Cessna. Safety modifications were high priorities but, very often, the model change consisted of a new paint design, a new shape for the windows, a swept tail or redesigned seat upholstery. Every three years or so, a major design improvement was introduced such as the all-round vision cabin of the 1963 models and the addition of retractable undercarriages to the Models 172, 177 and 182. They also offered different standards of upholstery and paint trim – with the standard models being known by their type designation only (eg, Cessna 172) and deluxe models by a name (eg, Skyhawk).

Good marketing of their private light aircraft together with manufacture of military aircraft and mundane products such as filing cabinets and other office furniture saw Cessna through the post-war recession of the late 1940s. During the next ten years they expanded into larger versions of the Cessna 180 to meet demands for increased performance and utility. The first development was the Model 210, developed with a stronger airframe from the Cessna 182 Skylane and fitted with a more powerful engine and an unusual rear-folding retractable undercarriage. It received its type certificate (3A21) on 20th April 1959. Cessna continued to develop the original Model 210, initially moving from a strut-braced wing to a full cantilever wing structure and then introducing the P.210 with a pressurized cabin and turbocharged engine to meet the increasing demands of serious business aircraft users who could justify the cost of this type of transportation. With a stretched fuselage and fixed undercarriage, the 210 became the Model 205 – followed by the refined Model 206 in 1963 and the stretched Model 207 that was certificated on 31st December 1968. These proved to be excellent utility designs and were frequently fitted with skis and floats by bush operators. Most of these general-purpose upper-class singles had optional turbocharged engines and were available with 'hard' utility interiors or deluxe trim with plush carpets, seats and headliners.

The utility aircraft group also included a range of agricultural aircraft that departed from the Cessna culture and had a strut-braced low

Cessna 140 NC81059

Cessna 150 LV-LBV

wing. The Model 188 Agwagon, which achieved its type certificate (A9CE) on 14th February 1966, used existing Cessna wing technology and the familiar spring steel undercarriage married to a new single-seat fuselage. Again, this was offered with a variety of engines of different horsepower and with progressively greater load-carrying capacity.

As the business aircraft market developed, Cessna moved into a range of low-wing twins. The first Cessna twin was the Model 310, which was approved on 22nd March 1954 under certificate 3A10 and was one of the fastest and most refined of light aircraft of that era. The Model 310 was expanded into the Model 320 and pressurized Model 340 both of which had longer cabins and increased power. The company also designed the unusual Model 336 Skymaster strut-braced high-wing 'push-pull twin' which had twin booms and engines at the front and rear of the pod fuselage. This was developed into the Model 337 Super Skymaster with a retractable undercarriage together with its pressurized P.337 derivative.

It was still necessary to offer a substantially larger 'cabin-class' model with a comfortable interior for four to six passengers, an airstair entry door and sufficient power, range and avionics to meet the stringent operating demands of company users. Cessna's answer was the Model 411, which first flew in July 1962 and was approved on 17th August 1964 (Certificate A7CE). This was an immediate success and it spawned numerous variants including the Model 402 and stretched 404 for third-level airline operation and the pressurized piston-engined corporate Model 414 Chancellor and 421 Golden Eagle. Later versions of these types abandoned the distinctive wingtip fuel tanks in favour of a new wet wing.

The undisputed market niche created by the turbine-powered Beech King Air soon induced Cessna to develop the 400-series airframe into the Model 441 Conquest, which was fitted with Garrett TPE331 turboprops and completed its certification process on 19th August 1977. In turn, this led to Cessna modifying the Model 421 Golden Eagle as the Model 425 Corsair (later Conquest I) with Pratt and Whitney PT6A turboprops.

The business had faced lean times when the commercial market had run into post-war recession, but Cessna's military contracts allowed it both to stay in business and to build up an important commercial base

for the future. An important outgrowth of the Model 170 was the Model 305 'Bird Dog' military liaison machine. This combined the wings of the Model 170/180 (modified with high lift flaps) with a new fuselage and all-round vision cockpit. The Model 305 was approved on 11th January 1951 – and some 2,526 examples left the Wichita production line during the next five years. In 1952, Cessna bid and won a contract to supply a new jet trainer for the US Air Force. The Model 318 went into production in 1955 as the T-37A and was sufficiently versatile also to become an effective ground-attack aircraft in Vietnam. Cessna also sold a number of O-2 support aircraft that were based on the Model 337 and a large batch of T-41 trainers based on the commercial Model 172 Skyhawk.

The company became involved in some abortive ventures. In 1956, there seemed to be a market opportunity for an 8/10-seat multi-engined business aircraft to replace the ageing fleet of corporate DC-3s. The four-engined Model 620 was designed and a prototype flown. Unfortunately, as development advanced, it was clear that surplus airline Convair 440s and Martin 404s were going to provide a much cheaper and more comfortable alternative – so Cessna abandoned the Model 620. Another move involved the acquisition, in 1952, of the Wichita-based Seibel Helicopter Company. Seibel's S-3 and S-4 designs led Cessna to the CH-1 light helicopter which flew in July 1954. It was an attractive machine with its engine mounted in the nose to give it an appearance similar to that of a conventional light aircraft, and, in its CH-1A version, it could accommodate four people. Sadly, Cessna found that the CH-1 was taking up production resource needed for the expanding line of fixed wing models and most of the production CH-1s were bought back by them and destroyed for reasons of product liability protection.

The main production base for the company has always been Wichita, Kansas where the single-engined models were built at the Pawnee Plant to the east of the city and the multi-engined and military aircraft came from the Wallace plant on the edge of Wichita Municipal Airport. Other plants were operated at Winfield and Hutchinson, Kansas. Other subsidiaries have included Aircraft Radio Corporation (ARC) and the Industrial Products Division at Hutchinson, which concentrated on industrial hydraulics systems. The company has been involved in vari-

Cessna 500 Citation N275GK

ous overseas manufacturing ventures. Between 1966 and 1976, airframes for three Cessna types were supplied for local assembly by DINFIA in Argentina. DINFIA built 48 of the Model A-150L and A-A150L, three P-172s, 148 Skylanes (A-182J to A-182N) and 34 of the A-A188B Ag Truck.

On 16th February 1960, Cessna acquired a 49% interest in Avions Max Holste in France and thereafter changed its name to Reims Aviation SA and started to build Cessna models for sale in Europe and the Middle East. Reims started by assembling the Model 172 from Wichita-built kits but full local production capability was soon established and, eventually, Reims built many of the Cessna types including the following models: F150F to F150M, FA150K and L, FRA150L and M, F152, FA152, FP172, F172D to F172P, FR172E to FR172K, F177RG, F182P and Q, FR182, F337E to H and FP337.

The Reims models were generally indistinguishable from the Wichita-built equivalents and incorporated all the annual model changes. However, there were certain models, such as the Reims Rocket (an uprated Model 172), which were peculiar to the French company. Cessna and Reims developed the Model F.406 Caravan II, which was based on the Cessna 404 and fitted with Pratt and Whitney PT6A turboprops. During the 1980s, production of Reims single-engined models progressively declined and in 1989 Cessna sold its interest in Reims Aviation to Compagnie Francaise Chaufour Investissement which discontinued the single-engined models in line with Cessna's own actions but continued to build around six of the F.406 each year.

1969 saw the first flight of the Cessna 500 Citation business jet. The Citation programme represented a huge investment for Cessna but it was successful as a result of the excellent marketing programme established by James B Taylor. It was certificated on 9th September 1971 (certificate A22CE). The Citation has been stretched and upgraded into a number of models including the US Navy's T-47A and the Citation I, Citation II and Citation V which are certificated for single-pilot operation. Cessna then went on to build the larger Model 650 Citation (Citation III, VI and VII), which was a new design with twelve seats and inter-continental range and gave the company a complete corporate jet line. When the Model 650 started to wane, Cessna replaced it with

the Citation Excel, which used a combination of elements of the Citation Ultra and Citation X. The two original Citation models were continuously upgraded and currently consist of the Model 550 Citation Bravo and Model 560 Citation Encore.

A new generation of small Citations was initiated with the CitationJet. This first flew in April 1991 and has been expanded to a family of three models including the basic CJ1 and the stretched CJ2 and CJ3. At the other end of the scale is the stretched high-performance Citation X, which was announced in October 1990 and was first delivered in 1996. Cessna has also developed the Citation Sovereign which fits between the Excel and the Citation X and received its type certificate I December 2003 with deliveries commencing in 2004. In October 2002, Cessna announced the Citation Mustang, which is a six-seat personal jet aimed at the market targeted by the Eclipse and first flown in April 2005. Production of the Mustang will take place at the Liberal, Kansas factory.

Together with the Citations, the other current production model from Wichita is the Model 208 Caravan I. This is the largest single-

Cessna 170A CC-PRE

Cessna F177RG Cardinal RG F-BVSN

engined Cessna to have been built and it achieved its type certificate on 23rd October 1984. The Caravan is a large high-wing machine designed for freight carrying and general utility roles and it is sold in standard or stretched versions powered by a single Pratt & Whitney PT6A turboprop. The majority of the early production Caravan Is were sold to Federal Express, who use the type extensively on mini-hub freight operations, but examples have also been sold in executive configuration, on amphibious floats and in Grand Caravan passenger layout.

In June 1986 the crisis over product liability had reached major proportions and, because of its size, resources and number of aircraft flying in the United States, Cessna was a major target for damage suits by accident victims and their dependants. Due to the size of these claims, Cessna suspended production of all the lower-value single-engined aircraft and, progressively over the next eighteen months, abandoned the other piston-engined models. They closed the Pawnee production plant and concentrated manufacture at the Wallace Plant at Wichita Municipal Airport. This left the company to concentrate on the Citations, the Caravan I and some military contracts. Cessna was acquired

by General Dynamics in September 1985 and on 20th January 1992 Cessna was, again, sold, to Textron Inc for $600m.

With the passing of the General Aviation Product Liability Reform Bill, Cessna re-established production of the Model 172, 182 and 206. A new factory at Liberal, Kansas was opened in August 1996 and the first production Model 172R was first flown on 6th November 1996. This was followed by a new Cessna 182S Skylane prototype on 16th July 1996 and a new Model 206H Stationair on 28th August 1996. The first customer deliveries of these aircraft started in 1997 and minor annual changes have been initiated subsequently, the most significant being the introduction of glass cockpits on the Skylane and Stationair in 2004. In the calendar year 2004, Cessna delivered the following new aircraft – 172R Skyhawk (32), 172S Skyhawk SP (204), 182T Skylane (196), T182T Turbo Skylane (133), 206H Stationair (22), T206H Turbo Stationair (67), 208 Caravan I (13), 208B Caravan IB (51), 525 CitationJet CJ1 (20), 525A CitationJet CJ2 (27), 525B CitationJet CJ3 (6), 550 Citation Bravo (25), 560 Citation Encore (24), 560XL Citation Excel (23), 560XLS Citation XLS (32), 680 Citation Sovereign (9), 750 Citation X (15).

Postwar Cessnas have been given model numbers in broad groups that are intended to indicate the general size of the type, measured by its horsepower rating. Broadly, the types have fallen into the following sections:

100 Series	Light single-engined aircraft up to 280hp (eg, Model 172)
200 Series	Larger single-engined aircraft over 280hp (eg, Model 210)
300 Series	Light twin-engined aircraft up to 600hp (eg, Model 310)
400 Series	Medium twin-engined aircraft over 600hp (eg, Model 421)
500 Series	Light turbofan-powered aircraft (eg, Model 500)
600 Series	Medium turbofan-powered aircraft (eg, Model 650)
700 Series	Larger high-performance turbofan aircraft (eg, Citation X)

Inevitably, these groups have become blurred as time has passed. For instance, the original Model 188 Agwagon came into the 100- series with its 230hp engine, but the heavier 300hp Agwagon 300 still came under the same type number. At the heavy end of the scale, the 600-series was used initially for the piston-engined Model 620, which was

Cessna 172S Skyhawk SP N5182Z

Cessna 180K Skywagon II N6TK

rather different from the later Model 650 Citation III. The system was also upset by the use of the type number 305 for the single-engined military Bird Dog and 318 for the T-37 jet trainer.

Following this broad classification, Cessna used a method of prefix and suffix letters to differentiate between models produced in each year. A letter was added to the numerical designation to denote each different annual version (eg, Model 172B, 172C, 172D etc). From 1957, each model tended to be given a new suffix letter every year, but after 1967 only major changes warranted an alteration to the designation. When the single-engined models were offered with retractable undercarriages, the letters 'RG' were added as a suffix to the basic type number (eg, 172RG). Fortunately, there was no need to further complicate this by adding an additional letter to denote a major sub-variant.

Prefix letters are given by Cessna to denote special features involved in certain models and these include:

A	Used on Model 185 (A185E et seq) to denote version with 300hp engine because both 300 and 260hp versions were produced together
A	Used on Model 188 to denote 300hp version
A	Used to identify the improved 1953/54 model of the Model 195
A	Used for DINFIA-built Argentinian aircraft
A	Used to identify the Aerobat version of the Models 150 and 152
F	Used to identify Reims-built French production
P	Used to identify P206 Super Skylane version of Model 206
P	Used to denote 'Powermatic' on geared engine P172
P	Used to denote 'Pressurized' model – eg, P337, P210
R	Used for the Reims Rocket, the higher-powered military T-41 and the R172K Hawk XP
T	Used to denote 'Turbocharged' model (eg, TU206F Turbo Stationair). In the data table, these models are identified thus †
U	Used on the U206 to denote Utility category certification

In addition to the designations, Cessna has generally given names to most aircraft models. These have changed, in some cases, during the life of the basic type. For instance, the original fixed-gear Model 205 had no name but became the Super Skywagon when it was re-engined in 1964. In 1971, it was renamed Stationair – and then, later, became the Stationair 6. Names were always given to the deluxe-trim models, but those delivered in basic finish often only carried the standard type number. For instance, the deluxe Model 177 was named Cardinal but the relatively small number of basic aircraft delivered just carried the title Cessna 177. These Cessna 177s were in bare metal finish with a simplified colour paint stripe, had vinyl seats and lacked wheel fairings and other deluxe additions. Cessna no longer offered these economy versions after the mid-1970s.

Cessna has always aimed to deliver fully factory-equipped aircraft to the customer, with packaged avionics produced for many years by their ARC avionics division at Boonton, New Jersey. From the mid-1970s, the various avionics options have been identified by the suffixes -I, -II, -III etc. Thus, the 1978 model of the Cessna 402 was known as the Utililiner II in fully equipped form with the ARC Series 300 and 400 'Nav-o-matic' system, dual Nav/Com, ADF, Glideslope, marker beacon and transponder as standard.

Finally, it should be said that Cessna has also used other model numbers outside the standard system. Firstly, there is a separate category of experimental designations, which gives a four-digit identity for projects. For instance, the Cessna XMC experimental twin-boomed research aircraft was the Model 1014, and the Model 177RG started out as the Model 1008. There are also some examples of one-off designations, such as the Model 195 fitted with a Continental flat-six engine and known as the X-210 and the Cessna Skyhook helicopter, which used its own unique identity as the CH-1.

Type numbers allocated by Cessna to date are shown in the following table:

Model	Name	Built	Notes
120	-	2,172	Economy Model 140 without flaps or rear side windows. 1,450 lb TOGW
140	-	4,907	High-wing side-by-side two-seater with metal fuselage and metal/fabric wings with flaps and V-bracing struts. 1,450 lb TOGW. Powered by one Cont C-85-12 piston engine. Prototype NX41682 (c/n 8000) FF 28 June 1945

Cessna 182P Skylane N9166M. Cessna

140A	-	525	Model 140 with all-metal wings, single wing support struts and optional 90hp Continental C-90-12 engine. 1,500 lb TOGW
142	-	1	Preliminary designation for Model 150
150	-	1,018	High-wing two-seat all-metal trainer developed from Model 140 with tricycle u/c, powered by one 100hp Continental O-200A. 1,500 lb TOGW. Prototype N34258 (c/n 617) FF 12 Sep 1957
150A	-	333	Model 150 with main u/c legs moved back, larger rear side windows and improved instrument panel
150B	-	350	150A with improved propeller and spinner plus minor changes
150C	-	387	150B with minor changes. Optional child seat
150D	-	686	150C with cut-down rear fuselage and omni-vision rear windows. 1,600 lb TOGW and increased useful load. FF 4 Feb 1963
150	-	760	150D with minor changes
150F	-	2,933	150E with swept vertical tail, larger cabin doors and electric flaps
F150F	-	67	Reims-built Model 150F
150G	-	2,666	150F with wider cabin interior and new instrument panel. Prototype N3763C
F150G	-	152	Reims-built Model 150G
150H	-	2,110	150G with minor changes
F150H	-	170	Reims-built Model 150H
150J	-	1,820	150H with new u/c fairings and new instrument panel
F150J	-	140	Reims-built Model 150J
150K	-	875	150J with cambered wingtips, new seats and trim tab on lower rudder
F150K	-	129	Reims-built Model 150K
150L	-	3,778	150K with enlarged fin fairing, tubular steel u/c legs, new wheel fairings (from 1974) and redesigned engine cowling
F150L	-	485	Reims-built Model 150L
A-150L	-	39	Argentine-built 150L by DINFIA
150M	-	3,624	150L with taller, narrower tail
F150M	-	285	Reims-built Model 150M
A150K to A150M	Aerobat	734	Aerobatic equivalent of standard 150 models with strengthened airframe, full harness, quick release doors and cabin skylight windows. FF 2 Jan 1969
FA150K	Aerobat	81	Reims-built Model A150K
FA150L	Aerobat	39	Reims-built Model A150L
FRA150L	Aerobat	141	FA150L with 130hp R-R Continental O-240-A
FRA150M	Aerobat	75	FRA150L with Model F150M modifications
152	-	6,628	150M with 110hp Lycoming O-235-L2C engine, new propeller, single piece engine cowling, 28-volt electrical system, electric flaps, new fuel tanks. 30° flap setting. 1,670 lb TOGW. FF 16 Jul 1976
F152	-	552	Reims-built Model 152
A152	Aerobat	315	Aerobatic version of Model 152
FA152	Aerobat	89	Reims-built Model A152
160	-	1	Experimental high-wing tricycle u/c four-seater with one Franklin engine. Prototype N5419E (c/n 643) FF 1962
170	-	730	Four-seater developed as an enlarged Model 140 with new two-panel fabric-covered wing, V-bracing struts, fixed tailwheel u/c, powered by one 145hp Cont C-145. 2,200 lb TOGW. Prototype NX41691 (c/n 18000) FF 5 Nov 1947
170A	-	1,536	170 with all-metal wings, dorsal fin fairing and single wing struts. Prototype NX41693 (c/n 18002)
170B	-	2,907	170A with larger slotted flaps and 145hp Continental O-300 engine
170C	-	1	Experimental 170A with new rectangular vertical tail, 155hp Continental O-300-A engine. Prototype N37892 (c/n 609). Developed into Model 172
172	-	3,757	170C with tricycle u/c, new square vertical tail and 145hp Continental O-300-C engine. 2,200 lb TOGW. Prototype N41768 (c/n 612) FF 12 Jun 1955
172A	-	994	172 with swept vertical tail
172B	Skyhawk*	989	172A with deeper fuselage, new windshield, revised engine cowling and propeller spinner, shorter u/c, external baggage door and new instrument panel. *Deluxe Skyhawk option with overall paint, spats etc
172C	Skyhawk*	810	172B with 2,250 lb TOGW and minor changes

Cessna A-188B AgTruck N731BY. Cessna

172D	Skyhawk*	1,011	172C with cut-down rear fuselage and omni-vision rear windows. 2,300 lb TOGW
F172D	-	18	Reims-built Model 172D
172	Skyhawk*	1,209	172D with electric flaps, optional rear child seat and minor changes
F172E	-	67	Reims-built Model 172E
172F	Skyhawk*	1,400	172E with O-200D engine and minor changes. USAF T-41A with 2 seats
F172F	-	94	Reims-built Model 172F
172G	Skyhawk*	1,474	172F with minor changes. USAF T-41A
F172G	-	140	Reims-built Model 172G
172H	Skyhawk*	1,586	172G with new nose u/c and spats, modified engine cowling, new instrument panel. USAF T-41A
F172H	-	435	Reims-built Model 172H
172I	Skyhawk*	649	172H with 150hp Lycoming O-320-E2D engine and 40 lb useful load increase
172J	-		Initial designation for Model 177
172K	Skyhawk*	2,055	172I with enlarged rear side windows, smooth dorsal fin fillet, rudder trim tab and cambered wingtips. USAF T-41A
F172K	-	50	Reims-built Model 172K
172L	Skyhawk*	1,535	172K with tubular steel u/c legs, nose-mounted landing light, new spats. 1972 model has longer fin fairing and shorter propeller
F172L	-	100	Reims-built Model 172L
172M	Skyhawk*	6,825	172L with wing leading edge camber. 1974 model has new spats and enlarged baggage area
F172M	-	610	Reims-built Model 172M
172N	Skyhawk 100*	6,425	172M with 160hp Lycoming O-320-H2AD engine, air conditioning, new seats etc
F172N	-	525	Reims-built Model 172N
172P	Skyhawk*	2,664	172N with Lycoming O-320-D2J engine, 89 lb useful load increase and 2,400 lb TOGW, modified elevator, reduced flap setting and optional long-range tanks
F172P	-	215	Reims-built Model 172P
172Q	Cutlass	391	172P with 180hp Lycoming O-360-A4N engine, 11 gal fuel increase and 2,550 lb TOGW. FF 15 Jul 1982
172R	Skyhawk	1,222	New 1996 production 172P with fuel-injected 180hp Lycoming IO-360-A4M, new fuel system, new interior details and instrument panel etc. Concept Prototype N6786R FF 21 Apr 1995. Production Prototype N5250K FF 16 Apr 1996
172S	Skyhawk SP	1,653	172R with fuel-injected 180hp Lycoming IO-360-L2A and 2,550 lb TOGW
R172E	T-41B	335	172F powered by one 210hp Continental IO-360-D engine with constant-speed prop. Strengthened u/c. T-41C variant has fixed pitch prop
FR172E	Reims Rocket	60	F172H powered by 210hp Continental IO-360-D
R172F	T-41D	74	R172E with 28-volt electrical system, 4 seats, constant-speed prop, wing hard points and simplified equipment for delivery to foreign air forces under MAP
FR172F	Reims Rocket	85	F172K powered by 210hp Continental IO-360-D
R172G	T-41D	35	R172F with minor changes and 2,550 lb TOGW. For USAF/MAP
FR172G	Reims Rocket	80	FR172F with minor modifications
R172H	T-41D	180	R172G with styling modifications of 172M and spring steel main u/c legs. USAF/MAP deliveries
FR172H	Reims Rocket	125	F172L powered by 210hp Continental IO-360-D
R172J	-	1	R172G with IO-360-H engine
FR172J	Reims Rocket	240	F172M with camber lift wing, tubular u/c legs and 210hp Continental IO-360-H engine
R172K	Hawk XP	1,455	172N with 195hp Cont IO-360-K engine, constant-speed prop, luxury interior and 116 lb useful load increase
FR172K	Reims Hawk XP	85	F172N powered by 210hp Continental IO-360-K. FF 29 Jan 1976
P172D	Skyhawk Powermatic	69	Model 172D with 175hp Cont GO-300-E geared engine, constant-speed prop and revised cowling with dorsal gearbox fairing. 2,500 lb TOGW

Cessna U206F Stationair OB-1616

FP172D	-	3	Reims-built Model P172D
172RG	Cutlass RG	1,191	Model 172N with retractable u/c, 180hp Lycoming O-360-F1A6 engine and 3-blade constant-speed prop. 2,650 lb TOGW. Prototype N7190C (c/n 690) FF 24 Aug 1978
175	-	1,237	Model 172 with 175hp Continental GO-300-A engine in redesigned cowling. 2,350 lb TOGW. Prototype N34260 (c/n 619) FF 23 Apr 1956
175A	Skylark*	539	Model 172A with GO-300-C engine. *Deluxe model Skylark with overall paint, spats etc
175B	Skylark*	225	172B with GO-300-C engine
175C	Skylark*	117	172C with GO-300-E engine and constant-speed prop. 2,450 lb TOGW
177	Cardinal*	1,164	Formerly 172J. Cantilever high-wing four-seater with fixed tricycle u/c and 150hp Lycoming O-320-E2D engine. 2,350 lb TOGW. *Deluxe model Cardinal with overall paint, spats etc. Prototype N3765C (c/n 660) FF 15 Jul 1966
177A	Cardinal*	206	177 with 180hp Lycoming O-360-A2F engine, new tailcone, and stabilator slots. 2,500 lb TOGW. FF 19 Jan 1968
177B	Cardinal*	1,381	177A with redesigned wing aerofoil, cambered wingtips, constant-speed prop and extra child seat. 1978 deluxe model named Cardinal Classic. FF 4 Dec 1968
177RG	Cardinal RG	1,366	177B with retractable tricycle u/c and 200hp Lycoming IO-360-A1B6D engine with constant-speed prop. 2,800 lb TOGW. Prototype N7172C (c/n 671) was Model 1008. FF 16 Feb 1970
F177RG	-	177	Reims-built Model 177RG
180	-	3,000	Model 170B with 225hp Continental O-470-A engine, rectangular vertical tail with dorsal fairing and reshaped side windows. 2,550 lb TOGW. Prototype N41697 (c/n 604) FF 26 May 1952
180A	-	356	180 with 230hp Continental O-470-K engine, stronger u/c, 2,650 lb TOGW and detail changes
180B	-	306	180A with revised engine cowling and minor detail changes
180C	-	250	180B with Continental O-470-L engine and constant-speed prop
180D	-	152	180C with minor detail changes
180	-	118	180D with increased fuel and minor detail changes
180F	-	129	180E with two optional extra seats and modified engine cowling
180G	-	133	180F with 2,800 lb TOGW, full six-seat capacity, extra side windows, 185 u/c and wings
180H	Skywagon 180	830	180G with detail changes including firewall from Skywagon 185. USAF U-17C
180J	Skywagon 180	486	180H with camber lift wing and minor detail changes
180K	Skywagon 180	433	180J with 230hp Continental O-470-U engine. Some fitted with A185E tail for float flying
182	-	843	Model 180 with fixed tricycle u/c and 230hp Continental O-470-R engine. 2,550 lb TOGW
182A	Skylane*	1,713	182 with 2,650 lb TOGW and minor changes. *Deluxe Skylane option available

Cessna 208B Caravan Floatplane N9382F

Cessna 195 N195AB

182B	Skylane*	802	182A with minor detail changes
182C	Skylane*	649	182B with swept vertical tail and third cabin window each side
182D	Skylane*	591	182C with minor detail changes. Canadian Army version designated L-19L
182	Skylane*	825	182D with cut-down rear fuselage and omni-vision rear windows, wider cockpit, electric flaps, 2,800 lb TOGW and O-470-R engine
182F	Skylane*	635	182E with minor changes
182G	Skylane*	786	182F with streamlined rear window structure and elliptical rear side windows
182H	Skylane*	840	182G with pointed prop spinner and minor changes
182J	Skylane*	885	182H with narrower vertical tail and other minor changes
A182J	-	56	DINFIA – built 182J
182K	Skylane*	840	182J with modified fin tip and minor changes
A182K	-	40	DINFIA – built 182K
182L	Skylane*	800	182K with minor changes
A182L	-	20	DINFIA – built 182L
182M	Skylane*	750	182L with minor changes
182N	Skylane*	770	182M with new instrument panel, enlarged baggage area, new spats, 2950 lb TOGW
A182N	-	33	DINFIA – built 182N
182P	Skylane*	4,350	182N with tubular steel u/c legs, cambered wing leading edge, nose-mounted landing light. Larger dorsal fin from 1973
F182P	Skylane	25	Reims-built Model 182P
182Q	Skylane*	2,540	182P with O-470-S engine, new spats and minor changes
F182Q	Skylane	145	Reims-built Model 182Q
182R	Skylane	900	182Q with optional turbocharged 235hp Lycoming O-540-L3C5D or standard Continental O-470-U engine
182S	Skylane	945	New 1996 production model with 230hp Lycoming IO-540, longer nose cowling, revised interior, panel & seats, standard avionics package. Special Millennium Edition for 2000
182T	Skylane	419	182S with design changes to wheel fairings, wingtips, strut fairings etc, minor changes to interior. Optional Garmin G1000 glass cockpit introduced 2004

T182T	Skylane	270	182T powered by one turbocharged 235hp Lycoming TIO-540-AK1A engine
R182	Skylane RG	2,041	182Q with retractable u/c and 235hp Lycoming O-540-J3C5D engine. Optional turbocharged O-540-L3C5D available from 1979. 3,100 lb TOGW
FR182	Skylane RG	67	Reims-built Model R182
185	Skywagon	237	180C with strengthened airframe, six seats, extra rear cabin side windows, enlarged dorsal fin and 260hp Cont IO-470-F engine. Prototype N34272 (c/n 632). Optional utility interior, belly cargo pod, skis & floats
185A	Skywagon	275	185 with optional long-range tanks and minor changes
185B	Skywagon	78	185A with minor changes. USAF U-17A
185C	Skywagon	89	185B with minor changes. USAF U-17A
185D	Skywagon	108	185C with minor changes. USAF U-17A
185	Skywagon	110	185D with enlarged baggage shelf and minor changes. USAF U-17A
A185E	Skywagon 185	723	185E with 50 lb TOGW increase and 285hp IO-520-D engine. Also special AgCarryall agricultural model from 1972. USAF U-17B
A185F	Skywagon 185	2,358	A185E with 3-blade prop and minor changes. USAF U-17B
	Super Cyclone		Kit-built copy of Cessna 185 supplied by St Just Aviation Inc of Montreal, Canada
187	-	1	Model 182 with cantilever wing. Prototype N7167C (c/n 666) FF 22 Apr 1968
188	Agwagon 230		Strut-braced low-wing single-seat all-metal agricultural aircraft with fixed tailwheel u/c and 3,800 lb TOGW. Powered by one 230hp Continental O-470-R. Prototype N5424E FF 19 Feb 1965
A188	Agwagon 300	317	Model 188 with 285hp Continental IO-520-D engine and 4,000 lb TOGW. Note: the production total is combined 188/A188
188A	Agwagon A & B		Model 188 with minor detail changes. 'B' model with increased wing dihedral, cambered wingtips, wire cutters on windshield and u/c, optional propeller spinner and new rear vision window
A188A	Agwagon A & B	515	A188 with minor detail changes and constant-speed prop. See 188A for other Agwagon B changes. Note: production total of 515 is combined 188A/A188A

Cessna T303 Crusader D-ICJL

188B	AgPickup	662	188A without rear window, spinner etc but fitted with camber-lift wing. Note: production total of 662 is combined 188B, A188B and T188C	P206A	Super Skylane†	146	P206 with minor detail changes and optional belly cargo pack. † TP206A has optional TSIO-520-C turbocharged engine
A188B	Agwagon C & AgTruck	.	A188A with camber-lift wing, drooped wingtips etc AgTruck fitted with much optional equipment and 280-gal hopper	U206B	Super Skywagon†	258	U206A with new instrument panel etc
T188C	Ag Husky		A188B AgTruck with 310hp Continental TSIO-520-T turbocharged engine, 4,400 lb TOGW and hydraulic chemical dispersal system	P206B	Super Skylane†	113	P206A with new instrument panel etc
A-A188B	AgTruck	34	DINFIA – built A188B	U206C	Super Skywagon†	319	U206B with minor detail changes
AC-05	Pijao	8	Agwagon 300 derivative manufactured by Aviones de Colombia with 4,200 lb TOGW and 300hp Continental IO-520D engine. Prototype HK-3631-X FF 10 Apr 1991	P206C	Super Skylane†	100	P206B with minor detail changes
190	-	1,083	All-metal high-wing five-seater with fixed spring-steel tailwheel u/c, powered by one 240hp Cont W670-23 radial engine. 3,350 lb TOGW. Prototype NX41681 FF 7 Dec 1945. Note: production total of 1083 is combined 190/195/195A	U206D	Super Skywagon†	210	U206C with minor changes. Float version has enlarged fin and rudder
				P206D	Super Skylane†	84	P206C with minor detail changes
195	-		190 powered by one 300hp Jacobs R755-A-2. Float version with elevator mounted finlets. Military LC-126A	U206E	Skywagon 206†	243	U206D with smoother lower nose cowling and minor changes. Deluxe 1971 model introduced as Stationair with further detail changes
195A	-		195 with 245hp Jacobs R755-9 engine	P206E	Super Skylane†	44	P206D with minor changes
195B	-	100	195 powered by 275hp Jacobs R755-B2	U206F	Stationair†	1,820	U206E with camber-lift wing, increased baggage area and new instrument panel. 3-blade prop standard from 1975. Stationair II with standard factory avionics fit
205	-	480	Model 210C with 3,300 lb TOGW, fixed tricycle u/c, extra port side door, two main doors, six seats, 260hp Cont IO-470-S engine. Prototype N5417E (c/n 641)				
205A	-	97	205 with minor detail changes	U206G	Stationair 6†	3,499	U206F with new nosewheel leg and detail changes. 1978 model has club seating option. Turbocharged engine changed to 310hp Continental TSIO-520-M
206	Super Skywagon	275	205 with 285hp Cont IO-520-A engine, 42in starboard double cargo door and pilot's (port) entry door only. 3,300 lb TOGW. Prototype N3753C (c/n 646)				
				T206H	Stationair TC	461	New 1996 production aircraft with turbocharged Lycoming TIO-580-A1A engine, new interior and instrument panel etc. Prot N732CP FF 28 Aug 1996
U206	Super Skywagon	162	206 with minor detail changes and utility category certification				
P206	Super Skylane	160	U206 with two main doors and port side rear door – but no cargo door. Deluxe interior, pointed spinner, spats and revised nose contours	206H	Stationair	215	T206H with fuel-injected 300hp Lycoming IO-540-AC1A engine
				207	Skywagon 207†	362	Stretched 206D with 18-inch baggage section ahead of windshield and 27-inch plug aft of wing to give seven seats in 4 rows. 3,800 lb TOGW. Powered by one 300hp Cont IO-520-F or † (turbocharged) TSIO-520-G engine. Prototype N1907F (c/n 665)
U206A	Super Skywagon†	219	U206 with minor detail changes, 3,600 lb TOGW, and optional belly cargo pack. † TU206A with TSIO-520-C turbocharged engine				

207A	Skywagon 207†	426	207 with minor changes and optional turbocharged engine changed to 310hp TSIO-520-M. From 1980 fitted with eight seats and named Stationair 8
208	Caravan I	376	Large all-metal high-wing utility aircraft with fixed tricycle u/c and 14-seat/cargo interior with 4 doors including port side double cargo door. Powered by one 600shp Pratt & Whitney PT6A-114 turboprop. 8,000 lb TOGW. Prototype N208LP (c/n 699) FF 9 Dec 1982. Military U-27A. Special Missions model has large roller-blind door
208	Caravan-675		Caravan 208/208A fitted with 675shp PT6A-114A engine. Introduced as standard, 1998
208A	Cargomaster		Model 208 for all-freight operation with hardened interior, no cabin windows or starboard rear door, taller vertical tail and belly pannier
208B	Super Cargomaster	1,103	208A with 4-ft. fuselage stretch aft of the wing, no windows and larger belly pannier. 675shp PT6A-114A engine. 8,750 lb TOGW. Prototype N9767F FF 3 Mar 1986
208B	Grand Caravan		208B with windows and passenger seating for passenger/cargo operations
208B	Pathfinder	1	Soloy-remanufactured 208B with 6-ft aft fuselage stretch, under-fuselage cargo section and Soloy Dual-Pac PT6A turboprop. Prototype N5010Y (c/n 208B-0304)
X210	-	1	Model 195 with 240hp Continental flat-six engine and redesigned forward fuselage, new flaps, square wingtips, square tail and tubular u/c legs. Prototype N41695 (c/n 602) FF Jan 1950
210	-	575	Four-seater developed from Model 182B with swept tail, new wing, retractable tricycle u/c, 260hp Cont IO-470-E engine. 2,900 lb TOGW. Prototype N1296 (c/n 616) FF 25 Feb 1957
210A	-	265	210 with third cabin window each side and higher rear cabin roof
210B	-	245	210A with cut-down rear fuselage, rear vision window, higher and wider cabin, new fuel system, IO-470-S engine and 3,000 lb TOGW
210C	-	135	210B with minor detail changes

Cessna 337G N53573. Cessna

210D	Centurion	290	210C with 285hp IO-520-A engine, redesigned control surfaces, two rear child seats and 3,100 lb TOGW
210E	Centurion	205	210D with minor detail changes
210F	Centurion†	300	210E with 3,300 lb TOGW and † optional 285hp turbocharged TSIO-520-C engine
210G	Centurion†	228	210F with strutless cantilever wing and modified rear window without wrap-round edges, 25 gal fuel increase. 3,400 lb TOGW
210H	Centurion†	210	210G with new flap system and instrument panel and detail changes
210J	Centurion†	200	210H with reduced wing dihedral, smooth lower nose profile and IO-520-J or † optional TSIO-520-H engine
210K	Centurion†	303	210J with full six seats, 3,800 lb TOGW and IO-520-L engine. U/c legs changed from spring steel to tube with bulged main gear doors. Enlarged cabin with single rear side window replacing previous two and larger externally-accessible baggage area
210L	Centurion†	2,070	210K with nose-mounted landing lights and minor detail changes

Cessna 340A D-IMHW

Model	Name	No.	Description
210M	Centurion†	1,381	210L with 310hp TSIO-520-R engine option and minor detail changes
210N	Centurion†	1,943	210M with open wheel wells for main u/c and minor changes
210R	Centurion†	112	210N with longer span stabiliser, cambered wingtips and detail changes. † Optional turbocharged TSIO-520-CE
P210N	Pressurized Centurion	834	Turbo 210N with pressurized cabin and four windows each side, powered by one 310hp TSIO-520-AF. 4,000 lb TOGW
P210R	Pressurized Centurion	40	P210N with longer span, stabiliser, cambered wingtips, 4,100 lb TOGW and 325hp Continental GTSIO-520-CE engine
303	-	1	Four-seat low-wing light twin with two 160hp Lycoming engines and 3,600 lb TOGW. Design replaced by T303. Prototype N303CP (c/n 687) FF 14 Feb 1978
T303	Crusader	305	All-metal low-wing six-seat cabin-class twin with retractable tricycle u/c, airstair door and two 250hp Continental TSIO-520-AE engines with counter-rotating props. 5,150 lb TOGW. Prototype N303PD (c/n 694). FF 17 Oct 1979. Initially named Clipper
305	-		Two-seat army cooperation aircraft based on Model 170 with cut-down rear fuselage, high-lift slotted wing flaps and 210hp Cont O-470-11. Prototype N41694 (c/n 601). FF Dec 1949
305A	Bird Dog	2,486	Model 305 with military equipment for US Army as L-19A-CE (later O-1) and USMC as OE-1 (later O-1B). Trainer variants include L-19AIT-CE and TL-19A. XL-19B fitted with 210shp Boeing XT50-BO-1 turboprop (52-1804, FF 2 Nov 1952) and XL-19C with XT51-T-1 turboprop (52-6311 and 52-6312, FF 1 Sep 1953)
305B	Bird Dog	310	305A for instrument training as TL-19D-CE (later TO-1D) with dual controls and 210hp O-470-15 engine with constant-speed prop
305C	Bird Dog	469	Improved 305A designated L-19E-CE with 2,400 lb TOGW and equipment changes
308	-	1	Six-seat high-wing all-metal utility aircraft with fixed tailwheel u/c and one 375hp Lycoming GSO-580-C. Prototype N41696 (c/n 603) FF 1952
309	-	1	Model 170 used for boundary layer control experiments. N5516C FF Dec 1951 Later Models 309B and 309C used chemical gas generating system to provide airflow
310	-	547	Five-seat all-metal low-wing light twin with retractable tricycle u/c, wingtip tanks and 3600 lb TOGW. Powered by two 240hp Continental O-470-B. Prototype N41699 (c/n 606) FF 3 Jan 1953
310A	Blue Canoe	160	Model 310 for USAF as L-27A (later U-3A) with aux fuel tanks, new instrument panel and military cabin trim
310B	-	225	310 with new instrument panel, 4,700 lb TOGW, O-470-M engines and minor changes
310C	-	259	310B with 260hp IO-470-D engines, 4,830 lb TOGW and other minor detail changes
310D	-	268	310C with swept vertical tail and minor detail changes
310	Blue Canoe	36	Military 310F as L-27B (later U-3B)
310F	-	156	310D with extra cabin window each side, pointed nose, new tip tank shape and minor changes
310G	-	156	310F with slimline canted 'stabila-tip' tip tanks, six-seat cabin, 4,990 lb TOGW
310H	-	148	310G with 5,100 lb TOGW and enlarged cabin interior
310i	-	200	310H with IO-470-U engines, baggage compartments in rear of engine nacelles and minor detail changes
310J	-	200	310i with minor detail changes
310K	-	245	310J with long 'vista view' side windows, 5,200 lb TOGW and IO-470-V engines
310L	-	207	310K with single-piece windshield, redesigned u/c, increased fuel capacity and minor changes
310M	-		Revised designation for 310E
310N	-	198	310L with new instrument panel, optional tanks in engine nacelles, IO-470-V-O engines and minor changes
310P†	-	240	310N with shorter nose u/c leg, ventral fin, optional † turbocharged 285hp TSIO-520-B engines
310Q†	-	1,160	310P with 5,300 lb TOGW and detail changes. From c/n 310Q-0401 fitted with bulged rear cabin roof with rear-view window
310R†	-	1,332	310Q with 3-blade props, lengthened nose with baggage compartment, 5,500 lb TOGW & 285hp IO-520-M engines
310S	-		Original designation for Model 320
318	XT-37	3	Two-seat XT-37 all-metal USAF military trainer powered by two 920 lbst Continental YJ69-T-9 turbojets. Prototype 54-716 (c/n 40001) FF 12 Oct 1954. Production variants included T-37A (Model 318A), T-37B (318B), T-37C (318C), A37A (318D), A-37B (318E). Total production 1,849
319	Bird Dog		Experimental L-19A modified for boundary layer research with '180 tail and new wings incorporating blowing fans. Prototype N37880 (c/n 608) FF 1953
320	Skyknight	110	310F with six seats, enlarged rear cabin extra window each side, 4,990 lb TOGW and two turbocharged Cont TSIO-470-B engines. Prototype N34262 (c/n 623)
320A	Skyknight	47	320 with stabila-tip fuel tanks, 5,200 lb TOGW and minor changes
320B	Skyknight	62	320A with nacelle baggage lockers etc
320C	Skyknight	73	320B with longer cabin, optional seventh seat and other minor changes
320D	Executive Skyknight	130	320C with reshaped rear side windows and 285hp TSIO-520-B engines
320	Executive Skyknight	110	320D with pointed nose, single-piece windshield modified u/c, 5,300 lb TOGW and minor changes
320F	Executive Skyknight	45	320E with minor changes
321	OE-2	25	Observation aircraft based on Model 305 for US Navy with Model 185 vertical tail, armoured panels, two hardpoints and 265hp Cont O-470-2 supercharged engine. Designated OE-2 (O-1C). Prototype N41767 (c/n 611) FF Sep 1954
325	-	4	Model 305 for agricultural use with enclosed rear cabin, hopper, underwing spraybars, 230hp engine with constant-speed prop
327	Mini Skymaster	1	Reduced-scale version of Model 337. Prototype N3769C (c/n 663) FF 4 Dec 1967. To NASA as full-scale wind tunnel research unit
330	-	1	Light twin based on Model 411. Prot N3764C (c/n 659)
335	-	65	Model 340 with non-pressurized cabin, 5,990 lb TOGW and 300hp TSIO-520-EB engines
336	Skymaster	195	Twin-boomed all-metal high-wing push-pull twin with six seats, fixed tricycle u/c and two 195hp Continental IO-360-A. 3,900 lb TOGW. Prototype N34273 (c/n 633) FF 28 Feb 1961
337	Super Skymaster	239	336 with retractable u/c, redesigned nose cowling, new rear engine air intake, 210hp IO-360-C engines, 4,200 lb TOGW. Prototype N5422E (c/n 647) FF 30 Mar 1964
337A	Super Skymaster	255	337 with minor detail changes
337B	Super Skymaster†	230	337A with 4,300 lb TOGW, optional belly cargo pack and optional † turbocharged 210hp TSIO-360-A engines
337C	Super Skymaster†	223	337B with new instrument panel and 4,400 lb TOGW (4,500 lb on Turbo 337C)
337D	Super Skymaster†	215	337C with minor detail changes
337	Super Skymaster†	100	337D with cambered wingtips and minor changes. Turbo 337E has 4,630 lb TOGW
F337E	Super Skymaster†	24	Reims-built Model 337E
337F	Super Skymaster†	114	337E with 4,630 lb TOGW for both models
F337F	Super Skymaster†	31	Reims-built Model 337F
337G	Super Skymaster	352	337F with split airstair entry door, smaller rear side windows, improved flaps, larger front prop, modified wing struts, optional long-range tanks and prop synchrophaser, Cont IO-360-G engine. No turbo version

Cessna 402B N766EA

F337G	Super Skymaster	29	Reims-built Model 337G
T337G	Pressurized Skymaster	292	337G with pressurized cabin, dual front seat windows, redesigned windshield with storm windows each side, 225hp TSIO-360-C turbocharged engines
FT337G	Pressurized Skymaster	22	Reims-built Model T337G
337H	Skymaster†	136	337G with minor changes and optional † turbocharged TSIO-360-H engine
F337H	-	1	Reims-built Model 337H
P337H	Pressurized Skymaster	64	T337G with minor changes
FP337H	Pressurized Skymaster	1	Reims-built Model P337H
FTB337G	Milirole	61	Reims-built military F337G with Robertson STOL mods and underwing equipment hardpoints. Powered by two 225hp Continental TSIO-360-D turbocharged engines
M337	-	513	USAF O-2A Forward Air Control aircraft with 4 underwing pylons, dual controls powered by two 210hp Continental IO-360-C engines
MC337	-		Civil Model 337s converted to USAF O-2B for psycho-warfare duties with three loudspeakers, leaflet dispensers etc. 31 aircraft converted
340	-	350	Low-wing six-seat pressurized light twin based on Cessna 330 with retractable tricycle u/c, tip tanks, port side rear entry airstair door. Powered by two 285hp Cont TSIO-520-K engines. Prototype N2340C (c/n 672)
340A	-	948	340 with better air conditioning, 15 lb TOGW increase, prop synchrophasers, 310hp Continental TSIO-520-N engines, and new seats
360			Initial designation for Cessna 402
382	Skylane		Unofficial designation for Cessna 182Q fitted with Porsche PFM.3200 engine
401	-	322	Model 411 with broader vertical tail, lower (6,300 lb) TOGW, six-seat executive interior and two 300hp Cont TSIO-520-E engines set further out on wings. (Note: Production total includes Model 402, qv)
401A	-	132	401 with minor changes
401B	-	91	401A with minor changes. Replaced by 402B
402	-		401 with utility interior for freight or nine-seat commuter use
402A	-	129	402 with 26ft³ baggage compartment in lengthened nose, optional crew entry door and other minor changes
402B	Utililiner/ Businessliner	835	402A with minor changes. 1973 model has larger cabin and five square cabin windows each side instead of four portholes. Businessliner has deluxe cabin trim
402C	Utililiner/ Businessliner	681	402B with 6,850 lb TOGW, longer-span bonded wet wing without tip tanks, new u/c similar to 414A without wheel well doors and 325hp TSIO-520-VB engines
404	Titan	396	Stretched 402B with enlarged vertical tail, dihedralled tailplane, trailing link u/c legs, 8,400 lb TOGW and two 375hp Continental GTSIO-520-M engines. Titan Courier has cargo interior; Titan Ambassador is 10-seater. Prototype N5404J (c/n 627) FF 26 Feb 1975
F406	Caravan II	67	14-seat development of 404 Titan with two P&W PT6A-112 turboprops. Built by Reims Aviation. Prototype F-WZLT FF 22 Sep 1983. Also sold as the Polmar II maritime surveillance aircraft and the Vigilant coastal patrol model
407	-		Projected pressurized five-seat cabin version of Model 318 (T-37) for executive use powered by two Cont C-356-9 turbojets Prot N34267 (c/n 627) not completed
411	-	252	All-metal eight-seat low-wing cabin business twin with retractable tricycle u/c, oval cabin windows, airstair door, tip tanks and two 375hp Cont GTSIO-520-M engines. Prototype N5418E (c/n 642) FF 18 Jul 1962
411A	-	50	411 with lengthened baggage nose and optional extra tanks in engine nacelles
414	-	516	401B with pressurized cabin, 6,350 lb TOGW, and two 310hp Continental TSIO-520-J engines. Prototype N7170C (c/n 667)
414A	Chancellor	554	414 with narrower vertical tail, longer-span bonded wet wing without tip tanks, lengthened nose, redesigned u/c, 6,750 lb TOGW and 310hp TSIO-520-N engines
421	-	200	411A with pressurized cabin, 6,800 lb TOGW, broader vertical tail, cockpit clear vision panel and smaller side

			windows. Powered by two 375hp Continental GTSIO-520-D engines
421A	-	158	421 with minor detail changes
421B	Golden Eagle/ Executive Commuter	699	421A with GTSIO-520-H engines set further out on longer span wings, strengthened u/c, longer nose with larger dual baggage compartment, longer cabin with toilet area, 5th window each side, 7450 lb TOGW
421C	Golden Eagle/ Executive Commuter	859	421B with narrower fin/rudder, longer span wet wing without tip tanks, redesigned u/c, larger props and GTSIO-520-L engines
425	Corsair	236	421C with two 450shp P&W PT6A-112 turbo-props, dihedralled tailplane, trailing link u/c, rounded nosecone and 8,200 lb TOGW Prototype N4089L (c/n 693)
425	Conquest I		Renamed Corsair with 8,600 lb TOGW
435	Conquest II	1	Model 441 with two P&W PT6A turboprops. Prototype N435CC (c/n 435-0001)
441	Conquest II	362	8-11-seat executive aircraft based on scaled-up Model 421 with 9,850 lb TOGW, two 635shp Garrett TPE-331-8-401S turboprops, semi-square cabin windows, retractable trailing link tricycle u/c. Prototype N441CC (c/n 679) FF Aug 1975
500	Citation	379	Eight-seat all-metal low-wing business jet powered by two 2,200 lbst UACL JT15D-1 turbofans. 4 cabin windows each side. Prototype N500CC (c/n 669). FF 15 Sep 1969. Later Citation I has high aspect ratio wing and JT15D-1A engines
501	Citation I/SP	313	FAR Part 23 certificated Citation I for single-pilot operation
510	Mustang	1	Six-seat entry-level light jet with two 1,350 lbst Pratt & Whitney PW615F turbofans. Prototype N27369 (c/n E510-712001) FF 25 Apr 2005
525	CitationJet	360	Six-seat light business jet with Citation I forward fuselage, new wings and T-tail, 10,000 lb TOGW, powered by two Williams/Rolls-Royce FJ44 turbofans. Prototype N525CJ FF 29 Apr 1991
525	Citation CJ1	180	CitationJet with 10,600 lb TOGW and Collins Proline 21 avionics
525	Citation CJ1+	1	Citation CJ1 with FADEC-controlled Williams FJ44-1AP engines and new ProLine 21 avionics. Prot N525AD FF 8 Oct 2004
525A	Citation CJ2	216	CitationJet with fuselage stretched 4ft 3in to give 6+2 seat interior, 3ft longer wingspan and modified tailplane, powered by two 2,400 lbst Williams FL44-2C turbofans. 12,300 lb TOGW Prototype N2CJ FF 27 Apr 1999
525A	Citation CJ2+	1	Citation CJ2 with FADEC-controlled Williams FJ33-3A-24 engines and new ProLine 21 avionics. Prot N2CJ FF 2 Apr 2005
525B	Citation CJ3	5	CJ-2 with 42-inch fuselage stretch and 2,780 lbst Williams FJ44A-3A turbofans. Prototype N3CJ (c/n 711) FF 17 Apr 2003
526		2	Tandem-two-seat twin-jet trainer based on Model 525 wing, engines and u/c with new tail and fuselage for USAF JPATS competition. Prototype N526JT (c/n 704) FF 20 Dec 1993. Second aircraft N526JP (c/n 705)
550	Citation II	604	Stretched Citation I with 12 seats and 6 cabin windows each side. Powered by two JT15D-4 turbofans. 13,300 lb TOGW. Prototype N550CC (c/n 686) FF 31 Jan 1977
550B	Citation Bravo	280	Citation II with two 2,750 lbst Pratt & Whitney PW530A turbofans with thrust reversers, longer range, improved short field performance, increased cruise speed, new avionics, trailing link u/c, new cabin interior, airstair door. Prototype N550BB FF 19 Apr 1995
S550	Citation S/II	160	550 with wing leading edge cuffs, new wing aerofoil, 14,300 lb TOGW and JT15D-4B engines. Prototype N550CC (c/n 686)
551	Citation II/SP	85	Model 550 for single-pilot operation
552	T47A	15	S550 equipped as T-47A US Navy trainer for UNFO/TSU program with modified wing, cockpit roof windows, JT15D-5 engines. Model OT-47B Tracker is version with APG-66 radar and WF-360TL imaging system
560	Citation V	260	Citation S/II with fuselage stretched 2ft, 7 cabin windows each side and two 2,900 lbst JT15D-5A turbofans. 15,900 lb TOGW. Introduced Oct 1987. Prototype N560CV (c/n 560-0001)
560	Citation Ultra	279	Citation V with EFIS, new autopilot, 16,300 lb TOGW. Powered by two 3,045 lbst JT15D-5D turbofans. Military UC-35A, UC-35C, OT-47B
560	Citation Ultra Encore	121	Citation Ultra with trailing link u/c, improved de-icing, increased fuel capacity and upgraded interior and air conditioning. Powered by two 3,400 lbst Pratt & Whitney PW535 turbofans. Prototype N560VU (c/n 707) FF 9 Jul 1998. Military UC-35B, UC-35D
560XL	Citation Excel	373	New design with Citation V wings, and tail, shortened 8-pax Citation III fuselage, two 3,800 lbst P&W PW545A turbofans, trailing link u/c and Citation X panel and avionics. 20,000 lb TOGW. Prototype N560XL FF 29 Feb 1996
560XLS	Citation XLS	8	Excel with 3,990 lbst PW545B turbofans, TOGW increased to 20,198 lb, improved interior furnishings and instrument panel
620	-	1	8-10-seat pressurized low-wing executive aircraft with four 320hp Cont GSO-526-A engines and retractable tricycle u/c. Prototype N620E (c/n 620) FF 11 Aug 1956
650	Citation III	204	8-12-seat low-wing intercontinental business jet with 19,500 lb TOGW, powered by two 3,650 lbst Garrett TFE731-3b-100S turbofans. Prototype N650CC (c/n 696) FF 30 May 1979
650	Citation VI	38	Low-cost Citation III with standard systems package
650	Citation VII	119	Citation III development with 4,000 lbst Garrett TFE731-4 turbofans, electrically-heated windshield and standard avionics package
670	Citation IV		Proposed intercontinental Citation III with 5ft 6in-longer wingspan and lower-set wing, no fuselage fuel tanks, 24-inch longer cabin, 24,000 lb TOGW and two 4,000 lbst TFE731-4 turbofans. Not built
680	Citation Sovereign	10	Super mid-size 2+8-seat business jet with two rear-mounted 5,686 lbst Pratt & Whitney PW306C turbofans, 30,000 lb TOGW. Prototype N680CS (c/n 709) FF 27 Feb 2002
700	-		Initial 1974 design for 3-engined T-tailed Citation III. Not built
750	Citation X	231	10-passenger business jet derived from Citation III with stretched fuselage, Mach 0.9 max speed. 31,000 lb TOGW, two 6,000 lbst Allison GMA.3007C turbofans, supercritical swept wing. From c/n 173 has increased gross weight and higher-thrust GMA-3007C-1 engines. Prototype N750CX (c/n 703) FF 21 Dec 1993
1,014	XMC	1	Twin-boomed two-seat experimental light aircraft with single pusher engine and fixed tricycle u/c. Prototype N7174C (c/n 674) FF 22 Jan 1971
CH-1	-	1	Two-seat light helicopter developed from the Seibel S-3, powered by one 260hp Cont FSO-470-A piston engine. Prototype N5155 (c/n 1) converted to four-seat CH-1A
CH-1B	-	13	CH-1A with 270hp Continental FSO-526-A engine. 10 sold to US Army as YH-41
CH-1C	Skyhook	30	CH-1B with revised systems and structure

A summary of Cessna's total post-war production by main models (including foreign-built aircraft) is as follows:

Model	No	Model	No	Model	No
120/140	7,604	205/206	8,905	400 srs	6,540
150/152	23,938	207	788	500/550/560	2,551
170	5,174	208	1,479	525 srs	820
172/172RG/175	45,039	210/P210	9,336	560XL	424
177/177RG	4,294	T303	315	650	361
180/185	10,171	305/321	3,294	680	54
182/182RG	23,580	310/320	6,314	750	241
188	1,528	335/340	1,363	CH-1	44
190/195	1,183	336/337	3,097	*Total*	*168,437*

Model 402B	1970/71	serial c/n 402B0001 to 402B0122
Model 402B	1972	serial c/n 402B0201 to 402B0249
Model 402B	1973	serial c/n 402B0301 to 402B0455
Model 402B	1974	serial c/n 402B0501 to 402B0640

The company has also built the 'knocked-down' airframes for assembly in Argentina and France. Here, aircraft that are substantially Wichita-built carry a normal Cessna serial number together with a local Reims or DINFIA number. For example, the 19th Reims Cessna F177RG started life at Wichita with the American serial number 00149.

Finally, there is the 600-/700- series of serials allocated to experimental aircraft. Frequently, Cessna has fabricated its prototypes from scratch, but sometimes the development department takes a standard production line example and modifies it into a new type with a new 600/700-series number. Details of all Cessna serial number batches are shown in this table:

Model 120/140

120/140	8000-15075	140A	15200 - 15724

Model 150/152

150	17001 - 17999	150J	15069309 - 71128
150B	15059351 - 59700	150M	15075782 - 79405
150E	15060773 - 61532	150A	15059019 - 59350
150H	15067199 - 69308	150D	15060088 - 60772
150L	15072004 - 75781	150G	15064533 - 67198
150	59001 - 59018	150K	15071129 - 72003
150C	15059701 - 60087	152	15279406 - 86033
150F	15061533 - 64532		

Reims F150 and F152 (serials prefixed F150/F152, eg, F15000530)

F150F	0001 - 0067	F150K	00530 - 00658
F150G	0068- 0219	F150L	00659 - 01143
F150H	0220 - 0389	F150M	01144 - 01428
F150J	0390 - 0529	F152	01429 - 01980

Model A150/A152

A150K	A1500001 - 0226	A150M	A1500524 - 0734
A150L	A1500227 - 0523	A152	A1520735 - 1049

Reims FA150/152 and FRA150 (serials prefixed FA150/152 or FRA150)

FA150K	0001 - 0081	FRA150M	
FA150L	0082 - 0120	FA152	0337 - 0425
FRA150L	0121 - 0261		

Model 170

170	18000 - 18729	170B	20267 - 20999
170A	18730 - 20266	170B	25000 - 27169

Model 172

172	28000 - 29999	172G	17253393 - 54892
172	36000 - 36999	172H	17254893 - 56512
172	46001 - 46754	172I	17256513 - 57161
172A	46755 - 47746	172K	17257162 - 59223
172B	47747 - 48734	172L	17259224 - 60758
172C	48735 - 49544	172M	17260759 - 67584
172D	17249545 - 50572	172N	17267585 - 74009
172E	17250573 - 51822	172P	17274010 - 76673
172F	17251823 - 53392		

Model 172 (new production – up to current c/n, 2004)

172R	17280001 - 81222	172S	172S8001 - 9653

Reims F172 & FP172 (serials prefixed F172 or FP172, eg, F17200805, FP172-0008)

F172D	0001 - 0018	F172K	00755 - 00804
F172E	0019 - 0085	F172L	00805 - 00904
F172F	0086 - 0179	F172M	00905 - 01514
F172G	0180 - 0319	F172N	01515 - 02039
F172H	0320 - 0654	F172P	02040 - 02254
F172H	00655 - 00754	FP172D	0001 - 0018

Model P172

Model P172		P172	P17257120 - 57189
Model 172RG		R172K	R1722000 - 3454
Model R172 Hawk XP		172RG	172RG0001 - 1191

Model 175

175	55001 - 56238	175B	17556778 - 17557002
175A	56239 - 56777	175C	17557003 - 17557119

Reims FR172 Rocket (serials prefixed by model number, eg, FR172E0045)

FR172E	0001 - 0060	FR172H	0226 - 0350
FR172F	0061 - 0145	FR172J	0351 - 0590
FR172G	0146 - 0225	FR172K	0591 - 0675

Model 177

177	17700001 - 01164	177B	17701371 - 02752
177A	17701165 - 01370		

Model 177RG / Model F177RG

177RG	177RG0001 - 1366	F177RG	F177RG0001 - 0177

Model 180 (from 1961 Model 180D all are prefixed 180, eg, 18051875)

180	30000 - 32661	180E	51064 - 51183
180A	32662 - 32999	180F	51184 - 51312
180A	50000 - 50355	180G	51313 - 51445
180B	50356 - 50661	180H	51446 - 52284
180C	50662 - 50911	180J	52285 - 52770
180D	50912 - 51063	180K	52771 - 53203

Model 182, F182, R182 and FR182

182	33000 - 33842	182K	18257626 - 58505
182A	33843 - 34999	182L	18258506 - 59305
182A	51001 - 51556	182M	18259306 - 60055
182B	51557 - 52358	182N	18260056 - 60825
182C	52359 - 53007	182P	18260826 - 65175
182D	18253008 - 53598	182Q	18265176 - 67715
182E	18253599 - 54423	182R	18267716 - 68615
182F	18254424 - 55058	F182P	F18200001 - 00025
182G	18255059 - 55844	F182Q	F18200026-00169
182H	18255845 - 56684	FR182	FR18200001-00070
182J	18256685 - 57625	R182	R18200001-02041

Model 182 (new production – up to current c/n, 2004)

182S	18280001 - 80945	T182T	T18208001 - 8270
182T	18280946 - 81364		

Model 185

185	185-0001 - 0237	185E	185-0968 - 1149
185A	185-0238 - 0512	A185E	185-1150 - 1599
185B	185-0513 - 0653	A185E	18501600 - 02090
185C	185-0654 - 0776	A185F	18502091 - 04448
185D	185-0777 - 0967		

Model 188

188/A188	188-0001 - 0572	188B/A188B	18800833 - 03968
188A/A188A	18800573 - 00832	T188C	T18803307T - 03968T

Note: Ag-Trucks have suffix T. T188C is included in same sequence as A188B.

Model 190 and 195

190/195	7001 - 7999	190/195	16000 - 16183

Model 205

205	205-0001 - 0480	205A	205-0481 - 0577

Model P.206

P206	P206-0001 - 0160	P206C	P206-0420 - 0519
P206A	P206-0161 - 0306	P206D	P206-0520 - 0603
P206B	P206-0307 - 0419	P206E	P20603522 - 07020

Model 206 & U206

206	206-0001 - 0275	206F	U20601701 - 03521
206B	U206-0657 - 0914	206A	U206-0438 - 0656
206E	U20601445 - 01700	206D	U206-1235 - 1444
206	U206-0276 - 0437	206G	U20603522 - 07020
206C	U206-0915 - 1234		

Model 206 (new production – up to current c/n, 2004)

206H	20599786	T206H	T20608001 - 08461

Model 207 and F207

207	20700001 - 00362	F207	F2070001 - 0009
207A	20700363 - 00788		

Model 208

208	20800001 - 00061	208B	208B0001 - 0303+
208A	20800062 - 00216+		

Model 210

210	57001 - 57575	210L	21059503 - 61573
210A	21057576 - 57840	210M	21061574 - 62954
210B	21057841 - 58085	210N	21062955 - 64897
210C	21058086 - 58220	210R	21064898 - 65009
210D	21058221 - 58510	P210N	P21000001 - 00834
210E	21058511 - 58715	P210R	P21000835 - 00874
210F	21058716 - 58818	T210F	T210-0001 - 0197
210G	21058819 - 58936	T210G	T210-0198 - 0307
210H	21058937 - 59061	T210H	T210-0308 - 0392
210J	21059062 - 59199	T210J	T210-0393 - 0454

Model T303   **Model 335**

T303	T30300001 - 00247	335	335-0001 - 0065
T303	T30300258 - 00315		

Model 310

310	35000 - 35546	310L	310L0001 - 0207
310B	35547 - 35771	310N	310N0001 - 0198
310C	35772 - 35999	310P	310P0001 - 0240
310C	39001 - 39031	310Q	310Q0201 - 1160
310D	39032 - 39299	310R	310R0001 - 0330
310F	310-0001 - 0156	310R	310R0501 - 0735
310G	310G0001 - 0156	310R	310R0801 - 1004
310H	310H0001 - 0148	310R	310R1201 - 1434
310i	310i0001 - 0200	310R	310R1501 - 1690
310J	310J0001 - 0200	310R	310R1801 - 1899
310K	310K0001 - 0245	310R	310R2101 - 2140

Model 320

320	320-0001 - 0110	320D	320D0001 - 0130
320A	320A0001 - 0047	320E	320E0001 - 0110

Cessna 310Q N6277Q. Cessna

320B	320B0001 - 0062	320F	320F0001 - 0045
320C	320C0001 - 0073		

Model 336, 337 and Reims F.337

336	336-0001 - 0195	F337E	F33700001 - 00024
337	33700001 - 00239	F337F	F33700025 - 00055
337A	33700240 - 00525	F337G	F33700056 - 00084
337B	33700526 - 00755	F337H	F33700085 - 00086
337C	33700756 - 00978	T337G	P3370001 - 0292
337D	33700979 - 01193	P337H	P3370293 - 0356
337E	33701194 - 01316	FT337G	FP33700001-00022
337F	33701317 - 01462	FP337H	FP33700023
337G	33701463 - 01815	FTB337G	FTB3370001 - 0061

Model 340

340	340-0001 - 0115	340A	340A0401 - 0562
340	340-0151 - 0260	340A	340A0601 - 0801
340	340-0301 - 0370	340A	340A0901 - 1045
340	340-0501 - 0555	340A	340A1202 - 1280
340A	340A0001 - 0125	340A	340A1501 - 1543
340A	340A0201 - 0375	340A	340A1801 - 1817

Model 401

401	401-0001 - 0322 (in common series with Model 402)		
401A	401A0001 - 0132	401B	401B0201 - 0221
401B	401B0001 - 0121		

Model 402

402	402-0001 - 0322 (in common series with Model 401)		
402A	402A0001 - 0129	402B	402B1201 - 1250
402B	402B0001 - 0122	402B	402B1301 - 1384
402B	402B0201 - 0249	402C	402C0001 - 0125
402B	402B0301 - 0455	402C	402C0201 - 0355
402B	402B0501 - 0640	402C	402C0401 - 0528
402B	402B0801 - 0935	402C	402C0601 - 0653
402B	402B1001 - 1100	402C	402C0801 - 1020

Model 404

404	404-0001 - 0136	404	404-0801 - 0895
404	404-0601 - 0695	404	404-0401 - 0460
404	404-0201 - 0246		

Model 411

411	411-0001 - 0250	411A	411A0251 - 0300

Model 414

414	414-0001 - 0099	414	414-0901 - 0965
414	414-0151 - 0175	414A	414A0001 - 0121
414	414-0251 - 0280	414A	414A0201 - 0340
414	414-0351 - 0437	414A	414A0401 - 0535
414	414-0451 - 0550	414A	414A0601 - 0680
414	414-0601 - 0655	414A	414A0801 - 0858
414	414-0801 - 0855	414A	414A1001 - 1212

Model 421

421	421-0001 - 0200	421C	421C0201 - 0350
421A	421A0001 - 0158	421C	421C0401 - 0525
421B	421B0001 - 0056	421C	421C0601 - 0715
421B	421B0101 - 0147	421C	421C0801 - 0910
421B	421B0201 - 0275	421C	421C1001 - 1115
421B	421B0301 - 0486	421C	421C1201 - 1257
421B	421B0501 - 0665	421C	421C1401 - 1413
421B	421B0801 - 0970	421C	421C1801 - 1807

Model 425   **Model 441**

425	425-0001 - 0236	441	441-0001 - 0362

Note: The serial batches for Model 400 Cessnas relate to separate model years. In many cases, there are missing serial numbers as a result of factory conversion of airframes built in one year but delivered in the specification of the following year.

Cessna 650 Citation III N398CW

Citation 500 series

500*	500-0001 - 0476	550*	550-0001 - 0734
501*	501-0001 - 0689	550 Bravo	550-0801 - 1110
525	525-0001 - 0553+	551*	551-0002 - 0617
525A	525A-0001-0226+	552	552-0001 - 0015
525B	525B-0001-0039+	S550	S550-001 - 0160

Note: There are many missing serial numbers in the batches marked * due to complications arising from the separate factory system of 'line numbers' and due to conversion of airframes from one model to another on the line. Latterly, the method of allocating serial numbers has been changed so that the serial and the line number coincide.

Model 560, 650, 680, 750

560	560-0001 - 0259	650 Cit III	650-0001- 0206*
560 Ultra	560-0260 - 0538	650 Cit VI	650-0207 - 0241†
560 Encore	560-0539 - 0684+	650 Cit VII	650-7001 - 7119
560XL	560-5001 - 5372	680 Cit Sov	680-0001 - 0053+
560XLS	560-5501 - 5551+	750 Cit X	750-0001 - 0240+

* Excluding 0200-0202; † Plus 0200-0202.

Experimental Serial Number Batches

Serial	Registration / Model		Serial	Registration / Model	
601	N41694	305A	657	N3758C	411
602	N41695	X210	658	N3759C	320E
603	N41696	308	659	N3764C	330
604	N41697	180	660	N3765C	172J
605	N41698	170B	661	N3766C	177
606	N41699	310	662	N3768C	182M
607	N37879	310	663	N3769C	327
608	N37880	319	664	N4000L	T310P
609	N37892	170B	665	N1907F	T207
610	N41783	172	666	N7167C	187
611	N41767	321	667	N7170C	414
612	N41768	170B	668	N7171C	210K, 210L
613	N41782	182	669	N500CC	500
614	N4599B	180	670	N501CC	500
615	N1295	172L	671	N7172C	177RG
616	N1296	210	672	N2340C	340

Serial	Reg	Model	Serial	Reg	Model
617	N34258	142/150	673	N4571L	340
618	N34259	210	674	N7174C	XMC
619	N34260	175	675	N7175C	182N
620	N620E	620	676	N7177C	TU206E
621	N620F	620	677	N7178C	T337G
622	N34261	172	678	N7180C	A188B
623	N34262	320	679	N7185C/N441CC	441
624	N34263	180C	680	N7186C	R172J
625	N34264	172	681	N7187C	152
626	N34265	175	682	N7188C/N5404J	404
627	N34267	407 (not flown)	683	N7188C	R182
628	N34268	150A	684	N7189C	P210N
629	N34269	310C	685	N4089L	414A
630	N34270	172B	686	N550CC	550
631	N34271	182C	687	N303CP	303
632	N34272	185	688	N303PD	303
633	N34273	336	689	N402CW	402C
634	N34266	182H	690	N7190C	172RG
635	N5411E	320E	691	N7191C	172RG
636	N5412E	336	692	N303LT	303
637	N5413E	210	693	N4089L	425
638	N5414E	172H	694	N303PD	T303
639	N5415E	175D	695	N303LT	T303
640	N5416E	175D (stat test)	696	N650CC	650
641	N5417E	205	697	N650	650
642	N5418E	411	698	N7192C	441
643	N5419E	160	699	N208LP	208
644	N5420E	150E	700	N208FP	208
645	N3762C	180H	701	N501CC	501-SP
646	N3753C	TU206	702	N525CJ	525
647	N5422E	337	703	N750CX	750
648	N5423E	150F	704	N526JT	526
649	N3763C	150G	705	N526JP	526
650	N5416E	172G	706	N560XL	560XL
651	N5424E	188	707	N560VU	560
652	N5425E	185E	708	N2CJ	525A (ex 702)
653	N3755C	188	709	N680CS	680
654	N3756C	188	711	N3CJ	CJ3
655	N3760C	402A	712	N27369	510
656	N3757C	337			

Cessna Annual Model Designations 1946 to 2005

Model	1946	1947	1948	1949	1950	1951	1952	1953	1954	1955	1956	1957
120	120	120	120	120								
140	140	140	140	140	140A	140A	140A					
170				170	170A	170A	170A	170B	170B	170B	170B	
172											172	172
180								180	180	180	180	180A
182											182	182A
190		190	190	190	190	190	190	190				
195		195	195	195	195	195	195	195				
195								A195B	A195B			
310										310	310	310

Model	1958	1959	1960	1961	1962	1963	1964	1965	1966	1967	1968	1969
150		150	150	150A	150B	150C	150D	150E	150F	150G	150H	150J
172 Skyhawk	172	172	172A	172B	172C	172D	172E	172F	172G	172H	172I	172K
175 Skylark	175	175	175A	175B	175C	P172D					FR172E	FR172F
177 Cardinal											177	177A
180	180A	180B	180C	180D	180E	180F	180G	180H	180H	180H	180H	180H
182 Skylane	182A	182B	182C	182D	182E	182F	182G	182H	182J	182K	182L	182M
185 Skywagon				185	185A	185B	185C	185D	185E	A185E	A185E	A185E
188 AgWagon/Pickup									188	188	188A	188A
188 AgWagon/Truck									A188	A188	A188A	A188A
205						205	205A					
206 Super Skywagon							206	U206	U206A	U206B	U206C	U206D
Turbo Super Skywagon									TU206A	TU206B	TU206C	TU206D
206 Super Skylane								P206	P206A	P206B	P206C	P206D
Turbo Super Skylane									TP206A	TP206B	TP206C	TP206D
207												207
210 Centurion			210	210A	210B	210C	210D	210E	210F	210G	210H	210J
Turbo Centurion									T210F	T210G	T210H	T210J
310	310B	310C	310D	310F	310G	310H	310i	310J	310K	310L	310N	310P
Turbo 310												T310P
320 Skyknight					320	320A	320B	320C	320D	320E	320F	
336 Skymaster						336						
337 Super Skymaster								337	337A	337B	337C	337D
Turbo Super Skymaster										T337B	T337C	T337D
401										401	401	401A
402										402	402	402A
411								411	411	411A	411A	
421 Golden Eagle										421	421	421A

Model	1970	1971	1972	1973	1974	1975	1976	1977	1978	1979	1980	1981
150/152	150K	150L	150L	150L	150L	150M	150M	150M	152	152	152	152
A150/152 Aerobat	A150K	A150L	A150L	A150L	A150L	A150M	A150M	A150M	A152	A152	A152	A152
172 Skyhawk	172K	172L	172L	172M	172M	172M	172M	172N	172N	172N	172N	172P
FR172 Reims Rocket	FR172G	FR172H	FR172H	FR172J	FR172J	FR172J	FR172J					
R172 Hawk XP								R172K	R172K	R172K	R172K	R172K
172 RG Skyhawk RG											172RG	172RG
177 Cardinal	177B	177B	177B	177B	177B	177B	177B	177B	177B			
177RG Cardinal RG		177RG	177RG	177RG	177RG	177RG	177RG	177RG	177RG			
180 Skywagon	180H	180H	180H	180H	180J	180J	180J	180K	180K	180K	180K	180K
182 Skylane	182N	182N	182P	182P	182P	182P	182P	182Q	182Q	182Q	182Q	182R
R182 Skylane RG									R182	R182	R182	R182
Turbo Skylane RG										TR182	TR182	TR182
185 Skywagon	A185E	A185E	A185E	A185F	A185F	A185F	A185F	A185F	A185F	A185F	A185F	A185F
188 AgTruck/Wagon	A188A	A188A	A188B	A188B	A188B	A188B	A188B	A188B	A188B	A188B	A188B	A188B
188 AgPickup	188A	188A	188B	188B	188B	188B						
188 Ag Husky										T188C	T188C	T188C
206 Stationair	U206E	U206E	U206F	U206F	U206F	U206F	U206F	U206G	U206G	U206G	U206G	U206G
Turbo Stationair	TU206E	TU206E	TU206F	TU206F	TU206F	TU206F	TU206F	TU206G	TU206G	TU206G	TU206G	TU206G
P206 Super Skylane	P206E											
Turbo Super Skylane	TP206E											
207 Stationair 7/8	207	207	207	207	207	207	207	207A	207A	207A	207A	207A
Turbo Stationair 7/8					T207	T207	T207	T207A	T207A	T207A	T207A	T207A
210 Centurion	210K	210K	210L	210L	210L	210L	210L	210M	210M	210N	210N	210N
Turbo Centurion	T210K	T210K	T210L	T210L	T210L	T210L	T210L	T210M	T210M	T210N	T210N	T210N
Pressurized Centurion									P210N	P210N	P210N	P210N
310	310Q	310Q	310Q	310Q	310Q	310R	310R	310R	310R	310R	310R	310R
Turbo 310	T310Q	T310Q	T310Q	T310Q	T310Q	T310R	T310R	T310R	T310R	T310R	T310R	T310R
335											335	
337 Skymaster	337E	337F	337F	337G	337G	337G	337G	337G	337H	337H	337H	
Turbo Super Skymaster	T337E	T337F							T337H	T337H	T337H	

Model												
Pressurized Skymaster					T337G	T337G	T337G	T337G	P337H	P337H	P337H	
340		340	340	340	340	340	340A	340A	340A	340A	340A	340A
401	401B	401B	401B									
402 Utililiner	402B	402B	402B	402B	402B	402B	402B	402B	402B	402C	402C	402C
404 Titan								404	404	404	404	404
414 Chancellor	414	414	414	414	414	414	414	414	414A	414A	414A	414A
421 Golden Eagle	421B	421B	421B	421B	421B	421B	421C	421C	421C	421C	421C	421C
425 Corsair												425
441 Conquest								441	441	441	441	441
500/501 Citation I		500	500	500	500	500	500	500	500/501	500/501	500/501	500/501
550/551 Citation II										550/551	550/551	550/551

Model	1982	1983	1984	1985	1986	1987	1988	1989	1990	1991	1992	1993
152	152	152	152	152								
A152 Aerobat	A152	A152	A152	A152								
172 Skyhawk	172P	172P	172P	172P	172P							
172 Cutlass		172Q	172Q									
R172 Hawk XP	R172K											
172RG Skyhawk RG	172RG	172RG	172RG	172RG								
180 Skywagon 180	180K											
182 Skylane	182R	182R	182R	182R	182R							
Turbo Skylane	T182R	T182R	T182R									
R182 Skylane RG	R182	R182	R182	R182	R182							
Turbo Skylane RG	TR182	TR182	TR182	TR182	TR182							
185 Skywagon 185	A185F	A185F	A185F	A185F								
188 AgHusky	T188C	T188C										
188 Ag Truck/Wagon	A188B	A188B										
206 Stationair	U206G	U206G	U206G	U206G	U206G							
Turbo Stationair	TU206G	TU206G	TU206G	TU206G	TU206G							
207 Stationair 8	207A	207A	207A	207A								
Turbo Stationair 8	T207A	T207A										
208 Caravan I			208	208	208	208	208	208	208	208	208	208
208A Caravan I			208A	208A	208A	208A	208A	208A	208A	208A	208A	208A
208B Caravan I							208B	208B	208B	208B	208B	208B
210 Centurion	210N	210N	210N	210N	210R							
Turbo Centurion	T210N	T210N	T210N	T210N	T210R							
Press. Centurion	P210N	P210N	P210N	P210N	P210R							
303 Crusader	T303	T303	T303	T303								
340	340A	340A	340A	340A								
402	402C	402C	402C	402C								
404 Titan	404											
F406 Caravan II			F406	F406	F406	F406	F406	F406				
414 Chancellor	414A	414A	414A	414A	414A							
421 Golden Eagle	421C	421C	421C	421C	421C							
425 Corsair	425	425	425	425	425							
441 Conquest II	441	441	441	441	441	441						
500/501 Citation I	500/501	501	501	501								
525 CitationJet												525
550/S.550 Citation II	550	550	550	550/S.550	550/S.550	550/S.550	550/S.550	550/S.550	550	550	550	550
551 Citation II/SP	551	551	551	551								
560 Citation V								560	560	560	560	560
650 Citation III		650	650	650	650	650	650	650	650	650		
650 Citation VI											650	650
650 Citation VII											650	650

Model	1994	1995	1996	1997	1998	1999	2000	2001	2002	2003	2004	2005
172 Skyhawk				172R	172R	172R	172R	172R	172R	172R	172R	172R
172 Skyhawk					172S	172S	172S	172S	172S	172S	172S	172S
182 Skylane				182S	182S	182S	182S	182T	182T	182T	182T	182T
182 Turbo Skylane								T182T	T182T	T182T	T182T	T182T
206 Stationair					206H	206H	206H	206H	206H	206H	206H	206H
206 Turbo Stationair					T206H	T206H	T206H	T206H	T206H	T206H	T206H	T206H
208 Caravan I	208	208	208	208	208	208	208	208	208	208	208	208
208B Cargomaster	208B	208B	208B	208B	208B	208B	208B	208B	208B	208B	208B	208B
525 CitationJet/ CJ1	525	525	525	525	525	525	525	525	525	525	525	525
525A Citation CJ2								525A	525A	525A	525A	525A
550 Citation Bravo	550	550	550	550	550	550	550	550	550	550	550	550
560 Citation V/Ultra	560	560	560	560	560	560						
560 Citation Encore								560	560	560	560	560
560XL Excel					560XL	560XL	560XL	560XL	560XL	560XL	560XL	560XL
650 Citation VI	650	650										
650 Citation VII	650	650	650	650	650	650						
680 Citation Sovereign											680	680
750 Citation X			750	750	750	750	750	750	750	750	750	750

Cessna T210L Centurion N2533S. Cessna

Cessna 421B N4001L. Cessna

Cessna 750 Citation X N444CX

CFA   France

In the 1930s the Société des Moteurs Salmson under M Deville had built the three-seat high-wing Phrygane tourer and the two-seat Cri-Cri, which was ordered by the French Government in large numbers for flying club use. When the war came to a close, the Compagnie Francaise d'Aviation (CFA), which was a long-term associate of Salmson, decided to reinstate the designs. Type numbers for these aircraft consisted of, firstly the Deville design number (eg, D1, D2 etc), secondly the role intended for that model (eg, T for Tourisme) and finally the number of seats (eg, T3).

Initially, CFA built a couple of Cri-Cris and then went on to produce a somewhat improved version – the D7 Cri-Cri Major, which had greater power and an enclosed cockpit canopy. CFA built single examples of two other designs, the D21 and the D211, which were both based on the original pre-war Phrygane. They also constructed a pair

of D57 Phryganets, which were side-by-side two-seat derivatives of the D7, but by 1951 the design of these machines had become very outdated and it was decided to abandon further production. Details of the post-war models are as follows:

Model	Built	Notes
D63T2 Cri-Cri	2	Open-cockpit tandem two-seat parasol-wing monoplane with 85hp Salmson 5AP-01 engine. Prototype F-WEAL
D7T2 Cri-Cri Major	10	D6 with enclosed cockpit and 90hp Salmson 5AQ-01 engine. Prototype F-WEAN FF 15 Mar 1949
D21T4 Phrygane	1	Four-seat high-wing cabin monoplane with 135hp Salmson 9NC. F-BEER FF 3 Oct 1949
D211T4 Super Phrygane	1	D21 with 135hp Salmson 7AQ engine. F-WBGA FF 27 Jul 1951
D57 Phryganet	2	D7 with side-by-side seating and modified u/c. Prototype F-WBBH FF 7 Nov 1950

CFA D63T2 Cri-Cri F-AZAB. M J Hooks

CFA D21T4 Phrygane F-BEER

CFM-Metalfax   United Kingdom

MetalFax Ltd (trading as CFM – Cook Flying Machines) was formed at Leiston, Suffolk, to develop and build the CFM Shadow ultralight that had been designed by David Cook. The (probably unregistered) prototype Shadow made its first flight in 1983 powered by a 43hp Cuyuna

engine. This was followed by a second aircraft (G-MJVF c/n 002), initially powered by a Robin EC.44 but later fitted with a Rotax 503. The aircraft was of tube and composite construction with a tandem two-seat pod fuselage and a tubular aluminium tailboom that mounts an inverted tailfin and tailplane. It had a fixed tricycle undercarriage and a fully enclosed cabin. In standard microlight form the initial produc-

CFM Shadow DD G-MZKH

tion Shadow and then the Shadow B (and dual control Shadow B-D) were powered by a 40hp Rotax 447 engine, fitted as a pusher immediately behind the rear fuselage bulkhead. Aircraft were sold either as factory-complete or in kit form. The Shadow C and C-D, which were introduced in 1990, used a 64hp Rotax 582. The Shadow D, which has standard dual controls, had an increased gross weight and optional 80hp Rotax 912UL engine and the Shadow E was similar but with long-range fuel tanks and an electric starter. The Streak Shadow, which first flew in June 1988, was a higher-performance aircraft with a further increased gross weight, a lighter structure and a redesigned shorter-span wing. This was subsequently supplemented by the Star Streak which first flew in 1992 and had a slightly narrower and longer wing and was powered by a 95hp Hirth F30 engine or by the 80hp Rotax 912UL or 64hp Rotax 582UL. Several specialised versions of the Shadow were also produced including the Shadow II equipped for aerial surveillance.

In 1996, CFM-MetalFax went into receivership but the business was reconstituted as CFM Aircraft Ltd Production continued until July 2002 when the company again called in a receiver. The business was then sold to Bella Aviation Ltd who established new production facilities at Bentwaters, Suffolk to build the Shadow D, Streak and Star Streak, but by late 2004 production had not restarted. In total, 306 Shadows have been completed. These have simple c/ns from 001 to 306 with some c/ns being suffixed with the aircraft model (eg, 306-DD). Kit-built aircraft have a K prefix to their serial number (eg, K.043) and aircraft built under UK PFA or BMAA authority have PFA or BMAA numbers in place of the CFM serials while a number of overseas-built machines have unique serial numbers.

Champion   United States

The current American Champion high-wing light aircraft have their origins in the designs of the Aeronautical Corporation of America ('Aeronca'), which was formed in 1928 to produce another of the 'flivver' designs aimed at the popular flying market. It was not the best time to start such a business but, in due time, the Aeronca C-2 and C-3 with their familiar bathtub fuselages became a fairly common sight in the United States.

In 1937, Aeronca introduced the high-wing Aeronca K with an enclosed cabin providing side-by-side seating for two, powered by a two-cylinder Aeronca engine. This was the forerunner of a series of Aeronca monoplanes including the Model 50 Chief and Model 65 Super Chief. All were of similar basic design and allowed the company to meet the wartime demands of the United States Army with the tandem two-seat O-58B (later L-3B) observation aircraft. Large numbers of Aeronca 'Grasshoppers' were built for army cooperation and training tasks – and some were also produced as TG-5 training gliders equipped with three seats. When the war was over, many L-3s found their way onto the civilian market and a good number of TG-5s were converted as powered aircraft.

Aeronca's principal early postwar production model was the 7AC Champion, based on the L-3 and certificated on 18th October 1945. Such was the demand that in 1946 alone 7,555 aircraft were built, making Aeronca the second largest manufacturer of light aircraft (after Piper). At about the same time (on 28th September 1945) Aeronca had also gained a type certificate for the Model 11AC Chief and this was introduced in 1947. It was a side-by-side two-seat development of the 7DC Champion, which was built with a number of engines ranging in power from 65 to 85hp.

The company acquired the rights to the Erco single-axis control system originally used on the Ercoupe. They used this system on their new design, the Model 12 Chum, which was virtually the same as an Ercoupe with a single fin and rudder assembly. Three prototype Chums were flown, powered by the 85hp Continental C-85 engine, but the design was eventually abandoned. Another abortive project was the Aeronca Model 9 Arrow. This side-by-side two-seater was fitted with a low wing and a 90hp engine. It had a fully enclosed cabin and resembled the Globe Swift in many respects. Only one prototype was flown and then, sadly, it was also forgotten. Aeronca did successfully complete certification (on 23rd September 1948) of the Model 15AC Sedan, four-seat derivative of the Champion. While it was much larger than the Champion, the Sedan shared the same tube-and-fabric construction and fixed tailwheel undercarriage. Most Sedans were powered by the 145hp Continental C-145 engine, but a few 165hp Franklin-powered aircraft were also delivered.

By 1951, the market for light aircraft had subsided to the point that Aeronca was forced to abandon aircraft production. The company continued with aerospace industry subcontract work and in 1980 was involved in the construction of the prototype Foxjet business aircraft. Production rights for the Model 7 Champion line remained with Aeronca until June 1954 when they were acquired by a new company – Champion Aircraft Corporation – which commenced production of the Model 7EC from a factory at Osceola, Wisconsin. The rights for the Model 11 were sold to E J Trytek of Syracuse, NY. Trytek did not build the Chief themselves, but the Indian company, Hindustan Aircraft constructed a number under licence as the HAL Pushpak and also used the Sedan design to produce their HAOP-27 Krishak army cooperation aircraft. The type certificate for the Model 11 was eventually sold to Bellanca.

Champion produced a variety of wing, fuselage and powerplant options for the basic Model 7 airframe. One of the earliest developments was the 7FC Tri-Traveler with a tricycle undercarriage. Another strange compromise was the 7JC Tri-Con, which had a reverse tricycle undercarriage, and Champion also produced various specialised crop dusting variants of the design. They tried to modernise the 7AC, building the rather angular 7KC Olympia – but buyers were increasingly interested in all-metal aircraft and the Champion's tube-and-fabric construction was becoming an anachronism. As a result, they turned to the specialised aerobatic market for which they developed the Citabria line.

At about the same time they also built the ultimate Champion – the Model 402 Lancer. The Lancer was a two-seat twin-engined development of the Citabria. It first flew in October 1961 and had a stalky tricycle undercarriage, cruciform tail unit and the two engines mounted on the high-wing. The Lancer was hailed as the new answer to twin-engined training, but only 25 were produced during 1963.

In September 1970, Champion's assets were purchased by Bellanca Aircraft Corporation who reintroduced the 7AC Champion in 1971 as the Franklin-powered 7ACA Champ. Bellanca also continued with the Model 7ECA, 7GCBC and 7KCAB Citabrias, but they soon decided to embark on a major updating of the Champion airframe. The result was the 8KCAB Decathlon – which was externally similar to the 7GCAA but was certificated to FAR Part 23 with an airframe stressed for unlimited aerobatics. A heavy-duty version, the 8GCBC Scout, was also produced for agricultural and general utility roles.

While working on the Model 8 series, Bellanca attempted to come up with a brand new trainer using the Model 11 Chief as a basis for the

Aeronca 7AC Champion N85163

Aeronca 11AC Chief NC9504E

design. The prototype (N9089E) was constructed from the airframe of a standard Chief (c/n 11AC-722) and it first flew on 26th October 1973. Compared with the Model 11AC, it had a tricycle undercarriage, cutdown rear fuselage and rear-view window and a swept tail. It was powered by one 115hp Lycoming O-235-C1 engine. After a long period of testing, Bellanca eventually abandoned this experiment.

In April 1980 Bellanca closed down its production lines and manufacture of the Champion aircraft ceased. On 1st November 1982, the type certificate with 26 partially-completed aircraft and tooling and parts were sold in a bankruptcy sale to B & B Aviation of Tomball, Texas. The new Champion Aircraft Company Inc completed a number of Model 7GCBC and 8KCAB Champions from acquired components but, in December 1989, all rights were sold to Jerry Mehlhaf who formed American Champion Aircraft (ACAC).

ACAC are building five designs. At the top of the range is the Super Decathlon 8KCAB-180 with a 190hp Lycoming AEIO-360-H1B engine. The first aircraft (N38AC c/n 643-90) first flew in July 1990 and new features include metal spars, a new design for windows and doors and a new instrument panel and ventilation system. They are also producing the ACAC Scout (8GCBC) with a 180hp Lycoming O-360-C1 and either

a fixed pitch or constant-speed propeller, the 7ECA Aurora, the 7GCAA Adventure and the 7GCBC Explorer. During 2004, American Champion delivered 12 7GCAA Adventures, two 7ECA Auroras, 38 8KCAB Super Decathlons, 24 7GCBC Citabria Explorers and 18 8GCBC Scouts.

Each separate Champion model has been given its own serial number sequence commencing at '1'. This serial was prefixed with the model designation (eg, 7DC-106, 7AC-3948) until the Model 7KC was introduced but, thereafter, the number has been used without any prefix. From 1970 onwards, Champion and ACAC serials have been suffixed with the year the aircraft was built. Examples are a 7GCBC, N8737V that had the serial 848-75 (indicating that it was the 848th 7GCBC and was built in 1975) and 7GCAA c/n 492-2004 (showing the full year suffix used from 2000 onwards). Serial blocks allocated to the end of 2004 have been:

Model	Batch	Model	Batch
7AC	7AC-1 to 7AC-7197	7JC	7JC-1 to 7JC-25
7ACA	1-71 to 71-73	7KC	7KC-1 to 7KC-4
7BCM	7BCM-1 to 7BCM-509	7KCAB	1 to 624-80
7CCM	7CCM-1 to 7CCM-226	8GCBC	1-74 to 467-2004*
7DC	7DC-1 to 7DC-184	8KCAB	1 to 975-2004*
7EC	7EC-1 to 7EC-773	11AC	11AC-1 to 11AC-1866
7ECA	1 to 1388-2003*	11ACS	11AC-S1 to 11AC-S100
7FC	7FC-1 to 7FC-472	11BC	11BC-2 to 11BC-181
7GC	7GC-1 to 7GC-171	11CC	11CC-1 to 11CC-277
7GCA/ 7GCAA	1 to 492-2004*	15AC	15AC-1 to 15AC-561
7GCB	7GCB-1 to 7GCB-195	402	1 to 25
7GCBC	1 to 1379-2004*		
7HC	7HC-1 to 7HC-39	Total	18,200

* Including current ACAC production.

A number of Champion prototypes have carried special serial numbers. This is generally the number '1' and it was normal for a prototype to bear the first serial of the production batch for that type. Champions have been certificated for floatplane operations and their designations have the letter 'S' added when this modification has been made (eg, 7DCS). The changes necessary include float pickup points and

Champion 7FC Tri-Traveler N7583E

additional tail finlets or ventral fins to give extra side area. In general, all seaplane Champions carry their normal basic serial number but the 11ACS seaplane version of the Chief has a unique series of its own (c/n 11AC-S1 to 11AC-S100). Details of all the Champion models are as follows:

Model	Name	Built	Notes
7AC	Champion	7,197	Tandem two-seat high-wing monoplane, powered by one 65hp Cont A-65. Prototype N39557 (c/n 7AC-1)
7ACA	Champ	71	Updated 7AC reintroduced in 1971 with spring steel u/c, 60hp Franklin 2A-120B engine. Prototype N9110L (c/n 1-71). Most converted to 7ECA standard
7BC			7AC with 85hp Continental C-85 engine. Certificated, not built
7BCM	L-16A	509	Military 7BC with extensive rear cabin glazing
7B-X	-	1	Prototype – no details known. N4084E (c/n 7-BX-1)
7CC			7BC with 90hp Cont C-90. Certificated, not built
7CCM	L-16B	226	Military 7CC with enlarged fin and auxiliary wing tanks
7DC	Champion	184	7BC with increased gross weight. Prototype N4340E (c/n 7DC-1)
7EC	Traveler	773	7CC with increased gross weight. Prototype N9838E (c/n 7EC-1)
7ECA	Citabria	1,388	7EC with modified fin, increased gross weight, no flaps, enlarged side windows and 100hp Continental O-200-A. From 1967 fitted with spring steel u/c. Prototype N9976Y c/n 1
7ECA	Aurora		American Champion version. Introduced 1998
7FC	Tri-Traveler	472	7EC with tricycle undercarriage. Prototype N1292H (c/n 7FC-1)
7FL	-	1	Prototype – no details known. N9888E (c/n 7FL-1)
7GC	Sky Trac	171	7EC with 140hp Lycoming O-290-D2B, three seats and increased TOGW
7GCA	Sky Trac	492	Agricultural version of 7GC with 150hp Lycoming O-320-A2B engine
7GCAA	-		7GCA with 7GCB engine mounting and various detail changes
7GCAA	Adventure		American Champion version. Introduced 1998
7GCB	Challenger	195	7GCA with flaps and larger wings
7GCBA	Challenger		Agricultural version of 7GCB
7GCBC	Citabria	1,379	7GCAA with 7GCB wings, flaps, 160hp Lyc O-320-D2A engine and other modifications as on the 7ECA
7GCBC	Explorer		American Champion version
7HC	DX'er	39	7GC with tricycle undercarriage and increased gross weight. Prototype N8503E (c/n 7HC-1)
7JC	Tri-Con	25	7EC with reverse tricycle u/c. Prototype N8940R (c/n 7JC-1)
7KC	Olympia	4	7GCA with smaller wings, more angular tail unit, general streamlining and detail changes. Prototype N8977R (c/n 1)
7KCAB	Citabria	624	7GCAA with new NASA-1412 aerofoil section aerobatic wing, no flaps, spring steel u/c, inverted fuel system and 150hp Lycoming IO-320-E2A injected engine. Prototype N5143T (c/n 1)
8GCBC	Scout	467	New FAR Part 23-certificated strengthened airframe similar to 7KCAB with longer wings and flaps. One 180hp Lycoming O-360-C1E engine and c/s or f/p prop. Prototype N41819 (c/n 1-74). Also built by American Champion
8KCAB	Decathlon	975	Fully aerobatic aircraft similar to 8GCBC with 150hpLyc. AEIO-320-E2B engine, short symmetrical wing, inverted fuel system and no flaps
8KCAB-180	Super Decathlon		8KCAB with 180hp Lycoming AEIO-360-H1A. Also built by American Champion
9	Arrow	1	Two-seat low-wing cabin monoplane with retractable tailwheel u/c. One prototype only, NX39581 (c/n 1)
11A	Chief	1	Side-by-side two-seat version of 7AC. Prototype NX39570 (c/n 11A-1)
11AC	Chief	1,866	Production Chief with 65hp Continental A-65-8 engine
11ACS	Chief	100	Seaplane version of 11AC
11BC	Chief	180	11AC with 85hp Continental C-85-12 engine
11CC	Super Chief	277	11BC with enlarged fin, new nose cowling, Continental C-85-8F engine etc
12AC	Chum	3	Two-seat low-wing monoplane with fixed tricycle u/c. Three aircraft: N2668E c/n 12AC-1; NX39637 c/n 12A-1; NX83772 c/n 12A-2
15AC	Sedan	562	Four-seat high-wing cabin monoplane of tube-and-fabric construction powered by one 145hp Cont C-145-2 engine. Prototype NX39800 (c/n 15AC-X1)
402	Lancer	25	Tandem two-seat high-wing light twin based on Citabria with two 100hp Continental O-200A engines and fixed tricycle u/c. Prototype N9924Y (c/n 1) FF Oct 1961

American Champion 8GCBC Scout N249SF

American Champion 8KCAB Super Decathlon G-YZMO

Aeronca 15AC Sedan N115H

Champion 402 Lancer N9957Y

Chrislea   United Kingdom

The Chrislea Aircraft Co Ltd was formed in 1936 by Richard Christopherides and Bernard Leak to develop the two-seat Chrislea Airguard. This did not reach production, but Christopherides designed the four-seat CH-3 Ace light aircraft for the post-war market. The prototype Ace, G-AHLG (c/n 100), made its first flight in September 1946 and was a fairly conventional high-wing strut-braced tube-and-fabric monoplane with a fixed tricycle undercarriage, powered by a 125hp Lycoming O-290 horizontally-opposed engine. What attracted most attention was the control system, which, like that of the Erco Ercoupe, aimed at a much simplified arrangement of interconnected controls which would allow the pilot to operate the aircraft through a single driving

wheel. The tail of the prototype was soon changed from a conventional single fin to a twin fin/rudder assembly. The CH-3 was found to be underpowered with the Lycoming and so the definitive production version was named Super Ace Srs 2 (prototype G-AKFD c/n 101) and this was powered by a 145hp Gipsy Major 10 in-line engine. It also incorporated metal construction for the wings and tail and a 2-ft increase in wingspan.

Revolutionary as it was, the patent control system did not find favour among customers and a more normal arrangement of rudder bar and control column was intended for the 22 Super Aces that were laid down at the Exeter works (c/n 101 to 122). From aircraft c/n 123 there was a change to a new version of the Ace – the Skyjeep. The prototype Skyjeep was actually c/n 126 (G-AKVS), first flown on 21st November

Chrislea Super Ace G-AKUW

1949. The Skyjeep was designated CH.3 Series 4 and was, essentially, an Ace fitted with a tailwheel undercarriage and a 155hp Blackburn Cirrus Major 3 engine. It featured a removable rear fuselage top decking for freight and ambulance work. Chrislea managed to keep going until 1950 but they finally abandoned production and scrapped the uncompleted airframes c/n 116 to 124 and c/n 130 to 131. The final production totals, excluding the prototype, were 15 Super Aces and six Skyjeeps.

Cirrus   United States

Cirrus Design, headed by Alan Klapmeier and based at Duluth, Minnesota, is the most successful of the new generation light aircraft producers and one of the first American companies to have applied composite technology to a high volume production light aircraft design. Its SR20 is a low-wing four-seater with a 200hp Teledyne-Continental IO-360-ES engine and a fixed tricycle undercarriage. It has side sticks instead of conventional control columns and a modern cockpit, initially with conventional instruments but later, from 2003, fitted with two Avidyne PFD/MFD screens. The cabin is entered through two gull-wing entry doors and the aircraft is fitted with a Ballistic Recovery System consisting of an emergency parachute housed in the rear cabin roof. The SR20 prototype (N200SR) made its first flight on 31st March 1995 and a total of eight flying and static airframes were built (c/n 0001 to 0008). It went into series production in 1999 with serial numbers starting at c/n 1001 and output had reached c/n 1476 by the end of 2004. After approximately 133 SR20s had been built, Cirrus improved the aircraft with a gross weight increase from 2,900 lb to 3,000 lb and minor changes including a new landing light. This variant has sometimes been referred to as the SR20A.

In April 2004, Cirrus announced the Cirrus SRV, which is a lower-priced SR20 without full IFR instrumentation and is produced within the same c/n range as the SR20.

In October 2000 Cirrus announced the SR22 (prototype N140CD), which has the higher-powered 310hp Continental IO-550-N engine. First deliveries started in February 2001 with production reaching 1259 aircraft (c/n 0001-1259) by the end of 2004. 100 examples of a 'Centennial Edition' SR22 were sold in 2003 with special trim and

Cirrus SR22 N677MB

accessories, a 6-point engine mount and a cream colour scheme. From March 2004, at approximately c/n 0864, production was upgraded to the SR22-G2 version with a modified fuselage structure, improved interior, a new door latching system, new engine cowling and 6-point engine mount and a Hartzell Scimitar Select propeller. The SR20 and SRV were subsequently upgraded with similar improvements, becoming the SRV-G2 and SR20-G2 and Special Edition versions launched in 2005 are designated SR20-GTS and SR22-GTS. Cirrus have also worked on development of the SR21 tdi which is a version with a 230hp SMA SR-305 turbo-diesel engine but this was shelved and had not been certificated by mid-2004. During 2004 Cirrus delivered three SRVs, 91 SR20s and 459 SR22s.

Classic Aircraft Waco YMF-5 N64JE

Classic Aircraft Corporation   United States

A small but enthusiastic market for classic pre-war biplanes led to the formation, in 1983, of Classic Aircraft Corporation at Lansing, Michigan by Richard Kettles and Michael Dow. The intention was to build the three-seat YMF-5 open-cockpit Waco biplane for discerning private owner-pilots. It was found that all Waco type certificates had been transferred to the custody of the Federal Aviation Administration and Classic eventually gained manufacturing authority under type certificate ATC.542 in February 1984.

The YMF-5 was a tailwheel biplane with dual controls and Classic Aircraft made several alterations in arriving at the production Waco

Classic F-5. The airframe was upgraded to 4130 steel tubing, a stainless steel firewall replaced the original aluminium, the tailwheel became steerable, modern disc brakes were fitted and a full IFR panel became a 'standard' option. The F-5 Classic is powered by a remanufactured 245hp Jacobs R-755 radial engine and a subsequent development was the F-5C 'YMF Super' with a slightly wider and longer fuselage providing a larger cockpit. The prototype YMF (N1935B c/n F5-001) first flew on 20th November 1985 and type certification was received on 11th March 1986. 35 production YMF-5s were built (c/n F5-002 to F5-036) followed by the F-5C of which 70 had been completed by December 2004 (F5C-037 to F5C-106).

Commander Aircraft   United States

Commander Aircraft was, until recently, the manufacturer of the Rockwell 114 – which was one of a group of four-seat light aircraft designed by Rockwell International in 1968/69. The Model 111/112/114 airframe, fitted with various engines and equipment, was intended as the basis for a comprehensive range to compete with existing light aircraft from the Piper Cherokee to the Beech Bonanza. It was designed by Aero Commander at Bethany, Oklahoma and had a cruciform tail, low wing and a much wider cabin than any of its competition.

The first version was the Model 112 with a retractable undercarriage, but Rockwell also flew two prototypes of the fixed-gear Model 111, although this did not go into production. One of the Model 112 prototypes was lost in a high-speed dive at Albany, Georgia during testing but the tail was re-engineered and the first production unit was delivered following certification on 1st June 1972. There were further problems, particularly with high noise levels, which required many modifications. Eventually, in 1978, the Model 112 was discontinued with production concentrated on the more powerful Model 112TCA and Model 114A.

The 112/114 designs passed to Gulfstream Aerospace with the sale of Aero Commander in February 1981 and for several years they

tried to sell the single-engined Commander line. In November 1982 there was an abortive deal with Evans-Auch Aircraft of Cody, Wyoming and eventually Randall Greene acquired all rights and formed Commander Aircraft Co to support existing aircraft and to build new 114Bs at a factory in Kenosha, Wisconsin although they eventually decided to stay in the existing plant at Bethany. Production started under the new owners (Special Investment Holdings Inc) and the first Model 114B was delivered in mid-1992 with a special trainer variant, the 114AT, being added in mid-1994. Subsequently, in 1995 the turbocharged Model 114TC was introduced and in 2000 the existing models were replaced by the improved Model 115, 115TC and 115AT. The 115 designations were for marketing purposes only and continued to be certificated as the related Commander 114 model.

Commander Aircraft was subsequently acquired by Aviation General Inc but production ceased at the end of 2001 and financial pressures led to it filing for Chapter 11 bankruptcy in December 2002. In early 2004 the business was acquired by Tiger Aircraft of Fredericksburg, Virginia who planned to restart production at Bethany. However, Commander went into liquidation in early 2005. Details of the Commander models are as follows.

Commander Aircraft 114B OO-MOM

Model	Built	Notes
112	125	Four-seat low-wing all-metal aircraft with retractable tricycle u/c, 2,550 lb TOGW and one 200hp Lycoming IO-360-C1D6 piston engine. Prototype N112AC (c/n 1) FF 4 Dec 1970 (w/o 25 Oct 1971)
111A	2	Model 112 with fixed tricycle u/c and 180hp Lycoming O-360-A1G6 engine. Prototypes N111NR (c/n 10001) and N5602X (10002)
112A	364	Structurally strengthened Model 112 to FAR23 (Amdt.7). Metal cabin doors and 2,650 lb TOGW. Introduced Sep 1975
112B	45	112A with 2,800 lb TOGW, 34-in wingspan increase, new propeller, larger wheels and improved soundproofing
112TC	109	112A with turbocharged Lycoming TO-360-C1A6D engine and 2,850 lb TOGW
112TC-A	160	112TC with 2,950 lb TOGW and wing, prop, undercarriage and soundproofing as on 112B. Later named Alpine Commander
114	405	112 with 260hp Lycoming IO-540-&4A3D (or T4B5D) engine, 2-blade prop and 3,140 lb TOGW
114A	41	114 with same airframe mods as 112B. 3-blade prop. 3,250 lb TOGW. Named Gran Turismo
114B	131	114A with strengthened airframe, new McCauley propeller, revised engine cowling with smaller intakes, new cooling induction and exhaust systems, Lycoming IO-540-T4B5 engine and interior restyling. 3,250 lb TOGW
114AT		Trainer version of 114B with dual controls and utility interior
114TC	35	114B with 270hp Lycoming TIO-540-AG1A turbocharged engine, 3,305 lb TOGW. Prototype N195TC (c/n 20001) FF Oct 1994
115	12	114B with detail improvements to systems and external drag factors, redesigned interior and package avionics
115TC	10	114TC with 115 improvements
115AT		114AT with 115 improvements
Total	1,439	

The prototype Commander 112s were given serial numbers 1, 2 (static test), 0003, 0004 and 0005. Thereafter, production aircraft were as follows:

Model	C/n batch	Model	C/n batch	Model	C/n batch
112	6 to 125	112TC	13000 to 13108	114A	14500 to 14540
112A	126 to 489	112TC-A	13150 to 13309	114B	14541 to 14683
112B	500 to 544	114	14000 to 14459*	114TC	20001 to 20045

* 114 excludes c/n 14135-14149, c/n 14320-14349, c/n 14429-14441 (but including 14431, 14434, 14437).

Commonwealth   United States

During the 1930s, Rearwin Aircraft and Engines Inc produced a series of high-wing light aircraft including the two-seat Model 8090 Cloudster powered by the 120hp Ken Royce 7F radial engine and the Model 8135 which was a three-seater and was powered by a 135hp Ken Royce 7G. These were conventional tailwheel aircraft constructed of tube and fabric and they formed the basis for the postwar Skyranger.

The Model 165 Ranger prototype (N25548) had first flown on 9th April 1940 and gained its type certificate (A-729) on 16th August of that year. It provided two seats, side-by-side, and used a 65hp Continental engine. Rearwin built 55 of the higher-powered production Model 175 Skyranger, which was powered by a 75hp Continental engine, and 9 Model 180 Skyrangers with the 80hp Continental. They also produced 17 of the Model 180F with an 80hp Franklin engine and a single 90hp

Commonwealth Rearwin 175 Skyranger G-RWIN

Model 190F. These 82 aircraft, built between 1940 and 1942, carried serials c/n 1501 to 1582.

On 7th January 1943, the owners of Rearwin – Rae, Kenneth and Royce Rearwin and Carl Dolan – sold out their interests and a new company was formed to manufacture the Rearwin line. As it turned out, the first products of the Commonwealth Aircraft Corporation were a batch of 1,470 Waco CG-4A Hadrian and 100 CG-3A troop-carrying gliders and it was not until 1945 that the Skyranger 185, powered by the 85hp Continental C-85-12 engine, went into production at Kansas City, Missouri. Commonwealth completed 296 examples (c/n 1601 to 1896) during the next eighteen months and the last Skyranger (N73837 c/n 1896) left the factory in October 1946.

Culver   United States

The design of the two-seat Culver Cadet originated with Dart Aircraft Co and their little Dart Model G, which was produced during the mid-1930s and was based on the Monocoupe Monoprep G Dart Aircraft, which had been formed by K K Culver and Al Mooney, was reorganised in 1939 as the Culver Aircraft Co based at Wichita. Mooney carried on the successful career he had established with Alexander Aircraft, Bellanca and Monocoupe and the Culver designs also carried Mooney design numbers M.12 to M.17. The initial model was the wood and fabric M.12 Culver Cadet, produced in two versions as the LFA and LCA, powered by the 80hp Franklin 4AC-176-F3 and Continental A-75-8 engine respectively. A total of 357 were built before the war forced the end of civilian production. In 1996, the Cadet was revived as an amateur-built design with a steel tube fuselage structure as the Cadet STF. The prototype, built by Aero Systems of Wichita, Kansas is registered N46TY and is powered by a 90hp Continental C.90 engine.

During the war, Al Mooney redesigned the Cadet for military use with a tricycle undercarriage under the designation LAR-90 (M-13). In military service this became the PQ-8 target drone – and, when fitted with the higher-powered Franklin O-300-3 engine and other refinements, it emerged as the Culver NR-D. In this form it was built in quantity for the USAAF as the PQ-14A (M-16) and for the US Navy as the TD2C-1. A number of these drones were sold to civil users and converted to personal aircraft after the war.

With hostilities over, Culver launched the new Culver V (M-17), which was a considerably developed version of the LAR. As with all the Culver Cadet series, it was a low-wing cabin monoplane with side-by-side seating for two. However, the tailwheel undercarriage was replaced with a retractable tricycle unit, the fuselage was much more streamlined and the Model V had redesigned wings with upturned outer panels. Powered by an 85hp Continental C-85 engine, some 378 examples of the Culver V were built but it was underpowered and neither it nor the improved Culver V-2 was very successful. Postwar production of the Culver V started with the prototype, N44504, c/n V-1 and ran as far as c/n V-357 together with additional aircraft numbered V-3A and V-10A to V-29A – making a total of 378 of the Model V-1. The V-2 aircraft were serialled V2-503 to V2-517 and it seems that c/n 518 to 525 were abandoned unfinished. Eventually, the Culver V was forced out of production when Culver went bankrupt in late 1946.

Culver V N80281

Culver LCA Cadet NC37818

Helton Lark G-LARK

The design was revived in 1956 when the Superior Aircraft Company was formed by Priestly Hunt Aircraft Corporation to purchase the assets of Culver and put the aircraft back into production as the Superior Satellite. The Satellite mainly differed from the Culver-built model in having a 95hp Continental engine – which gave it a cruise speed of 130mph. The prototype was N3157K (c/n 526) and four production aircraft (c/n 527 to 530) were built. Unfortunately, by 1959, the type had again fallen by the wayside.

One outgrowth of the Culver monoplanes was a development by the Jamieson Corporation of DeLand, Florida. In 1948 they built the prototype J-2-L1 Jupiter, which was based on the Culver Cadet with all-metal construction and three seats. The prototype Jupiter had a V-tail and a 115hp Lycoming O-235-C1 engine. After a protracted development period they built a new prototype (N39804), initially named the 'Take 1' (but later the Jamieson J-1) and first flown in December 1958. It was similar to the original Jupiter but was a four-seater with a single fin/rudder, tricycle gear and 150hp Lycoming O-320-A3C engine. It seems that a further prototype Jamieson (otherwise known as the J-2-L1B), N1859M c/n 1, was flown on 13th December 1962 (and certificated on 3rd July 1963) and that Jamieson built two further aircraft (c/n 2 and 3) and then abandoned further development. Jamieson had also obtained a new type certificate (2-584) on 3rd July 1963 for a programme to convert a number of Culver PQ-8As and TDC-2s to Jamieson J-1 standard with a tricycle undercarriage, enlarged vertical tail and a 140hp Lycoming O-290-B engine. It is understood that five aircraft were completed (and their serial numbers are identified by the suffix AR added to the Culver number, eg, c/n 350AR).

In 1966, California Aero of Tracy, California, who had secured the Culver LAR from Superior, produced a new model, the Helton Lark 95. The prototype was N9726C (c/n 9501) The Lark had a fixed tricycle undercarriage, side-by-side seating for two and a Continental C-90-16-F engine – and a new company, Lark Aviation Corporation, was formed to build it. Lark Aviation survived long enough to finish 16 production models (c/n 9502 to 9517) after which the Culver type certificate was taken over by Spinks Industries who have not revived production.

Dallach   Germany

Operating under the name of WD Flugzeugbau GmbH, this company builds the ultralight designs conceived by Wolfgang Dallach. His first design was the low-wing ultralight Sunrise II, first flown in 1968, which has been built in single and two-seat versions and is of wood and fabric construction with a fixed tailwheel undercarriage. It was kit or factory built with various engines in the 35hp to 80hp range, particularly the 40hp Lemon-Visa and the 80hp Verner SVS1400. 39 examples of the Sunrise are believed to have been completed. The D.3 Sunwheel is a further kit-built ultralight, which uses the Sunrise fuselage but is a tube-and-fabric biplane with tandem open cockpits for two and a fixed tailwheel undercarriage. The Sunwheel is powered by a 65hp Sauer ULM.2000 or 80hp Rotax 912 and approximately 50 have been built. The D.4 marked a change in the Dallach designs and was a highly streamlined high-performance aircraft built from tube, wood and fabric with some composite parts. The prototype, which was designed in 1993 and built in coopera-

tion with the Czech firm UL Jih sro, flew in the spring of 1995. The aircraft was marketed as the kit-built D.4 Fascination and manufactured by UL Jih with 41 being produced. It had a side-by-side two-seat cockpit enclosed by a large transparent bubble canopy and was fitted with a retractable tricycle undercarriage and equipped with flaps. The standard powerplant was the Rotax 912 fitted with a variable-pitch propeller but it could also be fitted with the 100hp DZ.100 engine. In 1996 Dallach and UL Jih flew the all-composite Fascination D4 BK (prototype D-MPMM), which replaced the D4 in 1999 as the standard version, sold as factory-complete or as a kit. Over 70 Fascination D4BKs have been sold to date and a new JAR-VLA version is available with a 650kg gross weight. The most recent design from WD Flugzeugbau is the D5 Evolution, which is, again, built from composites. This is a cantilever high-wing aircraft with a fully enclosed cabin and a retractable tricycle undercarriage. It utilises the tail unit and wings of the D4 BK Fascination and is powered by an 80hp Rotax 912UL. The prototype was first flown in 2001 and the type is now in production with six produced by mid-2005.

Dallach Sunrise D-MTHE

Dallach D.3 Sunwheel D-MOYO

Dallach D.4 Fascination PH-3P3

Dallach D.5 Evolution D-MPMM

Dassault   France

In 1947, the pre-war Marcel Bloch company was reconstituted as Avions Marcel Dassault. In the immediate post-war years it produced Ouragan and Mystère fighters and MD.300 Flamant piston-engined transports. Its civil prototypes included the MD-415 Communauté 8/10-seat turboprop feeder transport and the light business turboprop Hirondelle – neither of which reached production. However, Dassault was anxious to have a strong civil aircraft line and, in 1961, work started on the design of a pure jet business aircraft – the Mystère XX. The prototype achieved its maiden flight in May 1963 and during testing there were modifications to the vertical tail, wings and undercarriage. The engines were also changed from Pratt & Whitney JT12A-8s to the General Electric CF700 for the production model.

The first production Mystère XX (F-WMSH c/n 1/401) was flown on 1st January 1965 with the type certificate (A7EU) being issued on 9th June 1965 and deliveries to the United States distributors, Pan American Business Jets Inc, starting shortly afterwards. The name Fan Jet Falcon was given, initially, to American aircraft but this was shortened to Falcon 20 at a later stage. Dassault not only achieved significant sales of executive Falcon 20s but also found a market with Federal Express who put the Falcon 20 into service in 1972 as a high-speed transcontinental small package freighter. The basic Falcon 20C was followed by the higher-powered 'D' model in 1983 after which a series of improved variants appeared, culminating in the Mystère Falcon 200 which was announced in 1981. Dassault also developed the Falcon 20G fitted with Garrett ATF-3 turbofan engines. This was intended as a civil version to meet new noise regulations, but it was also aimed firmly at the US Coast Guard 'Medium-Range Surveillance' requirement. Dassault was successful in gaining the contract for 41 HU-25A Guardians which was placed in 1977 – and the Falcon Gardien became an additional model which was marketed by Dassault to other nations. The last of the Falcon 20 series was completed in mid-1990.

1973 saw the first flight of the Falcon 30. A 29-passenger commuter airliner based on the Falcon 20 (and originally known as the Falcon 20T), the Falcon 30 had a new, larger fuselage and a pair of Avco-Lycoming ALF502 turbofans. It was eventually shelved because the ALF502s were not entirely suitable and there was no viable alternative. A larger 40-passenger version was to have been built as the Falcon 40, but Dassault believed that the market was not yet ready for these aircraft, partly because of the world fuel crisis of 1973-74, and abandoned further development. As the Canadair RJ series has shown, the Falcon 40 was probably ahead of its time.

Attention turned to a new version of the Falcon 20 with intercontinental range. First designs for the Falcon 20-3 (later renamed Falcon 50) were started in 1974 and the prototype flew in late 1976. The aircraft was, essentially, a stretched Falcon 20 with an enlarged vertical tail, a large additional fuel tank situated behind the passenger cabin and three Garrett TFE731 turbofans mounted in the rear fuselage. The initial design was internally designated Falcon 50A and the prototype

Dassault Falcon 100 F-GPFD

Dassault Falcon 20 EC-HCX

flew on 7th November 1976 with a version of the Falcon 20 wing, but it was subsequently refined as the Falcon 50B with the production-standard supercritical wing. Extra cabin windows were fitted and the aircraft had a 3,470-mile range and nine to twelve-passenger seating capacity. After certification on 27th February 1979 (and subsequent issue of the American type certificate A46EU) Dassault was able to set up a production line backed by substantial orders, many of which came from the strong American market – built up through sales of the Falcon 20. The Falcon 50 was further developed as the 50EX which received its FAA certification on 20th December 1996, and has new engines with 24% higher thrust and increased range, faster climb and increased cruise speed. It remains in production at Bordeaux.

While the Falcon 20 was bringing in brisk sales in the mid-1960s, Dassault began design studies for the scaled-down Mini-Falcon with eight-passenger seats and using a pair of Turboméca Larzac turbofans. The prototype (soon named Falcon 10) had a smaller cabin with seven passenger seats, increased fuel capacity and two General Electric CJ610 jet engines. The second example, F-WTAL c/n 02, which flew on 15th October 1971 exchanged the CJ610s for two Garrett AiResearch TFE731-2 turbofans and this became standard for the production model. The first production Falcon 10 was flown on 30th April 1973

Dassault Falcon 900EX N498A

with the French Type Certificate being issued some five months later. The aircraft was later improved and renamed Falcon 100. Production ceased in 1990.

Dassault was merged with Breguet in 1971 to become Avions Marcel Dassault-Breguet Aviation and in 1979 the French State took up ownership of 21% of the equity of the company. In mid-1990 it changed its name to Dassault Aviation. By mid-1988, Dassault had produced 1,000 Falcons of all models. The current production line-up consists of the Falcon 50EX, 900DX, 900EX EASy, 2000 and 2000EX.

The three-engined Falcon 900 was first announced in May 1983 and was intended as a larger version of the Falcon 50 with a completely new wide-bodied fuselage to compete with the Gulfstream IV and Canadair Challenger intercontinental business jets. It flew in September 1984 and first deliveries took place at the end of 1986. It was later upgraded as the 900B in 1991 with TFE731-5B engines, and this was followed by the 900EX with 4,500nm range and TFE731-60 engines which was first rolled out in March 1995. The Falcon 900C which first flew in 1998 replaced the 900B and featured the avionics suite of the 900EX. During 2001/2003 Dassault developed their new high technology EASy flightdeck and this was introduced on the 900EX EASy and on the Falcon 900DX, which was announced in May 2004 and replaces the 900C.

In June 1989, Dassault announced the Falcon 2000, aimed at existing Falcon 20 owners. This offered a 3,000nm range and combined a fuselage with the same width (but shorter length) as the Falcon 900 and twin rear-mounted CFE738 engines. Certification to FAR25/JAR25 was achieved on 2nd February 1995. This base model was supplemented by the 2000EX, which was certificated on 21st March 2003 and provides a 25% increase in range and improved climb performance due to an engine change. The 2000EX EASy adds the new technology cockpit to this variant.

The NBAA Show in 1992 saw Dassault announcing the Falcon 9000 ultra-long-range business jet project with a new laminar-flow wing and 6,000nm range. This was to have been powered by CFE738 engines but the project was subsequently shelved. They also announced, in 1997, a study for a Falcon SST supersonic business jet with a targeted Mach 1.8 cruise speed but the lack of suitable engines caused this to be abandoned two years later. However, in July 2001 Dassault launched the FNX, a high-speed (Mach 0.9) three-engined business jet

Dassault Falcon 50 XA-GCH

which features a high-speed wing and a fuselage which is 20% longer than that of the Falcon 900EX. This is intended to go faster than its competitors, the Gulfstream 450 and Global 5000. It was subsequently renamed the Falcon 7X and the prototype first flew in May 2005

In the calendar year 2004, Dassault delivered 63 new aircraft including – Falcon 50EX (5), Falcon 2000 (11), Falcon 2000EX (10), Falcon 2000EX EASy (19), Falcon 900C (3), Falcon 900EX (1), Falcon 900EX EASy (14). Dassault has never given type numbers to its business jets although unofficial/flight plan designations such as MY-20 or DA-50 are sometimes referred to. Each separate primary model (the '10, '20, '50, 2000 and '900) has its own series of serial numbers commencing at c/n 1. Early Falcon 20s delivered outside the United States also carried an additional separate number that ran from c/n 401 to 557, but this created some confusion and was eventually dropped by Dassault. Serial number allocations for the various types have been:

Model	Prototypes	Production c/ns	Model	Prototypes	Production c/ns
10	01 to 03	1 - 191 (exc 183)	900B		103 - 178
100	183	192 - 226	900C		179 - 201+
20	01	1 - 515	900EX	1	2 - 146+
50	1	2 - 250	2000	1	2 - 220+
50EX		251-340+	2000EX	1	2 - 55+
900	1	2 - 102			

Dassault's business aircraft models have been as follows:

Model	Built	Notes
MD.320 Hirondelle	1	10/14-seat low-wing business aircraft or feederliner. Powered by two Turboméca Astazou XIV turboprops. Prototype F-WPXB (c/n 01) FF 10 May 1959
Falcon 10	193	Low-wing 7/9-seat business jet powered by two 3,230 lbst Garrett TFE731-2 turbofans. 18,740 lb TOGW. Prototype F-WFAL (c/n 01) FF 1 Dec 1970
Falcon 100	36	Falcon 10 with fourth starboard window, rear baggage compartment, EFIS cockpit and 19,300 lb TOGW. FF 10 Feb 1977
Mystère XX	1	Low-wing 8/10-seat business jet powered by two 3,300 lbst Pratt & Whitney JT12A-8 turbojets. 24,470 lb TOGW. Prototype F-WLKB (c/n 01) FF 4 May 1963

Falcon 20	1	Production Mystère XX with 10/12 seats, lengthened fuselage, taller tail, 26,450 lb TOGW and General Electric CF700 engines. Prototype F-WMSH (c/n 1/401)
Falcon 20C	176	Marketing designation for standard Falcon 20
Falcon 20CC	1	Falcon 20C with low-pressure tyres and dual-wheel landing gear for unprepared strips. F-WJML (c/n 73/419)
Falcon 20D	60	Falcon 20C with 80 gal fuel increase, 27,337 lb TOGW, improved brakes and 4,315 lbst CF700-2D turbofans
Falcon 20E	60	Falcon 20D with modified starter/generator, revised rudder and 28,660 lb TOGW
Falcon 20F	134	Falcon 20E with full leading edge slats and increased fuel capacity. Prototype F-WLCU (c/n 173) FF 20 Feb 1970
Falcon 20G Guardian	47	Maritime surveillance version of Falcon 20F fitted with two 5,300 lbst Garrett ATF3-6 turbofans. 40 delivered to USCG as HU-25. 32,000 lb TOGW. Prototype F-WATF (c/n 362) FF 28 Nov 1977
Falcon 20H	1	Falcon 20F with Garrett ATF3-6-2C turbofans and new rear fuselage fuel tank. Prototype F-WZAH (c/n 401) FF 24 Apr 1979
Falcon 20S		Revised designation for Falcon 20C
Falcon 200	36	Revised designation for Falcon 20H. FF 30 Apr 1980

Dassault Falcon 2000 HB-IGQ

Falcon 20-3		Initial designation for Falcon 50
Falcon 20-5		Falcon 20 retrofitted with Garrett TFE731-5AR engines. Prototype FF 1988
Falcon 30	1	30/32-seat light airliner based on Falcon 20 with larger fuselage and two 6,070 lbst Lycoming ALF 502D turbofans. 35,275 lb TOGW. Prototype F-WAMD (c/n 01) FF 11 May 1973
Falcon 40		Proposed 40-passenger Falcon 30. Not built
Falcon 50	250	10/12-seat intercontinental business jet based on Falcon 20 with longer fuselage and 7 windows each side. Powered by three 3,700 lbst Garrett TFE731-3 turbofans. 37,478 lb TOGW. Prototype F-WAMD/F-WNDB (c/n 1) FF 7 Nov 1976. Replaced by Falcon 50EX
Falcon 50EX	90+	Falcon 50 with three 3,700 lbst TFE-731-40 engines upgraded avionics and new engine management system. 39,700 lb TOGW. Prototype F-WOND (c/n 251) FF 10 Apr 1996
Falcon 50M		Maritime surveillance version of Falcon 50
Falcon 900	102	Scaled-up development of Falcon 50 with typical 13-passenger luxury interior or 36-seat high-density cabin. Powered by three 4,500 lbst Garrett TFE 731-5AR turbofans. 45,500 lb TOGW. Prototype F-WIDE (c/n 1) FF 21 Sep 1984
Falcon 900B	76	Falcon 900 with 4,750 lbst TFE731-5BR-1C engines and increased speed and range. 45,500 lb TOGW. Replaced Falcon 900 in Feb 1991. Prototype F-GIDE (c/n 1)
Falcon 900C	23+	900B with Honeywell Primus 2000 flightdeck of 900EX. 46,500 lb TOGW. Prototype F-WWFP (c/n 169) FF 17 Dec 1998
Falcon 900EX	146+	900B development with additional fuel/range, three 5,000 lbst TFE731-60 turbofans, new 5-tube EFIS avionics and HUD. 48,300 lb TOGW. Prototype F-WREX (c/n 1) FF 1 Jun 1995. Falcon 900EX EASy with advanced flightdeck. FF 21 Feb 2002
Falcon 900DX		900C with increased range and EASy cockpit. Prototype F-WWFA FF 13 May 2005
Falcon 2000	220+	Replacement for Falcon 20 with wide body fuselage based on shortened Model 900, giving maximum 19-passenger capacity and typical 10/12-pax executive interior, powered by two 5,725 lbst Garrett/GE CFE738 turbofans. 36,500 lb TOGW. Prototype F-WNAV (F-GNAV, c/n 1) FF 4 Mar 1993
Falcon 2000EX	55+	Extended range Falcon 2000 with 7,000 lbst Pratt & Whitney PW3087C turbofans and 36,500 lb TOGW. FF 25 Oct 2001. Falcon 2000EX EASy with advanced cockpit. Prototype F-WMEX (c/n 1) FF 29 Jan 2003
Falcon 9000		Proposed intercontinental business jet based on Falcon 900 with 7-ft fuselage stretch, three 7,200 lbst CFE738 turbofans, 6,000nm range, 68,000 lb TOGW and typical 12/14-pax long-range capacity. Not built
Falcon FNX		High-speed intercontinental business jet with longer fuselage than Falcon 900, fly-by-wire controls and new high-subsonic wing. Powered by three 6,100 lbst Pratt & Whitney PW307A turbofans
Falcon 7X	1	Revised designation for Falcon FNX. Prototype F-WFBW (c/n 1) FF 5 May 2005

De Havilland Australia   Australia

As part of its pre-war overseas expansion, the British De Havilland Aircraft Company Ltd established De Havilland Aircraft Pty Ltd (DHA) at Bankstown, NSW on 7th March 1927. DHA spent the war in production of Mosquito FB.40 fighter-bombers and other repair and production activities. When the war was over a requirement developed for a utility aircraft for use by the Royal Flying Doctor Service (RFDS) and DHA designed the DHA-3 Drover which embodied much of the design philosophy of the DH.104 Dove.

The prototype Drover (VH-DHA c/n 5001) made its first flight on 23rd January 1948. The Drover 1 was a six/eight-seat low-wing aircraft with a fixed tailwheel undercarriage and three 145hp Gipsy Major 10/2 piston engines with variable-pitch metal propellers while the Drover 1F had fixed pitch propellers. Between 1950 and 1954 a total of 20 Drovers were built (c/n 5001 to 5020). Five of these were Drover 2s with double-slotted flaps and most of the Mk 1s were converted to this standard. In 1960/61, six Drovers, notably those used by the RFDS, were re-engined with 180hp Lycoming O-360-A1A flat-four piston engines and redesignated Drover Mk 3.

DHA Drover Mk 3 VH-FPC

De Havilland Canada   Canada

In the 1920s, demand built up in Canada for air transport services to supply the isolated development communities that were being created. On 5th April 1928, the de Havilland Aircraft Company established a subsidiary known as The de Havilland Aircraft of Canada, Limited (DHC) to assemble and sell the aircraft produced by the British parent. Moths and Dragons were supplied during the next decade and the Tiger Moth, Avro Anson and Mosquito were built during the war years. The first postwar product was the DH.83C Fox Moth biplane, which used many Tiger Moth components and had a cabin for four passengers in the centre-fuselage and a pilot's cockpit atop the fuselage behind the wings. De Havilland had flown the original Fox Moth prototype in January 1932 but the first Canadian example (CF-BFI c/n FM.1) was delivered from the DHC factory at Downsview, near Toronto, in June 1946. Eventually, 53 Fox Moths were completed (c/n FM.1 to FM.52, together with FM.54 built from spares by Leavens Brothers) and the last delivery was made in February 1948.

During this period, DHC designed a new low-wing tandem two-seat trainer – the DHC-1 Chipmunk – to replace the ageing Tiger Moth. The Chipmunk was of all-metal construction and the prototype (CF-DIO-X c/n 1) first flew on 22nd May 1946. DHC built a total of 217 Chipmunks (c/n 1 to 217) and delivered large batches to India and the air forces of Canada, Thailand and Egypt. The Chipmunk was built in Britain by the parent company who constructed 1,000 (c/n C1-0001 to C1-1014, excluding 0955 to 0968) and in Portugal by OGMA who built 66 aircraft (c/n OGMA-1 to 66).

The Canadian Chipmunk, fitted with a single-piece clear-view bubble cockpit canopy was built in two models – the DHC-1B-1 with a 145hp Gipsy Major 1C and the DHC-1B-2 using a Gipsy Major 10-3 engine. The British versions had a framed canopy and a large number were built for the Royal Air Force as the Chipmunk T.10 with a Gipsy Major 8 engine – the civil equivalents being the Chipmunk Mk 22 and the Mk 22A, which had increased fuel capacity, and the Mk 21 with a Gipsy Major 10 Mk 2 engine. A few British Chipmunks were also converted as the crop-spraying Mk 23 with a single cockpit.

Mindful of the growing demand for bush aircraft, DHC used its experience to create the DHC-2 Beaver – which is still unsurpassed in this role. The Beaver was a high-wing all-metal STOL aircraft with a fixed tailwheel undercarriage (or floats or skis) fitted with a 450hp Pratt & Whitney R-985-AN-1 Wasp air-cooled radial engine. It could accommodate a pilot and seven passengers, but was mainly used to haul freight, which was loaded through large doors on either side of the cabin. The first Beaver (CF-FHB-X c/n 1) flew from Downsview on 16th August 1947 and DHC received a huge order for 970 examples (designated L-20 or U-6A) from the US Army and US Air Force. In total, 1,692 of the DHC-2 were built (c/n 1 to 1692). Of these, 60 were completed as DHC-2 Mk III Turbo Beavers with a 578shp Pratt & Whitney PT6A-6 turboprop, a lengthened fuselage to accommodate up to 11 seats and enlarged squared-off vertical tail surfaces. The prototype Turbo Beaver (CF-PSM-X c/n 1525) first flew on 30th December 1963 and the last production aircraft was completed in May 1968. In 2003, Beaver Aircraft Canada announced plans to open a new production line for the Beaver and Otter in the facility of Viking Air in Vancouver but this appears to have been shelved.

The success of the Beaver led to a demand for more of the same formula with greater capacity. The result was the DHC-3 Otter – and again the US Army was a big customer for the U-1 variant. The Otter was designed to carry 14 passengers or 2,240 lb of freight, which could be loaded through double doors on the starboard side and it was, like the Beaver, a strut-braced high-wing aircraft with fixed tailwheel gear. Fitted with a 600hp Pratt & Whitney R-1340-S1H1-G radial, the Otter could be equipped with standard or amphibious floats and many were used in this configuration for operations such as the Widerøes fjord-hopping airline service in Norway. The prototype Otter was CF-DYK-X (c/n 1) which first flew on 21st December 1951 and was followed by 465 production units (c/n 2 to 466). A number of Otters have been re-engined. The programmes include installation of the 1,000hp PZL ASz-621R-M18 radial engine in place of the existing R-1340 by Airtech Canada (of which 17 have been completed) and several turboprop

DHC-1 Chipmunk T.10 G-BCGC

DHC-2 Mk III Turbo Beaver N148KS

DHC-3 Otter N44NB

conversions. The most successful has been by Vazar Aerospace who fit the aircraft with a 750shp Pratt & Whitney PT6A-135A or -34 engine.

The DHC-4 and DHC-5 were both twin-engined military aircraft of which a few production examples and some military surplus machines were used by civil operators. The DHC-4 Caribou was the DHC answer to a US Army specification calling for a three-ton rear-loading tactical transport powered by two 1,450hp Pratt & Whitney R-2000-D5 piston engines. The first Caribou (CF-KTK-X c/n 1) was flown on 30th July 1958 and of the 253 examples built some 165 went to the US Army and others were delivered to the air forces of Malaysia, Australia, Kenya, Zambia, India, Ghana and Canada. Several ended up in the hands of the CIA operations: Air Asia, Air America and Pacific Architects & Engineers. As with other DHC designs there are now a fair number of ex-military Cariboux in service with commercial operators.

DHC-6 Twin Otter N40269

The prototype DHC-4 was transferred to the RCAF and in 1961 was fitted with two General Electric T64-4 turboprop engines. This led to the development of the Caribou II, again to a US Army requirement, which crystallised as the DHC-5 Buffalo. The Buffalo was a scaled-up Caribou with the T64 engines and a T-tail – and the prototype, carrying the US Army serial 63-13686, took to the air on 9th April 1964. As it turned out, only four evaluation CV-7A Buffalos went to the US Army and the main customers were the Canadian, Brazilian, Kenyan, Tanzanian and Peruvian air forces although the Buffalo was marketed to civil users as the 44 passenger DHC-5E Transporter. Later examples of the Buffalo were the DHC-5D version with more powerful 3,133shp CT64-820-4 turboprops. The last of 126 DHC-5s was delivered in December 1986.

At this point, DHC moved into the commuter airline market with the DHC-6 Twin Otter which was a strut-braced high-wing monoplane with a fixed tricycle undercarriage and two Pratt & Whitney PT6A tur-boprop engines. It entered production in 1965 following the first flight of the prototype, CF-DHC-X (powered by PT6A-6 engines) on 20th May of that year. While the early deliveries were to commuter air carriers the Twin Otter took on many utility roles including service with the British Antarctic Expedition. The initial model was the Series 100 with 578shp PT6A-20 engines and a short nose, and this was replaced in April 1968 by the Series 200 with a lengthened nose (though the float-plane continued with the short nose), increased aft baggage capacity and PT6A-20A engines. The Series 300 was similar but had 652shp PT6A-27 engines. The last Twin Otter (c/n 844) was completed in December 1988.

De Havilland Canada then moved on to develop the DHC-7 Dash Seven high-wing four-turboprop 48-seat airliner and the DHC-8 Dash Eight which is in current production by DHC's parent company, Bombardier. These airliners are considered to be outside the definition of General Aviation.

Diamond Aircraft
Austria/Canada

Diamond Aircraft Industries is the current name (introduced in 1997) for HOAC of Wiener Neustadt. The original company, Hoffman Flugzeugbau GmbH, was formed at Friesach in Austria in 1979 by Wolff Hoffman and it became one of the most successful producers in the motor glider field with its Hoffman H-36 Dimona. The first prototype Dimona (D-KDIM c/n 3001) was built at Dachau and first flown on 9th October 1980 with production commencing in the following year. The Dimona was a wholly glassfibre aircraft with side-by-side dual seating, a T-tail and a fixed glassfibre tailwheel undercarriage. It was powered by an 80hp Limbach SL2000-EB1 engine and achieved considerable sales success.

In addition to the Dimona, a number of other prototypes were built including the H-38 Observer. Based on the Dimona, this had a bulbous clear-view cockpit and a Limbach SL2000 engine mounted behind the cabin with a driveshaft passing between the two crewmembers. The H-39 Diana single-seat microlight was also tested and this was constructed of composite materials and used a König SD570 pusher engine. Neither of these designs was offered as a production model.

Following a financial crisis in 1984, Wolff Hoffman left and contin-

HOAC H.36 Dimona D-KOTO

ued separate development of light aircraft through a new company, Wolff Hoffman Flugzeugbau KG. His company flew the prototype of a new two-seater, H-40 D-EIOF, on 28th August 1988, this being a lighter version of the Dimona with shorter-span forward-swept wings, a tricycle undercarriage and a Limbach L2400 engine. Wolf Hoffman is now developing a new version of the H-40 with a 116hp Lyoming O-235-P1 engine for production in partnership with AAI-ABS Aircraft Industries at Mönchen Gladbach.

After the 1984 financial reconstruction, the original Hoffman company became a subsidiary of Simmering Graz Pauker. It was subsequently acquired in 1989 by Christian Dries and named HOAC-Austria Flugzeugwerke – and became Diamond Aircraft Austria (and later, in March 1996, Diamond Aircraft Industries GmbH). Manufacture was established at Wiener Neustadt. Initially, it built the HK-36R Super Dimona (the 'K' and 'R' designations identifying the designer – Kurdoi and the Rotax engine), which was a major redesign of the H.36. Later marketed as the Super Dimona HK36-TS, it was certificated to JAR-22 and had an 80hp Rotax 912A3 engine in a new engine cowling, strengthened undercarriage, redesigned single-piece cockpit canopy, improved cockpit ventilation and a new instrument panel. The later Super Dimona HK36-TTS had a turbocharged Rotax 914F3 engine and was fitted with glider towing equipment and both of these models were fitted with tailwheel undercarriages. Equivalent versions with tricycle gear were the Super Dimona HK36-TC and Super Dimona HK36-TTC. Subsequent motor glider developments included the Katana Xtreme and Katana Turbo Xtreme and the company's motor glider products, built in Austria, are currently the HK36 Motorglider and the HK36-MPX special missions surveillance aircraft.

On 16th March 1991, HOAC flew the first prototype LF.2000 Turbo (OE-VPX c/n 20001), which was a lightweight tailwheel short wing derivative of the Super Dimona. The definitive DV.20 Katana (OE-CPU c/n 20002) followed in December 1991 and was certified under the JAR-VLA rules with a lower gross weight than the Dimona (1,698 lb) due to its redesigned fuselage structure. Compared with the HK36, the Katana has a tricycle undercarriage, smaller rudder and a reduced span wing with flaps, constant taper and upturned tips. The DV.20 retained the 80hp Rotax 912.A.3 engine with a hydraulic constant-speed propeller and production commenced in March 1993. In that year, HOAC formed a Canadian company, Dimona Aircraft (later Diamond Aircraft Industries Inc) to operate a second production line in London, Ontario building the DA20-A1 Katana which featured a new instrument panel, revised seating, landing lights and upturned wingtips. The first aircraft (C-FSQN, c/n 10001) was rolled out in June 1994 and Austrian production of Katanas was discontinued in mid-1996.

Several variants of the DA20 have been produced. The prototype DV.22 Speed Katana Turbo (OE-ASP) was first flown at Wiener

Diamond DV20 Katana 100 D-ETLM

Neustadt in 1996 powered by a 115hp turbocharged Rotax 914F engine but no production was undertaken. This was followed by the DA20-C1, which was certified and entered production in 1998, and the DA20-C1 Eclipse that followed in 1999. Diamond has also developed the DA20-100 Katana and the DA20-C1 Evolution and these last three models remain in production in Canada for worldwide markets. In 1995, Diamond embarked on a cooperative venture with the Russian organisation, Sokol, to build and sell an updated version of the Frati F.15F Delfino. Known as the HOAC Excalibur, the first prototype (OE-VPY) was converted from the original General Avia prototype but the venture had come to a halt by mid-1996.

In 1997, Diamond initiated design of a four-seat derivative of the DA20 designated DA40. This was larger than the Katana but followed the same composite construction and T-tail layout with a high-aspect-ratio wing and fixed tricycle undercarriage. The first DA40 made its maiden flight on 5th November 1997 powered by a Rotax 914 engine. Eight prototypes were used for testing, powered by a variety of engines including the Continental IO-240 and, eventually, the Lycoming IO-360 that powers the production version. The DA40-180 Diamond Star was certificated and first deliveries started in 2000 with initial production in Austria but manufacture moved to Canada in 2001. Diamond has subsequently developed the DA40 DiamondStar TDI with a Thielert TA-125 diesel engine and this first flew in November 2001 and received JAA-JAR23 certification in 2002. A version of the DA40 with a fixed-pitch propeller and a non-injected O-360 engine was introduced in April 2004.

Diamond DA-40 Diamond Star G-CBFA

Diamond DA-42 Twin Star OE-VDA

In May 2002, Diamond unveiled the prototype of its DA42 Twin Star, which is, essentially, a DA40 with a faired-in nose and two Thielert TAE-125 engines mounted on the wings. It has retractable tricycle gear and the prototype made its first flight on 9th December 2002. It completed testing and received EASA certification on 13th May 2004. Diamond have also tested two Twin Stars (OE-VDC and -VPS) fitted with a pair of Lycoming IO-360-M1A engines and this may be offered as an alternative to the diesel variant. The latest Diamond project is the D-Jet: an all-composite five-seat light personal jet with a low wing and a single turbofan mounted in the rear fuselage. In early 2005, the prototype D-Jet was nearing completion at Wiener Neustadt but flight tests are to be carried out at the Canadian factory where the aircraft will be built.

During calendar year 2004, Diamond Aircraft delivered 58 DA20 Katanas and 203 DA40 Diamond Stars. Details of HOAC and Diamond designs are as follows:

Model	Built	Notes
H-36 Dimona	316	Side-by-side two-seat all-composite motor glider with cantilever fixed spatted tailwheel u/c, T-tail, mid-wing, powered by one 80hp Limbach SL2000-EB1 engine. Prototype D-KDIM (c/n 3001) FF 9 Oct 1980
HK36R Super Dimona	114	Redesigned H-36 with deeper forward fuselage, single-piece canopy, new u/c legs, modified wing and 90hp Limbach L2400EB engine
HK36TS Katana Xtreme	236	HK36R for glider towing with winglets and 81hp Rotax 913A-3 engine with c/s prop. Prototype OE-9415
HK36TC Katana Xtreme		HK36TS with tricycle u/c
HK36TTS Katana Turbo Xtreme		HK36TS with new carbon wingspar and 115hp Rotax 914F-3 engine
HK36TTS Super Dimona		HK36TTS renamed
HK36TTC Katana Turbo Xtreme		HK36TTS with tricycle u/c
TTC115 Super Dimona		HK36TTC renamed. US name Xtreme Turbo
TC100 Super Dimona		HK36TC fitted with 100hp Rotax 912S engine
HK36MPX		Special missions version of HK36TC with underwing surveillance pods, IR sensors and video-cam data collection equipment. Prototype C-GEPR
H-38 Observer	1	Two-seat observation aircraft based on H-36 with extensively glazed cockpit, tricycle u/c and 80hp Limbach L2000EBI or 105hp L2500EBI engine buried behind cockpit driving nose-mounted propeller. Prototype D-KOBS
H-39 Diana	1	Single-seat ultralight with a high wing and contoured fibreglass fuselage, powered by one König SD570 engine in pusher configuration
H-40	2	Composite side-by-side two-seater with T-tail, swept-forward wings, fixed tricycle undercarriage and powered by one Limbach 2400 engine. Prototype D-EIOF FF 28 Aug 1988
LF.2000 Turbo	1	HK36R with new short wing with flaps and upturned wingtips, extra rear cockpit glazing and turbocharged Rotax engine. Prototype OE-VPX (c/n 20001) FF 16 Mar 1991
DV20 Katana	160	LF.2000 with reduced-depth, wider chord vertical tail, fixed tricycle u/c, no rear cockpit glazing and 80hp Rotax 912A engine. Various canopy variations. Prototype OE-CPU (c/n 20002) FF Dec 1991. Austrian production until 1996
DV20 Katana 100		DV20/DA20 retro-fitted with 100hp Rotax 912S engine. Prototype OE-VPP
DA20-A1 Katana	331	Canadian-built version of DV20. 1,610 lb TOGW. Built 1995 to 1998
DA20-C1 Katana	305	Replacement for DA20-A1 with more streamlined engine cowl and cockpit canopy, optional rear cockpit windows, 125hp Continental IO-240-B engine. 1,720 lb TOGW. Prototype C-FDVA FF 1997
DA20-C1 Eclipse		Deluxe version of DA20-C1 with leather seats, Garmin avionics, autopilot, improved trim, rear windows. Prototype C-GKAQ (c/n C0001)
DA20-C1 Evolution		Rebranded DA20-C1 trainer with minor changes
DV22 Speed Katana	2	DV20 Katana with 115hp turbocharged Rotax 914F engine, new longer span wing with split flaps and wingtip winglets, new wheel fairings, external baggage door, fuel tanks in the wings instead of fuselage, revised seating. Prototype OE-ASP (c/n 22001). No production
DA40-180 Diamond Star	354	4-seat low-wing all-composite light aircraft with T-tail, fixed tricycle u/c, powered by one 180hp Lycoming IO-360-M1A engine. 2,535 lb TOGW. Prototype OE-VPC FF 5 Nov 1997. Built in Austria but production transferred to Canada from Jan 2002
DA40D Star TDI	152	DA40 powered by 135hp Thielert TAE135PS diesel engine in enlarged cowling. Prototype OE-KPP FF 28 Nov 2001. Austrian production
DA40-180FP Diamond Star		DA40-180 with 180hp normally aspirated Lycoming O-360A4D engine and fixed-pitch propeller
DA42 Twin Star	7	DA40 with faired nose and two Thielert TAE135PS diesel engines. Winglets and retractable tricycle u/c. Prototype OE-VPS (c/n 42.001)

DA42 Twin Star	1	DA42 with alternative Lyc IO-360-M1A piston engines. Prototype OE-VDC (c/n L001) FF 18 Dec 2004
DA42MPP		Twin Star 'multi-purpose platform' fitted with high-tech UOMZ camera system for surveillance
D-Jet		Low-wing all-composite light jet with five-seat cabin and powered by a single 1,400 lbst Williams FJ33 turbofan fed by wing root intakes. Prototype to fly in 2005

Serial numbers of the various production models are:

Model	C/n range	Model	C/n range	Model	C/n range
H-36	3501 - 3539	H-40	40001 - 40002	DA40	40.001 - 40.084
H-36	3601 - 36277	DV20	20001 - 20160	DA40*	40.201 - 40.470
HK-36R	36301 - 36414	DA20-A1	10001 - 10331	DA40D	D4.001 - D4.152
HK-36TTS	36415 - 36416	DA20-C1	C0001 - C0305	DA42	42.001 - 42.008
HK-36TTS	36501 - 36734	DV20	20.001 - 20.160	*Canadian	

DINFIA   Argentina

DINFIA (Dirección Nacional de Fabricaciones e Investigaciones Aeronáuticas) was a state-owned company derived from the original FMA and the Instituto Aerotécnico. In 1968 it reverted to the title FMA. In the mid-1950s, they developed a high-wing light aircraft for crop spraying and general club flying and glider towing. This IA.46 Ranquel first flew on 23rd December 1957 and went into production shortly afterwards at Cordoba. It was a fairly conventional tube-and-fabric aircraft with a forward pilot's seat and a rear bench seat for two passengers.

The IA.46 was powered by a 150hp Lycoming O-320-A2B engine and for crop spraying it used an external 88-imp gallon spray tank. The Super Ranquel was similar, but had a more powerful 180hp Lycoming O-360-A1A engine. A subsequent development was the IA.51 Tehuelche, which was a developed Super Ranquel with metal covering to the wings, larger flaps and agricultural load capacity raised to 110 imperial gallons. The prototype of this variant (LV-X-26, later LV-IMF and PG-416) first flew on 16th March 1963. Over 220 Ranquels were built and a number served in the Fuerza Aerea Argentina as glider tugs.

DINFIA also developed a six-seat light twin, the I.A.45B Querandi, which was powered by a pair of 180hp Lycoming O-360 engines buried in the wings and driving pusher propellers. The Querandi, which had a high wing and twin tail fins was first flown on 23rd September 1957 but was abandoned after testing. Between 1957 and 1960 FMA also produced a batch of I.A.-35-II Huanquero low-wing military piston-engined transport and crew trainer aircraft. This aircraft was intended for civil use as the 7-passenger Pandora, but DINFIA decided instead to marry the wings and twin-finned tail to a new 10-seat fuselage and use a pair of 858shp Turboméca Bastan IIIA turboprops to create the Guarani I. The prototype (LQ-HER) first flew on 6th February 1962. This was followed on 23rd April 1963 by the prototype IA.50 Guarani II (LV-X27) which had a shorter rear fuselage, swept single fin/rudder assembly, 1,005shp Bastan IVA turboprops and accommodation for up to 15 passengers. The Guarani G-II could be fitted with supplementary wingtip fuel tanks. A total of 41 Guarani IIs were built (c/n 01 to 41). The majority were delivered to the Argentine military establishment, but the Guarani saw service as a feeder airliner and for survey work and several military aircraft were transferred to the civil register.

DINFIA Guarani II LQ-MBS

DINFIA Super Ranquel LV-HOU

Dittmar   Germany

Heini Dittmar a well-known glider designer had developed the Condor single-seat glider in the 1930s and after the War developed the two-seat Condor 4 and the HD-53 Segelmöwe which flew in 1953. His company, the Heinrich Dittmar Condor-Flugzeugbau then used the base of the HD-53 to develop an ultralight aircraft that is understood to have made its maiden flight in 1955 after post-war restrictions on powered aircraft in Germany were lifted. This high-wing HD-153A-1 Motor Möwe had side-by-side seating for two, a fixed tricycle under-carriage and a 65hp Continental engine. The prototype HD-153V-1 (D-EMAD c/n 001) was subsequently tested with a 70hp Hirth HM.60 engine but the production HD-153, which flew in May 1956, was fitted with a 90hp Continental C90-12F engine. Eight production HD-156A-1 aircraft were produced (c/n WB3, 4, 10, 15,18, 19, 20, 39), the missing c/ns being airframes that were started but not completed. In addition, there were five amateur-built aircraft (c/n AB301, AB302 and AB304 to AB306). Dittmar also converted two to HD-156A-1 standard with a third rear seat and additional side windows. The first example was

Dittmar HD-153 Motor Möwe D-EKIH

D-EHYT (c/n WB20) and one other was flown (D-ELUR c/n 550 converted from WB39). Heini Dittmar was killed in an accident in April 1960 and the Motor Möwe project ceased.

Dornier Do 28A-1 G-ASUR

Dornier   Germany

During the immediate postwar years, while aircraft manufacturing was prohibited in Germany, Dr Claudius Dornier moved to Spain and established the Oficinas Tecnicas Dornier based in Madrid. In 1953, Dornier responded to a Spanish Air Ministry specification for a STOL liaison and observation aircraft. The resulting prototype was built by CASA and designated Do 25 (following on from the wartime Do 24 flying boat designation). It was an all-metal monoplane with a high cantilever wing, fixed tailwheel undercarriage and numerous high lift devices to facilitate its short field performance. All fuel was carried in underwing teardrop tanks and the machine was fitted with a 150hp ENMA Tigre G-4-B piston engine. The definitive Do 27 production version had an enlarged tail unit, 225hp Continental engine, modified cockpit transparencies and a slimmer rear fuselage.

The Do 27 prototype had been built by CASA but, by this time the German manufacturing embargo had been lifted and the aircraft was flown in April 1955 by Dornier Werke in Germany. The production Do 27 featured integral wing fuel tanks together with various detailed changes and its commercial success was assured by an initial order for 428 observation and communications versions for the new Luftwaffe. Many of these were subsequently passed on to other air forces around the world. Just over 140 commercial Dornier 27s were built and many were exported as civil and military aircraft with the type gaining a good reputation on account of its excellent STOL and slow flying capabilities. On 3rd December 1959, CASA flew their own production version of the Do 27 and subsequently built some 50 examples (which were similar to the Do 27A-1) for use by the Spanish Air Force as the C-27.

In 1959, Dornier developed the twin-engined version of the Do 27. On this Do 28 the designers replaced the nose-mounted engine with a stub wing set in the fuselage just ahead of the cockpit on which were mounted two Lycoming engines together with the main undercarriage units. The production Do 28 had 250hp engines and, with the exception of a few delivered to the Katangese, Turkish and Nigerian air forces, virtually all of the 120 aircraft built were sold to civil customers – although a number of these found their way into service with the CIA in Laos. Later models of the Do 28 were fitted with turbocharged engines and a version powered by Turboméca Astazou turboprops was also planned. A Do 27 had already been used by Turboméca as an Astazou testbed, but Dornier did not eventually adopt this engine for either the Do 27 or Do 28.

The next model to appear was the Do 28D, which, despite its designation, bore little similarity to the Do 28 that had gone before. The Do 28D Skyservant, which was aimed at both military and civil users, was a light utility aircraft with a square-section fuselage, an enlarged version of the Do 28 wing and two Lycoming IGSO-540 engines mounted on stub wings. From the outset, the Do 28D established itself with the German forces and the first examples were delivered to the Luftwaffe in 1970. A small number of civil Skyservants were sold, including 13 aircraft delivered to the United States. The company has also built a number of experimental aircraft, including the Dornier 24ATT development of the wartime Do 24 flying boat (now revived for use in the Philippines tourist trade) and these are all detailed in the table of models.

The Do 28D was also important to the company as the basis for a new group of commuter airliners – the Do 228 series. In the late 1970s Dornier carried out extensive research into new technology wing design and converted a Do 28D into its 'TNT' prototype for the advanced 'Tragsflugels Neuer Technologie' programme. The Do 228 (originally known as the Do 28E) was fitted with this wing and has been built in both standard and stretched fuselage versions. The Do 228 fuselage incorporated sections of Do 28D structure but was, essentially, a new design and the aircraft received its German type certificate on 18th December 1981 with the first delivery, to A/S Norving taking place on 3rd March 1982. The Do 228 has also been built by Hindustan Aeronautics to meet local Indian requirements.

Fairchild acquired an 80% stake in Dornier in June 1996, and they inherited the Do 328 turboprop 30-seat airliner programme, which used the TNT wing married to a completely new circular-section pressurized fuselage. The prototype Do 328-100, D-CHIC (c/n 3001), first flew in late 1991 and a few, marketed as the Fairchild Envoy, have reached corporate customers, the first example in 19-seat corporate shuttle configuration being delivered in early 1998. The 328JET is a largely identical airframe with the twin turboprops replaced by two 6,050 lbst Pratt & Whitney PW306/9 turbofans and the prototype (D-BJET, converted from the second 328 prototype, D-CATI) flew in January 1998. This aircraft has largely been delivered to airline customers but a few have made their way into the executive market (as the Fairchild Envoy 3). In mid-2003, following the April 2002 bankruptcy of Fairchild Dornier, the rights to the 328JET and proposed 428JET programmes were acquired by AvCraft together with 18 completed aircraft (of which four were in executive configuration). AvCraft marketed the 328JET to corporate buyers as the AvCraft Envoy Executive and Envoy Executive Shuttle and delivered nine aircraft in 2004. However, they were forced into administration in March 2005.

Each aircraft type was given its own block of serial numbers. The blocks known to have been used are as follows:

Dornier Do 28D YS-401P

A summary of Dornier models is as follows:

C/n Batch	Aircraft Type	C/n Batch	Aircraft Type
101 to 527	Do 27	4331 to 4349	Do 128-2
601 to 604	Do 27 (military)	4358/4359	Do 228-100
601 to 622	Fiat G-91-T1	6002 to 6022	Do 128-6
301 to 595	Fiat G-91R-3	7001 to 7168*	Do 228-100
2001 to 2141	Do 27 (civil/export)	8001 to 8245*	Do 228-200
3001 to 3120	Do 28	3001 to 3119†	Do 328
4001 to 4054	Do 28D-1	3120 to 3219	Do 328JET
4080 to 4200	Do 28D-2		

* The Do 228-100 & -200 are in a common series, differentiated only by the prefix 7 or 8.
† Includes 328JET c/n 3099, 3102, 3105, 3108, 3111, 3114, 3116, 3118.

Model	Built	Notes
Do 24ATT	1	Modern version of wartime Do 24 flying boat with three PT6A-50 turboprops. Prototype D-CATD (later RP-C2403) FF 25 Apr 1983
Do 25-P1	1	Four-seat cabin monoplane with single-piece cantilever high-wing, fixed tailwheel u/c and underwing fuel tanks. Powered by one 150hp ENMA Tigre G-IVB. Prototype FF 25 Jun 1954
Do 25-P2	1	Developed Do 25 with smaller glazed area and 225hp Continental O-470-J engine. Prototype EC-AKY FF 27 Jun 1955
Do 27	2	Do 25 with individual wings, larger cabin side windows, new doors, larger tail, new u/c and 275hp Lycoming GO-480-B1A6 engine. Prototype D-EKER (c/n 102)
Do 27A-1	177	Military Do 27 with 3,858 lb TOGW
Do 27A-2	2	Do 27A-1 with internal modifications
Do 27A-3	88	Do 27A-1 with TOGW increased to 3,858 lb
Do 27A-4	65	Military Do 27 with wide u/c and 4,078 lb TOGW
Do 27B-1	86	Dual-control training version of Do 27A-1
Do 27B-2	5	Do 27B-1 with internal modifications
Do 27B-3	16	Do 27B-2 with TOGW increased to 3,858 lb
Do 27B-5		Do 27B-3 conversions to Do 27A-4 standard
Do 27H-1		Do 27B-2 with 340hp Lycoming GSO-480-B1B6 engine, 3-blade propeller and larger tail. D-ENTE (c/n 2001)

Dornier Do 27Q-1 D-EJEX

Dornier Do 228-101 D-CALM

Do 27H-2	14	Do 27H-1 for Swiss AF with modifications similar to those on Do 27Q-1
Do 27J-1	12	Do 27A-4 for Belgian Army
Do 27K-1	16	Do 27A-4 for Portuguese AF
Do 27K-2	24	Do 27K-1 with minor mods for Portuguese AF
Do 27Q-1	16	Civil production Do 27A-1 with six seats
Do 27Q-3	1	Four-seat Do 27Q-1 with 230hp Continental O-470K engine
Do 27Q-4	34	Improved Do 27Q-1 with auxiliary fuel tanks
Do 27Q-5	12	Do 27Q-4 with internal modifications
Do 27Q-6	2	Do 27Q-5 with internal modifications for Guinea Bissau and Brazil
Do 27S-1	1	Twin float seaplane Do 27Q with ventral fin and enlarged rudder. Prototype D-EGUW (c/n 2023) FF 20 Apr 1959
Do 27T		Do 27Q-4 converted to Turboméca Astazou II turboprop testbed. F-WJRD (c/n 2068)
Do 28	1	Twin-engined version of Do 27 with faired-in nose and two 180hp Lycoming O-360-A1A engines fitted to forward fuselage beam. Prototype D-IBOB FF 29 Apr 1959
Do28A-1	60	Production Do 28 with 250hp Lycoming IO-540-A1A engines and new wing with 7-ft span increase. Prototype D-IHIL (c/n 3002) FF 20 Mar 1960
Do 28B-1	60	Do 28A with enlarged nose, additional fuel tanks, increased tailplane area, 295hp Lycoming IO-540-A1A5 engines
Do 28B-2	1	Do 28B-1 with turbocharged 350hp Lycoming TIO-540 engines
Do 28C		Proposed pressurized Do 28 with Astazou II turboprops
Do 28D	7	Skyservant. Redesigned Do 28 with box fuselage, larger wing, new tail, 7,700 lb TOGW and two 380hp Lycoming IGSO-540 engines. Prototype D-INTL (c/n V-1/4001) FF23 Feb 1966
Do 28D-1	54	Production version of Do 28D
Do 28D-2	121	Skyservant with 8,040 lb TOGW, lengthened fuselage, fin fairing, improved flaps and ailerons
Do 28D-5X	1	Turbo Skyservant. Do 28D-2 fitted with two Lycoming LTP101-600 turboprops in new engine installation with new fuel tanks. Prototype D-IBUF (c/n 4302) FF 9 Apr 1978
Do 28D-6X		Do 28D-5X with 400shp PT6A-110 turboprops. Became Do 128-6
Do 28E TNT	1	Do 28D fitted with high technology wing. Prototype D-IFNT (c/n 4330) FF 14 Jun 1979
Do 128-2	19	Do 28D-2 with improved engine installation, trim and performance
Do 128-6	21	Production Turbo Skyservant
Do 228-100	13	15/16-seat commuter aircraft, originally designated Do 28E-1, with TNT wing, two 715shp Garrett TPE331-5 turboprops, stretched fuselage and retractable tricycle u/c. 12,566 lb TOGW Prototype D-IFNS (c/n 4358) FF 28 Mar 1981
Do 228-101	22	228-100 with 13,184 lb TOGW and increased fuel. Also Hindustan-built
Do 228-200	18	19/20-seat 228-100 (formerly Do 28E-2) with 5-ft fuselage stretch and 776shp TPE331-5A engines. Prototype D-ICDO (c/n 4539) FF 9 May 1981
Do 228-201	53	228-200 with 13,184 lb TOGW and increased payload. Also Hindustan-built
Do 228-202	64	228-200 with 13,668 lb TOGW and increased fuel
Do 228-203F	5	Freighter version with 14,330 lb TOGW
Do 228-212	72	228-202 with 14,109 lb TOGW, improved systems and better short field performance
Do 328	111	33-pax high-wing airliner with T-tail, retractable tricycle u/c and two 2,180shp Pratt & Whitney PW119B turboprops. Executive shuttle Envoy version by Fairchild-Dornier. Prototype D-CHIC FF 6 Dec 1991

Dornier Do 328JET N328JT

Do 328JET	107	Do 328 fitted with two 6,050 lbt Pratt & Whitney PW306/9 turbofans. Also designated Do 328-300. Prototype D-BJET (c/n 3002), FF 20 Jan 1998. Executive Envoy by AvCraft	Do 31E	3	VTOL experimental transport with two Bristol Pegasus 5-2 turbofans and eight Rolls-Royce RB-162-4D lift jets. Prototype D-9530 (c/n E-1) FF 10 Feb 1967
Do 29	1	Experimental V-STOL research aircraft based on Do 28 with full glazed nose and two Lycoming GO-480-B1A6 engines in articulated pusher nacelles under wings. Prototype YD-101 (c/n E-1) FF 10 Feb 1967	Do 32E	3	Single-seat collapsible light helicopter. One 90hp BMW 6012L turbine. Prototype D-HOPF (c/n 320001) FF 29 Jun 1962
			Do 132		Developed Do 32E with enclosed cabin and new propulsion
			Do 34 Kiebitz	2	Tethered rotor military carrier system

Eagle   United States

The single-seat Eagle DW-1 was designed by Dean Wilson of Eagle Aircraft Company of Boise, Idaho and the prototype, N77001 (c/n DW-1-0001), first flew in 1977 powered by a Jacobs R-755-B2 radial engine. The Eagle was a single-seat agricultural biplane with high-aspect-ratio wings, an enclosed cockpit and tailwheel undercarriage. The production Eagle was initially powered by a Continental W670-6N radial engine, but the most popular model was the version with the 300hp horizontally-opposed Lycoming IO-540-M1B5D engine, which gave improved performance and reduced the visibility problems of the radial.

In July 1979, Eagle entered into a production agreement with Bellanca of Alexandria, Minnesota. When Bellanca ceased building its established lines it continued with the Eagle until 1983 by which time 95 production units had been completed. Eagle DW-1s carry serial numbers that run from c/n DW1-0002-80 to DW1-0014-80, DW1-0015-81 to DW1-0051-81, DW1-0052-82 and DW1-0053-83 to DW1-0096-83. In line with Bellanca practice the last two digits indicate the year of construction. The Eagle DW-1 type certificate was sold to Alexandria Aircraft LLC on 30th May 2002 but there has been no further production.

Eagle DW-1 N8809U

Eagle   Australia

The Eagle two-seat light aircraft is an all-composite design with a fixed tricycle undercarriage, side-by-side seating and a shoulder-mounted main wing with a second smaller front wing mounted just behind the engine. The Eagle has a conventional fin and tailplane. The prototype Eagle X, VH-XEG (c/n E2X-88-1-A-01), developed by Eagle Aircraft Pty Ltd, first flew in 1988 powered by a 78hp Aeropower engine. This was later replaced by a 100hp Continental O-200 and a second aircraft

(VH-XEP c/n PPT-1) was flown on 6th November 1992. Further redesign, particularly the wing, was required prior to JAR-VLA certification and the production prototype (VH-XPI c/n XPT-01) was fitted with a 120hp Continental IO-240 engine. The first production Eagle XT-S, VH-AHH c/n 001 (later redesignated Eagle XT-S 100), powered by the 125hp IO-240-A engine, flew on 23rd October 1993 and a total of ten were completed at the company's factory at Henderson near Perth in Western Australia (c/n 001 to 010). This was replaced by the Eagle XT-S 150A (c/n 011 to 015), also with the IO-540-A but with

N155EA Eagle XT-S 150B N155EA

altered weights, and then by the Eagle XT-S 150B (c/n 016 to 040) with the IO-540-B engine, which gave some performance improvement.

Eagle Aircraft became a wholly-owned subsidiary of Malaysian industrial holding company CTRM and Eagle Aircraft (Malaysia) Ltd and a Malaysian production line was established, the first aircraft (VH-PMI c/n M1001) first flew on 27th March 2001 with two more aircraft completed subsequently (c/n M1002 and M1003). In March 2000 it was announced that HGL Aero LLC of Augusta, Kansas would assemble and market the Eagle 150B for the American market but no further news is available. The current Eagle programme appears to be concentrating on an unmanned UAV version (the Eagle ARV) and a prototype (registered M51-02X), fitted with a belly-mounted surveillance turret, has been flown.

Eclipse   United States

The Eclipse 500 is an all-composite 5/6-seat light jet, aimed at private owners and the air taxi market, designed by Eclipse Aviation of Albuquerque, New Mexico. The prototype, N500EA (c/n EX500-100), first flew on 26th August 2002. It was powered by two 770 lbst Williams EJ22 small turbofans mounted on the rear fuselage but after initial flight trials it was determined that these had insufficient resilience and that there were possibly insurmountable development problems with the new engine. The prototype Eclipse 500 was retired and a conforming prototype, N503EA (c/n EX500-108), powered by 900 lbst Pratt & Whitney PW610F engines was flown on 31st December 2004. A further two aircraft (N502EA and N504EA) flew on 14th and 21st April 2005 and are to be used for certification which is targeted for the end of 2006. Eclipse claimed to hold over 2,200 orders for the aircraft at the end of 2004.

Eclipse 500 N500EA

Edgley   United Kingdom

In 1974, Edgley Aircraft Co Ltd was established to develop the revolutionary EA.7 Optica observation aircraft. The Optica was built around a ducted fan nacelle that mounted a pusher 160hp Lycoming O-320-B2B engine (later upgraded to a 180hp Lycoming IO-360). It had constant-chord high aspect ratio wings, twin booms mounting the fins, with the tailplane set on top, and a fixed tricycle undercarriage. The three-seat accommodation module was mounted ahead of the duct and was a helicopter-style unit with all-round vision. The first Optica prototype (G-BGMW c/n EA7/001) flew on 14th December 1979.

The first customer delivery was made in the spring of 1985 but this aircraft (G-KATY c/n 004) crashed shortly afterwards while on police patrol and this was a major factor leading to Edgley Aircraft calling in a receiver on 21st October 1985 after six EA.7s had been built (c/n 001 to 006). A new company, Optica Industries Ltd, was formed at the end of that year to buy the Edgley assets so that production of the Optica OA-7 could get under way. Production had reached c/n 015 by the end of 1986, but, on 17th January 1987 the company suffered an arson attack at its Old Sarum, Wiltshire works which destroyed all but one of the airworthy Opticas.

Edgley Optica OA7 N130DP

The company was reconstituted as Brooklands Aircraft Company Ltd (later Brooklands Aerospace Ltd) and the Optica Scout, which was renamed Scoutmaster, returned to production powered by a 260hp

Lycoming IO-540 engine. Brooklands production reached aircraft c/n 020 and they announced a new initiative to market the Scoutmaster in the United States. However, all of the Brooklands aircraft manufacturing projects were halted on 23rd March 1990 when the company was forced to call in a receiver.

The Optica was subsequently sold to Lovaux Ltd (part of the Danish company, FLS Aerospace) in August 1990 and they completed FAA certification in mid-1992, naming the aircraft 'Lovaux Optica Scout' and later the 'FLS Aerospace OA7 Optica Srs 300'. Changes made by FLS include a stronger centre-section mainspar to improve fatigue life, upturned wingtips and a new Hoffman ducted fan. A new production line was established at Bournemouth-Hurn in the late summer of 1992. FLS started building two new aircraft (c/n 024 and 025) but these were not completed and the line was then suspended pending sale of the programme. In 1996, FLS entered into an agreement for manufacture of the Optica OA7-300 initially by the British company, RCR, and later by Gegasi Industries in Malaysia. No further Optica production has occurred and all rights were sold to new UK owners in 2004. The development of the FLS Sprint light aircraft is referred to later under FLS.

El Gavilan   Colombia

The El Gavilan 358 is an all-metal bush aircraft designed with assistance from Piper Aircraft and built in Colombia by Aero Leaver of Guaymaral near Bogota. It is a slab-sided aircraft with a strut-braced high wing, a fixed tricycle undercarriage and a 350hp Lycoming TIO-540-W2A piston engine. The prototype (HK-3500-Z) first flew on 27th April 1990 and this was later modified with a 12-inch fuselage stretch. The second aircraft (HK-4120-Z and N358EL) was built in the USA and used for FAA FAR Part 23 certification, which was awarded in May 1998. By mid-2004, 11 aircraft had been built (c/n 1 to 11) including four for the Colombian Air Force and one (ARC.409 c/n 9) for the Colombian Navy. In 2003, Gavilan Aircraft Corporation of Canada was formed to build the aircraft in Montreal for North American sale. Production in Colombia is said to be continuing at a rate of three to four per annum.

El Gavilan 358 HK-4199-X

Emair   United States

The Murrayair (Emair) MA-1 is not strictly a new aircraft since it originated as an extensive modification of the Boeing Stearman 75 Kaydet biplane. Murrayair, a Hawaii-based operator contracted Air New Zealand to build a prototype of the MA-1, based on a Stearman frame and this machine (N101MA c/n 001) first flew on 27th July 1969. The MA-1 had a larger wing than the Stearman, a substantial 380-gallon chemical hopper fitted as an integral part of the forward fuselage and a 600hp Pratt & Whitney R-1340-AN1 Wasp radial piston engine. An enclosed cockpit with sealing to keep out chemical dust was provided, complete with a second jump seat for transport of a ground operative.

The MA-1 prototype was handed over to Emair in late 1969 and they obtained FAA certification in the following year.

Murrayair then established Emair Inc which set up manufacturing facilities at Harlingen, Texas and proceeded with series production of the MA-1 Paymaster, completing approximately 28 further examples (c/n 002 to 029). The company was subsequently taken over by George A Roth and was renamed Emroth Co The MA-1 was redesigned and emerged as the MA-1B Diablo 1200 with a re-shaped vertical tail, a larger hopper and a 1,200hp Wright R-1820 engine. Emroth built a further 23 aircraft (c/n 0030 to 0052) and several of the production MA-1s were converted to MA-1B standard. Production was completed in 1980.

Emair MA-1 Diablo N9919M

Embraer   Brazil

The Empresa Brasileira de Aeronáutica SA (otherwise known as Embraer) was formed with Brazilian government investment on 19th August 1969 and is based at Sao José dos Campos near Sao Paulo. Its first product was the EMB-110 Bandeirante which was developed from the experimental IPD-6504 design created by Max Holste at the Centro Tecnico Aerospacial (CTA). The low-wing turboprop Bandeirante was built in a number of variants and the majority went to commuter airlines in the United States although a substantial proportion of the 500 production examples were delivered as light transports to the Brazilian Air Force and to other military groupings.

With the Bandeirante well in production, Embraer designed the EMB-121 Xingu corporate aircraft. Aimed at the same market as the Beech King Air 90, the Xingu was an entirely new model showing only a general family resemblance to the EMB-110. It had a fairly short-span broad-chord wing with flared wingtips, a stocky fuselage and a dominant T-tail. The Xingu used a pair of 680shp Pratt & Whitney PT6A-28 turboprops and offered standard internal accommodation for five passengers and two crew, with an aft baggage and toilet area. A high-density nine-passenger layout was also available.

The prototype Xingu (PP-XCI c/n 01) was first flown on 10th October 1976 and the type gained its Brazilian airworthiness certificate in May 1979. Embraer delivered 29 of the initial production model, the EMB-121E Xingu I, including a batch of six VU-9s for the Brazilian Air Force – GTE. From c/n 030 they changed to the EMB-121A Xingu II which was fitted with higher-powered 750shp PT6A-135 turboprops driving four-bladed propellers, an improved interior and rear fuselage strakes. Major users were the French Aéronavale and Armée de l'Air (41 aircraft) and the Sabena flying training school (5). Embraer, having completed a total of 111 of the two Xingu models (c/n 001 to 111), discontinued production in late 1987.

Production of the Bandeirante was completed at the end of 1989 and it was succeeded by the EMB-120 Brasilia local service airliner, a few of which have been used by corporate operators as executive shuttles. Embraer also tested the CBA-123 Vector 19-seater corporate/commuter turboprop, based on the Brasilia. The prototype (PT-ZVE c/n

Embraer EMB-110P1 Bandeirante G-TABS

801), which first flew on 18th July 1990, was powered by a pair of pusher Garrett TFE731-20 turboprops mounted on the rear fuselage but, due to Embraer's financial difficulties in 1991, it was abandoned. Embraer has also built the Ipanema crop sprayer and various Piper aircraft under licence. Details of these are given under the entry for Neiva, which Embraer acquired on 11th March 1980.

The next generation of commuter airliners launched by Embraer was the EMB-145, a low-wing 40-seat regional jet with twin Allison AE3007A turbofans mounted on the rear fuselage. The prototype (PT-ZJA) first flew on 11th August 1995 and it was successfully launched into production, subsequently being titled ERJ-145. It was joined by the ERJ-135, which was a 37-seat version with a shortened fuselage. Several standard ERJ-145s and ERJ-135s have been used as executive aircraft. In July 2000, Embraer announced a business jet version of the EMB-135 designated EMB-135BJ Legacy and the prototype (converted from the second ERJ-135, PT-ZJC) flew as PP-XJO on 31st March 2001. The Legacy differs from the ERJ-135 in having an extended belly fairing housing additional fuel tankage, a recessed cabin floor and

Embraer EMB-121 Xingu PT-MCI

appropriate interior trim as the Legacy Executive or Corporate Shuttle (Legacy HC). The Executive has larger fuel capacity and range, 8,110 lbst Rolls-Royce AE3007A1E engines, winglets and a higher take-off weight than the Shuttle (48,479 lb as against 44,092 lb). Legacys have serial numbers in the standard ERJ-135/145 production sequence that started at c/n 145001 and had reached approximately c/n 14500890 by the end of 2004. Embraer has also developed the larger Embraer 170 regional jet and this will form the basis for an executive version in due course. During calendar year 2004, Embraer delivered 13 examples of the Legacy Executive and a total of 49 were in service by early 2005. In May 2005, Embraer announced development of two new light business jets – the (provisionally titled) VLJ, which is a straight-winged aircraft in the Cessna CJ1 class, and the larger LJ, which is a larger swept-wing machine competitive with the Cessna CJ3. The VLJ with two Pratt & Whitney PW617F turbofans is targeted for certification in 2008 and the LJ (with PW535/4 engines) in 2009.

Embraer EMB-135BJ Legacy N691AN

Emigh Aircraft United States

One of the large crop of postwar two-seat light aircraft built in the United States, the Emigh A-2 Trojan was the brainchild of Harold Emigh and was built by the Emigh Aircraft Company at Douglas, Arizona. The all-metal low-wing Trojan was designed for the maximum simplicity of construction with interchangeable tail surfaces and wings that incorporated external channel-section stiffeners to take the place of conventional wing ribs. It had a side-by-side enclosed cabin and a fixed tricycle undercarriage. The first Trojan (NX28390 c/n 1) was first flown on 20th December 1946 and the type certificate was issued on 21st December 1948. A total of 58 production Trojans were built (c/n 2 to 59) and the line finally closed in 1950.

Emigh A-2 Trojan N838AC

Enaer Chile

Enaer is the national aircraft manufacturer of Chile with a factory at El Bosque near Santiago. Their first original design was the Pillan, which was produced as a basic trainer for the Chilean Air Force and resulted from cooperation between Enaer and Piper Aircraft. The XBT prototype, produced by Piper flew on 6th March 1981 and had a cut-down version of the PA-32R Saratoga fuselage with a tandem two-seat cockpit enclosed by a large bubble canopy and a PA-28 Warrior wing. It was powered by a 300hp Lycoming IO-540-K1K5 piston engine and designated PA-28R-300. Piper provided kits for assembly by Enaer who built 80 T-35 Pillans for the Chilean Air Force, 10 for Panama (T-35D) and 15 for Paraguay. 41 have been built by CASA for the Spanish Air Force as the E.26 Tamiz. Other versions built as prototypes have included the T-35TX Aucan and the T-35DT both with a 420hp Allison 250B-17D turboprop and the T-35S single-seater, which has the rear cockpit deleted, but none of these have gone into production. Several Pillans have been civil registered in Chile, mainly to the manufacturer. Production of the Pillan had reached c/n 240 by mid-2004. In 1986, Enaer designed a small side-by-side two-seater for civilian club training and military ab initio training. The Namcu prototype (CC-PZI c/n 001), which first flew in April 1989, was a low-wing design of all-composite construction (glassfibre, carbon fibre and foam) with a fixed tricycle undercarriage and an enclosed cabin fitted with gull-wing doors. It was powered by a 115hp Lycoming O-235-N2C piston engine. A second prototype flew (CC-PZJ c/n 02) and two production standard aircraft (c/n 04 and 05), designated EE-10 Eaglet were produced. It was intended to sell the aircraft in Europe as the Euro-Enaer Eaglet with all basic components manufactured in Chile and final assembly being carried out in Holland by EuroEnaer. This version had a 160hp Lycoming O-320-D2A engine, modified cockpit and changes to the flaps and other control surfaces. In 2004, Enaer decided to suspend further development of the Eaglet. One further Eaglet has been amateur-built in the USA with Enaer components as the Hayman AM Special (N823SS).

Enaer T-35 Pillan CC-PZF

Enaer EE-10 Eaglet CC-PBZ

Erco Ercoupe 415C N94131

Erco   United States

Formed in 1930 in Washington, DC, The Engineering and Research Corp (known as Erco) built aircraft manufacturing machine tools and aircraft propellers. In 1937, Erco's Fred Weick developed a new two-seat monoplane of metal construction with fabric-covered wings and a tricycle undercarriage. This prototype Model 310 (NX19148 c/n 1) first flew on 1st October 1937 and was the basis for the Model 415C Ercoupe. NX19148 had a 37hp Continental A-40 engine, but this was later replaced with Erco's own 55hp Erco IL-116 engine. During development, the single fin of the Model 310 was replaced with twin fin/rudders set at the outward ends of the tailplane. The production Ercoupe, certificated on 25th March 1940 (Type Certificate 718), was equipped with a 65hp Continental A-65-8 engine.

Weick's research into light aircraft safety was employed in the Ercoupe's design and it featured a single-axis control system operated through a steering wheel similar to that of an automobile. Elimination of the normal rudder pedals was supposed to make the Ercoupe easier for new pilots who were more familiar with car driving. In practice, this system tended to confuse existing pilots and did limit the performance of the Ercoupe in difficult weather conditions. Consequently, all later model Ercoupes (and 'Aircoupes') were fitted as standard with conventional rudder bars and many earlier examples were converted to this configuration.

The first 415C (NC15692 c/n 1) appeared in 1940 from the Riverdale, Maryland factory and production continued until 1941 when aluminium supplies became limited to strategic needs. The line was halted with 112 aircraft having been built – although two experimental wooden examples were also completed by the company. While the Ercoupe was unsuited to any major military role three aircraft were tested in observation and target drone versions as the YO-55 and XPQ-13. It was not until October 1946 that the Ercoupe returned to production but during the next six years Erco built 5,081 aircraft of various models. In 1951, they ceased Ercoupe production – both because of falling demand and because the demands of the Korean war for their other products made light aircraft manufacture uneconomic.

At this point, the Ercoupe passed into the hands of a succession of small companies. Initially, Ercoupes were completed by Sanders Avia-

tion from Erco-built parts and aircraft in progress. This covered the models 415E, 415F, 415G and 415H (though there is no record of the 415F or 415H versions being built). In 1954 the type certificate was disposed of to J E Dyer's Vest Aircraft and in April 1955, it was sold on to the Forney Aircraft Manufacturing Co (sometimes referred to under the marketing name, Fornaire). They set up production at Fort Collins, Colorado and built 115 examples of their Forney F-1 Aircoupe during the three years up to 1959. In that year, Forney sold its aircraft division to the City of Carlsbad, New Mexico, complete with production facilities. This asset was handed on to Air Products Inc who started production of their Aircoupe F-1A. After another short run, Air Products ceased production in 1962.

The next producer of the design was Alon Inc, which was formed on 31st December 1963 by John Allen and Lee Higdon of Wichita, Kansas. The company bought the Ercoupe type certificate and started to build the Alon A-2 at McPherson, Kansas in late 1964, later moving to Newton, Kansas. The A-2 and the A-2A embodied some quite significant modifications and the design spawned two other experimental Alon models. The A-3 Argus 130 was an A-2A fitted with a 130hp Franklin engine and a 'two-plus-two' cabin. A prototype was flown (N5401F c/n

Mooney M-10 N9516V

C-1), but the company did not progress further with this model. The other A-2 development was the four-seat Alon XA-4, N6399V c/n 001, which was powered by a 150hp Lycoming O-320A engine. It featured a stretched A-2 fuselage, swept single fin and rudder, highly-contoured nose cowling and modified wings. The prototype was first flown on 25th February 1966 at McPherson, but Alon's financial situation could not support the cost of the XA-4 and it was abandoned.

Alon merged with Mooney Aircraft Corporation on 9th October 1967 and production of the A-2A was moved from Newton to Kerrville, Texas. There, Mooney redesigned the A-2A with a single Mooney-style fin to become the M-10 Cadet. After the acquisition of Mooney by Butler Aviation, the M-10 was marketed as the Aerostar 90, but only 61 of the M-10 had been completed when the production line closed in mid-1970. Ercoupe details are:

Model	Built	Notes
310	1	Low-wing all-metal side-by-side two-seat monoplane with fixed tricycle u/c, single fin/rudder (later replaced by twin fins) powered by one 37hp Continental A-40 engine. Prototype NX19148 FF 1 Oct 1937
415C	112	Basic model. One 65hp Continental A-65-8. Pre-war production
415C	4,408	Postwar version with a 75hp Continental C-75-12 engine, increased fuel, modified undercarriage and self starter
415D	77	415C with 10 US Gal extra fuel, modified up-elevator limit and 140 lb TOGW increase to 1,400 lb
415CD	275	415D with 1260 lb gross weight, revised elevator limit and modified nose gear and fuel venting system
415	139	415D with 85hp Continental C-85-12 engine. Sanders-built
415F		415D with 90hp Continental C-90 engine. Sanders version
415G	70	415E with modified windscreen and rear 'kiddie' seat. Named 'Club-Air'. Sanders-built
415H		Sanders 415G fitted with 75hp Continental engine
F-1	115	Forney-built Model 415G fitted with one 90hp Continental C-90-12F engine, revised engine cowling, new seats, instrument panel and trim, metal outer wing cladding, improved canopy. Prototype N6130C (c/n 5600). Later named Fornaire Explorer, Execta and Expediter
F-1A	50	F-1 built by Forney and Air Products with modified control runs, new rear spar and nosewheel leg. Gross weight increased by 50 lb. Prototype N3022G (c/n 5715)
A-2	244	Alon-built F-1A with Continental C-90-16F engine, sliding bubble canopy, improved fuel tanks and instrumentation
A-2A	52	A-2 with spring steel main u/c. Prototype N5646F (c/n B-246)
M-10	61	Mooney-built version of A-2A with single vertical tail unit, modified cockpit and new engine cowling. Prototype N5461F FF 23 Feb 1968
Total	5,604	

Serial number batches used by the various manufacturers have been:

Model	Manufacturer	Serial Batch
415C to 415H	Erco	1 to 5081
F-1	Forney	5600 to 5714
F-1A	Air Products	5715 to 5764
A-2	Alon	A-1 to A-245
A-2A	Alon	B-246 to B-297
M-10	Mooney	690001 to 690011
M-10	Mooney	700001 to 700050

Evangel   United States

Evangel Aircraft Corporation was established by Carl Mortensen of Orange City, Iowa to produce the Evangel 4500-300 twin-engined utility aircraft. Mortensen was a former missionary aviation pilot who saw the need for a reliable transport for use in the isolated conditions of South America. The prototype (N4501L c/n 001) was an all-metal high-wing twin with a fixed undercarriage and it first flew in 1965.

The performance of the Evangel I was less than satisfactory so it was dismantled and redesigned as the low-wing Evangel II. Using a large proportion of the original components, the seven/nine-seat Evangel II flew in August 1968. It was fitted with a pair of 300hp Lycoming

IO-540-K1B5 engines and had a retractable tailwheel undercarriage, a slab-sided fuselage with large cargo doors on both sides and large wings incorporating dihedralled outer panels and Booster Tips fibreglass drooping wingtips.

The first customer delivery took place in November 1972 and eight aircraft (including the prototype) were eventually completed (c/n 001 to 008). In 1984, Mortensen flew the prototype of a new aircraft – the Angel 44 (N44KE) powered by two pusher 300hp Lycoming IO-540-M1A5 engines and seating eight passengers. Angel Aircraft Corporation was formed to certificate and build the aircraft – again, for the South American missionary market – and two production aircraft were built in 2002 and 2003 (N442KB c/n 002 and N442KC c/n 003).

Evangel 4500 N4506L

Angel 44 N442KB

Walter Extra   Germany

In the early 1980s, with performance levels in competition aerobatics advancing rapidly, Walter Extra designed a new single-seat aircraft to the order of the Swiss Aero Club that would compete against the Sukhoi Su-26 and Yak-55 which were ready to break into the market. The Extra 230 was based on the successful mid-wing Stephens Akro but with a raised rear fuselage and faired-in canopy and a very precisely

constructed wing. Officially known as a Stephens Akro Laser EA.230, the first aircraft (D-EJNC c/n 83-05-002) flew on 14th July 1983 followed by c/n 83-05-001 (D-EKEW). Extra Flugzeugbau GmbH then put the EA.230 into limited production at Dinslaken and built 15 aircraft (including prototypes).

Extra then redesigned the EA.230 as a two-seater designated Extra 300 with a composite wing (as opposed to the wooden wing of the EA.230) and a 300hp Lycoming engine. The prototype was D-EAEW

Extra EA.230 N9750N

Extra 400 D-EXLH

and 67 aircraft have been built. Extra has also produced the EA.300 airframe in single-seat form as the EA.300S with a lower-set wing, 3-inch shorter fuselage and a four-blade Muhlbauer propeller. The prototype, D-ESEW (c/n V-1), was first flown in early 1992. The EA.300 airframe was then developed into the 300/L, introduced in 1995, which is, essentially, an EA.300S with a two-seat cockpit and this became the most popular version with 188 completed by mid-2004. It is now the only model in production. In the mid-1990s, Extra added the EA.200 which is a two-seater, based on the EA.300/L but intended as an entry-level model with a 200hp Lycoming AEIO-360 engine and a lighter weight airframe and lower gross weight. Other models include the EA.330 with a 330hp engine and the one-off EA.350 converted from an Extra 300 with an uprated 350hp engine.

In January 2003, Extra Flugzeugbau was declared insolvent and production was briefly suspended but restarted by the administrator when a new investor was found. It emerged from the receivership in August 2003, having been re-established as Extra Aircraft LLC based at Lancaster, Pennsylvania. Production and research and development remain at the existing Düsseldorf premises.

Model	Built	Notes
EA.230	15	Single-seat mid-wing aerobatic aircraft of tube-and-fabric construction with fixed tailwheel u/c and one 230hp Lycoming AEIO-360-A1E piston engine. 1,234 lb TOGW. Prototype D-EJNC c/n 83-05-002 FF 14 Jul 1983
Extra 300	67	EA.230 with tandem two-seat cockpit, composite wing and 300hp Lycoming AEIO-540-L1B5D engine. 1,808 lb TOGW. Prototype D-EAEW (c/n V-1) FF 6 May 1988
Extra 260	3	Non-certificated Extra 300 with single-seat cockpit and 260hp Lycoming IO-540 engine
Extra 300S	32	Extra 300 with lower-set shorter-span wing and single-seat cockpit. Prototype D-ESEW (c/n V-1) FF 4 Mar 1992
Extra 300/L	193	Extra 300S with tandem 2-seat cockpit. Prototype D-EUWH
Extra 200	31	Extra 300/L with 200hp Lycoming AEIO-360-A1E engine. 1,914 lb TOGW. Prototype D-ETEL (c/n 01) FF 2 Apr 1996
Extra 300LX		Extra 300/L with enlarged rudder and elevator with overhung tips
Extra 330	1	Extra 300S with strengthened airframe, enlarged ailerons and elevator and 330hp Lycoming AEIO-580 engine. Prototype D-ESEW c/n 01 FF Jan 1998
Extra 330L	1	Extra 330 with tandem 2-seat cockpit
Extra 330LX	1	Extra 330/L with enlarged rudder. Prototype D-EDGE c/n 03 FF 1999

Extra 300/L N168EX

Extra 500 D-EKEW

Extra serial numbers have been allocated separately for each model. The EA.230 was c/n 83-05-001 to -012 and c/n 83-05-011A, 012A and -014. The EA.300 was c/n 001 to 067, the EA.300S, c/n 001 to 032 and the EA.200 c/n 01 to 031. The current production Extra 300/L has had serials in the range c/n 01 to 170, 203 and 1171 to 1192. The later c/ns starting at c/n 1171 were adopted after the production line restarted following Extra's bankruptcy problems.

On 4th April 1996, Extra flew the prototype of its Extra 400 six-seat pressurized touring aircraft (D-EBEW, c/n 01). The Extra 400 is an all-composite cabin aircraft with a 350hp Continental Voyager TSIOL-550A piston engine and a tricycle undercarriage that retracts into fully enclosed fuselage wells. It has a cantilever high wing and a highly streamlined circular-section fuselage, which is fitted with a split airstair entry door giving access to the main air-conditioned cabin. Passenger accommodation is for four people in facing seats with a two-seat crew cockpit. The Extra 400 has a T-tail and is fitted with large Fowler flaps for approach control. The engine is a 350hp 6-cylinder Teledyne Continental TSIOL-550-A driving a three-bladed constant-speed propeller. First customer deliveries were made in early 1999 and 28 had been completed by mid-2004 (c/n 01 to 28). The prototype Extra 400 was re-engineered as the prototype Extra 500 (D-EKEW) with a 450shp Rolls-Royce Allison 250-B17 turboprop and flew in this form on 26th April 2002. Despite a crash landing during test flying the Extra 500 prototype and one further development aircraft (D-EHEW) are completing certification testing.

Fairchild   Canada

Following World War Two, there was considerable demand for air support in the Canadian outback. This role had been serviced by Fairchild Aircraft Ltd of Canada with the Fairchild 71 and later with the Fairchild 82 – the 24 production examples of which gained a reputation as the best bush aircraft produced for Canadian conditions. Fairchild had also built a prototype of the all-metal Super 71P and the design philosophy of this aircraft led to the post-war F-11 Husky. The Husky was primarily intended as a seaplane, although wheels or skis could be fitted, and it was a rugged all-metal, high-wing machine with a waisted rear fuselage, a freight-loading door on each side and a high-set tail unit. It could carry six to eight passengers and a crew of two. The prototype (CF-BQC c/n 1) made its first flight in June 1946 from the St Lawrence River near Montreal and was powered by a 450hp Pratt & Whitney Wasp R-985-SB3 radial engine. Fairchild delivered the first production aircraft from its Longueuil plant to Nickel Belt Airways in 1947 and a total of 12 Huskys (c/n 1 to 12) were completed during the next two years. A plan by Husky Aircraft Ltd to revive the design in 1956 was stillborn, but all rights to the design were acquired in 1970 by Industrial Wings Ltd, who

Fairchild F-11 Husky CF-SAQ

had intentions to revive the type. The prototype was converted by Industrial Wings with an Alvis Leonides engine as a basis for future production examples.

Fairchild-Swearingen   United States

Swearingen Aircraft was formed by Edward J Swearingen in 1959 and, at that time, it specialised in development projects for other manufacturers including the turboprop conversion of the Grand Commander and design of the Twin Comanche. The San Antonio plant also carried out engine conversions and aerodynamic cleaning-up on the Beech Twin Bonanza (Excalibur and Excalibur 800) and Queen Air (Queen Air 800).

In 1964, Swearingen designed its first all-new aircraft, drawing on experience with the Queen Air conversions. The SA-26 Merlin 1 was a low-wing twin-engined pressurized cabin monoplane which used a wing similar to that of the Twin Bonanza and had many Queen Air design features. The first prototype, N2601S c/n 26-1, was powered by a pair of 400hp Lycoming TIGO-41 turbocharged piston engines. However, it soon became clear that the aircraft would be an ideal application for turboprops and the prototype Merlin II (the SA-26T) first flew on 13th April 1965 powered by two PT6A turboprops. It was certificated on 15th July 1966 and went into production as the Merlin IIA in 1966.

After some 98 production Merlin IIAs had been delivered, Swearingen switched to the Model IIB. This mainly differed in having twin Garrett TPE331-1-151G engines that were higher-rated than the PT6As and were also favoured by AiResearch Aviation who were marketing the aircraft in the United States and preferred to have their own engines fitted to the Merlin. The substantially altered Merlin III followed in 1971. This version had a completely new fuselage, swept vertical tail, taller undercarriage new engines and a higher gross weight and useful load. The Merlin III, which was certificated on 27th July 1970, replaced the Merlin IIB on the San Antonio production line.

Since 1968, Swearingen had been in cooperation with Fairchild-Hiller on the joint development of a 22-seat turboprop commuter airliner. This was named the Metro and the prototype was first flown in the summer of 1969. It employed virtually the same nose and tail unit as the Merlin III but had a new circular-section centre-fuselage that would accommodate 19 passengers seated either side of a centre aisle. The engines were similar to those used on the Merlin III. First deliveries started in 1970 and Swearingen also took the opportunity to gain certification for the very similar Merlin IV for sale to corporate buyers.

Having cooperated on Metro development, it was arranged that a substantial amount of Metro subassembly would be done by Fairchild at Hagerstown, Md. The Metro programme also meant that Swearingen's financial and organisational resources were being stretched – which led to takeover talks with Piper Aircraft. These came to nothing, and eventually on 2nd November 1971 it was announced that Fairchild would take over Swearingen's assets. A new company, Swearingen Aviation Corporation, was formed by Fairchild to build the Merlin and Metro. On 5th January 1981 the name was again changed – to Fairchild Swearingen Corporation – and in October 1987 the company was sold to GMF Investments by Fairchild Industries. Fairchild Aircraft declared Chapter 11 bankruptcy on 1st February 1990 but this was resolved when the company was acquired by Fairchild Acquisition Inc in September 1990. Fairchild Aircraft continued to build the Metro 23 and delivered a substantial batch of 53 C-26A aircraft (SA227-DC) to the US National Guard. Production of the Metro series ceased in 2000 and the final aircraft was delivered to National Jet Aviation Services on 28th March 2001. It appears that total production of Merlins and Metros was 1,039 aircraft although Fairchild give a total of 1,053 (perhaps confused by the numerous conversions from one model to another) and the final aircraft was delivered on 28th March 2001.

Both the Merlin III and Merlin IV/Metro have undergone numerous model changes aimed at improving performance. In particular, the introduction of new airworthiness regulations SFAR-41 and SFAR-41B allowed Fairchild to bring in versions of the Metro and Merlin III with a 12,500 lb zero-fuel weight instead of the previous FAR-23 gross weight at this level. The different Merlin and Metro variants have been as follows:

Model	Built	Notes
SA26 Merlin I		Original Lycoming TIGO-41 piston-engined Merlin. Prototype N2601S
SA26-T Merlin II	1	Original prototype re-engined with PT6A turboprops
SA26-T Merlin IIA	35	Production Merlin II with PT6A-20 turboprops and 9,300 lb TOGW

Swearingen Merlin II N963BP

SA26-AT Merlin IIB	89	Merlin IIA with two AiResearch TPE331-1-151G turboprops. 10,000 lb TOGW. Prototype N1202S (c/n T26-100 conv from c/n T26-10)
SA226-T Merlin III	50	Redesigned Merlin II with new fuselage, u/c and tail. TPE331-3U-303G turboprops. 12,500 lb TOGW. Prototype N5292M (c/n T-201)
SA226-T Merlin IIIA	42	Merlin III with minor changes to cockpit controls, instrument panel, fuel system, air-conditioning. 2 extra starboard windows; 1 extra port window
SA226-T (B) Merlin IIIB	73	Merlin IIIA with revised wing root, modified tailplane, increased power, 4-blade props and synchrophasers. Improved interior fittings and air conditioning. Introduced 1978
SA227-TT Merlin IIIC	26	Merlin IIIB to SFAR-41 standard. Can be Merlin IIIC-23 at 12,500 lb TOGW or Merlin IIIC-41 at 13,230 lb TOGW
SA227-TP Merlin IIID		Proposed PT6A-powered Merlin IIIC
SA227-TT Fairchild 300	10	Merlin IIIC with winglets and modified controls
SA226-TC Metro	1	20-seat commuter airliner with low wing, retractable tricycle u/c, 12,500 lb TOGW and two 840shp AiResearch TPE331-3U-303 turboprops. Prototype N226TC (c/n TC200) FF 26 Aug 1969
SA226-AT Merlin IV	20	21-seat Merlin III with stretched fuselage similar to Metro but with differences in trim and some systems. TPE331-3U-303G engines
SA226-AT Merlin IVA	37	Merlin IV with minor changes to cockpit controls and fuel system. Rectangular cabin windows instead of round ones
SA227-AT Merlin IVC	44	Merlin IVA to SFAR-41 standard. 4-blade Dowty props, improved u/c doors, increased wingspan, new engine installation and TPE331-11U-601G engines. Available as Merlin IVC-41 or IVC-41B. Alternative cargo model without windows named Expediter
SA227-AT Fairchild 400	1	Merlin IVC with TPE331-14 engines, 16,000 lb TOGW, counter-rotating props. Prototype only
SA226-TC Metro II	202	Metro with modifications similar to Merlin IVA
SA226-TC Metro IIA		Metro to SFAR-41 standard. Replaced by Metro III
SA227-AC Metro III	271	Metro II to SFAR-41 standard with TPE331-11U-601G engines and changes similar to those on Merlin IVC. Offered as Metro III-41 and Metro III-41B. Military C-26A
SA227-BC Metro III	18	SA227-AC with TPE331-12 engines
SA227-PC Metro IIIA	2	Metro III with 14,500 lb TOGW and PT6A-45R turboprops for both commuter and executive use
SA228-AE Metro V		Proposed Metro III with T-tail, deeper cabin, heavier landing gear, stronger wing, 5-blade props and 1,100shp Garrett TPE331-12UA-701G engines. Not built
SA227-CC	5	Initial designation for civil Metro 23
SA227-DC Metro 23	112	Metro with 1,100shp TPE331-12UAR engines, 16,500 lb TOGW. Certificated to FAR.23 (Amendment 34). Initially known as Metro IV. Expediter 23 is all-cargo version. Military version designated C-26B
SA227 Metro VI		Proposed higher-powered Metro V. Not built
SA227 Metro 25		Proposed Metro III with belly baggage compartment, 25 seats and TPE331-12 turboprops. Project discontinued
SA227 MMSA		Multi-mission surveillance type based on any Metro model, fitted with belly-mounted multi-sensor surveillance pod and Mitsubishi IRM.500 FLIR in nose
SA-28T		1971 design for eight-seat supersonic business jet. Not built

In the early days, each Swearingen model had its own separate series of serial numbers and these continued until the Merlin IIIB had reached c/n T339 and the Metro II had reached TC339. At this point all models were merged into an integrated series with separate models being identified by the prefix letters to the serial number. For example, aircraft number 425 was a Metro III, c/n AC425 and it was followed by Merlin IIIC, c/n TT426. In the early production stages, the company changed from one model to another on the production line (for instance from Merlin IV to Metro) or inserted a priority order. Rather than bringing these into the normal serial sequence they allocated 'Extra' serial numbers consisting of the line number at the point of insertion with the letter 'E' as a suffix (eg, T205E). In some cases, several extra aircraft were

Fairchild SA227-TT Merlin IIIC N17VV

introduced and this led to more than one letter 'E' being added. The most notable occasion was a batch of four additional Metros that became c/n TC211E, TC211EE, TC211EEE and TC211EEEE.

It is also noteworthy that the prototype SA226TC Metro (c/n TC-200) was converted to Merlin standards in 1973 and became c/n AT-003E. This re-serialling applies to other aircraft with the result that there are gaps in the number sequences and in some cases the prefix letters change. Fairchild have also given an 'A' suffix to the Merlin IIIC to FAR Part 23 standard (eg, N3067W which was given c/n TT-486A). Metro III aircraft with heavy-duty landing gear have a 'B' suffix (eg, AC-650B) and military C-26As are suffixed 'M' (eg, DC-811M). The main serial number allocations are as follows:

Model	Serial Batches	Extra Numbers and Notes
SA26-T	T26-2 to T26-36	
SA26-AT	T26-100 to T26-179	T26-140E, 149E, 154E, 158E, 163E, 167E, 171E, 172E, 180E
SA226-T-III	T201 to T248	T205E, 215E
SA226-T-IIIA	T249 to T288	T290, 291
SA226-T-IIIB	T292 to T332	T289, 303E
SA226-T-IIIB	T336 up	Integrated series
SA227-TT-IIIC	TT421 up	Integrated series
SA227-TT-300	TT447 up	Integrated series
SA226-AT-IV	AT001 to AT074	003E, 038E, 062E, 064E, 071E. Some conv. From TC- c/ns. Some changed to Metros
SA227-AT	AT423 to AT695B	Integrated series
SA226-TC	TC201 to TC419	202E, 208E, 211E, 211EE, 211EEE, 211EEEE, 215E, 222E, 222EE, 227E, 228E, 229E, 234E, 238E, 239E, 331E, 334E
SA226-TC	TC340 to TC419	Integrated series
SA227-AC	AC422 to AC788B	Integrated series. Plus AC415, 416
SA227-BC	BC762B to 789B	Integrated series
SA227-CC	CC827B to 844B	Integrated series
SA227-PC	PC436 to PC562	Integrated series
SA227-PC	BC762B to BC789B	Integrated series
SA227-DC	CC827B to CC844B	Metro 23. Integrated series
SA227-DC	DC791B to DC904B	Metro 23. Integrated series
SA227-DC	DC784M to DC836M*	C-26A. Integrated series

Fairchild SA227-AC Metro III N98EB

Fantasy Air   Czech Republic

The Fantasy Air Allegro is a strut-braced high-wing 450kg ultralight aircraft designed by Oldrych Olsansky and manufactured in the Czech Republic. In 2004 there were two versions in production – the Allegro ST and the Allegro 2000. It has side-by-side seating for two, a T-tail and a fixed tricycle undercarriage, the fuselage being composite and the wings made of metal. The aircraft was originally produced by Jora SRO and known as the Jora with a 52hp Rotax 503 engine, and then became the Cora, around 30 of which are believed to have been completed at the Prague factory. Two versions of the Cora were produced – the Legato with long-span curved wings and full-span ailerons and the Allegro with shorter-span straight wings with a shallower aerofoil section. The Legato was discontinued in 1999 and the Allegro continued as the Allegro SW (Short Wing) with an 80hp Rotax 912UL engine. The triangulated main undercarriage was replaced by a new design with cantilever legs in 2001. At that time, a new version was added with a new longer-span wing with a straight centre section and tapered outer panels. This was available as the Allegro ST (64hp Rotax 582UL) and Allegro 200 (74hp Rotax 618UL) – both of which were replaced by the current Allegro 2000. Fantasy Air have also introduced the Arius F that has a longer-span version of the SW wing and first flew in November 1999. The Allegro is sold as a factory-complete aircraft and 170 Allegros are understood to have been completed by the end of 2004.

Fantasy Air Allegro N336FA

Serial numbers for European aircraft have a year prefix followed by the individual aircraft serial number (eg, 04-038). Aircraft in the USA and Australia and perhaps elsewhere) have local serial numbers consisting of the year built, the country code (eg, 2 for the USA) and the individual aircraft number for that country. A typical US example is 03-203 (the third aircraft, built in 2003 for the US market).

FFT   Germany

On 1st March 1990, the German company, Gesellschaft fur Flugzeugund Faserverbund Technologie (FFT), took over all the activities of the German business, Gyroflug Gmbh. together with the Swiss company, FFA and started to establish production facilities at Mengen. FFT ceased all production when it became bankrupt on 30th September 1992.

Of the constituent companies, FFA (Flug und Fahrzeugwerke AG, Altenrhein) was an important Swiss aircraft manufacturer, established in 1926. In 1967, FFA and SIAI-Marchetti agreed to cooperate in the manufacture of a two/three-seat trainer, the AS-202 Bravo. The first

prototype to be flown was HB-HEA (c/n V-2), built by FFA. It flew on 7th March 1969 and was followed by a second Swiss-built prototype, HB-HEC (c/n V-3). SIAI also built a prototype (I-SJAI c/n 01 or V-1) and flew it on 7th May 1969. The Swiss AS-202s were fitted with the 150hp Lycoming O-320 engine and the Italian prototype used a lower-rated 115hp Lycoming O-235-C2A. The AS-202 was a low-wing all-metal monoplane with a fixed tricycle undercarriage and two seats plus a rear bench seat. The cockpit was enclosed by a large sliding bubble canopy.

SIAI carried out prototype testing but, in 1973, FFA took full control of the project having gained Swiss type approval on 15th August 1972 and FAA certification on 16th November 1973. AS-202 models were built by FFA but marketed by the FFA subsidiary company, Repair AG.

FFA AS.202/15 Bravo HB-HEG

The majority of units delivered have been for military training with the air forces of Iraq (48), Oman (4), Morocco (10), Uganda (8) and Indonesia (40) but a batch of eleven AS-202/18As was delivered to the British Aerospace Flying College where it was known as the Wren. In total three prototypes (c/n 01, V-2 and V-3) and 170 production aircraft (c/n 001 to 030, 034, 101 to 238 and 243) were built. Airframes c/n 239 to 242 were partly complete when the production line closed. Several versions of the AS-202 have been marketed, as follows:

Model	Built	Notes
AS-202/15	34	Low-wing all-metal two-seat training and sporting aircraft with fixed tricycle u/c and 150hp Lycoming O-320-E2A engine. Prototype HB-HEA FF 7 Mar 1969
AS-202/18A	31	AS-202/15 with 180hp Lycoming AEIO-360-B1F engine. Prototype HB-HEY c/n 015 FF Aug 1974
AS-202/18A2	48	AS-202/18A for Iraq Air Force with lengthened canopy, electric trim and increased TOGW
AS-202/18A3	40	AS-202/18A2 for Indonesian Air Force with 24v electric system and manual trim
AS-202/18A4	15	CAA-certificated AS-202/18A2 for British Aerospace Flying College with modified instrumentation. Named Wren
AS-202/26A	1	AS-202/18 with 260hp. Lyc AEIO-540-D4B5 engine, 24v electrical system, enlarged fin. Prototype HB-HEY c/n 015
AS-202/32TP	1	AS-202/18A4 with extra wingtip fuel tanks, enlarged fin and 420shp R-R Allison 250-B17D turboprop engine with 3-blade prop. Prototype HB-HFJ c/n 243 FF Jul 1992

When FFA transferred all aviation activities to FFT in 1990, they included their new project – the Eurotrainer 2000A. This was a four-seater based on the Bravo layout but of composite construction with a retractable undercarriage, IFR equipment, variable-pitch propeller and a 270hp Lycoming AEIO-540L engine. The prototype (D-EJDZ) was first flown on 29th April 1991 from Mengen. An initial batch of eight aircraft was ordered by Swissair. FFA also carried out design work on a tandem two-seat trainer known as the AS-32T, which would have been powered by an Allison 250-B17 turboprop. However, this was abandoned after the company had spent some time testing an AS-202/32 (HB-HEC) fitted with this powerplant.

The other constituent part of FFT was the former Gyroflug Inge-nieurgesellschaft mbH which was the initiator of the SC-01 Speed Canard. Outwardly following similar design philosophies to those used by Burt Rutan on the VariEze, the glassfibre Speed Canard is a canard design with a swept wing mounting large wingtip fin/rudder assemblies and a horizontal control surface ahead of the tandem two-seat cockpit. The tricycle undercarriage uses a retractable nosewheel

The prototype (D-EEEX c/n A-1) was first flown on 2nd December 1980 and production started at Baden Baden-Oos in February 1984 with wings being built under contract by Glaser-Dirks. The modified

FFT Eurotrainer D-EJDZ

SC-01B with an enlarged fin and other minor changes was introduced from the 21st production unit. In standard form the aircraft was fitted with a 116hp Lycoming O-235-P2A pusher engine with a three-blade Hoffman constant-speed propeller. The later production version was the SC-01B-160 with a 160hp O-320-D1A powerplant. Speed Canard serials included the two flying prototypes, c/n A-1 and A-3 and a static test airframe c/n A-2. 59 series production aircraft ran from c/n S-4 to c/n S-62. One of these was an experimental single-seat aircraft (D-EEMX c/n XM-49). This was equipped for surveillance with advanced electronics equipment, but development was shelved.

Gyroflug Speed Canard D-EKSC

Fiat   Italy

Following World War Two, the Italian Air Force gradually re-equipped and Fiat built a number of military types. The only aircraft to have major civil impact was their standard basic/advanced trainer, the Fiat G.46, which was an all-metal low-wing monoplane with a retractable tailwheel undercarriage and a tandem two-seat cockpit. The prototype (MM52000, c/n 1) first flew in 1948. Several different versions were produced including the G.46-1 with a 205hp Alfa 115bis engine, the G.46-2 with a 250hp de Havilland Gipsy Queen 30 and the G.46-3, G.46-4 and G.46-5 all of which had the 225hp Alfa 115-1ter engine. The majority were two-seaters (and had a B suffix to their designation, eg, G.46-4B) but some single-seaters were built as aerobatic trainers and had an 'A' suffix (eg, G.46-4A). Many of these G.46s were allocated to civilian flying clubs and schools and those in full military service were sold to private owners in the 1950s. In total, Fiat built 223 G.46s and, in addition to the deliveries to the Italian Air Force, 30 went to the Argentine Air Force and the G.46 was in military service in Syria and five aircraft went to Austria.

Fiat G.46-2 Ea-441

Fläming Air Saphir D-MATR

Fläming Air Germany

This company, based at Oehna is the German importer of several Czech and Polish ultralights, but it has designed and developed its own FSU Saphir two-seater as a factory-complete or kit-built ultralight. This all-composite aircraft has a low wing based on that of the Urban Samba and the fuselage, which is based on the ATEC Zephyr, has an enclosed side-by-side cockpit and a fixed tricycle undercarriage. Three development aircraft were built, the first of which (D-MATR) first flew in early 2002. Three versions have been launched – the standard Saphir with a 472.5kg gross weight, the Super Saphir JAR-VLA kit aircraft with a shorter span wing (prototype D-EERJ) and the Smaragd touring motor glider version with a 600kg gross weight, a tailwheel undercarriage and longer span wings. The Smaragd is available as the Smaragd 100 (Rotax 912s engine), Smaragd 80 (Rotax 912UL), Smaragd J (Jabiru 2200) and

Smaragd D with a Diesel 280 engine. The Saphir has similar designations and engines (ie, Saphir 100, Saphir 80, Saphir J and Saphir D).

Production has, initially, concentrated on the Smaragd, seven of which had been built by the end of 2004 (c/n 01/03 to 07/04). The company has also flown the prototype Smaragd FA.01 (D-MFAK), which has a shorter fuselage and shorter wing, and the Smaragd FA.03 which is a soaring motor glider with a longer span wing and tailwheel undercarriage (prototype D-KERH). Fläming Air also sells the Trener Baby, which is an 80% scale version of the Zlin Z.126 tandem two-seat trainer powered by a Walter Mikron IIIB engine, and have flown the prototype (D-EETB) of the Trener Baby E which is a higher weight JAR-VLA certificated version with a retractable undercarriage. These are built of wood, tube and fabric by Thomas Podesva in Poland as either factory-complete or kit aircraft.

Fleet Canada

Well-known for their wartime production of Fleet 16B Finch biplanes, Fleet Aircraft of Canada Ltd turned its hand to light aircraft production when the war was over. In 1945, they acquired rights to the Noury N-75 high-wing two-seater (which was, itself, developed into the T-65 Noranda). This aircraft was powered by an 85hp Continental C85-12J engine and was a conventional strut-braced monoplane with a distinctive waisted rear fuselage and a fixed tailwheel undercarriage. The first Fleet 80 Canuck (CF-BYW c/n 001) flew on 26th September 1945 and differed from the Noury aircraft in having an enlarged vertical tail and revised instrumentation. In view of Canadian conditions, the Canuck was designed to operate on floats and skis. Fleet went into production and built 208 further aircraft (c/n 002 to 209) before the company found itself in financial trouble in 1947 and closed the production line. The tooling and many components were acquired by Leavens Brothers of Toronto, and they completed a further 26 Canucks (c/n 210 to 227 and c/n 300 to 307).

Fleet 80 Canuck C-FDZA

Flight Design
Germany

The Flight Design CT is one of the more efficient 450kg ultralight types in current production and was certified and first introduced in 1997. It has a large side-by-side two-seat cabin, docile handling and a maximum speed of 146kts using an 80hp Rotax 912UL engine. The all-composite CT has a cantilever high wing and fixed tricycle undercarriage and was initially sold in kit form as the ultralight CTX at 600kg gross weight or in standard category as the CTM factory-delivered model at 450kg (or 540kg for some countries). In 2001 these models were replaced by the CT2K, which is factory-complete and has a lighter-weight airframe and new wingtips. The CT2K airframe is fabricated in the Ukraine and the aircraft completed in Germany by ASO Flugsport. A special German ultralight version with a 2ft 6in shorter wingspan is known as the CTS. Approximately 440 CTs had been completed by late 2004. The serial number system used by Flight Design is unclear.

Flight Design CT2K G-CCHU

FLS
United Kingdom

The involvement of FLS Aerospace in the Edgley Optica programme has been detailed in the section on Edgley but, in 1989, Brooklands had also taken on responsibility for the Venture light aircraft. The Venture was originally designed by Sydney Holloway as the SAH-1 and the prototype (G-SAHI c/n 01) was built by Trago Mills Ltd at Bodmin in Cornwall. It made its first flight on 23rd August 1983 and received its certificate of airworthiness on 12th December 1985. Trago Mills had made various attempts at production arrangements for the SAH-1 including agreements with Hungary and, later, Yugoslavia to build the aircraft (as the Orca SAH-1), but these were unsuccessful. Lovaux took over responsibility for the design in November 1991. The SAH-1 is a low-wing all-metal trainer with a side-by-side cockpit and tricycle undercarriage. The engine used on the prototype was the 118hp Lycoming O-235-L2A. This was replaced by a 160hp Lycoming AEIO-320-D1B engine and FLS intended to offer both models as the FLS Sprint and FLS Sprint 160. The first production Sprint 160 (G-FLSI c/n 001) was first flown on 16th December 1993. By August 1994, FLS Aerospace had built four airframes (c/n 001 to 004) including the first Sprint Club (G-BVNU c/n 004), but they announced their intention of selling off the Optica and Sprint designs and a deal was concluded in mid-1999 with Sprint Aircraft Ltd whereby the Sprint would be assembled at North Weald from subassemblies manufactured at PZL (Okecie) in Poland. In the event, no further Sprint production took place and the rights and assets were sold with the Optica programme to new UK owners in 2004.

FLS Sprint G-SCLX

Fly Synthesis Texan Top Class OO-D63

Fly Synthesis   Italy

Based at Udine in northwestern Italy, Fly Synthesis builds three different
models of 450kg light aircraft built from composites. The first design was
originally produced as the Rodino Storch. It has a side-by-side two-seat
cabin equipped with twin stick controls and a braced high wing. The rear
fuselage consists of a slim tailboom carrying the tail surfaces and the
Storch is fitted with a fixed tricycle undercarriage. Versions of the Storch
have included the Pulcino with a 46hp Rotax 503, the Classic with an
80hp Jabiru 2200 or 64hp Rotax 582 and the Storch HS, which is the
Classic with lower empty weight and improved performance. Over 350
factory-complete examples of the Storch have been built together with
100 kits. In 1997, Fly Synthesis announced the Texan, which is a low-
wing light aircraft with a fixed tricycle undercarriage, a two-seat side-by-
side cockpit with a large blister canopy and a 100hp Rotax 912S engine.
Production of this model, known as the Texan Top Class, exceeded 70
by the spring of 2005 and the company also builds the Texan RG (of
which 5 have been built). This is the same airframe but with an electro-
pneumatically operated retractable undercarriage. A limited-edition
Texan RG Solaris is available with a deluxe leather interior. The third
main model, first flown in 1998, is the Wallaby which is a basic category
high-wing pod-and-boom aircraft which uses Storch wings and has a

Fly Synthesis Storch HS 28-YE

46hp Rotax 503 engine mounted on the wing centre section above the
cockpit. 100 Wallabies in complete or kit form have been built to date.
Fly Synthesis is developing a two-seat lifting body light aircraft named
Mansos for a first flight in 2006. Half of current Fly Synthesis production
is the Texan with the Storch representing 35% and the Wallaby 15%. Fly
Synthesis serial numbers vary in presentation but are normally the year
of construction followed by a simple serial number (eg, Texan c/n
2002/0021). Each model has its own number series.

FMP   Czech Republic

FMP sro, which was established in 1991, is an engineering company
specialising in metal valves and connectors. It has produced a small
series of the all-composite Qualt 200 side-by-side two-seat 560kg ultralight that first flew in 1996. The Qualt (also known as the Speedy
Mouse) has a low wing, fixed tailwheel undercarriage and a T-tail. It is
powered by a 100hp Rotax 912S and 27 have been completed. The
newest model is the Qualt 201, of which three had been built by early
2005, and this has a wider fuselage and is offered as the Q201J (80hp
Jabiru 2200 engine), Q201R582 (65hp Rotax 582), Q201R (80hp Rotax
912UL2) and Q201RS (100hp Rotax 912ULS2).

FMP Qualt 201J OK-JUU 44

Fokker S-11 Instructor PH-ACG

Fokker   Netherlands

The S.11 Instructor was Fokker's first postwar production aircraft, designed for the Royal Netherlands Air Force as a primary trainer. Constructed from steel tube and fabric, the Instructor had a broad chord low wing with dihedralled outer panels, a wide cockpit with two seats side-by-side and a large sliding canopy. The tailwheel undercarriage had distinctive main legs that were attached to the wing leading edges and designed with trailing link shock absorption. In total, Fokker built 81 examples (c/n 6191 to 6257 and c/n 6269 to 6282): of which 39 were built for the R Neth A F, two were civil-registered, and 40 went to the Israeli Air Force. The S.11 was built under licence in Italy by Macchi who built 120 (c/n 5918 to 5967, c/n 5995 to 6055, c/n 6073 to 6044 and c/n 6046 to 6082), and IMM who built 60 (c/n 1001 to 1060) as the M.416, and in Brazil by the Fabrica do Galeao. Fokker also re-engineered the S.11 as the S.12 with a tricycle undercarriage and this was built in Brazil as the T-22 for the Brazilian Air Force. 360 S.11s and 50 S.12s were completed by the parent factory and the licensees. Many were sold subsequently to private civil operators.

Fouga   France

Originally started at Aire-sur-Adour in the southwest of France in 1920, Fouga became established as an aircraft manufacturer in the mid-1930s when it took on a contract from M Pierre Mauboussin to build 100 examples of the M.123 Corsaire tandem two-seat trainer for the French Air Force. This low-wing aircraft was based on the PM.XII (F-ALVX) that had been flown in September 1931. When the war was over, the Corsaire returned to production as the M.129/48 and was used by many flying clubs. Details of the different Corsaire variants are as follows:

Model	Built	Notes
M.120	13	Low-wing tandem open two-seat trainer with fixed tailwheel u/c and 60hp Salmson 9Adr radial engine. Prototype F-AMHT
M.121	4	Corsaire Major with 75hp Cataract R engine
M.122	1	Corsaire Major with 75hp Salmson 9Aers
M.123	65	Main pre-war production version. Prototype F-APQA
M.124	1	Corsaire with 60hp Aster 4A engine. F-BAOF
M.125	5	Corsaire with 75hp Regnier 4JO engine
M.126	1	Corsaire with 80hp Salmson 5AP-1 engine
M.127	2	Corsaire with 95hp Regnier 4EO engine
M.128	1	Corsaire with 95hp Mathis G4-G engine
M.129	23	Postwar Corsaire with 75hp Minie 4DA-28 engine

Mauboussin also entered the field of glider production and this led to a number of powered gliders based on the Fouga CM.8-13 and using the light turbojets developed at that time by Turboméca. The powerplant was mounted on the top of the fuselage and the aircraft all had V-tails to allow free flow of the exhaust gases. The series included single examples of the CM-8-R-13 Sylphe 1 (F-WFOI, initially named Cyclone) with a Turboméca TR-011 which flew on 14th July 1949, the CM-8-R-13 Sylphe 2 (F-WFOJ, c/n 02) with a Turboméca Piméné flown on 23rd March 1950, the CM-8-R-9.8 Cyclope I (F-WCZO) with a Turboméca Palas and the similar Cyclope II (F-WFKM) which made its first flight on 28th April 1951. A batch of eight examples of the CM-8-R-8.3 Midjet, derived from the Cyclope 2, was built for competition and display work, the first (F-WGKF, c/n 1) flying on 30th May 1952. Fouga also built two of the CM-88R Gemeaux which use two Sylphe fuselages joined together. The prototype (F-WEPJ) had a Turboméca Piméné mounted on each of the fuselages, but the second aircraft used a single Turboméca Marboré 1 turbojet.

Mauboussin M-123 Corsaire F-PBHK. M J Hooks

Found Bush Hawk 300 C-GYWK

Found   Canada

Captain S R Found originally designed the four-seat FBA-1A light util-ity aircraft in 1948 and established Found Brothers Aviation to put it into series production. It was designed as a 'flying truck' and was a can-tilever high-wing monoplane with a fixed tricycle undercarriage, a 140hp Gipsy Major engine and steel tube and fabric construction. The prototype (CF-GMO-X) first flew on 13th July 1949, but its flight char-acteristics were very poor and the company went into a complete and prolonged redesign that resulted in the FBA-2A, which flew on 11th August 1960. This was of all-metal construction, had a five-seat slab-sided fuselage with large cargo doors on each side and was powered by a 250hp Lycoming O-540-A1D six-cylinder engine. The vertical and horizontal tail surfaces were designed to be interchangeable.

The first production FBA-2C (CF-NWT-X c/n 2) first flew on 9th May 1962 and it was substantially the same as the FBA-2A but had a length-ened cabin, a large dorsal fin and a tailwheel undercarriage. It went into production later that year and a further 25 (c/n 3 to 27) were built up to 1967. Found intended to replace the FBA-2C with the Centen-nial 100, which was slightly larger and had a 290hp Lycoming IO-540-G engine. The first Centennial (CF-IOO-X c/n 100) was first flown on 7th April 1967 and a further four examples were completed (c/n 101 to 104), but Found ran out of funds and ceased production in the autumn of 1968. In 1996, the design was revived by Found Aircraft

Found FBA-2C CF-SVD

Development Inc and an existing FBA-2C (CFSVD c/n 26) was flown with a 260hp Lycoming IO-540-D engine. This was considered under-powered and the updated FBA-2C1 (C-GDWO, c/n 28), named Bush Hawk 300 and powered by a 300hp Lycoming IO-540L, was flown in October 1998. With a number of further modifications, including a redesigned wing, an enlarged tail and modified undercarriage, this became the production Bush Hawk-XP, the first of which (c/n 30) flew on 2nd March 2000. By the end of 2004 a further 17 had been com-pleted (c/n 31 to 47).

Fournier   France

During the 1950s there had been various sporting aircraft developments in Germany based on motorised conversions of existing glider designs. In France, René Fournier set out to build a brand new aircraft that was designed from the outset as a motor glider. His RF-01, first flown on 30th May 1960, was a single-seat machine with a high-aspect-ratio wing and a Volkswagen car engine mounted in the nose. The RF-01 would take off under its own power and, once at altitude, the pilot would switch off its engine and operate as if it were a conventional sailplane.

Fournier subsequently built two RF-2 development machines (F-WJSR and F-BJSY) under an arrangement with Pierre Robin – but he did not stay with Pierre Robin's company (Centre Est), choosing instead to use his own resources to bring the 'Avion Planeur' to a commercially viable state. This led to him flying the further improved RF-3 (F-BKQV, c/n 1) in April 1963. This aircraft gained its type certificate on 7th June 1963 and René Fournier and the Comte d'Assche then proceeded to form the Société Alpavia, which set up operations and built 87 examples of the RF-3 (c/n 2 to 88) at the air-field of Gap-Tallard.

Fournier RF-7 G-LTRF

Fournier RF-5 D-KIFP

With the RF-3 and the Jodel D.117A (taken over from SAN) in full production, the company became increasingly involved with Alfons Pützer KG in Germany and when the strengthened aerobatic RF-4 appeared it was decided that production should be undertaken by a new company, Sportavia-Pützer GmbH, which was formed in 1966 by Pützer and the Comte d'Assche. Sportavia built 155 aircraft (c/n 4004 to 4158). Alpavia's factory was sold and the company was reorganised into a sales support role based in Paris.

At this point, René Fournier set up an independent design bureau and produced the design of a tandem two-seater based on the RF-4. This RF-5 was passed over to the Sportavia-Pützer organisation and subsequently achieved considerable success both in basic form (c/n 5001 to 5126) and as the Sperber (c/n 51001 to 51079). In 1991, the RF-5 was returned to production in Spain by Aeronautica de Jaen (AJI) who completed a prototype (EC-650 c/n E-0001) and ten production examples of the 'RF-5-AJ1 Serrania' (c/n E-002 to E-011) powered by the 80hp Limbach 2000 engine. Fournier also designed the side-by-side two-seat RF-6, which was much less like a motor glider than the previous types although it still had a high aspect ratio wing. The RF-6 was fitted with a fixed tricycle undercarriage and a blister canopy that had a hinge mechanism to open it upwards and backwards.

René Fournier decided to set up his own company to build this new model and he established Avions Fournier with premises at Nitray. The RF-6B prototype had a 90hp Continental O-200E but the production version was powered by a 100hp Rolls-Royce Continental O-200-A engine and the first series example (F-BVKS c/n 1) was rolled out in March 1976. Sadly, Fournier had adopted a production concept that incorporated a considerable degree of sub-contract manufacture and after 43 aircraft had been completed (c/n 01, 1 to 41 and c/n 44) the line had to be closed as it was financially unviable and the company collapsed.

Prior to the closure Fournier, in cooperation with the Société Indraero, had flown the prototype of the tandem two-seat all-metal RF-8. This led to the more commercially viable RF-9, which flew as a prototype (F-WARF c/n 01) on 20th January 1977. It was powered by a 68hp Limbach SL.1700E engine and featured a retractable tailwheel undercarriage and a side-by-side two-seat cockpit with a blister canopy. The prototype (redesignated c/n 02) was later fitted with wings which were foldable at mid-span for ease of hangarage. The RF-9 was shelved until the company recapitalised in 1978 as Fournier Aviation and 13 production aircraft were built at the Nitray factory (c/n 1 to 13). ABS Aviation of Dahlemer Binz in Germany also took a licence and built one RF-9 (D-KHGO c/n 9021), which first flew on 30th June

Fournier RF-6B F-GANB

Fournier RF-47 F-GRTA

Fournier RF-9 F-CAHM

1995, but responsibility was passed to Gomolzig Flug-und-Maschinenbau who had intentions of starting new production. Fournier also granted a licence for RF-6B production to the British company, Slingsby Engineering. Sportavia also built a handful of the RF-6C together with a developed version – the RS-180.

Fournier's next development of the basic formula was the RF-10, which was externally similar to the RF-9, of all-composite construction and the first of two prototypes (F-WARG c/n 01) first flew on 6th March 1981. During flight testing the prototype was lost during spinning tests and the design was revised with a deeper fin and rudder and a T-tail. Financial strictures at the Société Fournier resulted in the RF-10 being built by Société Aerostructure at Marmande from early 1984, but this company was unable to cope with the complex construction of the aircraft and eventually closed down in early 1985 after 12 production aircraft had been completed. Their output included four for the Portuguese Air Force. At this stage, the RF-10 design was sold to Aeromot in Brazil and development of their Ximango is detailed in the section devoted to that company. In the mid-1990s, Réne Fournier returned to light aviation with the RF-47 which was a side-by-side two-seat trainer with a fixed tricycle undercarriage and wood-and-fabric construction. The prototype (F-WNDF c/n 01) made its first flight on 9th April 1993 followed by a second aircraft (F-WWTJ/F-GSTJ c/n 02). The aircraft entered production with Euravial but the company went out of business after encountering problems connected with certification, having completed one further example (F-GRTA c/n 3). Details of the Fournier designs are:

Model	Built	Notes
RF-1	1	Single-seat motor glider ('Avion Planeur'). Volkswagen engine. Prototype F-WJGX FF 6 Jul 1960
RF-2	2	RF-1 with minor changes powered by Rectimo AR.1200 engine. Prototype F-WJSR FF Jun 1962
RF-3	89	Production Avion Planeur built by Alpavia. Prototype F-WJSY FF Mar 1963
RF-4	3	Redesigned RF-3 with strengthened aerobatic airframe. Prototype F-BMKA (c/n 1)
RF-4D	155	RF-4 built by Sportavia
RF-5	127	Tandem two-seat development of RF-4 with Limbach SL.1700 engine. Built by Sportavia. Prototype D-KOLT FF Jan 1968
RF-5-AJ1	5	RF-5 built by Aero Jaen with 80hp Limbach L.2000-E01
RF-5B	99	Sperber. RF-5 with longer wings and cut-down rear fuselage, built by Sportavia and by Helwan in Egypt (20 examples). Prototype D-KHEK FF 15 May 1971
RF-5D	1	Modified Sperber. D-KACM (c/n 53001)
RF-5S	1	Experimental quiet reconnaissance RF-5 built by Sportavia with Lycoming O-235-E2A engine. Prototype D-EAFA (c/n V-1) FF 1971
RF-6B	43	Side-by-side two-seat wooden light aircraft with fixed tricycle u/c and 100hp Rolls-Royce Continental O-200A. Built by Fournier at Nitray. Prototype F-WPXV (c/n 01) FF 12 Mar 1974
RF-6B/120	1	RF-6B with 115hp Lyc O-235-L2A. F-GANF (c/n 44) FF 16 Aug 1980
RF-6C	4	Four-seat RF-6 built by Sportavia as the Sportsman powered by one 150hp Lyc O-320-A2B. Prototype D-EHYO (c/n 6001) FF 28 Apr 1976
RS-180	18	Developed version of RF-6C. See Sportavia-Putzer
RF-7	1	RF-4D with 6-ft. wingspan decrease and Limbach 1700 engine. Prototype F-WPXV FF 27 Feb 1970
RF-8	1	All-metal tandem two-seat development of RF-4 with retractable tricycle u/c, powered by one 125hp Lycoming. Prototype F-WSQY FF 19 Jan 1973
RF-9	14	Side-by-side two-seat motor glider with retractable tailwheel u/c, powered by one 68hp Limbach SL 1700E. Built by Fournier. Prototype F-WARF (c/n 01). ABS Aviation version has carbon fibre components and Rotax 912 engine
RF-10	13	Plastic-composite version of RF-9 with T-tail. Powered by one 80hp Limbach L2000-EO-1. Prototype F-WARG (c/n 01) FF 6 Mar 1981. Later built as Aeromot Ximango
SFS-31	12	Sportavia development of RF-4D with Scheibe SF-27M wings and Rectimo AR.1200 engine. Named Milan. Prototype D-KORO (c/n 6601) FF 1 Aug 1969
RF-47	3	Low-wing side-by-side two-seat club trainer with fixed tricycle u/c and 90hp Sauer engine. Prototype F-WNDF FF 9 Apr 1993

Frati   Italy

Stelio Frati is one of the best known of Europe's independent designers. He started his career in aircraft design in 1941 at the Milan Polytechnic where he worked on sailplanes at the Centro per il Volo a Vela (CVV). After the war, Frati designed a number of aircraft with extremely clean lines and he granted production licences to other companies to produce these models. These constructors included Aviamilano Srl of Milan, Legnami Pasotti SpA, Aeromere SpA of Trento (and its successor, Laverda SpA) and Progetti Construzioni Aeronautiche SpA (Procaer) of Milan. In recent times, Stelio Frati has operated through his own company, General Avia, to construct prototypes. His most recent ventures have included the Promavia Jet Squalus jet trainer and the F.22 Pinguino trainer. Frati's main designs have been as follows:

FM.1 Passero	High-wing single-seat motor glider with a fixed tailwheel undercarriage and 20hp Macchi MB.2 pusher engine. Prototype I-MOVO built by Ditta Movo
F.4 & F.7 Rondone	Two-seat low-wing cabin monoplane. See entries for Ambrosini and Pasotti
F.5 Trento	Two-seat jet trainer. See entry for Caproni
F.6 Airone	Four-seat light cabin twin. See entry for Pasotti
F.8 Falco	Low-wing two-seater with retractable tricycle undercarriage. See entries for Aeromere, Aviamilano and Laverda. The F.8L was also supplied by Sequoia Aircraft Corporation of Richmond, VA, USA as a kit for amateur builders. Fitted with 135hp, 150hp or 160hp engines
F.9 Sparviero	Single-engined version of F.6 Airone. See entry for Pasotti
F.14 Nibbio	Four-seat light single-engined aircraft. See entry for Aviamilano

F.15 Picchio	Four-seat light single-engined aircraft. See entries for Procaer and General Avia
F.20 Pegaso	Four-seat light cabin twin. See entry for General Avia
F.22 Jet Condor	1972 project for an 8-seat low-wing executive jet powered by two Turboméca Astafan engines mounted on rear fuselage. Not built
F.22 Pinguino	Two-seat single-engined trainer/tourer. See entry for General Avia
D-130	Low-wing side-by-side two-seat trainer developed from the F.22 with 125hp Cont IO-240 engine. Under development, 2002 for 'I-I-I'
F.200	Aerobatic trainer version of D-130 with 200hp Lyc IO-360 engine
F.300	Four-seat touring development of D-130 powered by 300hp Lycoming IO-540
F220 Airone	Four-seat derivative of the F.22 Pinguino. See entry for General Avia
F.250 & F.260	Three-seat high-performance trainer/tourers. See entry for SIAI-Marchetti
F.30 Airtruck	Proposed 8/10-seat light freighter for production by Procaer. Not built but developed into F.600 Canguro
F.400 Cobra	Two-seat jet trainer. See entry for Procaer
F.600 Canguro	Ten-seat high-wing light transport. See entry for SIAI Marchetti
F.1000	Two-seat side-by-side jet trainer and personal transport with one FJ33 turbofan positioned in pod above rear fuselage. Not yet flown
F.1300 Jet Squalus	Two-seat all-metal jet trainer. See entry for General Avia
F.3500 Sparviero	19-seat twin-turbofan commuter aircraft project conceived in 1983 but not built

---

Fuji   Japan

The principal sporting aircraft to have come from Japan is the FA-200 Aero Subaru, which was manufactured by Fuji Heavy Industries between 1967 and 1986 having been initiated in 1964. The design concept was for a low-wing all-metal four-seat tourer with a fixed tricycle undercarriage. The prototype F.200-II (JA3241 c/n 1) was first flown on 21st August 1965 powered by a 160hp Lycoming O-320-B2B engine and it gained its Japanese type certificate on 1st March 1966. The production version was quite similar, but had a more extensively glazed cockpit canopy and the section between the cabin and the engine firewall was extended by three inches.

Fuji also had intentions of building several other models including the three-seat F-201, the two-seat F-202 aerobatic trainer, the crop spraying F-204 and a special STOL version known as the F-203. However, as it turned out, the four-seat FA-200-160 was the only version that went into production, although several engine options were available over the life of the design. In addition to the 160hp model, the FA-200-180 was offered with a fuel-injected 180hp Lycoming IO-360-B1B engine with a constant-speed propeller and an increase of 200 lb in gross weight.

Fuji FA-200-180 D-EITT

A low cost equivalent, the FA-200-180AO joined the line in 1974 and used a fixed pitch propeller and a standard non-injected O-360 engine. Total production of the FA-200 series was 274 aircraft. The first production aircraft was JA3263 which had serial c/n 1 and production ceased with c/n 274. The majority of FA-200s were exported with many going to Australia, Germany and the United Kingdom.

Funk (Akron)   United States

The Funk Model B was designed and built by the Funk Brothers as a prototype at the end of 1933. The first aircraft (NX14100 c/n 1) was powered by a 3-cylinder 45hp Szekley engine but this was replaced, firstly by a converted Ford Model A engine and then by a modified Ford

Model B engine which developed 63hp and was known as the Akron Model E-200-E4L. This particular aircraft was subsequently modified to full Funk B standard and became NC22683 (c/n 10).

The Funk B was a high-wing side-by-side two-seater with a rather tubby fuselage and tailwheel undercarriage. It went into production with the Funk Brothers' Akron Aircraft Inc at Akron, Ohio and the first

Funk B85C N89V

pre-production machine, c/n B-2 (NX90, later NX9000) together with the initial batch were fitted with the E-200 engine. This was followed by a further batch, upgraded to a 75hp Lycoming GO-145-C2 or -C3 engine and known as the Model B75L. Two aircraft were re-engined with a Continental A-75-8 engine as the Funk Model C (otherwise known as the Akron V), but this did not go into production.

In 1941, Akron Aircraft Inc ceased operation having built 151 aircraft consisting of 101 Model Bs (c/n 2 to 75 and c/n 176 to 202) and 50 Model B75Ls (c/n 176 to 210). Funk became the Funk Aircraft Co at Coffeyville, Kansas and production of the B75L restarted at c/n 211, (rolled out in February 1942), and continued to c/n 251. The aircraft then became the Funk B85C by virtue of a power upgrade to the 85hp Continental C-85-12F engine and Funk finally ceased production in 1948 after building 188 examples of this model (c/n 252 to 439). The last 20 aircraft were known as the 'Customaire' with minor changes to their internal trim. The type certificate was sold to Thomas H McClish and later to Dr Larry Smith of Canfield, Ohio but no further aircraft were built.

D D Funk   United States

The Donald D Funk Company of Broken Arrow, Oklahoma developed a single-seat low-wing crop spraying aircraft, the F-23, and flew the prototype (N55076 c/n 10434AE) in November 1962. It was of largely original construction but used the fuselage frame of the Fairchild M-62 Cornell and was powered by a 240hp Continental W-670-M radial engine. It carried the 200 US gal chemical load in a tank located between the cockpit and the firewall. Eleven production F-23A aircraft were built between 1964 and 1967 (c/n 2 to 12) of which one was exported to Guatemala. The final three aircraft were designated F-23B and fitted with a 275hp Jacobs R-755 engine. The design was taken over by Cosmic Aircraft of Norman, Oklahoma in May 1970 but no further aircraft were completed.

Fairchild Funk M62C/F-23A N1131Z. H B Adams

Yves Gardan   France

Yves Gardan was the designer of the Minicab and Supercab, built in the late 1940s and detailed in the section on Constructions Aéronautique de Béarn (CAB). He also designed the SIPA Coccinelle and the GY-80 Horizon which was built in quantity by Sud-Aviation together with the derivative Diplomate and is described in the section on Aérospatiale. His final design was the GY-100 Bagheera which was an all-metal low-wing light aircraft with a fixed tricycle undercarriage and four-seat fully enclosed cabin, closely resembling the Piper Cherokee. The prototype, F-WOFO, which was built by SITAR and first flew on 21st December 1967 powered by a 135hp Lycoming O-320 engine, was lost during flight-testing in 1969. However, the type was certificated and one higher-powered production example (F-WRGA/F-BRGN c/n 1) was built by SITAR and this is currently operational in France.

Gardan GY-100 Bagheera F-BRGN

General Avia   Italy

General Avia was established in 1970 by Stelio Frati in order to develop and prototype new aircraft designs. Initially, General Avia concentrated on development of the F.15 Picchio. This was a four-seat low-wing cabin monoplane with aluminium skinning over wooden construction and the initial F.15, F.15A, F.15B and F.15C were built in series by Procaer. General Avia subsequently developed the F.15E, which was an all-metal version of the F.15B with a 300hp Continental IO-520-K engine and larger side windows. The prototype, I-PROM (c/n 37), was built by General Avia and first flew on 21st December 1968. One further aircraft, I-PROD (c/n 38-GA) was completed. This was followed by the F.15F Delfino, which was a two-seat Picchio with a sliding bubble canopy, all-metal construction and a 200hp Lycoming IO-360-A1B engine. This aircraft (I-PROL, c/n 39-GA) first flew on 20th October 1977 and was damaged in 1986. No production ensued but a new company, Eurospace, was formed between HOAC-Austria and the Sokol factory at Novgorod in Russia to put a re-engineered Delfino back in production. A prototype was produced (OE-VPY, later I-EXCA) and the Delfino was to have been marketed by HOAC-Austria as the F.15F Excalibur but this plan collapsed in 1993. A 30-aircraft production line was laid down and one aircraft completed as a demonstrator. 10 airframes are believed to have been sold to China and two sold in

General Avia F.15F N24VK

the USA. One of the American airframes has been completed and flown under the experimental category (N24VK).

In the early 1980s, Stelio Frati produced the design of the F.30 Airtruck, a ten-seat light transport with a fixed undercarriage and two 310hp Lycoming TIO-540-A1B piston engines. In many respects it was similar to a larger version of the Britten-Norman Islander and it was intended that this would be built by Procaer. General Avia refined it into the F.600 Canguro and flew the prototype (I-CANG c/n 001) on

General Avia Pinguino F.22B Pinguino D-EDMJ

30th December 1978. SIAI-Marchetti SpA (then part of the Agusta Group) took a licence to build it but decided that it should be modified to turboprop power and the prototype, I-CANG was refitted with two 420shp Allison 250-B17C engines and re-flown as the SF.600TP in April 1981. SIAI built eight production aircraft (c/n 002 to 009) one of which (I-KANG c/n 003) was fitted with a retractable undercarriage. Another SF.600TP (c/n 007) was shipped to the Philippines as a pattern aircraft for possible local production, although this did not materialise. In 1997, after SIAI-Marchetti was sold to Aermacchi, rights to the SF.600TP passed to VulcanAir and the tenth example (I-VULA) was completed by them with a view to further production.

The company was also involved in design work on the F.1300 Jet Squalus, a side-by-side two-seat all-metal jet trainer developed by Promavia in Belgium. It had a broadly similar design layout to the Trento and Cobra and was powered by one Garrett TFE109-1 turbofan. The prototype, I-SQAL, first flown on 30th April 1987 and the project was later sold to Alberta Aerospace. General Avia's other main project was the F.20 Pegaso. This was an all-metal light cabin twin with 5/6 seats, a retractable tricycle undercarriage and two 300hp Continental IO-520-K engines. They built the prototype I-GEAV (c/n 001) and flew it on 21st October 1971. It was followed by two further aircraft (c/n 002 and 003). A four-seat military derivative, the F.20TP Condor, powered by two Allison 250-B17B turboprops and fitted with a bubble canopy and cut-down rear fuselage was built in prototype form (I-GEAC) and flown on 7 May 1983 but no further production took place.

Continuing the classic Frati design theme, the company then produced the F.22 Pinguino. This all-metal low-wing side-by-side two-seat trainer was generally similar to the SF.260 with a fixed tricycle undercarriage and powered by a 116hp Lycoming O-235-2NC. The prototype F.22A, (I-GEAD c/n 001), built by General Avia, first flew on 13th June 1989. The F.22B Pinguino (prototype, I-GEAG c/n 004) had a 160hp

Lycoming O-320-D2A and the F.22C Sprint (prototype I-GEAH c/n 005) was a version with a retractable undercarriage and 180hp Lycoming O-360-A1A engine with a c/s propeller. The F.22R Pinguino Sprint (prototype I-GEAE c/n 002) had a retractable undercarriage and the 160hp Lycoming O-320-A2D engine. First production deliveries of the Pinguino were made in March 1994. In 1996, General Avia completed the prototype F.220 Airone, which is a four-seat derivative of the F.22C Sprint fitted with a retractable tricycle undercarriage and a 200hp Lycoming IO-360 -A1A engine. Manufacture of the F.22 continued until 1998 when the General Avia factory was damaged in an earthquake and production ceased when the company was forced into administration. Up to that date, 26 aircraft, including prototypes, had been built (c/n 001 to 026).

General Avia SF.600TP Canguro I-KANG

Gippsland   Australia

The Latrobe-based Gippsland Aeronautics, which started as an aircraft maintenance organization in the 1970s, developed the GA-200 Fatman agricultural aircraft. This was based on the Piper PA-25 Pawnee airframe with a wider fuselage to accommodate two people side-by-side and an enlarged hopper. Seven Pawnees were converted as development aircraft, the first of which was VH-BCE (c/n 200-9101), and the type was certificated in Australia in March 1991. Powered by a 260hp Lycoming O-540-H2A5 engine, the GA-200 is fitted with a number of Gippsland's other agricultural improvements. From the 23rd aircraft the GA-200C was introduced with a 300hp IO-540-K1A5 engine and a small batch, designated GA-200B, have been assembled in the USA from Australian components. The aircraft remains in low-scale production with 45 completed by mid-2004 (up to c/n 200C-03-45). Serial numbers include the type prefix followed by the year of manufacture and a consecutive serial starting at 01. On 3rd March 1995, the company flew the prototype of the GA-8 Airvan high-wing single-engined utility aircraft. Using wings derived from those of the GA-200, the GA-8 has a square section six-seat fuselage with a fixed tricycle undercarriage and is powered by a 250hp Lycoming O-540 piston engine with a constant-speed propeller. A significant sale of nine aircraft for the US Civil Air Patrol has been achieved. Gippsland is testing a turbocharged variant with a Lycoming TIO-540 and has also been

Gippsland GA-200 Fatman ZK-CMC

considering a stretched turboprop version (the GA-10T Tasker), a version with a larger Lycoming 580 engine and a diesel-powered version. During 2004, Gippsland delivered 20 Airvans. Serial numbers for the Airvan consist of two digits for the year built, followed by the individual aircraft number (eg, GA8-02-012) and 69 aircraft have been built (c/ns 001 to 012 and 014 to 070) with 20 delivered during 2004.

Gippsland GA-8 Airvan N530AV

Globe   United States

Globe Aircraft was a subsidiary of the Globe Medicine Company of Fort Worth, Texas and before World War Two it was involved with the Bennett Aircraft Corporation, which intended to use a new Bakelite-bonded plywood for aircraft construction. In 1941, R S 'Pop' Johnson designed and built a small side-by-side two-seater (NX17688 c/n 1) fitted with an 80hp Continental A-80 engine that it was intended would be built by Globe. This GC-1 prototype was scrapped after a dispute between Johnson and Globe and Johnson left to produce virtually the same design as the Johnson Rocket. A second Swift was built (NX17690 c/n 2) and this was later substantially redesigned as the prototype GC-1A, NX17640 (c/n 1), still built of tube and fabric. The definitive

production Globe GC-1A Swift was NX33336 (c/n 2), which was an all-metal redesign of the earlier prototype and powered by an 85hp Continental C-85. Because of Globe's wartime production of the Beech AT-10 and other products, it did not fly until January 1945. The GC-1A was a high-performance low-wing monoplane with a fully enclosed side-by-side two-seat cabin and a tailwheel undercarriage incorporating retractable main units and a fixed tailwheel. In the course of development many changes took place, including a revised engine installation, longer engine cowling and extended firewall, but the type certificate was eventually issued on 5th July 1946.

Production of the Swift was subcontracted to the Texas Engineering and Manufacturing Co (later Temco) who built 428 GC-1As (c/n 2 to 429) before going over to production of the GC-1B Swift. Serial

Globe Swift GC-1B N80707

Temco TE-1 Buckaroo N904B

numbers of the GC-1B were c/n 1001 to 1527. This version was fitted with a 125hp Continental C-125 engine and was outwardly similar to the GC-1A except for the modified engine cowling. In July 1947, Globe was declared bankrupt with the result that Temco bought the assets of the business, including the Swift type certificate. They continued to build the GC-1B until 1951 and produced c/n 2001 to 2329 and c/n 3523 to 3760. Temco also converted a batch of 22 GC-1Bs (c/n 1505 to 1526) to GC-1A standard and issued them with new serials c/n 3001 to 3522. When production ceased a total of 1,521 production Swifts had been built.

In 1949, Temco used the basic Swift design to produce the TE-1 Buckaroo tandem two-seat trainer. The US Air Force took some interest in the Buckaroo and received three evaluation aircraft. 17 further Buckaroos were eventually constructed (including a batch of 10 for the Royal Saudi Air Force). After production of the Swift and Buckaroo had ceased, Temco sold the type certificate to Universal Aircraft Industries (Univair), which now supplies spares for the Swift.

Univair subsequently sold the type certificate to the loyal band of owners who comprise the Swift Association. During 1987, LoPresti-Piper Air-

craft Engineering Co developed an interest in possible production of an updated Swift. Under the late Roy LoPresti two Swifts were modified to become the SwiftFury and turboprop SwiftFire prototypes. The first aircraft (registered successively N207LP and N217LP – c/n 246) first flew on 27th February 1989 powered by a 200hp Lycoming IO-360 engine and featuring new flush-riveted wing skins, a reshaped rudder, wing fences and a sliding cockpit canopy. This aircraft was later known as the LoPresti Fury. The turboprop Swiftfire (N345LP) had a 425shp Allison 250 engine and LoPresti-Piper also considered a military Swift with a tricycle undercarriage but this development was abandoned as a result of financial pressures at Piper Aircraft. Roy LoPresti inherited all rights to the SwiftFury in 1999 on Piper's bankruptcy but died before further development could take place. Many Swifts have been modified with Nagel bubble cockpit canopies and other refinements.

In early 1997, it was announced that Aviat Aircraft of Afton, Wyoming had taken up a licence to build a new version of the Swift (the Millennium Swift), which was expected to be fitted with a 210hp Continental IO-360ES engine and a smaller laminar-flow wing. This project was subsequently suspended.

Great Lakes   United States

The Great Lakes biplane designed by Charles W Meyers and built by Great Lakes Aircraft Company of Cleveland, Ohio achieved considerable success in the 1930s. It was a tandem two-seat open-cockpit

biplane with a swept upper wing and straight lower wing surfaces and the initial Model 2T-1 was powered by an 85hp Cirrus Mk 3 in-line engine. This was followed by the Model 2T-1A with a 90hp or 100hp Cirrus. A fair number were used for aerobatic demonstrations with the front cockpit blanked off and, in many cases, these machines were

Great Lakes 2T-1A-2 N13SA

fitted with Warner radial engines of up to 200 horsepower or the 95hp Menasco B-4.

In 1932, Great Lakes succumbed to the Depression after building 258 production aircraft (c/n 7 to 264) and the type certificate for their range of biplanes remained in limbo until January 1972 – although plans had been made available to homebuilders for a number of years. All rights were then acquired by Doug Champlin's Windward Aviation Inc of Enid, Oklahoma and a new company – Great Lakes Aircraft Inc – was established. They built the Model 2T-1A-1 with a 150hp Lycoming O-320-E2A and the 2T-1A-2 with a fuel-injected 180hp Lycoming IO-360-B1F6. Basic construction was carried out in Wichita, Kansas with final assembly in Enid. Three pre-series aircraft were completed (c/n 0501 to 0503) and the first production aircraft, designated Model 2T-1A-2, was N703GL (c/n 0701). They continued until 1978 at which

time output had reached c/n 0838. Great Lakes also built one example of the turboprop Model X2T-1T 'Turbine Lakes' (N6187L c/n 0900), which was fitted with an Allison 250 and delivered astonishing aerobatic performance, but this was destroyed with the loss of the chief test pilot.

The following year, all rights were acquired by R Dean Franklin who relocated production to a new plant at Eastman, Georgia. His Great Lakes Aircraft Company built its first production aircraft in mid-1980 (c/n 1001) but ceased operations in 1982. On 3rd April 1984, Great Lakes became the property of John LaBelle and was moved to Claremont, New Hampshire. Production ceased at c/n 1012 in 1985 and the production jigs and engineering drawings were put up for sale and are now owned by Chaparral Motors of Palmer Lake, Colorado.

Grob   Germany

The initial products of Grob-Werke KG, which was formed at Mindelheim in 1971, were a range of fibreglass sailplanes. These included the Astir CS standard class single-seater and the Twin Astir two-seater and Speed Astir high-performance 15 metre sailplanes. In 1980, the G-109 powered glider was announced. This was a side-by-side GRP two-seater with a fixed tailwheel undercarriage, a T-tail and an 80hp Limbach engine. Production of the G-109 had reached 10 aircraft per month by the end of 1982 with 140 units produced by the end of that year. Grob's serial numbers for these types consist of a four-digit number in a different series for each model and G-109 serials were c/n 6001, 6003 and 6010 to 6159. G-109B serials ran from c/n 6200 to 6576, at which point production was suspended.

The company turned to full specification aircraft for flying clubs and private owners and in 1981 flew the prototype of the G-110 all-composite two-seat trainer. The G-110 first flew in the Spring of 1982 but it was written off on 29th July 1982 during the test programme and the project was abandoned. A rather more elegant two-seater, the G-112, was then tested but Grob further enhanced it as the G-115 which was a larger aircraft and has been built at Mindelheim-Mattsies with serial numbers for production aircraft in the range c/n 8006 to 8109 and

Grob G-109B D-KISI

82001 to 82184. A number of versions have been produced, as described in the data table. Current production versions are the G-115C, G-115D and the G-115E Tutor for use by the RAF at University Air Squadrons and air cadet units. In addition Grob has built the G-115EG, 74 of which have been delivered to the Egyptian Air Force

Grob G-115 HB-UGD

Grob G-520 Egrett II D-FGEE

(c/n 82200 to 82273). A retractable-gear version was designated G-115T and 15 have been built to date (c/n 8500 to 8514) including a small batch of 12 G-115TAs delivered to the UAE Air Force This model was replaced by the G-120A which has the same general layout as the 115TA but is fully aerobatic with a 260hp Lycoming AEIO-540 engine and an EFIS cockpit. The launch customer was the Lufthansa Flight Training School in Arizona and other flight-training customers for the Grob trainers include the China Southern Flying College (38 G-115C), Australian Flying School and the Norwegian Aviation College.

The G-115 formed the basis for the G-116 four-seater but this did not enter production and Grob decided instead to develop the GF-200 four-seat cabin-class aircraft with a tail-mounted pusher engine and an advanced wing. This was abandoned in favour of the less radical G-140 which was, again, a low-wing all-composite aircraft with retractable gear and a four-seat cabin with upward-hinged doors for the front and rear compartments. It is powered by the Rolls-Royce (Allison) 250 turboprop engine. The larger G-160TP, which was announced at the 2003 Paris Air Show, is a cabin-class aircraft with up to seven seats and a PT6A turboprop engine. In June 2005, Grob unveiled their new G-180 SPn, which is a multi-role aircraft which doubles as a business jet and utility aircraft with the ability to operate from rough strips. Powered by two Williams FJ44-3A engines, the 8/10-seat G-180 prototype made its first flight on 20th July 2005.

The company has also worked with E-Systems of Greenville, Texas to build a series of high-altitude surveillance aircraft, the first of which was the Egrett I. These are offered as a platform for military surveillance, police border patrol, mapping and geophysical survey. The latest variant is the Strato 2C, which is a completely new design and is intended for high-altitude research for the German BDLI. Details of Grob aircraft (including gliders for the sake of completeness) are:

Model	Built	Notes
G-101	1	Prototype 2-seat motor glider
G-102	1,241	Astir single-seat sailplane. Prototype FF 19 Dec 1974
G-103 Twin Astir	944	Twin Astir two-seat sailplane. Prototype FF 31 Dec 1976
G-103C Twin III	51	Powered sailplane powered by a 43hp Rotax 505
G-104 Speed Astir	108	Single-seat sailplane. Prototype FF 3 Apr 1978
G-109	151	Two-seat side-by-side motor glider with fixed tailwheel u/c, upward-hinged canopy and one 80hp Limbach L.2000-E1 engine. Prototype D-KBGF (c/n 6001) FF 14 Mar 1980
G-109B	377	G-109 with 100hp GVW.2500IT1 turbocharged engine. Production variant has 90hp GVW.2500 engine, variable-pitch prop, redesigned longer-span wings, larger sliding canopy with fixed windshield. Ranger has increased fuel capacity. Prototype D-KIRO FF 18 Mar 1983
G-110	2	Two-seat low-wing light aircraft with fixed tricycle u/c and one 118hp Lyc O-235-M1 engine. Prototype D-EBGF (c/n 8001) FF 6 Feb 1982. Second aircraft D-EEGW (c/n 8002)
G-111	1	Special missions G-109B certificated to FAR.23 standard with developed GVW.2500 engine, upward-hinged cockpit doors and increased fuel. Prototype D-EEGW (c/n 7001) FF 15 Apr 1984
G-112	2	Side-by-side two-seat GRP trainer developed from G-110 with cruciform tail and short span wings. 3 aircraft with 90hp GVW.2500-F1, 116hp Lyc O-235-P1 and 118hp Lyc O-235 engines respectively. Prototype D-EMKF (c/n 8003) FF 4 May 1984. Second aircraft D-EBGW (c/n 8004) FF 31 May 1985
G-115	4	Developed G-112 with longer fuselage, sliding canopy and 116hp Lycoming O-235-H2C engine. Production model with lowered tailplane on fuselage. Prototype D-EBGF (c/n 8005) FF 15 Nov 1985
G-115A	99	G-115 with minor modifications
G-115B	8	G-115A with 160hp Lyc O-320 engine. Prototype D-ELCF (c/n 8109) FF 28 Apr 1988
G-115C	19	G-115B with increased capacity fuel tanks in wings, improved 2-piece canopy, rear cockpit luggage area, 160hp O-320-D2A engine. 2,183 lb TOGW. Prototype D-EBGF (c/n 8006). Production prototype D-EPBG. FF 26 Jan 1993
G-115C-1 Acro	8	G-115C for aerobatics with provision for parachutes, g-meter
G-115C-2	42	G-115C powered by 180hp Lycoming AEIO-360-B engine

Grob G-140TP D-ETPG

G-115D	11	G-115C-2 with reduced useful load, wing fuel tanks and stressed for aerobatics. Named Bavarian for US Sale. Prototype D-EVSA FF 2 Mar 1993
G-115D-2	7	G-115D powered by 160hp Lycoming AEIO-320-D1B engine
G-115E Tutor	100	G-115D-2 for RAF with 180hp Lycoming AEIO-360-B1F
G-115EG	74	G-115E for Egyptian AF
G-115T	1	G-115B stressed for aerobatics, fitted with retractable tricycle u/c, modified tail and 260hp Lycoming AEIO-540D4A5 engine with 4-blade c/s prop. 2,866 lb TOGW. Prototype D-EMGT (c/n 8500) FF 11 June 1992
G-115TA Acro	15	Production G-115T for UAE AF
G-116	1	Four-seat version of G-115 with 200hp Lyc IO-360-A engine. Prototype D-EGRF (c/n 9001) FF 29 Apr 1988
G-120A	7	Development of G-115TA for airline training powered by 260hp Lycoming AEIO-540-D4D5 engine. 3,174 lb TOGW. Prototype D-ELHU FF 1999
G-120A-1	18	G-120 for Israeli AF, named Snunit
G-140 TP	1	Low-wing all-composite light aircraft for utility and training roles with four-seat cabin, retractable tricycle u/c and one 850shp Rolls-Royce 250-B17F turboprop. Prototype D-ETPG
G-145		Civil version of G-140TP for executive use with pressurized cabin and modified fuselage
G-160TP Ranger	1	7-seat all-composite cabin-class business aircraft powered by one Pratt & Whitney PT6A-42A turboprop. Prototype D-FTBG FF 24 Mar2004

G-500	1	Egrett I single-seat surveillance and meteorological sampling aircraft with high aspect ratio wing and fixed tricycle u/c, powered by one Garrett TPE331-14A turboprop. Prototype D-FGEI/N14ES (c/n 10001) FF 24 June 1987. Also known as Model G-117
G-520	3	Egrett II. Similar to Egrett I with 16ft 4in increase in wingspan, pressurized cockpit, retractable u/c, TPE331-14F engine and increased gross weight. Prototype D-FGEE (c/n 10002) FF 20 Apr 1989. Third aircraft is G-520D with shorter wingspan
G-520G	1	Strato I variant of Egrett II with wingtip winglets, improved equipment bay etc. Prototype D-FGRO (c/n 10005) FF 5 Jun 1991
G-520T	1	Tandem two-seat version of Strato I. Prototype D-FDST (c/n 10200)
GF-200	1	Four-seat low-wing composite aircraft with retractable tricycle u/c, T-tail, advanced design wing and one 275hp Lycoming TIO-540 engine in pusher configuration. Prototype D-EFKH (c/n 20001) FF 26 Nov 1991
GF-250		Proposed pressurized 5-seat GF.200 with full de-icing and 260Kw engine
GF-300		Proposed stretched GF-200 with 6/7 seats and Allison 250 turboprop engine
GF-350		Proposed GF-300 development with two Allison 250 turboprops mounted externally on the rear fuselage
Strato 2C	1	High-wing monoplane with T-tail and tricycle u/c with main units in fuselage sponsons. Powered by two pusher turboprop engines. Prototype D-CDLR FF 31 Mar 1995

Grob G-160TP D-FTBG

Grumman   United States

In 1944, as the War was approaching its end, Grumman Aircraft Engineering Corporation turned to possible civilian markets and built on its experience of the G-21A Goose and the G-44 amphibians with a new version of the Widgeon – the G-44A – with a redesigned hull and civilian trim. The G-44A was an all-metal high-wing five-seat amphibian powered by two 200hp Ranger 6-440-C5 piston engines. First deliveries were made in 1945 and a total of 76 aircraft (c/n 1401 to 1476) were delivered by the time the line was closed in 1947.

Grumman also licensed production to the French company, Société des Constructions Aéronavales (SCAN). They built approximately 40 airframes (c/n 1 to 41), but ran into difficulties as a result of the severe shortage of Ranger engines. The prototype (F-WFDM c/n 01) first flew on 14th May 1953 but it had to use a pair of Gipsy Queen IIs to get into the air. The production SCAN-30s employed a variety of powerplants, principally the horizontally-opposed Lycoming GO-435-C2, and most of those built ended up in the United States where they were often re-engined with the radial Lycoming R-680E or Continental W-670.

Grumman itself also built the much larger G-73 Mallard 'air yacht', which had the ability to carry 10 passengers and two crew in its streamlined hull. The prototype Mallard (NX41824 c/n J-1) was flown on 30th April 1946 and had the distinction of being the first Grumman amphib-ian to be fitted with a fully retractable tricycle undercarriage. The Mallard, which was certificated on 8th September 1947 (certificate number A-783), was a hand-built aircraft of high quality and 59 examples had flown (c/n J-1 to J-59) by the time the aviation recession forced its suspension in 1951. Later production by Grumman, including the G-159 Gulfstream, is covered under Gulfstream Aerospace.

Grumman G-73 Mallard N98BS

Guerchais Roche   France

In September 1944, Roche Aviation completed the prototype of a low-wing side-by-side two-seat cabin monoplane which was designated T-35 (F-BBCZ c/n 01). This was powered by a 140hp Renault 4Pei engine and it formed the basis for a small series of similar aircraft with various engines. The largest production batch was seven units of the T-35/II with a Renault 4PO-3 engine and they built single examples of the T-35/I (F-BFAY c/n 1) with a 100hp Renault and the T-35/III (F-BFKI c/n 01) with a 145hp Regnier 4L-00.

The T-35 was then modified as a three-seater and Roche built two of the T-39/I with the 175hp Mathis G7R engine (prototype F-WCEG) and two of the T-39/II with a 175hp Salmson 9ND. The final development was the T-55 (F-BFAA c/n 01) which first flew on 20th July 1950 and was a T-39 with a clear-view canopy, modified tail and a 160hp Walter Minor 6-111 engine.

Guerchais Roche T-35 F-BBSU. P Maclou

Gulfstream   United States

During the 1950s, Grumman Aircraft Engineering Corporation abandoned production of its well-respected line of amphibians and concentrated its activities on military production, in particular the S2F Tracker and TF-1 Trader naval types. This experience convinced the company that they could produce a civil executive transport based on the Tracker. In the event, the design which emerged, the G-159 Gulfstream, was considerably different. It was much larger, with accommodation for 21 passengers, had a low wing and was powered by two Rolls-Royce Dart turboprops. The prototype, N701G (c/n 1), first flew on 14th August 1958, followed quickly by two further prototypes, and the type certificate (1A17) was awarded on 21st May 1959.

The Gulfstream was the right design at the right time and demand was encouraging. Full-scale production soon got under way and Grumman eventually finished building the Gulfstream in early 1969 having completed 200 examples including nine TC-4Cs for the US

Grumman G-159 Gulfstream I VH-FLO

Gulfstream G-II XA-BRE

Navy. The Gulfstreams were allocated c/n 1 to 200 (excluding c/n 13 and 113) and c/n 322 and 323. In 1979, the company announced a new version of the G-159 aimed specifically at the commuter airline market. The GAC-159-C (later known as the G-159C) featured a fuselage stretch of 9ft 6in to allow a maximum payload of 38 passengers. The prototype (N5400C c/n 116) was converted from a standard Gulfstream and first flew in this form on 25th October 1979. Grumman converted a further five existing G-159s (c/n 27, 83, 88 and 123) but did not put the G-159C into full production. However, the surviving standard Gulfstreams became popular for commuter airline service.

With the appearance of the Dassault Falcon, HS.125 and Sabreliner, the corporate turboprop appeared to be an anachronism and Grumman embarked on the design of a large intercontinental business jet that would appeal to the most affluent sector of the market. The G-1159 Gulfstream II was the result. Powered by a pair of Rolls-Royce Spey 511-8 turbofans, the first production aircraft (there being no prototype as such) made its first flight in October 1966. The 'G-II', as it has become universally known, was a low-wing aircraft with twin jets hung onto the rear fuselage and the large oval windows that had become popular on the turboprop Gulfstream. The new aircraft received its type certificate (A12EA) on 19th October 1967 and the first delivery, to National Distillers, was made in the following December. As an option, the aircraft could be converted to Gulfstream IIER standard with additional long-range tanks giving 400 miles extra range.

In 1969, Grumman restructured its commercial business and formed a separate subsidiary to handle each of its activities. This allowed the acquisition of American Aviation Corporation on 2nd January 1973 and the formation of Grumman American Aviation Corporation. This entity took charge of the American Aviation single-engined models, the Gulfstream II, the Cougar and the Ag-Cat agricultural aircraft (see Schweizer). Subsequently, in 1978, Grumman sold its interest to Allen E Paulson's American Jet Industries who renamed the company Gulfstream American Corporation (changed to Gulfstream Aerospace Corporation on 15th November 1982). Gulfstream soon discontinued production of the single-engined aircraft, but acquired the Aero Commander twin-engined line from Rockwell in February 1981. Four years later, on 15th August 1985, Allen Paulson sold Gulfstream to the Chrysler Corporation. In December 1989 it was announced that the Chrysler Technologies operating division, which included Gulfstream, was up for sale and, in February 1990, it was acquired by Allen Paulson (who later disposed of his interest) and venture capitalists, Forstmann Little. In May 1999 Gulfstream was sold to

Gulfstream 100 CC-CWK

General Dynamics, which maintained its principal base in Savannah, Georgia.

When it acquired Grumman's general aviation interests in 1978 American Jet Industries was deeply involved in its Hustler 500 project. This was a six passenger low-wing business aircraft with a Pratt and Whitney PT6A-41 turboprop in the nose and a Williams Research WR.19-3 small fanjet in the tail. The Williams engine was subsequently replaced by a larger Pratt & Whitney JT15D-1 turbofan. The prototype Hustler, N400AJ, was flown on 11th January 1978 and extensively tested.

The main elements of the Hustler design were also used to produce a turbofan military trainer known as the Peregrine 600, the prototype of which (N600GA) made its first flight on 22nd May 1981 at Mojave, California. As it turned out, neither the Hustler nor the Peregrine trainer progressed further, but Gulfstream built a developed Peregrine six-seat business jet which was given the name Commander Fanjet 1500. This aircraft was powered by a single 2,900 lbst Pratt & Whitney JT15D-5 turbofan buried in the tail and was intended for the rich 'sportsman flyer'. The prototype, N9881S made its maiden flight on 14th January 1983 but Gulfstream eventually dropped further work on the Fanjet 1500 because it was clear that the market for the aircraft was insufficient to justify further development.

In 1976, Grumman American had announced that it was developing a brand new Gulfstream III. As it turned out, the planned redesign was far too ambitious but the G-1159A that did emerge was able to offer greater range, speed and fuel efficiency. This model replaced the Gulf-

Gulfstream 200 HB-IGP

Gulfstream G-V N914BD

stream II on the Savannah, Georgia production line. The owners of 43 G-IIs gained certain G-III advantages by having their aircraft converted to G-1159B Gulfstream IIB standard by fitting the new 'G-III' wing, and other third-party conversions have included winglets and tip tanks. The next development was the Gulfstream G-IV with a stretched fuselage and further improvements in speed, range, systems and operating costs. At this point, the original Grumman designation system was abandoned and the G-1159 designation was dropped in favour of the designation G-IV. The GIV-SP was announced in October 1991. This high-weight (Special Performance) variant replaced the standard G-IV from 1992 and offered a 53% improvement in payload/range, 13% reduction in landing distance, landing weight increased from 58,500 lb to 66,000 lb and an increase in range from 1,800 miles to 3,000 miles. A 'wide-body' configuration was introduced to increase interior space.

In 1992, Gulfstream embarked on development of the Gulfstream GV in partnership with Vought Aircraft. This received its Type Certificate on 11th April 1997. It is seven feet longer than the G-IV, giving a standard passenger capacity of 19, with a new wing of 13 feet greater span. It has BMW-RR BR710-48 turbofans, a gross weight of 89,000 lb and the ability to carry eight passengers for 6,500 nautical miles at Mach 0.8 which is almost twice the range performance of the G-IV. The cockpit was enlarged and upgraded and the vertical tail is taller with a prominent tip fairing. In October 2000 the improved Gulfstream GV-SP was announced and it first flew in August 2001. This model with greater range, increased power, a further enlarged cabin and Gulfstream's 'Plane View' enhanced vision system, replaced the GV on the production line at the end of 2002.

Many Gulfstreams have been ordered by the American and overseas military customers. US military Gulfstream IIIs, of which 17 were delivered, are designated C-20A (USAF Special Missions), C-20B (USAF VIP) and C-20C (USAF War Readiness Alert), C-20D (US Navy) and C.20E (US Army). The C-20F (US Army), C-20G (US Navy with a large cargo door and convertible passenger/cargo interior) and C-20H (a USAF-operated VIP aircraft for the US Vice-President) are based on the Gulfstream G-IV while USAF Gulfstream GVs are designated C-37A.

In June 2001, General Dynamics acquired Galaxy Aerospace (see entry for Israel Aircraft Industries) and immediately integrated the Galaxy and Astra SPX business jets into the Gulfstream product line, renaming them Gulfstream G200 and G100 respectively. They contin-

ued to be manufactured in Israel at IAI but completed in the USA. The new designation style was introduced to the whole Gulfstream line in September 2002 and, at the same time, the company announced three new models. The G150 is a developed version of the Astra SPX with a wider and taller cabin, which will replace the G100 when introduced in 2006. The G300 is a G-IV with a reduced gross weight, reduced fuel load (and range) and factory-standard interior, which was replaced by the G350 and the G500 is a lower-weight GV with reduced fuel capacity. Other new designations included the G550 (formerly GV-SP) and G400 (formerly GIV-SP).

A total of 256 Gulfstream IIs were built with serial numbers c/n 1 to 248, 250 to 251 and 253 to 258 (including c/n 87 changed to c/n 775). Gulfstream IIIs were c/n 249, 252 and c/n 300 to 498 and c/n 875. Gulfstream G-IVs started at c/n 1000 with the GIV-SP being phased in from c/n 1185. The GIV-SP was discontinued with c/n 1499 (in Dec 2002) and G300/G400 production continued from c/n 1500 reaching 1534 by the end of 2004. Gulfstream 350/450s are serialled from c/n 4001 (to, currently, 4036). The Gulfstream GV commenced at c/n 501 and production ceased at c/n 699 in mid-2003, with the GV-SP (Gulfstream 500/550) continuing from c/n 5001 and reaching 5075 at the end of 2004. Gulfstream 100 and Gulfstream 200 serial numbers are detailed under the entry for IAI. During 2004, Gulfstream Aerospace delivered 22 of the Gulfstream 100 and 200 series and 56 of the 300/400/500 series. The many Gulfstream variants are described in the following table:

Model	Built	Notes
G-1159 Gulfstream II	256	Max 19-passenger, all-metal, low-wing business jet powered by two RR RB163-25 Spey 511-8 turbofans. Prototype N801GA (c/n 001) FF 2 Oct 1966
G-1159 Gulfstream IISP		Conversion of G-1159 by Aviation Partners Inc with winglets etc
G-1159 Gulfstream IITT		18 aircraft built with wingtip fuel tanks
G-1159B Gulfstream IIB		43 conversions of G-1159 with G-1159A wing. First conv N711SC (c/n 70) FF 17 Mar 1981
G-1159A Gulfstream III	202	G-1159 with 24-inch fuselage stretch, improved wing with leading edge extensions and NASA winglets, new nose and cockpit. Prototype N901GA (c/n 249) FF 2 Dec 1979. Military C-20A, C-20B, C-20D, C-20E

Gulfstream G-IV	204	G-1159A with 54-inch fuselage stretch, one extra cabin window each side, modified wing, glass cockpit and two RR RB183-03 Tay 610-8 turbofans. Prototype N404GA (c/n 1000) FF 19 Sep 1985. US Army C-20F, US Navy C-20G and USAF C-20H
Gulfstream GIV-SP	296	G-IV with 1,400 lb TOGW increase (to 74,600 lb), higher landing weight, increased payload, minor changes to airframe and enlarged cabin. Prototype N476GA (c/n 1183) FF 24 Jun 1992
Gulfstream G-IV SRA-IV		Special missions variant with optional forward cargo door for medevac, ASW or surveillance duties. Prototype N413GA (c/n 1034)
Gulfstream GIV-X		Proposed upgraded GIV-SP. See G450
Gulfstream GV	193	G-IV with 7-ft fuselage stretch, 13ft wingspan increase, modified tail unit, increased fuel capacity and range, 23,000 lb TOGW increase and 14,750 lbst BMW-RR BR710-A1-10 turbofans. Prototype N501GV (c/n 501) FF 28 Nov 1995
Gulfstream GV-SP		GV with 7 cabin windows each side, entry door moved 24 ins forward and cabin lengthened internally, two 15,385 lbst RR BR700-710-C4-11 turbofans, reduced drag mods, PlaneView cockpit. 6,750nm range. 91,000 lb TOGW. Prototype N632GA (c/n 632) FF 31 Aug 2001. 1st production, N5SP (c/n 5001) FF 18 Jul 2002. Redesignated G550
Gulfstream G100		Galaxy Astra SPX redesignated (from June 2001)
Gulfstream G150		G100 with new fuselage and 25% larger cabin interior, reshaped nose section and oval windows. Prototype 4X-TRA (c/n 201) FF 7 May 2005
Gulfstream G200		Galaxy redesignated (from June 2001)
Gulfstream G300		Economy version of G400 with shorter range and 3 standard package interior options and standard avionics. 72,000 lb TOGW
Gulfstream G350		Replacement for G300, announced March 2004. Combines fuselage and engines of G450 with cockpit of G500/G550. Lower price, specification and shorter-range version of G450
Gulfstream G400	35	Revised designation for GIV-SP (from Oct 2002)

Gulfstream G-IV EC-HGH

Gulfstream G450	36	G400 with 12-in fuselage stretch, nose section of G550, entry door moved rearwards, increased range. Powered by two Rolls-Royce Tay 611-8C engines. Prototype N450GA (c/n 4001) FF 30 Apr 2003
Gulfstream G500		G550 without HUD and EVS and with 5,800nm range. 85,100 lb TOGW
Gulfstream G550	75	Revised designation for GV-SP (from Oct 2002)

Gulfstream product development included studies announced in September 1988 for a supersonic business jet 10/12-passenger capacity, Mach 2.0 maximum speed and a 4,000-mile range. A cooperative agreement between Gulfstream and the Soviet Sukhoi design bureau was shelved in 1992 but a later project was established with Lockheed-Martin. When they withdrew from the programme in 2000, Gulfstream widened their relationship with Israel Aircraft Industries (IAI) to include a supersonic aircraft. Gulfstream were also involved in the Gulfjet light business jet based on the SA-30 designed by Ed Swearingen. However, in September 1989 it was announced that the cooperation between Gulfstream and Swearingen had ceased. The Swearingen SJ-30 is described separately under the entry for Sino-Swearingen Aircraft.

Hamburger Flugzeugbau   Germany

Hamburger Flugzeugbau GmbH (HFB) was the postwar descendant of the former wartime Blohm und Voss company. In 1961, HFB embarked on the design of the HFB-320 Hansa business jet. The seven-to twelve-seat Hansa had swept-forward wings based on the principles of the wartime Junkers Ju.287 experimental bomber which had been designed by HFB's chief engineer, Hans Wocke. The first prototype (D-CHFB c/n V-1/1001) was flown on 21st April 1964 followed by D-CLOU (c/n V-2/1002) on 19th October 1964.

The first production Hansa, powered by two 2,950 lbst General Electric CJ610-5 turbojets, was delivered in September 1967 and a total of 45 aircraft were completed (c/n 1021 to 1065). Some 14 Hansas had been delivered to the Luftwaffe as transports for the VIP flight and as ECM aircraft. A small number were sold in the United States as executive aircraft but a poor marketing strategy resulted in a disappointing level of acceptance by American business users. Hamburger Flugzeugbau joined the MBB group on 14th May 1969 and the HFB.320 was discontinued shortly after that date.

MBB HFB-320 Hansa

HB Flugzeugbau   Austria

In 1949, the long-standing Brditschka company re-established itself in northern Austria as a manufacturer of jewellery. After a few years, enthusiasm for flying spurred Heinrich W Brditschka to build a Raab Krähe wood-and-fabric powered glider. The single-seat Krähe, designed by Fritz Raab, employed an unusual pusher engine arrange-

ment. The Puch TR.II engine was fitted in the centre fuselage with its propeller turning within a cutout in the fabric-covered rear fuselage. Some eight examples of the Krähe were built with HB-Brditschka GmbH & Co KG providing materials and support in the period from 1946 to 1966.

Brditschka realised the limitations of the Krähe and the possibilities for development as a full-scale light aircraft rather than a powered

Brditschka HB-23 Hobbyliner OE-9328

glider. This led to the design of the HB-3, which was a much-modified Krähe. The monowheel undercarriage was replaced by a fixed fibreglass tricycle gear and the HB-3 had a welded steel tube frame and glassfibre covering. The 40hp Puch engine was retained in the prototype, but the rear fuselage was redesigned with a lower top longeron that served as an axle for the propeller. Brditschka established a new factory at Linz in 1969 and started to build the production HB-3AR powered by a 41hp Rotax 642 two-stroke engine. The HB-3BR, which was the principal variant, benefited from a strengthening of the basic Krähe wing, which was still used. Eight of the HB-3 (c/n 051 and 055 to 061) were built and the prototype was converted to become the MB-E1, powered by an electric motor system designed by Fred Militky. Using the power of Varta batteries and a Bosch motor, the aircraft was first flown in this form on 21st October 1973.

Having marshalled its activities under the name HB Flugzeugbau and operating from a factory at Haid and their own airfield at Hofkirchen the company moved on to the HB-21. This was, essentially, a tandem two-seat HB-3 with a scaled-up wing and fuselage intended as a low-cost answer to the needs of flying and gliding clubs. The first HB-21 was flown in March 1974 and several engine installations were used including a 40hp Rotax and a 60hp Limbach – before HB Flugzeugbau settled on a 50hp Westermayer conversion of the Volkswagen car engine. The definitive production models became known as the Hobbyliner but HB Flugzeugbau (later renamed HB Flugtechnik and known as HB Flug) also built the glider-towing HB-21/2400 Hobbylifter with a 75hp Volkswagen G engine and increased fuel capacity. HB-21 serial numbers ran from c/n 21001 to 21029.

HB Flug's next move was to widen the forward fuselage of the HB-21 to provide side-by-side seating. The resultant HB-23 Hobbyliner had upward-opening gullwing doors and a completely redesigned T-tail. It retained the traditional wooden sailplane wing and glassfibre covering for the fuselage and went into production at Haid in 1984. A production licence was issued to Ciskei Aircraft Industries in Southern Africa who built the first of a batch of HB-23 Hobbyliners. The HB-23 has also been built in modified form as the Scanliner military observation aircraft with a large transparent nose section. HB-23 production totalled 47 aircraft (c/n 23001 to 23047) of which ten were Scanliners (c/n 23003, 11, 12, 13, 21, 23, 24, 28, 37 and 47).

The final development in the HB-23 series was the HB-202. The forward fuselage was largely unchanged, but the vertical tail was redesigned with broader chord and the tailplane is positioned at the base of the fin rather than in the 'T' position. HB Flug changed the wing, moving away from the high aspect ratio sailplane-inspired design. The HB-202 used a 110hp Volkswagen engine driving a five-bladed propeller in a fuselage slot but it was intended that production aircraft would have a 160hp O-320 powerplant although no production was undertaken. HB-23 serials commenced at c/n 23001 and reached c/n 23047. Scanliner serials were in this sequence but were suffixed by an additional 'S' serial (eg, c/n 23047-S9). In recent times, HB Flug has designed the HB-401 which is a Rotax 912 powered four-seater with a similar layout to the HB-202 but with a normal pod-and-boom fuselage with a pusher engine, but no prototype has flown to date. Details of all the Brditschka/HB Flug models are as follows:

Model	Built	Notes
HB-3AR	4	Single-seat powered glider with wooden wing and tube/fibreglass fuselage, fixed tricycle u/c, with one pusher 40hp Puch TR.II engine with propeller turning in fuselage slot. Prototype OE-9023 (c/n 051) FF 1968
HB-3BR	4	HB-3AR with strengthened wings
MB-E1		One aircraft – HB-3AR OE-9023 with Militky-Varta electric engine
HB-4	1	HB-3 fitted with Pilatus B4 wings. OE-9080

HB Flug HB 207 D-EAAJ

HB-21	26	Hobbyliner. HB-21 with 50hp VW-Westermayer engine. Prototype OE-9063 (c/n 21001) FF 22 Mar 1974
HB-21/2400	4	Hobbylifter. HB-21 fitted with 75hp VW-HB-2400-G engine for glider towing
HB-21R		HB-3 with longer tandem two-seat forward fuselage, side-hinged cockpit canopy 14-ft. longer wings with droop tips. 41hp Rotax engine
HB-21L		HB-21 with 60hp Limbach engine
HB-22	1	Single-seat development aircraft for HB-23 with streamlined fuselage, T-tail, retractable u/c and 110hp Renault engine
HB-23/2000	3	Hobbyliner. HB-21 with enlarged fuselage and side-by-side seating, T-tail, gull-wing doors and 2,000 cc. 50hp VW-Westermayer engine. Prototype OE-9200 (c/n 23001) FF 16 Dec 1982
HB-23/2400	34	Hobbyliner. HB-23 with 75hp VW-HB-2400-G engine
HB-23	10	Scanliner. HB-23/2400 with fully-glazed nose section for military surveillance. Prototype OE-9242 FF 1986
HB-202	1	Fledger. Developed HB-23 with redesigned 10-metre short-span wing, low-set tailplane and 110hp Volkswagen engine. Prototype OE-AHB (c/n 202-001)

On 14th March 1995 the company flew the prototype Alfa HB 207 (OE-CHC). This is a low-wing all-metal side-by-side two-seater available with either a retractable tricycle undercarriage (HB 207RG) or fixed gear (HB 207), and either a 110hp Porsche engine or a turbocharged Rotax driving a five-blade propeller. It is manufactured as a kit by HB Flugtechnik and more than 30 were flying by the end of 2004.

HB Flug/Let Mont Tulak 57-NK

In 2003, HB Flug also obtained rights to the LET-Mont Tulak and Piper UL high-wing two-seat ultralight designs produced in the Czech Republic. The Tulak (now named the Cubby) has side-by-side seating and the Piper UL (now named the Dandy) is a tandem-seat version. 31 Cubbys have been built. An adaptation of the Cubby, known as the TUL-03 Amigo, has a fixed tricycle undercarriage, a swept tail and cut-down rear fuselage with a rear vision window. This first flew in May 2003 and only the prototype has been completed (D-MBHB). HB Flugtechnik has also built a prototype of the unconventional HB 204 Tornado (OE-VPP), which has tandem seating and a centrally-mounted propeller that turns in a cutout fuselage slot.

Helio   United States

The remarkable take-off and landing characteristics of the Helio Courier have earned it a unique place in General Aviation. The type was the creation of Dr Otto Koppen and Dr Lyn Bollinger who researched high lift wing design during the early 1950s. Their first prototype 'Helioplane 2' was converted from a Piper PA-15 and first flew on 8th April 1949. This prototype had very short span wings with automatic leading edge slats and dual-purpose aileron/flaps, a lengthened fuselage, redesigned undercarriage and a modified rudder.

Its performance was sufficiently encouraging to prompt the designers to build the four-seat Helioplane Four (N74151) which was a cantilever high-wing tube-and-fabric monoplane powered by a 145hp Continental engine. This incorporated further high-lift modifications and showed outstanding low-speed performance. Helio went on to build three substantially similar tube-and-fabric production prototypes for the definitive model: which was named Helio Courier. The military significance of the aircraft's abilities was soon apparent, so one of these three prototypes was delivered as a YL-24 (military serial 52-2540) to the United States Army for evaluation.

In 1953, the all-metal prototype of the Courier (N9390H c/n 1) made its first flight and this was the first step towards full production of the type. Type certification was received on 5th August 1953 and the first five production aircraft were built in Canada as the Model 391B after which manufacture was moved to a plant at Pittsburg, Kansas. The Model 391B was the first of a series of single-engined Couriers which mainly differed from one another in respect of the powerplant employed. The Courier was used in large numbers by the United States armed forces and its short field performance made it especially useful in Vietnam and in the clandestine Air America operations in Laos.

In 1968, Helio announced the Twin Courier, which used the standard Courier airframe with the nose faired over to incorporate a retractable nosewheel (the main gear remained fixed) and two 290hp Lycomings mounted on the high wing. The production version had a shorter nose and fixed tailwheel undercarriage – and Helio subcontracted production of the centre fuselage to ALAR in Portugal. Licence production in Peru was contemplated but, in the event, only a small number of Twin Couriers was produced at the Pittsburg plant and all of these ended up on the Indian register during service with the CIA in Tibet.

Helio Aircraft Corporation was purchased by General Aircraft Corporation in 1969 and renamed Helio Aircraft Company. The company sought to develop the Courier by fitting a 317shp Allison 250-B15 turboprop engine to the standard H-391 airframe, but the aircraft they finally built was a completely new design named the Helio Stallion. The first prototype Stallion was flown on 5th June 1964. Powered by a Pratt & Whitney PT6A-27 turboprop, this was superficially similar to the Courier, but was much larger with ten-seat capacity and large cargo doors. The development aircraft were designated HST-550 but the production model, the HST-550A, was too expensive for the civilian market. Thus, the majority of production Stallions were delivered to the United States Air Force as the AU-24A under the 'Credible Chase' programme.

In December 1974 it was announced that General Aircraft Corporation was suspending all production, and that the production rights and tooling for the Courier (though not the Stallion) would be sold to John Roberts Ltd The exact outcome of this deal is obscure, but the Type Certificate for the Helio designs did eventually pass into the hands of Helio Precision Products who subsequently, in 1976, sold all the assets to Helio Aircraft Ltd of Pittsburg, Kansas. At about this time General Aircraft decided to take legal action against the United States Central Intelligence Agency on the grounds that they had brought about the

Helio H-295 Courier N99PM

company's financial downfall through a scheme to manufacture copies of the Courier without Helio's permission.

Helio Aircraft Ltd waited until the early 1980s to return to production. They designed a new version of the Courier, which was based on the H-295 Super Courier but with either a 350hp Lycoming flat-six engine or a 400hp Lycoming flat-eight. The Courier 700 and 800 could be operated on either skis or floats in addition to the newly-designed polymer composite land undercarriage. Output totalled eighteen aircraft but production was halted in 1984. One H-800 has been converted with a Vedeneyev M-14-P radial engine. Helio also tested the prototype of a low-wing agricultural aircraft using Courier components during 1982, but this project was abandoned. The business was subsequently acquired by Aircraft Acquisitions who declared their intention of reopening the H-295 line in a factory at Waynesburg, Pennsylvania but failed to get into production. In 1992 Helio Enterprises Inc was formed and the owners of this company formed Alliance Aircraft Group LLC in 1997 to acquire the type certificates and assets remaining from the old business and to return to production of two new versions, the HT-295C and HST-550B, through a new corporation titled Helio Aircraft Company of Bristol, Tennessee. Details of Helio models are as follows:

Helio HT-295 Courier N18JC

Model	Notes
H-391 Courier	Original basic Courier powered by one 260hp Lycoming GO-435-C2 engine. Prototype N242B (c/n 001)
H-391B Courier	Production version of H-391 with 260hp Lycoming GO-435-C2B engine
H-392 Strato Courier	H-391B for high-altitude photography with 340hp Lycoming GO-480-C1D6 engine
H-395 Super Courier	Model 391B with 295hp Lycoming GO-480-G1D6 engine. USAF model U-10A and U-10B
H-395A Courier	Lower-powered H-395 with 260hp Lycoming GO-435-C2B6 engine
H-250 Courier II	Model H-295 with lengthened fuselage and 250hp Lyc O-540-A1A5 engine
H-291	Single prototype Courier, N9757 (c/n 1238)
H-295 Super Courier	Courier powered by one 295hp Lycoming GO-480-G1D6 engine. USAF designation U-10D
HT-295 Super Courier	H-295 fitted with tricycle undercarriage
HT-295C Courier	Proposed new production version of HT-295 with modified u/c and 350hp Lycoming TIO-540-B2D engine. 4,000 lb TOGW
H-500 Helio Twin	Six-seat light twin powered by two 250hp Lycoming O-540-A2B engines mounted on the high wing. Prototype N92860 (c/n 1). Military U-5
HST-550 Stallion	10-seat high-wing monoplane powered by one UACL PT6A-6A turboprop. Prototype N550AA (c/n 001)
HST-550A Stallion	Production HST-550 with UACL PT6A-27 engine. Prototype N9550A (c/n 550A-001) converted from second HST-550 (N10038). Military AU-24A
HST-550B Stallion	Proposed new production version of HST-550A with tricycle u/c, 750shp Pratt & Whitney PT6A-34 turboprop. 6,100 lb TOGW
H-580 Twin Courier	Proposed H-500 with retractable nosewheel and two 290hp Lycoming IO-540-G1A5 engines
H-634 Twin Stallion	Proposed Stallion with two 317shp Allison 250 turboprops mounted on a beam in the nose ahead of the cockpit. Not built
H-700 Courier	H-295 with new undercarriage, wing carry-through structure, upturned wingtips and 350hp Lycoming TIO-540-J2B turbocharged piston engine in new cowling
H-800 Courier	H-700 with 400hp Lycoming IO-720-A1B engine. Prototype N4002M (c/n H-1) FF 24 Mar 1983

Helio HST-550 Stallion N550AA

| H-1201T Twin Stallion | Proposed version of Stallion with two turboprops mounted on underslung wing nacelles, retractable undercarriage, wingtip fuel tanks and wing cargo pods |
| H-21A Rat'ler | Low-wing single-seat agricultural aircraft with H-291 wing and tail, new fuselage with 400 US gal chemical hopper and 400hp Lycoming IO-720-A1B engine. Prototype N4405S (c/n A-1) |

Helio type numbers are generally derived from the horsepower of the engines used. Thus, the H-295 used the 295hp Lycoming GO-480 and the H-500 used two 250hp O-540 engines. This system became modified later when Helio introduced new models with the same horsepower as earlier versions of the Courier.

The serial number blocks allocated to Helio aircraft were:

Model	Built	Serial Batch	Model	Built	Serial Batch
H-250	41	2501 to 2541	H-395	138	502 to 639
H-291	1	1238	H-395A	7	1002 to 1008
H-295	173	1201 to 1295*	H-500	7	1 to 7
H-295		1401 to 1479	HST-550	2	1 to 2
HT-295	19	1701 to 1719	HST-550A	18	001 to 018
H-391	1	1	700/800	18	H-1 to H-18
H-391B	102	001 to 102	H-21A Ag-R	1	A-1
		* Excl c/n 1278	Total	528	

It seems probable that, in addition to the production total of 501 piston-engined Couriers, a significant number of other aircraft were built from spare parts and through the engineering resources of the CIA-sponsored Air Asia. At least 19 ex-military Couriers have been converted to civil configuration, ostensibly for missionary work in South America, by Jungle Aviation and Radio Service of Waxhaw, North Carolina.

A substantial proportion of Helio's production detailed in the serial number table consisted of military orders. Two Model 500s were evaluated as the U-5A and all but three of the Stallions built were military AU-24As. The military Courier variants were:

YL-24	Early model of the H-391 evaluated by the US Army in 1953. Later to US Army Museum, Fort Rucker, Alabama
L-28A	Three aircraft delivered in 1958 as pre-production evaluation models. These were standard H-395s, subsequently designated U-10A
U-10A	Similar to civil model H-395A with 260hp Lycoming GO-435-C2B6 engine and five-seat cabin
U-10B	Similar to Model H-295 with 295hp Lycoming GO480-G1D6 engine, 120 gal fuel capacity and six seats. Some with tricycle undercarriage
U-10D	U-10B with gross weight increased to 3,600 lb

Heliopolis   Egypt

In 1950, the Egyptian Government established Factory 72 of the National General Aero Organisation at Heliopolis near Cairo. One of its first projects was to produce a version of the Bücker Bü.181D Bestmann wartime German trainer for use by the Egyptian Air Force. Known as the Heliopolis Gomhouriya, it was an all-wood aircraft with a low wing, fixed tailwheel undercarriage and side-by-side seating for two in the enclosed cockpit. Some were fitted with a clear sliding canopy, and a version with a tricycle undercarriage is understood to have been tested. Total production was approximately 300 aircraft, some of which were used by civilian flying clubs. A number of military examples have also been sold to private owners in Germany. Several versions were built, as follows:

Gomhouriya Mk 1	Basic version powered by a 105hp Walter Minor 4-III
Gomhouriya Mk 2	Similar to Mk 1 but powered by a 145hp Continental
Gomhouriya Mk 3	Mk 2 with increased fuel and improved brakes and tailwheel
Gomhouriya Mk 4	Mk 3 without the increased fuel capacity
Gomhouriya Mk 5	Fully aerobatic Mk 1 with engine moved forward and small fuel tanks
Gomhouriya Mk 6	Mk 4 with limited aerobatic capability, 145hp Cont O-300 engine

It was intended that the Gomhouriya would be returned to production in 1995 for sale in the USA as the Shadin G.10 Aeropony powered by a

Heliopolis Gomhouriya D-EGBA

145hp Continental O-300D engine and fitted with IFR equipment. The development aircraft was N711TK, which was a reworked Gomhouriya Mk 6. Subsequently, in 1999 this project re-emerged as the KNR Aeropony G-10 and development was carried out with an Egyptian-built aircraft (SU-BNF). The Kader (Heliopolis) factory was scheduled to supply the aircraft in kit form, but it appears this project has collapsed.

HF Dorna   Iran

Tehran-based HF Dorna has started production of its Blue Bird two-seat light aircraft and had completed at least five examples by the end of 2004. It is an all-composite low-wing JAR-VLA two-seater with a fixed tricycle undercarriage, which appears to be a virtual copy of the Tri-R KIS kit aircraft. It is powered by a 115hp Rotax 914-F3 engine.

HF Dorna Bluebird EP-BDP

Hindustan HUL-26 Pushpak VT-DWA. J Wadia

Hindustan   India

Little known outside of India, Hindustan Aircraft Ltd was formed by
Walchand Hirachand on 23rd December 1940 to assemble Harlow
PC-5 trainers and Curtiss Hawk fighters and also as a repair and manufacturing organisation to support the allied forces. It was not until
well after the war that the company entered aircraft manufacture. The
first product was the Hindustan HT-2, which closely resembled the de
Havilland Chipmunk: an all-metal low-wing tandem two-seat trainer
with a fixed tailwheel undercarriage. The first prototype (VT-DFW c/n
HAL/BT/1) was fitted with a de Havilland Gipsy Major III engine for its
initial flight on 13th August 1951 but the other two prototypes and all
production HT-2s used the 155hp Blackburn Cirrus Major III in-line
engine. Starting in 1963, Hindustan built approximately 153 production HT-2s (c/n HAL-T-4 to T-156), which were delivered in quantity to
the Indian Air Force and Indian civilian flying clubs as well as the air
forces of Ghana (12), Indonesia (1) and Singapore (1).

During the mid-1950s a number of Aeronca 11AC and 11CC Chiefs
were imported into India. As a consequence, Hindustan decided to set
up a production line at Bangalore to build the Chief for flying clubs as
the HUL-26 Pushpak and they flew the first example (VT-XAA c/n
HAL/UL-1) on 28th September 1958. The Pushpak used a 90hp Continental C.90 engine and was, in virtually all respects, identical to the
Chief. It appears that 154 production Pushpaks were built (c/n PK.001
to PK.154) before production ceased in 1968.

Hindustan took a licence to build Aeronca's Model 15AC Sedan, two
prototypes of which were built as the four-seat Krishak. This first flew
in November 1959. It was later modified as a general-purpose 2/3-seat
military aircraft for artillery spotting and army liaison as the Kanpur 1
but was renamed the HAOP-27 Krishak Mk II and a small series of 68
examples was then completed by Hindustan for the Indian Army
together with a small batch of the similar Kanpur II which was fitted
with a 250hp Lycoming O-540-A1B5 engine. Hindustan also built the
prototype of a high-wing 10-seat 'Logistic Air Support Transport'
which resembled the DHC-3 Otter and this first flew in September

1960. After studies for a turboprop variant had been carried out the
design was shelved.

Hindustan was principally concerned with military production
including licence-built Aérospatiale Alouette helicopters, the Percival
Prentice, Vampire Trainers, the Folland Gnat and the indigenous Kiran
jet trainer, Marut fighter and HTT.34 primary trainer. However, the
needs of Indian agriculture did result in the Bangalore factory designing the HA.31 crop sprayer, which was first flown in 1969. The HA-31
Mk I performed poorly, and Hindustan redesigned the aircraft as the
HA-31 Mk II Basant (VT-XAO c/n HA-001) with the cockpit repositioned
further aft. It made its maiden flight on 30th March 1972. The Basant
closely resembled the Piper PA-36 Pawnee Brave and had a 2,000 lb
capacity fibreglass hopper situated ahead of the pilot's cockpit and a
low strut-braced wing and fixed tailwheel undercarriage. It was powered by a 400hp Lycoming IO-720-C1B engine and 39 examples were
built from 1976 onwards with serials from c/n HA-004 to HA-023 and
c/n 18501 to 18519.

Hindustan HA-31 Basant VT-XAN. Hindustan

Wolf Hirth   Germany

Wolf Hirth GmbH designed the Akrostar Mk II competition aerobatic aircraft to the requirements of aerobatic champion Arnold Wagner and flew the prototype (D-EMKB c/n 4001) on 16th April 1970. It was a streamlined low-wing aircraft with a fixed tailwheel undercarriage and single-seat cockpit with a full bubble canopy. Construction was largely of wood with ply covering and the mainspar was made of fibreglass. Nine Akrostars were completed by Wolf Hirth (c/n 4001 to 4009). Sold in Germany, Switzerland and Spain, they produced championship performances at international competitions in the 1970s. A single Akrostar Mk III was also built with a lighter airframe and detailed performance-improving modifications.

Hirth Akrostar Mk II HB-MSA

Max Holste   France

Avions Max Holste was originally formed in 1933 and was reorganised at the end of the war with the intention of producing light aircraft for the anticipated demands of peacetime France. The company's first design was the MH.52 – an all-metal two-seater with a side-by-side cockpit covered by a framed canopy with forward-opening doors and fitted with a twin fin tail unit and fixed tricycle undercarriage. The first aircraft was flown on 21st August 1945 and put into small-scale production, including a batch of three machines for Egypt. A variety of engines were used and one aircraft was fitted with a tailwheel undercarriage. Experiments were carried out to fit dual controls for the club trainer market and the company also planned a five-seat version with two 165hp engines (the MH.60) but neither of these developments went further. Serial numbers allocated to the MH.52 aircraft were c/n 01 to 13.

The various models of the MH.52 were:

Model	Built	Notes
MH.52M	2	Initial model powered by one 140hp Renault 4 engine (later changed to 150hp Potez 4D). Prototype F-WBBH (c/n 01)
MH.52G	6	MH.52M with 120hp Gipsy Major I engine
MH.52R	4	MH.52G with 140hp Renault 4P-01 engine
MH.53	1	MH.52G with tailwheel u/c. Named Cadet. F-BEEU (c/n 13)

Holste then built the prototype of the MH.152, which was, essentially, a four-seat high-wing MH.52 with an all-round-vision cabin and tailwheel undercarriage. The original Argus engine in the MH.152 was later replaced by a Turboméca Astazou turboprop, but the aircraft was considered to be too small for the utility role that Holste had in mind. Accordingly, they went into a scaling-up exercise that resulted in the MH.1521 Broussard.

The Broussard had a new slab-sided fuselage with six seats and a 450hp Pratt & Whitney Wasp R-985 radial engine. The first prototype (F-WGIU c/n 01) was flown on 17th November 1952. The main production variant was the MH.1521M for the French Army and Holste produced a total of 318 of this model and a further 52 examples of the civil MH.1521C which had a number of minor refinements and civilian interior trim. The company also experimented with the MH.1522, which was a conversion of an existing MH.1521M (No 10M) with full-span leading-edge slots and double slotted wing flaps to give enhanced short-field performance. The serial number system for Broussards was complicated and four numerical c/n sequences were used in parallel, covering five batches – prototypes, military pre-series, civil aircraft (divided into pre-series and production), military first group and military second group. Civil aircraft (suffixed C) were mixed with military aircraft (suffixed M) on the production line. The two prototypes were c/n 01 and 02 and c/n 03 was a test fuselage. Then followed pre-series military production (c/n 04M to 022M) and civil aircraft c/n 06C and

Holste MH.52R. via Air-Britain

Holste MH.1521 Broussard LX-MAX

07C followed by 1C to 5C, 20C to 45C, 48C and 50C to 53C. The main military batch was c/n 1M to 319M. In total, 376 Broussards were built (excluding prototypes) of which 38 were civil aircraft, 289 were for the Armée de l'Air, 3 were for the Aéronavale and 46 were for the ALAT.

Once involved in the production of Broussards, Max Holste studied a new twin-engined eight-seat 'Broussard Major' with Continental GIO-470A engines. This went no further than the drawing board, but it facilitated a move to the MH.250 Super Broussard, a light 17-seat transport that was flown in prototype form (F-WJDA c/n 001) on 20th May 1959. The French government was sufficiently interested to give Holste a development contract for 10 examples of the improved MH.260 but the company's resources were so stretched that, in October 1959, they entered into a co-production arrangement with Nord Aviation so that manufacture of these aircraft could get under way.

On 16th February 1960, as a consequence of the financial stresses, Cessna Aircraft Company acquired a 49% shareholding in the company, which became the Société Nouvelle Max Holste. This meant that the further development of the MH.260 was handed over completely to Nord. They subsequently developed the design into the Nord 262, which was built successfully for commuter airline and military use. Max Holste was renamed Reims Aviation SA and it embarked on production of Cessna aircraft for sale in Europe and the Middle East. These models are described under the Cessna Aircraft Company entry. In 1989 Cessna sold its interest in Reims Aviation to Compagnie Française Chauffour Investissement who continued low-volume production of the F.406 Caravan II. This was upgraded to F.406 Mk 2 standard with 635shp PT6A-135 engines (in place of the earlier PT6A-112s) and it is now mainly sold as a military aircraft under the name Vigilant and as the Polmar III for surveillance and maritime patrol. By the end of 2004 Caravan II production had reached 91 aircraft (F406-0001 to F406-0091)

Dee Howard   United States

In the post-war period there was a strong demand for fast executive transports to meet the demand of American business organisations. Conversions of piston-engined light bombers such as the On-Mark Marksman and Smith Tempo modifications of the B-26 Invader were a popular choice and the Dee Howard Co of San Antonio, Texas was successful with civil versions of the Lockheed PV-1 Ventura naval patrol bomber.

This led to the Howard 500, which was a new aircraft externally similar to the Ventura but actually only employing outer wing panels from that aircraft. The new longer and deeper pressurized fuselage could accommodate twelve passengers and the aircraft was powered by a pair of 2,500hp Pratt & Whitney R-2800-CB17 radial engines. Dee Howard built 17 examples of the Model 500 (c/n 500-101 to 500-117) but the design was short lived because more modern turboprop-powered designs were already starting to become available, making obsolete the complex, noisy Howard.

Howard 500 N511Y

Humbert Tetras

Humbert Aviation   France

Ets Humbert produces the Moto du Ciel and Tetras ultralights, the majority of which have been sold in the French market. Jacques Humbert designed the Moto du Ciel in 1980. It was a simple open-frame ultralight with a strut-braced high wing, pusher Rotax 582 engine and tandem seating in an open pod cockpit. In 1984 Sté Humbert Aviation was formed at Ramonchamp near Mulhouse in eastern France and the Moto du Ciel went into production with optional Rotax 582, 912 or

912S engines. Production quantities are unknown but it is thought that around 50 have been built to date. The little Tetras light monoplane, which first flew in 1991, is a side-by-side two-seat cabin monoplane similar to the Piper Vagabond with a strut-braced high wing and tailwheel gear. Several different versions are available, in both 450kg ultralight or 472kg JAR-VLA form, including the standard Tetras with an 80hp Rotax 912, the Tetras B with flaps and the alternative HW.2000 engine and the Tetras BS with a 100hp Rotax 912S. Over 100 have been completed, both as kits and factory-complete.

Hungarian Aviation Industry   Hungary

Hungary had a small aircraft manufacturing industry in the 1930s and 1940s, the main indigenous products being the Fabian Levente ('Hero') and the Varga Kaplar parasol-wing trainers and the two-seat M.25 Nebulo low-wing monoplane which was built in quantity by the Muegyetemi Sportrepulo Egyesulet. When the German forces withdrew, the base for the aviation industry was dispersed and Hungary was not designated as an aircraft-manufacturing nation under the planning process for Soviet satellites.

A light aircraft design competition was held in 1948 for the OMRE (Hungarian State Flying Association) which was won by the Samu-Geonczy SG-2 Kek Madar low-wing two-seater (prototype, I-001, first flown on 3rd January 1950) with the Nagy-Cserkuti Botond (a low-wing aircraft which never actually flew) in second place and the Lampich Pajtas HA-BAA, first flown in September 1955) in third place. Unfortunately, this did not lead to any significant production. The most prolific aircraft designer, however, was Ing Erno Rubik. He owned Aero-Ever Ltd, which became nationalised on 25th March 1948

as the Sportarutermelo Nemzeti Vallalat based at Esztergom. Rubik was responsible for the R.15 Koma, R.16 Lepke, R.17 Moka and R.22 Futar gliders together with the more recent R.26 Gobe. He also conceived the R.14 Pinty, which was a single-seat low-wing sporting aircraft powered by a 45hp Continental engine. Erno Rubik's main production powered aircraft was the R.18 Kanya. This was a strut-braced high-wing light aircraft with an enclosed cabin, intended for use as a glider tug and club trainer. It had a cut-down rear fuselage and a rear cabin window to allow a clear view of towed gliders and a tailwheel undercarriage with substantially strutted main legs braced to the engine firewall.

The Kanya, which first flew on 18th May 1949, was powered by a 105hp Walter Minor and the prototype carried the experimental registration I-002 (c/n E-524), although it was later registered HA-RUA. A second prototype (HA-RUB), with minor changes, was designated R-18B but the main production variant was the R-18C which was fitted with a 160hp Walter Major or 160hp M-11R engine and equipped with full glider towing equipment. In total, nine Kanyas were completed, including R-18Cs HA-RUC to HA-RUI.

Hurel-Dubois   France

One of the most distinctive aircraft seen in French skies was the Hurel-Dubois HD.34. Conceived by the Avions Hurel-Dubois SA at Villacoublay-Velizy, the HD.34 resulted from work by Maurice Hurel on very high aspect ratio wings using the tiny single-seat HD.10 research air-

craft (F-BFAN). In 1953, this research resulted in the first flight of the HD-31 (F-WFKU) which was a medium sized high-wing twin-engined transport intended as the forerunner of a range of passenger and freight carrying aircraft. However, the only order was for a mapping and aerial survey machine to be used by the Institut Geographique National (IGN). The long narrow wings of the HD.34 allowed it to

Hurel-Dubois HD.34 F-BHOO

cruise at low speeds for long periods and the IGN found it to be an ideal photo platform. It was powered by two 1,525hp Wright 982-C9 radial piston engines and fitted with a fixed tricycle undercarriage. The

prototype HD.34 (F-WHOO) first flew on 26th February 1957 and was followed by a further seven aircraft (F-BICP to F-BICV, c/n 2 to 8) which served with the IGN until the mid-1970s.

IAR   Romania

The Romanian aircraft industry can trace its origins back to 1906 and, in the years before World War Two, IAR (Regia Autonoma Industria Aeronautica Romana) built a number of light aircraft including the IAR-22 tandem open-cockpit trainer. During the war years, IAR built a range of military aircraft. When peace came and Romania became part of the Soviet bloc IAR was absorbed into a general manufacturing organisation named Sovromtractor.

The first post-war aviation project was licence manufacture of the Zlin 381 version of the Bücker Bestmann. Original designs were then put in hand starting with a small club two-seater, the IAR-811 and, under the design leadership of Radu Manicatide, this was followed by a light twin-engined local service airliner (the MR-2) and then a number of high-wing utility aircraft including the IAR-817 and IAR-818.

IAR operated from three factories. ARMV-1 at Medias and ARMV-2 at Bucharest were overhaul and repair units, while URMV-3 at Brasov was the main manufacturing plant for powered aircraft and gliders. The activities of URMV-3 were separated in 1959 with the engine overhaul and repair activities being transferred to IRMA (the former ARMV-2) at Bucharest-Baneasa while responsibility for all aircraft design and construction was given to ICA (Intreprenderea de Constructii Aeronautice) at Brasov.

Some ten years later, the whole aircraft industry was reorganised and brought under the control of CNIAR (Centrul National al Industriei Aeronautice Romane) with a subsidiary structure of five operating companies including ICA and IRMA. Marketing of Romanian aircraft overseas was handled by a state company known as ICE-CNA (Intre-

prenderea Comert Exterior – Centrul National Aeronautic). One of the main activities of IRMA is the subcontract production of the BN-2 Islander referred to under the section on Britten Norman.

ICA at Brasov embarked on a varied range of utility designs. The most important was the IAR-821 agricultural aircraft, which followed a classic low-wing layout with the chemical hopper between the single-seat cockpit and the engine firewall. It had a fixed tailwheel undercarriage, used a 300hp Ivchenko AI-14MRF radial engine and was constructed of steel tube with fabric and light alloy covering. This design led on to a range of derivatives that were built, largely to meet

IAR-823 N2114Z

IAR-46 HB-2321

domestic requirements, during the period from 1969 to 1982. In 1979 the organisation was redesignated I.Av.Bucuresti and later Romaero SA.

ICA also built a large range of sailplanes, including the IS-28M1, IAR-28MA and IAR-46 powered gliders and the IAR-823 and IAR-825TP military trainers. Numbers built are largely unknown, but the full range of aircraft types produced by ICA is as follows:

Model	Notes
IAR-811	Low-wing side-by-side two-seat cabin trainer with fixed tailwheel u/c, for flying club use, powered by one 60hp Train in-line engine. Prototype FF May 1949. No production
IAR-813	Developed IAR-811 with all-round vision canopy, squared-off tail and 160hp Walter Minor 6-III engine. Prototype YR-IAA FF 1955. 80 examples built
IAR-814	6-seat low-wing light transport with retractable tailwheel u/c, initially designated MR-2. Powered by two Walter Minor 6-III engines. FF 1953. 20 production aircraft completed
IAR-817	Cantilever high-wing light utility aircraft with pod-and-boom fuselage, fixed tricycle u/c and one 160hp Walter Minor 6-III engine
IAR-818	IAR-817 for ambulance, agricultural and light transport duties fitted with 210hp Walter M-337 engine and minor modifications including wing endplates. 104 built plus one IAR-818H seaplane variant
IAR-821	Low-wing single-seat agricultural aircraft with 175-gal hopper and fixed tailwheel u/c, powered by one 300hp Ivchenko AI-14MRF radial engine. Prototype YR-UAC. 20 built, 1966 to 1969

IAR-822 YR-MCD. M J Hooks

Model	Notes
IAR-821B	IAR-821 modified as agricultural trainer with tandem two-seat cockpit, increased fuel and reduced capacity chemical hopper. Prototype only. FF Sep 1968
IAR-822	IAR-821 powered by one 290hp Lycoming IO-540 engine for agricultural work, glider towing, light freighting and fish spotting. 20 built, 1968 to 1972
IAR-822B	IAR-821B with 290hp Lycoming IO-540 engine. 10 built, 1972 to 1974
IAR-823	Four-seat low-wing cabin tourer with retractable tricycle u/c and 290hp Lycoming IO-540-G1D5 engine. Approx 80 built
IAR-824	Six-seat high-wing all-metal utility aircraft with fixed tricycle u/c, swept tail and 290hp Lycoming IO-540 engine developed from IS.23. Prototype YR-ISB FF 24 May 1971
IAR-825TP	Tandem two-seat military trainer developed from IAR-823 with Pratt & Whitney PT6A-15AG turboprop engine. Prototype YR-IGB. FF 12 June 1982. Named Triumf
IAR-826	All-metal version of IAR-822. Prototype YR-MDA
IAR-827	Extensively modified IAR-826 with swept tail, new cockpit with optional mechanic's seat, increased payload and 400hp Lycoming IO-720-DA1B engine. Prototype only, YR-MGA (c/n 01)
IAR-827A	IAR-827 fitted with 600hp PZL-3S radial engine. Prototype YR-MGB. 6 built, 1976 to 1980
IAR-827TP	IAR-827 with 715shp Pratt & Whitney PT6A-15AG turboprop. Prototype YR-MGA
IAR-828	Revised designation for IAR-827TP
IAR-831	IAR-825TP fitted with 290hp Lycoming IO-540-G1D5 piston engine. Prototype YR-IGA. Named Pelican
IAR AG-6	Single-seat all-metal agricultural biplane with fixed tailwheel u/c and one 360hp M14-P radial engine. Prototype YR-BGX
IS-23A	Six-seat high-wing tube-and-fabric utility aircraft with fixed tricycle u/c and 300hp Ivchenko AI-14RF radial engine. Prototype only YR-ISA FF 24 May 1968
IS-24	Initial designation for IAR-824
IS-28M1	Motorised version of IAR IS-28B2 sailplane with T-tail, low-set wing and tandem two-seat cabin, powered by one 68hp Limbach SL.1700E1 engine
IS-28M2	IS-28M1 with side-by-side cabin and conventional twin leg u/c in place of monowheel
IAR-28MA	IS-28M2 with new wing fitted with split flaps and an 80hp Limbach L.2000 E01 engine
IS-29EM	Single-seat version of IS-28MA
IAR-46	Light trainer based on IS-28M2 with shorter span wing and 79hp Rotax 912A engine. Prototype YR-1037

Ibis Ae.270 OK-INA. Ibis Aerospace

Ibis Aerospace   Czech Republic

As a part of its diversification out of dependency on military aviation, the Czech company, Aero Vodochody joined with the Taiwanese company, AIDC to form Ibis Aerospace Ltd to develop the Ae-270 single-engined turboprop aircraft. The Ae-270 is a low-wing aircraft that closely resembles the Pilatus PC-12 and carries nine passengers in high-density layout. Two main versions have been planned – the Ae-270P which is a pressurized nine-passenger or cargo variant with a retractable tricycle undercarriage and an 850shp Pratt & Whitney PT6A-42A turboprop, and the Ae-270W which is a utility version without pressurization and having simplified systems, a fixed undercar-

riage and a Walter M-601E engine. A further Ae-270UP version of the Ae-270U is envisaged with a PT6A powerplant. The prototype Ae-270P, OK-EMA (c/n 001) was built in early 2000 and was followed by two static test airframes (c/n 002 and 004) and two flight test aircraft (OK-SAR, c/n 0003 and OK-LIB, c/n 0005), the second of which is a production standard Ae-270HP with a PT6A-66A engine. It first flew on 25th February 2003. Two further aircraft were used for testing (OK-INA c/n 0006 and OK-EVA c/n 0007). The executive version of the Ae-270P, fitted with winglets, is named Spirit for western marketing purposes. The Ibis partnership was dissolved in October 2004 when AIDC abandoned the project and Aero Vodochody continued on its own.

Ikarus   Germany

Originally formed in 1976, Ikarus (actually Comco-Ikarus GmbH) was one of the largest manufacturers of hang gliders, producing over 2,000 of four separate types. In 1982 they introduced the Ikarus Sherpa: a wire-braced high-wing pod-and-frame three-axis ultralight with two seats side-by-side and a 40hp Rotax 462 engine. This was a two-seat version of the Swiss-designed Gigax Fox and Ikarus also sold the single-seater as the Ikarus Fox. They then developed the Ikarus C 22 which was a tube-and-fabric high-wing design with an enclosed two-seat cabin, a tricycle undercarriage and an 80hp Rotax 912 (or 65hp Rotax 582) engine mounted on the wing centre section above the cabin. This continues to be offered by the Mengen factory as the C 22C and over 740 have been built. In 1995, the company flew the prototype C 42: a strut-braced high-wing 450kg three-axis ultralight built around an alloy tube central spine with glassfibre fuselage cladding and a tube-and-fabric wing. The prototype Ikarus C 42 is believed to have been D-MSOV (c/n 9507-0001). Production commenced in 1996 at c/n 9600-6002 and over 620 had been built by mid-2004, the aircraft being available as a factory-complete aircraft or a kit. The current C 42/B, which has an improved wing, new wingtips, a redesigned engine cowling and a faired undercarriage, is powered by a Rotax 912UL or ULS and the latest version, the C42/B Super Bison has a turbocharged Rotax 914

Ikarus C.42 G-EGGI

engine. Serial numbers for Ikarus production aircraft are prefixed by the year and month of construction followed by the aircraft number. Aircraft numbers are in the 3000 series for the C 22 and the 6000 series for the C42. By July 2004 the company had reached C 42/B c/n 0407-6623 but C 22 production appears to have ceased in 2001 at around c/n 0109-3747.

Ilyushin   Russia

The IL-103 was designed by the Ilyushin Design Bureau as a replacement for the large Russian fleet of Yak-18Ts. Design commenced in 1990 and the first of three prototypes (RA-10300 c/n 01-01) first flew on 17th May 1994. It is a modern low-wing five-seat light aircraft with a fixed tricycle undercarriage, designed to AP-23 Russian certification rules. The IL-103 is powered by a 210hp Continental IO-360ES2B engine and production aircraft are built by the MiG-MAPO factory at Lukhovitsy near Moscow. The first production-standard aircraft flew on 30th January 1995 and first customer deliveries started in 1997 with a batch of six being sold to the Peruvian Air Force. MiG-MAPO has announced three versions although these designations do not appear to be used. The standard VFR version for the Russian Federation is the IL-103-01, the export IFR model is the IL-103-10 and an export VFR-equipped version is the IL-103-11. A retractable gear IL-103RG model has been mooted but has not yet flown. A version with a ski undercarriage has also been tested and other models for basic two-seat training, crop spraying and atmospheric monitoring have been proposed. Aircraft are built in batches of 10 and it appears that four prototype airframes (c/n 01-01 to 01-04) and around 28 production IL-103s (c/n 02-01 to 02-10 and 03-01 to 03-011 and 04-01 to 04-07) had been built by the end of 2004, many being sold to military users including Peru, Bulgaria and North Korea.

Ilyushin IL-103

Indraero   France

The Société Indraero was founded in the early 1950s by Jean Chapeau and J Blanchet, who were active amateur aircraft builders. In 1950, they constructed the prototype of the Aero 101 all-wood open-cockpit two-seat biplane. This first aircraft (F-WBBK c/n 01) was fitted with a 75hp Minie 4DC-32 engine and Indraero received a small production order for the Aero 101 for the Service de l'Aviation Légère et Sportive (SALS). Eleven aircraft were built (c/n 1 to 11). The company also built

one example of the Aero 110 (F-WBBJ), which closely resembled the earlier aircraft but had a steel tube-and-fabric airframe and was powered by a 45hp Salmson 9Adb radial engine.

In the early 1960s, Indraero built prototypes of the Aero 20 tandem two-seat low-wing monoplane (F-PKXY) which was also fitted with a Salmson 9Adb, and the similarly powered Aero 30 (F-PPPA), which was a single-seat biplane with an enclosed cabin and a spring steel tailwheel undercarriage. Neither of these later designs reached production.

Indraero Aero 101 F-PGIC

Interavia   Russia

In 1988, the Russian design organisation, Interavia, designed the 2-seat SL-90 Leshii light aircraft and the prototype first flew in February 1991. In its production version, named the I-1, it had a modified wing with slight forward sweep, a spring steel tailwheel undercarriage and an extensively glazed cabin that has a rear upward-opening hatch for loading baggage or cargo. The production version is sold as a factory-complete aircraft or as a kit and was built by LMZ factory (part of MiG-MAPO) at Lukhovitsy. Versions offered have been the I-1L (also known as the E-1L) with a 140hp Lycoming O-320, the I-1R with a VAZ.4133-10A engine and the SL.39 with the 138hp LOM M332A Other possible powerplants are the three-cylinder 110hp M-3 radial or various American powerplants including the 125hp Continental IO-240. It was proposed that the aircraft should also be built and sold by the Bulgarian company, Aviotechnica but this does not seem to have materialised. It is believed that over 50 aircraft have been built to date.

The I-1 has also been built as the SL-A by the Zhukovsky-based Alpha-M Scientific company who built six examples (c/n 01001 to 01006) powered by the Walter LOM M332A engine. They also marketed a kit-built version designated Alfa A-211 but it is doubtful whether any were sold. Another derivative, apparently only produced as a prototype, is

Interavia I-1L N677A

the SL-39WM. This is fitted with a Walter M332A engine and has an enlarged tail and a tricycle undercarriage. Interavia was also the initial design authority for the Kondratiev-designed I-3 aerobatic aircraft and the Finist utility type, which are described under Technoavia.

Interplane   Czech Republic

The present Interplane sro, based at Zbraslavice was formed as the manufacturing arm of Gryf Development, a small company formed by a group of 16 engineers from the LET Kunovice factory in Prague. Interplane was subsequently acquired by American investor, Ralph Mandarino. Gryf designed and built a small single-seat ultralight aircraft, the Gryf ULM-1 and the prototype, OK-WUC-01 first flew on 17th March 1989. It was to have been powered by a Trabant car engine but eventually used an Astro 600 engine. A small series of Gryfs powered by the Rotax 447 was built by the TIB company at Kolin. It was further developed into the Griffon which was a three-axis single-seater with a pod fuselage fitted with a fixed tricycle undercarriage, a triangulated strut open rear fuselage structure mounting the tail and a pusher 40hp Rotax 447 engine. This has been produced in some numbers and sold in Europe and the USA.

Gryf then designed the side-by-side two-seat Skyboy which has a metal frame based round a main tube spine running from the nose and forming a tailboom which mounts the tail unit. It has a moulded glass-fibre fuselage pod with a fully faired trailing link tricycle undercarriage, a pusher engine and strut-braced metal and fabric high wings. It can be powered by a 56hp Rotax 503DC or a 64hp Rotax 582. The Skyboy EX has an 80hp Rotax 912UL and is not classified as an ultralight due to its higher weight. The Skyboy is available factory-built or as a kit. Serial numbers include the individual serial number followed by the year built and factory-completed aircraft production had reached c/n

Interplane XJ

084/2004 by mid-2004. Including kit-built aircraft, 107 examples were flying in the USA by the end of 2004. In 2005, the Skyboy for American sale was renamed the S-1 Cobra with modified brakes, internal trim and other detailed improvements. In April 2004, Interplane unveiled the Interplane XJ which is similar to the Skyboy but has a nose-mounted engine and modified undercarriage but this project was shelved after a single prototype was completed in favour of an all-composite machine, the S-3 Eagle, which is expected to fly in 2005. Another aircraft built in prototype form is the Gryf P11, which is an all-metal low-wing two-seater with a fuselage similar to that of the Interplane XJ, fixed tricycle undercarriage and a forward-hinged blister cockpit canopy. The Gryf designers have also designed a new line of all-metal two-seaters designated MD-1 to MD-4. The first of these, the strut-braced high-wing MD3 Rider, has been developed for Flyitalia srl. It is a side-by-side 450kg two-seater with foldable wings, a fixed tricycle undercarriage and either a Rotax 912UL or 912ULS engine. The prototype (OK-JUR 06, c/n 001) flew on 25th February 2004 and, by the end of April 2005, eight further aircraft had been built (c/n 002 to 009, including static test c/n 003) by Kunovice-based Aerospool. Of these seven have been sold to Italian customers.

Interplane Skyboy N2069V

Flyitalia MD3 Rider OK-KUR 07

Israel Aircraft Industries   Israel

Following its acquisition by Rockwell Standard, Aero Commander Inc embarked upon the design of the Model 1121 Jet Commander twin-engined business jet. It was seen as a natural step-up aircraft for owners of the Grand Commander/Courser and the turboprop Turbo Commanders with similar internal capacity and general design. It had a straight, tapered, mid-set wing positioned at the rear of the cabin section, a cruciform tail and two General Electric CJ610-1 turbojets mounted on the rear fuselage. The first test example of the Jet Commander was flown in early 1963 and the definitive version with a 2.5-inch fuselage stretch received its type certificate (A2SW) on 4th November 1964 and went into production at Bethany.

In 1967 North American Aviation and Rockwell were merged. This prompted a review by the United States Justice Department under anti-trust legislation which ruled that Rockwell was in an unduly dominant position in the business jet market through ownership of both the Jet Commander and the Sabreliner – and one of the designs should be terminated. Rockwell decided to sell the Jet Commander in view of the long-term military support commitment posed by the T-39A Sabreliner and, in 1967, the whole Model 1121 production line was offered as a going concern.

The only serious potential acquirer was Israel Aircraft Industries Ltd, originally formed in 1952, which was active in aircraft overhaul and repair and had built Slingsby sailplanes and a large batch of Fouga Magisters for the Israeli Air Force. They had also done design studies on the Bedek B.101 business jet – but had abandoned this project. IAI acquired the Jet Commander in September 1967 and production commenced at Lod in mid-1968 once the necessary tools and jigs had been installed. At this point, Aero Commander/Rockwell had completed some 150 airframes (c/n 1 to 150) including the prototype and a static test airframe. Some of these were incomplete and IAI used them to start the new production line. These were sold in the United States as 'Commodore Jets'.

IAI developed an updated version of the Jet Commander designated IAI-1123 Westwind with a longer fuselage, more powerful CJ610-5 engines, wingtip fuel tanks, a larger stabiliser and wing modifications to improve slow-speed performance. Two Jet Commanders were used as Model 1123 prototypes and the first Westwind delivery took place in September 1972. Production ran from c/n 151 to 186 after which a further 40 of the Model 1124 Westwind with Garrett TFE731 turbofans were built (c/n 187 to 236). The 1124 was later fitted with additional internal fuel capacity and known as the Westwind I – and was supplemented by the even longer range Westwind 2 which used a new 'Sigma' wing section and was distinguished by the winglets fitted to the tip tanks. Both of these models are included in the same serial number sequence – which ran from c/n 237 to 442.

The successor to the Westwind was the IAI-1125 Astra which only bears a superficial resemblance to the original Jet Commander. The Astra has a swept wing using the Sigma section technology and this is mounted beneath the fuselage rather than centrally – thus improving cabin volume and giving the Astra very economical high-speed/long-range performance. The Astra went into production in 1985 and, from 1997 marketing was handled by Galaxy Aerospace (which was a joint venture between the Hyatt Corp/Prtizker family and IAI). From c/n 42 the aircraft became the Astra SP with improved range and speed and a new Collins autopilot and EFIS. In mid-1994 IAI flew the first Model 1125A Astra SPX (4X-WIX c/n 073) which had greater speed and range and was fitted with uprated Allied Signal (formerly Garrett) TFE731-40R-200G turbofans, a new interior and small wingtip winglets. In 2001, Galaxy Aerospace was acquired by General Dynamics and incorporated into their Gulfstream Aerospace subsidiary with production continuing at IAI in Israel. The Astra SPX was rebranded as the Gulfstream G100. To date, 148 Astras have been built, comprising three prototypes (c/n 01, 02 and 04), a static test airframe (c/n 03), 30 Astras (c/n 011 to 040), 37 Astra SPs (c/n 041 to 072 and 074 to 078), 66 Astra SPXs (c/n 073 and 079 to 145 – less 139 and 142) and 11 Gulfstream 100s (c/n 139, 142 and 146 to 154). A development of the Gulfstream 100, designated Gulfstream G150, with a wider fuselage and modified nose/cockpit section is under development and first flew on 18th May 2005.

IAI announced their IAI-1126 Astra Galaxy (initially the Astra IV) in September 1992. Initially a cooperative project with Yakovlev Aircraft it is a transatlantic mid-sized business jet powered by two 6,040 lbst

Pratt & Whitney PW306A engines with a standard 8-passenger executive interior or maximum 18-passenger corporate shuttle capacity. The prototype (4X-IGA, c/n 003) made its first flight on 25th December 1997 and a second prototype (c/n 004) followed on 21st May 1998. Two further airframes were used for static tests (c/n 001 and 002). Following certification in December 1998 the aircraft was marketed by Galaxy Aerospace and approximately 52 had been built when the aircraft was rebranded as the Gulfstream G200. By mid-2004, 100 aircraft had been completed (c/n 005 to 104). The gross weight of the G200 was reduced from c/n 52 onwards in order to improve its range. IAI continues to manufacture the G200 and G100 and will build the new G150.

Details of all executive jet models from Aero Commander, IAI and Gulfstream are as follows:

Model	Built	Notes
1121 Jet Commander	119	8/10-seat mid-wing business jet built by Aero Commander/ Rockwell. Two 2,850 lbst General Electric CJ610-1 turbojets, 17,500 lb TOGW. Prototype N610J (c/n 1) FF 27 Jan 1963
1121A	11	Unofficial designation for improved 1121 with better wheels and brakes, modified fuel system and upgraded interior
1121B Commodore Jet	16	1121A with 2,950 lbst CJ610-5 engines, 18,500 lb TOGW, stronger u/c
1121C Commodore Jet	3	1121B with 18,500 lb TOGW and extra rear fuselage tank. Built by IAI
1122		Proposed 1121 developed by Aero Commander with system changes. Two test aircraft only. No production
IAI 1123 Westwind	36	1121B built by IAI with 20,700 lb TOGW, 3,100 lbst CJ610-9 engines, wingtip fuel tanks, high lift wing with double slotted flaps and drooped leading edges, fuselage stretched 22 inches with entry door moved forwards and two extra cabin windows. Test a/c 4X-COJ (c/n 29) FF 28 Sep 1970
IAI 1124 Westwind	50	1123 with 3,700 lbst Garrett TFE731-3-1G turbofans, improved systems, avionics, u/c and wing leading edge and dorsal fin fairing. 23,500 lb TOGW
IAI 1124 Westwind I	116	1124 with additional 101 US gal long-range fuel tank

IAI-1124A Westwind N53WW

IAI 1124A Westwind 2	90	1124 with further wing mods, winglets on tip fuel tanks, new autopilot. Prototype 4X-CMK (c/n 239) FF 24 Apr 1979
IAI 1125 Astra	33	9/11-seat business jet based on 1124 with new low-set swept wing, deeper fuselage, longer cabin, 23,500 lb TOGW (opt. 24,650 lb) and two 3,650 lbst Garrett TFE731-3B-100G turbofans. Prototype 4X-WIN (c/n 01) FF 19 Mar 1984. Astra SP has improved wing, new autopilot and EFIS, new interior. Astra SPX has TFE731-40R-200G turbofans, revised interior and winglets
IAI 1125A Astra SPX	66	1125 with increased speed/range, Allied Signal (formerly Garrett) TFE731-40R-200G turbofans, FADEC, new interior & avionics and wingtip winglets. Prototype 4X-WIX (c/n 073) FF 18 Aug 1994
G100	11	Gulfstream version of Astra SPX
G150	1	G100 with wider fuselage and modified forward fuselage and flightdeck
IAI 1126 Astra Galaxy	52	Mid-size 8-pax business jet with low-wing, cruciform tail, retractable tricycle u/c and two rear-mounted 6,040 lbst Pratt & Whitney PW306A turbofans. Prototype 4X-IGA (c/n 003) FF 25 Dec 1997
G200	42	Gulfstream version of Galaxy

At about the same time that IAI introduced the Model 1123 it also started production of the IAI-101 Arava light utility transport. This was a classic strut-braced high-wing twin-boomed aircraft with a circular section fuselage and a fixed tricycle undercarriage. The prototype (4X-IAI c/n 002) was first flown on 27th November 1969. It could accommodate 20 passengers and a crew of two but was primarily viewed as a military freighter – for which purpose it had a hinged rear fuselage for cargo loading. The IAI-101 was powered by a pair of 715shp Pratt & Whitney PT6A-27 turboprops but the production IAI-102 was upgraded to the 783shp PT6A-34. The IAI-101B, which had an improved interior and better hot and high performance, had PT6A-36 engines. IAI's largest volume model was the IAI-201 military version and they also produced the IAI-202, which was longer and fitted with a wet wing and large dual wingtip winglets. By mid-1994, IAI had built two IAI-101 prototypes (c/n 002 and 003), a static test airframe (c/n 001) and 101 standard production Aravas (c/n 003 to 103). The majority of these have been for military customers, including Thailand, Colombia, Venezuela, Ecuador, Guatemala, Mexico, Honduras and El Salvador, although a number of civil deliveries were made including several to the United States.

Issoire Aviation   France

On 1st February 1978 a new company, Issoire Aviation, was established to acquire the assets of Wassmer (see separate section) and it set up operations at Issoire building E-75 and D-77 gliders and providing support for Wassmer aircraft in the field. However, no further production of the Wassmer powered aircraft line was undertaken. In 1995, Issoire Aviation was acquired by Rex Composites and it continues to manufacture the APM-20 Lionceau two-seat club trainer. The Lionceau was designed by Philippe Moniot, General Manager of Issoire Aviation and a specialist in composite construction. The prototype, F-WWMP, was first flown on 21st November 1995 and JAR-VLA certificated on 17th

May 1999. It is constructed, principally, from carbon fibre and has a side-by-side two-seat cockpit with a large sliding canopy and a fixed tricycle undercarriage. The production standard aircraft has a larger tail unit than the prototypes and higher useful load. The Lionceau is fitted with an 80hp Rotax 912A with a fixed pitch propeller but can use engines of up to 120hp There have been four development aircraft (c/n 01 to 04, of which c/n 02 was a static test airframe) and a further nine production examples (c/n 5 to 14) had been completed by mid-2004. The APM-21 Lion is a further development which is fitted with a 98hp Rotax 912ULS and the original prototype has been converted to this standard.

Issoire APM-21 Lion F-WWMP

Itoh N-62 Eaglet JA3255. P R Keating

C Itoh   Japan

The Itoh N-62 Eaglet four-seat light aircraft has its origins in research carried out by the Nihon University under Dr Hidemasa Kimura. The university's students developed a new STOL wing and tested this on its N-58 Cygnet (JA3133) which was based on a Piper Tri Pacer airframe and first flew on 28th November 1960. The Cygnet, which was built by C Itoh Aircraft Maintenance and Engineering Co (a subsidiary of the C Itoh industrial conglomerate), had a 140hp Lycoming O-290-D2 engine. This led to a new original design – the N-62 – which used the new strut-braced wing and had an all-metal airframe with a fixed tricy-

cle undercarriage and a 160hp Lycoming O-320-B2B engine. The prototype (JA3216) made its first flight at Chofu Airport near Tokyo on 8th August 1964. Japanese type approval was awarded on 17th December 1965 and a production line was set up by C Itoh. Several versions were planned including the two-seat N-62-100 with a 100hp Continental, the N-62-160 (Lycoming O-320) and the N-62-250 with a 250hp engine. The first production N-62-160 Eaglet (JA3251 c/n 0101) flew on 23rd October 1965 and it was claimed that five Eaglets had been completed by the end of 1966 although only two further examples have been identified (c/n 0102 and 0103). Production ceased at this point and none of the N-62s are still airworthy.

Jodel   France

Jodel low-wing club training and touring aircraft have been built by many individuals and companies since the early 1950s. The name Jodel is a contraction of the names of the test pilot (Edouard Joly) and his son-in-law, the designer, Jean Delemontez. Their company, Société des Avions Jodel based at Beaune, was formed as a design bureau and a provider of plans for the many Jodel variants. Separate details of specific commercially produced models are given under each of the main manufacturers, but the main Jodel variants have been as follows:

Jodel DR.1050 D-EBFE

Model	Builder	Notes
D.9 Bébé	Amateur	Single-seat low-wing open-cockpit monoplane with upturned outer wing panels and fixed tailwheel u/c, powered by one 25hp Poinsard engine. Prototype F-WEPF FF 21 Jan 1948
D.91 Bébé	Amateur	F-WEPF re-engined with 34hp ABC Scorpion engine
D.92 Bébé	Amateur	D.9 powered by one 27hp. or 45hp. Volkswagen
D.921 Bébé	Amateur	D.9 powered by one 40hp Hepu
D.93 Bébé	Amateur	D.9 powered by one 35hp Poinsard
D.94 Bébé	Amateur	D.9 powered by one 35hp Minie
D.95 Bébé	Amateur	D.9 powered by one 44hp Echard Lutétia
D.96 Bébé	Wassmer	D.9 powered by one 25hp Dyna-Wassmer Panhard
D.97 Bébé	Amateur	D.9 powered by one 32hp Sarolea Vautour
D.98 Bébé	Amateur	D.9 powered by one 25hp AVA-40-A.00
D.99 Bébé	Survol	D.9 powered by one 32hp Mengin 2A
D.10		Projected three-seat Jodel with new wing
D.11	Various	Two-seat enlarged version of D.9 with enclosed cockpit and 45hp Salmson 9ADb engine. Prototype F-WBBF FF 4 Apr 1950
D.111	Amateur	Jodel D.11 powered by one 75hp Minie 4DC engine. FF 8 May 1950
D.112	Various	D.11 powered by one 65hp ContA65 engine. Principal variant of D.11 as built by Wassmer, SAN, Valladeau, Denize, Dormoy and amateur constructors
D.112A	Wassmer	D.112 fitted with air brakes
D.112T	Amateur	D.112 fitted with tricycle u/c
D.113	Amateur	D.11 powered by one 100hp Continental O-200-A

SAN-Jodel D.117 G-BIOU

D.114	Amateur	D.11 powered by one 70hp Minie 4DA.28
D.115	Amateur	D.11 powered by one 75hp Mathis 4-GF-60
D.116	Amateur	D.11 powered by one 60hp Salmson 9ADR
D.117	SAN	D.11 powered by one 90hp Continental C90 and fitted with revised electrical equipment
D.117A	Alpavia	Alpavia-built D.117
D.118	Amateur	D.11 powered by one 60hp Walter Mikron II
D.119	Amateur	Mainly amateur-built equivalent of D.117. D.119D produced by Valladeau
D.119T	Amateur	D.119 fitted with tricycle u/c
D.120	Wassmer	Wassmer equivalent of D.117. Named Paris-Nice
D.121	Amateur	D.11 powered by one 75hp Continental A75
D.122	Amateur	D.11 powered by one 75hp Praga engine
D.123	Amateur	D.11 powered by one 85hp Salmson 5AP.01
D.124	Amateur	D.11 powered by one 80hp Salmson 5AQ.01
D.125	Amateur	D.11 powered by one 90hp Kaiser 4K
D.126	Amateur	D.11 powered by one 85hp Continental A85
D.127	E.A.C.	D.112 with sliding canopy and DR.100 u/c
D.128	E.A.C.	D.119 with sliding canopy and DR.100 u/c
D.1101	Amateur	D.11 powered by one JPX.2050
DR.100	SAN/CEA	Ambassadeur. Four-seat D.112 development. See SAN, Robin
DR.105	SAN/CEA	Ambassadeur development. See SAN, Robin
DR.1050	SAN/CEA	Ambassadeur development. See SAN, Robin
D.12		Delemontez design for tandem two-seat low-wing trainer
D.13		Delemontez design for four-seat low-wing aircraft with 140hp Renault 4PO-2 engine and retractable u/c
D.140	SAN	Mousquetaire. Four-seat touring aircraft. See SAN
D.150	SAN	Two-seat trainer/tourer. See SAN
D.160		Six-seat tourer planned by SAN but not built
D.18	Amateur	Two-seat lightweight Jodel design with hinged canopy and one 58hp Volkswagen engine
D.19	Amateur	D.18 fitted with tricycle u/c
D.20 Jubilé	Amateur	Two-seat lightweight Jodel with tricycle or tailwheel u/c and 85hp JPX-4T engine
DR.200	CEA	Development of DR.1050M. See Robin
DR.220	CEA	Two-seat trainer. See Robin
DR.250	CEA	Four-seat development of DR.200. See Robin
DR.251	Amateur	Four-seater similar to DR.250
DR.253	CEA	Enlarged DR.250 with tricycle u/c. See Robin
DR.300	CEA	Range of 3/4-seat tricycle u/c aircraft developed from DR.200/DR.253. See Robin
DR.400	CEA	Improved DR.300 models with forward sliding cockpit canopy. See Robin
D.1190S	A.S.A.	D.119 built in Spain by Aerodifusion SA 68 built (c/ns E.56 to E.123)
U.2V	Uetz	D.119 with non-cranked wing. See Uetz
U2-MFGZ	Uetz	Uetz-built D.119

Johnson   United States

Johnson Aircraft Inc was formed by R S 'Pop' Johnson in 1944 to develop the Rocket 185 high-performance light aircraft. This was a development of the Swift, which Johnson had built in 1940 and later became the Globe Swift. Johnson fell out with the owners of Globe and left at an early stage to build a new prototype named the Rocket (NX41674). This closely resembled his original machine and had a tailwheel undercarriage and a fully-enclosed side-by-side two-seat cabin. It had a fabric-covered tube fuselage, wooden wings and a 185hp Lycoming O-435-A engine. NX41674 made its first flight in mid-1945. The definitive Johnson Rocket (NX41662), which was more streamlined and had tricycle gear, was certificated on 9th October 1946 and the first deliveries were made later that year. 19 examples were built at Fort Worth, Texas (c/n 1 to 19) but sales were poor and the company was taken over and renamed Rocket Aircraft Inc. No further

Johnson Rocket NC90204

Rockets were built and the type certificate (A-776) passed into the hands of J C Pirtle.

In 1950 The Aircraft Manufacturing Company produced a refined version of the Rocket known as the AMC Texas Bullet 205. It was a full four-seater and in addition to its higher-powered 205hp Continental E185-1 engine it differed from the Rocket in having a redesigned vertical tail and a metal covered fuselage and a lower gross weight. The prototype was N72404 (c/n 101) and five further Bullets were completed (c/n 102 to 106) before production was abandoned. Attempts were later made by the Gem Aircraft Co to revive the Bullet but no further production occurred and the type certificate (4A2 awarded on 20th November 1950) was acquired by Richard P Schutze.

AMC Texas Bullet 205 N78852

Jordan Aerospace Industries — Jordan

This company was established in 2001 and has undertaken manufacture of a number of existing designs under licence. The Sama-CH2000 is a licence-built version of the Zenair-designed CH2000 Alarus, the first example of which flew on 14th December 2003. Jordan Aerospace Industries (JAI) obtained an initial order for four aircraft for the Middle East Flight Academy. The company is also licensed to build the Remos G3 ultralight, which it markets as the RaLi. Another ultralight produced by the company is the all-metal X-32 RumBird which was originally designed by the Lilienthal company in the Ukraine and is built by them as the X-32 Bekas. This is a tandem two-seater of pod-and-boom construction with a fixed tricycle undercarriage and a Rotax 582, 618 or 912 pusher engine. A three-seat version is known as the Gulf Bird X-32T. JAI has launched the Hawk-I, which is a Zenair CH.801 powered by a Lycoming O-360 or LOM M.332 engine and also sells a range of small gyrocopters including the Vortex S Copter, the Sea S Copter, the Barq S Copter and the Vortex 2S Copter. It is not known how many of any of these aircraft have been built.

Kappa 77 — Czech Republic

Kappa 77 AS was established in 1991, operating from Jihlava. Their first aircraft was the KP-2U Sova which is an all-metal side-by-side two-seat light aircraft with a 450kg gross weight to allow it to come within ultralight rules. It has a low wing with Fowler flaps and retractable tricycle undercarriage and is powered by an 80hp Rotax 912UL engine. The prototype (OK-BUU 230) was first flown on 26th May 1996. By mid-2004 the company had sold 156 aircraft including 24 for the domestic market, 16 to Holland, 18 to Germany, 19 to the USA, 29 to Italy, 5 to Finland, 4 to South Africa, 4 to Poland, 7 to Spain, 16 to France, 2 to Brazil, 1 to Ecuador, 3 to Portugal and 8 to Australia. In 2004, Kappa 77 became insolvent and was taken over by Jihlavan Airplanes who have relaunched the Sova as the KP-2U Rapid with a redesigned engine cowling and new cockpit canopy. The company has been developing a single-seat aircraft designated KP-4 and has also introduced the KP-5 which is a 544kg KP-2U with a fixed tricycle undercarriage and ground-adjustable propeller to meet American Sport Aircraft requirements. The prototype is N225KP (c/n 5100115J). A JAR-VLA version of the KP-2U is designated KP-6. The c/n system used by the company is unclear.

Kappa 77 Sova OK-FUU 54

Krunichev T-411 Aist RA-01585

Krunichev   Russia

The design of the T-411 utility aircraft was initiated in September 1992 by Aeroprogress. The first T-411 flew on 10th November 1993 and the production prototype (RA-01585) was first flown on 15th August 1997. Another T-411 was produced in 1994 as a kit for an American private owner ('N01522') and named the T-411 Wolverine. The T-411 is a strut-braced high-wing aircraft built of steel tube with fabric and light alloy covering with a fixed spring-steel tailwheel undercarriage and a large five-seat cabin with a rear baggage compartment and external

hatch for air ambulance operations. It is powered by a Voronezh M-14P radial engine. Responsibility for development of the T-411 Aist was taken over by Krunichev and they have produced two further prototypes – the T-411 Turbo which is an Aist with a Walter M.601B turboprop engine and the T-415 Snegir (RA-01522) which is a strengthened six-seat utility aircraft based on the T-411 airframe. Krunichev also manufactures parts for the Sherpa utility aircraft, which was designed and is marketed in the USA as a kit by Sherpa Aircraft. Sherpa Aircraft also sells the T-411 in the USA as a kit and at least three had been imported by the end of 2003 (believed to be c/n 63101 to 63103).

Lake   United States

Colonial Aircraft Corporation was formed in 1946 at Sanford, Maine by David B Thurston and Herbert P Lindblad. Both men had been employees of Grumman working on the G-65 Tadpole two-seat amphibian (NX41828) which was first flown in December 1944. When this project was discontinued, Thurston and Lindblad designed the three-seat Colonial C-1 Skimmer. This showed great similarity to the G-65 although it employed a novel pylon-mounted engine installation in place of the Grumman's integral pusher engine housing. The XC-1 Skimmer flew for the first time on 17th July 1948 and the Type Certificate (1A13) was awarded on 19th September 1955. Colonial quickly started a production line and the first delivery was made in 1956. The initial batch of 150hp Skimmers totalled 24 units and then Colonial changed to the higher-powered C-2 that had four seats. After building a further 18 aircraft, Colonial went into bankruptcy in 1959 and production ceased.

In 1960 Lindblad formed a new company, Lake Aircraft Corporation to acquire the assets of Colonial. Under his guidance, the G-2 was extensively altered. An existing C-2 (N261B c/n 121) was modified and flown in November 1959 as the LA-4P with a 48-inch increase in wingspan. This was followed by two similar LA-4As that had improved rear wing attachments and a strengthened wing carry-through structure. Lake then went into production with the LA-4 and built a number of variants as shown in the data table.

Lake's poor financial condition resulted in its being taken over by Consolidated Aeronautics Inc in 1962. They formed a marketing division entitled 'Lake Aircraft Division' and Aerofab Inc, at Sanford, Maine to build the Lake LA-4. Herb Lindblad subsequently acquired Aerofab, but sold it to Armand Rivard, (who also acquired the type certificate for the Lake designs) in September 1979. Lake built the basic aircraft at Sanford, Maine; painted and finished them at nearby Laconia, New Hampshire; and marketed them from both Laconia and Kissimmee, Florida. In August 1983, Lake gained certification for the enlarged LA-250 Renegade, which had a stretched fuselage and larger cabin and an increase in power. The standard LA-4 was phased out in 1987 and the LA-250 and LA-270, together with the military Seawolf, remained in production until 1993 when the production line was closed.

In 2001 there was an abortive acquisition of Lake by Archedyne, linked to the NauticAir 450 amphibian project, but in September 2002 the Lake companies were acquired by Wadi Rahim's LanShe Aircraft who also acquired Micco Aircraft. They intended to market the aircraft through Sun Lake Aircraft in Florida and use a new company, ManAero to take over manufacture from Aerofab. Two LA-270s were completed from existing components (c/n 235 and 236): the first (a SeaWolf) being delivered to the Galapagos Islands for coastal patrol and the second being a SeaFury. Additionally, the company announced that the LA-4-200EP would be returned to production. However, LanShe ran into financial trouble in April 2004 and production has been suspended.

Lake LA-250 N1402C

Serial numbers given to the Lake series as at June 1992 have been:

Model	Built	Serial Batch	Model	Built	Serial Batch
XC-1	1	1	LA-4-200	614	463 to 1076
C-1	24	2 to 25*	LA-200EP/EPR	41	1077 to 1118
C-2	18	126 to 143	LA-250	131	1 to 130 plus 234
LA-4A	2	244 to 245	LanShe LA250	2	235 & 236
LA-4-180	217	246 to 462	Seawolf	7	SW101 to SW107

* C/n 15 and 21 converted to Model C-2 with new c/ns 115 and 121. C/n 410 was LA-4S.

Details of Lake models are as follows:

Model	Name	Notes
XC-1		Three-seat light amphibian with retractable tricycle u/c, cruciform tail and one pusher 125hp Lyc O-290-D engine mounted on pylon above fuselage centre section. Prototype NX6595K (c/n 1) FF 17 July 1948
C-1	Skimmer	Colonial-built production version of XC-1 powered by a 150hp Lycoming O-320-A2A engine
C-2	Skimmer IV	Model C-1 with four seats, 180hp Lycoming O-360-A1A engine in redesigned mounting, modified horizontal tail and floats
LA-4P	-	Model C-2 with 4ft wingspan increase, enclosed nose u/c recess, new hydraulic system and detail changes. Prototype N261B (c/n 121) FF Nov 1959
LA-4A	-	LA-4P with strengthened wing mainspar and modified wing attachment points
LA-4S	-	Pure seaplane version of LA-4 with 211 lb useful load increase. One aircraft N7637L (c/n 410)
LA-4T	-	LA-4 with Rayjay-supercharged Lycoming O-360-A1D engine. One aircraft, N7637L
LA-4-180	-	Production LA-4A with 180hp Lycoming O-360-A1A
LA-4-200	Buccaneer	LA-4 with 200hp Lycoming IO-360-A1B engine. Wing root trailing edge fairings eliminated
LA-200EP	-	LA-4-200 with extended propeller shaft, redesigned engine cowling and exhaust manifolds, large aft wing root fairings and Lycoming IO-360-A1B6 engine
LA-200EPR	-	LA-200EP with reversible 2-blade Hartzell prop
LA-250	Renegade	LA-4 with 38-inch fuselage stretch, six-seat cabin, swept vertical tail, starboard cabin entry hatch, and a 250hp Lyc IO-540-C4B5 engine. Prototype N250L (c/n 1)
LA-250	Turbo Renegade	LA-250 fitted with 250hp turbocharged Lycoming TIO-540-AA1AD engine
LA-270	Turbo Renegade 270	Turbo Renegade with engine uprated to 270hp
LA-250	Seawolf	Military/governmental LA-250 with strengthened wing with four hardpoints, engine-nacelle-mounted radar and 290hp Lycoming TIO-540 engine. Prototype N1402J (c/n 19)
LA-270	Seafury	Renegade/Turbo Renegade for salt-water operation with improved corrosion proofing and survival gear stowage compartment and hardened interior

Lake LA-4-200 N5052L

Lancair Columbia 300 N143LC

Lancair   United States

The Lancair Columbia is manufactured by The Lancair Company, which was formed by Lance Neibauer as a separate organisation from Lancair International Inc that supplies the kit-built market. The original kit/homebuilt Lancair goes back to June 1984 when Neibauer made the first flight of his Lancer 200 (N384L) powered by a 100hp Continental O-200 engine. This was a fibreglass aircraft with a retractable tricycle undercarriage and a fully enclosed side-by-side two-seat cabin. Neico Aviation was formed at Redmond, Oregon in 1985 to build the aircraft and the main model to be sold was the Lancair 235, which had flown as a prototype in September 1985 and was powered by a 160hp Lycoming O-320. This was later supplemented by the Lancair 320 and the Lancair 360, which uses a 180hp Lycoming.

Lancair also developed the Lancair IV. This first flew in 1990 and is a four-seater with a 350hp Continental TSIO-550-B engine and a retractable tricycle undercarriage. The Lancair IV design led to the less demanding four-seat Lancair ES, which first flew in July 1992. This was a simplified Lancair IV, built from epoxy/glass composites, with a larger wing, fixed tricycle undercarriage and a 210hp Continental IO-360-ES engine. Lancair International has sold over 200 kits for the ES and the optional Super ES is also available with a 300hp IO-550G engine. More than 2,000 Lancair kits have been sold.

It was the Lancair ES design that formed the basis for the production factory-complete Lancair Columbia. The prototype LC-40 Columbia 300 first flew in early 1996 and it has a similar airframe and the same fixed undercarriage as the 'ES but is powered by a 310hp Continental IO-550-N. It has a modern cockpit with sidestick controls and modern avionics. The Lancair Company was established at Bend, Oregon and Lance Neibauer sold Lancair International (the kit operation) to Joseph C Bartels. The first certification test prototype LC-40 (N140LC, c/n 4001) first flew in early 1997. The first customer delivery of a Columbia was made in 1999 and this first model was designated Columbia 300 (Lancair LC40-550FG). In 2002, Lancair also announced the Columbia 350 (Lancair LC42-550FG), which is a Columbia 300 with all-electric systems. The other Columbia model is the Columbia 400 (Lancair LC41-550FG), which was certificated in April 2004. It is a version of the Columbia 350 with a 310hp turbocharged Continental TSIO-550 engine and a 200 lb gross weight increase (to 3,600 lb).

Despite a financial hiatus in 2002, Lancair has geared up its production and during 2004 the company delivered 28 Columbia 350s and 50 Columbia 400s. At the end of 2004 production totalled 210 aircraft and had reached c/n 40078 (Columbia 300), c/n 41069 (Columbia 400) and c/n 42063 (Columbia 350). In July 2005, The Lanair Company changed its name to Columbia Aircraft Manufacturing Corporation.

Laverda   Italy

The motor scooter manufacturer, Laverda, took over production of the F.8L Falco from Aeromere in 1964. Their version was the F.8L Falco IV, otherwise known as the 'Super' and built with a 160hp Lycoming O-320-B3 engine. 20 were completed (c/n 401 to 420) between 1964 and 1968 and these were the last production versions of the popular Frati design.

Learjet   United States

The name Learjet has come to be a generic term for any and all business jets. The name comes from William P Lear – a prolific inventor whose achievements included the first successful car radio, the first eight-track stereo system, navigational radio systems and direction finders for general aviation aircraft. Bill Lear formed the Radio Coil and Wire Corporation in 1962, created the Motorola Corporation and founded Lear Siegler – before setting up Lear Inc In the mid-1960s, this company became known for its conversions of Lockheed Lodestars to executive Learstar configuration. In 1960, Bill Lear publicly announced his most famous development – the Learjet. He had sold out his interest in Lear Inc for $ 14.3 million and 'retired' to Switzerland where he conceived the design of a small jet business aircraft and, in November 1959, set up the Swiss-American Aircraft Corporation. The SAAC-23 Execujet was inspired by the single-seat FFA P-16 (P-1604) fighter which had been flown in prototype form by the Flug und Fahrzeugwerke AG on 28th April 1955.

Lear moved back to the United States to set up development and production of his Lear Jet and settled on Wichita, Kansas as the base for operations. In October 1963, the prototype Lear Jet Model 23 made its first flight from Wichita's Mid-Continent Airport. This aircraft

Learjet 40 N40LJ. Bombardier

crashed during testing in the following June but, nevertheless, the type certificate to FAR. Part 3 was granted on 31st July 1964. Lear Jet Corporation quickly put the Model 23 into production, and with a price much lower than the competing Falcon it was an immediate success. However, it did gain a reputation for being very demanding for the average pilot and much of the later Learjet development concentrated on improvement to the low-speed handling characteristics of the type following an initial rash of accidents.

The Model 23 was replaced by the Model 24 in 1966. This had an airframe that was virtually identical to that of the Model 23 but it was certificated under FAR Part. 24, allowing the gross weight to be raised to 13,500 lb. It was soon joined on the production line by the stretched Model 25 with maximum of ten seats – still powered by General Electric CJ610 engines. Both were offered in alternative long-range versions with reduced passenger capacity. Bill Lear also designed the Model 40 Lear Liner, which came very close to the specification adopted by Grumman for the Gulfstream II, but this project was discontinued as financial pressures increased.

In 1966, the name of the company was changed to Lear Jet Industries and on 10th April 1967, the Gates Rubber Company bought a controlling interest. The Learjet was undoubtedly successful, but enormous operating losses had built up. The 1966 acquisition of Brantly Helicopters and the development cost of the Twinjet Helicopter (an aircraft of Sikorsky S-76 size) only served to fuel the financial crisis. On 2nd April 1969, Bill Lear resigned as Chairman of the Board. He went on to develop the LearAvia steam-powered car, the Learstar 600 (later to become the Canadair Challenger) and the revolutionary Learfan – before his death on 14th May 1978.

Gates renamed the company Gates Learjet Corporation and, in 1969, sold Brantly to Aeronautical Research and Development Corporation. Increasing pressure from the environmentalist lobby and competition from the Cessna Citation now prompted the company to refit the Learjet with turbofan engines. This resulted in the Models 35 and 36 – both based on the Model 25 with a small fuselage stretch and a pair of Garrett TFE731 engines. Following the previous formula, the

Model 35 was a short-range aircraft and the Model 36 was its long-range sister. In practice, the Model 35 outsold the Model 36 by two-to-one because the five-hour endurance of the long-range model was more than most customers required.

The next major development for the Learjet was the introduction of the 'longhorn' wing – first tested on a Model 25, N266GL (c/n 25-064) and a Model 24, N682LJ (c/n 24B-218). The NASA-designed supercritical wing was fitted with winglets at the tips – and as a consequence all fuel had to be internally housed due to the deletion of the wingtip tanks. The first aircraft to be fitted with the production wing was the Model 35 prototype, N351GL and the production versions were the Models 28 and 29 – respectively short- and long-range variants. Very few were built – largely because there was relatively little performance gain and the cost of wing manufacture was high.

The Longhorn wing was mainly intended for the new, larger, Model 54/55/56 series of Learjets. These aircraft were designed to combat criticism about the small Learjet cabin. They were scaled-up versions of the previous types with a stand-up cabin capable of carrying up to ten passengers. Most orders were for the mid-range Model 55, and the Model 54 and 56 designations were later abandoned. The final version was the Model 55C, introduced in 1988 with 'delta fins' mounted on the lower rear fuselage to improve low-speed handling but this has now been replaced in production by the Model 60. Also introduced at the same time was the Model 31 which was a Model 35 with delta fins and the Longhorn wing, aimed at users stepping up into jet aircraft for the first time.

Learjet's latest aircraft is the completely new Model 45, which was announced in September 1992. It falls between the Model 31 and the Model 60, and features a redesigned wing and a larger fuselage than the Model 31. The Model 45 made its first flight in 1995 and it received full FAA certification in May 1998 with first deliveries taking place in July of that year. Major production takes place at Short Bros in Belfast with final assembly in Wichita. It has been joined by the Model 40, which is a shortened Model 45 (the prototype Model 45 being converted to serve as the Model 40 prototype). The 6-passenger Model 40 replaces the Model 31A and was certificated on 11th July 2003.

Learjets have been delivered to a number of governmental operators and have been used for target towing, high-altitude mapping and photography. Air forces that have bought Learjets include Bolivia, Ecuador, Argentina, Mexico, Peru and Yugoslavia. The US Air Force has acquired Learjet 35As, designated C-21A, for communications, medical evacuation and high-priority cargo duties to replace their obsolete T-39A Sabreliners. Records achieved by Learjets include the round-the-world flight of the Model 36, N200Y, in May 1976 when Arnold Palmer and Jim Bir travelled 22,985 miles in 57 hours, 25 minutes. A number of special conversions have been carried out on Learjets, particularly the Dee Howard XR modification that includes a new swept-wing centre-section, wing leading edge, and engine pylons so as to improve high-speed performance, increase useful load and give longer range.

In 1979, Gates Learjet relocated a significant part of its production in Tucson while continuing with some completion, service and marketing functions in Wichita. With the slow-down in the business jet market, Learjet sales fell and Gates came under pressure over the financial position. On 22nd August 1986, Gates announced that it would sell its stake in Gates Learjet to M J Rosenthal & Associates for $ 62.7 million. This deal collapsed later in 1986 and, in December Cobey Corporation announced that it would acquire Learjet. This transaction also failed and was followed by abortive deals with AVAQ Investments and Interconnect Capital. Finally, on 5th August 1987 it was confirmed that Integrated Resources would be the new owner of Learjet and this led to the moving of all production from the Tucson factory back to Wichita. In mid-1989 a financial crisis in its property businesses forced Integrated Resources to seek buyers for Learjet once again. On 29th June 1990, it was acquired by the Canadian company, Bombardier Inc and the name was changed to Learjet Inc and later to Learjet Corporation. It is now referred to as Bombardier Aerospace Learjet.

Learjet serial numbers are all prefixed with the exact model number (eg, 24F-337) and each major model has its own unique series of serials. In a few cases additional serials have been added on the production line. The batches allocated have been as follows:

Model	Built	Serial Batch	Notes
23	105	23-001 to 23-099	Also c/n 015A, 028A, 045A, 050A, 065A, 082A. Some converted to Model 24
24 & 24A	81	24-100 to 24-180	Model 24 and 24A, mixed
24B	49	24B-181 to 24B-229	
24D	99	24D-230 to 24D-328	
24E & 24F	29	24E-329 to 24F-357	Model 24E and 24F, mixed
25	64	25-001 to 25-064	c/n 25-065 to 25-069 not built
25B & 25C	136	25C-070 to 25B-205	Model 25B and 25C, mixed
25D	168	25D-206 to 25D-373	
28	5	28-001 to 28-005	
29	4	29-001 to 29-004	
31	38	31-001 to 31-034	Also c/n 033A, 033B, 033C and 033D
31A	208	31-035 to 31-242	
35	66	35-001 to 35-066	
35A	610	35A-067 to 35A-676	
36	17	36-001 to 36-017	
36A	47	36A-018 to 36A-064	
40	12	45-2002 to 45-2013 up	Current Production
45	254	45-001 to 45-254 up	Current Production
55	126	55-001 to 55-126	Includes two Model 55ER
55B	8	55B-127 to 55B-134	
55C	13	55C-135 to 55C-147	
60	33	60-001 to 60-275 up	Current production
Total	2,172		

A detailed list of models built by Learjet is as follows:

Model	Notes
23	Original Learjet to FAR.3 with 12,500 lb TOGW, powered initially by two CJ610-1 turbojets then, from c/n 23-028, by CJ610-4. 8-place max seating. Prototype N801L (c/n 23-001) FF 7 Oct 1963. w/o 4 Jun 1964
24	Model 23 certificated to FAR 24. Redesigned tip tanks and thicker windshield, new engine fire control system and 13,500 lb TOGW. CJ610-4 engines. 11 aircraft converted from Model 23 to Model 24 or 24A. FF 24 Feb 1966

Learjet 25XR N225TJ

Learjet 60. Bombardier

24A	Model 24 with optional 12,499 lb TOGW at lower fuel load
24B	Model 24 with 13,500 lb TOGW and revised systems and interior. Powered by 2,950 lbst CJ610-6 engines. Model 24B-A has 12,500 lb TOGW
24C	Economy Model 24B with no fuselage tank and reduced range and performance. Three rectangular windows each side, no tail 'bullet' fairing, 12,499 lb TOGW
24D	Model 24C with 13,500 lb TOGW and increased range
24	24B with modified cambered wing and reduced stall speed powered by two CJ610-8A engines
24F	24E with additional fuselage fuel tank and 18% longer range
25	Stretched Model 24 with CJ610-6 engines and 52-inch fuselage plug to give 10-place interior. Prototype N463LJ (c/n 25-001) FF 12 Aug 1966
25B	Model 25 without tail 'bullet' fairing and four rectangular cabin windows each side. 910 US gal fuel capacity
25C	Long-range Model 25B with shorter passenger cabin and additional fuselage fuel tank to give max. 1,103 US gal fuel capacity
25D	Model 25B with CJ610-8A engines, and new wing to improve short field and low-speed performance. FAR.36 noise standard approved. 15,000 lb TOGW
25E	Not built. 'E' suffix not used due to 'Economy' implication
25F	25D with eight-place seating and increased fuel and range
25G	Model 25D with 16,300 lb TOGW, higher range and wing modifications
26	Proposed Model 25 with TFE731 engines. Not built. Became Model 35/36
28	Model 25D with supercritical wing, no tip tanks and Whitcomb winglets. 10-place seating. Operating ceiling raised to 51,000ft. Prototype N9RS (c/n 28-001) FF 21 Aug 1978
29	Long-range version of Model 28
31	Model 35 with Model 55 wings incorporating winglets (but without tip tanks) and rear fuselage delta fins. Powered by two TFE731-2 turbofans. Five port and six starboard cabin windows. Max range 1,202nm. Prototype N311DF (c/n 31-001) FF 11 May 1987
31A	Model 31 with new EFIS cockpit and avionics, FBW ground steering, increased (Mach 0.81) speed. Replaced Model 31 in mid-1991
31A/ER	Model 31 with additional fuel to give 1,526nm range
35	Model 25 with 13-inch fuselage stretch, increased wingspan and two Garrett TFE731-2 turbofans. 17,000 lb TOGW. Eight-seat cabin with various window

	arrangements (max. six starboard, five port windows). Prototype N26GL (c/n 26-001) FF 9 Jan 1973
35A	Model 35 with redesigned wing resulting in better short field and low-speed handling
35ZR	Learjet 35 modified by Raisbeck Engineering with inboard wing cuffs, wingtip fairings, modified flaps
36	Long-range Model 35 with six-seat cabin, increased fuel, 18,000 lb TOGW. Japanese ASDF version, U36A
36A	Model 36 with same wing modifications as Model 35A
40	Original model was Lear Liner project. Not built
40	Replacement for Learjet 31A. Based on Model 45 with 24.5-in shorter fuselage, smaller rear fuselage fuel tank, 6-seat main cabin, 7 windows each side. Prototype N40LX (c/n 45-001) FF 31 Aug 2002
45	Mid-sized redesigned Learjet with 8-passenger main cabin, eight windows each side, 20,500 lb TOGW and two 3,500 lbst TFE 731-20AR turbofans. Prototype N45XL (c/n 45-001) FF 7 Oct 1995
45XR	Higher-performance Model 45 with Honeywell TFE731-20BR turbofans
54	Enlarged Learjet with 10-passenger cabin using Model 28/29 wing married to new fuselage and powered by two Garrett TFE731-3-100B engines. Short-range version of 50 series with 866 US gal fuel
55	Main production 50 series. Similar to Model 54 with 1,001 US gal fuel capacity. Powered by two 3,700 lbst TFE731-3A turbofans. Prototype N551GL (c/n 55-001) FF 19 Apr 1979
55B	Model 55 with electronic flight instrumentation, new autopilot, increased gross weight, systems changes and thrust reversers
55LR	Model 55 with seven-passenger cabin and 1,141 US gal fuel capacity
55XLR	Model 55 with six-passenger cabin and 1,231 US gal fuel capacity
55C	Model 55B with delta fins similar to those on Model 31 and redesigned engine pylons. Also Model 55C/ER with 2,079nm range and 55C/LR with 2,052nm range. Discontinued 1991 and replaced by Model 60
60	10-passenger development of Model 55C with 43-inch fuselage stretch, two 4,600 lbst Pratt & Whitney PW.305 turbofans, electronic FBW ground steering etc. Prototype N60XL (c/n 55-001) FF 13 June 1991. Replaced Model 55 in 1992

Leopoldoff   France

The little Leopoldoff biplanes with their tandem open cockpits have been a significant part of the French light aviation scene for many years. The L-3 was originally designed in 1932 as an economical private and club machine by M L Leopoldoff, a Russian emigré. Powered by a 35hp Anzani engine this aircraft (F-ANRX c/n 01) first flew at Toussus-le-Noble on 27th September 1933. The production Colibri was built by Aucouturier-Dugoua & Cie and, later, by the Société des Avions Leopoldoff and some 33 were completed – fitted with the 45hp Salmson 9Adb radial engine. The L.31 was an L-3 retrospectively fitted with a 50hp Boitel 5Ao engine, and the L.32 had a Walter Mikron III.

After the war, the Colibri continued in production with the Société des Constructions Aéronautiques du Maroc who built six aircraft under the designation CAM-1, and the L.53 and L.55 were variants with minor alterations and the 75hp Minié and Continental C.90 engines respectively. Serial numbers of production L-3 series Colibris ran from c/n 2 to 33 and the L.5 series were c/n 1 to 8.

Leopoldoff L-55 Colibri F-PRJJ

LET (Letecky Narodny Podnik) Czech Republic

As mentioned under the section covering Aero, responsibility for the Aero 45 light twin was passed over to LET in 1951. The initial LET version was the Aero Ae-45S Super. It was similar to the Ae-45 but had a 200kg-higher gross weight in order to allow for full IFR instrumentation and some internal refinements together with changes to the cabin and window structure. As a consequence of this the performance and range suffered somewhat. A total of 228 aircraft was built.

The Aero Ae-45S was followed by 142 examples of the Super Aero 145, which used a pair of 140hp Walter M-332 engines. This improved the performance of the aircraft and permitted larger tanks to give greater range. The rudder of the Aero 145 was slightly enlarged. In addition, the Aero 145 was built in China by the Kharbin Engineering Works. They flew their prototype of the 'Yungari No 1 Nokadaun' in 1958 and it had a stepped windscreen and longer cabin than the standard Super Aero.

LET used a batch serial system for their production of the Aero series with a prefix indicating the batch number followed by a serial number. Aero 45S batches generally contained around 16 aircraft with serial numbers falling into the range c/n 01-001 to approximately 13-016. Serial numbers of the Ae-145 were c/n 14-001 to approximately 20-020 (although the 17- batch of serials included an extra '2' digit: eg, 17-2003).

By 1955, LET was well into production of the Super Aero and there was a clear need for a more modern replacement for use as an air taxi and to meet a Soviet requirement. This emerged as the L-200 Morava – an all-metal low-wing design with a retractable tricycle undercarriage, domed cabin structure with a door on each side and twin tail fins. Accommodation consisted of two front seats and a three-passenger rear bench. A large port-side rear-fuselage hatch was also provided to allow a stretcher to be loaded. Part of the Morava's fuel capacity was contained in wingtip tanks. The prototype XL-200 (c/n XL-001) carried the initial identity '300' and was later registered OK-LNA. Equipped with two 160hp Walter Minor 6-III in-line engines, it was first flown on 9th April 1957.

With some detail modification this went into production at Kunovice as the L-200. However, it was concluded at an early stage that the Morava was underpowered and, after building an initial pre-series batch of L-200s, LET (later renamed SPP – Strojirny Prvni Petiletky) re-engined it with 210hp M-337 engines in which form it was built as the L-200A from 1960 onwards. A further refinement came with the L-200D, which differed from the L-200A in having electrically-driven V-506 constant-speed propellers and an increase in useful load. A large number of Moravas were supplied to Aeroflot and some of these were operated on skis during the winter.

SPP also tested a prototype of the six-seat L-210 Morava (OK-PHB c/n 170814) which used 245hp M-338 engines and considered a developed Morava (the L-300) with a fully integrated cabin. The second prototype (OK-LNB c/n XL-003) was converted into the experimental E-33 with a T-tail and an engine in the rear cabin for boundary layer experiments. However, none of these developments resulted in new production variants.

SPP built two Morava prototypes (c/n XL-001 and XL-003), a static test airframe (XL-002) and ten pre-series L-200 aircraft (c/n 00-001 to 00-010). Thereafter, they built 160 of the L-200A and 197 of the L-200D in batches of approximately 30 aircraft. Serial numbers consisted of the prefix '17' followed by the 2-digit batch number and an individual 3-digit serial number. These ran from c/n 1701001 to c/n 1714030. A small batch of five L-200D Moravas was assembled from kits in Yugoslavia by LIBIS with serial numbers c/n 301-01 to 305-05.

The Brigadyr in its agricultural role was a compromise and by 1960 it was clear that a dedicated cropsprayer was required in Czechoslovakia. The first design proposed by the VZLU (Vyzkumny a Zkusebni Letecky Ustav) was the XL-36, a low-wing aircraft with a belly-mounted hopper, but this was abandoned in favour of the SPP-designed XZ-37 which had its hopper mounted in the fuselage immediately behind the cockpit. The Z-37 Cmelak had a low wing with dihedralled outer panels, fixed tailwheel undercarriage and provision for a second mechanic's seat facing rearwards in the back of its enclosed cockpit. The hopper area could be used to carry light freight if necessary and, for ease of maintenance, construction was tube-and-fabric.

The Cmelak went into production as a joint venture between Moravan and SPP in 1966 and output continued until 1977. The production line at Kunovice was reopened in 1981 to build a further batch of 40 piston-engined Cmelaks. Subsequently, the Otrokovice factory of Moravan went into production with a turboprop model – the Z-37T Agro Turbo. The variants of this versatile aircraft were as follows:

LET Z-37 Cmelak OM-OJN

XZ-37	Low-wing agricultural aircraft with fixed tailwheel u/c, powered by one 310hp Ivchenko AI-14VF radial engine. Prototype OK-60 (c/n 00-01) FF 29 June 1963
Z-37	XZ-37 fitted with 315hp Walter M-462RF radial engine and 143-gal hopper
Z-37-2	Z-37 with hopper replaced by second cockpit fitted with dual controls for agricultural pilot training. Named Sparka
Z-37-2C	Z-37-2 with twin rear passenger seats. 2 aircraft only
Z-37A	Z-37 with strengthened airframe, improved systems and improved corrosion-proofing
Z-37A-2	Tandem two-seat trainer version of Z-37A
Z-37C	Z-37 fitted with 300hp Continental IO-520-D flat-six engine. FF 9 Sep 1967
XZ-37T	Z-37 fitted with 690shp Walter M-601B turboprop, increased TOGW and 2ft-longer fuselage. Prototype OK-145 FF 3 Sep 1981
Z-37T	XZ-37T with 485shp Motorlet M-601Z turboprop, wingtip winglets and large dorsal fin fairing. Named Agro Turbo. Prototype OK-072 FF 12 Jul 1983
Z-37T-2	Z-37T trainer with second cockpit equipped with dual controls in place of hopper behind main seat. Prototype OK-RJO
Z-137T	Revised designation for Z-37T
Z-237	Revised designation for Z-37-2
Z-437	Z-37 with twin rear-facing rear seats. Named Kurier. Prototype only OK-UJG (c/n 009P)

Serial number of Cmelaks started with a batch of six prototypes (c/n 00-01 to 00-06) and then ran from 1966 to 1977 in batches of approximately 30 aircraft from c/n 01-07 to 25-26 with a production total of 713 piston-engined aircraft. These batches included 26 two-seat models. Output of Agro Turbos ran from c/n 001 to the most recent production aircraft at c/n 0044.

In 1966, LET designed the 15-passenger XL-410 utility aircraft and light feederliner. This flew in the spring of 1969 and, as the LET-410A Turbolet, entered production at Kunovice. While initial production aircraft went to the domestic operator, Slov-Air, the main production was for Aeroflot and these deliveries started in 1972. Early L-410As used the Pratt & Whitney PT6A turboprop but, in 1974 the L-410M, powered by the Walter M-601 was introduced. 1979 saw the Turbolet updated as the L-410UVP with a larger fuselage and tail, dihedralled tailplane, longer-span wing and improved systems including an anti-skid braking system, automatic pitch trim and a modified propeller feathering system. It was widely used for freight operations, sport parachuting, navaid calibration, mapping and survey and an ambulance variant with room for 6 stretcher cases. The subsequent Let-410UVP-E featured increased fuel capacity and a 19-passenger interior.

LET L-200D Morava D-GULL

LET Super Aero 145 OM-NHS

The Turbolet continued in production well into the 1990s but the Eastern Bloc economic hiatus resulted in production of the LET-410 coming to a close at the beginning of 1996. The company continued to develop the LET-420 version of the Turbolet. In August 1998, the American company, Ayres Corporation acquired a 93.6% interest in LET-Kunovice and intended to market the LET-410 and the larger LET-610 in the USA. They also intended to produce major components of the Ayres LM-200 Loadmaster at Kunovice. This restructuring failed to meet its objectives and LET was declared bankrupt in the wake of Ayres' own problems. LET was subsequently acquired by Moravan.

Serial numbers for the LET-410 followed the standard eastern bloc system including the year built and the production batch with an individual aircraft serial. The prototype Let XL-410 was c/n 69001 (the year built, 1969, plus the batch, 00, and the individual aircraft identity, 01) followed by four prototypes. Production aircraft started in 1971 at c/n 710101 with most production batches containing twenty aircraft and the last L-410M having serial number c/n 781120. With introduction of the L-410UVP, LET started a new series of batches with production aircraft starting at c/n 770101. By 1994, L-410UVP production had reached Batch 27 (922730) although the Kunovice factory completed a number of additional airframes for later completion when orders are received. In detail, the Turbolet models were as follows:

Model	Name	Built	Notes
XL-410		5	High-wing 15-pax civil or light tactical military transport with retractable tricycle u/c, cruciform tail and powered by two 715shp Pratt & Whitney PT6A-27 turboprops. 11245 lb TOGW. Prototype OK-YKE (c/n 690001) FF 16 Apr 1969
L-410A	Turbolet	30	Initial production L-410 for max 19-pax with PT6A-27 engines, seven (instead of eight) cabin windows each side, port rear pax/cargo door and minor changes. 11905 lb TOGW
L-410AB	Turbolet		L-410A fitted with 4-blade Hartzell propellers
L-410AF	Turbolet	1	One L-410A (HA-YFA) with nine cabin windows each side and extended glazed nose for aerial photo-survey work
L-410AS	Turbolet		L-410A with avionics as required by Aeroflot
L-410M	Turbolet	115	L-410A with two 550shp Motorlet M601A turboprops
L-410FG			Special military version for Czech AF. Also L-410T
L-410MA	Turbolet		L-410 with two 730shp. M601B engines
L-410MU	Turbolet		L-410M with avionics & equipment required by Aeroflot
L-410UVP	Turbolet	950	L-410M with 19-in fuselage stretch, enlarged wing with spoilers, larger vertical tail and dihedralled tailplane, anti-skid braking, prop auto-feather and improved cockpit systems. Prototype OK-166 (c/n 770001) FF 1 Nov 1977
L-410UVP-E	Turbolet		L-410UVP with wingtip fuel tanks, four extra seats and repositioned toilet, improved systems, increased flap deflection and 750shp M.601E engines with 5-bladed Avia V.510 propellers. 14110 lb TOGW. Sub-variants designated UVP-E1, UVP-E2, UVP-E3, UVP-E4, UVP-E9, UVP-E20 etc depending on customer
L-410UVP-E20		1	L-410UVP-E with two 778shp Motorlet M.601F engines, central point refuelling, auto beta-range propeller locks, and Bendix-King avionics. 14550 lb TOGW. Prototype OK-150 FF 15 Nov 1993. Redesignated L-420
L-420			Revised designation for L-410VP-E20
L-430			Proposed L-410UVP-E with PT6A turboprops and increased weights

LET L-410UVP Turbolet UR-67439

Liberty Aerospace

United States

In September 1992, Ivan Shaw's Europa homebuilt light aircraft made its first flight in the United Kingdom and over 1,000 kits had been sold by 2004 when the Europa company went into receivership. The Europa was a high-performance all-composite two-seater that could be fitted with long-span glider wings and had a retractable monowheel undercarriage or an optional fixed tricycle gear. In 1997, Ivan Shaw sold Europa to new owners and started the design of a new two-seat private aircraft that was broadly based on the Europa and would be built and certificated in the USA. The Liberty XL-2 is a low-wing aircraft with a gross weight of 1,575 lb, side-by-side seating for two and a fixed tricycle undercarriage. It has a composite fuselage and tail and metal wings and is powered by a 125hp Continental IOF-240 engine, although an alternative XL-2R version with the 100hp Rotax 912S is also available. The Rotax-powered prototype, N202XL (c/n 0001P), first flew at Montrose, Colorado on 2nd April 2001 followed by two development aircraft (N203XL c/n 0002P and N204XL c/n 0001). Early plans were for the manufacture of the XL-2 to be handled by Scaled Technology Works but this company ceased business in 2002 and Liberty moved operations to Melbourne, Florida. The XL-2 received its

Liberty XL-2 N204XL

approved type certificate in February 2003 but difficulties with new production arrangements resulted in first deliveries being delayed until April 2005, at which time production had reached c/n 0005.

LIBIS

Yugoslavia

One of the mainstays of club flying in Yugoslavia during the 1950s and 1960s was the LIBIS Matajur. LIBIS was a new company formed by the amalgamation of the Institu LZS Branko Ivanus and the Letalski Konstrukcijski Biro at Ljubljana. The all-wood low-wing Matajur was similar in appearance to the Druine Condor and was built in the following versions:

KB-6D Matajur	Side-by-side two-seat club trainer with fixed tailwheel u/c and sliding bubble canopy. Powered by one 136hp Regnier 4L00 engine. Prototype FF 4 Jun 1952
KB-6T Matajur	Matajur Trised – production model with third rear seat. Powered by 160hp Walter Minor JW6-III engine. 8 aircraft built
LIBIS-160	KB-6T with swept vertical tail and minor structural changes. No production
LIBIS-180	LIBIS-160 with 185hp Lycoming O-435-1. Production total believed to be 11 (c/n 289-09 to 299-19)

Using much of the design layout of the Matajur, LIBIS went on to design a four-seat model, the KB-11 Branko. The prototype Branko (YU-CGE) was flown in December 1959. It was an all-wood aircraft with a low wing, retractable undercarriage and a 185hp Lycoming O-435-1 engine. A total of four Brankos were completed (including the prototype). In addition, LIBIS, which had become the Letalski Institut Branko Ivanus in 1960, formed an association with the Czech SPP company and built a batch of five L-200 Moravas from kits supplied from Czechoslovakia.

LIBIS KB-11 Branko YU-CNB

Lockheed JetStar -6 N198DL

Lockheed   United States

The immediate post-war production effort of Lockheed Aircraft Corporation was entirely concentrated on military training and combat aircraft for the Korean War and the highly successful Constellation and, later, Hercules transports. In early 1957, however, the Georgia company announced that it was developing a small twin-jet transport to meet the US Air Force's UCX requirement. The first of the two prototype L-1329 JetStars (N329J c/n 1001 and N329K c/n 1002) was first flown on 4th September 1957. It had a ten-passenger maximum capacity and was powered by a pair of Bristol Orpheus turbojets mounted on the rear fuselage. This method of fitting jet engines had been introduced on the Caravelle but was, nevertheless, highly unusual at the time.

The two JetStar prototypes were tested extensively and, during this period, acquired large wing slipper fuel tanks. In 1959, N329J was fitted with four Pratt & Whitney JT12A turbojets fitted in paired nacelles. This raised the combined thrust of the JetStar's engines from 9,700 lbst to 12,000 lbst and the production JetStar was built to this specification. The type certificate (2A15) was issued on 28th August 1961 and first deliveries to customers started in September with aircraft being delivered to the United States Air Force as well as to commercial purchasers.

A total of 16 C-140 JetStars reached the USAF for use as VIP aircraft (C-140B) and for navaid calibration (C-140A). The initial civil JetStar was the L-1329-23A JetStar Dash-6 with JT12A-6 or the L-1329-23D with JT12A-6A engines. However, from the 97th aircraft (N300L c/n 5097) the higher-powered JT12A-8 engines were fitted and the type was known as the L-1329-23E JetStar Dash-8. Serial numbers of JT12A powered JetStars ran from c/n 5001 to 5162.

On 18th August 1976, Lockheed flew the prototype L-1329-25 JetStar II (N5527L c/n 5201) which had the JT12A turbojets replaced by four TFE731-3 turbofans. This went into immediate production at Atlanta with the first aircraft being delivered to Esmark Corporation. The last JetStar was delivered on 23rd April 1980 and the line was closed, with 40 examples of the JetStar II having been built. JetStar II serial numbers ran from c/n 5201 to 5240.

A number of JetStars have been converted to turbofan power by AiResearch and are known as JetStar 731s. In addition, American Aviation Industries of Van Nuys, California developed the FanStar which was fitted with two 9,150 lbst General Electric CF34-3A high bypass turbofans. The prototype (N380AA c/n 5131) made its first flight on 5th September 1986.

Luscombe   United States

The post-war Luscombe monoplanes originated with the Luscombe Phantom, which first flew in 1934. This all-metal two-seater was created by Donald A Luscombe who had formed his own company, the Luscombe Airplane Development Corporation, to build a high-performance machine for the discerning flyer. In practice, there were few private owners who could afford the sophisticated Phantom and only 22 production units left the factory (c/n 101 to 108 and 110 to 123). It was followed, in 1937, by the simpler and less expensive Model 90 (otherwise known as the Luscombe 4) and four (c/n 401 to 404), together with the prototype (NX1017), were built before the lighter and cheaper Luscombe 50 (Luscombe Model 8) was offered to the market in 1938.

The Model 8 had an all-metal structure with strut-braced, fabric-covered wings, a fixed tailwheel undercarriage and a variety of engines.

Renaissance Luscombe 8F N999RA

Luscombe 11A Sedan N1625B

During the years 1938 to 1942, some 1,112 production examples of the Luscombe 8A to 8D were built. Serial numbers were in the 800 series (which was intended to be an indicator of the type number, just as the Luscombe 4 had started at c/n 400). The two prototypes were c/n 800 and 801 and production aircraft ran from c/n 803 to c/n 1923 – but some serial numbers were not used (eg, c/n 806, 827, 829, 830, 834, 922, 1134, 1263, 1321). With the entry of the United States into the war, Luscombe was forced to cease production and concentrate on output of components for other military aircraft and the ownership of the company passed out of the hands of Don Luscombe.

In 1945, Luscombe resumed production at c/n 1925 in a factory in Dallas, Texas offering all the familiar pre-war models. A number of changes were made shortly thereafter. The primary change was the use of single (rather than twin V-) wing bracing struts and a simplified metal wing (at c/n 3200 – although some fabric winged aircraft were built up to c/n 3517). It was intended to designate all post-war aircraft as the Luscombe 9 but this was abandoned due to certification problems. The company also produced the highest-powered Silvaire of all – the Model 8F and its specialised tandem-seat variant, the T8F. Many aircraft were delivered with the optional extra rear window on each side and with a roof skylight transparency. With the introduction of the 85hp Model 8E, the vertical fin was given a squarer profile and, in 1947, at aircraft c/n 5078 the rudder was also squared-off. From c/n 6730, they introduced flaps on the Model 8F and this greatly aided the landing characteristics of the Luscombe which was prone to 'float' and was difficult to get on the ground. The main versions were as follows:

Model	Notes
8	Initial model with 50hp Continental A-50 engine, built in 1938/39. Prototype NX1304 (c/n 800) FF 18 Dec 1937
8A	Higher-powered Model 8 with 65hp Continental A-65. Known as the Luscombe Master. Prototype N22066 (c/n 892)
8B	Luscombe Trainer. Model 8A powered by a 65hp Lycoming O-145-B
8C	Silvaire Deluxe. Model 8A with 75hp Continental A-75 engine
8D	Silvaire Deluxe Trainer. Identical to Model 8C with steerable tailwheel, main wheel brakes, engine starter etc
8E	Silvaire Deluxe. Developed Model 8C with metal wing, 85hp Continental C-85 engine, increased gross weight etc
8F	Model 8E with 90hp Continental C-90 engine
T8F	Luscombe Observer. Tandem two-seat version of Model 8F for pipeline patrol, based on XT-8E prototype (NX2788K). Some built as Crop Master with spray equipment
8G	Proposed Model 8F with tricycle u/c. Mockup only

In 1948, Luscombe went bankrupt and its assets were acquired by Temco Engineering, which saw the Silvaire as a good companion for the Globe Swift. However, Temco was not in much better financial condition and they eventually produced only 50 Silvaires (c/n 6730 to 6774) before terminating production in October 1951. Up to that date some 4,778 post-war Luscombe 8s had been built (c/n 1925 to 6774, excluding 72 serial numbers not used).

1955 saw the Model 8 type certificate being sold to Otis T Massey who formed the Silvaire Aircraft Company which commenced production of the Model 8F at Fort Collins, Colorado. The first aircraft, N9900C (c/n S-1) flew on 9th October 1956 and production continued as far as c/n S-86, although six serial numbers were unused. Silvaire Aircraft Company ceased production in 1960 and in 1985 the type certificate passed on to Moody Larsen of Fort Collins, Colorado who formed Larsen Luscombe Inc and then to Luscombe Aircraft Corporation of Atlanta, Georgia. Ultimately, in 1994, all the type certificates were acquired by the Don Luscombe Aviation History Foundation of Chandler, Arizona. In 1999, Renaissance Aircraft LLC of Cape Girardeau, Mo. produced a working prototype of the new Luscombe Renaissance. This aircraft (N999RA, c/n RA999) was a rebuilt Luscombe 8F airframe with a 150hp Lycoming O-320 engine and Renaissance intended to sell new aircraft, major components of which will be built by Czech Aero Works. By mid-2004 the company had completed one further aircraft but suspended further activities for financial reasons.

In addition to the Silvaire, the post-war Luscombe company produced two other aircraft in an attempt to widen the base of its operations. The Luscombe 10 (NX33337 c/n 10-1) was an all-metal low-wing single-seat light plane with a fixed tailwheel undercarriage that was designed for aerobatic competition and first flew in January 1946. It had a Continental A-65 engine and used a number of Silvaire components but was abandoned following its maiden flight.

e other new aircraft was the Model 11A Sedan four-seater. Con-
..uing the Luscombe strut-braced high-wing design layout the Sedan
was of all-metal construction with a fixed tailwheel undercarriage and
the cabin had all-round vision. The prototype was NX72402 (c/n 11-1)
which first flew on 11th September 1946 powered by a 165hp Continental E-165 engine. The company only built 198 aircraft (c/n 11-3 to
11-6 and 11-104 to 11-199) and production was terminated in 1949. In
1970, an attempt was made to revive the Sedan. Alpha Aviation Co of
Greenville, Texas redesigned it as the Alpha IID with a swept tail unit
and tricycle undercarriage. The engine was to be upgraded to a 180hp
Lycoming O-360 – but the project never advanced beyond the drawing
board. The type certificate then passed to Classic Air of Lansing, Michigan who planned production with a substantially redesigned version,
the Luscombe 185-11E Spartan. The prototype 11E was converted
from Luscombe Sedan N1674B (c/n 11-180) with an enlarged tail, tricycle undercarriage and a 185hp Continental IO-360-ES4 engine. This
was followed by two conforming development aircraft, N747BM
(c/n 11E-00995, later N11XE) and N11XA (c/n 11E-00996) which had
a smaller rear vision window, larger entry doors and other minor
changes. Further test airframes are c/n 11E-00997 to 11E-01000 and
new production is due to start at c/n 11E-01001. The Spartan 210 is a

Luscombe 11E Spartan 185 N11XE

proposed version with a 210hp IO-360. Partly due to continued legal
wrangles and lack of finance, Luscombe anticipates first deliveries will
not take place until the end of 2005 although a tentative order for 10
or more is held for the Civil Air Patrol.

Maule   United States

Maule Aircraft Corporation was formed by Belford D Maule at Jackson,
Michigan to develop, certificate and produce the Maule M-4 Bee Dee.
Maule was a producer of light aircraft ventilation units and tailwheel
assemblies and had previously built two light aircraft prototypes: the
1930 Model M-1 mid-wing single-seat monoplane with a 27hp Henderson motorcycle engine (NC12634 c/n M-1) and the M-2 single-seat
ornithopter (NC34105 c/n M-2) completed in 1944.

The M-4 was a classic steel tube-and-fabric high-wing light aircraft
with a fixed tailwheel undercarriage. The prototype Maule Bee Dee
(N40001 c/n 1) was first flown in February 1957 and Maule intended
that it would meet customer demand from those who preferred conventional fabric-covered aircraft to those all-metal designs that were

beginning to appear. In fact, the M-4 is covered in 'Razorback' fibreglass material and is, therefore, more durable than most traditional
fabric-covered types. The M-4 received its type certificate on 10th
August 1961 and went into production at Jackson, Michigan powered
by a Continental O-300A engine. It provided full four-seat capacity with
very favourable short field performance.

Maule then developed the M-4 airframe by installing a variety of
powerplants and airframe modifications. The fuselage was altered to
include a cargo door on the rear starboard side and machines with this
feature have a 'C' as a suffix to the designation (eg, M-4-210C). They
also produced a two-seat trainer that had 'T' as a designation suffix and
had no rear seating or rear door. The prototype was N9822M, but
Maule only built two further aircraft and did not produce the proposed
180hp, 210hp or 220hp versions. In addition, the specially equipped

Maule M4-220C N51359

Maule MX-7-235 HB-KDS

M-4S was also produced, but only three examples were flown. The M-4 was also certificated for operation on floats. In 1963, an arrangement was set up for licence production in Mexico by Servicios Aereas de America SA The Mexican M-1 Cuauhtemoc was a standard M-4 powered by a 180hp Lycoming O-360 engine. Only three production aircraft (c/n 101 to c/n 103) are thought to have been built. The original M-4 was resurrected in 2003 with the objective of competing in the emerging Sport Aircraft category market in the USA.

In September 1968, Maule moved its expanding operations to a new factory at Moultrie, Georgia. 1975 saw the Maule M-5 being introduced to replace the M-4. This had similar engine options, but the vertical tail was enlarged, the flaps extended and numerous other improvements introduced. By 1984, Maule Aircraft Corporation was in financial trouble, and it went into Chapter 11 bankruptcy. A new company, Maule Air Inc, was formed to continue trading and the new M-7 was introduced. This has been produced in two versions with both a standard and an extended cabin. More recent Maule developments are a tricycle-undercarriage option for the M-7 and MX-7 and several turboprop models using the Rolls-Royce Allison 250 powerplant. In addition, Maule have become one of the first manufacturers to use the SMA SR.307 diesel engine in their new M-9-230. The founder of the company, B D Maule died on 2nd September 1995 at the age of 83, but the company continues very much as a family concern. During 2004, Maule delivered 27 aircraft including the MXT-7-180 (6), MXT-7-180A (2), MX-7-180AC (3), MX-7-180B (1), MX-7-180C (1), M-7-235B (2), M-7-235C (6), MT-7-235 (1), M-7-260C (3), MT-7-420 (2).

The profusion of Maule models can be extremely confusing and there are numerous combinations of undercarriage, powerplant, cabin size and wings. The designation of the current M-7/MX-7 models is intended to explain the individual features. All designations start with 'M' (for Maule) and models without the deeper fuselage but with an extended cabin are designated MX-. The 'M' or 'MX' is followed by 'T' (eg, MXT-) if the aircraft has a tricycle undercarriage. Then comes the basic type number (currently '7' for most production types) followed by the engine horsepower (eg, -180). Finally, there are up to two letters, these being 'A' to denote a fixed-pitch propeller and 'B' to indicate the tailwheel undercarriage with oleo strut main legs or, alterna-

tively, 'C' for the tailwheel undercarriage with spring aluminium main legs. Thus, an MXT-7-180A has the extended cabin, tricycle gear, a 180hp engine and a fixed-pitch propeller. All M-7/MX-7 series models have a wingspan of 32ft 11ins, except for the M-7-420AC, which has a longer 33ft 8in wing, and the turboprop models have a greater overall length. These differences are tabulated on page 186.

Maule gives a separate sequence of serial numbers to each production model. The following numbers of aircraft built and relevant construction number batches have been used up to mid-2004:

Serial Batch	Model	Built	Serial Batch	Model	Built
1 to 94	M-4	94	17001C to 17008C	MXT-7-160	8
1C to 11C	M-4C	11	18001C to 180085C	MT-7-235	85
1S to 3S	M-4S	3	19001C to 19046C	MX-7-160	46
1T to 3T	M-4T	3	20001C to 20058C	MX-7-180A	58
101 to 103	Cuauhtemoc		21001C to 21087C	MXT-7-180A	87
1001 to 1045	M-4-210	45	22001C to 22021C	MX-7-180B	21
1001C to 1117C	M-4-210C	117	23001C to 23084C	M-7-235B	84
2001C to 2190C	M-4-220C	190	24001C	M-7-235A	1
2001S	M-4-220S	1	25001C to 25102C	M-7-235C	102
3001C to 3007C	M-4-180C	7	26001C to 26015C	M-7-260	15
4001C to 4132C	M-7-235	132	27001C to 27010C	MT-7-260	10
5001C to 5057C	M-5-220C	57	28001C to 28020C	MX-7-180C	20
6001C to 6206C	M-5-210C	206	29001C to 29007C	M-7-420AC	7
7001C to 7374C	M-5-235C	374	30001C to 30034C	M-7-260C	34
7375C to 7541C	M-6-235C	167	31001C	MX-7-205C	1
8001C to 8094C	M-5-180C	94	33001C to 33009C	MX-7-180AC	9
9001C to 9010C	M-5-210-TC	10	34001C	MX-7-160	1
100001C to 10122C	MX-7-235	122	35001C	M-7-420A	1
11001C to 11097C	MX-7-180	97	36001C	M-7-420AC	1
12001C to 12002C	M-7-420	2	44001C	M-9-230	1
13001C to 13003C	MX-7-420	3	47003T	M-4-180V	1
14000C to 14116C	MXT-7-180	117	51001C	MT-7-420	1
15001C to 15005C	M-8-235	5	53001C	M-4-180V	1
16001C	MXT-7-420	1			
Total		*2,455*			

Post-War Maule Production

Model	Landing Gear	TOGW	Engine	Notes
Initial Tailwheel Models				
Bee Dee	Oleo t/w	2100 lb	145hp Cont O-300A	Four-seat high-wing light aircraft. Introduced 1962. Prototype N40001 (c/n 1)
M-4	Oleo t/w	2100 lb	145hp Cont O-300A	Production Bee Dee
M-4C Jetasen	Oleo t/w	2100 lb	145hp Cont O-300A	M-4 with cargo door. Prototype N9827M (c/n 1C)
M-4S	Oleo t/w	2100 lb	145hp Cont O-300A	M-4 'Standard' with upgraded equipment. Prototype N9834M (c/n 1S)
M-4T	Oleo t/w	2100 lb	145hp Cont O-300A	Dual-control trainer. No rear seats or rear entry door. Prototype N9822M (c/n 1T)
M-4-180C Astro Rocket	Oleo t/w	2300 lb	180hp Franklin 6A-335-B1A	Higher-powered M-4C
M-4-210 Rocket	Oleo t/w	2300 lb	210hp Cont IO-360A engine.	
M-4-210C Rocket	Oleo t/w	2300 lb		M-4-210 with cargo door.
M-4-220C Strata Rocket	Oleo t/w	2300 lb	220hp Franklin 6A-350-C1 engine.	Development of M-4C
M-4-220S	Oleo t/w	2300 lb	220hp Franklin 6A-350-C1	Development of M-4S
M-4 Sport 100	Oleo t/w	1320 lb	100hp Rotax 912S	2-seat sport category version of M-4 without flaps. Prototype N5505C
M-4-180V	Oleo t/w	2300 lb	180hp Lycoming O-360	2-seat version of M-4 introduced 2004. Prototype N799ZZ (53001C)
M-5-180C	Oleo t/w	2300 lb	180hp Lycoming O-360-C1F	M-4C with enlarged swept tail, larger flaps, optional extra fuel, drooped wingtips, four cabin doors. Prototype N6262M (c/n 8001C)
M-5-200	Oleo t/w	2300 lb	200hp Lycoming IO-360-J1A6D	Experimental 200hp M-5, N5643T (c/n A8015C)
M-5-210C Strata Rocket	Oleo t/w	2300 lb	210hp Cont IO-360D	M-5-180C with revised engine cowling. Prototype N51449 (c/n 6001C)
M-5-210TC Luna Rocket	Oleo t/w	2300 lb	210hp turbocharged Cont TIO-360	Prototype N56294 (c/n 9001C)
M-5-220C Luna Rocket	Oleo t/w	2300 lb	220hp Franklin 6A-350-C1.	
M-5-235C Luna Rocket	Oleo t/w	2300 lb	235hp Lycoming O-540-J1A5D	
M-6-235C Super Rocket	Oleo t/w	2500 lb	235hp Lycoming O-540-J1A5D	M-5-235C with 3ft longer wingspan, smaller ailerons, larger multi-position flaps, increased fuel and optional rear seat. From c/n 7473C has larger ailerons. Prototype N5631R (c/n 7249C)
M-7 Models with 3-in higher rear fuselage and extended rear cabin with extra 5th seat				
M-7-205C	Oleo t/w	2500 lb		Experimental M-7
M-7-235 Super Rocket	Oleo t/w	2500 lb	81in c/s prop. 235hp Lyc O-540-B4B5	M-6-235 with longer interior cabin, optional 5th seat and extra windows. Prototype N5656A (c/n 4001C)
M-7-235B Super Rocket	Oleo t/w	2500 lb	81in c/s prop. 235hp Lyc O-540-B4B5	
M-7-235C Orion	Spring t/w	2500 lb	81in c/s prop. 235hp Lyc O-540-B4B5	
M-7-260 Super Rocket	Oleo t/w	2500 lb	78in c/s prop. 260hp Lyc IO-540-V4A5	
M-7-260C Orion	Spring t/w	2500 lb	78in c/s prop. 260hp Lyc IO-540-V4A5	
M-7-250 Starcraft	Oleo t/w	2500 lb	250hp Allison 250-B17 turboprop	
M-7-420 Starcraft Turboprop	Oleo t/w	2500 lb	RR Allison 250-B17C turboprop	
M-7-420C Starcraft	Spring t/w	2500 lb	RR Allison 250-B17C turboprop	Prototype N5671K
M-7-420AC	Spring t/w	2500 lb	RR Allison 250-B17C	33ft 8in wings
MT-7-420AC	Tricycle	2500 lb	RR Allison 250-B17C	33ft 8in wings
MT-7-235 Super Rocket	Tricycle	2500 lb	81in c/s prop. 235hp Lyc IO-540-W1A5	Prototype N9226Y (c/n 18001C)
MT-7-260 Super Rocket	Tricycle	2500 lb	78in c/s prop. 260hp Lyc IO-540-V4A5	
M-8-235 Star Rocket	Spring t/w	2500 lb	235hp Lyc. O-540-J1A5D	M-7-235 with mod flaps & ailerons. Prototype N6135Z (c/n 15001C)
MX-7 Models with standard short four-seat cabin				
MX-7-160 Sportplane	Oleo t/w	2200 lb	74 in f/p prop. 160hp Lyc O-320-B2D	
MX-7-160C Sportplane	Spring t/w	2200 lb	74 in f/p prop. 160hp Lyc O-320-B2D	
MX-7-180 Star Rocket	Oleo t/w	2400 lb	76 in f/p prop. 180hp Lyc O-360-C4F	Prototype N5653R (c/n 11001C)
MX-7-180A Sportplane	Oleo t/w	2400 lb	76 in f/p prop. 180hp Lyc O-360-C4F	
MX-7-180AC Sportplane	Spring t/w	2400 lb	76 in f/p prop. 180hp Lyc O-360-C4F	
MX-7-180B Star Rocket	Oleo t/w	2500 lb	76 in c/s prop. 180hp Lyc O-360-C1F	
MX-7-180C	Spring t/w	2500 lb	76 in c/s prop. 180hp Lyc O-360-C1F	
MX-7-180C Millennium	Spring t/w	2500 lb	76 in c/s prop. 180hp Lyc O-360-C1F	
MX-7-235 Star Rocket	Oleo t/w	2500 lb	235hp Lyc. IO-540-W1A5	Prototype N5657Y (c/n 10001C)
MX-7-250 Starcraft	Oleo t/w	2500 lb	250hp Allison 250-B17 turboprop	Prototype N5666K
MX-7-420 Starcraft Turboprop	Oleo t/w	2500 lb	RR Allison 250-B17C	
MXT-7-160 Comet	Tricycle	2200 lb	74 in f/p prop. 160hp Lyc O-320-B2D	
MXT-7-180 Star Rocket	Tricycle	2500 lb	76 in c/s prop. 180hp Lyc O-360-C1F	Prototype N6133A
MXT-7-180A Comet	Tricycle	2400 lb	76 in f/p prop. 180hp Lyc O-360-C4F	
MXT-7-420 Starcraft Turboprop	Tricycle	2500 lb	RR Allison 250-B17C	
MX-9-230	Spring t/w	2800 lb	230hp SMA SR.305 diesel engine	Prototype N305SR (c/n 44001C) FF 18 Jul 2003

Maule MX-7-420FP N9210Q

Meyers   United States

Formed at Tecumseh, Michigan by George F Meyers in 1936, the Meyers Aircraft Company went into production initially with the Meyers OTW. This two-seat biplane was unusual in having an all-metal fuselage and wooden wings and was produced in 125hp and 145hp Warner Super Scarab-powered versions – and, latterly, with a Kinner R-56 engine. A total of 102 OTWs were built between 1936 and 1943, most of these being delivered to the flying training schools.

Production of the OTW gave way to other war work in 1943, but after the war Meyers determined to get back into the aircraft manufacturing business. A small side-by-side two-seat prototype was constructed. This all-metal aircraft (NX34358 c/n 1001) had a retractable tailwheel undercarriage and a 125hp Continental engine. From the engine power came its designation – the Meyers MAC-125C. Only one further MAC-125C was built and this was followed by the MAC-145C, which mainly differed in having a 145hp engine and a modified engine cowling and enlarged fin. The first aircraft (N34360 c/n 203) was delivered in 1949 and production continued until 1956 by which time 20 MAC-145s had been built (ending at c/n 222). Meyers subsequently had ideas about building the type as the MAC-145T with a tricycle undercarriage but did not continue with this because they were fully occupied with the Model 200. The type certificate for the OTW is still owned by Meyers Industries Inc

The MAC-145 certificate and tooling was acquired by Meyers Aircraft Company of Fayetteville, North Carolina and they reworked an existing airframe (N145RH c/n 1) as the prototype Meyers 145 Spark powered by a 145hp Continental O-300 engine. Under the reconstituted New Meyers Aircraft Company this was further developed into the

SP-20 proof of concept prototype (N520SP) converted from an existing MAC-145 with a 200hp Lycoming IO-360, enlarged bubble cockpit canopy and modified vertical tail. The production prototype (N34372) had a modified sliding canopy, a redesigned wing centre section, retractable tailwheel and further modifications to the vertical tail. It was planned that it would be built at Fort Pierce, Florida together with a new version of the Aero Commander 200 known as the New Meyers M200 with a 310hp Continental IO-550 engine.

Eventually, in January 1995 the company was acquired by the Seminole Indian tribe and renamed Micco Aircraft Company in 1997. A further redesign with many detail changes used N520SP and a prototype of the definitive Micco SP.20 (N720SP which first flew on 17th December 1997) was built. The SP.20 (MAC-145A) gained its Type Certificate on 15th January 2000. Micco also developed the SP.26 (MAC-145B) which was a higher-powered version of the SP.20 and first deliveries were made early in 2001. At the end of that year the slowdown in US light aircraft sales resulted in Micco suspending production and in 2002, internal decisions in the Seminole tribe resulted in the Micco business being sold to Wadi Rahim's LanShe Aircraft (who also acquired Lake Aircraft). However, LanShe ran into financial trouble in April 2004 and production has been suspended. Up to that point, eight SP-20s (c/n 301 to 308) and eleven SP-26s (c/n 26001 to 26011) had been completed.

The Meyers Model 200 was, essentially, the MAC-145 with a 31-inch fuselage extension providing room for a lengthened four-seat cabin. The aircraft had a retractable tricycle undercarriage and was powered by a 240hp Continental engine. Meyers built one prototype followed by two examples of the basic Model 200. The type certificate was issued on 6th March 1958, but it was soon evident that the Model 200 was

Micco SP-26 N179MA

underpowered so the definitive Model 200A was fitted with a 260hp Continental engine.

First customer deliveries took place in 1959. Production continued at Tecumseh until 12th July 1965 when Meyers was taken over by Rockwell's Aero Commander Division. The Model 200 seemed to be an ideal choice as Rockwell's competitor against the Bonanza, Cessna 210 and Comanche and the construction of the Meyers 200 fitted into the quality image fostered by Aero Commander. In reality, however, the Model 200 was more expensive than the Comanche and less flexible than the Bonanza. Aero Commander only built 88 aircraft by mid-1967 at which time they discontinued production. Production serial numbers have been c/n 203 to 222 (MAC-145-C), c/n 1 and 251 to 252 (200), c/n 253 to 263 (200A), c/n 264 to 280 (200B), c/n 281 to 289 and 291 (200C), c/n 290 and 292 to 383 and 385 (200D). Micco's SP-20s have been c/n 301 to 308 and the SP-26, c/n 26001 to 26011. In detail, the post-war Meyers aircraft were:

Model	Built	Notes
125-C	2	Two-seat all-metal low-wing monoplane powered by one Continental C-125. N34358 (c/n 1001) and N34359 (c/n 202)
145-C	20	Model 125-C with 145hp Continental C-145-2H and cowling and tail modifications. Prototype N34360 (c/n 203)
SP-20	8	Model 145 with bubble cockpit canopy, Model 200 vertical tail and 200hp Lycoming. Certificated designation MAC-145A. Prototype N520SP (c/n 215)
SP-26	11	SP-20 built as MAC-145B with 260hp Lycoming IO-540-T4B5 engine
200	3	Four-seat development of Model 145 with retractable tricycle u/c and 240hp Cont O-470-M engine. Prototype N3441M (c/n 1) FF 8 Sep 1953
200A	11	Production Model 200 with fuel-injected 260hp Continental IO-470-D. Fuel increased from 40 gal to 80 gal with auxiliary wing tanks. Prototype N485C (c/n 253)
200B	17	Model 200A with detail changes and improved performance
200C	10	Model 200B with 285hp Continental IO-520A and detail changes
200D	93	Model 200C as produced by Aero Commander with improved trim etc. Named Aero Commander Spark for a short while

Meyers 200 N108M

Rockwell was already developing its own single-engined line, the Model 112 and 114 series that replaced the Model 200, but they did intend to use the Model 200 airframe as the basis for a light twin. The penultimate airframe (c/n 384) was rebuilt as the T200E with two Continental engines and a new swept vertical tail. This aircraft, N4001X, was flown by Product Development Group Inc under a subcontract arrangement, but the type did not advance further.

Having discontinued production of the Model 200, Rockwell sold the type certificate and all tooling to Interceptor Corporation. This was a new company, formed in November 1968 for the purpose of turning the type into a high-performance turboprop business aircraft. Interceptor built two prototypes (N400TP c/n 001 and N400HS c/n 2) powered by Garrett TPE-331 engines and the first of these flew on 27th June 1969. Full type approval was gained on 20th August 1971 and Interceptor went ahead with plans for full manufacture. As it turned out, however, only two aircraft (N5008A c/n 401 and N74166/N840PJ c/n 402) were built before the company ran into financial difficulty – partly caused by an accident in which N5008A was destroyed.

Subsequently, in 1982, the type certificate was sold to another company – Prop Jets Inc of Boulder, Colorado. The owner, Paul M Whetstone, had plans to build the Model 400A with an 840shp Garrett TPE331-6 engine and the 400B with a 1,000shp TPE331 variant.

Miles Aircraft   United Kingdom

Miles aircraft had its origins in Phillips & Powis Ltd, a light aircraft overhaul company based at Woodley near Reading, which progressed to building the pre-war Hawk series of single-engined monoplanes and the cabin Falcon and Whitney Straight. During the war, Miles was well known for the M.14 Magister two-seat primary trainer many of which were civilianised after the war as the Hawk Trainer III.

In 1939, George Miles had designed the M.28 Mercury – a low-wing four-seat cabin monoplane with a twin fin tail unit, retractable tailwheel undercarriage and a 130hp Gipsy Major I engine. The first prototype (U-0232) made its first flight on 11th July 1941 and five further prototypes were built with various powerplants. The M.28 was not built in quantity but the prototype was fitted with a new wing and fixed undercarriage to become the M.38 Messenger. This was intended for Air Observation Post duties, but the 21 Messengers delivered to the Army were actually used for general communications. The production Messenger had a triple fin tail unit and a 140hp Gipsy Major engine. Peace cut short the Messenger's military career, but it was an ideal type for sale to civilian buyers and a new factory was set up at Newtownards in Northern Ireland to turn out postwar commercial models with Cirrus Major III engines.

The Messenger airframe, constructed of resin-bonded plywood, was a good starting point for Miles to produce a light twin. The result was the M.65 Gemini, which was powered by a pair of 100hp Blackburn Cirrus Minor engines but was, in most other respects, identical to the Messenger except for having twin fins and an electrically-retractable undercarriage. The prototype, G-AGUS, flew in October 1945 and shortly afterwards the Gemini went into production and proved to be an immediate success – although its single-engine performance left much to be desired.

Miles also saw postwar opportunities for freighter aircraft for military and civil use. Their answer was a group of three major designs of which the main production variant was the all-wood M.57 Aerovan. This had a 'pod-and-boom' fuselage with a rear loading door, triple-finned tail unit, fixed tricycle undercarriage and a high wing mounting two 150hp Cirrus Major engines. The production Aerovan was very similar to the prototype except that it had a lengthened fuselage and round windows rather than the square ones used on the first aircraft. Many export sales were achieved with deliveries to Iraq, Switzerland, New Zealand and Colombia.

A four-engined Aerovan (the M.72) was planned by Miles but the prototype was never completed. However, the company did build and fly the M.68 Boxcar, which was an enlarged Aerovan with four engines and a detachable cargo pod that formed the centre fuselage. They also built the M.71 Merchantman, which was a scaled-up all-metal Aerovan powered by four Gipsy Queen 30 engines. To speed up development, the Merchantman used the wings that Miles had designed for the Miles

Miles M-38 Messenger G-AKVZ

Miles M.65 Gemini OO-RLD

Marathon transport, and the first flight of this prototype took place in August 1947.

Perhaps the most ambitious of the Miles designs was the M.60 Marathon – a four-engined, high-wing, 14-passenger airliner with a retractable tricycle undercarriage. It was the outcome of a long trail of Miles design studies starting with the M.51 Minerva of 1943 and using many of the concepts contained within the 'X' projects that had occupied the company for a number of years. The Marathon was the winner of a Ministry of Aircraft Production design specification and the first of three prototypes was flown in May 1946. There was considerable political argument and bureaucratic delay over the M.60 specification and this led to very slow progress in getting the aircraft into production – a situation that was to prove disastrous for Miles.

Miles had produced numerous studies for new aircraft during the immediate postwar period and was committed to prototype or production work on the M.38, M.57, M.60, M.65, M.68 and M.71 together with complex wind tunnel research on the supersonic M.52 project. They also became involved with the Biro ballpoint pen, prefabricated housing, the Copycat photocopier and numerous other areas of diversification. It turned out that they had become financially over-stretched with all these activities and the severe winter of 1946 brought disruption that proved to be more than the company could bear. Creditors petitioned for Miles to be wound up in November 1947.

The Marathon was the only project to survive and it was taken over with the other aviation assets by Handley Page who established Handley Page (Reading) Ltd and built a batch of 40 aircraft for the RAF and civil customers. The Miles brothers set up their own organisation and built the M.100 Student and the HDM.105, which was a cooperative venture with the French company Hurel Dubois. This design was ultimately used as the basis for the Shorts Skyvan. The Miles brothers later joined the new Beagle company which was set up in 1960. The remainder of Miles Aircraft – largely consisting of the property at Woodley and the engineering plant and equipment – became the Western Manufacturing Company and then, after merger with Adamant Engineering in 1955, was named Adamant and Western Co Ltd It subsequently became the Adwest Group plc, operating from Woodley.

Serial numbers of pre-war Miles aircraft ran from c/n 1 to 43 and from c/n 101 to 332. These batches of numbers included several mock-ups, spare fuselages and demonstration units that cannot be counted as proper aircraft. M.14 Hawk Trainers started at c/n 333 and wartime production ceased at around c/n 6264. Postwar aircraft were numbered from c/n 6265 up to c/n 6729 but many serial numbers were not used. The principal postwar civil Miles designs that reached the prototype or production stage were:

Model	Built	Notes
M.38 Messenger 1	21	M.28 with fixed u/c, new wing with trailing edge flaps and triple fins. 140hp DH Gipsy Major engine. Military production but many civilianised postwar. Prototype U-0223 FF 12 Sep 1942
M.38 Messenger 2A	65	Four-seat civil M.38 with 150hp Blackburn Cirrus Major III engine and oval rear windows
M.38 Messenger 2B	1	Three-seat version of Messenger 2A
M.38 Messenger 2C	1	Messenger 2A with 145hp Gipsy Major 1D engine
M.48 Messenger 3	1	M.38 with electrically-operated split trailing edge flaps and 155hp Cirrus Major III engine
M.38 Messenger 4	4	Messenger 2A with 145hp Gipsy Major 10 engine
M.38 Messenger 4A		Civil conversions of Messenger 1
M.38 Messenger 5		Messenger 1 RH420 (G-2-1) converted to 180hp Blackburn Bombardier 702 engine
M.57 Aerovan I	1	Wooden freighter aircraft with pod-and-boom fuselage, four square windows each side and two 150hp Cirrus Minor III engines. Prototype U-0248 (later G-AGOZ) (c/n 4700) FF 26 Jan 1945
M.57 Aerovan II	1	Aerovan I with 18-inch longer fuselage and five round windows. U-8 (later G-AGWO) (c/n 6432)
M.57 Aerovan III	7	Aerovan II with modified rear cargo door
M.57 Aerovan IV	41	Aerovan III with four windows each side
M.57 Aerovan V	1	Aerovan IV with 145hp Gipsy Major 10 engines
M.57 Aerovan VI	1	Aerovan IV with 195hp Lycoming O-435-4A engines and enlarged tailfins
M.60 Marathon I	2	High-wing all-metal transport with retractable tricycle u/c and four 330hp Gipsy Queen 71 engines. Prototype U-10/G-AGPD (c/n 6265). FF 19 May 1946. 40 built by Handley Page (Reading) Ltd
M.64 L.R.5	1	Two-seat side-by-side low-wing trainer with fixed tricycle u/c and one 100hp Cirrus Minor engine. Prototype U-0253 FF 3 Jun 1945
M.65 Gemini 1	1	Twin-engined development of M.38 with two 100hp Cirrus Minor engines, twin fins, square rear windows and retractable tailwheel u/c. Prototype G-AGUS (c/n 4701) FF 26 Oct 1945
M.65 Gemini 1A	133	Production Gemini with oval rear windows and 3,000 lb TOGW
M.65 Gemini 2		G-AGUS re-engined with 125hp Continental C-125-2s
M.65 Gemini 3	9	Gemini 1A with 145hp Gipsy Major 1C engines
M.65 Gemini 3B	1	Gemini 3C with retractable flaps

M.65 Gemini 3C	4	Gemini 1A with 145hp Gipsy Major 10-II engines
M.65 Gemini 4	1	Gemini 1A ambulance version
M.65 Gemini 7		Gemini 3C modified to M.75 standard. 3,500 lb TOGW
M.65 Gemini 8		Mk 7 with 155hp Cirrus Major III engines
M.68 Boxcar	1	Four-engined Aerovan derivative with detachable cargo pod and four Cirrus Minor II engines. Prototype G-AJJM (c/n 6696) FF 22 Aug 1947
M.69 Marathon II	1	M.60 with two Armstrong Siddeley Mamba turboprops. Prototype G-AHXU (c/n 6541) FF 23 Jul 1949
M.71 Merchantman	1	All-metal freighter based on scaled-up Aerovan powered by four 250hp Gipsy Queen 30 engines. Prototype U-21 (c/n 6695) FF 7 Aug 1947
M.75 Aries	2	M.65 development after Miles liquidation with enlarged fins and two 155hp Cirrus Major III engines. Prototype G-35-1/G-AMDJ (c/n 75/1002)
M.77 Sparrowjet	1	Sparrowhawk G-ADNL converted with two Turboméca Palas jet in wing roots. FF 14 Dec 1953
M.100 Student	1	Two-seat light jet trainer with twin fins, retractable tricycle u/c and Turboméca Marboré light jet mounted on centre section. Prototype G-APLK, later G-MIOO (c/n 1008) built by F G Miles. FF 15 May 1957
HDM.105	1	Test aircraft for Hurel Dubois high aspect ratio wing with Aerovan fuselage and tail. Prototype G-35-3 /G-AHDM (c/n 1009) FF 31 Mar 1957

Mitsubishi   Japan

Mitsubishi Heavy Industries can recall a distinguished wartime record of production of military aircraft, not least of which was the famous A6M Zero fighter. It was not until 1959, however, that it was possible for Mitsubishi to return to aircraft manufacture. They decided to aim at the developing business aircraft market and were one of the first manufacturers to see the possibilities of turboprop engines. On 13th September 1963 the company flew the first of three prototypes of the MU-2A business turboprop.

The MU-2 was a high-wing aircraft with a circular section fuselage, retractable tricycle undercarriage, large wingtip fuel tanks and two Turboméca Astazou engines slung on pylons below the wings. What was remarkable was the high-speed performance of the MU-2, aided by a unique wing design that abandoned conventional ailerons in favour of a system of retractable spoilers that extended in sections across the centre of the wing upper surfaces. This made it possible to fit full span flaps without concession to the other control surfaces so that the MU-2 could also offer low landing speeds and short take-offs.

The Turboméca engines were soon abandoned in order to meet American market conditions and the production MU-2B was fitted with Garrett TPE331 turboprops mounted directly on the wings and was certificated in Japan on 15th September 1965. Mitsubishi entered into a marketing and production agreement with Mooney which resulted in early production MU-2s being delivered to Kerrville, Texas for sale

in the United States – which was considered to be the prime market for this aircraft. This relationship was short-term and unsuccessful although it did result in beneficial improvements to the finish and soundproofing of the aircraft. Eventually, Mitsubishi set up Mitsubishi Aircraft International Inc at San Angelo, Texas where 'green' MU-2s were delivered for completion, with a high level of American added value, and sale to all western hemisphere customers.

The MU-2B was joined by the stretched MU-2G, which featured external main undercarriage housings to provide greater internal cabin volume. Thereafter, there was a succession of long and short fuselage variants that used TPE331 turboprops of varying power and a steadily improving standard of internal trim and equipment. A non-pressurized MU-2 was built for the Japanese Ground Self Defence Forces and served in various roles including search and rescue and general communications.

Mitsubishi enjoyed a period of good sales for the MU-2 with the majority of deliveries going to American corporate customers. The aircraft gained a questionable reputation for its high-performance handling as a result of a number of accidents. An FAA Review eventually exonerated it but this sounded the death knell of MU-2 production. Mitsubishi started to reduce the build rate and the last MU-2 left the production line at the end of 1983. Many Mu-2s have found a new role as high-speed overnight package freighters. The different MU-2 types were all certificated as variants of the basic MU-2B and given an appropriate Type Number. However, a separate marketing designation was

Mitsubishi Mu-2B-60 Marquise. MHIA

Type No	Designation	Built	Notes
MU-2A	MU-2A	3	7/9-seat high-wing pressurized business twin with retractable tricycle u/c and two under-slung 562shp Turboméca Astazou IIK turboprops. Prototype JA8620 FF 14 Sep 1963
MU-2B	MU-2B	34	MU-2A with numerous systems and internal changes and two Garrett TPE331-25A turboprops. 8,930 lb TOGW. Prototype JA8627 (c/n 004) FF 11 Mar 1965
MU-2C	LR-1	20	Unpressurized MU-2B for JGSDF. FF May 1967
MU-2D	MU-2B-10	14	MU-2B with 9,350 lb TOGW and internal improvements
MU-2DP	MU-2B-15	3	MU-2D with 665hp TPE331-1-151A engines
MU-2E	LR-1		MU-2C for JASDF with nose radome, electronic search equipment, sliding entry door and observation windows
MU-2F	MU-2B-20	103	MU-2DP with larger wingtip tanks, 9,920 lb TOGW and systems changes
MU-2G*	MU-2B-30	47	9/11-seat MU-2B with 1.9m fuselage stretch, 10,800 lb TOGW, two more windows each side, lavatory, larger vertical tail, rear entry door, external u/c fairings and TPE331-1-151A engines. Prototype JA8737 (c/n 501) FF 10 Jan 1969
MU-2J*	MU-2B-35	112	MU-2G with 724shp TPE331-6-251M engines and improved soundproofing
MU-2K	MU-2B-25	69	MU-2F with 724shp TPE331-6-251M engines
MU-2L*	MU-2B-36	55	MU-2J with 11,575 lb TOGW and improved internal trim
MU-2M	MU-2B-26	25	MU-2K with 10,470 lb TOGW and improved internal trim
MU-2N*	MU-2B-36A	16	MU-2L with quieter 776shp TPE331-5-252M engines and new low-rpm gearbox, 4-blade props and new interior
MU-2P	MU-2B-26A	94	MU-2M with engines and modifications as MU-2N
MU-2S	LR-1	29	MU-2E for Japanese military search and rescue role. See MU-2E
Marquise*	MU-2B-60	138	MU-2N with 778shp TPE331-10 engines, 11,575 lb TOGW, increased fuel capacity
Solitaire	MU-2B-40	5	MU-2P with 10,450 lb TOGW and modifications and engines as on Marquise

Note: the long-fuselage variants are marked * in the above table.

In total, 767 Mu-2s of all models, including prototypes, were completed. Serial numbers for the MU-2 started at c/n 001 (the prototype) and ran to c/n 038 and then consecutively from c/n 101 to c/n 347 (except c/n 237 and 238) covering a mixture of MU-2B, MU-2C, MU-2D and MU-2F models. From c/n 348 civil model serials were suffixed 'SA' (eg, c/n 348SA) although the military MU-2C and MU-2S did not have this suffix. This serial batch, covering the short-fuselage models, continued to c/n 459SA (plus 463 to 466). The long-fuselage MU-2G started with the prototypes c/n 501 and 502 (ex c/n 152 and 153) and continued from c/n 503. They also picked up the SA suffix at c/n 689SA and

Mitsubishi Mu-2K N290GC

ran on to c/n 799SA. The batches c/n 801 to 818 and c/n 901 to 955 were all military MU-2C, MU-2S and MU-2J aircraft which were originally allocated numbers in the normal production runs and then re-serialled. The final batch of civil Marquises was serialled c/n 1501SA to 1569SA.

In 1977, Mitsubishi embarked on the design of a new business jet known as the MU-300 and flew the first prototype in August 1978. This aircraft, subsequently named Diamond, was a conventional low-wing design with a T-tail and two JT15D turbojets mounted on the rear fuselage. The standard cabin interior accommodated eight passengers and had a toilet and baggage area. After initial testing in Japan, the two prototypes were transferred to San Angelo where they completed FAA testing to FAR Part 25 and were awarded Type Certificate A14SW on 6th November 1981. Thereafter, production Diamond Is were assembled at San Angelo from components manufactured in Nagoya.

The performance of the Diamond I was somewhat lacklustre and the type went through a number of engine changes in order to improve this. Eventually, in late 1985, Beech Aircraft acquired the MU-300 from Mitsubishi and renamed it the Beechjet 400. Mitsubishi had built 100 MU-300s which carried the serials c/n 001 and 002 (prototypes), c/n A003SA to A092SA (Diamond I and IA) and c/n A1001SA to A1008SA (Diamond II). The initial 65 Beechjets were built from Japanese-supplied components, but Beech soon took over full manufacture at Wichita. Details of the various MU-300 models are as follows:

Model	Built	Notes
MU-300	2	8/10-seat low-wing all-metal business jet with T-tail, tricycle u/c and two 2,500 lbst P&W JT15D-4 turbojets. Prototype JQ8002 (c/n 001SA) FF 29 Aug 1978
MU-300 Diamond I	63	MU-300 with minor production changes including deletion of one port rear cabin window and increased TOGW to 14,100 lb
MU-300 Diamond IA	27	Diamond I with JT15D-4D engines, 16,230 lb TOGW, Sperry EFIS, extra port side window and new interior trim
MU-300 Diamond II	8	Diamond IA with 2,900 lbst JT15D-5 engines, 15,780 lb TOGW, increased fuel capacity and new interior trim

Monocoupe   United States

During the 1930s, Mono Aircraft (later the Monocoupe Corporation) had built the well-known range of Monocoupe high-wing two-seat light aircraft. They were steel tube-and-fabric designs powered by a variety of small Lambert, Lycoming and Franklin radial and horizontally-opposed engines. The most prolific version was the Model 90, which continued in production until 1942 when Monocoupe's parent company, Universal Moulded Products, abandoned aircraft production for other war tasks. In 1945, Universal revived the Monocoupe and built one Model 90AF (N52271 c/n 860) powered by a Franklin 4AC-199, but, in 1947, they sold Monocoupe to Robert G Sessler & Associates. Sessler formed Monocoupe of Florida Inc based at Melbourne, Florida and started production of the Monocoupe 90AL-115 which was powered by a 115hp Lycoming O-235-C1 engine. They com-

Aviat/Monocoupe 110 Special N110XZ

Monocoupe 90AL NC11760

pleted ten aircraft (c/n 861 to 870) between 1947 and 1950. In 1998, Aviat Aircraft of Afton, Wyoming announced plans to return a modified Monocoupe 110 Special to production and they flew the prototype of their new version (N110XZ, c/n 7001) on 25th July 1999. The Monocoupe 110 Special was powered by a 200hp Lycoming IO-360A-1B flat-four engine. Aviat subsequently shelved their plans for the aircraft.

During the period 1950 to 1954, Monocoupe built the prototype Monocoupe Meteor five-seat light twin which used a large number of non-structural plastic components. It was powered by two 180hp Lycoming O-360-A1A engines. Monocoupe subsequently sold it to Saturn Aircraft & Engineering of Oxnard, California who fitted a swept tail and renamed the aircraft 'Saturn Meteor II'. They abandoned the project in 1961, but the Meteor was last known to be under restoration at Chino, California by a private owner.

Mooney   United States

Albert W Mooney was the former Chief Designer of the Culver Aircraft Corporation, and had formerly worked for Alexander Aircraft, Marshall Aircraft, Bellanca and Monocoupe. When Culver ceased business in 1946, Al Mooney left to design the C-1 Mite. This became the M-18, which followed on from the M-17 Culver V in Al Mooney's personal number series. It was intended as an ultra-low-cost single-seater with superior performance and had a plywood-covered steel-tube framed fuselage, an all-flying tail, wooden wings and a retractable tricycle undercarriage. Mooney decided to power the prototype with a 25hp Crossley Cobra motorcar engine.

Mooney Aircraft Corporation was formally incorporated on 18th June 1948 and M-18 production got under way from a small factory on Rock Road on the east side of Wichita. The Crossley engine proved to be inadequate and the M-18 was soon re-engined with 65 horsepower Continental or Lycoming engines. Mites were popular with sportsman pilots and today are so sought-after that they can be built by home-builders from plans supplied by Mooney Mite Aircraft Corp of Charlottesville, Virginia. Mooney also experimented with a military ground-attack version of the Mite, designated M-19, but this did not progress beyond prototype stage.

In 1953, Mooney was forced to abandon Wichita and a new factory was established at Kerrville, Texas. However, the full force of general aviation recession hit the company in July 1954. It had accumulated creditors for around $350,000 and was on the brink of filing bankruptcy papers when it was rescued by two external investors – Hal Rachal and Norm Hoffman. In August 1953, Al Mooney had flown the prototype of a new four-seat light aircraft based on the Mite and the new investment allowed this aircraft to be certificated on 24th August 1955. Shortly afterwards, Al Mooney retired from the company and went to work for Lockheed where he designed the LASA-60 and the Hummingbird VTOL research aircraft.

As with the M-18, the new four-seat aircraft had tube-and-plywood construction, a laminar-flow wing, adjustable tailplane and a swept-forward vertical tail. Al Mooney had intended to fit a new 170hp Lycoming engine into the M.20 but this engine was not available and the 150hp Lycoming O-320 was used instead. Nevertheless, the per-

Mooney M.18C N4160

Aerostar Mooney M.20C N6827V

formance of the M.20 was outstanding and the company soon built up a strong order book. In due course, with the assistance of the new chief designer, Ralph Harmon, Mooney moved away from the plywood structure for the M.20 and the new all-metal M.20B, competing with the Piper Comanche, was introduced in 1961.

The M.20 broadened into a range of models with various power-plants, including the M.20D Master. This had a fixed undercarriage and a commensurately low price – but could be converted to retractable gear as a later option for the purchaser. By 1966, almost 800 Mooneys had been delivered and the company was looking at expansion of their product range. They developed a twin-engined version of the M.20, which was unofficially referred to as the M.22, and flew the prototype quite extensively before abandoning the project. They also entered a joint venture with Mitsubishi Heavy Industries in 1966 under which the MU-2 twin-turboprop would be marketed by Mooney from a new centre at San Angelo, Texas. Much money and effort went into this, but eventually Mitsubishi took over and set up their own independent marketing organisation. Mooney also acquired the Ercoupe designs from Alon in October 1967 and developed the M-10, which was fitted with a Mooney-style tail instead of the earlier twin-fin design.

Ralph Harmon had also been experimenting with an up-market pressurized single-engine machine: the M.22 Mustang (the name was

Mooney M.20C N6754U

dropped after objections from North American). Mooney spent almost $5 million on its development, including flying a T-tailed version, and when it did enter production it was too expensive to attract many buyers. Even at the very substantial price (for those days) of $46,000, Mooney was losing money on it and only 39 units (including the static test airframes) were built.

Mooney reached a crisis on 17th February 1969 when the financial pressures forced it to declare bankruptcy. Fairly soon, however, a new investor was found in the shape of American Electronic Laboratories (AEL) who introduced enough money to enable Mooney to carry on in production. This was a short-lived situation because AEL was reluctant to make sufficient investment and it soon allowed Mooney to go bankrupt again. In November 1969, the remnants of Mooney were sold to Butler Aviation, which was an established general aviation fixed base operator. Butler was already in the aircraft manufacturing business, having bought Ted Smith Aerostar from American Cement in 1969. They changed the company name to Aerostar Aircraft Corp in July 1970 and embarked on a marketing drive which gave each Mooney model an Aerostar name and new paint schemes and styling, including 'bullet' fairings on the fin tips of some models. Aerostar ran into trouble in 1971, and the three Mooney models were, again, suspended.

Mooney remained out of production until 4th October 1973 when Republic Steel Corporation of Columbus, Ohio took control and renamed the company Mooney Aircraft Corporation. They built the Chapparal, Ranger and Executive but they had recruited Roy LoPresti from Grumman and he set about improving the M.20F Executive to give substantially better performance. In January 1974 the first delivery was made of the new M.20J Model 201. LoPresti also designed a new pressurized single-engined aircraft known as the MX and later as the M.30. A prototype was flown in April 1983, but the project was eventually suspended in favour of the TBM700 single-engined turbo-prop jointly developed by Aérospatiale and Mooney. In May 1991, it was announced that the TBM700 programme was being taken over by Aérospatiale.

By 1984, Republic Steel had been taken over by LTV Corporation and it was decided to dispose of the aviation interests. Accordingly, Mooney was sold to a group of private investors named Mooney Holding Corp This led to acquisition of the company by French investors, Alex Couvelaire and Michel Seydoux. Under their ownership the M.20J was followed by a succession of modernised Mooney variants includ-

Mooney M.22 N7727M

ing the stretched Porsche-powered M.20L and the similarly stretched TLS with a 270hp turbocharged Lycoming engine. The company was sold in 1997 to AVAQ Partners (Paul and Christian Dopp) who rationalised models, dropping the short fuselage M.20J Allegro and M.20K Encore and concentrating on the stretched airframe of the M.20M for all three models in the line (the turbocharged M.20M TLS, normally-aspirated M.20R Ovation and lower-powered Eagle which effectively replaced the Allegro). However, by July 2001, Mooney's financial situation had become acute and it filed Chapter 11 bankruptcy.

In April 2002 it was acquired by AASI (Advanced Aerodynamics & Structures Inc), which subsequently changed its name to Mooney Aerospace Group and established Mooney Airplane Company as the operating subsidiary. AASI had started its JetCruzer 500 project in 1983; this was a new technology business aircraft of mixed construction with a graphite carbon composite fuselage, accommodating six including two crew, and aluminium wings and tail. It had a canard layout and was initially powered by an Allison 250 turboprop in a pusher installation driving a five-blade propeller, although this was later changed to a 450shp Pratt & Whitney PT6A-27. The proof of concept prototype JetCruzer 450 (N5369M) first flew on 11th January 1989 followed by the pre-production prototype (N102JC) in April 1991. The production-standard prototype, N450JC was flown on 13th September 1992. Eventually, N102JC was modified as the pressurized JetCruzer 500 powered by an 850shp PT6A-66, flying in this form in August 1997 and N450JC was also similarly upgraded. One further Model 500, N136JC, was built together with N500JC, which is believed to have been only a mock-up. A later derivative, the Stratocruzer 1250, was planned as a stretched 11-seat version with two rear-fuselage-mounted Williams/Rolls FJ44-2 turbofans. When AASI acquired Mooney it almost immediately abandoned the JetCruzer project even though certification of the Model 450 had been gained and the Model 500 certification was well advanced. The assets were acquired by Jetcruzer LLC in 2004 and they intend to sell a redesigned kit version powered by a small turbofan.

The arrival of AASI did not stem Mooney's difficulties and foreclosure by the secured bondholders of AASI resulted in Mooney Airplane Co being sold to Allen Holding Finance in 2004. In early 2005, Mooney was in production with the Bravo DX and GX and the Ovation 2DX and

GX, the GX models being fitted with Garmin G.1000 glass cockpit technology. Total deliveries in 2004 were 37 aircraft consisting of nine of the Bravo DX and 28 of the Ovation 2 DX.

Mooney has pursued numerous diversification options including acquisition of the Bonanza and Baron from Raytheon, development of a pressurized single and purchase of the Century CA-100 business jet project. In mid-2003 Mooney negotiated with CAG in Spain to acquire rights to the Toxo II two-seater, which would be built by Mooney as the Speedster, both in factory-complete and kit form and would lead to a four-seat version. However, this was abandoned in 2004. Mooney's model line over the years has comprised:

Model	Name	Notes
M-18	Mite	Single-seat low-wing monoplane with retractable tricycle u/c and one 25hp Crossley Cobra engine. Prototype NX12512 (C/n 1) FF 18 May 1947
M-18L	Mite	M-18 with 65hp Lycoming O-145-B2 engine
M-18C	Mite	M-18 with 65hp Continental A-65-8 engine
M-18LA	Mite	M-18L with gross weight increased 70 lb to 850 lb
M-18C-55	Mite	M-18C with 850 lb TOGW, larger cockpit canopy, taller fin and minor changes. Deluxe 'Wee Scotsman'
M-19	-	Military version of M-18 fitted with 30-calibre machine guns
M.20	-	Four-seat low-wing steel tube and wood cabin monoplane with retractable tricycle u/c, powered by one 150hp Lyc O-320. Prototype N4199 (c/n 1001) FF 10 Aug 1953
M.20A	-	M.20 with 180hp Lycoming O-360-A1A engine.
M.20B	Mark 21	M.20A re-engineered to all-metal construction. Prototype N6099X (c/n 1700X)
M.20C	Mark 21	M.20B with O-360-A1D engine and 125 lb increase in TOGW with provision for optional higher fuel capacity. PC wing-leveller and electric gear introduced in 1965
M.20C	Ranger	Mark 21 with squared-off windows and new windshield
M.20C	Aerostar 200	Ranger with bullet tail fairing and minor internal trim changes. Prototype N78911 (c/n 1940)
M.20D	Master	M.20C with non-retracting u/c, introduced in 1963 as an economy model. Prototype N6606U (C/n 101)
M.20E	Super 21	M.20C with 200hp Lyc IO-360-A1A engine. 2,525 lb TOGW

Mooney M.20L P4-ING

M.20E	Chapparal	Super 21 with squared-off windows and new windshield
M.20E	Aerostar 201	Chapparal with bullet tail fairing. This feature removed in 1974 version. Prototype N6729U (c/n 101)
M.20F	Executive	M.20E with 10-inch fuselage stretch and longer cabin with 3 windows each side. Powered by 200hp Lyc IO-360-A1A
M.20F	Aerostar 220	Executive with bullet tail fairing. 2,740 lb TOGW
M.20G	Statesman	Economy M.20F with reduced power 180hp Lyc O-360-A1D and 2,525 lb TOGW. Also named Aerostar 202
M.20J	Mooney 201	M.20F with cleaned-up nose cowling, 2 windows each side, new windshield, double u/c doors and numerous detail changes. Powered by 200hp Lyc IO-360-A3B6D. Prototype N201M (c/n 24-0001)
M.20J	Mooney 201LM	'Lean Machine' no-options lower-specification version of Model 201
M.20J	Mooney 201SE	'Special Edition' with improved interior trim
M.20J	Mooney 205	Replacement for 201SE with rounded-edge side windows, new wingtips, new u/c doors etc
M.20J	Mooney 205SE	Mooney 205 introduced 1986 with higher specification seats and trim as in 252TSE, improved electrical system
M.20J	Mooney ATS	Reduced specification trainer version of Mooney 205
M.20J	Mooney MSE	Modified Mooney 205 with 160 lb useful load increase and IFR equipment
M.20J	Mooney MSE Ltd	Lower-cost special edition version of MSE
MT.20	TX-1	Experimental two-seat military trainer based on M.20J with sliding clear view roof canopy, and four underwing pylons, powered by a Continental TSIO-360 turbocharged engine. Prototype N231TM (c/n 22-1179)
M.20K	Mooney 231	M.20J with turbocharged 210hp Cont. TSIO-360-GB-1 engine. 2,900 lb TOGW and increased fuel capacity
M.20K	Mooney 231SE	'Special Edition' with improved interior trim
M.20K	252 TSE	Mooney 231 with same window and other mods as Model 205 and improved 210hp Cont TSIO-360-MBI engine and instrument panel

Mooney M.20J MSE N201VB

M.20K	Encore	Mooney MSE with Ovation interior and 220hp/ Continental TSIO-360-MB7B engine. Prot N20MK (c/n M20K-25-2001) FF Mar 1997
M.20L	Mooney PFM	Model 252 with 12-inch longer fuselage and cabin and a 217hp Porsche PFM.3200 engine with single-lever power control. Prototype N20XL (c/n 26-0001). Production terminated 1991 when Porsche ceased building PFM.3200
M.20M	Mooney TLS	Turbo Lycoming Sabre version of M.20L with 270hp turbocharged Lycoming TIO-540-AF1A, long rear side windows with extra rear panel, 3-blade prop, 3,200 lb TOGW, extra fuel. Prototype N20XM (c/n 27-0001)
M.20M	Bravo	Mooney TLS with TIO-540-AF1B engine
M.20M	Bravo DX	Bravo with DX mods (enlarged instrument panel, Garmin avionics, new McCauley 2-blade prop etc)
M.20M	Bravo GX	Bravo with Garmin G1000 2-screen 'glass' cockpit instrument panel
M.20R	Ovation	M.20M fitted with 280hp Cont IO-550G engine with 3-blade prop, LoPresti cowling and luxury interior. 3,368 lb TOGW. Prototype N20XR (c/n 29-0001)
M.20R	Ovation2	Ovation with 2-blade McCauley prop and detail changes
M.20R	Ovation2DX	Ovation2 with enlarged instrument panel, Garmin avionics, new McCauley 2-blade prop and other minor changes
M.20R	Ovation2GX	Ovation2DX fitted with Garmin G1000 2-screen 'glass' cockpit instrument panel. Introduced Feb 2004
M.20S	Eagle	Reduced specification economy version of Ovation with 244hp Cont IO-550G engine, lower performance, reduced fuel, reduced specification avionics and 3,200 lb TOGW
M.20S	Eagle 2	Eagle with 3-blade propeller and 100 lb increased useful load
M.20T	Mooney EFS	Two-seat trainer for USAF EFS competition based on M.20J with sliding bubble canopy, firewall moved back 5 inches, 6 inch taller fin and 260hp Lycoming AEIO-540-D4B5 engine. Prototype N222FS (later N20XT) (c/n 28-0001). Renamed Predator
M.22	-	Unofficial designation for experimental twin-engined version of M.20A flown in Oct 1958 with two 150hp Lycoming O-320 (later 180hp O-360) engines. Prototype N5299B (c/n 6000)
M.22	-	Five-seat pressurized cabin monoplane with M.20 wings and tail unit, powered by a turbocharged 310hp Lycoming TIO-541-A1A. Initially named Mustang. Prototype N9122L (c/n 650001) FF 24 Sep 1964
M-10	Cadet	Mooney-built version of Alon A-2A with single vertical tail, modified cockpit and engine cowling. Prototype N5461M (c/n 690001)
M.30	Mooney 301	Six-seat pressurized low-wing business aircraft with retractable tricycle u/c and powered by one turbocharged 360hp Lycoming TIO-540-X27 piston engine. Prototype N301MX (c/n 000) FF 7 Apr 1983
TBM700	-	Single-engined turboprop business aircraft. See also Aérospatiale

Serial numbers allocated to Mooney aircraft were, initially, in a simple numerical sequence for the M-18 series. When the M.20 went into production, a completely new series was started, commencing at c/n 1001 and running up to c/n 3466 – including the models M.20, M.20A, M.20B and M.20C. For the M.20D and M.20E, new batches were started – each commencing at c/n 101. Aircraft were identified by M20D- or M20E- before the number.

In 1966, a new system was introduced. This gave each model its own serial range commencing at 0001. A new sequence was used for each model year – with the model year being identified as the first part of the total serial number. For instance, the 1967 M.20Fs ran from 670001 to 670539 and then the 1968 model started at 680001. This system continued until the Butler Aerostar takeover in 1970. From then onwards, each model was given a numerical prefix and serial numbers ran consecutively from 0001 without any separation of model years. M.20Cs started at 20-0001, M.20Es started at 21-0001 and M.20Fs started at 22-0001. The present Mooney company has used the prefix 24- for the M.20J, 25- for the M.20K, 26- for the M.20L, 27- for the M.20M, 28- for the M.20T, 29- for the M.20R and 30- for the M.20S. All the serial number allocations are detailed in the following table:

Mooney Aircraft Serial Allocations

Model	Name	Serial From	Serial To	Number Built	Years Built	Notes
M.20	Mark 20	1001	1200	200	1955-1958	
M.20A	Mark 20	1201	1700	500	1958-1960	
M.20B	Mark 21	1701	1939	238	1961	excluding 1852
M.20C	Mark 21	1940	2276	337	1962-1964	plus 1852
M.20C	Mark 21	2297	3466	1170	1964-1966	
M.20C	Mark 21	670001	670149	149	1967	
M.20C	Ranger	680001	680198	198	1968	
M.20C	Ranger	690001	690098	98	1969	
M.20C	Ranger 200	700001	700091	91	1970	
M.20C	Ranger 200	20-0001	20-0009	9	1971	
M.20C	Ranger	20-0010	20-0046	37	1974	
M.20C	Ranger	20-1147	20-1258	212	1975-1978	
M.20D	Master	101	260	160	1963-1966	
M.20E	Super 21	101	1308	1208	1964-1966	
M.20E	Super 21	670001	670062	62	1967	
M.20E	Chaparral	690001	690073	73	1969	
M.20E	Chaparral 201	700001	700061	54	1970	excluding 700040, 44, 53, 54, 57-59
M.20E	Chaparral 201	21-0001	21-0060	60	1971	
M.20E	Chaparral	21-1161	21-1180	20	1974	
M.20F	Executive 21	660003	660004	2	1966	
M.20F	Executive 21	670001	670539	539	1967	
M.20F	Executive 21	680001	680206	206	1968	
M.20F	Executive 21	690001	690092	92	1969	
M.20F	Aerostar 220	700001	700070	67	1970	excluding 700062, 64, 65
M.20F	Aerostar 220	22-0001	22-0078	78	1971	
M.20F	Executive	22-1179	22-1439	260	1975-1977	
M.20G	Statesman	680001	680164	164	1968	
M.20G	Statesman	690001	690020	20	1969	
M.20G	Statesman	700001	700006	6	1970	
M.20J	201	24-0001	24-1499	1493	1977-1984	excluding 24-0758 to 763
M.20J	201LM	24-1500	24-1685	186	1985-1988	
M.20J	ATS	24-1686-14	24-1706-14	21	1989-1990	
M.20J	205	24-3000	24-3078	79	1987-1988	
M.20J	201	24-3079	24-3375	296	1989-1995	excluding 24-3374
M.20J	MSE	24-3376	24-3412	38	1996-1997	plus 24-3374
M.20J	201	24-3413	24-3431	19	1998	
M.20K	231	25-0001	25-0999	999	1979-1985	
M.20K	TSE	25-1000	25-1230	230	1986-1990	excluding 25-1212
M.20K	Encore	25-2000	25-2032	34	1997-1998	plus 25-1212
M.20L	PFM	26-0001	26-0041	41	1988	
M.20M	TLS	27-0002	27-0208	207	1989-1995	
M.20M	TLS Bravo	27-0209	27-0333	125	1996-	current
M.20R	Ovation	29-0001	29-0199	198	1994-1999	excluding 29-0183
M.20R	Ovation 2	29-0200	29-0341	142	2000-2003	plus 29-0183
M.20R	Ovation 2DX	29-0300	29-0316	17	2003-	current
M.20S	Eagle	30-0001	30-0065	65	1999-2000	
Total				10500		
M-18	Mite	2	12	11	1949	
M-18L	Mite	13	81	69	1949-50	
M-18L	Mite	201	203	3	1950	
M-18C	Mite	82&101		2	1950	
M-18C	Mite	204	324	120	1950-53	excluding 277
M-18LA	Mite	102	145	44	1953-54	excluding 108, plus 277
M-18C-55	Mite	325	357	33	1955-56	
M.10	Cadet	690001	690011	11	1969	
M.10	Cadet	700001	700050	50	1970	
M.22	Mark 22	650001	650003	3	1965	
M.22	Mark 22	660004	660006	3	1966	
M.22	Mark 22	670001	670004	4	1967	
M.22	Mark 22	680001	680015	15	1968	
M.22	Mark 22	690001	690005	5	1969	
M.22	Mark 22	700001	700006	6	1970	
Total				379		

GRAND TOTAL				**10879**		

Moravan   Czech Republic

As explained in the section describing Aero, Czechoslovakia's entry into Soviet influence resulted in a 1949 reorganisation, which brought motor vehicle and aircraft manufacturing under the state holding company, CZAL (Ceskoslovenske Zavody Automobilove a Letecke). Under the CZAL umbrella, light aircraft continued to be built by the original Otrokovice factory of Zlinska Letecka A.S. (known as Zlin) but in 1950, this situation was rationalised by the establishment of three new companies – which included Moravan to take on the former Zlin civil aircraft activities. All marketing of their aircraft was handled by a national Foreign Trade Corporation (Omnipol).

During the war, Zlin had been producing the Bücker 181 Bestmann low-wing trainer for the Luftwaffe and during 1945-46 they continued to build some 72 of their Z-181 version, powered by a 105hp Hirth HM.504 engine. These were used by flying clubs and by the Czech Air Force, which designated them C.6. This gave way to the Z-281, 79 of which were completed with a 105hp Toma 4 engine, and then the Z-381 (military C.106) with a Walter Minor 4-III powerplant which added a further 314 examples to total production.

The first original postwar design from Zlin was the Z-20 – a six-seat low-wing twin with a fixed tailwheel undercarriage, which closely resembled the British Percival Q-6. The Z-20 prototype (OK-ZCA) was powered by a pair of 240hp Argus 10c engines and first flew on 14th March 1946. However, development of the Aero 45 light twin was also proceeding and it was decided that the Z-20 and its developed version, the Z-120 with a retractable undercarriage, should be abandoned.

Zlin directed its attentions towards a Bestmann replacement and Karel Tomas designed an attractive low-wing two-seat club trainer designated Z-22 and powered by a 57hp Zlin Persy III engine. The prototype Junak (OK-AOA) made its maiden flight on 28th April 1946 and the type went into production in 1949 with 170 examples being completed by the time output ceased in 1952. A number of these were the Z-22D version with a 75hp Praga D engine and Zlin also built a Z-22M model with a third seat, powered by a 105hp Walter Minor 4-III. The company also built two prototypes developed from the Z-22. These

were a four-seater – the Z-122 which used the 105hp Toma engine – and a single example of a side-by-side two-seat trainer, the Z-33 or PLK-5 (OK-FNA) which was a Junak with a cut-down rear fuselage and a bubble canopy. Neither of these models advanced beyond the development stage.

The design of the Z-22 made a perfect basis for Zlin to develop a new trainer to a specification issued in 1946 by the Czech Air Force. The Z-26 Trener used a refined version of the Z-22 wing but had a new fuselage with two seats in tandem under a framed sliding canopy. Zlin was successful in the competition and won an order for 113 units of the Z-26, which were put into service with the primary flying schools as the C.5. The Trener was a tube-and-fabric aircraft with a wooden wing and it gained a reputation for docile behaviour in its training role and for outstanding aerobatic qualities.

In both single and two-seat versions the Zlin became the standard mount in the 1950s and 1960s in world competition aerobatics. It was progressively developed with increasingly powerful engines. Single-seat Akrobat versions were built for each new basic model and later versions of the Akrobat were fitted with sophisticated wings and control surfaces to enhance their aerobatic performance. At an early stage, the Trener was equipped with a retractable undercarriage. The Zlin Trener series was widely exported and a small number of the Lycoming engined Z-526L were built in an attempt to improve its appeal in western markets. The Zlin Trener variants were as follows:

Z-26 Trener	Tandem two-seat low-wing dual control trainer of tube-and-fabric construction with fixed tailwheel u/c, powered by one 105hp Walter Minor 4-III. 1,653 lb TOGW. Prototype OK-COA FF 20 Oct 1947
Z-126 Trener 2	Z-26 with metal wings and rear decking, new metal tail unit, new brakes and new tailwheel. 1,686 lb TOGW. Z-126T is modification with 160hp Walter Minor 6-III engine
Z-226B Bohatyr	Z-126 with 160hp Walter Minor 6-III, glider-towing hook, single set of controls. 1,697 lb TOGW. Extra 40 litre fuel tank. Prototypes OK-JFA (c/n 830) FF 19 Apr 1955 & OK-JFB (c/n 831)

Moravan Zlin Z-126 Trener N247D

Z-226T Trener 6	Dual-control Z-226B without extra fuel tankage. Prototype OK-JEB converted from Z126 (c/n 870) FF 12 Apr 1956
Z-226A Akrobat	Single-seat Z-226T for competition aerobatics with front cockpit faired over. 1,642 lb TOGW
Z-226AS Akrobat	Z-226A with hydraulically-controlled Avia V503 metal prop, automatic elevator trim and new u/c fairings. 1,587 lb TOGW
Z-326 Trener Master	Z226T with 12in longer wings, tip tanks, electric retractable u/c, new cockpit canopy with fewer frames, larger rudder. 2,149 lb TOGW. Prototype OK-090 (c/n 301) FF 12 Aug 1957
Z-326A Akrobat	Single-seat version of Z-326 with hinged cabin entry. 1,873 lb TOGW. Prototype OK-OND FF 13 Apr 1960
Z-326TM	Z-326A with mods for East German competition team
Z-426	Agricultural version of Z-326. Not built
Z-526 Trener Master	Z-326 with Avia V503 prop, rear seat moved back, new engine cowling, new instrument panel. 2,149 lb TOGW. Prototype OK-SND (c/n 869) FF 3 Sep 1965
Z-526A Akrobat	Single-seat version of Z-526. 2,006 lb TOGW
Z-526AS Akrobat	Z-526A with sliding canopy, no flaps, strengthened forward fuselage. Prototype OK-WKA FF 29 Mar 1968
Z-526F Trener Master	Z-526 with 180hp Avia M-137A engine, low-pressure fuel injection, new engine cowl, larger oil tank. 2,149 lb TOGW. Prototype OK-SNA FF 24 Apr 1969. Model 526FI with mods for Iraq AF
Z-526AF Akrobat	Single-seat version of Z-526F. 1,829 lb TOGW. Prototype OK-WXA
Z-526AFS Akrobat Special	Z-526AF with shortened forward fuselage, wings cropped by 43in, large root fairings, larger rudder and differential flaperons, smaller fuel tank. 1,851 lb TOGW Prototype OK-YRA FF 25 Sep 1970
Z-526L Skydevil	Z-526F with 200hp Lycoming AIO-360-B1B engine and Hartzell C2YK-4 c/s prop. New canopy with reduced framing. 2,149 lb TOGW. Prototype OK-95 FF Aug 1969
Z-626	Z-526F with 210hp Avia M-337AK engine
Z-726 Universal	Z-526F with Avia M-137AZ engine, 2204 lb TOGW, metal control surfaces, 28in wingspan reduction. Prototype OK-082 (c/n 1331)

Moravan Zlin Z-526AF Akrobat N526ZZ

Z-726K Universal	Z-726 with 210hp Avia M-337AK engine and V500A c/s prop. Prototypes OK-95 (c/n 1069) FF 22 Aug 1973 & OK-078 (c/n 1075)

It should be noted that a number of Z-226, Z-326 and Z-526 series aircraft have been modified with the M-337 engine and their designations are suffixed 'M' (eg, Z-226M, Z-326M, Z-526AFM).

A substantial number of Zlin Treners of all models were exported to western countries. In 1970, it was even intended that Reims Aviation in France should build a batch of 250 of the Z-526L under licence with Reims Cessnas being marketed in the Eastern bloc by Omnipol. However, Reims finally decided not to proceed with this deal. Production of the Zlin Trener series is believed to total 1,493 examples in the following serial batches:

Type	Built	C/n Batches	Type	Built	C/n Batches
Z-26	162	1 to 12 & 501 to 650	Z-326	431	1 to 427 & 501 to 504
Z-126	171	701 to 870 & 883	Z-526/626	330	1001 to 1330
Z-226	366	1 to 370	Z-726	32	1331 to 1363

Moravan Zlin Z-326 HB-TCC

Moravan Zlin Z-50LX OK-XRB

By 1973, the Zlin Trener had reached the end of its development cycle and aerobatic pilots were searching for a more agile highly-stressed aircraft that could perform negative-G manouevres. Moravan designed the completely new all-metal single-seat Z-50L which had a straight, slightly tapered wing and fixed tailwheel undercarriage and was powered by a 260hp Lycoming. The Z-50L was sold in Europe as well as in the Eastern bloc and it went through a number of variants, as follows:

Type	Notes
Z-50L	Single-seat all-metal competition aerobatic aircraft powered by one 260hp Lycoming AEIO-540-D4B5. 1763 lb TOGW. Can be fitted with additional wingtip fuel tanks. Prototype OK-070 (c/n 0001) FF 18 July 1975
Z-50LA	Z-50L with a propeller-speed governor and pitch control
Z-50LE	Z-50L with lighter airframe and shortened wings with pointed tips. Prototype OK-VZA (c/n 51)
Z-50LS	Z-50L powered by a 300hp Lycoming AEIO-540-L1B5D engine with 1852 lb TOGW. Z-50LX has additional special equipment
Z-50M	Z-50L fitted with a 210hp Avia M-137AZ in-line engine. 1719 lb TOGW. Prototype OK-090 FF 25 Apr 1988

To date, Moravan have completed 80 examples of the Z-50 series from c/n 0001 to 0080.

In 1966, Moravan embarked on the design of a new light trainer for the flying clubs and the Ceskoslovenske Letectvo (Czech Air Force) that would offer rather less spartan conditions than the Z-326. This emerged as the Z-41 – an all-metal low-wing aircraft of similar layout to the Piper Cherokee. The intention was to use the airframe as a universal platform for a family of types, which would include an aerobatic aircraft, a crop sprayer, a turboprop utility transport and even a light twin. In the event, Moravan only went into production with the three basic models (the Z-42, Z-43 and Z-142) but have progressively developed them. Moravan was financially reorganised as the Moravan Akciova Spolecnost at Otrokovice but, in 1994, it was announced that the company was to be privatised and was available for sale. In 1999 a 55% interest was acquired by the American company, SDC International but it is understood that financial pressures have forced suspension of production. Details of different models are as follows:

Model	Notes
Z-41	Low-wing side-by-side two-seat aerobatic cabin monoplane with fixed tricycle u/c and Avia M-132 engine
Z-42	Production Z-41 with taller vertical tail, enlarged cockpit canopy with small additional side windows, powered by one 180hp Avia M-137A. Prototype OK-41/OK-ZSB FF 17 Oct 1967
Z-42M	Z-42 with V-503A c/s prop and dorsal fin extension
Z-42MU	Z-42 retrofitted with V-503A c/s prop
Z-42L	Z-42M with 160hp Lycoming AIO-360-B1B engine. Prototype only OK-YSA FF 10 Aug 1971
Z-43	Four-seat Z-42 with 27' fuselage plug and lengthened cabin. Powered by one 210hp Avia M-337A. Prototype OK-XKN FF 10 Dec 1968. Production aircraft has dorsal fin similar to Z-42M
Z-43L	Z-43 fitted with Lycoming engine and 3-blade prop. Prototype OK-LOW (c/n 0084)
Z-43R	Proposed Z-43 with retractable undercarriage
Z-43S	Z-43 modified to carry stretcher for ambulance work. Prototype OK-076/OK-XKN FF 1974
Z-44	Proposed single-seat aerobatic Z-42 with tailwheel u/c and M-137A engine
Z-45	Proposed single-seat crop sprayer with 500 litre hopper and 210hp M-337 engine
Z-46	Proposed high-wing 8-seat light twin
Z-47	Proposed high-wing utility aircraft with PT-6 turboprop engine
Z-48	Proposed twin-boomed 6-seat pusher turboprop

Moravan Zlin Z-43 D-EWFB

Z-52	Proposed 2-seat mid-wing trainer
Z-61L	Proposed tandem 2-seat, 300hp military trainer
Z-90	Proposed low-wing four-seat tourer with retractable u/c and 200hp Lycoming IO-360 engine. 1991 project. Not flown
Z-142	Z-42 with modified forward-sliding bubble canopy, new instrument panel and 210hp M-337AK engine and V-500A prop. Prototype OK-078 FF 27 Dec 1978
Z-142C	Z-142 fitted with western avionics etc
Z-143L	Four-seat Z-242 powered by 235hp Lycoming O-540-J3A5 engine. Prototype OK-074 FF 24 Apr 1992
Z-242L	Z-142 fitted with a 200hp Lyc AEIO-360-A1B6 with 3-blade Muhlbauer MTV-9 prop, modified wings with no forward sweep, u/c spats and new wingtips. Prototype OK-VNP (c/n 0490) FF Feb 1990. US certification awarded July 1994

Moravan has built 48 of the Z-42 (c/n 0001 to 0048), 149 of the Z-42M (c/n 0049 to 0190) and 114 of the Z-43 (c/n 0001 to 0114). The Z-142 was in current production with 368 built (c/n 0201 to 0568) and some 44 of the Z-143L had also been completed by the time production was suspended (c/n 0001 to 0006). Z-242L production commenced at c/n 0651 and reached c/n 0746.

Moravan Zlin Z-142 N48LK

Morrisey

United States

The Morrisey 1000C Nifty was designed by William J Morrisey and first flown in 1948. The prototype (NX5000K c/n 1A) was a low-wing monoplane built of wood and fabric with a fixed tricycle undercarriage. It used a 90hp Continental C-90 engine and the two occupants were housed in a tandem cockpit with a sideways-hinged canopy. The Morrisey Aircraft Company was formed in 1949 to exploit the design and a second aircraft, the Model 2000C (N5100V c/n 1B), was built and flown with a 108hp Lycoming O-235 engine.

The company was recapitalised and became Morrisey Aviation Inc in order to put the aircraft into production. It took some time for the new factory at Santa Ana, California to get into operation and the production aircraft was much different from the prototypes. Designated the Model 2150, it was re-engineered for all-metal construction, had an enlarged tail unit without the large fin fillet of the Nifty and was powered by a 150hp Lycoming O-320-A2A engine. Morrisey built nine aircraft during 1958 and 1959 (c/ns FP-1 to FP-9) and then sold the production rights to Shinn Engineering Inc who used the tenth airframe as the prototype for their improved Shinn 2150A (N5151V c/n MS-1-P). Shinn built 35 units (c/n SFP-11 and SP-12 to SP-45) before

ceasing production in 1962 due to demands of the other sections of their engineering business.

In 1967, Morrisey sold the type certificate for the Models 2150 and 2150A to George Varga who set up the Varga Aircraft Corporation to manufacture the Varga 2150A Kachina. A factory was established at Chandler, Arizona and first deliveries were made in mid-1975. The 2150A was joined, in late 1980, by the Model 2180 powered by a 180hp Lycoming O-360-A2D engine (the first aircraft being N8440J c/n VAC-171-81). The Kachina was also sold with a tailwheel undercarriage as the Varga 2150TG and 2180TG, and existing aircraft were modified to tailwheel undercarriage configuration by Hibbard Aviation of Oakland, California. Serial numbers of Varga aircraft carried a suffix indicating the year of construction and 121 of the Model 2150A were built as c/n VAC-50-74 to VAC-170-81. Varga 2180 production totalled 18 (c/n VAC-171-81 to VAC-188-82).

Varga eventually ceased production in 1982 and Bill Morrisey later reacquired the type certificates. Morrisey, based at Las Vegas, Nevada, launched a 'certified kit' version of the original Morrisey 2000C which could be completed by a homebuilder but would be regarded as a certificated aircraft after FAA inspection.

Varga 2150A Kachina G-BLHW

Mudry   France

Auguste Mudry formed CAARP (Cooperatives des Ateliers Aéronautiques de la Region Parisienne) in 1965 at Beynes-Thiverval to the south of Paris. It was, at first, primarily a design bureau with a number of ex-Scintex employees including Claude Piel, Louis de Goncourt and Nenad Hrissatovic. The initial production activity of the company was to build the CP.1310-C3 Super Emeraude, which had been transferred to the Beynes factory by Scintex. 11 examples were completed (c/n 932 to 942).

In August 1966, CAARP flew the prototype of the Piel CP.100, which was a 160hp development of the Super Emeraude with a larger nose and taller fin and rudder. Sadly, it was destroyed in an accident that killed Gérard Verette and Jacques Gomy and a second CP.100 was built in 1967 for static testing after the crash. With a broader chord rudder and various other modifications, the CP.100 later emerged in production form as the CAP-10 two-seat trainer. Encouraged by a French Air Force order for 26 aircraft, the company started building the CAP-10 in 1970. They also flew the prototype of the CAP-20, a single-seat aerobatic aircraft based on the CAP-10, and a small series of this type was produced including six aircraft for use by the Equipe de Voltige Aérienne of the Armée de l'Air.

Société Aéronautique Normande (SAN) had gone into receivership in November 1970. This gave Auguste Mudry the opportunity to expand by acquiring the SAN assets, so he set up a new company, Avions Mudry & Cie, and liquidated CAARP In 1978, the CAP-10 and CAP-20 assembly line was moved to the old SAN factory at Bernay but Avions Mudry also continued to fulfil the remaining orders for SAN D-140s and other models. Eventually, these Jodel designs were discontinued and the factory concentrated on the CAP-10 and CAP-20. It should be mentioned that amateur builders have also built at least four CAP-10s together with two aircraft using the CAP-10 fuselage and different wings (the AJBS.10 and the CAPDOL).

Mudry CAP-222 F-WWMX

The single-seat CAP-20 was much developed as demand increased for ever more sophisticated aerobatic aircraft. The first production batch of seven CAP-20s was followed by the lighter CAP-20L and then the CAP-21 with a completely new wing. The CAP-230 and CAP-231 were much enhanced developments to meet world aerobatic demands and Mudry built six CAP-231EX aircraft fitted with Extra-built wings with carbon fibre mainspars, this being eventually discontinued in favour of the CAP-232 with a new Mudry-built wing. Several other designers, notably Gérard Feugray with the ASA.200, used the CAP-20 airframe as the basis for custom aerobatic machines.

In addition to these models, the company also built fuselages for two sailplanes – the single-seat CAP-1 and the Rolladen-Schneider LS-1. Sadly, the CAP-1, which was an active project during 1974, did not get beyond the prototype testing stage. However, the company did build

Mudry CAP-10B G-BXRB

Mudry CAP-231EX F-GKKF

a new side-by-side two-seater, the CAP-X, which first flew in September 1982 and was followed by a further two prototypes. The CAP-X was of GRP construction and was powered by an 80hp Buchoux engine. They also built the Zenith Baroudeur microlight. On the night of 15th December 1995 Mudry suffered an arson attack that destroyed the production hangar at Bernay and three aircraft following which, in July 1996, Mudry declared bankruptcy. On 7th July 1997, the business passed into the hands of the Pellisier brothers and the CAP designs were taken over by Akrotech Europe (and by CAP Aviation in the following year). The line of CAP aircraft was expanded by the addition of the American Giles G-202 and eventually the designs were absorbed into Robin (Apex Aviation) and production was moved from Bernay to Dijon where they are built by CAP Aviation. The latest variant of the designs is the CAP-10C, which has a carbon fibre wing and larger ailerons and this wing can be retrofitted to existing CAP-10Bs. The company also built a prototype of the CAP-222 that was a re-engineered version of the American-designed Giles G-202 but this was abandoned in the face of uneconomic certification costs.

Each primary model from the Mudry factory had its own serial number series. The main production model was the CAP-10, serialled from c/n 01 to 04 (prototypes) and c/n 1 to 282 (the last Bernay-built CAP-10). This run included two spare fuselages (c/n 94 and 98) and one aircraft sold as a kit. As the Dijon-built CAP-10C, production has continued from 300 to 314 (at late 2004). CAP-20s were c/n 01 and 02 plus c/n 1 to 7. The CAP-20L was c/n 001 (prototype) and c/n 01 to 12 and CAP-21s were c/n 001 and c/n 01 to 17. The CAP-232 was c/n 001 and 02 to (currently) 45. and eleven CAP-230s were completed (c/n 001 and 01 to 10) with the CAP-231 following (c/n 11 to 24). The CAP-231EXs were c/n 001 and 02 to 06 and, finally, the CAP-232s were c/n 001 and 02 to 45 (in production in 2004). Details of these models are:

Type	Built	Notes
CP-100	1	Aerobatic two-seater based on Piel CP.301 with modified tail and wing and 160hp Lycoming. Prototype F-WNTD FF 12 Aug 1966
CAP-10	4	CP-100 with enlarged rudder, bigger canopy and 180hp Lyc IO-360-B2F engine. Prototype F-WOPX (c/n 01) FF 22 Aug 1968
CAP-10B	280	Production version of CAP-10
CAP-10C	12	CAP-10B with new carbon fibre reinforced mainspar, larger ailerons. Prototype F-WWNN (c/n 300) FF 2 Mar 2001
CAP-20	1	Single-seat competition aerobatic derivative of CAP-10 with 200hp Lycoming AIO-360-B1B engine. Prototype F-WPXU FF 29 Jul 1969
CAP-20A	3	CAP-20 without main wing dihedral
CAP-20B	4	CAP-20 with 1.5 degree dihedral and enlarged ailerons
CAP-20E	1	CAP-20 with 260hp Lycoming AEIO-540-D4B5 engine
CAP-20L-180	1	CAP-20 with simplified structure, modified tail, nil dihedral and 180hp Lycoming AEIO-360 engine. Prototype F-WVKY (c/n 001) FF 15 Jan 1976
CAP-20LS-200	12	CAP-20L with 200hp Lycoming AEIO-360-B1B engine. Prototype F-WZAJ
CAP-21	18	CAP-20LS-200 with cantilever u/c and redesigned wing. Prototype F-WZCH (c/n 001) FF 23 Jun 1980
CAP-202	1	Initial designation for CAP-222
CAP-222	1	Tandem 2-seat low-wing aerobatic aircraft based on Akrotech Giles G-202 with fixed tailwheel u/c and 200hp Lyc AEIO-360-A1E engine. Prototype F-WWMY (c/n 001) FF 12 June 1997
CAP-230	11	CAP-21 with 300hp Lycoming AEIO-540-L1 engine and fitted with angular tail. Prototype F-WZCH (c/n 001) FF 8 Oct 1985
CAP-231	14	CAP-230 with extended wingroot leading edges, elevator servo tab and Muhlbauer 3-bladed prop
CAP-231EX	6	CAP-231 with carbon fibre components including the wing built by Walter Extra. Prototype F-WZCI FF 18 Dec 1991
CAP-231C		CAP-231 retrofitted with CAP-232 wings
CAP-232	45	CAP-231 with new Mudry-designed carbon fibre wing with thinner section and modified ailerons. Prototype F-WZCH FF 7 Jul 1994
CAP-X	3	Side-by-side two-seat trainer with fixed tricycle u/c powered initially by 80hp Buchoux MB4-80. 4th prototype to have tailwheel u/c. Production version fitted with 112hp Lyc O-235. Prototype F-WZCJ (c/n 001) FF 10 Sep 1982
Total	420	

Myasishchev M-101T Gzhel RA-15101

Myasishchev
Russia

The M-101 Gzhel is a single-turboprop business and utility aircraft of conventional layout with a pressurized cabin, low-wing and retractable tricycle undercarriage. Standard accommodation is for seven passengers and one pilot. The production M-101T is powered by a 760shp Walter M601F turboprop but a westernised version, designated M-101PW, is planned with a Pratt & Whitney PT6A-64 engine. The prototype first flew on 31st March 1995 followed by three further development aircraft (c/ns 150001 to 1500040). At least eight production M-101Ts are known to have flown (c/n 1501001 to 1501008) at Myasishchev's Zhukovsky factory.

National Aerospace Laboratories
India

In 1992, the National Aerospace Laboratories (NAL) designed a new two-seat trainer for use by Indian flying clubs. The Hansa-2 was an all-composite aircraft with side-by-side seating, a fixed tricycle undercarriage and a 100hp Continental O-200 engine. The aircraft's wing was unusual in having pronounced sweep on the front edge of its outer panels. The prototype, VT-XIW, first flew on 17th November 1993 and was subsequently re-engined with a 125hp Continental IO-240 to become the Hansa-2RE. The production version, known as the Hansa-3 was further modified with longer-span wings, flaps and cabin rear side windows. The prototype Hansa-3I (VT-XAL c/n 001) first flew on 26th November 1996 and was followed by the Hansa-3II (VT-XBL/HBL c/n 002) in May 1998 powered by a 113hp Rotax 914-F3 engine which is the production standard powerplant. The Hansa-3 is being built in series by Taneja Aerospace and Aviation Ltd at Bangalore, the first example (VT-HNS c/n 001) flying on 14th May 1999. Eight production aircraft had been built by mid-2004 (c/n 001 to 008). The next version will be the Hansa-4, which would be powered by an SMA SR.305-230 diesel engine. NAL has also developed the Saras 14-seat turboprop business and general utility aircraft in cooperation with Myasishchev (who designated it M-102 Duet). This is now at prototype

NAL Hansa 3 VT-HBL. J Wadia

stage and being managed by the CSIR (Council for Scientific and Industrial Research). The prototype, VT-XSD made its maiden flight on 29th May 2004 powered by two Pratt & Whitney PT6A rear-fuselage-mounted pusher turboprop engines.

Neiva   Brazil

The Sociedade Construtora Aeronáutica Neiva Ltda. was established in postwar aircraft manufacturing by José Carlos de Barros Neiva on 12th October 1953 with the aim of building the BN-1 and Monitor gliders and, later, the CAP-4 Paulistinha. The Paulistinha was a near-copy of the two-seat high-wing Piper Cub. The original prototype (PP-TBF), known as the EAY-201 Ypiranga, was built in 1935 by the Empresa Aeronautica Ypiranga and used a Salmson radial engine. This was soon replaced by a 65hp Franklin engine, but only four production aircraft were completed before the company was taken over, in 1942, by the Companhia Aeronáutica Paulista. An improved model, known as the CAP-4 Paulistinha, was then built in series for civil and military use and 782 examples, including two CAP-4Bs and a single CAP-4C, were completed during the period up to 1949 (c/n 1 to 782). The company then fell into financial trouble and abandoned further manufacture.

The Neiva version of the Paulistinha differed from the CAP-4 in having a larger 90hp or 100hp engine, more modern instrumentation, re-shaped cabin windows and improved soundproofing. The initial production batch was largely constructed from Paulista-produced parts acquired when the original production line closed. Variants of this Neiva 56 included an agricultural model and the L-6 military observation version, which was delivered in small numbers to the Brazilian Air Force. Neiva built a total of 240 of the Model 56 (c/n 1001 to 1240) including a number known as the 'Luxo' with a factory-fitted radio and electric starter, and details of all the Paulistinha models are as follows:

Neiva CAP-4 Paulistinha PP-GSP

Model	Notes
Paulistinha 56B	Neiva-built CAP-4 with styling changes, new instrument panel and 100hp Lycoming O-235-C1 engine. Military L-6
Paulistinha 56C	Paulistinha 56 with 90hp Continental C90-8F engine
Paulistinha 56D	Paulistinha 56 with 150hp Lycoming O-320-A1A engine for glider towing and agricultural use (Agricolo)
IPD-5802 Campeiro	Military observation version of Neiva 56D. One aircraft only, PP-ZTT, FF 2 Feb 1960. Military L-7

Model	Notes
CAP-4 Paulistinha	Tandem two-seat high-wing light aircraft of mixed construction with fixed tailwheel u/c and one 65hp Franklin 4AC-176-B2 engine. Paulista-built
CAP-4B Ambulancia	CAP-4 with hinged upper rear fuselage decking to accommodate stretcher case
CAP-4C	Military observation CAP-4 with cut-down rear fuselage, all-round vision cockpit and rear-facing observer seat. Known as the 'Paulistinha Radio'
CAP-5 Carioca	Side-by-side two-seater based on CAP-4 and powered by one 90hp Franklin. 7 built. Prototype PP-RHN
CAP-9D	No details known. 10 built

Neiva now moved on to an original design – the N-591 Regente. It was a modern high-wing all-metal light aircraft with four seats, a fixed tricycle undercarriage and a 180hp Lycoming O-360-A1A engine. The prototype, PP-ZTP, made its first flight on 7th September 1961 and the type was ordered in quantity by the Brazilian Air Force as the L-42 liaison aircraft and the C-42 light transport. Some 120 are understood to have been completed and, although it was not sold as a commercial model, several Regentes subsequently appeared on the Brazilian civil register. Following the Regente, Neiva built a long production run of N-621 and N-622 Universal military trainers at their factory at Sao José dos Campos near Sao Paulo and on 11th March 1980, the company was acquired by Embraer who passed over responsibility for their light aircraft production.

Neiva N-591 Regente

Embraer/Neiva EMB-201 Ipanema PT-GTB

enlarged (950-litre) hopper, 550 lb higher gross weight, three-blade propeller, a new crop dusting system and large wingtip winglets. Ipanema production continues, with virtually all aircraft going to the Brazilian coffee-farming market and the 1,000th aircraft was delivered in March 2005. A version of the EMB-202 with a Lycoming engine modified to operate using alcohol has also been introduced. The serial batches to the end of 2004 have been c/n 200001 to 200998 with reservations extending to c/n 20001062 for 2005. These include three glider-towing EMB-201Rs, used by the Brazilian Air Force as the U-19.

The largest of all Embraer's general aviation programmes was the assembly of Piper aircraft for sale in Brazil. This agreement was established in August 1974 with several models being supplied in kits of progressively smaller subassemblies. Piper aircraft assembly was handed over to Neiva in 1980 and it continued until the supply of kits from Piper ceased in 1992. The various Piper models built by Embraer/Neiva have been:

In the late 1960s, the CTA had designed the IPD-6901 low-wing agricultural aircraft to specifications drawn up by the Ministry of Agriculture. Embraer built the prototype of this design (PT-ZIP) powered by a 260hp Lycoming O-540-H1A5 engine and it was first flown on 31st July 1970. With minor alterations, it went into production in 1972 as the EMB-200 Ipanema and 49 of the initial model were built followed, in February 1974, by 24 of the EMB-200A with larger wheels and a variable-pitch propeller. In September 1974, the EMB-201 was introduced and this used a 300hp Lycoming IO-540-K1J5D engine and had increased agricultural payload. 203 examples were delivered before it was replaced in 1977 by the EMB-201A, which has a new wing design to improve slow-speed handling. After Neiva was acquired by Embraer on 11th March 1980 and Neiva took over light aircraft responsibility they transferred production of the Ipanema and Piper types to their factory at Botucatu. The latest version of the Ipanema is the EMB-202 Ipanemão which has a 40%

Embraer/Neiva Model	Piper Model	C/n Batch
EMB-710C Carioca	PA-28-235 Dakota	710001 to 710264
EMB-710D Carioca	PA-28-236 Dakota	710265 to 710288
EMB-711C Corisco	PA-28R-200 Arrow II	711001 to 711219
EMB-711B Corisco	PA-28R-201 Arrow III	711220 to 711251
EMB-711S Corisco II	PA-28RT-201 Arrow IV	711252 to 711443
EMB-711ST Corisco Turbo II	PA-28RT-201T Turbo Arrow IV	inc in 711252 to 711443
EMB-712 Tupi/Carioquinha	PA-28-181 Archer II	712001 to 712145
EMB-720C Minuano	PA-32-300 Saratoga	720001 to 720126
EMB-720D Minuano	PA-32-301 Saratoga	720127 to 720291
EMB-721C Sertanejo	PA-32R-300 Saratoga SP	721001 to 721150
EMB-721D Sertanejo	PA-32R-301 Saratoga SP	721151 to 721205
EMB-810C Seneca	PA-34-200T Seneca II	810001 to 810452
EMB-810D Seneca	PA-34-220T Seneca III	810453 to 810846
EMB-820 Navajo	PA-31-350 Chieftain	820001 to 820168
EMB-821 Carajah	Schaefer Comanchero 500	821-001 to 821-034

Noorduyn   Canada

Canada has been famous for breeding excellent bush aircraft. One of the best known is the Noorduyn Norseman, which was designed by Robert B Noorduyn and owed much to his past experience at Bellanca.

It was put into production by Noorduyn Aviation Ltd. The prototype Mk I (CF-AYO c/n 1) first flew in November 1935, powered by a 420hp Wright R-975-E3 radial and was followed by three Mk IIs (c/n 2 to 4) and two Mk IIIs, upgraded to a 450hp Pratt & Whitney Wasp SC (c/n 5 and 6).

CCF Norseman Mk V N45TG

The Norseman was a classic high-wing tube-and-fabric monoplane with a fixed tailwheel undercarriage and a capacious cabin that could carry eight passengers or large quantities of freight. During the war, Noorduyn built 762 of the C-64 Norseman for the United States Air Force comprising 13 of the Mk IV (6 YC-64s and 7 C-64Bs) and 749 of the Mk VI (UC-64A). These all used an even larger powerplant – the 550hp Pratt & Whitney R-1340-AN-1 or S3H1 radial. They were included in a production run which covered 93 Mk IVs (c/n 7 to 99) and 750 of the Mk VI (c/n 100 to 849).

At the end of the war production of the Norseman was continued by Noorduyn Norseman Aircraft. They introduced some minor changes and started to build the new civil Norseman V – still fitted with the R-1340-AN-1 Wasp engine. The first Norseman V (CF-OBG c/n N29-1) was delivered to Ontario Provincial Air Service in 1945. Production continued until February 1959 by which time 53 examples of the Norseman V had been completed. These carried serial numbers N29-1 to N29-48, N29-50 to N29-53 and N29-55. One of these aircraft (CF-GOQ-X c/n N29-49 – later CCF 129-1) was converted by Canadian Car & Foundry (CCF) to Norseman VII standard with a longer cabin and all-metal wings and horizontal tail, but this prototype was destroyed in a hangar fire and the version was not developed further. CCF also converted two Mk IVs to Mk V configuration (c/n CCF-52 and CCF-55).

Norman Aircraft   United Kingdom

Following the collapse of the original Britten-Norman company in 1970, Desmond Norman left and formed NDN Aircraft Ltd. One of the light aircraft designs which had been produced in prototype form by Britten Norman was the BN-3 Nymph all-metal high-wing light aircraft. The prototype (G-AXFB c/n 5001) was first flown on 17th May 1969 powered by a 115hp Lycoming O-235-C1B piston engine. It was intended for local assembly in under-developed countries under a 'technology transfer' system. NDN intended to build the Nymph as the re-engined NAC-1 Freelance with a lengthened cabin, redesigned wing, integral fuel tanks and a 180hp Lycoming O-360-A engine. They flew the reworked prototype (G-NACI c/n NAC.001) on 30th September 1984 and this was followed by a further NAC-2 Freelance 180 (G-NACA c/n 2001) but, although at least four further airframes were manufactured, Freelance production did not progress any further. NDN Aircraft Ltd also designed and built the NDN.1 Firecracker turboprop military trainer which was unsuccessfully entered in the RAF trainer competition via a partnership with Hunting Aircraft.

Another project was the NDN.6 Fieldmaster agricultural aircraft which was originally designed by Desmond Norman's NDN Aircraft Ltd under the sponsorship of the National Research and Development Council (NRDC). The first prototype (G-NRDC c/n 004) was first flown on 17th December 1981. It was powered by a 750shp Pratt & Whitney PT6A-34AG turboprop and was able to carry 698 US gallons of liquid dressing or firefighting chemical retardant in its hopper. The Fieldmaster, which had a second seat to allow for the transport of a ground crewman, went into production at the Cardiff factory of Norman Aircraft Company (renamed from NDN Aircraft Ltd in July 1985) and five production examples of the NAC.6 (c/n 6001 to 6005) were built before NDN went into receivership in August 1988.

Croplease Ltd then acquired all rights to the aircraft and contracted with Brooklands Aerospace to develop a more powerful version – the Firemaster 65. The prototype was converted from an existing Fieldmaster (G-NACL c/n 6001) and was fitted with a 1,230shp PT6A-65 engine and five-bladed Hartzell propeller. This first flew from Old Sarum in the new configuration on 28th October 1989 and Croplease went ahead and re-engined at least two other Fieldmasters (G-NACN and G-NACO). They planned to construct a further five new aircraft and intended that major components should be made by UTVA in Serbia for final assembly by Croplease at Sandown, Isle of Wight. An agricultural Fieldmaster 65 variant was also to be available – but none of these plans reached fruition. Desmond Norman passed away on 13th November 2002.

NDN Firemaster G-NACM

Oberlerchner   Austria

The Josef Oberlerchner Holzindustrie was an Austrian company that established a pre-war reputation for building sailplanes. In 1957, the company built the prototype of the JOB-5 side-by-side two-seat light aircraft (OE-VAF/OE-CAF, c/n 01) powered by a 95hp Continental C90-12F piston engine. It first flew on 2nd December 1958 and was of mixed wood, tube, fabric and glassfibre construction with a low wing and fixed tailwheel undercarriage. It had a blister cockpit canopy that was subsequently enlarged.

In its production version, as the JOB-15, the wing was redesigned, the cabin modified for three seats and many detail changes were made including enlargement of the tail unit. Oberlerchner decided to produce two models – with either a 135hp Lycoming O-290 engine or a 150hp Lycoming O-320-A2B, but in practice only the first aircraft (OE-VAL/OE-CAL, c/n 051) had the 135hp powerplant. This was first flown on 21st March 1961 and the type went into production at Spittal-Drau with a total of 22 JOB-15/150s being produced (c/n 052 to 073). From c/n 062 the aircraft were built to JOB-15-150/2 standard with an enlarged rear seat so that total accommodation was increased

Oberlerchner JOB-15-150 D-EFNI

to four people. Three examples were re-engined with a 180hp Lycoming O-360-A3A engine and redesignated JOB 15-180/2. The last JOB-15 was completed in 1966.

OMF   Germany

In 1998, OMF was formed at Neu Brandenburg to develop a production light aircraft based on the Stoddard-Hamilton GlaStar. The GlaStar is a strut-braced high-wing aircraft with a side-by-side two-seat cabin and a fixed tricycle or tailwheel undercarriage and the prototype (N824G) first flew at Arlington, Washington on 29th November 1994. The GlaStar, which has a composite fuselage and metal wings, has been sold as a kit to amateur builders by Stoddard-Hamilton and, subsequently, New GlaStar LLC. The OMF-100-160 Symphony is a JAR.23 certificated version and the prototype (D-ETCW c/n P1) first flew in May 1999. Compared with the GlaStar the Symphony has substantially redesigned control surfaces including electrically-driven flaps, a redesigned tricycle undercarriage and a 60 lb increase in gross weight. It is powered by a 160hp Lycoming O-320-D2A engine. Production by OMF GmbH commenced at Trollen-hagen in 2001 and a Canadian subsidiary, OMF Aircraft, was also formed to build the aircraft. In December 2003 the company declared bankruptcy and the assets in Germany were sold to OMFDE. The Canadian business was reconstituted at Trois Rivieres by Symphony Aircraft Industries Inc (SAI) in February 2004 and the assets repurchased from OMFDE. Aircraft from c/n 0001 to 0042 had been completed by mid-2004, the majority being sold in the USA. The first of these (D-EMVP c/n 0001) has been converted as the prototype OMF-100-135-TDI powered by a 135hp Thielert Centurion 1.7 diesel engine and first flew as such in June 2003. The first example of the SAI Symphony SA160 (C-GUSA, c/n S-0001) flew in March 2005 at Trois Rivieres and is similar to the OMF-100-160 with options of a ballistic parachute and a glass cockpit. The Symphony 250 (formerly Symphony 4) is a four-seat version powered by a 250hp Lycoming IO-540 engine which was being developed but has been suspended until the new production line is established.

SAI Symphony SA160 C-GUSA

Orlican L-40 Meta Sokol G-APUE

Orlican   Czechoslovakia

One of the strongest pre-war light aircraft companies was the Benes-Mraz Tovarna na Letadla which was based at Chocen. During the 1930s, the company was well known for its training and touring aircraft, particularly the Benes-Mraz Be-50 and Be-51 tandem two-seat trainers and the Be-550 Bibi two-seat cabin tourer. During the war, Benes-Mraz was employed on German war production but, under Ing Zdenec Rublic, they secretly designed a new two-seat low-wing light aircraft – the M-1A Sokol – which was based on the Bibi and the Zobor design but was fitted with a retractable undercarriage.

Soon after the defeat of Germany, Automobilov Zavody absorbed the former Benes-Mraz factory (renaming it Orlican Narodny Podnik) and built a prototype of the Sokol. This went into production at Chocen in 1946 alongside a batch of 138 Mraz-built Fieseler Storchs (known as the K-65 Mraz Cap). Five different versions of the Sokol were built during the period 1946 to 1950, as follows:

Model	Notes
M-1A	Side-by-side all-wood two-seat low-wing cabin monoplane with retractable tailwheel u/c and one 105hp Walter Minor 4-III engine. Prototype OK-ZHA FF 9 Mar 1946
M-1B	M-1A fitted with 105hp ZLAS Toma 4 engine. One prototype only OK-ZHB FF 19 May 1947
M-1C	M-1A with increased gross weight, longer cabin and third rear seat, extra rear side windows and swept wing leading edges. Prototype OK-BHD FF 16 Feb 1947
M-1D	M-1C with single-piece clear view main cockpit canopy hinged on left side and larger rear windows. Prototype OK-CEF FF 4 Oct 1948
M-1E	M-1D fitted with twin floats at increased gross weight. One known aircraft: OK-DHR (c/n 277)

A total of 287 Sokols were completed. Exact serial batches are uncertain, but it seems that there were 183 examples of the M-1C (c/n 101 to 273) and 104 of the M-1D (c/n 274 to 387).

While the Sokol was in full production, Ing Rublik designed a new two-seat trainer: the M-2 Skaut. This had the Sokol tail and a derivative of its wing married to a new fuselage with a large bubble canopy. The Skaut prototype (OK-CEB) was powered by a 75hp Praga D engine and had a fixed tricycle undercarriage. It was extensively tested from the summer of 1948 onwards but did not reach production status.

The next major development from Orlican was the M-3 Bonzo which led to the L-40 Meta Sokol. The Bonzo was, essentially, a Sokol airframe using a modified wing without the Sokol's swept leading edge and the fuselage enlarged to provide an additional rear seat. The rear fuselage was cut down to allow for a large 360° cabin canopy and a retractable tricycle undercarriage was fitted. The Bonzo was powered by a 160hp Walter Minor 6-III engine and OK-CIZ, the prototype, first flew at Chocen in April 1948.

The Bonzo still used a wooden airframe and it was decided to develop the concept as an all-metal aircraft. The result was the XLD-40 Mir which was virtually a new design. The 3-seat Mir prototype, OK-EKZ (c/n 1), which first flew on 30th July 1950, reverted to the Sokol wing but had a V-tail, a large rear-sliding bubble canopy and a 105hp Walter Minor 4-III engine. Its 'reverse tricycle' undercarriage consisted of main legs retracting backwards as on the Sokol and a small retracting rear wheel placed under the fuselage at rear wing root level.

The V-tail on OK-EKZ was subsequently replaced by a conventional fin and tailplane, the surfaces of which were interchangeable. Three prototypes (OK-KHA, KHN and KHO c/n 01 to 03) were built, the first of which was flown on 29th March 1956. Initial production aircraft were powered by the Walter Minor 4-III engine and operated as three-seaters but the majority used a 140hp Walter M-332 which allowed a fourth occupant. 107 Meta Sokols were produced (including the three prototypes), of which at least half were exported. These included a number of extended range variants with wingtip fuel tanks. Production serial numbers followed a similar system to that used for the Chocen-built Brigadyr. They were in batches with a prefix '15' followed by a batch number and two digits. Batches were 150001 to 150003, 150201 to 150207, 150301 to 150309, 150401 to 150410 and five further batches of 15 aircraft commencing at c/n 1505001 and ending at 150915.

Benes Mraz Sokol M-1C Sokol

MAI-890 '07'

OSKBES-MAI   Russia

This organisation (the Otraslevoye Spetsialnoye Konstruktorskoye Byuro Eksperimentalnogo Samolyotostroyeniya – Moskovskogo Aviatsionnogo Instituta) is the light aircraft development department of the Moscow Aviation Institute whose activities go back to 1967. Its earliest flying design was the Kvant single-seat aerobatic machine, two of which were built in 1977. OSKBES-MAI has been responsible for a number of military UAVs and the Foton experimental lift-augmentation aircraft but the best-known aircraft, now built in quantity, are the series of designs based on the Aviatika 890. This design started as the Yunior: a single-seat pusher-engined ultralight biplane built round a steel tube spine to which were attached the engine/wing support pylon, a fixed tricycle undercarriage and the tail unit. The Yunior flew in July 1987 powered by a 45hp KhAI-45 engine. In 1989, the prototype MAI-89, fitted with a Rotax 582 engine was flown and this resulted in production of the MAI-890, initially under the auspices of Aviatika but eventually in association with MAPO (RSK-MiG). Production quantities and serial numbers are not known but details of the MAI-890 and a range of other civil light designs are as follows.

MAI-890 Single-seat 450kg ultralight biplane with fixed tricycle u/c, partly-enclosed cabin pod and powered by a pusher 64hp Rotax 582UL, 50hp Rotax 503UL or 100hp Rotax 912ULS

MAI-890U MAI-890 with enlarged cabin pod with side-by-side seating for two and dual controls. 80hp Rotax 912UL. FF Aug 1991. JAR-VLA certified. 540kg gross weight

MAI-890SKh MAI-890 fitted with 27.7 gal chemical tank and spraybars for crop spraying. Fully enclosed cockpit. JAR-VLA certified. 540kg gross weight

MAI-890USKh Two-seat MAI-890SKh for agricultural pilot training

MAI-890S MAI-890 powered by a 100hp Rotax 912ULS engine

MAI-205 Autogyro version of MAI-890 without wings and fitted with rotor pylon and 2-blade rotor. 100hp Rotax 912ULS or 64hp Rotax 582 engine. Some equipped for crop spraying. Prototype designated MAI-890A. MAI-205 FF 26 Jan 2001

MAI-217 Side-by-side two-seat multi-purpose mid-wing light aircraft with fixed tricycle u/c and Rotax 912ULS engine

MAI-290 Single-seat training glider using MAI-890 fuselage/tail, monoplane wing and monowheel u/c

MAI-223 Strut-braced/pylon mounted parasol-wing light aircraft with enclosed two-seat cabin, fixed tailwheel u/c. Powered by Rotax 582UL or Rotax 912ULS engine. Prototype FF 20 Oct 2004

MAI-900 Acrobat. Single-seat low-wing aerobatic aircraft with fixed tailwheel u/c and powered by one 360hp Vedeneyev radial engine. FF 1992

MAI-910 Interfly. Side-by-side two-seat all-metal light aircraft with fixed tricycle u/c and extensively glazed enclosed cabin. Powered by an 80hp Rotax 912UL engine. FF 22 Jun 1995

Pacific Aerospace   New Zealand

Pacific Aerospace (PAC) was formed in Hamilton, New Zealand on 1st July 1982 as a result of a reorganisation of New Zealand Aerospace Industries Ltd – which was, itself, the result of the amalgamation of Air Parts (NZ) Ltd and Aero Engine Services Ltd on 1st April 1973. Pacific Aerospace became owned by ASTA (75%) and Lockheed Aeronautical Systems Corp (now Lockheed Martin) but the ASTA share was acquired by the New Zealand company, Aeromotive Ltd in 1996. PAC widened its activities in 1984 with the takeover of another prominent company, James Aviation Ltd In addition to subcontract component manufacture and turnkey aerospace engineering projects, PAC builds three aircraft

types – the FU24 (and Pacific Aerospace Cresco) agricultural aircraft, the CT4 Airtrainer and the PAC.750XL utility aircraft.

The FU24 design goes back to 14th June 1954 when the Sargent – Fletcher Company of El Monte, California flew the prototype of this low-wing all-metal agricultural aircraft (N6505C c/n 1 – later ZK-BDS). This was specifically designed by John Thorp (as the T-15) for the needs of the New Zealand top-dressing market, which had been using Tiger Moths for this work. Fletcher was awarded a type certificate on 22nd July 1955 and, initially, they built complete aircraft and shipped them to Hamilton, New Zealand. However, after eleven units had been completed the FU24 started to be shipped in kit form for assembly by Cable-Price Corporation at Hamilton's Rukuhia Airport.

The task of manufacture of the FU24 passed to Air Parts (NZ) Ltd in 1962 and eventually, in 1964, they bought out all manufacturing rights from Fletcher (by this time renamed Flair Aviation). The FU24 was produced with a 300hp Continental IO-520-F engine in either standard form or as the FU24A with dual controls. The hopper was situated in the large rear fuselage with a filler hatch on top, but Air Parts also experimented with a six-seat passenger-carrying model (ZK-CVW c/n 139) with oval portholes in the rear fuselage and at least one other aircraft was converted to this layout.

A total of 257 examples of the basic FU24-950 (c/n 1 to 257) were built and Pacific Aerospace then changed to the FU24-954, which has a 1,360 lb increase in gross weight and is powered by a 400hp Lycoming IO-720-A1A piston engine. By June 1992 production of this model had reached 40 (c/n 258 to 297). A number of additional aircraft were built either from spare parts or from the remains of crashed Fletchers with various one-off serial numbers, and James Aviation has produced at least seven, numbered c/n JAL-FU-1 to JAL-FU-7. At least three Fletchers in kit form (c/n 3001 to 3003) were delivered to the United States. Some FU24s have been modified under an STC by Super Air in New Zealand with a 550hp Ford 460 converted automotive engine fitted with a three-blade reversible Hartzell propeller.

In July 1967, James Aviation flew the prototype Fletcher 1060 (ZK-CTZ c/n 1001), which was powered by a 500shp Pratt & Whitney PT6A-20 turboprop and had a stretched fuselage and longer wings. In February of the following year, another Fletcher (ZK-BHQ c/n 2001) was fitted with a Garrett AiResearch TPE331 turboprop and this received the designation Fletcher 1160. Neither of these models went into production but they did lead the way for Pacific Aerospace's turboprop model – the Cresco 08-600. This was similar to the FU24-954 but with a longer nose housing a Lycoming LTP-101-700A-1A turboprop, a large dorsal fin and a port side rear cargo door. The prototype (ZK-LTP c/n 001) was first flown on 28th February 1979 and production had reached c/n 039 by mid-2004. From the tenth aircraft, Pacific Aerospace changed the engine to the Pratt & Whitney PT6A-34AG. The Cresco airframe formed the basis for the larger PAC.750XL, which married the Cresco tail, wings and undercarriage to a new deeper fuselage with large square windows to the passenger cabin. It is aimed at the sport parachuting market and as a competitor for the Cessna Caravan as a 9-passenger (17-parachutist) general utility aircraft. The 750XL is powered by a 750shp Pratt & Whitney PT6A-34 turboprop. Design work started in January 1999 and the prototype (ZK-XLA c/n 101) first flew in September 2001. FAA certification was received on 10th March

Victa Air Tourer ZK-VTR

2004 and total production had reached c/n 115 by the end of 2004 with ten aircraft delivered during that year.

The CT4 Airtrainer has its origins in Australia with the Victa Airtourer design. In 1952, the British Royal Aero Club sponsored a design competition for a new two-seat light club trainer. The winner was the low-wing Airtourer, designed by Dr Henry Millicer, chief aerodynamicist of the Australian Government Aircraft Factory. After some years a wooden prototype was constructed by members of the Australian ULAA and this Airtourer Mk 1 (VH-FMM) made its first flight on 31st March 1959 powered by a 65hp Continental A-65 engine. Two years later, the Airtourer was taken over by Victa Ltd and redesigned as an all-metal aircraft for commercial production.

The basic Victa Airtourer was fully aerobatic and featured an unusual centrally-mounted control column with a spade grip so that the aircraft could be flown from either seat. It was powered by a 100hp Continental engine but Victa also built a version with a 115hp Lycoming. They completed a total of 170 aircraft before production ceased in 1966 as a result of the poor profit margin that was being achieved.

Victa sold the Airtourer design, in 1967, to Aero Engine Services Ltd (AESL). The sale included all the necessary jigs and tooling and seven incomplete airframes which formed the initial batch of production by AESL. AESL was successful in gaining substantial orders with 24 going to Britain, a batch to Thailand and military deliveries to Singapore.

Fletcher FU24-950 ZK-CTS

They also sold several to the Airtourer's birthplace, Australia, and rebuilt a number of damaged Victa-built aircraft (which then received new AESL serial numbers). After PAC had moved on to the Airtrainer, rights to the Airtourer were obtained by Edge Aviation of East Sale in Australia. They built one new aircraft (VH-CTU, c/n 036), which was titled Edge Tourer 160 and first flew in August 2001.

As a follow-on to the Airtourer, Dr Millicer had designed a four-seat derivative called the CT2 Aircruiser which had a 210hp Continental IO-360-D engine, a fixed cabin roof (instead of the Airtourer's sliding canopy) and a modified wing. The sole prototype Aircruiser (VH-MVR c/n 07-1) was built by Victa as the Victa 210CS and flown on 18th July 1966, but Victa decided not to go ahead with production. AESL took over the rights to the Aircruiser and redesigned it with a strengthened airframe and a rear-hinged clearview canopy as a fully aerobatic military trainer.

The prototype of this new variant was first flown at Hamilton in early 1972. As the CT4 Airtrainer this gained military orders from Australia (38 units) where it replaced the Winjeel basic trainer, from New Zealand (19), Thailand (24) and from Switzerland (14). The latter were not delivered and eventually went to the RAAF. The first delivery (to Thailand) took place in October 1973 and production continued until all orders were completed in 1977. In mid-1990, the Airtrainer production line was reopened with orders for CT4Bs for the RAAF and the Royal Thai Air Force. PAC has also flown the prototype of the CT4C variant with an Allison 250 turboprop engine, which was undergoing certification testing in late-1996. The CT4E is a higher-powered variant that was unsuccessfully entered in the US Air Force basic trainer competition but is now in production for military use and six were delivered in 2004. Airtourer and Airtrainer variants were as follows:

Model	Built	Notes
Victa production		
Airtourer 100	110	Two-seat side-by-side all-metal low-wing trainer with sliding bubble canopy and fixed tricycle u/c. Prototype VH-MVA (c/n 1) FF 12 Dec 1961 with 95hp engine. Production model fitted with 100hp Continental O-200-A engine
Airtourer 115	60	Airtourer 100 with 115hp Lycoming O-235-C1B engine and 1,650 lb TOGW
AESL production		
Airtourer T1	30	AESL-built Airtourer 115
Airtourer T2	1	T1 with strengthened airframe and increased gross weight
Airtourer T3	2	T1 with 130hp RR Continental engine
Airtourer T4	5	T1 with 150hp Lycoming O-320-E1A and 1,750 lb TOGW
Airtourer T5	16	T4 with Hartzell constant-speed propeller. Also named Airtourer Super 150
Airtourer T6	26	T5 with 1,850 lb TOGW. Later T6/24 has 1,900 lb TOGW and 24-volt electrical system
Airtourer T7		Proposed T4 with increased aerobatic weight
Airtourer T8		Proposed competition aerobatic version with 160hp fuel-injected Lycoming AEIO-320 engine
Pacific Aerospace production		
Airtrainer CT4	1	Two-seat aerobatic military trainer derived from Victa Aircruiser, powered by one 210hp Continental IO-360-D. Prototype ZK-DGY (c/n 001) FF 23 Feb 1972
Airtrainer CT4A	77	Production CT4 for military use with IO-360-H engine, enlarged dorsal fin fairing, longer cockpit canopy etc
Airtrainer CT4B	36	CT4A certificated for civil use with minor modifications
Airtrainer CT4C		CT4A fitted with 350shp Allison 250-B17D turboprop. Prototype ZK-FXM (c/n 088, ex NZ1940) FF 21 Jan 1991
Airtrainer CT4C/R		Proposed CT4C with retractable u/c
Airtrainer CT4E	40	CT4B with wing moved further forward, 300hp Lycoming AEIO-540L engine with 3-blade prop. Prototype ZK-EUN (c/n 065) FF 16 Nov 1991

Serial numbers of Victa-built Airtourers ran from c/n 1 to c/n 170, of which the last five were assembled with Victa serials by AESL. C/n 171 and 172 became the first two full AESL production aircraft as c/n 501 and 502. AESL production continued from c/n 503 to c/n 580. A new series was started for Airtrainer production with an initial batch running from c/n 002 to 096 and a second batch from c/n 097 to 114. Early aircraft (c/n 002 to 077) were CT4As and the remainder CT4Bs The CT4E started at c/n 200 and had reached c/n 240 (excluding c/n 213) by mid-2004. A number of Victa aircraft were rebuilt by AESL and their serial numbers carry the suffix 'R' (eg, ZK-DSZ c/n 60R).

Partenavia   Italy

Partenavia was formed shortly after the war under the leadership of Professor Luigi Pascale of Naples University. Prior to 1957 several Pascale prototypes had been flown successfully, but in that year a factory was acquired at Arzano and Partenavia Costruzione Aeronautiche became a limited company in 1959.

The first major model was the P.57 Fachiro, a four-seat high-wing aircraft of mixed steel tube-and-fabric construction with a 150hp engine for aero club use. The production Fachiro had a swept tail and was upgraded to a 160hp power unit – and the later Fachiro IIf had a further power increase to 180 horsepower. 36 Fachiros were eventually built (c/n 01 to 36). The company then followed this with the prototype Fachiro III (I-LRAS), which used a completely metal wing, had a slimmer rear fuselage, and a taller fin and modified tailplane. It also incorporated a revised undercarriage that was moved back several inches. Eventually, this aircraft was given a metal fuselage and an all-round vision cockpit, in which form it was known as the Oscar B and replaced the Fachiro on the Arzano production line.

Partenavia later produced prototypes of the P.59 Jolly and the P.70 Alpha to meet aero club training needs, but it was the Oscar that continued to be built and appeared in various P.64 and P.66 models. Partenavia also exported some 21 P.64s to South Africa where they were assembled and marketed by AFIC Pty Ltd as the RSA-200. In July 1981, the company was absorbed into the Aeritalia Group (now Alenia) and it subsequently built a substantial batch of the P.66C Charlie that were delivered for use by the various units of the Aero Club d'Italia. Partenavia abandoned further development of the Oscar line in 1987 but a prototype of the P.66D Delta (a slightly modified P.66B) was built and flown by Aviolight SpA although no production ensued.

Partenavia P.66C Charlie I-IADX

In 1970, Partenavia flew the prototype of its most successful design – the P.68. Known initially as the Victor, the P.68 was a high-wing light piston twin with a fixed-tricycle undercarriage and was aimed at a range of business and utility users. The prototype was built in the limited facilities at Arzano, but Partenavia moved to a new factory at Casoria where P.68 production started in 1972. The majority of P.68s have been exported and the aircraft has been flown on floats and is also sold with turbocharged engines. In Germany, Sportavia-Putzer produced the prototype of the Observer, which involved replacement of the existing P.68 nose section with a glazed structure so that the aircraft could be used by police forces and maritime agencies for patrol and observation tasks. Initially, Observers were converted from existing aircraft, but Partenavia then started to build them on the production line.

The P.68 offered opportunities for further development and Partenavia flew the prototype of a version with a retractable undercarriage in 1976. They did not go into production with this P.68R, but it was useful in the development of the turboprop versions of the aircraft. The first of these was the AP.68TP, which was a P.68R powered by a pair of Allison B.250 engines and developed in cooperation with Aeritalia. The definitive aircraft, however, emerged with a somewhat deeper fuselage, modified cockpit windows and an additional 14-inch fuselage section and longer rear window added behind the wing. Named the AP.68TP-300 Spartacus, this model reverted to the fixed undercarriage and eleven were completed.

Partenavia subsequently built the prototype of the Spartacus RG which was fitted with the retractable undercarriage of the P.68R and had a lengthened nose to accommodate maritime surveillance equipment. This was further refined as the AP.68TP-600 Viator with a further 25-inch fuselage stretch and an extra pair of cabin windows. A small run of seven aircraft was completed and, following the takeover of Partenavia by Alenia, they also worked on a pressurized derivative named Pulsar but development was abandoned. Under Alenia, production of all P.68 models had been reduced to a trickle by early 1993 when the company was taken over by Aercosmos of Milan. Aercosmos entered into an agreement with Tajena Aerospace and Aviation of Bangalore, India under which Tajena assembled an initial batch of four P.68s and a Viator from kits and then produced a further 20 P-68Cs and Observers but appear to have ceased production due to disagreement with VulcanAir. The first example of the Taneja Observer 2 (VT-TAA) first flew from Bangalore on 17th March 1994. Partenavia was also involved in the original design (through Professor Pascale) of the P.92 ultralight two-seater and this is covered in the section on Tecnam.

After the Aercosmos takeover in March 1993, P.68 production virtually ceased and the company subsequently went into receivership. The business was bought by VulcanAir SpA in April 1998 and they have continued to produce the P.68C, P.68 Observer 2 and P.68 Observer 2TC at the Casoria factory (near Naples) and have plans to revive the retractable undercarriage version of the P.68 (P.68C RG). They have

Partenavia P.68B D-GEMB

also flown the prototype of a diesel-engined version of the P.68C fitted with the 230hp SMA SR305-230 powerplant. VulcanAir has also taken on responsibility for the SF.600TP Canguro (now referred to as the SF.600A) and the tenth Canguro (I-VULA) was completed by them with a view to further production which may include a diesel powered variant designated VA.300. The earlier history of the Canguro is described under General Avia. VulcanAir has also designed the VF-600W Mission high-wing 10-16 passenger utility aircraft, which is broadly based on the Canguro but has a stretched fuselage and a single 778shp Walter M.601F-11 turboprop engine. The prototype (I-VAVF c/n 01) made its first flight in December 2002. Details of all models are:

Model	*Built*	*Notes*
P.48 Astore	1	Strut-braced high-wing tandem two-seat cabin monoplane with fixed tailwheel u/c and one Continental A.65 engine. Prototype I-NAPA (c/n 1) FF 1952

Vulcanair VF.600W Mission I-VAVF

Model	Qty	Description
P.52 Tigrotto	1	All-wood side-by-side two-seat cabin monoplane with retractable tailwheel u/c and one 85hp Continental C85-12F engine. Prototype I-CARB FF 1953
P.53 Aeroscooter	0	All-metal single-seat low-wing 'pod and boom' monoplane with fixed tricycle u/c and pusher 22hp Ambrosini P-25 engine. Prototype I-REDI
P.55 Tornado	1	Streamlined side-by-side two-seater with mid wing and retractable tricycle u/c. Powered by one 140hp Lycoming O-290-D2 engine. Prototype I-REGJ FF 1955
P.57 Fachiro II	3	High-wing four-seat cabin monoplane with 160hp Lycoming O-360-B2A and fixed tricycle u/c. Prototype I-NORI FF 7 Nov 1958 with 150hp Lycoming O-320
P.57 Fachiro IIf	33	Fachiro II with swept vertical tail and 180hp Lycoming O-360-A2A engine
P.59 Jolly	2	High-wing side-by-side two-seat cabin trainer with fixed tailwheel u/c and 90hp Continental C90-12F engine. Prototype I-THOR (c/n 01) FF 2 Feb 1960
P.64 Fachiro III	1	Development of P.57 Fachiro with metal wing, taller fin, new elevator, revised u/c and 180hp Lycoming O-360-A1A engine. Later named Oscar. Prototype I-LRAS FF 2 Apr 1965
P.64B Oscar B	64	All-metal aircraft based on P.64 with cut-down rear fuselage and all-round vision. 2,425 lb TOGW. Oscar B-1155 has 1,155kg (2,546 lb) TOGW
P.64B Oscar 200	9	Oscar B with 200hp Lycoming IO-360-A1B engine
P.66B Oscar 100	80	Two-seat P.64 with 3,880 lb TOGW and 100hp Lycoming O-235-C1B engine. Prototype I-DOCE FF 1966
P.66B Oscar 150	50	Three-seat P.66B with 150hp Lycoming O-320-E2A engine. Prototype I-ACTV (c/n 01)
P.66C Charlie	107	Four-seat P.66B with 160hp Lycoming O-320-H2AD engine. Introduced 1977
P.66D Delta	1	P.66B with minor changes, 2,050 lb TOGW and 150hp Lycoming O-320-D2A engine. Built by Aviolight. Prototype I-AVLT (c/n 001) FF Sep 1988
P.66T Charlie	1	Two-seat trainer version of P.66C with upturned wingtips, 113hp Lycoming O-235-N2A engine and 1,808 lb TOGW. Prototype I-TRAY (c/n 7001) FF Jan 1976
P.68	12	High-wing cabin monoplane with fixed tricycle u/c and two 200hp Lycoming IO-360-A1B engines. Prototype I-TWIN (c/n 01). Named Victor. FF 25 May 1970
P.68 Observer	41	P.68B with 4321 lb TOGW and fully glazed nose section. Prototype D-GERD (c/n 16)
P.68 Observer 2	24	Observer with IO-360-A1B6 engines, 4,594 lb TOGW, 70% increased fuel, nose cone to house camera or FLIR
P.68 Observer 2TC	5	Observer 2 with 210hp Lycoming TIO-360-C1A6D turbocharged engines
P.68B	190	P.68 with 6-inch fuselage stretch, 443 lb TOGW increase to 4,387 lb. Standard six-seat interior
P.68C	104	P.68B with longer nose, integral wing fuel tanks and 200hp Lycoming IO-360-A1B engines
P.68C-TC	47	P.68C with 210hp Lycoming TIO-360-C1A6D turbocharged engines
P.68CJet	1	P.68C powered by two SMA SR305 diesel engines. Prototype I-DJET FF 24 Feb 2005
P.68R	1	P.68B equipped with retractable tricycle u/c. Prototype I-VICR (c/n 40) FF Dec 1976
P.68T	3	P.68R with lengthened fuselage, larger fuel tanks, larger tail and two 330shp Allison 250-B17B turboprops. Prototype I-PAIT (c/n 6001) FF 11 Sep 1978. Production aircraft designated AP.68TP-100
AP.68TP-300 Spartacus	13	P.68T with fixed u/c, redesigned tailplane, better soundproofing and upturned wingtips. Prototype I-RAIP (c/n 8001) FF 20 Nov 1981
AP.68TP-600 Viator	6	Spartacus with retractable u/c, lengthened nose, stretched fuselage and Allison 250-B17C engines. Prototype I-RAIL (c/n 9001)
VA-300		Proposed development of Spartacus with two Zoche ZO-02A diesel engines
P.70 Alpha	1	Metal and plastic low-wing two-seat trainer with fixed tricycle u/c and one 100hp Continental O-200-A engine. Prototype I-GIOY (c/n 01) FF 27 May 1972
P.86 Mosquito	1	Side-by-side two-seat all-metal trainer with pod-and-boom fuselage, tricycle u/c and twin fin tail unit powered by one 60hp KFM.112M engine. Prototype FF 27 Apr 1986
P.92J		See Tecnam
PD.93 IDEA		Projected 4-seat high-wing utility aircraft with P.68 wing and rear fuselage and one 200hp Lycoming IO-360-A1B6
VF-600W Mission	1	High-wing 17-seat utility aircraft with fixed tricycle u/c and one 778shp Walter M.601F-11 turboprop. Prototype I-VAVF (c/n 01) FF 4 Dec 2002

Serial nos of Partenavia and VulcanAir models have been as follows:

Model	C/n batch	Notes	Model	C/n batch	Notes
P.57	01 to 36	Exc c/n 17	P.68	01 to 436+	See note
P.64(B)	01 to 69	Exc c/n 17	Taneja P.68	C-3006 to 3025	Plus 001 to 005
P.64-200	01 to 10		AP.68TP-100	6001 to 6003	
P.66B-100	01 to 81	Exc c/n 17	AP.68TP-300	8001 to 8011	
P.66B-150	01 to 51	Exc c/n 17	AP.68TP-600	9001 to 9007	
P.66C	01 to 107				

Note: P.68 production aircraft carry serial numbers in the range c/n 02 to (currently) c/n 436 but these are suffixed with a separate number (indicating its position in the sequence of that particular model) if the aircraft is an Observer, an Observer 2, a Turbocharged Observer 2 or a P-68C-TC or a Turbocharged model (eg, c/n 331-21-OB, c/n 411-17-OB2, c/n 415-05-OTC or c/n 352-37-TC).

Pasotti   Italy

The Legnami Pasotti SpA, based at Brescia and formed by Dott Ing Piero Pasotti, was responsible for production of a number of light aircraft types designed by Ing Stelio Frati. Their first model was the F.7 Rondone II, a developed version of the two-seat Rondone I that was in production by Ambrosini. The Rondone II had three seats in an extended rear cabin with extra side windows. The prototype F.7 (I-ADRJ c/n 2-01) first flew on 10th February 1954 and 9 further examples were built by Pasotti (c/n 02 to 010). In addition, one F.4 was converted to F.7 standard. Pasotti continued with their work on Frati designs with the F.6 Airone low-wing all-wood four-seat light cabin twin. It had a retractable tricycle undercarriage and was powered by two 90hp Continental C.90 engines. Only one prototype (I-PUPI c/n P.001) was completed and first flown on 13th July 1954. The company also built a single prototype of the F.9 Sparviero, which was a single-engined version of the F.6 Airone with a 240hp Hirth V.8 engine (later a 250hp Lycoming GO-435-C2). This prototype (I-HAWK, c/n D.02) made its first flight on 27th July 1956.

Pasotti F.9 Sparviero I-HAWK

Percival P.50 Prince 4 F-BJAI

Percival
United Kingdom

Captain Edgar W Percival formed the Percival Aircraft Co Ltd in 1932 and the company built the Gull series and the twin-engined Percival Q.6 for private owner customers. The Vega Gull of 1935 became the wartime Proctor, which was used for various tasks including radio training and general communications. 90 Vega Gulls were built (c/n K.20 to K.109) followed by wartime Proctor Is and IIs (plus around six Proctor IVs) built by Percival at Luton (c/n K.110 to approximately K.437) and Proctor Is, IIs, IIIs and IVs by F Hills & Sons at Manchester (c/n H.1 to H.812). The Proctor was an all-wood low-wing cabin monoplane with a fixed tailwheel undercarriage and a 210hp Gipsy Queen II in-line engine. After the war many were declared surplus and flew with civilian owners. Percival, which had become part of the Hunting Group in 1944, decided to build the four-seat Proctor as a commercial model and they completed 139 examples of the P.44 Proctor V of which many were exported. These carried serial numbers c/n As.1 to As.3 and Ae.1 to Ae.143 (of which Ae.133 to Ae.137 were not completed).

Percival went on to develop the Prentice military trainer (some of which were later civilianised) and in May 1947, flew the prototype of the P.48 Merganser light twin-engined transport. With a change of engines and fairly minor systems modifications, this aircraft went into production at Luton as the P.50 Prince and was also built for the Royal Navy as the P.57 Sea Prince. Percival was, itself, renamed Hunting Percival Aircraft Ltd on 26th April 1954 and became Hunting Aircraft Ltd on 5th December 1957. The Prince was further developed as the military Pembroke and attracted large orders from the Royal Air Force and from the air forces of Belgium, Sweden, Denmark, West Germany, Finland and Sudan. Many of these military Pembrokes were subsequently civilianised and a handful of the civil equivalent – the P.66 President – were built. However, by the early 1960s more modern American business twins were becoming available and Hunting transferred their attentions to production of the Jet Provost trainer.

Designations of pre-war Percival aircraft were based on design letters (eg, the Mew Gull had the design letter 'E' and the Vega Gull and the wartime Proctors had the letter 'K') and these letters were reflected in the construction numbers allocated to them (eg, E.20, K.26). The later types had two-letter designations such as 'Au' (the Merganser) and 'Ae' (Proctor V). Following the acquisition of Percival by the Hunting Group a new system of type designations was started. These consisted of the letter 'P' followed by a sequential type number. The Merganser, which had been allocated the designation 'Au', became the P.48 and Hunting allocated retrospective 'P' designations to all prior Percival types. Capt Edgar Percival went on to design the EP.9 utility aircraft that is described under Edgar Percival.

Serial numbers of production P.50 and P.54 Princes were c/n P.50/1 to P.50/71. The P.66 series were c/n P.66/1 to P.66/109 and P.66/114 together with c/n 1000 to 1021, c/n 1040 and c/n 1071 built after the change to the Hunting Aircraft Ltd organisation. Details of the various Prince variants are as follows:

Model	Built	Notes
P.48 Merganser	1	5/8-seat high-wing all-metal transport with retractable tricycle u/c and two 296hp Gipsy Queen 51 radial engines. Prototype G-AHMH/X.2 (c/n Au.1) FF 9 May 1947
P.50 Prince 1	3	Merganser with modified fin and u/c and two 520hp Alvis Leonides 501/4 engines. Prototype G-ALCM (c/n P.50/1) FF 13 May 1948

Percival P.34A Proctor III G-ALJF

P.50 Prince 2	5	Prince 1 with sloping windscreen, stronger mainspar and 3,700 lb TOGW increase
P.50 Prince 3	12	Prince 2 with 550hp Leonides 502/4 engines and lengthened nose on some aircraft
P.50 Prince 4		10 conversions to Leonides 503 engines
P.50 Prince 5		Initial designation for P.66 President
P.50 Prince 6		Conversions to Leonides 504 engines
P.54 Survey Prince	6	Prince 2 with lengthened transparent nose and camera hatches. Prototype G-ALRY (c/n P.50/6)
P.57 Sea Prince C.1	3	Prince 2 Royal Navy staff transport

P.57 Sea Prince T.1	41	Prince 3 with long nose, twin wheel main u/c and lengthened engine nacelles for anti-submarine training
P.57 Sea Prince C.2	4	Transport version of Sea Prince T.1
P.66 Pembroke	128	Prince 3 with 8ft wingspan increase, 2,000 lb increase in TOGW and u/c and engine mods similar to Sea Prince T.1. Prototype WV698 (c/n P.66/1) FF 20 Nov 1952
P.66 President	5	Civil version of Pembroke with longer engine nacelles and deluxe interior. Prototype G-AOJG (c/n P.66/79) FF 26 Aug 1956

Edgar Percival   United Kingdom

Edgar Percival, who had resigned from Percival Aircraft Ltd in 1939, returned to aircraft designing in 1954 with the light utility EP.9. This was aimed at the Australian market where a combination light freighter, passenger or agricultural type was in demand. The EP.9 was a strut-braced high-wing monoplane of tube, fabric and light alloy construction with a pod-and-boom fuselage that incorporated rear clamshell doors for the freight role. A fixed tailwheel undercarriage was fitted and, in passenger layout, six seats could be installed. Powered by a 270hp Lycoming GO-480-B1 engine, the prototype (G-AOFU c/n 20) first flew at Stapleford Tawney on 21st December 1955 and, with minor modifications, entered production in 1956. Edgar Percival Aircraft Ltd finally built 21 production examples (c/n 21 to 41).

In 1958, the company was sold to Samlesbury Engineering and renamed Lancashire Aircraft Co Ltd Production was moved to Samlesbury, Lancashire where G-APWX (c/n 41) was completed as an LAC Prospector with a higher-powered 295hp Lycoming GO-480-G1A6 engine. The company built a further five additional Prospector airframes (c/n 42 to 46 – including one uncompleted aircraft c/n 45) and

Edgar Percival EP.9 G-APWZ

a single Prospector 2 (G-ARDG c/n 47) which was fitted with a 375hp Armstrong Siddeley Cheetah 10 radial engine. At this point it was decided to cease production with a grand total of 27 EP.9s having been completed. Capt Edgar Percival died on 23rd January 1983.

Petrolini El Boyero LV-ZFW

Petrolini   Argentina

In 1940, the Argentine state company, Fabrica Militar de Aviones (FMA) flew the prototype El Boyero high-wing side-by-side two-seater from their Cordoba headquarters. Designed by Juan Peretti, this aircraft was very similar to a Taylorcraft BC in appearance and was powered by a 50hp Continental A-50 engine. As it turned out, FMA was heavily committed to military production and the rights to the El Boyero were sold to Sfreddo y Paolini. In turn they transferred the design to Petrolini Hermanos SA.

Petrolini set up a small production line in Buenos Aires to meet an order for 150 examples placed by the Argentine Government. The first eight El Boyeros were delivered in January 1949 for use by aero clubs and by the Argentine military forces as spotter aircraft. Two versions were built, using either a 65hp Continental A65 engine or a 75hp Continental C75. By 1951, Petrolini was experiencing great difficulty in obtaining the necessary materials and it was announced that El Boyero production would be suspended. Total production is believed to have been 129 aircraft (c/n 01 to 129) and a handful of aircraft still fly with private owners.

Piaggio   Italy

Piaggio SpA can trace its origins back for over a hundred years, but the design and manufacture of aircraft started in 1915. This activity embraced a wide variety of aircraft types including the hydro-ski Schneider Trophy entrant, the P.7, and the FN.305A two-seat trainer that was built on behalf of Nardi. Numerous military aircraft were produced during the war. In 1948, the company designed the P.136 five-seat light amphibian. This was of conventional appearance except for its gull wing, which mounted two Franklin engines in a pusher installation. The P.136 had a retractable tailwheel undercarriage with the main wheels rotating upwards into the fuselage sides.

A production batch of the P.136 was ordered by the Italian Air Force for air sea rescue and these differed from the prototype primarily in the design of the rear hull keel which extended further back and also in the cockpit area where additional side windows were installed. In 1954, the higher-powered P.136L appeared. This version was sold in the United States by Kearney and Trecker, who imported the bare airframes and completed them for sale as the 'Royal Gull'. Production finally ceased in 1967 with 63 examples completed.

The next Piaggio project was the two-seat low-wing P.148 trainer that was built for the Italian Air Force. This was developed into the four-seat P.149 that had a retractable tricycle undercarriage and became the standard trainer for the West German Luftwaffe. The prototype (I-PIAM c/n 171) first flew on 19th June 1953 and Piaggio built

88 examples with a further 190 being built under licence by Focke-Wulf. A handful of civil P.149s were constructed – notably five P.149Es that were acquired by Swissair for pilot training. A number of military P.149s have been sold to the private owner market.

The success of the Beech Queen Air and the Aero Commander twins prompted Piaggio to use the basic P.136 structure to create a new unpressurized executive twin – the P.166. A new fuselage and tail unit were married to the P.136 wing and engines and the prototype P.166 (I-RAIF, later I-PIAK) first flew in late 1957 at Villanova d'Albenga and went into production in 1959. The P.166A was followed, in 1962, by the higher-powered P.166BL2 Portofino (the L2 designation indicating that a different Lycoming engine was used) and Piaggio also built the P.166C, which was fitted with external main undercarriage nacelles, and the P.166M for the Italian Air Force.

On 1st March 1964, the Industrie Aeronautiche e Meccaniche Rinaldo Piaggio SpA was formed as a separate company under Armando Piaggio to operate the aviation and transport activities of the Piaggio group. Eventually, in 1975, Piaggio decided to redesign the P.166 and fit Avco Lycoming LTP-101 turboprop engines. Initial deliveries were made to the Alitalia Flying School, Iraqi Airways and the Somali Air Force who used two for maritime patrol duties. The Italian Navy has also taken a batch fitted with external search radar dishes. Some efforts were made to sell the P.166DL3 in the United States as a corporate aircraft, but this was unsuccessful due to its lack of pressurization. In 2004, Piaggio started an upgrade programme for existing P.166DL3s to P.166DP1 standard with Pratt & Whitney PT6A engines substituted for the Lycomings. They delivered 16 examples of the Avanti during 2004. Details of the P.136 and P.166 variants are as follows:

Piaggio P.136L N40022

Model	Built	Notes
P.136	18	Five-seat gull-wing amphibian with retractable u/c and two 215hp Franklin 6AB-215-B9F engines. Prototype c/n 100 FF 29 Aug 1948
P.136L-1	29	P.136 with larger squared-off fin, deeper windscreen and 260hp Lycoming GO-435-C2 engines. Prototype I-PIAG (c/n 103)
P.136L-2	16	P.136L-1 with 320hp Lycoming GSO-480-B1C6 engines and enlarged dorsal fin
P.166	3	High-wing 6/10-seat cabin monoplane developed from P.136 with retractable tricycle u/c, 8,155 lb TOGW and two 340hp Lycoming GSO-480-B1C6 pusher engines. Prototype I-RAIF (c/n 341) FF 26 Nov 1967
P.166AL1	29	Production P.166 with non-slanted cockpit side windows
P.166ML1	51	Military version of P.166AL1 with additional cockpit door, stronger floor and larger main loading door
P.166BL2	6	P.166A with 380hp Lycoming IGSO-540-A1C engines and 8,377 lb TOGW. Prototype I-PIAS (c/n 411) FF 27 Mar 1962 Named Portofino
P.166CL2	4	P.166B with external u/c pods, max 13 seats including seats in baggage area with extra windows, 8,708 lb TOGW. Prototype I-PIAS

FW-Piaggio P.149D N5316W

Piaggio P.166 VH-FSA

Piaggio P.180 Avanti D-IJET

P.166DL3	20	P.166B fitted with two Lycoming LTP101-700A-1A turboprops, large tip tanks, ventral fin, double cabin doors etc. 9,480 lb TOGW. Prototype I-PIAP (c/n 371) FF 3 Jul 1976
P.166 DL3SEM		P.166DL3 for Italian Coast Guard with chin-mounted radar pod and underwing FLIR sensors
P.166DP1		Upgraded P.166DL3 for Guadia Finanza re-engined with two 615shp Pratt & Whitney PT6A-121 turboprops, new avionics and air conditioning, strengthened wing and 9,000 lb TOGW
P.166S	20	Albatross. For South African Air Force with long P.166B radar nose and larger tip tanks. 8,113 lb TOGW
Total	*196*	

Following the P.166, Piaggio embarked on the PD.808 business jet. The PD.808 was the outcome of a joint venture with Douglas Aircraft Company who carried out the basic design work on the nine-seat low-wing aircraft – which was initially known as the 'Vespa Jet' in honour of the motor scooter which was one of Piaggio's main products. Piaggio built the prototype PD.808 (MM577 c/n 501), which first flew on 29th August 1964 powered by a pair of Bristol Siddeley Viper 525 jets. One further PD.808-525 was built at Finale Ligure. This was followed by two civil demonstrators and a batch of 20 aircraft for the Italian Air Force (MM61948 to MM61963 and MM 62014 to MM62017) all powered by the 3,330 lbst Viper 626 engine. Attempts were made to market the aircraft to commercial customers, but the PD.808 did not gain any further orders.

The strategy of joint venture with American companies took a new turn in October 1983 when Gates Learjet and Piaggio joined forces to design the GP-180 Avanti twin-turboprop business aircraft which would be competitive with the Beech Starship – but would use only relatively small segments of composite construction. In January 1986, Learjet pulled out of the partnership but Piaggio continued with the project and flew the prototype Avanti (I-PJAV c/n 1001) on 23rd September 1986 and a second aircraft (I-PJAR c/n 1002) on 15th May 1987. The seven-passenger P180 Avanti, which went into production in Genoa, has a straight high-aspect-ratio wing set well to the rear of the fuselage, mounting a pair of 800shp Pratt & Whitney PT6A-66 turbo-

props in pusher configuration. It has a T-tail and there is a canard fore-plane in the extreme nose.

In 1993 the company (Industrie Aeronautiche e Meccaniche Rinaldo Piaggio SpA) started on a succession of financial crises and was restructured with Alenia having a 31% stake. In March 1994, Piaggio entered into an abortive sales and development partnership with Grumman to market the Avanti but eventually, in 2000, formed a marketing subsidiary, Piaggio America Inc. In November 1994 Piaggio went under bankruptcy protection and since November 1998, when the Ferrari and DiMase families invested in Piaggio (and the company was renamed Piaggio Aero Industries SpA.), ownership control has shifted several times because of increasing capital investment. This initially involved the Turkish company, Tushav but was followed by further major investment in June 1999 from Italian investment group, Aero Trust with the Italian Government investment agency, Sviluppo Italia, acquiring more than 20% in September 2003. This restructuring resulted in an increase in orders and production of the P.180 Avanti was raised to 18 aircraft per annum from mid-2003 and 22 planned for 2005. In October 2004 an upgraded Avanti II was announced with upgraded PT6A-66 engines, gross weight raised from 11,550 lb to 12,500 lb and ProLine 21 avionics.

Postwar Piaggio serial numbers commenced at c/n 100, which was allocated to the first P.136, and a sequential numbering system has been used to include all models built by the company. Generally, aircraft types have been allocated numbers in blocks, but this has not been followed absolutely. The main blocks of serials have been:

C/n Batch	Model	C/n Batch	Model
C/n 100 to 118	P.136	C/n 341 to 342	P.166
C/n 119 to 191	P.148	C/n 343 to 353	P.149
C/n 192 to 193	P.149	C/n 354 to 464	P.166
C/n 194 to 249	P.136L*	C/n 465 to 499	P.166DL3
C/n 250 to 324	P.149	C/n 501 to 524	PD.808
C/n 325 to 340	P.149 fuselages for FW	C/n 1001 to 1095+	P.180

* Some not completed.

Claude Piel   France

One of the best-known French light aircraft designers, Claude Piel started out as an amateur constructor but also worked full time in the aircraft industry with Lignel, Matra and Boisavia. In 1952, Piel left Boisavia and joined Roland Denize. He then designed the single-seat CP.20 Pinocchio, which looked like a miniature Spitfire and became the basis for his most famous design – the CP.30 Emeraude two-seater. Piel became a prolific designer with many sets of plans being sold, and the Emeraude, in particular, has been popular with amateurs, fitted with a variety of engines and with many personal modifications. Other

homebuilt designs included the CP.40 Donald which was Piel's only high-wing design, the CP.60 Diamant three-seat derivative of the Emeraude, the CP.70 Beryl which was a tandem two-seater, the CP.80 single-seat racer and the CP.150 Onyx which was a tandem-wing design following Mignet principles.

The Emeraude was adopted by Jean-Michel Vernhes whose company, Coopavia, embarked on a series of aircraft for commercial sale. Claude Piel went to work for the Société des Constructions Aeronautiques du Nord (SCANOR) where the Emeraude also entered production and Piel also entered into a licence agreement with Ets Claude Rousseau at Dinard who built their own modified version of the air-

Menavia Piel CP.301A Emeraude G-BKNZ

craft. In 1959, following his time at SCANOR, Claude Piel moved to Scintex who built the Super Emeraude and he then joined CAARP at Beynes where the CP-100 and the CAP-10 derivatives of the Emeraude were developed.

Serial numbers for Piel designs are generally in a simple numerical sequence commencing at c/n 1 and issued for each major design as a plans number. Accordingly, there are many gaps in the production sequences for aircraft that were not built and Binder Aviatik issued its own c/ns (and a series of AB-prefixed numbers for their amateur-built variants). Details of the commercially-built CP.301 Emeraude models are shown below. The other Piel designs built by Scintex and CAARP are shown under the chapters on those companies.

Model	Built	Notes
CP.30	1	Side-by-side two-seater with fixed tailwheel u/c and fixed cockpit canopy with forward-hinged doors, powered by one 65hp Continental A.65 and developed from CP-20. Prototype F-WFVY (c/n 01) FF 19 Jun 1954
CP.301A	118	Commercial production Emeraude powered by one 90hp Continental C90-14F. Later aircraft had sliding canopy. Built by Coopavia (96 aircraft), SCANOR (4), SOCA (9), Rouchaud (5) and Renard (4). Prototype F-BHOD (c/n 24)
CP.301B	23	CP-301A with smaller control surfaces, sliding cockpit canopy, spatted u/c and numerous constructional improvements. Built by Rousseau, c/n 100 to 119 (plus c/n 120 to 125 completed by amateurs)
CP.301C	84	CP-301A with large bubble canopy, pointed wingtips, modified tail and new engine cowling. Built by Scintex, c/n 511 to 594
CP.301S	25	Smaragd. Built by Schempp Hirth for Binder Aviatik at Donaueschingen, Germany with sliding canopy, dorsal fin etc and Cont C90-12S engine. c/n 100 to 124. Prototype D-EBIA (c/n 100)
Linnet	5	CP-301A with C90-14F engine built by Garland-Bianchi at White Waltham, UK Last three built by Fairtravel Ltd at Blackbushe with sliding canopies. Prototype G-APNS (c/n 001)
Ariel II	11	CP-301A built in South Africa by Genair

Claude Piel's homebuilt designs are outside the scope of this book but a summary of his known designs is as follows:

Model	Engine	Notes	Model	Engine	Notes
CP.10	25hp Poinsard	Pinocchio	CP.60	90hp Cont	Diamant*
CP.20	25hp VW	Pinocchio I*	CP.601	100hp Cont	Diamant*
CP.210	45hp Salmson	Pinocchio I*	CP.602	105hp Potez	Diamant*
CP.211	45hp Salmson	Pinocchio I*	CP.603	108hp Lyc	Diamant*
CP.212	65hp Cont	Pinocchio I*	CP.604	145hp Cont	Diamant*
CP.215	80hp Jabiru	Pinocchio I*	CP.605	150hp Lyc	Diamant*
CP.220	65hp Cont	Pinocchio I*	CP.606	140hp Lyc	Diamant*
CP.40	25hp VW	Donald*	CP.607	130hp Cont	Diamant*
CP.41	45hp Percy	Donald*	CP.608	180hp Lyc	Diamant*
CP.401	65hp Cont	Donald*	CP.70	65hp Cont	Béryl*
CP.402	40hp Rectimo	Donald*	CP.701	90hp Cont	Béryl*
CP.30	65hp Cont	Emeraude	CP.702	100hp Cont	Béryl*
CP.301A	90hp Cont	Emeraude*/†	CP.703	108hp Lyc	Béryl*
CP.301B	90hp Cont	Emeraude†	CP.750	150hp Lyc	Béryl*
CP.301C	90hp Cont	Emeraude†	CP.751	180hp Lyc	Béryl*
CP.301D	90hp Cont	Emeraude†	CP.760	150hp Lyc	Béryl*
CP.301S	90hp Cont	Smaragd†	CP.761	180hp Lyc	Béryl*
CP.302	90hp Salmson	*	CP.100	160hp Lyc	†
CP.303	85hp Salmson	*	CP.200	180hp Lyc	†
CP.305	108hp Lyc	*	CAP-10	180hp Lyc	†
CP.308	75hp Cont	*	CP.80	90hp Cont	*
CP.315	105hp Potez	*	CP.801	108hp Cont	*
CP.320	100hp Cont	*	CP.802	65hp Cont	*
CP.321	105hp Potez	*	CP.803	105hp Potez	*
CP.322	108hp Lyc	*	CP.90	90hp Cont	Pinocchio II*
CP.323	150hp Lyc	*	CP.901	100hp Cont	Pinocchio II*
CP.325	100hp Cont	*	CP.902	65hp Cont	Pinocchio II*
CP.330	125hp Lyc.	*	CP.903	108hp Lyc	Pinocchio II*
CP.1310	100hp Cont	Super Emeraude	CP.1320	150hp Lyc	Saphir*
CP.1315	105hp Potez	Super Emeraude	CP.1321	180hp Lyc	Saphir*
CP.1330	108hp Lyc	*	CP.150	18hp Solo etc	Onyx*

† = Commercial; * = Homebuilt.

Pilatus   Switzerland

On 16th December 1939, the Pilatus Flugzeugwerke AG was set up by the proprietors of Oerlikon Buehrle and it subsequently built its first major design – the SB-2 Pelikan. This rather ungainly high-wing six-seat utility aircraft was powered by an Argus radial engine and the prototype (HB-AEP) first flew in May 1944. The SB-2 did not progress beyond the prototype stage but Pilatus went on to build a series of 57 P-2 military trainers for the Swiss Air Force and these were followed by 80 examples of the more advanced P-3 that first flew in September 1953. The company also built the prototype of the P-4 high-wing five-seat light aircraft – which, again, failed to gain commercial orders.

In 1959, Pilatus made a new attempt at the market for general-purpose utility light aircraft and completed the prototype of the PC-6 Porter which was a STOL aircraft drawing heavily on the experience gained with the P-4. The all-metal PC-6 was powered, initially, by a 340hp Lycoming piston engine. It went into production at Stans in 1960 and quickly captured orders from all over the world due to its rugged construction and good short field performance. It was soon apparent, however, that the PC-6 would be much improved by turbo-prop power and this led to the first flight of the PC-6A Turbo Porter in 1961, powered by a 562shp Turboméca Astazou. Some 45 of the piston-engined Porters had been built before this model was phased out in favour of the turboprop versions. Several piston Porters were subsequently re-engined with turboprops.

The Astazou engine improved the Turbo Porter's performance greatly, but it was not completely satisfactory and in any case Pilatus felt an American powerplant would make the aircraft more saleable. Accordingly, they produced the PC-6/B version with a United Aircraft of Canada PT6A-6 turboprop and this has been the standard powerplant since 1966. 1965 saw Pilatus entering into a licence production agreement with Fairchild-Hiller of Germantown, Pennsylvania. Under this a new variant, the PC-6/C equipped with the Garrett AiResearch TPE331 engine, would be built by them for North American sale. A batch of ten airframe sets was delivered to the United States to get production under way and Fairchild subsequently built a total of 92 of the Garrett-engined 'Heli-Porters'.

At least a third of production Turbo Porters were delivered to military users including the air forces of Australia, Peru, Switzerland and the Argentine. Fairchild also built 20 examples for the US Air Force under the designation AU-23A for close support forward combat duties. A considerable number of the civil-registered Turbo Porters were acquired by Air America and its associate companies (Bird Air, Pacific Architects etc) for use in a great range of transport and clandestine missions in Laos and Vietnam.

By the late-1980s production of the PC-6/B2-H4 Turbo Porter had ceased at Stans and the construction of small batches of airframes was subcontracted to the Czech Republic. Pilatus are still willing to produce additional aircraft but production has virtually ceased at c/n 945. In total, 437 Pilatus examples have been completed (c/n 337 to 350, c/n 513 to 603 and c/n 614 to 945) together with at least 92 aircraft completed by Fairchild (c/n 2001 to 2092) including ten built from Pilatus kits (c/n 604 to 613). Details of the variants are as follows:

Model	Notes
PC-6	Basic Piston Porter. Seven-seat all-metal high-wing STOL utility aircraft with fixed tailwheel u/c, 4,320 lb TOGW and one 340hp Lyc GSO-480-B1A6 piston engine or supercharged 350hp Lyc IGO-540-A1A. Prototype HB-FAN (c/n 337) FF 4 May 1959. Some converted to PC-6/A standard
PC-6/A-H1	Initial Turbo Porter model. PC-6 with 523shp Turboméca Astazou IIE turboprop and 4,850 lb TOGW
PC-6/AX-H2	PC-6/A with 630shp Turboméca Astazou X turboprop
PC-6/A1-H2	PC-6/A with 700shp Turboméca Astazou XIIE turboprop
PC-6/B1-H2	PC-6/A with 550shp Pratt & Whitney PT6A-20 turboprop
PC-6/B2-H2	PC-6/A with 550shp Pratt & Whitney PT6A-27 turboprop
PC-6/B2-H4	PC-6/B with 6,173 lb TOGW, stronger airframe, enlarged dorsal fin, extended wingtips, new tailwheel
PC-6/C1-H2	PC-6/A with 575shp Garrett TPE331-1-100 turboprop

A number of other Porter developments have been proposed over the years, including the PD-01 Master Porter and the PC-10 Twin Porter with a fixed tricycle undercarriage, rear loading ramp and PT6A engines. Pilatus did build the prototype of the PC-8D Twin Porter (HB-KOA) which first flew on 28th November 1987 and was a ten-seat

Pilatus PC-6/B2-H4 Turbo Porter N908PL

Pilatus PC-12 N507PB

development of the basic airframe with a swept tail and two 290hp Lycoming IO-540 piston engines mounted on the wing. This was demonstrated to various potential users, but was eventually abandoned.

The PC-12 (initially named PC-XII), which was launched in October 1989, is a single-engined multi-purpose utility aircraft for commercial, governmental and private customers. It has a low wing, retractable tricycle undercarriage and a T-tail and is powered by a 1,200shp Pratt & Whitney PT6A-67B turboprop. The nine-passenger pressurized fuselage has an internal capacity of 330 cubic feet and is fitted with a large cargo hatch behind the wing. Available configurations include a mixed four passenger and cargo (PC-12 Combi) model, a six passenger PC-12 Executive layout or an All-Cargo version. Two prototypes of the PC-12 (HB-FOA and 'FOB, c/n P-01, P-02) were built, the first of which first flew on 31st May 1991. Production modifications included an 8-ft wingspan increase, wingtip winglets, an increase in the pressurization level and a tail bullet fairing. The first production aircraft, delivered in October 1994, was N312BC (c/n 101). 516 had been completed by the

end of 2004 (c/n 101 to 616). The current production variant is the PC-12/45, which has an increased gross weight of 9,920 lb and was introduced in 1997. A military variant, the PC-12 Eagle, is fitted with an under-fuselage pod containing surveillance equipment including the Northrop-Grumman WF-160DS dual sensor system. In 2004, Pilatus delivered 70 examples of the PC-12.

For a while, Pilatus was the owner of the former Britten Norman company, based at Bembridge, Isle of Wight but this was sold (full details appear under the Britten Norman entry). Pilatus Aircraft Ltd was, for many years, a subsidiary of Unaxis, but it was sold to a private investor group in January 2001. The company recorded its 1,500th aircraft delivery in November 2001 at which time it had produced 469 PC-6s, 525 PC-7s and PC-7 Mk IIs, 245 PC-9s and 261 PC-12s. The company continues to build the PC-12 together with the PC-7 and PC-9 turboprop military trainers and is developing the PC-21 advanced military turboprop trainer (of which two prototypes had been completed by the end of 2004). A few examples of the PC-7 are used by civilian flying schools and private owners.

Piper   United States

The modern New Piper Aircraft originated with the Taylor Brothers Aircraft Corporation, which was originally formed by C G Taylor and his brother, G A Taylor, in September 1927. They designed and built the A-2 Chummy – a small parasol-wing side-by-side two-seat monoplane – but the company went bankrupt after six of the derivative B-2 Chummy had been built. In 1930, William T Piper bought Taylor's assets and started to build a much-altered tandem two-seat version of the Chummy – the Taylor E-2 Cub. This aircraft had an enclosed cockpit and was powered by a Continental A-40 engine, but later variants (the F-2, G-2 and H-2) used other powerplants. Some 353 aircraft were built between 1931 and 1936.

The E-2 Cub formed the basis for the J-2 which was designed by Walter Jamoneau with a new undercarriage and general cleaning-up of the airframe. Taylor Aircraft built some 695 examples of the J-2 at its Bradford, Pennsylvania plant before a fire forced relocation to Lock Haven, Pennsylvania – and a change of the Taylor name to Piper Aircraft Corporation. With the J-3 Cub, introduced with further refinements in 1937, Piper created the ultimate light aircraft legend – and built a range of Cubs with engines ranging from 40hp to 65hp The onset of war brought huge orders for the Continental-powered J-3C-65, delivered

to the US forces as the L-4. A total of 20,290 Cubs were built between 1938 and 1947 including a batch of TG-8 glider versions. Piper also built 1,251 of the side-by-side J-4 Cub Coupe and 1,507 of the three-seat Cub Cruiser. The J-3 has been resurrected by several companies

Cub Crafters PA-18-150 Top Cub N105CC

Piper PA-15 Vagabond

in recent times, the latest being the American Legend J-3 of which the prototype (N23787) flew on 10th March 2005.

Following the war, with civilian Cubs pouring out of Lock Haven, Piper designed and built a number of prototypes such as the Skycoupe, the Skysedan and the Skycycle, aimed at the new light aircraft market, but the postwar slump in sales came before any of these could be exploited. From delivering 7,817 aircraft in 1946 Piper's output fell to just over 1,000 units in 1951. The company managed just to stay in business during the next ten years by producing variants of the tube-and-fabric J-3 and J-4 – including the PA-11 Cub Special, PA-12 Super Cruiser and PA-14 Family Cruiser. A desperate move to find a new low-cost product that would exploit the large stocks of components that had built up resulted in the two-seat Vagabond that was certificated on 1st July 1948 (T C A-800) and its dual-control derivative, the PA-17. These designs led to the four-seat Clipper and the PA-20 Pacer and PA-22 Tri Pacer which were the main output of the 1950s. Piper stayed with the Cub, in improved PA-18 Super Cub form, but eventually ceased production in 1994. In 1999, the PA-18-150 reappeared as the 'remanufactured' Top Cub, built by Cub Crafters of Charleston, South Carolina. From early 2005, Cub Crafters has built brand new aircraft under a new type certificate designated CC18-180 in two versions – the Legend and utility Ranger. They also intend to produce a 100hp Sport Cub version for the American Sport Aircraft category.

In November 1948, Piper acquired Convair's Stinson division. In addition to the Model 108 Voyager, which continued in production until the PA-20 came on stream, Piper gained the design of the Twin Stinson. This four-seat light twin was to be fabricated in tube and fabric with twin fins and a retractable tricycle undercarriage – and Stinson had flown a prototype (N1953A) prior to the takeover. Piper eventually redesigned it with metal cladding over a tubular frame and gave it a single fin and larger 150hp engines. It received its type certificate (1A10) on 29th January 1954 and immediately went into production in 1954 as the PA-23 Apache. As a result, the company was weaned off its traditional tube-and-fabric construction methods. In 1961, the Apache was modified with a swept tail and larger engines into the higher-powered 250hp Aztec. This continued in production until the last example of the Aztec F was delivered in November 1981, although the company did have intentions of producing a pressurized version and had flown a prototype of the PA-41P during 1974.

The all-metal construction was next applied to one of Piper's most attractive models, the four-seat single-engined Comanche. This was built with various engines ranging from 180hp to 400hp and was certificated on 20th June 1957 (certificate 1A15), reaching a production total of 4,865 units. Piper engineers also produced the highly successful PA-30 Twin Comanche by replacing the single Lycoming in the nose of the Comanche with two 160hp Lycomings mounted on the wings. Later models of Twin Comanche had engines with opposite rotation to reduce torque. Piper also built three prototypes of an improved Twin Comanche – the PA-40 Arapaho – but this project was cancelled.

Piper was now firmly committed to all-metal monocoque construction although there were exceptions – such as the PA-18 and the agricultural Pawnee and Pawnee Brave. The Pawnee was developed from a design study carried out at Texas A & M by Fred Weick (creator of the Ercoupe) and known as the AG-1. The prototype AG-1 (N222) first flew in January 1950 and, though it was far from perfect, Piper saw the opportunity to take a new initiative in agricultural aviation and they employed Weick as a consultant. The resultant Pawnee low-wing single-seater with its hopper situated ahead of the cockpit became the standard for agricultural models produced by many other manufac-

Piper PA-16 Clipper G-BSWF

turers. It gained its type certificate (2A8) on 6th January 1959 and appeared with a range of powerplants. The later PA-36 Pawnee Brave was larger but somewhat less successful – although Piper still sold almost 1,000 of this model.

In 1957, John Thorp (designer of the Sky Skooter) joined Piper and designed the single-engined PA-28 Cherokee which was approved on 31st October 1960. It was intended for low-cost production to compete with the Cessna 172, but was so flexible that eventual Cherokee variants spanned the range from two-seat trainers (PA-28-140) to high-performance business aircraft such as the range of Cherokee Arrows, which had an automatically-sensing retractable undercarriage system. In between were PA-28s with different engine options and varying standards of interior fitting and equipment including special edition models. Later, Piper fitted the PA-28 with a new wing incorporating tapered outer panels and larger ailerons. This first appeared on the PA-28-151 Warrior in 1973, but was later extended to the other PA-28 models. They also built the stretched PA-32 Cherokee Six airframe, which was approved on 15th November 1965 and grew into the retractable gear Saratoga SP. It also formed the basis for the twin-engined PA-34 Seneca which appeared in September 1971.

At the heavier end of the product line, Piper built the prototype of an eight-seat cabin-class twin that received type certificate A20SO on 24th February 1966. It went into production the following year as the PA-31 Navajo and was the design basis for all Piper's subsequent large twins. This basic airframe was sold in stretched form as the PA-31-350 Navajo Chieftain and with a pressurized cabin as the PA-31P Pressurized Navajo. The PA-31P, fitted with PT6A turboprops, gave Piper the opportunity to compete with the Beech King Air. The prototype of this PA-31T Cheyenne first flew in October 1969 and, eventually, the Cheyennes were built with either standard or stretched fuselages and various different models of the PT6A powerplant. The ultimate variant of the Cheyenne was the T-tailed Cheyenne III, which was equivalent to the King Air 200 and had lengthened wings and fuselage. Equipped with two 1,000shp Garrett TPE-331-14 turboprops, this became the top-of-the-range Cheyenne 400LS which started to be delivered to customers in 1984.

Back in 1957, when the Cherokee project was starting up, Piper established a new development and production centre at Vero Beach in central Florida. The PA-28 and most subsequent new models were built at Vero Beach although Lock Haven continued for many years with the tubular-framed models and some of the early Navajos. They also built the PA-38 Tomahawk at Lock Haven. The company had attempted, on several occasions, to start up a new two-seat trainer and had experimented with all-plastic construction on the PA-29 Papoose. In the end, they came up with the all-metal Tomahawk and this saw a five-year production run which ended in 1982. It was one of the last types to come out of the old factory, because, over the years Piper had suffered a series of damaging floods caused by the Susquehanna river bursting its banks and the worst of these destroyed over 100 aircraft in June 1972. Lock Haven was closed in 1984 and all operations were moved to Vero Beach and to a new factory at Lakeland, Florida. The Lakeland factory was closed in October 1985.

An unusual move by Piper was the acquisition of the Aerostar programme from Ted Smith Aerostar Corporation in March 1978. The history of the Aerostar is described elsewhere, but Piper continued to include these aircraft in its line until 1984. Another most profitable activity was the production of components for the licence production of Piper models by Embraer and its Neiva subsidiary in Brazil (and also by Chincul in Chile, Aero Mercantile in Colombia and Pezetel in Poland). One application of this has been the hybrid Enaer Pillan (PA-28R-300) two-seat military trainer which was designed by Piper for production in Chile and consisted of a modified Saratoga fuselage with a Warrior wing and a 300hp Lycoming IO-540 engine. Piper kits have been delivered abroad in progressive stages of subassembly enabling the licence manufacturer eventually to manufacture the entire airframe locally. Brazilian production is described separately under Neiva.

One of the most successful designs to come from Piper has been the six-seat PA-46 Malibu single-engined pressurized business aircraft which first flew in November 1979. Later re-engined as the Malibu Mirage, the PA-46 was seen as the basis for a new generation of Piper medium-sized aircraft and it was expected that the company might develop a turboprop Malibu to challenge the TBM700 and also a Malibu Twin. In the event, the twin-engined version did not materialise but the turboprop development was to eventually come as the Malibu Meridian.

In 1977, Piper was caught up in a bitter and long-running takeover battle between Chris Craft and the eventual victor, Bangor Punta. Bangor Punta continued as Piper's parent until January 1984 when it was acquired by Lear Siegler, which saw benefits in bringing Piper's prod-

Piper PA-23-150 Apache N992 (C-FLAD)

Piper PA-22-108 Colt G-ARNJ

ucts together with its other aerospace activities. This ownership lasted through several years of losses until Piper had suspended almost all of its product line in the face of the product liability crisis. Lear Siegler then passed into the hands of Forstman Little, and Piper again came onto the market.

In May 1987 the company was acquired by M Stuart Millar, who restored many of the previous models to production. Millar's company, Romeo Charlie Inc, also had plans for several new types including a modernised version of the Globe Swift (the SwiftFury developed by Roy LoPresti) and an updated Comanche. However, the advancing threat from product liability actions again found Piper in financial difficulties and, by mid-1990, discussions were under way for the company to be acquired by Aérospatiale. These negotiations were abandoned and on 1st July 1991 the company declared Chapter 11 bankruptcy. There followed a number of abortive reorganisation and reinvestment initiatives during which time production was reduced to a trickle and assets were divested – including the sale of a number of type certificate rights and spares to Cyrus Eaton Group who intended to build Pipers in Russia and Canada. Romeo Charlie Inc was eventually taken over by Stone Douglass but there were further legal compli-

Piper PA-24-260 Comanche G-ATIA

cations connected with bankruptcy reorganisation. In 1993 the Bankruptcy Court ruled in favour of Pilatus as a preferred acquirer favoured by the bankruptcy court but they were eventually rejected by creditors as Piper's trading fortunes started to improve and in January 1994 a sale to Vero Holdings was announced.

Eventually, a deal was struck in mid-1994 for Piper to be taken over by its creditors and at last it appeared that a stable situation had been achieved. A new holding company was formed with Dimeling Schreiber & Park Inc (a Philadelphia-based investment group) owning 50%, Teledyne Industries owning 25% and The Piper Aircraft Corporation Irrevocable Trust Fund owning 25% on behalf of Piper's other creditors and shareholders. On 17th July 1995, The New Piper Inc took over all manufacture of the aircraft line. By mid-2003, New Piper had two major shareholders (Dimeling Schreiber & Park with 46% and Allegheny Technologies with 28%) and American Capital Strategies as major debt holder. Sales, which had declined to less than 100 units in 1993, reached a peak of 441 aircraft in 2001 but the impact of the '9-11' terrorist crisis brought a decline to 229 units in 2003. Production of the PA-28 series, the PA-32R, the PA-34, the PA-44 and PA-46 has continued and 189 aircraft were delivered in 2004. These included the Warrior III (18), Archer III (19), Arrow (12), Saratoga IIhp (9), Saratoga II TC (31), Piper 6X (24), Piper 6XT (14), Seneca V (10), Seminole (11), Malibu Mirage (15) and Malibu Meridian (26).

Several of the company's models have been given cosmetic upgrades. In 2003, the company reintroduced the fixed-gear PA-32 (Cherokee Six) as the Piper 6X and turbocharged Piper 6XT. They also successfully developed and brought to market the Piper Malibu Meridian turboprop version of the Malibu. The Malibu has also found a new lease of life as the JetPROP DLX conversion which involves replacement of the standard TSIO-520 piston engine with a Pratt & Whitney PT6A-35 and 145 of these conversions had been carried out by JetPROP LLC of Spokane, Washington by mid-2004. Another turboprop conversion under development is the GM-17 Viper produced by the Swiss company, Intracom General Machinery Co and manufactured in Russia. The GM-17 is a Piper PA-31P Pressurized Navajo airframe with the twin engines removed and refitted with a nose-mounted Walter M601E turboprop. A full list of Piper models is as follows:

Model	Notes
PWA-1 Skycoupe	Low-wing twin-boomed two-seat cabin monoplane with 113hp pusher Franklin 4ACG-199-H3 engine and fixed tricycle u/c. Prototype NX4500 (c/n 1). See also PA-7
P-1	Applegate Duck experimental two-seat high-wing light amphibian named Cub Clipper and fitted with Cub wings and re-engined by Piper with a pusher 90hp Franklin 4AC engine (later 130hp). Two a/c only, N17866 and NX27960 (c/n P1)
PT-1 Trainer	Low-wing tandem two-seat tube-and-fabric trainer with retractable tailwheel u/c. Powered by one 130hp Franklin 6AC-298-D engine. One a/c NX4300 (c/n 1). Currently preserved at Piper Museum, Lock Haven
P-2 Cub	High-wing tube & fabric two-seater built in 1941 derived from J-3 Cub with enclosed cowling, new tail, single right hand door. Powered by one 75hp Continental A-75-8 engine. One a/c only NX33281 (c/n 0)
J-3 Cub	Tandem two-seat high-wing monoplane built pre- and post-war and fitted with a variety of engines, most commonly the 65hp Continental A-65. Military L-4. Prototype NC16792 (c/n 1999) FF Oct 1937
Legend Cub	J-3 Cub copy by American Legend Aircraft. Prototype N23787 FF 10 Mar 2005
P-4 Cub	Four-seat development of P-2 with adjustable tailplane and 120hp Lycoming O-290 engine. One a/c only, NX38300 (c/n 1) FF 1941
P-5 Cub	J3C-65 Cub fitted with strutless cantilever wing. One a/c only, NX42111 (c/n 9110) otherwise known as J-3X. FF 29 Nov 1944
PA-6 Sky Sedan	Four-seat low-wing tube-and-fabric cabin monoplane derived from PT-1 with retractable tailwheel u/c and powered by one 165hp Continental E-165. Prototype NX580 (c/n 6-01) FF1945. Second aircraft, NC4000M (c/n 6-1) of all-metal construction with 205hp Continental E-185
PA-7 Skycoupe	Proposed production version of PWA-1. Not built
PA-8 Skycycle	Single-seat low-wing all-metal light aircraft of pod-and-boom layout. Fuselage of Prototype NX47Y (c/n 1) built from ex-military drop tank with 2-cylinder Franklin engine. Second aircraft, NX47Y (c/n 2), fitted with 37hp Continental A-40 engine and FF 29 Jan 1945
PA-9	High-wing military liaison aircraft. Not built
PA-10	Design similar to Thorp Skyskooter. Not built
PA-11 Cub Special	J-3C-65 Cub fitted with fully-enclosed engine cowling, divided landing gear, stronger airframe and wing fuel tanks. Some civil aircraft and the military L-18B fitted with 95hp Continental C90-8F engine. Prototype NC91913 (c/n 11-1)
PA-12 Super Cruiser	J-5C Cub Cruiser three-seat high-wing tube-and-fabric monoplane with improved trim, new engine cowling etc and 100hp Lycoming O-235-C engine. Prototype NX41333 (c/n 5-1309)
PA-13	Type number not used
PA-14 Family Cruiser	PA-12 with wider cabin and four seats, powered by one 115hp Lycoming O-235-C1 engine. Prototype NC2658M (c/n 14-1)
PA-15 Vagabond	Side-by-side two-seater developed from the P-2 with short span wing and one 65hp Lycoming O-235 engine. Prototype NX5000H (c/n 15-1) FF 29 Oct 1947
PA-16 Clipper	PA-15 with enlarged four-seat fuselage, improved interior trim and one 108hp Lycoming O-235 engine. Prototype NC4000H (c/n 16-1) FF 1948
PA-17 Vagabond	Deluxe version of PA-15 with dual controls and 65hp Cont A-65-8 engine. Prototype NC4153H (c/n 17-1, ex 15-36) FF 5 May 1948
PA-18-95 Super Cub	PA-11 with enlarged vertical tail, flaps, twin wing tanks etc, 95hp Cont C-90-8F engine and 1,400 lb TOGW. Prototype N5410H (c/n 18-1) FF 23 Nov 1949. L-18 is military liaison aircraft based on PA-18-95 with fully transparent rear cabin
PA-18A	Agricultural version of PA-18 with hopper in rear seat position and underwing spraybars or under-fuselage fertiliser spreader mostly based on PA-18-150 specification

Piper PA-25-150 Pawnee ZS-CSE

PA-18S	Seaplane version of PA-18 with twin floats and 1,474 lb TOGW
PA-18-105 Super Cub	PA-18 with 105hp Lycoming O-235-C1, no flaps, toe brakes and larger tailplane
PA-18-125 Super Cub	PA-18 with 125hp Lyc O-290-D engine. Military L-21A
PA-18-135 Super Cub	PA-18 with 135hp Lyc O-290-D2 engine. Military L-21B
PA-18-150 Super Cub	PA-18 with 150hp Lyc O-320 and modified wings, u/c and fuel system. 1,760 lb TOGW
PA-18-150 Top Cub	PA-18-150 'rebuilds' by Cub Crafters from 1999. Prototype N901CC (c/n 9901C). 74 built by early 2005 (to c/n 9974CC). New certificated CC18-150 Top Cub Legend and Top Cub Ranger from 2005 (from c/n CC18-0001)
PA-19 Super Cub	Designation used for 3 prototypes of military L-21 with modified wing centre section, 90hp Cont C90-12F engine. Production aircraft all designated in PA-18 series. Prototype N5011H (c/n 19-1) FF 25 Mar 1949
PA-20 Pacer	PA-16 with enlarged tailplane, modified u/c, increased fuel, wheel-type control columns, 1,750 lb TOGW and 115hp Lycoming O-235-C1 engine. Variants included PA-20-125 and PA-20-135 with Lyc O-290-D2 and 1,950 lb TOGW and seaplane variants with 1,738 lb TOGW. Prototype N7000K (c/n 20-01) FF Jul 1949
PA-21	Designation not used due to confusion with L-21 military Super Cubs. Originally intended as designation for Piper's uncompleted tractor-engined version of Baumann Brigadier (prototype N30025, c/n 1)
PA-22 Tri Pacer	PA-20 fitted with fixed tricycle u/c and 125hp Lycoming O-290-D engine. 1,800 lb TOGW. Also seaplane PA-22S. Prototype N7700K (c/n 22-1)
PA-22-108 Colt	Two-seat trainer version of Tri-Pacer without rear side windows and powered by one 108hp Lycoming O-235-C1 engine. Prototype N4500Z (c/n 22-8000) FF Sep 1960
PA-22-135 Tri Pacer	PA-22 with 135hp Lycoming O-290-D2 and 1,950 lb TOGW
PA-22-150 Tri Pacer	PA-22 with 150hp. Lycoming O-320-A2A and 2,000 lb TOGW. Economy Caribbean model introduced 1958

Piper PA-28-161 Warrior II N8461U

Piper PA-23-250 Aztec C N6588Y

PA-22-160 Tri Pacer	PA-22 with 160hp Lycoming O-320-B2A
Twin Stinson	Four-seat low-wing twin of tube/fabric construction with twin tail fins, fixed tricycle u/c and two 125hp Lycoming O-290-D engines. Design taken over in Stinson acquisition. One a/c only, N1953A (c/n 23-01) FF 22 Mar 1952
PA-23 Apache	Light twin developed from Twin Stinson with single fin/rudder, retractable u/c, metal cladding, 3,500 lb TOGW and powered by two 150hp Lycoming O-320 engines. Prototype N23P (c/n 23-1) FF 29 Jul 1953. Minor changes annually to systems and trim. Fifth seat intro 1955. Many upgraded to Seguin/Vecto Geronimo, Miller Jet Profile etc
PA-23-160 Apache E	PA-23 with 160hp Lyc O-320-B engines and 3,800 lb TOGW
PA-23-160 Apache G	PA-23 with longer internal cabin, extra rear window each side
PA-23-160 Apache H	Apache G with O-320-B2B engines and minor refinements
PA-23-235 Apache 235	Aztec with five seats and 235hp Lycoming O-540 engines. Prototype N4914P (c/n 27-460) FF 11 Dec 1961
PA-23-250 Aztec	Apache G with modified rear fuselage, new swept fin/rudder, stabilator horizontal tail and 4,800 lb TOGW, powered by two 250hp Lycoming O-540-A1D engines. Prototype N4250P (c/n 27-1) FF 1 Oct 1958. US Navy UO-1 (later U-11A)
PA-23-250 Aztec B	Aztec with longer nose incorporating 150 lb baggage compartment, six-seat interior, new instrument panel and systems changes
PA-23-250 Aztec C†	Aztec B with IO-540-C4B5 engines or † optional turbocharged TIO-540-C4B5 engines, streamlined engine nacelles and modified u/c
PA-23-250 Aztec D†	Aztec B with revised instrument panel and controls, styling changes
PA-23-250 Aztec E†	Aztec D with longer pointed nose, single piece windshield etc
PA-23-250 Aztec F†	Aztec E with improved brakes, fuel system, improved instruments, cambered wingtips and tailplane tip extensions
PA-24-180 Comanche	Low-wing all-metal four-seat cabin monoplane with retractable tricycle u/c, 2,550 lb TOGW and one 180hp Lycoming O-360-A1A engine. Prototype N2024P (c/n 24-1) FF 24 May 1956
PA-24-250 Comanche	PA-24-180 with one 250hp Lycoming O-540-A1A engine and 2,800 lb TOGW. Annual minor trim and equipment changes. Originally designated PA-26
PA-24-260 Comanche	PA-24 with one 260hp Lycoming O-540-E4A5 engine and 2,900 lb TOGW
PA-24-260 Comanche B	PA-24-260 with longer interior cabin and optional fifth/sixth seats, extra cabin window each side. 3,100 lb TOGW
PA-24-260 Comanche C†	Comanche B with extended propeller shaft, streamlined 'Tiger Shark' cowling, improved controls and 3,200 lb TOGW. † Optional turbocharged IO-540-R1A5 engine from 1970
PA-24-300 Comanche 300	Experimental PA-24 with 300hp Lycoming IO-540-L1A5 engine. Prototype N9300P (c/n 24-6000) FF 1967
PA-24-380 Comanche	PA-24-250 fitted with 380hp Lycoming IO-720 engine. Prototype N5316P (c/n 24-357)
PA-24-400 Comanche 400	PA-24-380 fitted with 400hp Lycoming IO-720-A1A, 3-blade propeller, enlarged horizontal tail, modified engine cowling, 3,600 lb TOGW. Prot N8380P (c/n 26-1) FF 7 Mar 1961
PA-25-150 Pawnee	Low-wing single-seat strut-braced agricultural aircraft of tube-and-fabric construction with fixed tailwheel u/c, 800 lb hopper, 2,300 lb TOGW and one 150hp Lycoming O-320-A1A engine. Based on Texas A&M AG-3 (Prototype N888B, FF Nov 1954). Prototype N9100D (c/n 25-1)
PA-25-235 Pawnee	PA-25-150 with 235hp Lycoming O-540-B2B5 engine and 2,900 lb TOGW. Prototype N74829 (c/n 25-02)
PA-25-235 Pawnee B	PA-25-235 with improved spray gear and enlarged hopper
PA-25-235 Pawnee C	Pawnee B with better cockpit comfort and ventilation, removable fuselage rear decking, oleo strut u/c and improved oil cooler and alternator
PA-25-260 Pawnee C	Pawnee C with 260hp Lycoming O-540-G1A5 engine
PA-25-235 Pawnee D	Pawnee C with wing-mounted fuel tanks and minor detail changes
Gippsland Fatman GA-200	Two-seat conversion/new build of Pawnee by Gippsland in Australia
PA-26 Comanche	Initial designation for PA-24-250
PA-27 Aztec	Initial designation for PA-23-250
PA-28 Cherokee	Low-wing all-metal four-seater with fixed tricycle u/c, developed from PA-10 design study. Prototype N9315R (c/n 28-01) FF 10 Jan 1960

PA-28-140 Cherokee	PA-28 with two seats, 2150 lb TOGW and one 150hp Lycoming O-320-A2B engine. Prototype N6000W (c/n 28-20000). Four-seat PA-28-140-4 with O-320-A2B engine available from 1965	PA-28-180 Cherokee F	PA-28-180E with separate rear seats replacing bench seat, new fuel selector system, optional air conditioning and minor detail changes
PA-28-140 Cherokee B	Model 140 with new instrument panel, Dynafocal engine mounting and minor detail changes	PA-28-180 Challenger	PA-28-180F with 5-inch fuselage stretch and longer cabin, 2-ft. wingspan increase, enlarged all-moving stabilator, redesigned vertical tail with leading edge fillet, enlarged glareshield, 2450 lb TOGW. Prototype N4273T (c/n 28-E10) FF 1971
PA-28-140 Cherokee C	140B with instrument panel and minor cosmetic changes		
PA-28-140 Cruiser	140E/F with four-seat interior, baggage area and modified cabin ventilation/heating system		
PA-28-140 Cherokee D	140C with new cabin heat system and minor changes to front seats, colours, trim and controls	PA-28-180 Archer	Challenger with modified window profile and minor detail changes
PA-28-140 Cherokee E	140D with fin fillet and minor cosmetic changes	PA-28-181 Archer II	Archer with new wing incorporating tapered outer panels, 180hp Lycoming O-360-A4A engine, 2550 lb TOGW, new u/c fairings and improved trim. Prototype N33413 (c/n 28-7690001) FF 28 Mar 1975
PA-28-140 Fliteliner	140E/F two-seat trainer with full instrumentation for use in Piper Flite Centers		
PA-28-140 Cherokee F	140E with new instrument panel and coaming, new front seats, optional air conditioning and minor cosmetic changes	PA-28-181 Archer III	Archer II with new cowling with 'axisymmetric' air inlets, squarer side windows, 3-inch fuselage stretch and 6-inch wingspan increase, O-360-A4M engine, new instrument panel overhead switch panel etc and 28-volt electrics
PA-28-150 Cherokee	PA-28 with four seats and 150hp Lyc O-320-A2A engine. Trim options included Standard, Custom, Super Custom		
PA-28-150 Cherokee B	PA-28-150 with minor detail changes	PA-28-235 Cherokee	PA-28-180 with longer wings containing extra fuel tankage, one 235hp Lycoming O-540-B2B5 engine, streamlined engine cowling, 2900 lb TOGW. Prot N2800W FF 9 May 1962.
PA-28-150 Cherokee C	Cherokee B with minor detail changes		
PA-28-151 Cherokee Warrior	PA-28-180 Challenger with new wing incorporating tapered outer panels. Powered by one 150hp Lyc O-328-E2D engine. Prototype N4273T (c/n 28-E-10) FF 17 Oct 1972	PA-28-235 Cherokee B	Cherokee 235 with minor detail changes and optional c/s prop
		PA-28-235 Cherokee C	235B with third cabin window each side, new engine console etc
PA-28-160 Cherokee	PA-28-150 with 160hp Lycoming O-320-D2A. Equivalent Cherokee B and C models with minor detail changes	PA-28-235 Cherokee D	235C with minor cosmetic changes
PA-28-161 Warrior II	PA-28-151 with one 160hp Lycoming O-320-D2G engine. Prototype N6938J (c/n 28-7716001) FF 27 Aug 1976	PA-28-235 Cherokee E	235D with separate rear seats replacing bench seat, improved soundproofing, optional air conditioning etc
PA-28-161 Cadet	2 + 2-seat VFR/IFR trainer version of Warrior II powered by one 160hp Lycoming O-320-D3G engine, with reduced trim standard & no rear side windows. Prototype N9142S (c/n 2816066) FF 24 Jun 1988	PA-28-235 Cherokee F	235E with redesigned vertical tail with leading edge fillet, new instrument panel and minor changes
		PA-28-235 Charger	PA-28-180 Challenger with 235hp Lyc O-540-B4B5 engine, enlarged windows and door, 3000 lb TOGW, Hartzell HC-2YK-1 constant-speed prop, improved instrument panel and trim. Prototype N2673T (c/n 28-E11)
PA-28-180 Cherokee B	PA-28-160B with 180hp Lycoming O-360-A2A engine and 2400 lb TOGW		
PA-28-180 Cherokee C	PA-28-180B with streamlined engine cowling incorporating buried landing light, new prop spinner and minor detail changes	PA-28-235 Pathfinder	Charger with restyled windows and minor detail changes
		PA-28-236 Dakota	Pathfinder with semi-tapered Warrior wing, 235hp Lycoming O-540-J3A5D engine, new u/c fairings, revised engine cowling and minor detail changes. Prototype N38505 (c/n 28-7911001)
PA-28-180 Cherokee D	PA-28-180C with third window each side, new engine control console, instrument panel and control column		
PA-28-180 Cherokee E	PA-28-180D with improved engine mount, new instrument lighting etc	PA-28-201T Turbo Dakota	Dakota with turbocharged 200hp Lycoming TSIO-360-FB engine, 2,900 lb TOGW

Piper PA-28RT-201T Turbo Arrow IV D-ERIF

Piper PA-31T1 Cheyenne I D-IAPA

PA-28R-180 Cherokee Arrow	PA-28-180 with third cabin window each side, extra baggage space, one 180hp Lycoming IO-360-B1E engine with constant-speed prop, 2,500 lb TOGW and retractable tricycle u/c with automatic extension system. Prototype N9997W (c/n 28-30000) FF 1 Feb 1967
PA-28R-200 Cherokee Arrow	PA-28R with 200hp Lycoming IO-360-C1C engine and 2600 lb TOGW. Prototype N4603J (c/n 28R-30482) FF 12 Jul 1968
PA-28R-200 Cherokee Arrow B	Arrow with new fuel system, optional autopilot and improved ventilation. Also 180hp version
PA-28R-200 Cherokee Arrow II	Arrow B with 5in fuselage stretch, larger cabin door, air conditioning, larger stabilator tail and other cosmetic changes
PA-28R-201 Arrow III	Arrow II with 3-ft longer semi-tapered wing, increased fuel, 2750 lb TOGW and 200hp Lycoming IO-360-C1C6 engine. Prototype N1169X (c/n 28R-7535264) FF 16 Sep 1975
PA-28R-201T Turbo Arrow III	Arrow III with turbocharged 200hp Cont TSIO-360-F engine, 3,000 lb TOGW, modified engine cowling etc. Prototype N3918X (c/n 28R-7635018) FF 1 Dec 1976
PA-28RT-201 Arrow IV	Arrow III with redesigned longer rear fuselage and new vertical T-tail with all-moving tailplane. Prototype N2970M (c/n 28R-7837107) FF 20 Mar 1978
PA-28RT-201T Turbo Arrow IV	Arrow IV with turbocharged 200hp Cont TSIO-360-F engine. Prototype N2251M (c/n 28R-7803114/28R-7931001) FF 14 Mar 1978
PA-28R-300 Pillan XBT	Tandem two-seat military trainer with Arrow wing and cut-down Saratoga fuselage for production in Chile as T-35 Pillan. Powered by one 300hp Lycoming IO-540-K. 2 a/c only. Prototype N300BT (c/n 28R-300-01) FF 6 Mar 1981. Production aircraft shipped in kit form to ENAER
PA-29 Papoose	Side-by-side two-seat low-wing all-plastic trainer with fixed tricycle u/c and one 108hp Lyc. O-235-C1B engine. One a/c only, N2900M (c/n 29-1) FF 30 Apr 1962
PA-30 Twin Comanche	PA-24 with engine removed and nose faired in, powered by two 160hp Lyc. IO-320-B1A engines in streamlined nacelles. 3,600 lb TOGW. Development prototype N5808P (c/n 24-888) FF 12 Apr 1961. Production prototype N7000Y (c/n 30-1) FF 7 Nov 1962
PA-30 Twin Comanche B†	PA-30 with third cabin window each side and optional fifth/sixth seats. † Optional Turbo Twin Comanche B with turbocharged Lycoming TIO-320 engines
PA-30 Twin Comanche C†	Twin Comanche B with improved IO-320 engines with higher power output, new instrument panel, improved seats and optional wingtip fuel tanks. †Optional Turbo Twin Comanche C
PA-30-200 Twin Comanche B	Experimental PA-30 with two 200hp Lycoming engines One a/c only, N8300Y (c/n 30-4000)
PA-31 Navajo†	6-8-seat all-metal low-wing cabin-class twin. Prototype N3100E (c/n 31-1) named Inca FF 30 Sep 1964. 6,200 lb TOGW. Powered by two 300hp Lycoming IO-470-M engines or † optional turbocharged 310hp TIO-540-A engines
PA-31 Navajo B	PA-31 with turbocharged 310hp TIO-540-E engines, optional pilot entry door, engine nacelle baggage lockers, better air conditioning etc. 6,500 lb TOGW
PA-31 Navajo C	Navajo B with TIO-540-A2C engines and minor changes
PA-31-325 Navajo C/R	Navajo B with counter rotating 325hp TIO-540-F2BD engines and extended nacelles
PA-31-350 Chieftain	PA-31 with 2ft fuselage stretch, one extra window each side, cargo door, 10-seat interior and 7,000 lb TOGW. Powered by two counter-rotating 350hp Lycoming TIO-540-J2BD engines. Originally named Navajo Chieftain. Prototype N7700L (c/n 31-5001) FF 22 Jan 1971
PA-31-350 T-1020	Chieftain for commuter use with 11-seat hard interior, improved u/c, new fuel system, crew entry door
PA-31-353 Chieftain II	PA-31-350 with 4-ft longer span wings, PA-31T tailplane, 350hp TIO-540-X48 counter rotating engines. 2 a/c only. Prototype N353PA(c/n 31-8458001)
PA-31P-425 Pressurized Navajo	PA-31 with pressurized fuselage, one window less on port side, smaller windshield and windows and two 425hp Lycoming TIGO-541-E1A6 engines. Prototype N9200Y (c/n 31P-1) FF 26 Mar 1968
PA-31P-350 Mojave	Pressurized piston twin with Cheyenne I fuselage, wings from the PA-31-353 and Chieftain tail. Powered by two 350hp Lycoming TIO-540-V2AD engines. Prototype N9087P (c/n 31P-8314001) FF 20 Apr 1982
GM-17 Viper	PA-31P Pressurized Navajo rebuilt by Intracom General Machinery Co in Russia with a single nose-mounted 750hp Walter M601E turboprop, wingtip winglets etc. Prototype RA-01559 (c/n 31P-7530007) FF 6 Dec 2000
PA-31T Cheyenne	PA-31P fitted with two 620shp P&W PT6A-28 turboprops, wingtip fuel tanks new flight control system. 9050 lb TOGW. Unpressurized prototype N3100E (c/n 31-1) used to test concept. Prototype N7500L (c/n 31T-1) FF 20 Aug 1969. Later, in 1978, renamed Cheyenne II
PA-31T1 Cheyenne I	Cheyenne with lower-powered 500shp PT6A-11 engines, 8,750 lb TOGW
PA-31T1 Cheyenne IA	Cheyenne I with improved engine performance, new engine cowlings, improved interior and cockpit layout
PA-31T2 Cheyenne IIXL	Cheyenne II with 2ft fuselage stretch, 620shp PT6A-135 engines and extra cabin window each side. Prototype N2446X (c/n 31T-8166001) FF 29 Feb 1980
PA-31T3 T-1040	Chieftain with wings, tail and nose of PA-31T1 and two 500shp PT6A-11 engines, 9,050 lb TOGW. Prototype N2389Y (c/n 31T-8275001) FF 17 Jul 1981
PA-32 Cherokee Six	PA-28-235 with 30-inch rear fuselage stretch and forward baggage compartment inserted between firewall and cabin. Six seats with (from 1967) optional seventh seat. Powered by one 250hp Lyc O-540. Prototype N9999W (c/n 32-01) FF 6 Dec 1963
PA-32-260 Cherokee Six	Production PA-32 with 260hp Lycoming O-540-E engine
PA-32-260 Cherokee Six B	Cherokee Six with new instrument panel, redesigned cabin interior etc
PA-32-260 Cherokee Six C	Cherokee Six B with detail changes
PA-32-260 Cherokee Six D	Cherokee Six C with detail changes
PA-32-260 Cherokee Six E	Cherokee Six D with revised instrument panel, optional air conditioning
PA-32-300 Cherokee Six	Cherokee Six with 300hp Lycoming IO-540-K engine
PA-32-300 Cherokee Six B	PA-32-300 with Cherokee Six B mods
PA-32-300 Cherokee Six C	PA-32-300 with Cherokee Six C mods
PA-32-300 Cherokee Six D	PA-32-300 with Cherokee Six D mods
PA-32-300 Cherokee Six E	PA-32-300 with Cherokee Six E mods
	Note: after 1972 no letter suffix used for Cherokee Six. Various mods each year inc extra side windows in 1974
PA-32-301 Saratoga	PA-32 with 300hp Lycoming IO-540-K1G5 engine and new semi-tapered wing based on that of PA-28-151 Warrior. Prototype N2114C (c/n 32-8006001) FF 1 Nov 1978
PA-32-301T Turbo Saratoga	Saratoga with turbocharged 300hp Lycoming TIO-540-S1AD engine in new cowling. Prototype N9326C (c/n 32-8024001) FF 15 Mar 1979
PA-32-301FT Piper 6X	Saratoga IIHP with fixed undercarriage, powered by one 300hp Lycoming IO-540-K1G5. Prototype N1326X (c/n 3232001) FF 24 Feb 2003
PA-32-301XTC Piper 6XT	Piper 6X with 300hp turbocharged Lycoming TIO-540-AH1A engine. Prototype N326XT (c/n 3255001)

PA-32R-300 Cherokee Lance	PA-32-300 with retractable tricycle u/c based on PA-34 gear. Prototype N44256 (c/n 32R-7680001) FF 30 Aug 1974. Known just as Lance from 1977	PA-35 Pocono	16/18-seat unpressurized low-wing cabin commuter twin with retractable tricycle u/c powered by two 475hp Lycoming TIO-720-B1A engines. One a/c only, N3535C (c/n 35-E1) FF 13 May 1968. Later fitted with 520hp Lycoming TIO-720-B1A engines. Sold to Poland 1976. Derelict at Widelka-Rzeszow, 1996
PA-32RT-300 Lance II	Lance fitted with T-tail. Prototype N44256 FF 28 Aug 1975		
PA-32RT-300T Turbo Lance II	PA-32RT-300 Lance II fitted with turbocharged 300hp Lycoming TIO-540-S1AD engine		
PA-32R-301 Saratoga SP	PA-32-301 (without T-tail) with Lance II retractable u/c	PA-36-285 Pawnee Brave	Single-seat low-wing agricultural aircraft dev. from PA-25 with 38ft³ hopper and one 285hp Cont Tiara 6-285 engine. Prototype N36PA (c/n 36-E1) FF 17 Nov 1969
PA-32R-301T Turbo Saratoga SP	PA-32R-301 with turbocharged 300hp Lycoming TIO-540-S1AD engine		
PA-32R-301 Saratoga IIHP	Saratoga SP with 300hp Lycoming IO-540-K1G5 engine, new cowling with round air intakes, reduced-depth side windows and new instrument panel. Prototype N9197X (c/n 3213042) FF 27 Mar 1993	PA-36-300 Brave 300	Pawnee Brave fitted with 300hp Lyc IO-540-K1G5 engine
		PA-36-375 Brave 375	Pawnee Brave fitted with 375hp Lyc IO-720-D1CD engine
		PA-37	Projected pressurized 6-seat light twin. Not built
PA-32-3M Cherokee Six	Three-engined Cherokee Six with two 115hp Lycoming O-235 engines mounted on wings. N9999W used as test vehicle for PA-34 development	PA-38-112 Tomahawk	Side-by-side two-seat low-wing all-metal trainer with fixed tricycle u/c. and T-tail. Powered by one 112hp Lycoming O-235-L2C engine. Prototype with conventional tail, N56346 (c/n 38-7320001) FF 17 Jul 1973. Production T-tail prototype N38PA (c/n 38-7738001) FF 11 Jun 1977
PA-33	PA-24 Comanche with pressurized cabin, PA-30 u/c and 260hp Lycoming O-540 engine. One a/c only, N4600Y (c/n 33-1) FF 11 Mar 1967		
PA-34-180 Twin Six	PA-32 with nose engine removed and two 180hp Lyc O-360 engines. One a/c only, N3401K (c/n 34-E1) FF 25 Apr 1967	PA-39 Twin Comanche C/R	PA-30 fitted with counter-rotating 160hp Lycoming IO-320-B1A engines and modified wing leading edges. Also turbocharged option with TIO-320-C1A engines
PA-34-180	Twin Six with retractable tricycle u/c, 2ft increase in wingspan and larger vertical tail. One a/c only, N3407K (c/n 34-E3) FF 30 Aug 1968	PA-40 Arapaho	Developed version of PA-39 with enlarged six-seat fuselage, modified hydraulic u/c, larger windows. 3 a/c only. Prototype N9999P (c/n 40-1) FF 16 Jan 1973
PA-34-200 Seneca	PA-34-180 fitted with 200hp Lycoming IO-360-A1A engines. 4,000 lb TOGW. 1974 model has extra window each side	PA-41P Aztec	PA-23-250 with pressurized cabin and two 270hp Lycoming TIO-540 engines. One a/c only, N9941P (c/n 41P-1) FF 21 Feb 1974
PA-34-200T Seneca II	Seneca with two turbocharged 200hp Cont TSIO-360-E engines in new nacelles. Optional club seating, seventh seat. Prototype N34PA (c/n 34-E4). 4,570 lb TOGW. Polish licence-production version PZL-M20	PA-42 Cheyenne III	11-seat pressurized low-wing cabin turboprop based on 8ft 8in-stretched Chieftain fuselage with PA-31T wings and large T-tail. Powered by two 720shp P&W PT6A-41 turboprops. 11,080 lb TOGW. Prototype N420PA (c/n 42-7800001) FF 15 Mar 1978
PA-34-220T Seneca III	Seneca with two turbocharged 220hp Cont TSIO-360-KB2A engines. 4,773 lb TOGW, single piece windshield, new instrument panel etc. Prototype N8181C (c/n 34-8133001)		
PA-34-220T Seneca IV	Seneca III with reduced depth side windows, new engine cowlings with round air intakes, upgraded interior trim and new instrument panel	PA-42-720 Cheyenne IIIA	PA-42 with 720shp P&W PT6A-61 engines, extra window each side new internal trim etc, 11,285 lb TOGW
		PA-42-1000 Cheyenne IV	Cheyenne III with two counter-rotating 1,000shp Garrett AiResearch TPE331-14 turboprops, 12,135 lb TOGW and changes to interior trim and systems. Prototype N400PT (c/n 42-842001) FF 23 Feb 1983
PA-34-220T Seneca V	Seneca IV with counter-rotating 220hp Cont L/TSIO-360-RB plus redesigned instrument panel and cabin executive console. Prototype N9183N (c/n 3448033) FF 1 Dec 1995		
		PA-42-1000 Cheyenne 400LS	Cheyenne IV renamed by Lear Siegler in Sep 1984

Piper PA-32RT-300T Turbo Lance II N646JR

Piper PA-38-112 Tomahawk II ZK-JCZ

PA-43	Chieftain derivative with T-tail. Not built. Prototype c/n 43-7800001
PA-44-180 Seminole	Four-seat low-wing light twin developed from Arrow with two 180hp Lyc O-360-E1A6D engines. Prototype N998P (c/n 44-7812001) FF May 1976. Also PA-44-180T optional turbocharged model with Lyc TO-360-E1A6D engines
PA-45	6-seat Aztec replacement. Not built
PA-46-310P Malibu	Low-wing pressurized six-seat single-engined cabin-class aircraft with retractable tricycle u/c and rear air stair door, powered by one 310hp Cont TSIO-520-BE engine. 4,118 lb TOGW. Prototype N35646 (c/n 46-E1) FF 30 Nov 1979
PA-46-350P Malibu Mirage	Malibu fitted with 350hp Lycoming TIO-540-AE2A engine, new electrical system and improved interior trim. 4,318 lb TOGW. Prototype N9134F (c/n 4622001) FF 21 Dec 1987
PA-46 JetPROP DLX	PA-46 re-engined with a 560shp Pratt & Whitney PT6A-34 (c/n 1 to 88), PT6A-35 (from c/n 89) or PT6A-21 turboprop. 145 conversions to date (conv c/n 1 to 145)
PA-46-500TP Malibu Meridian	PA-46 with lengthened inboard wing, larger tail, fuel increase, strengthened u/c, MAGIC instrumentation. 4,850 lb TOGW (later inc to 5,092 lb). Powered by one 500shp Pratt & Whitney PT6A-42A turboprop. Prototype N400PT (c/n E1) FF 21 Aug 1998
PA-47	Design not yet built
PA-48 Enforcer	Close-support turboprop aircraft utilising P-51 Mustang airframe. Prototype N201PE (c/n PE1-1001) FF 28 April 1971. Later PA-48 Enforcer with lengthened fuselage and 2,455shp Lycoming T55-L-9 turboprop (N481PE, c/n 48-8301001) FF 9 Apr 1983
PA-60 Aerostar	See section on Ted Smith

Total numbers of Piper aircraft built, up to mid-2004, are:

Model	Total	Model	Total	Model	Total
J-3	19,888	PA-28-150, 160, 180	7,472	PA-32-301	561
PA-11	1,541	PA-28-181	4,252	PA-32-6X	36
PA-12	3,760	PA-28-140	10,089	PA-32-6XT	27
PA-14	238	PA-28-151/161	5,498	PA-32R	3,399
PA-15	387	PA-28-235/236	2,947	PA-34	4,936
PA-16	736	PA-28R	6,897	PA-36	923
PA-17	214	PA-30	2,001	PA-38	2,519
PA-18	10,329	PA-31	1,785	PA-39	155
PA-20	1,120	PA-31-350	1,827	PA-42-III/IIIA	149
PA-22	7,641	PA-31 T-1020	23	PA-42-400	43
PA-22-108	1,849	PA-31P	259	PA-44	675
PA-23	2,047	PA-31P-350	50	PA-46	964
PA-23-235	118	PA-31T	178	PA-46-500TP	211
PA-23-250	4,812	PA-31T-I/IA	215	Other models	32
PA-24	4,717	PA-31T-II	348		
PA-24-400	148	PA-31T-IIXL	82		
PA-25-150	731	PA-31T T-1040	24		
PA-25-235	4,438	PA-32	3,876	*Total*	*127,167*

The postwar system of serial numbers used by Piper consists of the Model number followed by a chronological serial identity. Over the years, several different methods have been used to allocate these numbers. The table of serial numbers gives the batches for all Piper models. It should be noted that there are many missing serial numbers in these batches due to aircraft not being built, aircraft being re-serialled into a later year, airframes built as kits for overseas assembly and aircraft lost in the floods which affected the Lock Haven factory.

The first system used a simple sequence commencing at '1'. Under this arrangement the first production PA-22, for example, was c/n 22-1 and production of Tri Pacers continued to c/n 22-7642. One of the first

Piper PA-36 Pawnee Brave ZS-KWI

complications came with the Apache (PA-23) and its development – the Aztec. The Aztec was designated PA-23-250 and certificated under the Apache type certificate but it was built by Piper in parallel with the Apache so it was given 27- serial numbers. Similarly, the Comanche 400 was allocated 26- series serials but was designated PA-24-400 for certification purposes.

The second system was introduced when the Cherokee (PA-28) was introduced. Because it started to appear with 140, 160, 180 and 235 horsepower engines, it was obvious that Piper had to change the serial number policy. Therefore, while the Cherokee 180 continued with the basic series of 28- numbers (starting at c/n 28-1), the Cherokee 140 received numbers commencing at 28-20001 and the Cherokee 235 was serialled from 28-10001 upwards. In the case of the Cherokee 140, the serial number batch was changed each year (ie, to 28-21***, 28-22*** etc). This method was used from 1964 to 1970 on a number of models including the PA-28-140 Cherokee 140 (28-20*** up), PA-28-235 Cherokee 235 (28-10***up), PA-28R-180 Cherokee Arrow (28R-30***up), PA-28R-200 Cherokee Arrow (28R-35***up) and PA-32-300 Cherokee Six (32-40***up).

The third serial system came in 1971 when Piper brought in an additional refinement for Vero Beach production (with Lock Haven following in 1975). They included the model year in the serial number and started a new series of numbers (commencing at 001) for each model year. This '1971' system was changed in minor ways as the years went by so as to make sure that each model had a separate identifying serial number. An example of how this worked can be illustrated by the case of HB-OML – a PA-28-140 Cherokee E built in 1972. This aircraft was allocated the serial number 28-7225130. This number can be broken down as follows: 28- (aircraft type); 72 (model year); 25 (identifying code for Cherokee 140); 130 (3-digit individual aircraft serial).

From 1973, Lock Haven models (PA-18, PA-23, PA-25, PA-31 etc) had the model year identity (Part 'B') placed in front of their existing serial number. An example of this is PA-18 Super Cub c/n 18-7309016. In 1975, Piper reorganised the Identification Code (Part 'C') and allocated a new set of individual codes to all models. This resolved the '1971' system problem of several models using the same code. The change also allowed the company to absorb the Aerostar line and to include a fairly large number of new models during the busy period of the late-1970s and early 1980s. In the case of the PA-38 Tomahawk, an alpha-numeric Identity Code was used, incorporating a letter 'A' in the serial number, but this was not used on other aircraft. Not surprisingly, in this complicated system there were exceptions to the rule. The PA-42 Cheyenne III had been using the standard system until 1983 when the PA-42 Cheyenne 720-IIIA came into production. The new model started on a new series of numbers commencing at c/n 42-5501003 which ran on until c/n 42-5501060. The PA-42-1000 Cheyenne 400LS used numbers running from c/n 42-5527001 to 42-5527044.

The fourth and latest serial system, in use at Piper since 1986, leaves out the model year identification and runs consecutively without any re-starting of the series at annual break points. The first two digits are

the basic model number, the next two digits identify the individual model and the final three digits are the individual aircraft number. This system only allows 999 aircraft in each serial allocation but it is assumed that a new model number will be allocated for any type which exceeds this volume.

Piper prototypes have generally carried the first serial number applicable to their type number (eg, 18-1). With the new system of serials, prototypes have had serials identifying their year of construction – and normally ending with 0001 etc. Some prototypes have had unique serials, often with an 'E' suffix (for instance c/n 34-E1), and some of the early post-war types had the first prototype numbered -01 and the first production aircraft serialled -1. Serial numbers of prototypes are not referred to in the Model Table.

Post-War Piper Serial Number Batches

PA-11 Cub Special

11-1 to 11-1111	11-1249 to 11-1678

PA-12 Super Cruiser

12-1 to 12-3625	12-3901 to 12-4036

PA-14 Family Cruiser

14-1 to 14-204	14-490 to 14-523

PA-15 and PA-17 Vagabond

15-1 to 15-35	15-37 to 15-388
17-1 to 17-215	

PA-16 Clipper

16-01	16-2 to 16-736

PA-18 Super Cub

18-1 to 18-9004	18-7909001 to 18-7909200
18-7309016 to 18-7309025	18-8009001 to 18-8009061
18-7409026 to 18-7409151	18-8109001 to 18-8109086
18-7509001 to 18-7509142	18-8209001 to 18-8209025
18-7609001 to 18-7609157	18-8309001 to 18-8309025
18-7709001 to 18-7709198	1809001 to 1809113
18-7809001 to 18-7809188	9901CC to 9954CC (Top Cub)

PA-20 Pacer

20-01, 20-1	20-3 to 20-1121

PA-22 Tri-Pacer, Caribbean and Colt

22-1 to 22-7642	22-8000 to 22-9848 (Colt)

PA-23 Apache-150/160 and -235

23-1 to 23-2046	27-505 to 27-622 (PA-23-235)

PA-23-250 Aztec

27-1 to 27-504	27-7754001 to 27-7754163
27-2000 to 27-4916	27-7854001 to 27-7854139
27-7304917 to 27-7305234	27-7954001 to 27-7954121
27-7405235 to 27-7405476	27-8054001 to 27-8054059
27-7554001 to 27-7554168	27-8154001 to 27-8154030
27-7654001 to 27-7654203	

PA-24 Comanche

24-1 to 24-3687	24-4000 to 24-5034
26-1 to 26-148 (PA-24-400)	

PA-25 Pawnee

25-1 to 25-731	25-7656001 to 25-7656122
25-2000 to 25-5498	25-7756001 to 25-7756095
25-7305522 to 25-7305554	25-7856001 to 25-7856072
25-7305522 to 25-7405821	25-7956001 to 25-7956042
25-7405555 to 25-7405821	25-8056001 to 25-8056051
25-7556001 to 25-7556233	25-8156001 to 25-8156024

Piper PA-42-720 Cheyenne IIIA N141TC

PA-28 140 Cherokee

28-20000 to 28-24945	28-7325001 to 28-7325674
28-25001 to 28-26331	28-7425001 to 28-7425444
28-26401 to 28-26946	28-7525001 to 28-7525340
28-7125001 to 28-7125641	28-7625001 to 28-7625275
28-7225001 to 28-7225602	28-7725001 to 28-7725290

PA-28-150, -160, -180 Cherokee, Challenger and Archer and PA-28-181 Archer II and III

28-1 to 28-5499	28-8090001 to 28-8090372 (181/II)
28-5601 to 28-5859	28-8190001 to 28-8190318 (181/II)
28-7105001 to 28-7105234	28-8290001 to 28-8290178 (181/II)
28-7205001 to 28-7205318	28-8390001 to 28-8390090 (181/II)
28-7305001 to 28-7305601	28-8490001 to 28-8490112 (181/II)
28-7405001 to 28-7405280	28-8590001 to 28-8590092 (181/II)
28-7505001 to 28-7505260	28-8690001 to 28-8690062 (181/II)
28-7690001 to 28-7690467 (181/II)	2890001 to 2890205 (181/II)
28-7790001 to 28-7790607 (181/II)	2890206 to 2890239 (181/III)
28-7890001 to 28-7890551 (181/II)	2843001to 2843608 + (181/III)
28-7990001 to 28-7990594 (181/II)	

PA-28-151 and 161 Warrior/Cadet

28-7415001 to 28-7415703 (151)	28-8216001 to 28-8216226 (161)
28-7515001 to 28-7515449 (151)	28-8316001 to 28-8316112 (161)
28-7615001 to 28-7615435 (151)	28-8416001 to 28-8416131 (161)
28-7715001 to 28-7715314 (151)	28-8516001 to 28-8516099 (161)
28-7716001 to 28-7716323 (161)	28-8616001 to 28-8616062 (161)
28-7816001 to 28-7816680 (161)	2816001 to 2816125 (161)
28-7916001 to 28-7916598 (161)	2841001 to 2841365 (Cadet)
28-8016001 to 28-8016373 (161)	2842001 to 2842230 + (161)
28-8116001 to 28-8116322 (161)	

PA-28-235 and -236 Cherokee/Charger/Pathfinder/Dakota and 201T Turbo Dakota

28-10001 to 28-11255	28-7911001 to 28-7911335 (236)
28-11227 to 28-11255	28-7921001 to 28-7921095 (201T)
28-11301 to 28-11378	28-8011001 to 28-8011151 (236)
28-7110001 to 28-7110028	28-8111001 to 28-8011097 (236)
28-7210001 to 28-7210023	28-8211001 to 28-8211050 (236)
28-7310001 to 28-7310176	28-8311001 to 28-8311026 (236)
28-7410001 to 28-7410110	28-8411001 to 28-8411031 (236)
28-7510001 to 28-7510135	28-8511001 to 28-8511020 (236)
28-7610001 to 28-7610202	28-8611001 to 28-8611009 (236)
28-7710001 to 28-7710089	2811001 to 2811050 (236)

PA-28R-180, 200, 201 Cherokee Arrow and -201T Turbo Arrow

28R-30000 to 28R-31135 (180)	28R-7918001 to 28R-7918267 (201/IV)
28R-31251 to 28R-31270 (180)	28R-7931001 to 28-7931310 (201T/IV)
28R-35001 to 28R-35392 (200)	28R-8018001 to 28R-8018106 (201/IV)
29R-35601 to 28R-35820 (200)	28R-8031001 to 28-8031178 (201T/IV)
28R-7130001 to 28R-7130013 (180)	28R-8118001 to 28R-8118082 (201/IV)
28R-7135001 to 28R-7135229 (200)	28R-8131001 to 28-8131208 (201T/IV)
28R-7235001 to 28R-7135320 (200)	28R-8218001 to 28R-8218026 (201/IV)
28R-7335001 to 28R-7335446 (200)	2837001 to 2837054 plus 2837061 (201)
28R-7435001 to 28R-7435323 (200)	2844001 to 2844113 + (201)
28R-7535001 to 28R-7535383 (200)	28R-8231001 to 28-8231081 (201T/IV)
28R-7635001 to 28R-7635473 (200)	28R-8331001 to 28-8331051 (201T/IV)
28R-7703001 to 28R-7703427 (201T)	28R-8431001 to 28-8431032 (201T/IV)
28R-7737001 to 28R-7737178 (201)	28R-8531001 to 28-8531015 (201T/IV)
28R-7803001 to 28R-7803373 (201T)	28R-8631001 to 28-8631006 (201T/IV)
28R-7837001 to 28R-7837317 (201)	2831001 to 2831038 (201T/IV)

PA-30 Twin Comanche and PA-39 Twin Comanche C/R

30-1 to 30-2000	39-1 to 39-152

PA-31-300 and -31-325 C/R Navajo

31-1 to to 31-900	31-7812001 to 31-7812129
31-7300901 to 31-7300976	31-7912001 to 31-7912124
31-74000977 to 31-7400996	31-8012001 to 31-8012102
31-7401201 to 31-7401268	31-8112001 to 31-8112077
31-7512001 to 31-7512072	31-8212001 to 31-8212036

31-7612001 to 31-7612110	31-8312001 to 31-8312019
31-7712001 to 31-7712103	

PA-31P Pressurized Navajo and PA-31P-350 Mojave

31P-1 to 31P-109	31P-7630001 to 31P-7630019
31P-7300110 to 31P-7300172	31P-7730001 to 31P-7730012
31P-7400173 to 31P-7400230	31P-8314001 to 31P-8314002 (350)
31P-7530001 to 31P-7530028	31P-8414003 to 31P-8414050 (350)

PA-31-350 Chieftain and T-1020

31-5001, -5003	31-8152001 to 31-8152203
31-7305005 to 31-7305125	31-8252001 to 31-8252085
31-7405126 to 31-7405257	31-8253001 to 31-8253017 (T1020)
31-7405401 to 31-7405497	31-8352001 to 31-8352045
31-7552001 to 31-7552132	31-8353001 to 31-8353007 (T1020)
31-7652001 to 31-7652177	31-8452001 to 31-8452024
31-7752001 to 31-7752192	31-8453001 to 31-8453004 (T1020)
31-7852001 to 31-7852171	31-8553001 to 31-8553002 (T1020)
31-7952001 to 31-7952250	31-8558001 (T1020/353)
31-8052001 to 31-8052221	31-8557001 (T1020/353)

PA-31T Cheyenne, PA-31-T1, PA-31-T2 IIXL and T-1040

31T-7400002 to 31T-7400009	31T-7920001 to 31T-7920094 (T2)
31T-7520001 to 31T-7520043	31T-8020001 to 31T-8020095 (T2)
31T-7620001 to 31T-7620057	31T-8120001 to 31T-8120072 (T2)
31T-7720001 to 31T-7720069	31T-8120101 to 31T-8120104 (T2)
31T-7804001 to 31T-7804011 (T1)	31T-8166001 to 31T-8166076 (IIXL)
31T-7904001 to 31T-704057 (T1)	31T-1166001 to 31T-1166008 (IIXL)
31T-8004001 to 31T-8004057 (T1)	31T-1122001 to 31T-1122002 (IIXLa)
31T-8104001 to 31T-8104073 (T1)	31T-8275001 to 31T-8275025 (T1040)
31T-8104101 (T1)	31T-8375001 to 31T-8375005 (T1040)
31T-8304001 to 31T-8304003 (T1/1A)	31T-8475001 (T1040)
31T-1104004 to 31T-1104017 (T1/1A)	31T-5575001 to 31T-5575002 (T1040)
31T-7820001 to 31T-7820092 (T2)	

PA-32-260 and PA-32-300 Cherokee Six, PA-32-301/301T Saratoga and Piper 6X (301FT) and 6XT (301XTC)

32-1 to 32-1075	32-7440001 to 32-7440172 (-300)
32-1111 to 32-1194	32-7540001 to 32-7540188 (-300)
32-1251 to 32-1297	32-7640001 to 32-7640130 (-300)
32-7100001 to 32-7100028	32-7740001 to 32-7740113 (-300)
32-7200001 to 32-7200045	32-7840001 to 32-7840202 (-300)
32-7300001 to 32-7300065	32-7940001 to 32-7940290 (-300)
32-7400001 to 32-7400051	32-8006001 to 32-8006106 (301)
32-7500001 to 32-7500043	32-8106001 to 32-8106100 (301)
32-7600001 to 32-7600024	32-8206001 to 32-8206043 (301)
32-7700001 to 32-7700023	32-8306001 to 32-8306033 (301)
32-7800001 to 32-7800008	32-8406001 to 32-8406019 (301)
32-40000 to 32-40545 (-300)	32-8506001 to 32-8506021 (301)
32-40566 to 32-40777 (-300)	32-8606001 to 32-8606023 (301)
32-40851 to 32-40974 (-300)	3206001 to 3206098 (301)
32-7140001 to 32-7140078 (-300)	3232001 to 3232036 + (301FT)
32-7240001 to 32-7240137 (-300)	3255001 to 3255027 + (301XTC)
32-7340001 to 32-7340191 (-300)	

PA-32R-300/300T Lance, Saratoga SP and Saratoga II-HP

32R-7680001 to 32R-7680525	3246001 to 3246222 + (301/II-HP)
32R-7780001 to 32R-7780549	32R-7887001 to 32R-7887289 (300T)
32R-7880001 to 32R-7880068	32R-7987001 to 32R-7987126 (300T)
32R-7885001 to 32R-7885285	32R-8029001 to 32R-8029121 (301T)
32R-7985001 to 32R-7985106	32R-8129001 to 32R-8129114 (301T)
32R-8013001 to 32R-8013139 (301)	32R-8229001 to 32R-8229071 (301T)
32R-8113001 to 32R-8113123 (301)	32R-8229001 to 32R-8229071 (301T)
32R-8213001 to 32R-8213061 (301)	32R-8329001 to 32R-8329040 (301T)
32R-8313001 to 32R-8313030 (301)	32R-8429001 to 32R-8429028 (301T)
32R-8413001 to 32R-8413024 (301)	32R-8529001 to 32R-8529020 (301T)
32R-8513001 to 32R-8513016 (301)	32R-8629001 to 32R-8629005 (301T)
32R-8613001 to 32R-8613006 (301)	32R-8629001 to 32R-8629008 (301T)
3213001 to 3213041 (301)	3229001 to 3229003 (301T)
3213042 to 3213108 (301/II-HP)	3257001 to 3257372 + (301/II-TC)

Piper PA-46-500TP Malibu Meridian N402MM. New Piper Aircraft

PA-34-200, -200T and -220T Seneca

34-7250001 to 34-7250360	34-8233001 to 34-8233205 (220T)
34-7350001 to 34-7350353	34-8333001 to 34-8333133 (220T)
34-7570001 to 34-7570327 (200T)	34-8433001 to 34-8433088 (220T)
34-7670001 to 34-7670371 (200T)	34-8533001 to 34-8533069 (220T)
34-7770001 to 34-7770441 (200T)	34-8633001 to 34-8633031 (220T)
34-7870001 to 34-7870474 (200T)	3433001 to 3433238 (220T)
34-7970001 to 34-7970530 (200T)	3448001 to 3448085 (220T)
34-8070001 to 34-8070367 (200T)	3447001 to 3447029 (220T/IV)
34-8170001 to 34-8170092 (200T)	3449001 to 3449311+ (220T/V)
34-8133001 to 34-8133277 (220T)	

PA-36-285 Pawnee Brave 300 and 375

36-7360001 to 36-7360073	36-7902001 to 36-7902051 (375)
36-7460001 to 36-7460041	36-8060001 to 36-8060026
36-7560001 to 36-7560134	36-8002001 to 36-8002041 (375)
36-7660001 to 36-7660135	36-8160001 to 36-8160023
36-7760001 to 36-7760142	36-8102001 to 36-8102029 (375)
36-7860001 to 36-7860123	36-8202001 to 36-8202025 (375)
36-7802001 to 36-7802074 (375)	36-8302001 to 36-8302025 (375)
36-7960001 to 36-7960078	

PA-38-112 Tomahawk

38-78A0001 to 38-78A0844	38-81A0001 to 38-81A0210
38-79A0001 to 38-79A1179	38-82A0001 to 38-82A0124
38-80A0001 to 38-80A0198	

PA-40 Arapaho

40-7300001	40-7400002 to 40-7400003

PA-42 Cheyenne III, IIIA, 400 and 400LS

42-7800001 to 42-7800002	42-8301001 to 42-8301002 (IIIA)
42-7801003 to 42-7801004	42-5501003 to 42-5501010 (IIIA)
42-8001001 to 42-8001096	42-5501011 to 42-5501060 (IIIA)
42-8001101 to 42-8001106	42-5527001 to 42-5527044 (400)

PA-44-180 and -180T Seminole

44-7995001 to 44-7995329	44-8207001 to 44-8207020 (180T)
44-8095001 to 44-8095027	4495001 to 4495013
44-8195001 to 44-8195026	4496001 to 4496203+
44-8107001 to 44-8107066 (180T)	

PA-46-310P and -350P Malibu and PA-46-500TP Malibu Meridian

46-8408001 to 46-8408087	4622001 to 4622220 (350P)
46-8508001 to 46-8508109	4636001 to 4636365+ (350P)
46-8608001 to 46-8608088	4697001 to 4697210+ (500TP)
4608001 to 4608140	

Piper Aerostar 600A, 601B, 601P, 602P, 700P

60-500-162 to 60-0560-182 (600A)	61-0844-8162153 to 61-0880-8162157 (601B)
60-0563-7961183 to 60-0713-7961221 (600A)	61P-0498-204 to -0562-243 (601P)
60-0715-8061222 to 60-0824-8061236 (600A)	61P-0564-7963244 to -0825-8063433 (601P)
60-0833-8161237 to 60-0933-8161262 (600A)	61P-0826-8163434 to -0860-8163455 (601P)
61-0497-128 to 61-0537-132 (601B)	62P-0750-8165001 to -0932-8165055 (602P)
61-0573-7962133 to 61-0698-7962143 (601B)	60-8265001 to 60-8265057 (602P)
61-0717-8062144 to 61-0838-8062152 (601B)	60-8365001 to 60-8365021 (602P)
61-0717-8062144 to 61-0838-8062152 (601B)	60-8423001 to 60-8423025 (700P)

Note: Some aircraft in the above batches were not built, re-serialled, supplied as kits or destroyed in the Lock Haven floods.

Model	1946	1947	1948	1949	1950	1951	1952	1953	1954	1955	1956	1957
J3C Cub	J3C-65	J3C-65										
PA-11 Cub Special	11-65	11-65	11-90	11-90								
PA-12 Super Cruiser	12	12	12									
PA-14 Family Cruiser			14	14								
PA-15 Vagabond			15									
PA-16 Clipper				16	16							
PA-17 Vagabond			17	17								
PA-18 Super Cub					18-95	18-95	18-95	18-95	18-95	18-95	18-95	18-95
PA-18 Super Cub					18-105	18-125	18-125	18-135	18-135	18-150	18-150	18-150
PA-20 Pacer					20-115	20-125	20-125	20-135	20-135			
PA-22 Tri Pacer						22-125	22-125	22-135	22-135	22-150	22-150	22-150
PA-23 Apache									23-150	23-150	23-150	23-160

Model	1958	1959	1960	1961	1962	1963	1964	1965	1966	1967	1968	1969
PA-18 Super Cub	18-95	18-95	18-95	18-95								
PA-18 Super Cub	18-150	18-150	18-150	18-150	18-150	18-150	18-150	18-150	18-150	18-150	18-150	18-150
PA-22 Colt				22-108	22-108	22-108						
PA-22 Caribbean	22-150	22-150	22-150									
PA-22 Tri Pacer	22-160	22-160	22-160									
PA-23 Apache	23-160	23-160	23-160G	23-160H	23-160H	23-235	23-235	23-235				
PA-23 Aztec			23-250	23-250	23-250B	23-250B	23-250C	23-250C	23-250C	23-250C	23-250C	23-250C
PA-24 Comanche	24-180	24-180	24-180	24-180	24-180	24-180						
PA-24 Comanche			24-250	24-250	24-250	24-250	24-250	24-250	24-260	24-260B	24-260B	24-260B
PA-24 Comanche							24-400	24-400				
PA-25 Pawnee		25-150	25-150	25-150	25-235	25-235	25-235	25-235B	25-235B	25-235C	25-235C	25-235C
PA-28 Cherokee							28-140	28-140	28-140	28-140	28-140B	28-140C
PA-28 Cherokee					28-160	28-160	28-160B	28-160B				
PA-28 Cherokee							28-180B	28-180B	28-180C	28-180C	28-180C	28-180D
PA-28 Cherokee							28-235	28-235	28-235B		28-235C	28-235D
PA-28R Arrow										28R-180	28R-180	28R-180
PA-30 Tw. Comanche						30-160	30-160	30-160	30-160B	30-160B	30-160B	30-160C
PA-31 Navajo										31-300	31-300	31-300
PA-32 Cherokee 6								32-260	32-260	32-260	32-260	32-260
PA-32 Cherokee 6								32-300	32-300	32-300	32-300	32-300

Model	1970	1971	1972	1973	1974	1975	1976	1977	1978	1979	1980	1981
PA-18 Super Cub	18-150	18-150	18-150	18-150	18-150	18-150	18-150	18-150	18-150	18-150	18-150	18-150
PA-23 Aztec	23-250D	23-250E	23-250E	23-250E	23-250E	23-250E	23-250F	23-250F	23-250F	23-250F	23-250F	23-250F
Turbo Aztec					23-250E	23-250E	23-250F	23-250F	23-250F	23-250F	23-250F	23-250F
PA-24 Comanche	24-260C	24-260C	24-260C	24-260C								
PA-25 Pawnee	25-235C	25-235C	25-235C	25-235C	25-235D	25-235D	25-235D	25-235D	25-235D	25-235D	25-235D	25-235D
PA-25 Pawnee	25-235C	25-260C	25-260C	25-260C	25-260D	25-260D	25-260D	25-260D				
PA-28 Cherokee	28-140C	28-140D	28-140E	28-140	28-140	28-140	28-140	28-140				
PA-28 Cherokee				28-150	28-151	28-151	28-151	28-151				
PA-28 Warrior								28-161	28-161	28-161	28-161	28-161
PA-28 Cherokee	28-180E	28-180F	28-180G	28-180	28-180	28-180	28-181	28-181	28-181	28-181	28-181	28-181
PA-28 Cherokee	28-235D	28-235E	28-235F	28-235	28-235	28-235	28-235	28-235	28-236	28-236	28-236	28-236
Turbo Dakota										28-201T		
PA-28R Arrow	28R-200	28R-200	28R-200	28R-200	28R-200	28R-200	28R-200	28R-201	28R-201	28RT-201	28RT-201	28RT-201
Turbo Arrow								28R-201T	28R-201T	28RT-201T	28RT-201T	28RT-201T
PA-31 Navajo	31-310	31-310	31-310B	31-310B	31-310B	31-310C	31-310C	31-310C	31-310C	31-310C	31-310C	31-310C
PA-31 Navajo						31-325	31-325	31-325	31-325	31-325	31-325	31-325
PA-31 Chieftain				31-350	31-350	31-350	31-350	31-350	31-350	31-350	31-350	31-350
PA-31P Navajo	31P-425	31P-425	31P-425	31P-425	31P-425	31P-425	31P-425	31P-425				
PA-31T Cheyenne					31T-620	31T-620	31T-620	31T-620	31T-620	31T	31T	31T
PA-31T Cheyenne									31T1	31T1	31T1	31T1
PA-31T Cheyenne												31T2
PA-32 Cherokee 6	32-260C	32-260D	32-260E	32-260	32-260	32-260	32-260	32-260	32-260			
PA-32 Cherokee 6	32-300C	32-300D	32-300E	32-300	32-300	32-300	32-300	32-300	32-300	32-300	32-301	32-301
Turbo Saratoga SP											32-301T	32-301T
PA-32R Saratoga							32R-300	32R-300	32RT-300	32RT-300	32R-301	32R-301

Piper PA-31 Navajo VH-CLU

Piper PA-30-160 Turbo Twin Comanche C I-NASA

Piper PA-11 Cub Special NC1402N

Continued	1970	1971	1972	1973	1974	1975	1976	1977	1978	1979	1980	1981
Turbo Saratoga										32RT-300T	32R-301T	32R-301T
PA-32R Saratoga							32R-300	32R-300	32RT-300	32RT-300	32R-301	32R-301
Turbo Saratoga									32RT-300T	32RT-300T	32R-301T	32R-301T
PA-34 Seneca		34-200	34-200	34-200	34-200	34-200T	34-200T	34-200T	34-200T	34-200T	34-200T	34-200T
PA-36 Brave				36-285	36-285	36-285	36-285	36-300	36-300	36-300	36-300	36-300
PA-36 Brave									36-375	36-375	36-375	36-375
PA-38 Tomahawk									38-112	38-112	38-112	38-112
PA-39 Tw Comanche	39CR	39CR	39CR									
Turbo Tw Comanche	39CR	39CR	39CR									
PA-42 Cheyenne III											42-720	42-720
PA-44 Seminole										44-180	44-180	44-180
Turbo Seminole												44-180T
600A Aerostar									600A	600A	600A	600A
601B Aerostar									601B	601B	601B	601B
601P Aerostar									601P	601P	601P	601P
602P Aerostar												602P

Model	1982	1983	1984	1985	1986	1987	1988	1989	1990	1991	1992	1993
PA-18 Super Cub	18-150						18-150	18-150	18-150			18-150
PA-28 Warrior II	28-161	28-161	28-161	28-161	28-161	28-161	28-161	28-161	28-161	28-161	28-161	
PA-28 Cadet						28-161	28-161	28-161	28-161		28-161	28-161
PA-28 Archer II	28-181	28-181	28-181	28-181	28-181	28-181	28-181	28-181	28-181		28-181	28-181
PA-28 Dakota	28-236	28-236	28-236	28-236	28-236	28-236	28-236	28-236	28-236			28-236
PA-28R Arrow IV	28RT-201						28R-201	28R-201	28R-201			
Turbo Arrow IV	28RT-201T	28RT-201T	28RT-201T	28RT-201T	28RT-201T	28RT-201T	28R-201T	28R-201T	28RT-201T	28RT-201T		
PA-31 Navajo	31-310C	31-310C										
PA-31 Navajo C/R	31-325	31-325										
PA-31 Chieftain	31-350	31-350	31-350	31-350								
PA-31P Mojave		31P-350	31P-350	31P-350								
PA-31T Cheyenne	31T	31T										
PA-31T Cheyenne	31T1	31T1	31T1									
PA-31T Cheyenne	31T2	31T2	31T2	31T2								
PA-31 T-1040	T-1040	T-1040	T-1040	T-1040								
PA-32 Saratoga	32-301	32-301	32-301	32-301	32-301	32-301	32-301	32-301	32-301	32-301		
Turbo Saratoga	32-301T	32-301T	32-301T									
PA-32R Saratoga SP	32R-301	32R-301	32R-301	32R-301	32R-301	32R-301	32R-301	32R-301	32R-301	32R-301		32R-301
Turbo Saratoga SP	32R-301T	32R-301T	32R-301T	32R-301T	32R-301T	32R-301T			44-180			
PA-34 Seneca III	34-220T	34-220T	34-220T	34-220T	34-220T	34-220T	34-220T	34-220T	34-220T	34-220T	34-220T	34-220T
PA-36 Brave	36-375	36-375										
PA-38 Tomahawk	38-112											
PA-42 Cheyenne III	42-720	42-720	42-720	42-720	42-720	42-720	42-720	42-720	42-720	42-720	42-720	42-720
PA-42 Cheyenne LS				400LS	400LS	400LS	400LS	400LS	400LS	400LS		
PA-44 Seminole	44-180T						44-180	44-180				
PA-46 Malibu			46-310P	46-310P	46-310P	46-310P	46-310P	46-350P	46-350P	46-350P	46-350P	46-350P
PA-60 Aerostar			602P	602P	602P							
PA-60 Aerostar					700P							

Model	1994	1995	1996	1997	1998	1999	2000	2001	2002	2003	2004	2005
PA-18 Super Cub	18-150											
PA-28 Warrior II/III	28-161	28-161	28-161	28-161	28-161	28-161	28-161	28-161	28-161	28-161	28-161	28-161
PA-28 Archer II/III	28-181	28-181	28-181	28-181	28-181	28-181	28-181	28-181	28-181	28-181	28-181	28-181
PA-28 Dakota	28-236	28-236										
PA-28R Arrow		28R-201	28R-201	28R-201	28R-201	28R-201	28R-201	28R-201	28R-201	28R-201	28R-201	28R-201
PA-32 Piper 6X										28-301FT	28-301FT	28-301FT
PA-32 Piper 6XT										28-301XTC	28-301XTC	28-301XTC
PA-32R Saratoga	32R-301	32R-301	32R-301	32R-301	32R-301	32R-301	32R-301	32R-301	32R-301	32R-301	32R-301	32R-301
PA-32R Saratoga IITC			32R-301T	32R-301T	32R-301T	32R-301T	32R-301T	32R-301T	32R-301T	32R-301T	32R-301T	32R-301T
PA-34 Seneca III/V	34-220T	34-220T	34-220T	34-220T	34-220T	34-220T	34-220T	34-220T	34-220T	34-220T	34-220T	34-220T
PA-44 Seminole		44-180	44-180	44-180	44-180	44-180	44-180	44-180	44-180	44-180	44-180	44-180
PA-46 Malibu/Mirage	46-350P	46-350P	46-350P	46-350P	46-350P	46-350P	46-350P	46-350P	46-350P	46-350P	46-350P	46-350P
PA-46 Meridian							46-500TP	46-500TP	46-500TP	46-500TP	46-500TP	46-500TP

Piper PA-34-220T Seneca IV PT-WJO

Piper PA-44-180 Seminole N82549

Piper PA-46-310P Malibu N286CM

Pipistrelle — Slovenia

The Slovenian company Pipistrel D.o.o. has produced a range of ultra-light aircraft including the Spider and Twister flexwings of which over 300 have been produced. In 1994 they built the prototype Pipistrel Sinus (S5-NBP) which was a 450kg side-by-side two-seat cantilever high-wing light aircraft of all-composite construction. It had a high aspect ratio glider wing, a T-tail, a very narrow rear fuselage and a fixed tailwheel or (from 2005) optional tricycle undercarriage. Two versions have been manufactured – the Sinus 912 powered by a 72hp Rotax 912 engine and the lower-cost and performance version, the Sinus 503 with a 50hp Rotax 503UL engine. In 2002, Pipistrelle added the Virus 912 and Virus 582, which are higher-performance versions of the Sinus with a shorter wing and a tricycle undercarriage, powered by either the Rotax 912 or Rotax 582 engine. The Sinus and Virus are both supplied factory-complete with dual controls. Production to date is unknown but believed to be approximately 130 aircraft. The serial numbers for the Sinus and Virus are also unclear but an example is c/n 068S9120402 which is thought to break down as – Individual Number

Pipistrelle Sinus

(068), Model (S=Sinus), Engine (Rotax 912), Batch (04) and unit within the batch (02). Pipistrelle has also flown the prototype (S5-P1102) of the new Taurus single-seat sailplane with a retractable 53hp Rotax 503 engine fitted in the centre fuselage.

Potez — France

Though primarily a manufacturer of military aircraft, Ets Henri Potez launched a new 16/24-seat business and light commercial aircraft in 1961. The Potez 840 was an all-metal low-wing monoplane of generally conventional appearance with a retractable tricycle undercarriage and four Turboméca Astazou II engines. The prototype (F-WJSH c/n 01) first flew at Toulouse on 29th April 1961 and was followed by a second prototype (F-WJSU c/n 02) on 11th June 1962. This was fitted with more powerful Astazou XII engines, additional cockpit windows and a longer nose. It was envisaged that the Potez 840 would be built at Baldonnel in Ireland, but, in fact, the four production aircraft were constructed in France. Two of these (F-WLKR c/n 1 and N3430L c/n 2) were Potez 841s, powered by four Pratt & Whitney PT6A-6 turboprops and the other two (F-BNAN c/n 3 and CN-MBC c/n 4) were the Potez 842 with Astazou XII engines. In the end, Potez found that the economics of the 840 were poor and, due to cancellation of American contracts for the 840, the project was terminated.

Potez 841 F-BNAN

Pottier — France

The French light aircraft designer, Jean Pottier conceived the P.220S Koala homebuilt and the first amateur-built example, F-PYZM was flown in July 1987 powered by a 75hp Volkswagen. The P.220S was subsequently produced under licence as both a kit aircraft and as a factory-complete machine by Evektor-Aerotechnik (the EV-97), Aero (AT-3) and the Italian company SG Aviation (SG Storm) as described elsewhere.

Praga — Czechoslovakia

Better known for its range of small aero engines, CKD-Praga (formerly Ceskomoravska-Kolben-Danek) built a number of military biplanes before the war together with a small sporting aircraft – the E-114 Praga Air Baby. The E-114 was a two-seater with a cantilever high wing, rearwards-hinged cockpit canopy and fixed tailwheel undercarriage. The prototype, OK-PGA first flew in September 1934 and this was followed by 63 examples of the E-114 powered by a 40hp Praga B engine or 45hp Praga B-2. In addition, 39 aircraft were built in England by F Hills & Sons Ltd at Barton using Praga B engines, licence-built by Jowett Cars Ltd.

Following the war, Praga decided to return the Air Baby to production as the E-114D. The prototype E-114D (OK-PGF) had flown before the war with the higher-powered 60hp Praga D engine together with an improved version, the E-115, which had a shorter wing and other

Praga E-114 HB-UAD. M J Hooks

refinements. The postwar version of the E-114D had a larger tail, moulded windscreen, strengthened fuselage, increased wing dihedral and improved braking. The first of these was OK-AFJ which first flew on 14th September 1946.

Praga built 10 examples of the E-114D, but production was concentrated on the E-114M, which was equipped with a 65hp Walter Mikron III engine. The first E-114M (OK-AFM) made its first flight on 29th January 1947 and was followed by 95 production aircraft. Subsequently,

responsibility for the E-114M passed to the Rudy Letov company which completed a further 26 units. Praga also flew a postwar prototype of the E-117 (OK-AFU) that had a reshaped vertical tail, tricycle undercarriage and cabin doors to replace the hinged windscreen, but this did not go into production. Similarly, they built two prototypes of the Praga E-211 high-wing light twin, the first of which (OK-BFA) flew on 1st June 1947. The performance of the E-211 was considered inferior to that of the Aero 45 and further development was abandoned.

Procaer   Italy

Procaer was another Milan-based company formed to exploit the designs of Stelio Frati. The first design to be undertaken was the F.15 Picchio, which was a three-seat low-wing cabin monoplane of similar layout and construction to the Aviamilano-built F.14 Nibbio. Its construction consisted of wooden basic construction with aluminium skinning. It was built by Procaer between 1959 and 1963 in the following versions:

Model	Built	Notes
F.15 Picchio	5	Three-seat model with 160hp Lycoming O-320-B1A engine. Prototype I-PICB FF 7 May 1959. Production c/ns 01 to 05
F.15A Picchio	10	Four-seat Picchio with 180hp Lycoming O-360-A1A. Production c/ns 06 to 15
F.15B Picchio	20	F.15A with larger wings and fuselage fuel tank replaced by wing tanks. Prototype I-PROG. Production c/ns 016 to 036
F.15C	1	F.15B (I-RAIC/I-PROI c/n 028) built in 1964 with 260hp Continental IO-470-E engine and wingtip tanks
F.15D		Proposed F.15B with 250hp Franklin engine. Not built

The F-15E and F-15F were further versions of the Picchio that were developed by General Avia (see separate entry). Procaer's next project was the F.400 Cobra, again designed by Frati. This was a side-by-side two-seat jet trainer using the same construction of wood with aluminium cladding. It was fitted with retractable tricycle undercarriage and powered one 880lbst Turboméca Marboré II turbojet. The prototype, I-COBR (c/n 1) was built by Procaer and flown on 16th November 1960 but written-off in August 1965. A second aircraft, the four-seat F.480 prototype with a 1,058lbst engine was started but not completed. Procaer were also involved in the development of Frati's F.30 Airtruck utility aircraft which was a proposed 8/10-seat light passenger transport and freighter. In the event, this was not built but it was developed into the F.600 Canguro, which saw limited production by SIAI-Marchetti and has now been adopted by Vulcanair (see Partenavia). The SIPA S.251 Antilope single-engined turboprop business aircraft was also a project initiated by Frati and Procaer.

Procaer F.15B Picchio D-ECZA

PZL   Poland

Formal manufacture of aircraft in Poland goes back to the formation of Aviata in 1911, but Poland's principal manufacturer was formed, following the country's independence, as the Central Aircraft Workshops (CWL) in 1918. Following a decade of production of aircraft such as the P-11 and P-24 fighters and the P-23 Karas bomber, the national aircraft manufacturing organisation was reconstituted in 1928 as the State Aircraft Works – PZL (Panstwowe Zaklady Lotnicze)

and more than 5,000 aircraft of various types were manufactured prior to the outbreak of World War Two. These included sporting aircraft such as the PZL-5a biplane and the PZL-19 and PZL-26 three-seat tourers.

Other manufacturers such as PWS, Lublin, Bartel and LWS (which was absorbed into PZL in the mid-1930s) built military aircraft and RWD (Rogalskie – Wigury – Drzewieckiego) developed a large range of light aircraft. The RWD production total of some 800 aircraft included the RWD-5, RWD-9 and RWD-15 high-wing cabin tourers, the RWD-8 tandem open two-seat trainer (of which 570 were built) and the eight-seat RWD-11 light twin.

Following the war, PZL was reconstituted and it commenced postwar operations in 1948, firstly at Mielec and then at Okecie. Initially, it operated under the PZL name but this was changed to WSK (Wytwornia Sprzetu Komunikacyjnego – or Transport Equipment Manufacturing Works) in 1949. In 1957, the name became WSK-PZL with aircraft manufacture being carried out by PZL-Mielec and PZL-Okecie. Helicopters were manufactured by PZL-Swidnik A number of other PZL factories produced engines, instruments, components and gliders. All foreign marketing of PZL products was handled by a separate organisation – Pezetel.

In the immediate postwar period, there were still several independent aircraft companies, all of which were eventually merged into PZL. In 1944 the old PZL-Mielec factory became the base for a new company – LWD (Lotnicze Warsztaty Doswiadczalne) headed by the pre-war designer, Professor Tadeusz Soltyk. It built a series of trainers that served with the Polish Air Force and with national flying schools. The principal models were as follows:

Model	Built	Notes
LWD Szpak-1	-	Low-wing open-cockpit side-by-side two-seat trainer with fixed t/w u/c and 125hp M-11D radial engine. Not built
LWD Szpak-2	1	Tandem two-seat trainer of mixed construction with low-set Pulawski strut-braced dual taper wing transparent cockpit canopy, and fixed tailwheel u/c. powered by a 160hp Bramo-Siemens Sh.14-A4 radial engine. Prototype SP-AAA FF 28 Oct 1945
LWD Szpak-3	1	Szpak-2 with fixed tricycle u/c. SP-AAB. FF 17 Dec 1946
LWD Szpak-4A	1	Single-seat open-cockpit aerobatic version of Szpak-3. SP-AAD. FF 20 May 1947
LWD Szpak-4T	10	Production Szpak-2 with raised framed canopy, modified wing struts. Prototype SP-AAF (c/n 48-002) FF 5 Jan 1948
LWD Zak-1	1	Low-wing side-by-side two-seat trainer with enclosed cockpit and fixed tailwheel u/c powered by one 65hp Walter Mikron 4-III. Prototype SP-AAC FF 23 Mar 1947. Followed by 9 examples of modified Zak-3
LWD Zak-2	1	Zak-1 with open cockpit and 65hp Continental C.65 engine. Prototype SP-AAE FF 27 Nov 1947
LWD Zak-3	10	Zak-2 with enclosed cockpit and 65hp Walter Mikron III. SP-AAX
LWD Zak-4	1	Zak-2 with 105hp Walter Mikron 4-III. SP-BAE. FF 20 Oct 1948

All of these aircraft used wings derived from the designs of Ing Pulawski, which had been used on the PZL high-wing pre-war fighters. This embodied an inboard section, which tapered from a narrow root to a wide centre rib, and an outer section, which tapered down to the wingtip. Such a design was also used on the Zuraw (SP-GLB) that first flew on 16th May 1951. This was a high-wing army cooperation aircraft, owing much to the design of the Fieseler Storch. LWD also built the prototype of the LWD Mis twin-engined transport (SP-BAF), but neither design reached production.

LWD continued the development of tube-and-fabric trainers with the Junak (Cadet), which had many features of the Szpak but used a conventional wing with constant taper. A total of 255 Junaks and its

PZL Junak 2 SP-ABL. J Blake

Zuch (Daredevil) derivative were built for aero clubs and military use by PZL Okecie and the variants were as follows:

Model	Notes
Junak 1	Tandem two-seat low-wing trainer with fixed tailwheel undercarriage, powered by one 125hp M-11G radial engine. Prototype only SP-GLA FF 22 Feb 1948
Junak 2	Junak 1 with 160hp M-11FR engine. Prototype SP-ACZ FF 24 Nov 1949. Approx 110 built, 1951-54
Junak 3	Junak 2 with fixed tricycle u/c. Approx 145 built, 1953-56
Zuch 1	Junak 1 stressed for aerobatics with non-braced spatted u/c, enlarged rudder and 160hp Walter Minor 6-III in-line engine. Prototype only SP-BAD FF 1 Sep 1948
Zuch 2	Zuch 1 with modified cockpit and 160hp SH-Bramo Sh-14 radial engine. Prototype SP-BAG FF 1 Apr 1949. 6 built, 1949-51
TS-8 Bies	Developed all-metal Junak 3 with retractable u/c, modified wing and 340hp Narkiewicz WN-3 piston engine. 239 built

Light aircraft were also built by the Centralne Studium Samolotow (CSS) at Okecie, which designed a group of low-wing tandem two-seaters. The CSS-10A (SP-AAP) first flew on 3rd September 1948 powered by a 65hp Walter Mikron II engine. The second machine, the CSS-10C (SP-BAK) followed on 24th April 1949 and had the higher-powered 105hp Walter Minor 4-III powerplant. 40 examples of the CSS-10C were ordered (but not built) and CSS subsequently built two prototypes of the larger CSS-11 (SP-BAH) with a 160hp Walter Minor 6-III.

The CSS-13 was a licence-built version of the Russian Polikarpov Po-2. Some 180 examples were produced by Mielec as trainers and a few were converted to the S-13 enclosed air ambulance version. A further 372 were produced by PZL-Okecie (including 53 S-13s). CSS also built a prototype of the CSS.12 10-passenger feederliner (SP-BAR) but this did not reach series production.

PZL-Mielec   Poland

The Mielec factory of PZL was originally established to build the PZL-37 Los and became the largest factory in the PZL Group. It had occupied itself in the immediate postwar years with production of the CSS-13 (Polikarpov PO-2) followed by a series of 1,502 examples of the Lim-1 (MiG-15) jet fighter and its derivatives. It also built 239 examples of the TS/8 Bies trainer and the M-2 and M-4 Tarpan prototypes. The range of aircraft produced since then has included the AN-2, the Dromader, the M-28 Skytruck and the Piper Seneca-derived M-20. WSK-PZL Mielec was reorganised in 1998 under a Polish Government plan that created the new Polskie Zaklady Lotnicze Sp.z o o (Polish Aviation Works Ltd) and it continues under this structure.

In 1959, Mielec was given sole responsibility for building the Antonov An-2 utility biplane under the Soviet policy of transfer to Poland of light and utility aircraft designs. Production is now complete with at least 11,961 examples having been built by them, the great majority being exported to the former Soviet Union. Production virtually ceased in 1990 but was resumed in 1996, initially using a large supply of spare components stockpiled at the Mielec factory, and the last delivery (of four aircraft) was made to Vietnam in January 2002.

The An-2 was originally designed by Oleg K Antonov as an agricultural aircraft and first flown in the Soviet Union on 31st August 1947 with, reportedly, 3,670 examples being built between 1947 and 1964 at Kiev-Syvatoshino. It is an all-metal aircraft with a fixed tailwheel undercarriage and a capacious fuselage that is able to accommodate 14 passengers or freight or a large hopper for crop spraying. The powerplant is a 987hp PZL-built Shvetsov ASz-621R nine-cylinder air-cooled radial piston engine. The

An-3T is an upgraded refurbished An-2 with a 1,450shp Glushenkov TVD-20 engine and, after prototype conversions at Kiev, a further 21 have reportedly been completed at the Novosibirsk Factory 153.

The versions built in Poland and in Russia are generally externally identical. Different designations are given to aircraft off the production line as shown in the following table. It is very common for individual aircraft to be re-equipped in service without any change to their original model number because, in general, the differences between models come down to interior trim and minor equipment specifications.

Antonov Model	PZL Model	PZL Built	Notes
-	An-2T	1,370	Utility 12-seat utility passenger or 1500kg load cargo model
-	An-2TD	10	Version for training of parachutists
An-2T	An-2TP	1,609	Local service airline 10-pax model with improved trim compared with An-2T. Some with rectangular windows
An-2P	An-2P	764	12-passenger transport with improved level of interior trim, carpet, soundproofing and toilet compartment
An-2Skh	An-2R	2,056	Agricultural model with lengthened u/c, cabin hopper and spray bars under lower wings or under-fuselage duster
-	An-2Geo		Geophysical survey model conv of An-2T with TS-1230 infrared survey system
-	An-2PK		VIP An-2P with six passenger seats
-	An-2PF		Aerial photographic version of AN-2P
-	An-2PR		An-2T fitted with TV relay equipment
An-2S	An-2S		Ambulance version of An-2TP with provision for six stretchers and attendants
An-2F	-		Experimental night reconnaissance version, also known as An-2RK or An-2K
An-2ZA	-		High-altitude meteorological research model with observer cockpit on rear fuselage
An-2V	-	152	Twin-float seaplane also known as An-4
-	An-2W		An-2TP with twin floats, skis or wheels. Sometimes referred to as An-2M
An-2M	-		Improved agricultural model with square tail
An-2L	-		Chemical-tank equipped version for fire fighting
An-3T	-		An-2 rebuilt for agricultural work with 1,450shp Glushenkov turboprop engine, repositioned air-conditioned cockpit etc. Prototype CCCP-37901 (c/n 01-01)
An-6	-		Utility An-2 for high-altitude operations

Aircraft built in the Soviet Union used two different serial number systems. The first (eg, c/n 113647316) consisted of up to nine digits consisting of '1' followed by a two-digit batch number, the factory code number '473' (not included on export aircraft) and a two-digit number indicating the individual aircraft in the batch. The second system (eg, 5 003 08) consisted of a single digit indicating the year built, a three-digit batch number and a two-digit individual aircraft number. A total of around 1,000 An-2s was also built in China as the Y-5 at the Hua Bei Machine Plant in Shijiazhuang (Factory 134) and a further 727 at Nanchang (Factory 32). Serial numbers followed several different systems but followed a batch system of up to 50 aircraft and generally included the Batch Number, Factory Number and individual aircraft number in the batch. The Chinese also developed a turboprop variant powered by a 1,450shp Glushenkov TVD-20 engine. The PZL-built An-2 has generally been built in batches of 60 aircraft – although early batches are smaller and there have been some that have been as high as 65 or 70 with the largest batch being 95. When production ended PZL had reached the end of Batch 240 at 1G240-60 and c/n 1G241-01 to -03 are also believed to have been completed.

In 1971, PZL joined with a team of Soviet engineers to design a new large agricultural aircraft that would carry approximately 3,000 litres of liquid fertiliser. The result was the LLP-M-15 which first flew on 30th May 1973. The M-15 was a large twin-boomed high aspect ratio biplane with two large hoppers fitted between the upper and lower wings. It had a fixed tricycle undercarriage and upper wings derived from the Antonov An-14 Pchelka and a three-seat cabin – but, most unusually, it was powered by a 3,300 lbst Ivchenko AI-25 turbofan in a pusher installation above and behind the cockpit. By 1975, PZL had delivered five pre-production M-15 Belphegors to the Soviet Union and followed this with a production batch of approximately 150 aircraft as part of an order from Aeroflot for 3,000 aircraft. However, production stopped after around 175 had been completed (at approximately c/n 1S.020-30) because the Belphegor became unacceptably expensive to operate following the 1973 fuel crisis and because of the sensitivity of the duster system to granule size and humidity.

PZL-Mielec then turned its attention to a smaller-capacity agricultural aircraft which emerged as the M-18 Dromader. This was designed in cooperation with Rockwell International to FAR Part 23 standards and it used outer wing panels which were identical to those of the S-2R Thrush Commander. The Dromader was a conventional all-metal single-seat cantilever low-wing aircraft with the chemical hopper ahead of the cockpit and it was powered by a PZL-built Shvetsov radial engine. It was fitted with a 550-imp gal hopper which meant that it could take on tasks which were too great for the smaller Kruk including firefighting. The first M-18 Dromader was followed by two further prototypes, two fatigue test examples and eight pre-production prototypes. Production serial numbers started at 1Z001-01 and it seems that batches of 30 aircraft have been built, although some batches have been up to 50. Over 730 of the M-18 and M-18A have been completed to date and current serial numbers are in Batch 28 (eg, 1Z-028-16). In due course, PZL developed the Dromader design to include the smaller M-21 Dromader Mini and the scaled-up M-24 Dromader Super. It appears that only two prototypes of the M-21 and five of the M-24 have been built. A number of Dromaders have been converted to turboprop power by American companies with Pratt & Whitney PT6A engines. Details of the Dromader family are as follows:

Model	Notes
M-18 Dromader	Basic low-wing single-seat all-metal agricultural aircraft with 550 gal hopper, powered by one 1,000hp PZL ASz-621R radial engine. Prototype SP-PBW (c/n 1Z-P01-02) FF 27 Aug 1976
M-18A Dromader	M-18 with additional rearward-facing seat behind main cockpit to permit ferrying of ground crew
M-18AS Dromader	Dual control training version of M-18 with extended canopy and additional cockpit in place of hopper. Prototype SP-PBC (c/n 1Z007-06) FF 21 Mar 1988. 10 built
M-18B Dromader	M-18A with modified flaps and ailerons, increased payload and other performance improvements. Two-seat M-18BS FF Nov 1997
M-18C Dromader	M-18B fitted with 1,200hp Kalisz K-9 engine. Prototype only
M-21 Dromader Mini	M-18 with shorter forward fuselage and wings, smaller 375-gal hopper, triangulated undercarriage, and 600hp PZL-3SR radial engine. Two Prots. SP-PDM (c/n 1ALP01-01) FF 18 Jun 1982 and SP-PDN (c/n 1ALP01-02)

PZL M-18A Dromader D-FOMG

PZL M-28 Skytruck SP-FYV

M-24 Dromader Super	M-18A with longer-span wings of new aerofoil section giving greater swathe, larger cockpit, 600-gal hopper, greater range. Prototype SP-PFA (c/n 1AKP01-01) FF 14 Jul 1987 plus 4 further prototypes (1AKP01-02 to -05)
M-24T Turbo Dromader	Proposed M-24 powered by one Pratt & Whitney PT6A-65AG turboprop
M-25 Dromader Mikro	Proposed scaled-down version of M-21 with 150-gal hopper

PZL-Mielec took responsibility for another Antonov design, the An-28 light freighter, in 1978 and flew the first Polish production aircraft on 22nd July 1984. The An-28 had been developed as an enlarged and re-engined version of the piston-engined An-14 Pchelka light military transport (and was originally designated An-14M). It was, in effect, a completely new 15-passenger design with a full-depth rear fuselage fitted with clamshell loading doors, redesigned twin tail fins a pair of 810shp Isotov TVD-850 turboprop engines. The prototype

PZL M-15 Belphegor CCCP-15187

(CCCP-1968) flew in September 1969. Later development saw the air-craft fitted with uprated 960shp Glushenkov TVD-10 engines. The An-28 was sold widely to Aeroflot and to operators in former Soviet countries and a number were delivered for military use. It was followed by the M-28 Skytruck which was aimed at Western customers and is in current production powered by 1,100shp Pratt & Whitney PT6A-65B turboprops. The Mielec factory also builds a range of military variants for Polish forces powered by the TVD-10 engines and these include the M-28M for the Polish Navy, An-28TD Bryza with a modified rear loading door and the M-28B Bryza 1R, again for the Polish Navy.

In 1976 PZL had negotiated with Piper Aircraft to produce the PA-34 Seneca II from Piper-provided kits. Powered by two PZL-built 220hp Franklin 6A-350-C engines the aircraft was titled the M-20 Mewa. The first prototype Mewa was a Piper-built aircraft (SP-GKA c/n 34-7670279) that was re-fitted with Franklin engines. PZL subsequently built four production prototypes (c/n 1AHP01-01 to 1AHP01-04) followed by 25 production aircraft. The type was marketed for export customers by Gemini Aircraft of Oklahoma City as the M.20 Gemini fitted with two Teledyne Continental TSIO-360-KB turbocharged engines.

PZL-Mielec also developed the M-26 Iskierka military and civil trainer and marketed it in the USA through Melex USA. The M-26 was a tandem seat low-wing aircraft with a retractable tricycle undercarriage that used a modified version of the Seneca (M-20) wing and its tail and undercarriage. The first of two prototypes (SP-PIA c/n 1APP01-01) flew on 15th July 1986, powered by a 205hp PZL F6A-350CA piston engine. The production version was fitted with a 300hp Lycoming AEIO-540-L1B5D. Only seven production aircraft and two prototypes were produced and M-26 production has been suspended.

Different serial number systems have been used by the PZL Mielec and Okecie factories. PZL-Mielec has allocated serial numbers under a batch system to everything it produces (including components for other aircraft such as tail units, slats, engine pods, control surfaces and outrigger units for the IL-86 and IL-96-300 and the Melex golf carts, SW-680 diesel engines and TS-11 Iskra and An-28 aircraft). These are based on a prefix number/letter followed by the batch number and the individual serial number. The serial system started with the prefix 1A and included 1A (MiG-15/LIM-1), 1B (MiG-15bis/LIM-2), 1C (MiG-17F/LIM-5), 1D (MiG-17PF/LIM-5P), 1E (TS/8 Bies), 1F (LIM-5M), 1H (Iskra), 3H (Iskra), 1J (LIM-6bis) and 1AN (I-322 Irydia). In addition there were civil models, which are shown in greater detail in the table which follows:

Model	Built	C/n example	Notes
An-2	11,961	1G208-22	Prefix 1G followed by batch No (01 to 241) and number in batch
M-15	175?	1S014-17	Prefix 1S followed by batch No (001 to ?020) and number in batch
Dromader	736	1Z005-06	Prefix 1Z followed by batch No (001 to 028) and number in batch (normally 30 aircraft)
M-20	4	1AH-P01-01	Prototypes 1AH-P01-01 to 1AHP01-04
M-20	25	1AH2-009	1AH002-01 to -17 and 1AH003-01 to -08
An-28	190	1AJ002-10	Prefix 1AJ followed by batch No (001 to 010) and number in batch (normally 25 aircraft)
M.28 Skytruck	32	AJE001-08	Prefix AJE followed by batch No (001 to 003) and number in batch
M.28 military	17	AJG002-08	Prefix AJG followed by batch No (001 to 002) and number in batch
Iskierka	9	1AP002-05	Prototypes 1APP01-01 to -02 and c/n 1AP002-01 to -07

PZL-Okecie — Poland

PZL-Okecie is located at the main Warsaw Airport site and its early activities have been described under the main section on PZL. Today it concentrates on parts manufacture for other aviation companies and limited production of the Wilga and Koliber. It was reorganised on 2nd January 1995 into a new joint-stock company, initially 100% owned by the Polish Ministry of Trade and Industry. The company is now a subsidiary of EADS.

By 1955, production of the CSS-13 and the Junak was drawing to a close and the Okecie factory commenced licence production of the Russian Yakovlev Yak-12 high-wing light aircraft. The majority of Yak-12s were destined for export to the Soviet Union and for Polish Air Force use, but a large number entered service with civilian aero clubs or were used for civil transport, ambulance and agricultural work. Between 1955 and 1960 PZL built 1,196 aircraft consisting of 137 of the Yak-12A and 1,059 of the Yak-12M. The Okecie factory then embarked on a major redesign of the Yak-12 as a specialised crop sprayer and utility aircraft. This model, the PZL-101 Gawron, was the first aircraft to use the new model designation system adopted by the Okecie factory. Type designations started at PZL-101 and have now reached PZL-130 (the Orlik trainer) for production types. The Gawron, of which 325 were completed, was used in a variety of utility applications. Details of all the Yak-12s and its variants are as follows:

Model	Notes
Yak-12	Four-seat strut-braced high-wing cabin monoplane of mixed construction developed from Yakovlev Yak-10 with fixed tailwheel u/c and one 145hp Shvetsov M-11FR radial engine. Soviet built
Yak-12R	Yak-12 with enlarged wings, lengthened fuselage and 240hp Ivchenko AI-14R radial engine in smooth cowling. Soviet production
Yak-12M	Yak-12R of all-metal construction with fin leading edge fairing and longer fuselage. Also specialised ambulance model
Yak-12A	Yak-12M with new wing incorporating taper on outer wing panels but without leading edge slats. Modified vertical and horizontal tail surfaces and additional rear windows
PZL-101G.1 Gawron	Yak-12M with new slightly swept wing with endplates, enlarged elevator, rear fuselage chemical hopper and uprated 260hp Ivchenko AI-14R-VI engine. Prototype SP-PAG FF 14 Apr 1958

PZL-101 Gawron SP-CKF

PZL-104 Wilga 35A YR-VIS

PZL-101G.2 Gawron	Four-seat transport version of Gawron with additional rear side windows. Prototype SP-PAO
PZL-101A Gawron	Production model of PZL-101G.1
PZL-101AF Gawron	PZL-101A with increased useful load and a 300hp AI-14RF engine
PZL-101B Gawron	Production model of PZL-101G.2

The next model to appear from Okecie was the PZL-102 Kos – a side-by-side two-seat low-wing trainer. This neat little aircraft was of all-metal construction and had a fixed tailwheel undercarriage. The prototype, SP-PAD (c/n 02), was first flown on 21st May 1958, powered by a 65hp PZL-65 engine. On production models, known as the PZL-102B, the engine was changed to the 90hp Continental C90-12F and an enlarged vertical tail was fitted. The Kos was not very successful and only 11 production examples were built.

Success with the Gawron prompted PZL to look at a more modern replacement. This emerged as the PZL-104 Wilga 1 – an all-metal cantilever high-wing monoplane with a fixed tailwheel undercarriage, a conventional square-section fuselage, four seats and a 195hp WN-6 engine. SP-PAZ, the prototype Wilga 1, was first flown on 21st July 1962. Testing of the Wilga showed that it had a poor useful load, limited range and a high stall speed – so PZL entered into a complete redesign. The PZL-104 Wilga 2 had the same gross weight as the Wilga 1 – but with a 20% decrease in empty weight providing a 55% increase in useful load. The fuselage was sharply waisted behind the cabin module, the vertical tail was swept and the wing structure was redesigned. The Wilga 2 was fitted with a distinctive undercarriage embodying trailing links. The principal versions of the Wilga 2 which have been built are as follows:

Model	Notes
PZL-104 Wilga 2	4-seat high-wing all-metal cantilever-wing monoplane with fixed t/w u/c, powered by one 195hp WN-6B engine. Prototype SP-PAR FF 11 Oct 1963. 5 built

PZL-104 Wilga 2C	Wilga 2 fitted with 230hp Continental O-470-13A engine. 7 sold to Indonesia
PZL-104 Wilga 3	Wilga 2 fitted with 260hp PZL AI-14RA radial engine. 14 built
PZL-104 Wilga 3A	Wilga 3 fitted for flying club use
PZL-104 Wilga 32	Wilga 2C with shorter landing gear and redesigned tailwheel, new front seats and new propeller
Lipnur Gelatik 32	Indonesian-built version of Wilga 32
PZL-104 Wilga 35	Wilga 3 with shorter landing gear and redesigned tailwheel, new front seats and new propeller
PZL-104 Wilga 35A	Aero club version of Wilga 35 with glider towing hook
PZL-104 Wilga 35AD	Wilga 35 with special exhaust system to meet German noise regulations
PZL-104 Wilga 35R	Agricultural version of Wilga 35 with under-fuselage chemical tank
PZL-104 Wilga 35H	Wilga 35 equipped with twin CAP-3000 floats.
PZL-104 Wilga 40	Wilga 40 with 260hp AI-14R engine, automatic leading edge slats, and all-moving tailplane. Prototypes SP-PHB c/n 59090 (FF 17 Jul 1969), SP-PHC c/n 59091
PZL-104 Wilga 43	Wilga 40 with Continental IO-470K engine. SP-PHE
PZL-104 Wilga 80	Wilga 35 modified to FAR Part 23 standards including modified carburettor
PZL-104 Wilga 80-1400	Wilga 80 with 280hp PZL AI-14RD engine, increased wingspan with modified tips and 3,086 lb TOGW. Prototype only
PZL-104 Wilga 550	Wilga 80 fitted with 300hp Continental IO-550 engine and enlarged passenger step and wheel fairings. Prototype only, N7131G c/n CF20890885
PZL-104 Wilga 80A	Aero club version of Wilga 80 with glider towing hook
PZL-104M Wilga 2000	Wilga 80 with 300hp Lycoming IO-540 engine, modified wing with increased fuel capacity and enlarged u/c fairings. Prototype SP-PHG FF 20 Aug 1996

The great majority of Wilga production has concentrated on the Wilga 35A and only a handful of the Continental and Lycoming-engined variants have been built. In an attempt to develop the Wilga, PZL produced prototypes of the PZL-105 Flamingo. This was originally referred to as the Wilga 88 but was really a completely new design. It was a six-seat high-wing utility aircraft with a more conventional box-section fuselage than the Wilga 35 and powered either (as the PZL-105M) by a 360hp Vedeneyev M-14P radial engine or (as the PZL-105L) by a 400hp Lycoming IO-720-A1B flat-eight engine. Two prototypes were built, the first of which (SP-PRC) was first flown on 19th December 1989. PZL also proposed to build the PZL-105T with either a Pratt & Whitney 110 or Allison 450 turboprop engine but the whole Flamingo programme has been shelved due to PZL's financial pressures.

Licence production of the Piper Seneca by PZL-Mielec was mirrored by the Okecie factory. The purchase of the Franklin line of aircraft powerplants resulted in a project to build the French SOCATA Rallye (which was about to be replaced by the TB light aircraft range) and fit it with a 126hp PZL-Franklin 4A-235-B1 engine. Three French-built examples of the Rallye 110ST were imported as pattern aircraft and the first PZL-110 Koliber I was flown on 18th April 1978. The first production Koliber I of an initial batch of ten was flown on 23rd May 1979 and a further batch of 20 was built during 1983-1985. Batches 3 and 4 followed but production slowed in the late-1990s and the most recent example (No 88) was completed in 2002. Difficulty with supply of Franklin engines and the need to export aircraft with western powerplants prompted PZL to test a prototype (SP-PHA) of the PZL-110 Koliber 150 fitted with a 150hp Lycoming O-320-E2A engine. PZL and the US distributor, Cadmus Corporation, offered a kit-assembled two-seat spinnable trainer version with reduced fuel capacity known as the Model 150B. The Koliber 160A is a further development which replaced the Model 150A in production in 1998 and it is fitted with a 160hp Textron Lycoming O-320-D2A and detailed changes including extra rear cabin side windows. Another specialised glider tug version of the Koliber made its first flight in mid-1995. This GM-01 (later GM-2) Gniady (SP-PBN c/n YL-003SH) was designed by Aviata and built by YALO Repair Company of Warsaw. It uses the wings and tail of the Koliber married to a new fuselage with a single pilot seat and power is from a PZL AI-14 radial engine.

In 1992, PZL started construction of the prototype of new version of the Koliber, designated PZL-111 Senior (prototype SP-PHI c/n 00950001). This flew in November 1995 and was developed as the PZL-111 Koliber 235A with a 235hp Lycoming O-540-B4B5 engine, strengthened structure, higher gross weight, redesigned vertical tail and a luggage compartment. 180hp and 200hp versions were planned together with a Koliber IV with a retractable undercarriage, and an IFR aircraft with a 290hp engine and 4/5-passenger capacity. Plans were also announced for a six-seat single-engined turboprop based on the PZL-130 Orlik military trainer (the PZL-140 Orlik 2000) and an agricultural biplane with an Orlik-based fuselage and a PT6A turboprop engine (the PZL-240 Pelikan). Financial pressures meant that none of these aircraft progressed further. A further Koliber derivative was the PZL-112 Junior which was built in prototype form. Intended as a club trainer, this had a much-modified fuselage and swept tail and a straight low wing based on that of the Koliber but without the automatic wing

slats. The sole prototype (SP-PRG c/n 00000001) first flew in 2002, powered by a 116hp Lycoming O-235-L2C engine.

PZL also assembled a batch of SOCATA TB9s and TB10s. The first aircraft was a TB10 built in 1991 (SP-DSA c/n P-001) followed by three TB9s and another two TB10s were built (c/n P-002 to P-006). From the seventh aircraft a batch system was introduced and by March 1994 a further 18 TB9s had apparently been completed (c/n BKA001-07/P07 to BKA001-09/P009 and c/n BKA002-01/P010 to BAK002-15/P024).

Manufacture of agricultural aircraft has been largely the prerogative of PZL-Mielec. However, in 1972 PZL-Okecie embarked on its own crop sprayer – the PZL-106 Kruk – as a replacement for the Gawron and as a means of offering greater spray volume than the Wilga 35R. The first of four prototype Kruks was first flown in April 1973, powered by a 400hp Lycoming IO-720 flat-eight engine but the third and fourth prototypes were fitted with the locally-produced PZL-3S radial and this was used on most production Kruks. Later aircraft were offered with the Walter M-601 Turboprop. Production started in 1975 and Kruk production is thought to have ceased in the early 1990s although specific orders for the PZL-106 BTU-115AG, powered by a Pratt & Whitney PT6A-15AG turboprop, have been filled from stock airframes. Total output of the Kruk (including prototypes) has reached 276. The Kruk is equipped with a second rearwards-facing seat to accommodate a ground crew member for transport to the operating site. Details of all the Kruk variants are as follows:

Model	Notes
PZL-106/I	Strut-braced low-wing agricultural monoplane with enclosed cockpit, fixed tailwheel u/c, T-tail and hopper between cockpit and engine. Powered by one 400hp Lycoming IO-720 engine. Prototype SP-PAS (c/n 03001) FF 17 Apr 1973
PZL-106/III	PZL-106 with tailplane positioned on rear fuselage and powered by one 600hp PZL-3S engine
PZL-106A	PZL-106 with increased hopper capacity
PZL-106A/2M	Experimental PZL-106A with additional instructor seat covered by a light canopy in place of hopper. Prototype SP-WUL FF 20 May 1977
PZL-106AR	PZL-106A with 600hp PZL-3SR engine
PZL-106AS	PZL-106A converted for tropical operation with 1,000hp Shvetsov ASz-621R uncowled radial engine and increased useful load. Prototype SP-PBD (c/n 48053) FF 19 Aug 1981
PZL-106AT	Turbo Kruk. PZL-106A re-engined with 760shp Pratt & Whitney PT6A-34AG turboprop. Prototype SP-PTK (c/n 26009) FF 22 Jun 1981
PZL-106B	PZL-106A with redesigned longer-span wing, smaller bracing struts and trailing edge flaps. Prototype SP-PKW (c/n 61116) FF 15 May 1981
PZL-106BR	Production PZL-106B with 600hp PZL-3SR engine
PZL-106BS	PZL-106B with 1,000hp Shvetsov ASz-621R uncowled radial engine and increased useful load. Prototype SP-PBK (c/n 07810129) FF 8 Mar 1982
PZL-106BT	PZL-106B with swept wing, larger vertical tail, increased useful load and 730shp Walter M-601D turboprop. Prototype SP-PAA FF 18 Sep 1985

PZL-106BT Turbo Kruk SP-ZPE

PZL-102 Kos ZS-UDI. K Smy

PZL-112 Junior SP-PRG

PZL-106BTU -15AG   PZL-106BT fitted with one 550shp Pratt & Whitney PT6A-15AG turboprop and fitted with enlarged hopper

Other activities of PZL-Okecie have included the PZL-130 Orlik and PZL-106T Turbo Orlik military trainers which may be fitted with PT6A engines for sale to American civil buyers (Orlik 130TD). PZL also studied a family of pressurized 6/9-passenger all-weather civil aircraft with turboprop or turbocharged piston engines grouped under the project name 'Orzel', but this project has been shelved. On 20th April 1990, the factory also flew the prototype (SP-PMA) of the PZL-126 Mrowka. This is a small low-wing single-seater with a fixed tricycle undercarriage and a T-tail. It was intended as a light crop sprayer fitted with wingtip-mounted chemical pods but no production has been undertaken.

As noted under the section on PZL-Mielec, different serial number systems have been used by the PZL Mielec and Okecie factories. The first aircraft at Okecie, the Yak-12 and Gawron, set the pattern for later models with serial numbers made up of three segments. The first one or two digits were a batch number, the next digit(s) indicated the year of construction and the last group of up to four digits was the individual aircraft sequence number. A batch of Gawrons is said to have been built by Nurtanio in Indonesia and serial numbers up to c/n IN024 are known. Wilgas used the same system, but, inevitably, there are some anomalies in batches. For instance, some Russian military deliveries in Batch 9 overlapped commercial aircraft in Batch 8 and c/ns 13945 to 13947 fell in the middle of Batch 12. A number of Wilga 80s carry a prefix 'CF' to the serial number (eg, CF14800561), which indicates aircraft intended for North American export. In Indonesia, Nurtanio produced Wilgas for the military forces as the Lipnur Gelatik 32, but no information is available on the serial number system used. Details of Okecie's civil aircraft allocations are:

Model	Built	C/n example	Notes
Yak-12	137	30137	First two digits are batch number (from 19 to 30) and last three digits are individual aircraft
Yak-12M	1,059	9127206	First one or two digits are Batch number (1 to 21), next two digits are type (12), next digit is year (eg, 9 = 1959 and 0 = 1960), last digits are serial (001 to 1196). Later batches, c/n 98207 to 2101057, omitted the '12'
PZL-101	4	101701	Prototypes/test airframes c/n 101701 to 101704
PZL-101	325	52065	First one or two digits are Batch number (2 to 11), next digit is year (1 = 1961 to 9 = 1969), last digits are serial (001 to 325)
PZL-102	13	208	c/n 204 to 214 plus c/n 01 to 03 as a static test and two prototypes
PZL-104	962	11780374	First two digits are Batch number (00 to 21), second two are year (eg, 78 = 1978), last four individual serial. Batches vary, normally 40 or 50 aircraft
Wilga 2000	9	00960001	First batch (00) followed by year (1996 to 1999) and 4-digit individual serial
Koliber 1	30	24018	First digit is Batch number (1 or 2), next digit is year (9 = 1979 to 5 = 1985), last digits are serial (001 to 030)
Koliber 150	82	04990088	First two digits are Batch number (03 or 04), next two digits are year (85 = 1985 to 1999), last digits are serial (31 to 0088)
PZL-106	8	05008	Prototypes c/n 03001 to 05008
PZL-106	128	60103	First digit is Batch number (2 to 6), next digit is year (5 = 1975 to 1 = 1981), last 3 digits are serial (001 to 0128)
PZL-106B	140	11960249	First 2 digits are Batch number (07 to 11), next 2 digits are year (81 to 02), last 4 digits are serial (0129 to 0268)

PZL-Bielsko and PZL-Swidnik Poland

The PZL factory at Bielsko-Biala has built a very large number of gliders designed by the Glider Experimental Establishment (SZD – Szybowcowego Zakladu Doswiadczalnego). On 29th May 1973 they flew the prototype of the SZD-45 Ogar powered glider (registered SP-0001, c/n X-107). This was a side-by-side two-seater with a cantilever high wing, pod-and-boom fuselage, T-tail and monowheel main undercarriage with supporting outrigger wheels. Of predominantly wooden construction, it was powered by a 68hp Limbach SL-1700EC engine in a pusher installation behind the wing. 66 production SD-45A Ogars have been built (serialled c/n B-598 to -606, B-643 to -663, B-751 to -775 and B-818 to -828 within Bielsko's overall serial number system).

The Swidnik factory has been tasked with helicopter design and manufacture, but it has been involved in the development of the PZL I-23 light aircraft from the Warsaw Institute of Aviation. This four-seater, initially known as the Ibis (and later as the Manager) is a low-wing aircraft of composite construction with a retractable tricycle undercarriage and a 180hp Lycoming O-360-A1A engine. The prototype (SP-PIL c/n 002) first flew on 20th February 1999 but no production has taken place to date.

SZD-45A Ogar G-BEBG

Raj Hamsa India

This company, based at Bangalore, produces a range of hang gliders (the Mosquito, Javelin XC and Racer III), powered hang gliders (Clipper and Voyager) and 450kg three-axis ultralights (the X-Air and Hanuman). The X-Air is a kit-only aircraft but the X-Air F and Hanuman are available in some markets in factory-complete form. The X-Air is a strut-braced high-wing side-by-side two-seat aircraft with a fixed tricycle undercarriage, constructed from tube with a fabric cover. It was designed by Joel Koechlin (a French citizen resident in India) who had started Raj Hamsa in 1980 (as a subsidiary of Aurelec Trust) to build hang gliders and expanded into powered hang gliders in 1986. The X-Air was introduced in 1993 and the X-Air F (also known as the X-Air Mk 2 Falcon) is a later version with Lexan side doors, a longer fuselage allowing for a baggage compartment behind the seats and a new smaller wing with flaps. It is known as the Gumnam in the Indian market. X-Airs fitted with a range of engines include the X-Air 502T

Raj Hamsa Hanuman 44-ACB

Raj Hamsa X-Air F 56-GL

(Rotax 503DCDI), X-Air 602T (Rotax 582DCDI), X-Air 604T (HKS.700E), X-Air 702T (AMW.540L70) and X-Air 804TJ (Jabiru 2200) with others fitted with the Rotax 912 and the BMW R.100. In 2003, Raj Hamsa flew the prototype Hanuman, which is a high-wing tube-and-fabric two-seater similar to the Rans Coyote and the Sky Ranger. It has been renamed X-Air Hawk and is available in kit or complete form as

the Hawk 602T (Rotax 582) or Hawk 804TJ (Jabiru 2200). It appears that Raj Hamsa has produced nearly 1,000 aircraft to date including around 600 X-Airs. There is a simple serial number system covering all kit and complete machines. This has reached around c/n 900 but these serials are often replaced by BMAA (UK) numbers or the equivalent in other countries.

Rawdon   United States

Among the aviation pioneers working in Wichita, Kansas in the 1920s was Herb Rawdon who was Chief Engineer of Travel Air and the creator of the Travel Air 'Mystery S'. After leaving Beech, he and his brother, Gene, established Rawdon Brothers Aircraft Inc and set up operations next to the Beech factory on Central Street.

In 1938, they designed a low-wing two-seat trainer, the Rawdon R-1 (N34770 c/n 1), which was intended for the Civil Pilot Training Programme but was not selected for a production order. This was followed by a similar, but higher-powered model – the Rawdon T-1 – that was built by the company from 1951 onwards for a variety of roles including crop spraying. These aircraft carried serial numbers from T-1 to T-36 with a suffix letter to indicate the exact model (eg, T1-12M, T1-28SD). In 1979, Herb Rawdon died and the Rawdon works was closed,

with Rawdon Field becoming part of the Beech facility. The T-1 type certificate passed to Spinks Industries of Fort Worth, Texas. Production versions of the T-1 were:

Model	Built	Notes
T-1	13	Strut-braced low-wing tandem two-seat tube-and-fabric trainer powered by one 125hp Lycoming O-290-C2. Some converted to open cockpit. Prototype N41776 (c/n T1-1)
T-1CS	2	Crop-spraying version of T-1 with belly tank and spray equipment buried in wing structure
T-1M	4	Military version delivered to Colombian Air Force
T-1S	9	Crop spraying model similar to T-1CS
T-1SD	7	Single-seat crop sprayer with chemical hopper in place of rear seat. Squared-off wingtips with endplates and modified vertical tail

Rawdon T-1 N6810D

REMOS   Germany

REMOS Aircraft was formed in 1990 in Germany as a subsidiary of the REMOS electronics and high-tech manufacturing conglomerate. Its principal product is the REMOS G-3 Mirage, which was developed from the earlier Racek strut-braced high-wing two-seater that had been designed in the early 1980s by Adam Kurbiel of the SZD-Bielsko glider manufacturing company. The Racek 450-UL, which first flew in May 1998, had a fixed tricycle undercarriage, an enclosed cabin and a Rotax engine. Construction was primarily of composites but early models had fabric covering on the rear part of the wings.

SZD-Bielsko offered the Racek as a standard design to a number of organisations who would market it under their own identity. These included Aerotrade in the Czech Republic who have sold it as the Racek 99 and it has also appeared as the SF-45SA Spirit. The Polish company

REMOS G-3 Mirage D-MRIZ

Zaklady Lotnicze 3Xtrim Sp z o o offer it as the 3Xtrim 450-VLA ultra-light category model with an 80hp Rotax 912UL engine or as the 550-VLA with a 99hp Rotax 912ULS. The prototype 3Xtrim was SP-YUC (c/n E-01.1) and 50 examples of the 3Xtrim have been built (c/n E-01 to E-50). REMOS was another company which adopted the design, with airframes being supplied by SZD-Bielsko and their G-2 Gemini (later Gemini Ultra) was marketed as a factory-complete aircraft, pow-ered, initially, by various engines including the Rotax 582, Guzzi-4 and Wankel AE.50R although later models used the 80hp Rotax 912.

The REMOS G-3 Mirage, which replaced the Gemini and first flew on 20th September 1997, is a more elegant aircraft with a redesigned streamlined fuselage and modified fully composite wings that fold for transport and storage. In standard form it uses the Rotax 912 UL engine but a higher-powered version, the Mirage RS with a 100hp Rotax 912ULS has also been built. By mid-2004 more than 154 Mirages had been delivered. REMOS have also designed the REMOS G-4 Veloc-ity, which is a low-wing aircraft with a fuselage similar to that of the Gemini and featuring a large blister canopy to enclose the two-seat cabin. To date, this aircraft has not flown.

3Xtrim 78-SM

Republic   United States

For the company that built the wartime Thunderbolt, a civil aircraft involved a totally new approach to design, production technique and costing. Nevertheless, as the war was ending Republic Aviation Cor-poration produced the prototype of the C-1 Thunderbolt Amphibian – a four-seat high-wing amphibian with a 175hp pusher Franklin 6ALG-365 engine mounted on the wing centre section, a retractable tailwheel undercarriage and a rear fuselage which was sharply cut away to provide propeller clearance. The first aircraft (NX41816 c/n 106-1) first flew in November 1944.

It was soon clear that the C-1 was underpowered and the second prototype (the RC-2 NX87451, c/n 1) had a 215hp Franklin 6A8-215-B7F engine, a strut-braced wing, modified floats, deeper fin and rud-der and main wheels which swung backwards and upwards rather than fully retracting into the fuselage as had been the case with the C-1. In total, 10 RC-2s were built as development machines for the production version – the RC-3 Seabee. Externally, the RC-3 was very similar to its predecessors although the engine nacelle was extensively modified. However, Republic had almost completely redesigned the Seabee to simplify the structure and reduce weight and the cost of manufacture. The first RC-3 Seabee was NX87461 (c/n 11) and, after the type certifi-cate (A-769) had been issued on 15th October 1946, deliveries started at a price of $ 3,995.

With Seabee production in full swing, Republic looked at develop-ment of the airframe in various ways. The five-seat 'Twinbee' was an enlarged RC-3 with two Franklin 6A8 engines mounted in a single nacelle driving one propeller. The 'Landbee' was similar to the RC-3

Republic RC-3 Seabee N565CB

United Consultants Twin Bee N87589

by a 215hp Lycoming O-425-5 engine but the expected order for 12 aircraft was not forthcoming.

Republic was losing money on every Seabee it built and in 1947, faced with a falling civil market and pressure on production space due to the start of Thunderjet production, the Seabee production line was closed with effect from the 1050th production RC-3 (CF-GRL, c/n 1060). The type certificate was subsequently sold to STOL Amphibian Corporation of Key Biscayne, Florida. Republic Aircraft Manufacturing of Arlington, Washington had plans to build a modernised Seabee with a new single-step hull, larger wings, retractable floats, six seats and a 300 or 350 horsepower engine but this project has been dormant for the past two years.

The underpowered Seabee has always been a prime candidate for re-fitting with larger engines. The most satisfactory conversion has been produced by United Consultants Corp of Norwood, Massachussetts (now STOL Aircraft Corporation). The first Twin Bee (N87589 c/n UC-1R158) was converted in 1966 with two 180hp Lycoming IO-360-B1D engines mounted as tractor units on the upper wing surfaces. This permitted a fifth seat to be fitted beneath the old engine installation and, because of the position of the new propellers, the rear cabin windows on each side were reduced in area and small portholes were fitted at the back of the cabin. 24 conversions have been completed (UC-1R to UC-3R and UC-004 to UC-024).

without the seaplane hull – and the more radical 'Beebee' was a smaller two-seat trainer with a 100hp engine. In practice, none of these got beyond the drawing board stage. Republic also presented the RC-3, in 1947, for evaluation by the US Army. The YOA-15 was to be powered

Rhein Flugzeugbau   Germany

In 1955, Rhein-West-Flug Fischer (RWF) produced a prototype of the Fibo 2a light aircraft in order to test the aerodynamic principles propounded by the company's founder, Herr Fischer. This was succeeded by the prototype of the RW-3A Multoplan (D-EJAS c/n 1) which was a tandem two-seat light aircraft of mixed construction with a high aspect ratio wing, retractable tricycle undercarriage and a T-tail. A 65 horsepower Porsche 678/0 engine was buried in the centre fuselage and drove a pusher propeller mounted in a slot between the fin and rudder. The two occupants were housed beneath a long blister canopy.

The prototype Multoplan was followed by a second aircraft, the RW3A-V2 (D-EKUM c/n 2), and RWF then granted a production licence to Rhein Flugzeugbau GmbH (RFB) who built an initial batch of Mul-

toplans at their factory at Krefeld-Uerdingen. The first production machine (D-ELYT c/n 001) was flown on 8th February 1958 and this and all subsequent aircraft were designated RW3.P75 to identify the 75hp Porsche 678/4 engine which was used. Rhein built a total of 22 Multoplans (c/n 001 to 022) and abandoned a further three when production was discontinued in 1961. However, one further machine (D-EFTU c/n AB601) was built by an amateur. They also built two examples of a higher-powered version, the RW3C-90 Passat (c/ns 091 and 092) and on these and all other RW3s they offered optional wingtip extension panels which enabled the Multoplan to be flown as a power-assisted sailplane.

RFB next turned its attention to the radical RF-1 all-metal six-seat touring and business aircraft. It had a high wing with STOL devices and was equipped with a pair of 250hp Lycoming O-540-A1A piston

Rhein RW-3 Multoplan D-EIFF. M J Hooks

engines. These were mounted in the wing roots and drove a large fan propeller mounted in an integral duct set in the rear fuselage behind the cabin. The tail was carried on a slender boom and the tricycle undercarriage featured an unusual retraction system. The prototype, D-IGIR (c/n V-1), first flew on 15th August 1960 but the RF-1 was too complex to be a practical production model.

In 1968, RFB became part of the VFW-Fokker Group and, in the following year, it bought an interest in Sportavia-Putzer. Based on experience with the RF-1, RFB was convinced that ducted fans were beneficial and, under its new parent, it was able to pursue its research with the RFB Sirius I powered sailplane. This used the wings and tail of the VFW-Fokker FK.3 glider and had two Fichtel & Sachs engines buried behind the single-seat cockpit driving propellers fitted within an integral louvred circular fuselage duct. D-KIFB, the prototype, made its maiden flight on 5th July 1971 and was followed, on 18th January 1972, by the Sirius II (D-KAFB) which used parts from a Caproni Calif glider and was powered by a pair of Wankel rotary engines.

These experiments allowed RFB to build the side-by-side two-seat Fanliner (D-EJFL), which flew on 8th October 1973 and incorporated Grumman AA-2 wings and an integral ducted fan with power being provided by a Wankel KM.871 engine as used in the NSU RO-80 motor car. On 4th September 1976 RFB flew a much-improved version and this second Fanliner (D-EBFL), with a futuristic cockpit 'pod' seating two people in reclining seats. Powered by a 150hp KM.871 engine, it was intended as a type for joint production between RFB and Grumman-American.

Despite several marketing initiatives in North America, the Fanliner failed to find a sponsor, but the company built a tandem two-seat

Rhein Fantrainer D-EATP

model – the AWI-2 Fantrainer (D-EATJ). This was, again, powered by two Audi-NSU rotary engines. The second prototype (D-EATI), designated ATI-2, which was flown on 31st May 1978, was powered by an Allison 250-C20B turboshaft and marketed as the Fantrainer 400. With the higher-powered Allison 250-C30 engine it became the Fantrainer 600 and RFB subsequently delivered 47 examples to the Royal Thai Air Force. The Fantrainer is also in service with Lufthansa for pilot training and formed the basis for the Fan Ranger, which was unsuccessfully proposed by Deutsche Aerospace (MBB) and Rockwell International as a contender in the USAF JPATS competition. The Fan Ranger 2000 prototype (D-FANA) first flew at Manching on 15th January 1993 and is powered by a Pratt & Whitney JT15D turbofan and fitted with a Collins EFIS.

Robin   France

The famous line of Robin light aircraft was the creation of Pierre Robin – an amateur builder who started originally by constructing a Jodel D.11 and progressed to production of a range of Jodel-inspired low-wing monoplanes. In 1956, he built the Jodel-Robin (F-PIER) which used the wing designed by Jean Delemontez for the D.10 project married to a three-seat fuselage which was, essentially, a stretched version of the D.11 structure. The prototype Robin first flew in 1957 and was followed by a definitive production prototype (F-WIFR) which was designated DR.100 and introduced a new engine cowling, smoother moulded cockpit canopy and numerous bits of general streamlining. In that year, Pierre Robin established the Centre Est Aéronautique at Dijon-Darois and the DR.100 went into production with the higher-powered DR.105 joining it soon afterwards.

Pierre Robin brought Jean Delemontez into his team at Dijon and soon expanded the basic Jodel design into a new range that was much more sophisticated than the original designers had foreseen. Robin allowed a production licence for the DR.100 to be taken up by SAN at Bernay, and the two organisations produced a number of variants in parallel. Personally, Pierre Robin gained fame through his dominance of the 1961 Tour of Sicily in which he flew an improved version of the DR.100. As a result, this DR.1050/DR.1051 Sicile replaced the DR.100 and was later fitted with a swept tail to become the Sicile Record (and the Excellence as built by SAN). These were followed by three experimental DR.200s that were DR.1050Ms with a lengthened fuselage and strengthened wing – and this led to the production DR.250 Capitaine, which flew in 1965 and was powered by a 160hp Lycoming engine. The exceptionally good finish that Robin had now achieved gave these aircraft quite remarkable performance and the company built up a respectable rate of production.

Still dedicated to wood and fabric construction, Robin came out with a two-seat variant of the DR.250, designated DR.220 and, with its later DR.221 version, this type sold well to aero clubs in France and abroad. The next major development, however, was the DR.253 Regent, which set the pattern for the line of tricycle-undercarriage Jodel designs that formed Robin's principal product range from the late 1960s onwards. The four-seat DR.253 flew in prototype form in March 1967 and featured a generally enlarged fuselage that provided

greater passenger comfort and was powered by a 180hp Lycoming engine. To a similar theme, although with a fuselage more akin to that of the DR.250, Centre Est followed the Regent with the '300 Series' 108hp Petit Prince, the 140hp Major and the 160hp Chevalier. The prototypes of all three flew during the early part of 1968 and, with the Regent, went into production later that year.

In 1970, Centre Est changed its name to Société des Avions Pierre Robin. This company became the manufacturing section of the business and separate sales and marketing companies were established in France, Germany and the United Kingdom. Through these companies and a wide-ranging dealer network Robin achieved a high level of export sales and good penetration in France in competition with Reims Aviation and SOCATA.

The designation system for the Jodel designs was changed to DR.300- followed by the engine horsepower rating (eg, DR.300-108). To some degree, the expansion was held up in April 1972 when a major fire destroyed the Darois production line, but this problem was soon resolved and in the same month they introduced the DR.400. Essentially, this new model was similar to the DR.300 but a forward-sliding cockpit canopy/windshield replaced the conventional doors that had been used before. Once again, numerous engine combina-

Centre Est DR.250 Capitaine HB-EEZ

Robin DR.400-140B Dauphin 4 F-GGQZ. Avions Robin

tions were offered with the basic DR.400 airframe giving rise to a rather confusing series of names and designations. The most recent ('new generation') DR.400 models incorporated increased cabin window area and the top end of the line now features the DR.500 President with a 200hp Lycoming IO-360 powerplant. Despite the attractions of all-metal aircraft, the wooden DR.400 has continued in production and is now the primary product following sale of the R.2160 to New Zealand. The overall development of these wood-and-fabric designs is illustrated in the family tree.

The Robin Jodels were wooden aircraft with a remarkably smooth finish achieved through superior craftsmanship but, in 1969, Pierre Robin concluded that the company should move into all-metal airframes and he used a young designer, Chris Heintz, to develop these designs. The prototype HR.100 was a low-wing monoplane closely resembling the Piper Cherokee with a fixed spatted tricycle undercarriage and an enclosed four-seat cabin. In general design it was clearly a Robin, but it abandoned the cranked Jodel wing in favour of a conventional constant-chord wing. The prototype HR.100 was powered by a 180hp Lycoming O-360 engine but the production HR.100 Royal (also known as the Safari) used a 210hp Continental powerplant and entered production in 1971. As with the DR.400, the HR.100 had a forward-sliding canopy.

The HR.100-210 was developed into the HR.100-180 which first flew in February 1976 and this, in turn, led to the first of the R.1000 range – the R.1180 Aiglon. This had detailed improvements including enlarged rear windows and it replaced the Royal in production. The HR.100 also formed the basis for other models including the retractable undercarriage HR.100-235 and the HR.100-285 – the latter being one of the few production aircraft to use the new Continental Tiara engine. Problems with this engine resulted in the model being discontinued and most of this version of the HR.100 were delivered to the French SFACT organisation. Robin also built one prototype of the HR.100-320 '4+2' which could accommodate six people, but this did not go into production.

In addition to building the four-seat HR.100, Robin had also launched the all-metal HR.200 trainer, which flew as a prototype in July 1971. This was designed by Chris Heintz, based on his Zenith home-

built, and had the appearance of a scaled-down HR.100 with a bubble canopy over the side-by-side two-seat cockpit. It was sold in a Club version powered by either a 108hp or, later, a 120hp Lycoming. An aerobatic 'Acrobin' model with a 125hp or 160hp engine was also announced but few were built. The HR.200 was subsequently redesigned with a larger tail to become the R.2100 and R.2160. This R.2000 series received its French certification on 13th September 1977 and in 1981 the company set up a jointly owned subsidiary in Canada, Avions Pierre Robin Inc, which undertook production of this particular range, building the R.2160 between 1983 and its closure in 1985.

By 1978, the R.1000 and R.2000 series were well established and Robin moved on to the new R.3000 models, which were all-metal aircraft of quite advanced concept and wholly new design. Using the same basic airframe the range was planned to cover applications from the simple two-seat trainer to the deluxe four-seat tourer with a retractable undercarriage. The first prototype was flown in 1980 and was fitted with a constant-chord wing, but the second aircraft (F-WZJZ) had tapered outer wing panels and upturned wingtips.

In early 1981, Robin was experiencing reduced orders and the R.2000 line was closed down in the early part of the year. In August the financial pressure forced the company to call in a receiver, under whose supervision production continued at a reduced level. Close links were established with SOCATA under a marketing agreement that created 'spheres of influence' for the products of each company and development of the R.3000 was continued under subsidy from the French Government.

Robin was able to advance with its new ATL project. This 'Avion Très Léger' was a very light weight two-seat machine with wooden wings and a composite fuselage that went into production at Dijon and sold in reasonable numbers to French aero clubs, but production finished following certification problems limiting export sales. Eventually, in 1988, the Compagnie Francaise Chaufour Investissements (CFCI) acquired a majority stake in Robin through its subsidiary, Aéronautique Services, which also took major participation in Reims Aviation and the sailplane manufacturer, Centrair. Under CFCI the company expanded and the R.2160 and HR200/120B returned to production at Dijon in 1993. In 1996, a new group structure was created. Avions

The Robin Family Tree of Jodel Wooden Airframe Designs

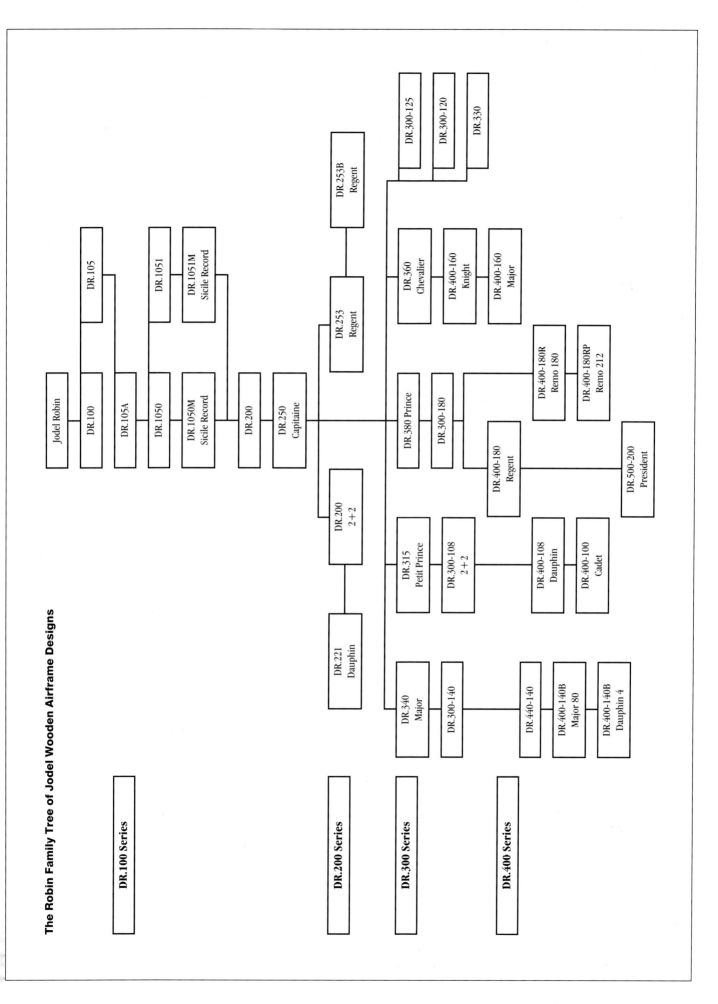

Robin SA was tasked as design bureau and with sales and after-sales service, Constructions Aéronautiques de Bourgogne (CAB) took over all manufacturing, Robin Gestion assumed administration responsibility and Bourgogne Ultra-Léger Aéronautique (Bul Aero) was formed to develop ultralight aircraft.

A further development was the acquisition of the assets of Avions Mudry by Robin and the formation of CAP Aviation, which resulted in the transfer of CAP-10 and CAP-232 production to Dijon. Robin and CAP Aviation merged in November 2001 to form Apex Aircraft as a holding company for four subsidiaries: CAB, Bul Aero, Apex Maintenance and Apex Parts. In September 2002 a sharp drop in sales resulted in Apex going into receivership but it emerged from this on 1st July 2003 and was released from court supervision in August 2003. At this time, the group structure was merged and responsibility for the CAP-222 and CAP-232 aerobatic aircraft was hived off to a new subsidiary run by Dominique Roland at Bernay with Apex as a minority shareholder. In 2004, all rights to the Robin R.2160 were sold to Alpha Aviation of Hamilton, New Zealand, leaving Apex with manufacture of the DR.400/500 series and the CAP-10.

Serial numbers for Robin aircraft have generally been simple sequential numbers with a new series for each main model. The initial series of DR.100 aircraft was given serial numbers from the main Jodel allocation in the range c/n 1 to 634 and those allocated to CEA are shown below. The largest allocation of serial numbers applies to the DR.300 and DR.400 series and, within these blocks, the many individual variants are scattered according to the flow of orders. A few DR.300/400 aircraft are believed to have not been built, or the c/ns may have been allocated to spare fuselages. A number of prototypes have also been constructed with individual serial numbers. The individual serial batches are:

Robin HR.100/210 Royal G-BBIO

Model	Serial Block	Model	Serial Block
DR.100 srs	c/n 1 to 50	HR.200, R2100 srs	c/n 01 to 211
DR.100 srs	c/n 201 to 250	HR.200, R2100 srs	c/n 250 to 377*
DR.100 srs	c/n 301 to 350	HR.100/200	c/n 01 to 09
DR.100 srs	c/n 401 to 450	HR.100/210	c/n 111 to 130
DR.100 srs	c/n 501 to 634	HR.100/210F	c/n 138, 142 to 213
DR.220/221	c/n 1 to 145	HR.100-285, -250	c/n 500 to 560
DR.250	c/n 1 to 100	R.1180	c/n 215 to 283
DR.253	c/n 101 to 200	R.3000	c/n 100 to 172
DR.300 & DR.400	c/n 301 to 673	ATL	c/n 01 to 135
DR.300 & DR.400	c/n 681 to 2568+		
DR.500	c/n 0001 to 0041+		* last Robin-built R2100

Details of all Robin models are as follows:

Model	Notes
D.11 Robin	Three-seat development of Jodel D.112 powered by one Continental C90 engine. Prototype F-PIER (c/n 01) FF 1957
DR.100	3/4-seat certificated development of Robin with streamlined canopy and engine cowling. Prototype F-WIFR FF 14 Jul 1958
DR.100A Ambassadeur	Production version of DR.100 with air brakes, hydraulic braking and minor detail changes
DR.105A Ambassadeur	DR.100A with 100hp Continental O-200-A. 1,654lb TOGW
DR.1050 Ambassadeur	DR.105A with improved fuel system and electrics. 1,654lb TOGW. Sicile has new u/c spats and modified engine cowling and 1,698lb TOGW

Robin R200/120B F-GOVJ

DR.1051 Ambassadeur	DR.1050 with 105hp Potez 4E-20 engine. Also Sicile model
DR.1050M Sicile Record	DR.1050 with all-flying tailplane, swept fin and separate rudder, new windshield and air intake design. 1,720 lb TOGW. Prototype F-WMGZ FF 16 May 1964. DR.1050MT is amateur-converted tricycle-gear version
DR.1050M1 Sicile Record	DR.1050M with minor changes to fin/rudder. FF May 1964
DR.1051M Sicile Record	DR.1050M with Potez 4E-20 engine
DR.1051M1 Sicile Record	DR.1050M1 with Potez 4E-20 engine
DR.1052M	DR1050M converted with 115hp Lycoming O-235 engine
DR.1053M	DR1050M converted with 120hp Lycoming engine
DR.200	DR.1050M development with 22-inch longer fuselage, full four-seat cabin and Potez 105E engine. 3 aircraft only. Prototype F-WLKV (c/n 01) FF 7 Nov 1964
DR.220 2 + 2	DR.250 with fully glazed cabin, two seats plus rear 'kiddie seat', taller tail and 108hp Continental O-200-A engine. 1,720 lb TOGW Prototype F-WNGP (c/n 01) FF 5 Feb 1966
DR.221 Dauphin	DR.220 with full four seats, 115hp Lycoming O-235-C2A engine and all-flying tailplane. 1,830 lb TOGW. Prototype F-WOFF (c/n 49) FF 16 Feb 1967
DR.250 Capitaine	DR.200 with extended wing inboard leading edges, all-flying tailplane and 160hp Lycoming O-320-E engine. 2,116 lb TOGW. Prototype F-WLKZ (c/n 01) FF 2 Apr 1965
DR.250-180	DR.250 with 180hp Lyc O-360-A. One aircraft, F-BMZT
DR.253 Regent	DR.250 with enlarged fuselage, tricycle u/c and 180hp Lyc O-360-D2A engine. 2,440 lb TOGW. Prototype F-WOFG (c/n 01) FF 30 Mar 1967
DR.253B Regent	DR.253 with improved mainspar and wing design
DR.315 Petit Prince	Development of DR.221 with tricycle u/c and 115hp Lyc O-235-C2A engine. Prototype F-WOFT FF 21 Mar 1968
DR.330 Acrobat	Experimental aerobatic DR.315 with 130hp Cont O-240A engine. 2,072 lb TOGW Prototype F-WPXX FF 25 Mar 1970
DR.340 Major	DR.250 with clear view canopy, tricycle u/c and 140hp Lyc O-320-E2A engine. Prototype F-WOFP FF 27 Feb 1968
DR.360 Chevalier	DR.340 with solid cabin roof and 160hp Lyc O-320-D2A engine. Prototype F-WOFS FF 27 Mar 1968

Robin R.1180T Aiglon G-VECD

DR.380 Prince	Experimental DR.360 with 180hp Lyc. O-360-A3A engine. F-WPXC (c/n 1) FF 10 Oct 1969
DR.300-108 2 + 2	Low cost successor to DR.315 with improved u/c and 2/4-passenger capacity
DR.300-120	Four-seat DR.300 with 120hp Lycoming O-235-L2A engine
DR.300-140	DR.300 with 140hp Lycoming O-320-E2A engine
DR.300-180	DR.300 with 180hp Lycoming O-360-A3A engine Glider tug version DR.300-180R (Prototype F-WPXY) FF 26 Jun 1970
DR.400-100 Cadet	Two-seat version of DR.400-108. 1,764 lb TOGW. and 112hp Lyc O-235 engine. *Note: Production is all DR400 models
DR.400-108 Dauphin 80	DR.300-108 with forward-sliding canopy, 1,980 lb TOGW. '2 + 2' is club trainer. FF 24 Nov 1972
DR.400-120 Petit Prince	DR.300-120 with forward sliding canopy. 118hp Lycoming O-235 engine
DR.400-120 Dauphin 2 + 2	Petit Prince with extra cabin windows and 1,984 lb TOGW
DR.400-125	DR.400-120 with 125hp Lycoming O-235-F. 1,990 lb TOGW. Prototype F-WSQT FF 15 May 1972

Robin ATL F-GGHG. Avions Robin

Robin R.3000-140 F-GDYI. Avions Robin

DR.400-135TDI	DR.400-120 with Thielert Centurion 1.7 diesel engine. Named Robin 135CDI. Prototype D-ECDI (c/n 2531)
DR.400-140 Major/Earl	DR.300-140 with forward sliding canopy. 2,170 lb TOGW. FF 16 Nov 1972
DR.400-140B Major 80	DR.400-140 with 160hp Lycoming O-320-D2A, 2,315 lb TOGW. Later named Dauphin 4
DR.400-160 Chevalier	Initial designation for DR.400-140B. 2,330 lb TOGW. Also known as the Knight. FF 29 Jun 1972
DR.400-160 Major	Revised Major 80 with extra cabin windows
DR.400-180 Regent	DR.300-180 with forward sliding canopy, 2,440 lb TOGW. Prototype F-WSQO FF 27 Mar 1972. Later with extra cabin windows
DR.400-180 Regent III	DR.400 'Nouvelle Generation' with longer and higher fuselage, extra rear cabin glazing etc. Prototype F-WGXT FF 19 Apr 1989
DR.400-180R Remorqueur	DR.400-180 glider tug with clear canopy and 2,205 lb TOGW. Later named Remo 180. -180RD is German version. FF 6 Nov 1972
DR.400-180RP Remo 212	DR.400-180R fitted with 212hp Porsche PFM.3200 engine and 3-blade prop. Prototype F-WEIQ
DR.400-200R Remo 200	DR.400 glider tug with 200hp Lyc IO-360-A1-B6 engine and without extra rear side windows. Prototype F-WLKN
DR.400-V6	Experimental DR.400 with 212hp Porsche PFM3200 engine. Prototype F-WGXT FF 7 Jun 1995
DR.400-200i President	Deluxe DR.400 with 200hp Lycoming IO-360-A1B6 engine. Prototype F-WZZY (c/n 2354) FF 29 May 1997. Became DR.400/500 and then DR.500-200i
DR.500-200i President	DR.400-200i redesignated and modified with reshaped rear cabin windows etc. 2,536 lb TOGW
DR.500-180 Grand Regent	DR.500 with 180hp Lycoming O-360-A1P engine and fixed-pitch prop. 2,235 lb TOGW. Prototype F-WZZY (c/n 027)
HR.1	Experimental all-metal low-wing four-seater with fixed tricycle u/c and constant-chord (non-cranked) wing with one 180hp Lycoming O-360 engine. Prototype F-WPXO FF 3 Apr 1969
HR.100/200A	HR.1 in production form with solid cabin roof, 200hp Lyc IO-360-A1D6 engine. Prototype F-WVKU FF 3 Feb 1976
HR.100-200B Royal	HR.100/200A with modified wing profile. 2,646 lb TOGW
HR.100-210F Safari	HR.100 with 210hp Continental IO-360-D. 2,755 lb TOGW. Special German version designated HR.100-210D. Also named Royal
HR.100-285TR	Experimental HR.100 with enlarged tail, retractable u/c and 285hp Continental Tiara 6-285-B3B engine. One aircraft. Prototype F-WSQV FF 18 Nov 1972
HR.100-235	HR.100-285TR with 235hp Lycoming O-540-B4B5 engine. Prototype F-WVKA (c/n 500) FF 7 Mar 1974
HR.100-250 President	HR.100-235 with 250hp Lyc IO-540-C4B5 engine, 3,040 lb TOGW. Prototype F-WVKA (c/n 500) FF Oct 1974
HR.100-320 '4+2'	Stretched six-seat HR.100 with 320hp Continental Tiara 6-320 engine. Prototype F-WSQV
R.1180 Aiglon	Modified HR.100 with lighter airframe, new wing aerofoil, new fin/rudder and 180hp Lycoming O-360-A3AD engine. Prototype F-WVKU (c/n 01) FF 25 Mar 1977
R.1180T Aiglon	Production R.1180 with longer cabin side windows and increased fuel. 2,540 lb TOGW
R.1180TD Aiglon II	R.1180T with new instrument panel, new cabin furnishings, external baggage locker door and engine silencer
HR.200/100	All-metal low-wing side-by-side two-seat trainer derived from Heintz Zenith with fixed tricycle u/c and one 100hp Lycoming O-235C. Prototype F-WSQP FF 29 Jul 1971
HR.200/100 Club/Ecole	HR.200 with 108hp Lyc. O-235-H2C engine. Prototype F-WSQR (c/n 01) FF 6 Apr 1973
HR.200/100S	Production low-cost HR.200 with minimum equipment
HR.200/120B	HR.200 with 118hp Lycoming O-235-L2A. Prototype F-WVQB (c/n 03)
R.200/120B	New production version of HR.200 introduced in 1993 with revised instrument panel, new prop spinner etc
HR.200/125 Acrobin	HR.200 stressed for aerobatics with 125hp Lycoming O-235-G1 engine
HR.200/160 Acrobin	Experimental HR.200 with 160hp Lycoming O-320-D engine. F-WSQS (c/n 02) FF 19 May 1973
R.2100 Super Club	Redesignated HR.200 with full aerobatic stressing, enlarged tail etc. Powered by one 108hp Lycoming O-235-H2C
R.2100A	Deluxe tourer version of R.2100
R.2112 Alpha	R.2100 with 112hp Lycoming O-235-L2 engine

R.2120U Alpha 120T	R.200 trainer with 118hp Lycoming O-235-L2A engine and 1,764 lb TOGW
Alpha 120T	Alpha Aviation (NZ-built) model with 118hp Lyc O-235-L2A
Alpha 160A	Alpha Aviation (NZ-built) model with 160hp Lyc O-320
Alpha 160Ai	Alpha Aviation (NZ-built) model with 160hp Lyc AEIO-320
R.2160 Alpha Sport	R.2100 with 160hp Lyc. O-320-D2A. Prototype F-WZAC (c/n 01)
R.2160 Srs II	New production R.2160 intro 1994 with modified ailerons and carburettor. Production inc 22 built in Canada
R.2160i	Revised designation indicating injected engine
R.2160 Acrobin	R.2160 with full aerobatic equipment
R.2160D	R.2160 with silencer etc for German sale
R.2160U	Aerobatic trainer version of R.2160
R.3000/100	All-metal low-wing two-seat monoplane with T-tail, fixed tricycle u/c and 143hp Lycoming O-235. Prototype F-WZJY (c/n 01) FF 8 Dec 1980
R.3000/120	R.3000 with new wing incorporating tapered outer panels and upturned wingtips, 2+2 seating, faired u/c and 118hp Lyc O-235 -N2A engine. 1,984 lb TOGW. Formerly R.3120
R.3000/140	Full four-seat R.3000 with 140hp Lycoming O-320-D2A engine. 2,315 lb TOGW. Formerly designated R.3140. Prototype F-WZJY
R.3000/160	R.3000 with 160hp Lycoming O-360 engine and 2,535 lb TOGW. Redesignated R.300/160
R.300/160S	R.3000 to Swiss certification requirements
R.3000-V6	R.3000 with enlarged fin and 185hp Renault PRV France-Aeromotors V6 engine with ventral radiator. Prototype F-WEIA
R.3000-200R	Proposed version of R.3000 with 200hp engine and retractable undercarriage
R.3000/235 4+2	R.3000 with lengthened fuselage and cabin with two extra rear seats. Powered by one 235hp Lycoming. Prototype F-WEIK
ATL Club	Mid-wing side-by-side two-seat trainer with wood wings and GRP fuselage, V-tail, fixed tricycle u/c and one JPX-4T-60A engine. Prototype F-WFNA (c/n 001) FF 17 Jun 1983
ATL Voyage	ATL with JPX-4T-75B engine. Swiss-certificated ATL-S
ATL-L	ATL with 70hp Limbach L2000-D2A engine. Prototype F-GGHQ
X-4	Experimental all-composite low-wing four-seat trainer/tourer with fixed tricycle u/c. powered by one 116hp Lycoming O-235. Prototype F-WKQX FF 25 Feb 1991

Total Robin production, excluding prototypes, to mid-2004 can be summarised as follows

Model	Built	Model	Built	Model	Built
DR.100A	9	DR.300-180R	31	HR.100 4+2	1
DR.1050	114	DR.400-100	14	HR.200-100	69
DR.1051	161	DR.400-108	128	HR.200-100S	10
DR.1050M	25	DR.400-125	423	HR.200-120	96
DR.1051M	24	DR.400-125/i	2	HR.200-125	1
DR200	2	DR.400-135TDI	1	HR.200-160	7
DR.220	83	DR.400-140	63	R.2100/A	24
DR.221	62	DR.400-140B	178	R.2112	15
DR.250	100	DR.400-160	177	R.2120	2
DR.253	100	DR.400-180	429	R.2120U	15
DR.315	104	DR.400-180R	362	R.2160	100
DR.340	59	DR.400-180RP	22	R.1180T	26
DR.360	30	DR.400-200R	13	R.1180TD	42
DR.380	21	DR.500-200i	40	R.3000-120	20
DR.300-108	87	HR.100-200B	31	R.3000-140	16
DR.300-120	22	HR.100-210	55	R.3000-160	37
DR.300-125	14	HR.100-210D	16	ATL	135
DR.300-140	4	HR.100-250TR	41		
DR.300-180	19	HR.100-285	21	Total	3,702

Rockwell International   United States

The Rockwell Sabreliner mid-sized business jet started life in the early 1950s when North American Aviation Inc produced the design of a light twin-jet aircraft, mainly aimed at the UTX high-speed transport and training requirement issued by the US Air Force. This aircraft, which became the Sabreliner, met both the needs of the USAF and US Navy and the requirements of the expanding business jet market. The prototype first flew in 1958 and deliveries of the military T-39A commenced in 1960. A total of 159 military examples were delivered including the T-39A (North American model numbers NA265 and NA276), T-39B (NA270) and T-39D (NA277).

The initial civil Sabreliner was the Model 40, which was certificated on 17th April 1963 and was similar to the T-39A but with reduced power. It retained the unusual triangular cabin windows of the T-39 but had a suitably high quality interior and improved avionics. On 22nd September 1967, North American Aviation Inc merged with Rockwell-Standard Corporation and the Sabreliner became part of the larger Rockwell product line. The Model 40 was followed by the stretched Model 60 (certificated in April 1967) and later, in June 1970, by the Model 75 with a deeper fuselage that allowed for a stand-up cabin and greater passenger comfort. The Model 75 also featured larger square windows. Production continued at El Segundo, California under the Aerospace Systems Group of North American Rockwell Corporation and this was later refined down into The Sabreliner Division of Rockwell.

In 1978, Raisbeck Engineering flight-tested their 'Mark Five System' for the Sabreliner series. This consisted of a new 6ft-longer supercritical wing, larger horizontal tail and additional fuel tankage and it was tested on Sabreliner 60, N605RG (c/n 306-116). Subsequently, conversions were made to 13 Sabreliner 60s (60A) and 12 Sabreliner 75As (80A). A similar conversion (from 40A to 40B) was proposed but it does not appear that any conversions were carried out. The Raisbeck wing was fitted to the new production Sabre 65, which was certificated on 30th November 1979 and offered much reduced noise levels as a result of its Garrett-AiResearch TFE731 turbofan engines. By mid-1981, only the Sabreliner 65 was in production and this had been suspended by 1st January 1982 due to the termination of the lease on the El Segundo plant as at that date. Rights to the aircraft were sold to Sabreliner Corporation (a company formed by New York investment bankers, Wolsey & Co) on 1st July 1983.

A three-engined enlarged Sabreliner with JT15D engines was also considered – but this proposal did not advance any further. Sabreliner Corporation, which took over the rights to the aircraft in 1983, proposed a new Sabreliner variant – the Model 85, powered by twin Garrett TFE731-5 turbofans and having a supercritical wing with winglets and a 5-ft fuselage stretch, but this was not progressed.

Sabreliners have always been certificated with a type number consisting of NA265 – followed by a subsidiary designation (eg, NA265-40

Rockwell Sabre 65 N45NP

or NA265-60). However, North American had a system of batch designations for its aircraft and these have been used as part of the serial number system. The designation NA265 was only the production batch number for the initial series of T-39As. Both the batch number and the certificated designation are given in the following table of types:

Batch	Model	Name	Notes
NA246	NA265	Sabreliner	Prototype Sabreliner N4060K (c/n 246-1) powered by two General Electric J85-GE-X turbojets. FF 16 Sep 1958
NA265 NA276	NA265	T-39A-1-NA	NA246 with lengthened nose and equipment. Two 3,000 lbst J60-P-3 turbojets. Standard US Air Force crew trainer and communications aircraft. First aircraft 59-2868 (c/n 265-1). Some conv. To T-39F electronic warfare trainers
NA270	NA265-20	T-39B	Radar trainer version of T-39A for F-105 training
NA277	NA265-30	T-39D	US Navy version (T3J-1) of T-39A
NA282	NA265-40	Sabreliner 40	Initial civil Sabreliner with 11-place maximum seating and two 3,300 lbst JT12A-6 turbojets. Two cabin windows each side. 20,172 lb TOGW. Prototype N7820C (c/n 282-1). US Navy CT-39E
NA285	NA265-40A	Sabreliner 40A	Upgraded Sabreliner 40 with Sabre 75 wing, 3 cabin windows each side, improved systems and two GE CF700 turbofans
NA285	NA265-40	Sabreliner 40B	Sabreliner 40A with Raisbeck Mark Five system
NA287	NA265-50	Sabreliner 50	Sabreliner 60 with Model 40 engines. Prototype N287NA (c/n 287-1)
NA306	NA265-60	Sabreliner 60	12-place stretched Model 40 with JT12A-8 engines, five cabin windows each side, 20,372 lb TOGW. Prototype N306NA (c/n 306-1). US Navy CT-39G
NA306	NA265-60	Sabreliner 60A	Sabreliner 60 with Raisbeck Mark Five system
NA370	NA265-70	Sabreliner 75	Model 60 with raised cabin roof giving 8 inches of additional headroom. 21,000 lb TOGW. Prototype N7572N (c/n 370-1)
NA372		CT-39G	US Navy version of Sabreliner 60
NA380	NA265-80	Sabreliner 75A	Sabre 75 with 4,500 lbst GE CF700-2D-2 turbofans and strengthened tail and engine mountings. 23,200 lb TOGW. Prototype N7572N (c/n 370-1) FF 18 Oct 1972
NA465	NA265-65	Sabreliner 65	Model 60 development with Raisbeck supercritical wing and 3,700 lbst Garrett TFE-731-3R-1D turbofans. Systems and internal fittings changes. Prototype N65R (c/n 306-114)
-	-	Sabreliner 40R	Factory modified Model 40 with Model 60 interior
-	-	Sabreliner 60/TF	Factory modified Model 60 with Garrett TFE731 turbofans
NA380	-	Sabre 80A	Sabreliner 75A with Raisbeck Mark Five system

The batches of serial numbers allocated to Sabreliners were:

Model	Built	Serial Batch	Model	Built	Serial Batch
NA246	1	246-1	40A		40 incl in 282- srs
T-39A	88	265-1 to 265-88	50	1	287-1
T-39B	6	270-1 to 270-6	60	130	306-1 to 306-146
T-39A	55	276-1 to 276-55	60/TF		Incl in 282- series
T-39D	10	277-1 to 277-10	75	9	370-1 to 370-9
T-39D	32	285-1 to 285-32	75A	66	380-1 to 380-726
CT-39G		13 incl in 306- srs	65	76	465-1 to 465-76
40	137	282-1 to 282-137	*Total*	611	

Rockwell Standard Corporation was a leading manufacturer of motor industry components – originally formed by Col Willard F Rockwell as the Rockwell Spring and Axle Company. Over the years, Rockwell had diversified into a number of industries and, in June 1958 acquired Aero Design (manufacturer of the Aero Commander twins). This led to the creation and the dispersal of an empire that, at one time, had a range to rival that of Cessna, Beech or Piper but, by the end of 1981, found Rockwell out of the General Aviation business. The separate types brought in by acquisition are dealt with under their respective original manufacturers, but the key events were as follows:

June 1958	Aero Design bought by Rockwell Spring & Axle
June 1958	Rockwell changes name to Rockwell Standard
1960	Aero Design changes name to Aero Commander Inc
July 1965	Meyers Aircraft Company acquired
July 1965	Volaircraft Inc acquired
November 1965	Snow Aeronautical Corp acquired
December 1966	Callair designs acquired from IMCO

Rockwell Sabre 75A N818LD

Rockwell 700 C-GBCM

It should not be supposed that Rockwell only built aircraft acquired from other companies. Rockwell-designed models filled two notable gaps in their range. These were the four-seat single-engined Model 112 and 114 and the cabin-class piston twin Model 700/710. The Model 112 was intended to compete across a fairly wide range from Cherokees up to the Bonanza and is described in the chapter on Commander Aircraft. The Model 700 was the result of a cooperative design and manufacturing venture between the Japanese Fuji Heavy Industries and Rockwell's General Aviation Divisions. The 700 was known in Japan as the Fuji FA-300 and was a pressurized low-wing twin powered by a pair of 340hp Lycoming TIO-540-R2AD turbocharged piston engines with standard seating for two crew and four passengers in a comparatively wide cabin. The first aircraft to fly was the Fuji prototype, JQ5001 (c/n 30001) on 13th November 1975, followed by Rockwell's prototype, N9901S (c/n 70001) on 25th February 1976. A second Bethany-built prototype (N700RE c/n 700-1) was subsequently tested and the aircraft received its American type certificate in November 1977.

The first Model 700 delivery was made in August 1978, but Rockwell and Fuji were already looking at the higher-powered Model 710, which was fitted with two 450hp Lycomings. There was little doubt that the Model 700 was underpowered in its basic version. Rockwell built two prototype Model 710s (N710RC c/n 710-01 and N710AB c/n 710-02) but time was running out for the whole programme and, in December 1978, Rockwell and Fuji terminated the joint venture agreement. By that time, the Bethany factory had built 32 units (c/n 700-01 to 70032) and had a further 13 shipsets of parts awaiting assembly.

Rollason   United Kingdom

Rollason Aircraft Services Ltd was founded in the 1930s by Capt William Rollason as an aircraft service and overhaul company. It was based at Croydon Airport and after the war had specialised in overhauling ex-RAF aircraft, particularly Tiger Moths, for civil use.

In 1957, prompted by Norman Jones, founder of the Tiger Club, Rollasons built the first of a series of Druine D-31 Turbulents. This aircraft (G-APBZ c/n PFA/440) was a low-wing open-cockpit single-seat ultra-light sporting aircraft of wood and fabric construction, originally designed by Roger Druine in France. The Rollason prototype was powered by a 30hp air-cooled Volkswagen but a fair number of the 29 aircraft built were given the 45hp Rollason-Ardem conversion of the Volkswagen car engine. The last three examples were designated D.31A and received full category certificates of airworthiness rather than the permits to fly of the earlier machines. These received serial

Rollason Druine D-31 Turbulent G-APTZ

Rollason Druine D-62B Condor G-AYFD

Druine design, the D.62 Condor, which was a side-by-side two-seat trainer with a fixed tailwheel undercarriage. The original Druine prototype (F-WBIX) had flown in France in 1956. The first Rollason aircraft (G-ARHZ c/n PFA/247) made its maiden flight in May 1961 powered by a 75hp Continental A75 engine but this was changed later to a 90hp Continental C90-14F. The first two production aircraft (c/n RAE/606 and RAE/607) were designated D.62A and used the 100hp Rolls-Royce Continental O-200-A engine but, from c/n RAE/608 Rollasons shortened the fuselage by four inches and, from aircraft c/n RAE/612, the Condors were fitted with flaps. In this form it was designated D.62B. Four production Condors were fitted with the 130hp Continental O-240-A engine to become D.62Cs. Production of all Condor models by Rollasons totalled 48 (c/n RAE/606 to RAE/653) plus three uncompleted airframes (RAE/654 and RAE/656).

The last production aircraft to emerge from the Rollason works was the Luton Group Beta – a single-seat Formula One racer that had been the winner of a 1964 competition sponsored by Mr Jones. Four Betas were built by Rollasons (serialled c/n RAE/01 to RAE/04). The first was G-ATLY, which was a Model B.1 with a 65hp Continental engine, and the other three examples included two of the B.2 model with a 90hp Continental C90-8F and one B.4 with a 100hp Continental O-200-A. In addition, a further three B.2 aircraft were built by amateur constructors (c/n JJF.1, PFA/02-10169 and PFA/02-12369).

numbers in the Rollason series (c/n RAE/578, RAE/100 and RAE/101) rather than the Popular Flying Association numbers (eg, G-ASAM was PFA/595) which had been allocated before.

In September 1959, Croydon Airport was closed and eventually Rollasons moved to Shoreham. They launched production of their second

Ruschmeyer   Germany

In 1985, Horst Ruschmeyer's Ruschmeyer Luftfahrttechnik GmbH embarked on the design of an all-composite low-wing four-seater which was initially designated MF-85. The MF-85 was a high-performance tourer with a retractable tricycle undercarriage and it was powered by a 212hp Porsche PFM.3200N engine fitted with a three-bladed MTV.9 constant-speed propeller. Ruschmeyer flew the prototype (D-EEHE, c/n V001) on 8th August 1988 from their home airfield at Melle and intended this as the first of a range of models based on the same airframe but offering different power options.

The discontinuation of aero engine production by Porsche resulted in a change to a 230hp Lycoming IO-540-C4D5 engine with a four-blade Muhlbauer propeller. In this form, on 25th September 1990

Ruschmeyer flew the second prototype, designated R90-230RG, (D-EERO, c/n V002) and achieved German certification on 12th June 1992. A further three aircraft (c/n V003, 004 and 05) had been completed by the autumn of 1992 at Melle and production was transferred to Dessau. It was intended that there would be two flying club versions; these being the fixed-undercarriage IO-360-powered R90-180FG and R90-230FG (prototype D-EECR). Ruschmeyer also started developing the turbocharged R90-300T-RG, the R90 Aerobat and the R90-420AT fitted with a 400shp Allison 250-B20 turboprop. The R90-420AT prototype (D-EERO re-engined) first flew on 2nd November 1993.

Longer-range plans included the R95 five-seat turboprop with a longer fuselage and rear cabin entry door, but Ruschmeyer declared bankruptcy in June 1996 before these ideas could mature. By this time, total production had reached 28 aircraft (c/n 001 to 028) all of which

Ruschmeyer R90-230RG Solaris N230S

were the R90-230RG. In 1999, the assets of Ruschmeyer were acquired by Solaris Aviation of West Palm Beach, Florida and in 2003 they announced the relaunch of the aircraft as the Sigma 230 powered by the IO-540 engine and had plans to add further models at a later date including the Sigma 310 with a 310hp Continental IO-550-N and the

Sigma 250 with an uprated Lycoming IO-540. This development did not progress but a new company, Aircraft Technology Construction, has taken over the design and has built two new R90-230s (c/n 029 and 030) at Melle. Future planned developments include higher gross weight and fuel capacity, a 300hp model and a glass cockpit.

Ryan   United States

With the end of wartime production, North American Aviation Inc designed a new light aircraft – the NA-143 – to meet postwar civil aviation demand. The NA-143 was an all-metal low-wing monoplane with four seats and a sliding bubble canopy. It had a retractable tricycle undercarriage and was powered by a 185hp Continental engine. Two prototypes were built and, as might be expected, the aircraft was engineered to a high specification, drawing on the company's long experience of military design. The two prototypes were followed by the production version, the NA-145 Navion, which featured minor changes to the vertical tail, nose cowling and internal systems. Production units started rolling down the line at Inglewood, California in mid-1947. In addition to the Continental E-185-3 engine the aircraft was also offered with a 205hp E-185-9 powerplant.

In June 1947, North American had already built over 1,000 Navions and the market was slowing down – to the extent of leaving the company with a large unsold inventory. At the same time, work was building up in preparation for F-86 Sabre production and North American decided to stop building the Navion. The field inventory was reduced by a delivery of 83 L-17As to the US Army. These were designated NA-154 and were virtually identical to the standard civil aircraft.

The type certificate was sold to Ryan Aeronautical Corporation of San Diego and production resumed in the latter part of 1947. On 3rd February 1949, the Navion A was certificated and this differed from the basic model in having improved ventilation and insulation, a revised fuel system and provision for an extra 20 US gallons of additional fuel tankage. A further batch of this model was delivered to the Army as the L-17B (later U-18B) and 35 of the previous L-17As were upgraded to this standard with the designation L-17C (U-18C). In 1950, Ryan further improved the Navion to produce the Navion B (approved in March 1950), which was also known as the Super Navion 260. This had a 260hp Lycoming GO-435-C2 engine, but only 222 examples were built before Ryan terminated production in the face of a slump in market demand.

Ryan delivered two Navion Bs to the US Army as XL-22As and these were later redesignated XL-17D – but they also converted a Navion B as a two-seat trainer to compete with the Temco Plebe in a US Navy competition held in 1953. This Model 72 (N4860K) had a 48-inch increase in wingspan, extra cabin transparencies, increased fuel tankage and a constant-speed propeller. The project was unsuccessful and the prototype later reverted to Navion B standard.

The next owner of the Navion type certificate was the Tulsa Manufacturing Co (Tusco). This company did not build any new airframes, but did convert existing aircraft to Navion D, Navion E or Navion F standard. In 1961, Tusco formed a separate division known as the Navion Aircraft Company that radically redesigned the aircraft as the Navion G Rangemaster with an integral cabin seating up to five people and it was approved on 5th May 1961. In 1965, production rights were again sold – to the Navion Aircraft Co, which was set up at Seguin, Texas by the American Navion Society to manufacture the Rangemaster. The engine power was increased once again and the new version called the Navion H Rangemaster. The company was acquired, in 1970, by Janox Corporation but Navion Aircraft only managed to survive until 1972 before declaring bankruptcy and abandoning further production. The type certificate and tooling were bought by Cedric Kotowicz who set up the Navion Rangemaster Aircraft Co and managed to build just one Navion H (N2553T) in 1974.

The holder of the type certificate to actually build aircraft was Consolidated Holding Inc, which restarted the Navion H line in 1975, but only eight aircraft were completed and the operation was suspended in the following year. The type certificate was sold to Jimmy Thomp-

Ryan Navion A N9TF

son Enterprise of Alexandria, Louisiana and then in 1982 to Diamond Aero Enterprises. No further production was undertaken although there were plans for a Navion J equipped with a turbocharged 350hp Lycoming engine and featuring an enlarged six-seat cabin and 'wet' wings. In 1995 the type certificate and assets were acquired by Navion Holdings Inc of Perrysburg, Ohio. Details of Navion models are:

Model	Built	Notes
NA-143	2	Original North American prototypes NX18928 (c/n 143-1) and NX18929 (c/n 143-2)
NA-145	1,027	North American production Navion fitted with 185hp Cont E-185-3 or 205hp Cont E-185-9. 2,750 lb TOGW
Navion	600	Ryan production
Navion A	602	Refined Navion with improved systems and 205hp Continental E-185-9 engine
Navion B	222	Navion A powered by 260hp Lycoming GO-435-C2. Known as the Super Navion 260. 2,850 lb TOGW
Navion D	-	Tusco conversion. 240hp Continental IO-470-P and tip tanks. 3,150 lb TOGW
Navion E	-	Tusco conversion. 250hp Continental IO-470-C and tip tanks
Navion F	-	Tusco conversion. 260hp Continental IO-470-H and tip tanks
Rangemaster G	121	Redesigned Navion B with integral cabin, tip tanks, 260hp Cont IO-470-H. Modified fin on Rangemaster G-1. 3,150 lb TOGW
Rangemaster H	60	Navion G with 285hp Cont IO-520-B engine. 3,315 lb TOGW

Navions have been subjected to many modifications over the years, ranging from the Northrop Aeronautical Institute's proposal to fit a 350 lbst turbojet to the more routine options aimed at improving performance through altered cooling systems, changes to stabiliser incidence and cleaning up the canopy area. However, the most radical changes have been the twin-engine conversions.

Navion Rangemaster G N2437T

Temco D-16A Twin Navion N108N

The best-known was originally developed by the Dauby Equipment Company of Los Angeles in 1952. This was designated the X-16 Bi-Navion and it involved the removal and fairing-over of the existing powerplant installation and the mounting of two 130hp Lycoming engines on the strengthened wings. Dauby did not do the production conversions, but passed this to the Riley Aircraft Co who decided to use 150hp Lycoming O-320 engines and to fit a larger vertical tail. After completing 19 aircraft, Riley passed over the rights to Temco who produced a further 46 of this D-16 model and a further 45 D-16As with 160hp Lycoming O-340-A1A engines. Temco was, incidentally, also involved in the conversion, during 1957, of six L-17A military Navions into QL-17A remote controlled drones for the US Air Force.

The other twin conversion of the long-suffering Navion was the Camair 480, produced by Cameron Aircraft Co – a subsidiary of Cameron Iron Works. The 35 units produced by Camair from their Galveston factory had a variety of Continental engines ranging from 225hp to 260hp and these aircraft can be distinguished from the Temco/Riley Twin Navion in having a similar but slightly taller fin to that of the standard Navion.

Serial numbers of the first two North American Navion prototypes were 143-1 and 143-2. Thereafter, production aircraft started at NAV-4-2 (NAV-4-1 is believed to have been a static test airframe) and continued to NAV-4-1627. Navion As and Bs were included in a common production line that ran from NAV-4-1628 to NAV-4-2350. The Rangemaster G started at NAV-4-2351 and continued to NAV-4-2370 at which point the Rangemaster G-1 was introduced with numbers from NAV-4-2401 to NAV-4-2502. The prototype Navion H was NAV-4-2501 and production ran from NAV-4-2503 to NAV-4-2561. Twin Navion conversions were serialled TN-1 to TN-19 when carried out by Riley and Temco conversions ran from TTN-1 to TTN-90. Camair's Model 480 conversions were numbered 1-050 to 1-083 and their prototype was c/n 101.

SAAB   Sweden

Svenska Aeroplan Aktiebolaget (SAAB) was formed by the Bofors company in 1937 at Trollhattan and it built a range of military aircraft during the 1930s and 1940s. During 1945, SAAB designed the Model 91 Safir, the prototype of which first flew in November of that year. The Safir was designed by Anders J Andersson, who had been chief designer of Bücker Flugzeugbau GmbH in Germany. The aircraft was an all-metal low-wing monoplane with three seats, which closely resembled an enlarged Bücker Bestmann with a retractable tricycle undercarriage. It was intended for civil and military flying training and was powered by a De Havilland Gipsy Major in-line engine.

Some 48 examples of the initial S.91A Safir were built before the company brought out the Model 91B which used a 190hp Lycoming engine. This model was ordered in quantity by the Swedish Air Force and 120 examples, which formed the bulk of production, were built by the De Scheldt factory in Holland because the SAAB factories were fully committed at that time. Safir production returned to Sweden in 1954 and SAAB announced the S.91C, which had been modified to provide a fourth seat. In 1957, the S.91D with a smaller engine joined the S.91C on the production line. Substantial civil deliveries of Safirs were made, but the bulk of production went to military users including the air arms of Sweden, Finland, Norway, Ethiopia, Tunisia and Austria. The aircraft were built in six production batches (c/n 91101 to 91148, 91201 to 91275, 91276 to 91290, 91291 to 91320, 91321 to 91345 and 91346 to 91474). Details of serial numbers and numbers completed are as follows

Model	Built	Serial Numbers	Model	Built	Serial Numbers
S.91	1	91,001	S.91C*	11	91276, 91311 - 91320
S.91A	48	91101 - 91148	S.91C	28	91385 - 91408, 91471 - 91474
S.91B*	109	91201 - 91275, 91277 - 91310	S.91D	99	91346 - 91384, 91409 - 91444, 91447 - 91470
S.91B-2	27	91321 - 91345, 91445 & 91446	Total	323	*De Scheldt built

In March 1968 SAAB acquired A B Malmo Flygindustri (MFI). During the 1960s, MFI had been involved in development of two light aircraft types – the MFI-10 Vipan and the MFI-9 Junior. The Vipan was a four-seat high-wing air observation aircraft, which had some novel features and was demonstrated extensively. While it did not then reach production, the Vipan was briefly revived in 1993 by RFB (DASA). More successful was the MFI-9. It was derived from the BA-7 prototype (N2806D/SE-COW) that first flew on 10th October 1958 and was built by Malmo's chief designer, Bjorn Andreasson. The Junior was a small all-metal shoulder-wing aircraft with an enclosed side-by-side two-seat cabin and a fixed tricycle undercarriage. The prototype flew in May 1961 and the production MFI-9 was constructed both at MFI's Malmo plant and under licence in Germany by Bölkow. Compared with the MFI-9, the Bölkow version had a straight nosewheel leg rather than a trailing link unit and had a wider fuselage instead of the fuselage bulge beside the cockpit. In addition to the production total of 70 MFI-9s, four aircraft were built by amateurs from kits and a further two completed from leftover MFI components. One MFI-9B (SE-XDK) was rebuilt with a Lycoming O-235 engine and designated MFI-11.

MFI also used the Junior airframe to develop the Militrainer with a hardened wing allowing it to carry light support weapons when used by military forces. It also formed the basis for the larger T-tailed MFI-15 Safari, which was originally intended as a trainer for the Swedish Air Force to meet the requirement eventually filled by the Scottish Aviation Bulldog. In the event, the MFI-15 was built for the air forces of Sierra Leone, Norway, Ethiopia and Zambia and the ground-attack version (the MFI-17 with a hardened wing) was produced for Denmark and Norway. MFI also delivered 15 MFI-15s to Pakistan and these were followed by kits for a further 117 aircraft which were completed to MFI-17 standard by Pakistan Aeronautical Complex (AMF) as the Mushshak. Further examples of the Mushshak have been built by AMF from scratch and it is reported that the Pakistan forces operate more than 220 aircraft (including the higher-powered Super Mushshak) and further examples have been delivered to Iran (25), Syria (6) and Oman (3).

The small batch of Juniors was serialled c/n 1 to 23 (MFI-9) and c/n 024 to 070 (MFI-9B and MFI-9C). MFI-15 and MFI-17 aircraft have all had serials prefixed 15 and running sequentially from 15.001 to 15.024 (plus kits c/n 15.025 to 15.141), c/n 15.201 to 15.270 (including 15.233 to 15.250 produced as spare parts), c/n 15.901 to 15.902 and c/n 15.801 to 15.851 of which the last five were built from spare parts. 19 aircraft from the final batch were destroyed in a hangar fire at Malmo in September 1979. Details of the SAAB aircraft are as follows:

SAAB S-91B Safir PH-RJB

Model	Built	Notes
S.91 Safir	1	All-metal three-seat low-wing cabin monoplane with retractable tricycle u/c and one 145hp Gipsy Major 10 engine. 2,415 lb TOGW. Prototype SE-APN (c/n 91001) FF 20 Nov 1945
S.91A Safir	48	S.91 with modified cockpit structure and detailed system changes
S.91B Safir	136	S.91A powered by 190hp Lycoming O-435-A engine. 2,736 lb TOGW
S.91C Safir	39	S.91B with four-seat interior, 2,678 lb TOGW. Prototype SE-BYZ (c/n 91276)
S.91D Safir	99	S.91B with 180hp Lycoming O-360-A1A engine
MFI-9 Junior	23	All-metal two-seat light aircraft with fixed tricycle u/c and one 100hp Continental O-200 engine. 1,367 lb TOGW. Prototype SE-CPF became D-EBVA with Bölkow
MFI-9B Trainer	46	MFI-9 with larger tail, lengthened cabin and electric flaps. Mili-Trainer has wing hardpoints
MFI-9C	1	MFI-9 with 130hp Continental engine and 1,268 lb TOGW. One aircraft, SE-FIG (c/n 69)

SAAB MFI-17 T-409

MFI-10 Vipan	1	High-wing all-metal army cooperation aircraft with one 160hp Lycoming O-320-B2B engine. Prototype SE-CFI FF 25 Feb 1961
MFI-10B	2	MFI-10 with 180hp Lycoming O-360-A1D engine
MFI-15 Safari	101	Enlarged MFI-9 military aircraft with third seat in centre fuselage compartment, T-tail and 200hp Lycoming IO-360-A1B6 engine. Prototype SE-XCB/SE-301 (c/n 15.001) FF 11 Jul 1969

MFI-17 Supporter AMF Mushshak	36	Military MFI-15 with four underwing hardpoints MFI-17 built by Pakistan AMF from MFI kits and then locally. 2,645 lb TOGW. Approx 285 built to date
AMF Super Mushshak		Mushshak powered by 260hp Lycoming IO-540-V4A5 engine and 2,755 lb TOGW. Approx 16 built to date
AMF Shahbaz		AMF Mushshak fitted with 210hp TSIO-360-MB engine. Approx 4 built to date

SAI (Skandinavisk Aircraft Industri) Denmark

The Skandinavisk Aero Industri (SAI) was started by Viggo Kramme and Karl Zeuthen in August 1937 to build the KZ-II Kupe two-seat light sporting aircraft. This basic airframe formed a basis for SAI to develop a sport version with tandem open cockpits. The Danish Naval Air Service placed an order for four aircraft, but, on 9th April 1940, Denmark was occupied by the German forces and these aircraft were impressed together with a number of other civilian examples. Most of them failed to survive the war, but the design was revived when peace came and a new version – the KZ-IIT Trainer – was produced. This featured a strengthened airframe and was built in some numbers for the Danish Air Force.

SAI was only permitted to follow 'approved' activities during the war, but they were able to develop two completely new aircraft designs. The first of these, the KZ-III, was a high-wing aircraft that was ostensibly for use as an air ambulance. It made its first flight in the summer of 1944 from Kastrup and a second aircraft (SE-ANY) was delivered to Sweden where the majority of the flight-testing was carried out. The KZ-III went into production in 1945 by which time hostilities had ceased and SAI was fully back in operation. Also under the 'air ambulance' cover story the company built the prototype KZ-IV twin-engined monoplane, which was intended for use by the Zone Redningskorpset (Red Cross). The KZ-IV was a very attractive machine with twin fins and one additional example was built after the war had finished.

Post-war production of the KZ-III reached a respectable level with most units being built in a factory owned by F L Smidth at Slusehol-

SAI KZ-IIT Trainer OY-FAK

men in the docks area of Copenhagen and then taken to Kastrup for flight-testing. The KZ-III was expanded to a full four seats as the KZ-VII Laerk and could be purchased with either a 125hp or 145hp Continental engine. Regrettably, the initial batch of KZ-VIIs was destroyed in a factory fire on 2nd February 1947 and, as a result, SAI set up a new factory at Kastrup where all aircraft from c/n 148 were built. A small batch of KZ-Xs was also constructed for the Danish Army. This was an army cooperation development of the KZ-VII but a series of crashes of

SAI KZ-III OY-DGV

early examples resulted in only 12 being completed rather than the 14 originally ordered. Subsequent investigation did not uncover any serious design deficiencies, but the remaining KZ-Xs were eventually scrapped in 1960 and replaced by the Piper L-19.

SAI aircraft were give serial numbers in a strict numerical sequence running from c/n 1 to 217. The main production models fell into the following serial blocks:

Model	Serial Numbers	Model	Serial Numbers
KZ-II	c/n 3 to 27; c/n 37 to 41	KZ-IV	c/n 43 and 70
KZ-IIT	c/n 109 to 123	KZ-VII	c/n 124, 135, 148 to 201
KZ-III	c/n 42 to 108 (excl 43,44,70)	KZ-X	c/n 205 to 217

Details of all designs by Skandinavisk Aero Industri are as follows:

Model	Built	Notes
KZ-I	1	Single-seat low-wing monoplane powered by a 38hp ABC Scorpion. OY-DYL (c/n 2) FF 24 Feb 1937
KZ-IIK Kupe	14	Two-seat side-by-side cabin monoplane powered by a 90hp Cirrus Minor. Prototype OY-DAN (c/n 3) FF 11 Dec 1937
KZ-IIS Sport	14	KZ-IIK with tandem open cockpits and 105hp Hirth 504A engine. Prototype OY-DAP (c/n 10) FF 10 Oct 1938
KZ-IIT Trainer	16	Trainer development of KZ-IIS with 145hp Gipsy Major X engine. Prototype OY-DRO (c/n 37) FF Apr 1946
KZ-III	64	Two-seat high-wing cabin monoplane with fixed tailwheel u/c and one 100hp Cirrus Minor II engine. Prototype OY-DOZ (c/n 42) FF 11 Sep 1944
KZ-IV	2	All-wood low-wing ambulance aircraft with fixed tailwheel u/c, twin fins and two 145hp Gipsy Major X engines. Prototype OY-DIZ (c/n 43) FF 4 May 1944
KZ-V		Twin-engined light transport design. Not built
KZ-VI		Four-seat light aircraft design. Not built
KZ-VII Laerk	58	Four-seat development of KZ-III with 125hp Cont C-125-2 or 145hp C-145-2 engine. Prot OY-DUE (c/n 124) FF 11 Oct 1946
KZ-VIII	2	Single-seat low-wing aerobatic aircraft with 145hp Gipsy Major X engine. OY-ACB and D-EBIZ (c/n 202, 203). FF 14 Nov 1949
KZ-IX	1	Replica of 1909 Ellehammer standard monoplane with Cirrus Hermes III engine. OY-ACE (c/n 204)
KZ-X	13	Tandem-two-seat AOP version of KZ-VII with clearview cabin and one 145hp Cont C-145 engine. Prototype OY-ACL (c/n 205) FF 29 Sep 1951
KZ-XI		Single-seat agricultural aircraft. Not built
Total Built	185	

SAN   France

Lucien Querey, an enthusiastic aeromodeller and glider pilot, formed SAN on 1st May 1948 as an 'Aviation Service Station' following the pattern of his garage business in the French town of Bernay. The Société Aéronautique Normande (SAN) was based at Bernay-St Martin and first entered the aircraft manufacturing business with a Piper Cub conversion (F-WFRA) and then with an original two-seater, similar to the Cub, which was known as the SAN-101. This aircraft did not offer sufficient promise as a production model but, instead, Querey decided to build a small batch of Jodel D.11s.

From 1952 onwards, SAN built a series of Jodel variants, all with the distinctive 'bent' wings, under licence from Jean Delemontez – commencing with the Jodel D.112 and following on with the improved D.117. Compared with the competitive D.112 built by Wassmer, the SAN aircraft featured a small fin fillet, somewhat larger cockpit transparencies and a moulded windscreen. SAN also designed a distinctive red or blue colour scheme with a scalloped edge to the rudder.

The D.117 was phased out in 1958 in favour of the DR.100 and, from 1st January 1959, Alpavia built the type at Gap as the D.117A. Jean Delemontez had become associated with Pierre Robin in his development of the 3/4-seat DR.100 Ambassadeur and Lucien Querey took a licence to build this aircraft at Bernay. The first SAN-built DR.100 was, in fact, a DR.100A (F-BIZI c/n 51), which was powered by a 90hp Continental. SAN followed this with a parallel version, the DR.105A, which had a 100hp engine. At the same time as the DR.100 was coming on-stream, SAN was developing the D.140 Mousquetaire – a scaled-up 4/5-seat version of the D.117. Powered by a 180hp Lycoming, the prototype D.140 first flew in July 1958 and entered production as the D.140A later the same year. It was followed by a series of D.140 variants culminating in the D.140R Abeille, which had a cut-down rear fuselage and was primarily used as a glider tug. 18 examples of the D.140E and 14 of the D.140R were built for the Armée de l'Air.

Regrettably, the company suffered a serious fire in November 1959 which put them out of production for some time and in the following month Lucien Querey died. Under the leadership of Mme Querey, SAN went on with the Mousquetaire and Ambassadeur – and introduced its own versions of the improved DR.100 models that were being announced by Centre Est.

The second design, which was exclusive to SAN, was the D.150 Mascaret. This was a two-seat Jodel with a fuselage similar to that of the D.117, the Ambassadeur wing with extended leading edges and a neat swept fin. The prototype was flown in the summer of 1962 and SAN went on to build a total of 60 units with optional Continental or Potez engines. By the mid-1960s, however, SAN was in deep financial trouble and, in November 1968, the company was forced into receivership. A small order for D.140s was in hand at that time and the factory was purchased by M Auguste Mudry, who kept the operation going and completed the final batch of Mousquetaires before moving on to production of the Piel designs produced by CAARP.

Serial numbers used by SAN for the D.11 models and the Ambassadeur variants were issued as 'plan numbers' by Avions Jodel, but the D.140 and D.150 had their own separate SAN serial numbers. Early D.112s built by the company had various Jodel serials allocate randomly. The other batches allocated to SAN aircraft were:

Model	Serial Batch	Model	Serial Batch	Model	Serial Batch
D.117	416 to 445	D.117	750 to 761	DR.100	451 to 494
D.117	493 to 511	D.117	799 to 848	D.140	1 to 215
D.117	588 to 612	D.117	899 to 916	D.140R	501 to 528
D.117	623 to 652	DR.100	51 to 200	D.150	01 to 61
D.117	686 to 705	DR.100	251 to 300		
D.117	719 to 738	DR.100	351 to 400		

Details of SAN aircraft models are:

Model	Built	Notes
101 SAN.B	1	Two-seat high-wing cabin monoplane similar to Piper Cub, powered by one 65hp Continental C.65. Prototype F-WFUP FF 19 Nov 1950
D.112	10	Jodel D.112 built under licence

SAN D-150 Mascaret G-OABB

SAN D-140 Mousquetaire G-TOAD

D.117	223	D.112 with electrical equipment and 90hp Continental C.90 engine. D.117A built by Alpavia
D.140 Mousquetaire	1	4/5-seat enlarged D.117 with triangular fin/rudder, powered by one 180hp Lycoming O-360 engine. Prototype F-BIZE FF 4 Jul 1958
D.140A Mousquetaire	45	Production D.140 with new cabin ventilation
D.140B Mousquetaire II	56	D.140A with improved brakes, redesigned engine cowling and improved ventilation
D.140C Mousquetaire III	70	D.140B with enlarged swept tail. Prototype F-BKSO
D.140E Mousquetaire IV	43	D.140C with further enlarged tail, all-flying elevator/tailplane and modified ailerons
D.140R Abeille	28	D.140E with cut-down rear fuselage and all-round vision canopy. Fitted with glider towing equipment. Prototype F-WLKK FF Jun 1965

D.150 Mascaret	44	Two-seat Jodel derivative based on D.117 with modified DR.100 wing and swept tail, powered by 100hp Cont O-200A engine. Prototype F-WJST FF 2 Jun 1962
D.150A Mascaret	17	D.150 with 105hp Potez 105E engine. Prototype F-WLDA
DR.100A	54	SAN-built version of Jodel DR.100A
DR.105A		SAN-built version of Jodel DR.105A
DR.1050 Ambassadeur	211	SAN-built version of Jodel DR.1050
DR.1051 Ambassadeur		SAN-built version of Jodel DR.1051
DR.1050M Excellence	29	SAN-built DR.1050M Sicile Record (see Robin)
DR.1051M Excellence		SAN-built DR.1051M Sicile Record (see Robin)
DR.1052	1	DR.1050 converted to full four-seat configuration. F-WJQM (c/n 27)
Total Production	*833*	

Sauper-Aviation   France

The J-300 Joker ultralight originated as the Tempest open-cockpit parasol-wing light aircraft, designed and built by Tony Minguet and first flown at Ponlevoy in 1984. A small series of 400kg Tempests were built by ULM Technic Aéromarine from 1987 onwards, but in 1990 the cabin was enclosed and the new J300 Joker was produced by Arno-Chereau Aviation (ACA) under Jean-Claude Chereau. The company was reconstituted in 1992 as Sauper-Aviation and it is now based at Blois-Le Breuil Airport in central France. The J300 is of classic steel tube and fabric construction with composite wing structure and is fitted with a triangulated steel tube undercarriage with elastic damping. It has side-by-side seating for two in an enclosed cabin and can be powered either by the 79hp Rotax 912ULS or various other Rotax, JPX, BMW or Limbach engines in the 70 to 120hp range. A new version, the Joker III was introduced in 2000 with a new instrument panel and enlarged tail. Sauper has a subsidiary in Madagascar that has supplied and operated the J300 with spraybars and chemical tanks for locust eradication and they have also tested a J300 with a tricycle undercar-

Sauper J300 Joker

Sauper ADV.01 Papango F-WWNO

riage. Sauper-Aviation's latest model is the ADV.01 Papango which is a larger JAR-VLA aircraft, again powered by a Rotax 912S, but with a large cockpit and good short field performance. The prototype, F-WWNO first flew on 30th November 2002 and this was followed on 8th June 2004 by the prototype Papango ULM, which meets ultralight rules. Sauper-Aviation has built 90 examples of the J300.

Scheibe   Germany

Egon Scheibe formed the Scheibe Flugzeugbau GmbH in Munich in late 1951 for the purpose of building the Mü-13E Bergfalke tandem two-seat sailplane. This design was soon followed by a further two-seat training glider, the Specht; by the single-seat L-Spatz; and, in 1955, by the high-performance Zugvogel. These sailplanes established a strong reputation for Scheibe, which enabled the company to contemplate the production of powered aircraft. It should be noted that several Bergfalkes were fitted with one-off retractable engine conversions and D-KOLT was converted as the Bergfalke IV BIMO with a pair of 22hp Lloyd LS-400 engines buried in the rear inboard wings.

In 1955, Scheibe designed the SF-23 Sperling – a high-wing side-by-side two-seat cabin aircraft powered by a 65hp Continental A-65 engine. The Sperling was largely sold to German aero clubs and, fitted with either the 90hp Continental C90 or 100hp Lycoming O-200A, was in production between 1958 and 1961 with serials running from c/n 2001 to 2018 (SF-23/-23A), c/n 2019 to 2022 (SF-23B) and c/n 3000 to 3003 (SF-23C). Three others were built by amateur constructors (c/n 2500, 3500 and 3501). Scheibe had, however, become impressed with the motor glider concept and before the war flew an Mu-13 Merlin glider fitted with a 13hp Kroeber M4 engine. In 1957, Scheibe built the SF-24 Motor Spatz which was, essentially, an L-Spatz fitted with a two-cylinder Zink-Brandl engine located in the nose. Later versions of the Motor Spatz had other engines – in particular the 26hp Hirth Solo.

The Motor Spatz was successful, but was little more than a power-assisted glider. Therefore, Scheibe took the Bergfalke and re-engineered it to produce a genuine low-powered light aircraft. The SF-25 Motorfalke was, again, a side-by-side two-seater and was broadly based on its glider forerunner but had an entirely new forward fuselage which contained an enclosed cockpit and Hirth F12A2C engine derived from the earlier Solo. It soon went into production and became known simply as the Falke.

With the SF-25B the wing position was lowered and several variants followed with various engines including the current production SF-25C, which was modified with a conventional tailwheel undercarriage and numerous other improvements in the late 1970s. A tricycle undercarriage version of the C-Falke 2000 is also offered. Falkes were also built by amateurs and by various other manufacturers including Sportavia-Putzer, Aeronautica Umbra in Italy, Loravia in France and Slingsby in the United Kingdom. The latest version is the SF-41 Merlin, which has a shorter fuselage and shorter wing and will be certificated in the JAR-VLA category. Scheibe subsequently also built the SF-28A Tandem Falke which was structurally similar to the SF-25C but had tandem seating and a long clearview canopy.

In 1967, Scheibe built the first SF-27M. Based on the SF-27 Zugvogel, this was fitted with a Hirth Solo engine on a retractable pylon mounted on the wing centre section. The SF-27M was able to take off

Scheibe SF-25C Falke C-2000 HB-2189

and manouevre using the engine and then retract it when the operating altitude was reached and normal soaring flight could be undertaken. Another single-seater was the SF-29, which emerged in 1973 and was powered by a Hirth two-stroke snowmobile engine. Neither this nor the SF-33, which was developed from it, achieved production status. The most recent Scheibe model is the SF-36 – a side-by-side development of the SF-H34 two-seat glider with a nose-mounted Limbach SL.2000 engine. This aircraft employs extensive glassfibre construction and has a forward sliding canopy for crew access.

Each Scheibe model has its own serial number series. Early gliders had numbers starting at c/n 101 and these continued chronologically to the Zugvogel which came into the c/n 1000 to 2000 range. Thereafter, serial numbers have consisted of a two-digit prefix followed by a sequential number starting at 01. A number of SF-25B Falkes have been converted to SF-25C or SF-25D standard – and their serial numbers carry a suffix to indicate this (eg, c/n 46107D). A total of 35 SF-25s were built by Slingsby and were allocated Slingsby serial numbers within the range c/n 1723 to 1778. Aeronautica Umbra aircraft carried serial numbers c/n 001 to 010. Details of Scheibe serial batches are:

Model	Serial Batch	Model	Serial Batch
SF-24A	c/n 4001 to 4024	SF-25C	c/n 44100 to 44704
SF-24B	c/n 4025 to 4046	SF-25E	c/n 4301 to 4362
SF-25A	c/n 4501 to 4556	SF-25K	c/n 4901 to 4906
SF-25B	c/n 4601 to 4699	SF-27MA	c/n 6301 to 6330
SF-25B	c/n 46100 to 46259	SF-28A	c/n 5701 to 57118
SF-25B	c/n 46301 to 46308*	SF-36	c/n 4101 to 4106
SF-25B	c/n 4801 to 4868†	SF-37	c/n 5201 to 5220
SF-25C	c/n 4201 to 4255†	SF-39	c/n 3401 to 3404
SF-25C	c/n 4401 to 4556	SF-40	c/n 3101 to 3105

* Amateur-built; † Sportavia-Putzer built.

Glider designs by Scheibe include the SF-26 Standard, SF-27, SF-30 Club Spatz and the SF-34 Delphin. Details of Scheibe's powered aircraft designs, with total production by all manufacturers, are as follows:

Model	Built	Notes
SF-23A Sperling	19	Two-seat side-by-side high-wing cabin monoplane with fixed tailwheel u/c and one 95hp Cont C90-12F engine. Prototype SF-25V-1 D-EBIN (c/n 2001) FF 8 Aug 1955
SF-23B Sperling	4	SF-23A with 100hp Lycoming O-200-A engine
SF-23C Sperling	6	SF-23A with 115hp Lycoming O-235-C1 engine
SF-24A Motor Spatz	24	L-Spatz single-seat glider with 21hp Brandl ZB300-S two-stroke engine in nose. Prototype D-EHUK later D-KHUK (c/n 4001) FF Aug 1957
SF-24B Motor Spatz	22	SF-24A with 25hp Hirth Solo 560A engine. Prototype D-KEBI
SF-25A Motor Falke	56	Scheibe Mu-13E Bergfalke side-by-side two-seat glider with nose-mounted 30hp Hirth F10A2c engine. 1,069 lb TOGW Prototype D-KEDO (c/n 4501) FF Apr 1963
SF-25B Falke	480	SF-25 with lower-set wings of reduced span, modified u/c and 45hp Stark Stamo 1500/1 engine. 1,224 lb TOGW. Prototype D-KOCO
SF-25C Falke	816	SF-25B with 65hp Limbach 1700A engine and electric starter. 1,345 lb TOGW. Prototype D-KBIK (c/n 4401). FF Mar 1971. Some fitted with Rotax 912 engine
SF-25C Falke 76		SF-25C with swept tail, optional spring steel u/c instead of monowheel, clear blown canopy and higher gross weight
SF-25CS Falke		SF-25C with feathering propeller. 1,279 lb TOGW.
SF-25C-2000 Falke		Falke '76 with 80hp Limbach L.2000-EA engine and optional tricycle undercarriage. 1,433 lb TOGW
SF-25D Falke		SF-25B conversions to Limbach 1700A engine
SF-25E Super Falke	62	SF-25CS with extended wing, air brakes, narrow-chord swept vertical tail, modified u/c and raised bubble canopy. 1,433 lb TOGW Prototype D-KLAC (c/n 4301) FF May 1974
SF-25K K-Falke	6	SF-25C with folding wings, larger canopy and GRP forward fuselage covering. 1,389 lb TOGW. Prototype D-KDBK (c/n 4901) FF Dec 1978
SF-27M-A	30	SF-27 Zugvogel V sailplane with manually retractable pylon-mounted Hirth F.10A engine. Prototype D-KOCI (c/n 6301) FF Apr 1967
SF-27M-B		SF-27M with Hirth 171R4E engine

Scheibe SF-23A Sperling D-EBYZ

SF-27M-Ci	1	SF-27M with Hirth 028 engine and Cirrus glider wings. D-KAFK (c/n 6401)
SF-28A Tandem Falke	118	Tandem two-seat version of SF-25C. Prototype D-KAFJ (c/n 5701) FF May 1971
SF-28B Tandem Falke	1	SF-28A with minor changes. D-KDCB (c/n 5401)
SF-29	1	Single-seat low-wing motor glider with fixed monowheel u/c and 28hp Hirth 194R engine. Prototype D-KOCH (c/n 6701) converted to SF-33
SF-32	1	Single-seat powered sailplane developed from SF-27M with electrically driven retractable Rotax 642 engine. D-KOJE (c/n 6501) FF May 1976
SF-33	1	SF-29 with 35hp BMW engine. D-KOCH FF Apr 1977
SF-35	1	Motor glider. No further details known. Prototype D-KDGM (c/n 4701) FF Dec 1979
SF-36	6	Two-seat side-by-side motor glider developed from SF-H34 sailplane with low wings, normal tailwheel u/c and 80hp Limbach SL.2000 engine. SF-36R has Rotax 912 engine. Prototype D-KOOP (c/n 4101) FF Jul 1980
SF-37	20	Open-frame single-seat ultralight. D-MXFI
SF-38		Two-seat version of SF-37. Probably not built
SF-39 Ultra/Uli	4	Side-by-side high-wing two-seat utralight with 62hp Rotax 462 mounted on wing centre section. D-MEMO
SF-39B Coach	1	Parasol-wing side-by-side two-seat ultralight with 35hp Gobler Hirth F2702 engine. D-MYAC FF 1985

SF-40 Mini Falke	5	Two-seat low-wing ultra-light monoplane with fixed tricycle u/c powered by a 60hp Sauer 1800UL engine. Prototype D-MOPE FF May 1994. SF-40B has improved performance. SF-40C fitted with 80hp Rotax 912
SF-41 Merlin		JAR-VLA version of SF-25C with shorter fuselage, shorter wings, fixed tricycle u/c and 100hp Rotax 912S2 engine. Prototype D-EESF due to fly June 2005
Total Production	*1,685*	

Scheibe SF-28A Tandem Falke F-CFTM

Schweizer   United States

Schweizer was originally formed in the 1930s as the Schweizer Metal Aircraft Corporation by three brothers – Ernest, Paul and William Schweizer. Renamed Schweizer Aircraft Corporation in 1939, it was owned and run by members of the same family until acquired by Sikorsky in mid-2004 and is based at Elmira, New York. For many years, Schweizer was the principal United States producer of single and multi-seat gliders and sailplanes. It acquired rights to the Model 269 piston-engined helicopter from Hughes on 2nd November 1983 and now builds this as the Schweizer 300C. It has also developed the larger Schweizer 330 turbine helicopter based on the 300C.

The glider business allowed Schweizer to develop a powered glider known as the SGM 2-37 (the designation signifying '2-seat Schweizer Glider – Motorised' and the 37th Schweizer design). The prototype (N36221) first flew on 21st September 1982. The SGM 2-37 combines the rear fuselage of the SGS 2-32 sailplane with SGS 1-36 wings and the 112hp Lycoming O-235 engine module of a Piper Tomahawk. It has a two-seat cockpit with a sliding canopy and a fixed tailwheel undercarriage. A total of 12 have been built (c/n 1 to 12) all of which were delivered as the TG-7A to the USAF Academy at Colorado Springs.

A further development, the SA 2-37A, has been built for specialised law enforcement and quiet surveillance work. The prototype, N3623C (c/n 1), first flew in 1986, and it has a 235hp Lycoming IO-540-W3A5D engine with extensive silencing, increased fuel capacity, a longer wing and a larger cockpit incorporating an underside equipment bay to carry cameras and sensors. 14 production examples have been completed (c/n 2 to 0015) together with four SA.2-37Bs (c/n 0017 to 0020) and deliveries have been made to the United States Coastguard, the CIA and Colombian and Mexican Air Forces as the RG-8A Condor. A variant of the SA 2-37A was unsuccessfully entered in the USAF EFS basic flight trainer competition. Schweizer has also re-engineered three RG-8As (c/n 2, 9 and 0011) as twin-boomed pusher aircraft designated RU-38A Twin Condor with two push-pull 350hp Continental GIO-550 engines mounted on the central pod fuselage and surveillance equipment fitted in the front section of each boom. The first of these (N61428) first flew on 31st May 1995. A further Twin Condor development is the SA.2-38B of which three have been built (c/n 001 to 003) and Schweizer are considering an unmanned surveillance version of the SA.2-37B.

Schweizer's major powered aircraft production programme was the Grumman G-164 Ag-Cat. This agricultural biplane was designed by Grumman in the mid-1950s and certificated on 20th January 1959. It

Schweizer TSC-1A Teal C-GOAE

is a steel tube aircraft covered by largely removable aluminium panels and was powered, initially, by a Continental W-670 radial engine. The early Ag-Cats had open cockpits, but this was soon changed to an enclosed cabin. From the outset, Schweizer built the aircraft under license. When Gulfstream American was established, it took over the Ag-Cat and prepared to move production to Savannah, Georgia, but, in early 1981, Schweizer acquired the type certificate and tooling and moved manufacture back to Elmira.

Schweizer G-164D Turbo Ag-Cat D/ST ZS-KPT

Schweizer SGM2-37 N26AF

A licence arrangement was set up for the Ag-Cat to be built by Admas Air Service in Ethiopia as the Eshet and at least eleven aircraft (c/n 001E to 011E) were completed from kits supplied by Schweizer. A number of independent conversions have been carried out. Most have involved the fitting of alternative powerplants but several aircraft have been converted for exhibition work and several have been fitted with floats and a dual passenger cockpit in place of the hopper for pleasure flights. Three Ag-Cats were converted as Twin-Cats with two Lycoming TSIO-540 engines mounted side-by-side on the nose, and the first of these (N8761H) first flew in this form in 1979. In May 1995 Schweizer sold the Ag-Cat rights to Ag-Cat Corporation owned by Jim Krepps of Malden, Missouri and the first aircraft to be built at the new factory was c/n 835B (N910MG). They completed seven aircraft but ceased production and went into receivership in 1997. The production variants of the Ag-Cat and some of the independent conversions carried out by other companies are as follows:

Schweizer G-164B Ag-Cat B 7Q-YCT

Model	Built	Notes
G-164 Ag-Cat	400	Basic aircraft with various 220hp to 450hp engines including the Continental or Gulf Coast W-670 or Pratt & Whitney R-985. 215 US gal hopper. Aircraft c/n 301 to 400 with 300hp Jacobs R755 and 245 US gal hopper. Prototype N74054 (c/n X1) FF 22 May 1957. Second prototype (N74055 c/n X2) and prod c/n 1 to 400
G-164A Super Ag-Cat	1,330	Refined model with improved performance, 300 US gal hopper and enclosed cockpit. Powered by 450hp P&W R-985 or 600hp R-1340. Production: c/n 401 to 1730
G-164B Ag-Cat B	841	G-164A with 6ft 3in longer span wings, new spray bar system and broad-chord fin. Prototype N8834H. Production: c/n 1B to 841B
G-164B Ag-Cat Super B Turbine		G-164B with 500, 680 or 750shp AG version of Pratt & Whitney PT6A turboprop
G-164C Super Ag-Cat C	44	Developed G-164A with 50-inch longer fuselage and 500 US gal hopper. Same engines as G-164A plus 525hp Continental/Page R-975. Prototype N48444 (c/n X1C) FF 27 Feb 1976. Production: c/n 2C to 44C
G-164D Ag-Cat D	24	G-164C with lengthened forward fuselage fitted with PT6A turboprop. Variants known as Turbo Ag-Cat D/T (PT6A-15), Turbo Ag-Cat D/ST (PT6A-34) and Turbo Ag-Cat D/SST (PT6A-41). Prototype N6868Q. Production: c/n 1D to 24D
G-164 Marsh Turbo Cat		Converted to Garrett TPE-331-101 turboprop
G-164 Harker Leo-Cat		Converted to Alvis Leonides piston radial
G-164 Frakes Turbo-Cat		Converted to P&W PT6A-34AG turboprop
G-164 Stage II Ag-Cat		Converted to Chrysler Stage II V-8 piston engine
G-164 Page Ag-Cat		Converted to Lycoming 600shp LTP-101 turboprop
G-164C Mid-Continent King Cat		Converted to Wright Cyclone R-1820

Another aircraft built by Schweizer was the Thurston TSC-1A Teal. This small two-seat amphibian was created by David B Thurston, based on his experience of designing Grumman's G-65 amphibian and the Colonial Skimmer (which became the Lake LA-4). Thurston set up Thurston

Aircraft Corporation at Sanford, Maine and built the TSC-1 prototype (N1968T c/n 1), which made its first flight in June 1968 powered by a 150hp Lycoming O-320-A3B engine.

The Teal gained its type certificate on 28th August 1969 and Thurston Aircraft delivered the first TSC-1A production unit (N2002T c/n 2) at the end of that year. This was followed by 13 further TSC-1As before the introduction of the TSC-1A1, which had new wing leading edge fuel tanks, a retractable tailwheel and an optional hull fuel tank.

At about this time, Schweizer bought the design and production rights and built 12 further examples (c/n 20 to 31). The Schweizer ver-sion was the TSC-1A2 Teal II and it incorporated slotted flaps, a higher gross weight and many detail changes to systems and trim. In 1976, Schweizer sold the whole project, including airframes c/n 32, 33 and 34, to Teal Aircraft Corporation of Canada. Teal moved production to St Augustine, Florida, and announced that a higher-powered version – the 180hp Marlin – would soon be available. However, by the time air-craft number 38 had been completed, Teal was in financial trouble and production was suspended. One further aircraft to the Teal design was built in South Africa. Named the Patchen Explorer 2000, this was fitted with a fixed tricycle undercarriage and a large omnivision cabin.

Scintex   France

The Société Scintex was formed by Jean-Michel Vernhes in 1956 and a production line was established to build the Piel CP.301 Emeraude for French club and private owners. Initially, the Scintex aircraft was a standard Emeraude with upward-opening cabin doors but, in 1960, the CP.301C was introduced and this featured a single-piece clearview sliding canopy. Claude Piel, who had been working for SCANOR joined Scintex in 1959 and the company went on to introduce the Super Emeraude which had a strengthened airframe for aerobatic certifica-tion and a generally cleaned-up layout. The majority of Scintex Emer-audes and Super Emeraudes were built in the Menavia factory at Clermont Ferrand and several CP.320s were constructed by amateurs. The following Super Emeraude variants were built commercially:

Scintex CP.1310-C3 Super Emeraude G-ASNI

Model	Built	Notes
CP.1310-C3	23	Strengthened Emeraude with revised canopy, tail and engine cowling, powered by one 100hp Continental O-200-A. Prototype F-BJVJ (c/n 900) FF 20 Apr 1962
CP.1315-C3	17	CP.1310 with 105hp Potez 4E-20 engine
CP.1330	3	CP.1310 with 116hp Lycoming O-230-C2A engine

Scintex attempted to broaden its product base in the early 1960s and flew the first ML-145 Rubis (F-BJMA) on 24th May 1961, powered by a 145hp Continental O-300-B engine. The Rubis was a four-seat low-wing cabin tourer and, unusually, featured a retractable tailwheel undercarriage at a time when most competing types were using tricy-cle gear. In its production version it was designated ML-250 with a 250hp Lycoming O-540-A1D5 engine, larger tail surfaces and a five-seat interior. Only five production aircraft were sold and Scintex aban-

Scintex ML-250 Rubis F-BJMG

doned production in late 1964. At the same time, they subcontracted all Super Emeraudes to CAARP at Beynes and eventually CAARP built the Super Emeraude in its own right.

Emeraude serial numbers were allocated by the Piel bureau and small batches were used by Scintex for the early CP.301A production.

The CP.301C production started at c/n 511 and continued to c/n 594. Menavia-built Super Emeraudes had serials running from c/n 900 to 932 and CAARP-built aircraft were c/n 933 to 942. The Scintex-built Rubis prototypes were c/n 01 to 03 and production aircraft were c/n 101 to 105.

Scottish Aviation — United Kingdom

Prestwick-based Scottish Aviation was formed in 1935 and shortly after the war they moved into aircraft production with the five-seat high-wing Prestwick Pioneer. The prototype (VL515 c/n 101) made its first flight on 5th November 1947. Five examples of the Pioneer were registered as civil aircraft for demonstration purposes, but the majority of the 58 units built (c/n 102 to 159) were delivered to the Royal Air Force and the Malaysian and Ceylon Air Forces as utility transports powered by a 550hp Alvis Leonides radial engine.

The success of the Pioneer encouraged Scottish Aviation to move on to a rather larger transport – the Twin Pioneer. This was a high-wing design with good short field performance, a fixed tailwheel undercarriage and 16 passenger seats in its square-section fuselage. The prototype (G-ANTP c/n 501) first flew at Prestwick on 25th June 1955 and was fitted with a pair of 570hp Alvis Leonides 503/8 radial piston engines. During later development, these were replaced by 640hp Leonides 531/8B engines and this was the version that the company sold to the RAF as the Twin Pioneer CC.2. Some 86 production aircraft were completed (with serial numbers c/n 502 to 590, excluding c/n 569, 585 and the static test c/n 506). A batch of 15 went to the Malaysian Air Force while 32 were sold to civil customers, mainly in the Middle and Far East and Australia.

In February 1970, Beagle Aircraft Ltd went into liquidation and Scottish Aviation took over the B.125 Bulldog military trainer project that had, by this time, been chosen for an order from the Swedish Air Force. The Scottish Aviation prototype Bulldog (G-AXIG c/n 002) was first flown on 14th February 1971 after which 331 production units were completed for sale to various military users including the RAF (135 aircraft), Sweden (78), Nigeria (37), Malaysia (15) and Ghana (13). Production Bulldogs were serialled from c/n 101 to 431. The company

Scottish Aviation Bulldog NX516BG

also built a single prototype of the Bullfinch, the prototype of which (G-BDOG c/n BH200-381) was flown on 20th August 1976. It had a longer fuselage with four seats, increased wingspan and a retractable tricycle undercarriage – but Scottish Aviation was not successful in finding either military or civil customers for it.

Apart from primary aircraft manufacture, Scottish Aviation had achieved a reputation for overhaul and subcontract work having refurbished many Sabres, Beech 18s, Canadair T-33s and CF-100s for the Canadian Armed Forces and through building subassemblies for Lockheed's C-130 Hercules. One major subcontract was for manufacture of wings for the Handley Page Jetstream business aircraft. The pressurized 18/20-seat HP.137 was powered by a pair of 850shp Turboméca Astazou XIV.C constant-speed turboprops and Handley Page flew the first Jetstream (G-ATXH c/n 198) at Radlett on 18th August 1967. While it was a most attractive design and gained good advance orders, a great

Scottish Aviation Twin Pioneer G-APRS

deal of re-engineering and weight reduction took place before Jet-streams could start to be delivered to customers. Consequently, by mid-1969, Handley Page was in the midst of a financial crisis.

Cammell Laird, the parent company of Scottish Aviation, agreed to invest new working capital of some £1.25 million but, on 8th August 1969, Handley Page was forced to call in a receiver and Jetstream production was temporarily carried on by a new operating company named Handley Page Aircraft Ltd. Great hopes of returning to solvency rested on an order for Garrett TPE331-powered C-10 Jetstreams placed by the US Air Force but this was cancelled – with the result that all the Mk 3M airframes which were in course of completion had to be abandoned and the financial rescue operation foundered. In addition to the Jetstream prototypes (c/n 198 to 201) Handley Page had built 40 complete aircraft and 33 incomplete airframes including the USAF order. These carried serial numbers c/n 202 to 251 and c/n 281 to 287.

The Official Receiver had been called in at the end of February 1970 and, later that year, all the stocks of production components and design documentation were sold to Terravia Trading Services who formed Jetstream Aircraft Ltd The intention was to build Mark 1 aircraft from existing components and the Mark 200 (powered by Astazou XVI engines) as a completely new model. Terravia was not able to establish the complex production facility necessary to meet future production demands but a contract was awarded for 26 Jetstream T.1 trainers for the RAF. In February 1972 all production rights were transferred to Scottish Aviation.

Scottish Aviation was able to fulfil the RAF order by using the incomplete airframes from the Handley Page line together with five new fuselages (c/n 422 to 426) that were built from scratch. The Jetstream T.1 had higher-powered 996shp Astazou XVI.D engines, more extensive cockpit glazing and numerous detail improvements. Some 12 aircraft were later converted as T.2s for the Royal Navy with nose-mounted MEL-E190 radar units. The impetus of the RAF order allowed Scottish Aviation to develop the aircraft into the civil Jetstream 31, which used the wing designed for the Jetstream 3M with new environmental and electrical systems and 940shp Garrett TPE331-10UG-514H engines. The prototype Jetstream 3001 (G-JSSD c/n 227) was converted from an existing airframe purchased in the United States and it was first flown in its new form on 28th March 1980.

The CAA type certificate was awarded to the Jetstream 31 in June 1982 and production aircraft commenced with G-TALL (c/n 601). While a few corporate aircraft have been built, most Jetstream 31s have been sold to third-level commuter carriers in the United States. British Aerospace introduced the Jetstream Super 31 (Model 3201) in 1987, the first production unit being c/n 790. The last standard Jetstream 31 was c/n 839 and production was suspended in 1994 at c/n 986. The Super 31 has 1,020shp TPE331-12 engines with four-blade Rotol pro-

Scottish Aviation Jetstream 31 LV-ZPW

pellers, a redesigned wing, increased fuel capacity and an increase of 882 lb in take-off weight. The Super 31 was sold in corporate transport form as the 'Grand Prix Formula I' with a luxury cabin with 8 to 10 seats and as the 'Formula III' fitted with 12 to 18 seats. Jetstream 31 designations identify the country of delivery and include the following models:

3100 Various	3109 Italy	32EP United States
3101 United States	3110 Sweden	3202 United Kingdom
3102 United Kingdom	3111 Saudi Arabia (AF)	3206 France
3103 Germany	3112 Canada	3207 Australia
3104 United Kingdom	3116 Switzerland	3212 Canada
3106 France	3117 Japan	3216 Switzerland
3107 Australia	3200 Various	3217 Japan
3108 Netherlands	3201 United States	

The final Scottish Aviation development was the stretched 29-seat Jetstream 41 with a generally scaled-up airframe and using a pair of 1,500shp Garrett TPE331-14 engines. The prototype Jetstream 41 (G-GCJL c/n 41001) was first flown on 25th September 1991 and production had reached c/n 41104 by the time production ceased in 1997. Virtually all the 104-aircraft production run went to commuter airlines as the Model 4101 (USA), 4102 (UK), 4112 (Canada), 4121 (South Africa), 4122 (Thailand Army), 4124 (Hong Kong Govt) and 4100 (other customers). A further stretched model, the Jetstream 51, was planned but not built.

Seabird   Australia/Jordan

Seabird Aviation Australia Pty Ltd designed the Seabird Seeker as a dedicated surveillance aircraft for civil and military use to fulfil roles met by helicopters – but at lower cost. The Seeker is a strut-braced high-wing aircraft with a low-set tubular boom rear fuselage, a tailwheel undercarriage and a pusher engine installation. The main fuselage module, fitted with side-by-side seating for two, is set well ahead of the wing with extensive cabin glazing to give maximum vision for search missions. The prototype SB5 Sentinel (VH-SBI, c/n 89001) was first flown on 1st October 1989 powered by a Norton rotary engine and the later SB5E (VH-SBU, c/n 90003) had an Emdair engine. The definitive production version, which has been certificated to FAR Part 23, is the SB7L-360 Seeker, powered by a 160hp Lycoming O-360-B2C and the first example (initially with a 116hp O-235 engine) flew on 6th June 1991. In September 2003 Seabird Aviation entered a joint venture with the Royal Jordanian Air Academy and formed Seabird Aviation Jordan to assemble the SB7L at Marka Airport near Amman. The first two deliveries were made to the Iraq Air Force in November 2004. At that time six aircraft had been built including prototypes (c/n 89001, 90002, 90003, 91004, 92005 and 070006). The individual serial number is normally prefixed by the year built. Future developments include the

SB-9 Stormer, a light ground-attack version and the Seahawk five-seat surveillance model, both of which will be powered by the R-R Allison 250 turboprop engine.

Seabird Seeker SB7L-360 VH-ZIG

SECAN
France

The Société d' Etudes et de Constructions Aéronavales (SECAN) was the aircraft manufacturing subsidiary of the Société des Usines Chausson and, in 1946, it built the prototype of the all-metal four-seat SUC-10 Courlis. This first aircraft (F-WBBF c/n 01) took to the air on 9th May 1946. It was a high-wing touring monoplane with twin booms supporting the tail unit and a 190hp Mathis G8R engine in the rear fuselage pusher installation. The Courlis was fitted with a fixed tricycle undercarriage but it was intended that this should be made retractable in later variants of the aircraft.

The Courlis eventually went into production at Genevilliers and Le Havre and a total of 144 airframes were completed of which a number went to South America. It appears that, because of considerable difficulty with the Mathis engine, many of the airframes were never completed with engines and were probably eventually scrapped. Indeed, the problems and incidents that arose from the Mathis engine installation in the Courlis resulted in the type certificate for this powerplant being withdrawn by the French Air Ministry. One aircraft was flown with a 220hp Mathis but this did nothing to help SECAN arrest the declining fortunes of the Courlis and production was discontinued.

A production batch of 500 Courlis was launched but only 144 were completed (c/n 1 to 144) and only 53 machines were actually regis-

SECAN SUC-10 Courlis F-BBXY

tered in France. A 1961 move by the Bureau d'Etudes Navales et Aéronautiques to revive the design as the SUC-11G Super Courlis with a 240hp Continental O-470M engine was abandoned with only a prototype (F-WEVZ) being built.

SG Aviation
Italy

Now one of the foremost producers of light aircraft in Europe, SG Aviation (named after founder Giovanni Salsedo) is based at Sabaudia near Rome. It started in 1989 by adopting the Pottier P.220 all-metal two-seat design (which has also been built as the Evektor Eurostar, Aero AT-3 etc) and they flew a prototype of their SG Storm engineered to JAR/VLA standards in March 1991. The Storm is produced either as a factory-complete or kit aircraft and approximately 800 have been sold including 33 Storm RGs. It is an all-metal, low-wing aircraft with side-by-side seating and a fixed undercarriage (except in the RG version), which can be either tailwheel or tricycle to the customer's requirement. A number of models have been produced as follows:

Model	Notes
Storm 280E	Standard Storm powered by one 110hp Cont O-200. 1,144 lb TOGW
Storm 280G	Storm 280E powered by one 80hp Rotax 912
Storm 280SI	Storm 280E with 992 lb (450kg) TOGW and 80hp Rotax 912 engine
Storm 280RG	Storm 280SI with modified short-span wings and retractable tricycle undercarriage. Powered by 100hp Rotax 912S
Storm 300 Special	Storm with redesigned high-speed wing with Fowler flaps and frise ailerons. Rotax 914 or Midwest AE.110 engine. 1,255 lb TOGW
Storm 320E	Storm 300 Spl. With 100hp Cont O-200 engine, 1,144 lb TOGW
Storm Century	Storm 300 Special with wing tanks, rear cabin baggage compartment, longer engine cowling, 1,232 lb TOGW.
Storm 400 Special	Storm 300 Special with optional two rear seats, 1,870 lb TOGW. Powered by one Lycoming O-320

SG Aviation Storm 300

Storm 400TI	Storm 400 with single rear seat and 1,587 lb TOGW powered by 116hp Lycoming O-235-N2C

In addition, SG Aviation supplies the SG Sea Storm, which is a kit-built amphibian with a pusher engine and a glassfibre hull with strut-braced metal wings. An all-composite version has also been made available. The Sea Storm, which was introduced in 1999, is sold in two versions – the two-seat Sea Storm Z2 powered by a 100hp Rotax 912ULS engine and the four-seat Sea Storm Z4 that has longer-span wings and uses a 210hp Lycoming O-360. 29 Sea Storms had been sold by the end of 2004. The third model from SG Aviation, first announced in 2003, is the Rally 105, which is, again, sold as a kit. It is a strut-braced high-wing two-seater with a fixed tricycle undercarriage. The 450kg ultralight model is powered by an 80hp Rotax 582 engine although a higher-weight version with a turbocharged 100hp Rotax 912S engine is also available. It has a composite fuselage and either composite or metal wings.

Short Brothers   United Kingdom

The long-established company, Short Brothers & Harland Ltd, emerged from World War Two with specialised experience in building flying boats. Their first postwar design was a light civil amphibian – the SA.6 Sealand.

The Sealand was a seven-passenger all-metal aircraft with a high wing and a tailwheel undercarriage whose main units retracted into the fuselage sides. The prototype (G-AIVX c/n SH.1555) was first flown on 22nd January 1948 and was powered by a pair of 345hp Gipsy Queen 70-2 in-line engines. The production Sealand, using 340hp Gipsy Queen 70-4 engines, was built at the Short Bros. factory at Rochester and a total of 24 aircraft was built (c/n SH.1562 to SH.1575 and c/n SH.1760 to SH.1769) between 1949 and November 1953. Customers included the Indian Navy (10) and the Yugoslav Air Force together with Shell Petroleum who used the Sealand in Borneo and Venezuela.

Shorts' next civil project was the SC.7. In 1958, the company had acquired the rights to the Miles-designed HDM.105. This was an aerodynamic vehicle to test the high aspect ratio wing concepts of the French Hurel Dubois company and it used the fuselage and tail of a Miles Aerovan married to the long, narrow HDM wings. Shorts went into a complete redesign, based on the HDM.106 studies carried out by Miles and abandoned all but the basic concepts of the HDM.105 to produce a light freighter, known initially as the PD.36 and then christened the SC.7 Skyvan. The SC.7 had a square section fuselage with a rear loading ramp, fixed tricycle undercarriage and twin fins – and the prototype (G-ASCN c/n SH.1828), which flew on 17th January 1963, was powered by a pair of 390hp Continental GTSIO-520 piston engines. In fact, Shorts had already concluded that turboprops should be used on the Skyvan and G-ASCN was soon re-engined with 554shp Turboméca Astazou IIs.

In its production form, with square windows and modified rudders and nosewheel, it became the Turbo Skyvan (later Skyvan 2), fitted with the 637shp Astazou X – and seventeen of this initial version were completed (c/n SH.1829 to SH.1845). The Astazou engine had certain shortcomings, however, and the Skyvan 3 (and its 22-passenger equivalent, the Skyliner) was soon developed with 757shp Garrett TPE331-201A engines. A total of 136 of this model (c/n SH.1846 to SH.1981) were built and ten of the Skyvan 2s were refitted with the Garrett powerplant to upgrade them to Series 3 standard.

The Skyvan gave Shorts an ideal entry into the light commuter aircraft market that was developing in the early 1970s and the design of the Skyliner was stretched to 33-passenger capacity to become the SD.330. This also involved some alterations to the wings, a retractable undercarriage embodying external gear pods, and installation of 1,120shp United Aircraft of Canada PT6A-45 turboprops. The SD.330

Shorts SC-7 Skyvan 9M-PIH

Shorts SD.360 G-SSWE

prototype (G-BSBH c/n SH.3000) made its maiden flight at Sydenham on 22nd August 1974 and was followed by a production prototype (c/n SH.3001) in December 1975. Full production followed and the SD.330 achieved good acceptance in America with commuter carriers and with the United States Air Force who took delivery of an initial batch of 18 C-23A Sherpa freighters. The main production run consisted of 123 civil and military aircraft (c/n SH.3002 to SH.3124) the last of which was completed in March 1988. A new series of 16 aircraft (c/n SH.3201 to SH.3216) was initiated in 1990 to cover an order for additional C-23B Sherpas for the United States Air Force. A further batch of serial numbers (c/n SH.3401 to SH.3428) was allocated to 28 SD.360s acquired in the commercial market and converted to C-23B Sherpas by the fitting of a new rear fuselage and twin fin tail unit. The SD.360 was a development of the SD.330 with a longer 36-passenger fuselage, swept fin and 1,327shp PT6A-65R engines and this sold well

to the commuter air carriers. The prototype SD.360 was G-BSBH (c/n SH.3600), which was first flown on 1st June 1981, and production ran from c/n 3601 to c/n 3764 (a final batch from c/n 3765 to 3771 not being completed). As noted earlier, 28 of these were converted to C-23B Sherpa standard.

During 1987, Shorts released details of two advanced local service turboprop airliners, the NRA-90A and NRA-90B, which it was working on in cooperation with De Havilland Canada. One of these featured a large pusher turboprop in the tail, but this cooperation was limited and Shorts went on to develop the design of its FJX 48-seat fanjet-powered regional airliner. As it turned out, in October 1989 Shorts was acquired by Bombardier Inc. This resulted in abandonment of the FJX project and Shorts became involved in production of the competitive Bombardier-Canadair 'RJ' Regional Jet together with Bombardier's successful Learjet 45 series

SIAI-Marchetti   Italy

Postwar Italy offered few opportunities for aircraft manufacturers but the Societa Idrovolanti Alta Italia Savoia Marchetti, a company established in 1915 and famous for its wartime SM.79 Sparviero three-engined bomber, had been fortunate in securing orders for its SM.95 airliner for Alitalia and for the SM.102 light communications aircraft. In March 1959, however, the company entered into a licence arrangement to build the Nardi FN.333.

The FN.333, designed by Nardi in Milan, was originally a three-seat amphibian with twin booms, a pusher engine and a forward fuselage that was reminiscent of the Republic Seabee. The prototype (I-KISS), powered by a 145hp Continental engine, flew on 4th December 1952 and on 8th December 1954 Nardi flew the enlarged four-seat FN.333S, which had a 225hp Continental C-125 engine and a rather unusual wing-folding arrangement. Two further prototypes (I-EUST and I-RAIG), with 240hp Continental O-470H engines and without the wing folding, were built by Fiat for Nardi, the first of which flew on 14th October 1956. In March 1959, Nardi granted a manufacturing licence to SIAI-Marchetti who proceeded with a series of 23 production examples powered by the 250hp Continental IO-470-P engine. Many of these went to the USA and SIAI reached agreement with the North Star Co of New Jersey to import and assemble the aircraft for North American customers. The Lane-SIAI Company of Dallas, Texas marketed the FN.333 Riviera during the mid-1960s with limited success and the Riviera production line closed in 1966. Serial numbers allocated to production Rivieras were c/n 001 to 009, 12bis and 101 to 111 – a total of 21 aircraft.

SIAI-Marchetti produced a batch of 83 SM.1019 turboprop versions of the Cessna Bird Dog (c/n 1-001 to 1-083), all but three of which went to the Italian Army, but it also turned its attention to the four-seat light aircraft sector in 1964 and produced the all-metal S.205. This was somewhat larger than the competing Piper Cherokee and was offered with 180hp or 200hp Lycoming engines and the option of either a fixed or retractable tricycle undercarriage. Production of the S.205 built up rapidly with over two-thirds of the first delivery batch going to export customers. SIAI was again anxious to sell in the United States so an agreement was reached with Alexandre Berger.

Berger had brought together the Waco company and the engine manufacturers, Jacobs and Franklin under the umbrella of his holding company, Allied Aircraft Industries. The newly-constituted Waco Aircraft Company was to assemble the S.205 and to market it as the S.220 Sirius powered by a 220hp Franklin engine. SIAI eventually delivered over 60 'green' airframes to the Pottstown, Pa. factory of Waco and later aircraft were sold as the five-passenger S.220-5 Vela. At least two Velas (N952W, c/n 4-152 and C-FWRJ, c/n 387) were fitted with a swept tail, modified windshield and turbocharged Franklin engine.

A new version of the S.205 was announced in May 1967. This was the S.208, which featured a standard S.205 airframe with five seats and the retractable undercarriage. A 260hp Lycoming engine was standard equipment and, of the 97 built by SIAI, some 45 were delivered to the Italian Air Force as the S.208M. Production of the S.205 and S.208 came to a halt in 1972 but SIAI reopened the line in 1977 when the Aero Club d'Italia placed an order for 40 of the S.205/20R model and this batch was completed in 1979. A total of 346 of all the S.205/208 variants were built (excluding three prototypes). Details of the S.205 and S.208 variants are as follows:

Model	Notes
S.205/18F	Low-wing all-metal four-seat touring aircraft with fixed tricycle undercarriage, powered by one 180hp Lycoming O-360-A1A engine. Prototype I-SIAK (c/n 001) FF 4 May 1965
S.205/18R	S.205/18F with retractable undercarriage
S.205/20F	S.205/18F with 200hp Lycoming IO-360-A1A engine
S.205/20R	S.205/20F with retractable undercarriage
S.205/22R	S.205/20R with 220hp Franklin 6A-350.C1 engine. Also known as the Sirius or Vela in the USA
S.206	Proposed six-seat S.205. Not built
S.208	S.205/20R with five seats and 260hp Lycoming O-540-E4A engine. Prototype I-SIAG (c/n 1-01 formerly c/n 391)
S.208M	Military S.208 for Italian Air Force

S.205 aircraft were approved for production and built in batches, and the first digit of the serial number identifies the batch concerned. The three prototypes were c/n 001 to 003 and the production aircraft were – c/n 101 to 110, c/n 211 to 240, c/n 341 to 399, c/n 3-100, c/n 4-101 to 4-301 and c/n 5-320 to 5-306. The new 1977 production ran from c/n 06-001 to 06-040. It is believed that all production S.208s were re-serialled within the above mentioned blocks with new numbers c/n 1-01 to 1-15, 2-16 to 2-50, 3-51 to 3-90, 4-51 to 4-52 and 4-60 to 4-64.

The S.205 airframe also gave rise to the S.210, which was, essentially, a twin-engined version with a full six-seat fuselage and a swept vertical tail. The prototype (I-SJAP, c/n 001) was fitted with a pair of turbocharged 200hp Lycoming TIO-360-A1B engines and first flew on 18th February 1970. It later appeared as the S.210M military version and was followed, in 1971, by a second flying prototype (I-SJAW c/n 003), which had larger rear windows, de-icing boots and wingtip tanks. SIAI had plans for selling the S.210 in the United States as the Waco TS-250-6 Nova, but this was abandoned and no further S.210s were built. SIAI also decided that it needed a two-seat trainer for its expanding light aircraft line and joined with FFA in Switzerland to design the S.202 Bravo. The S.202 was a low-wing two-seat all-metal monoplane with a fixed tricycle undercarriage and two seats plus a rear bench seat

SIAI-Marchetti S.205-22/R D-EGEE

with the cockpit enclosed by a large sliding bubble canopy. It was prototyped by both SIAI-Marchetti and FFA and the first prototype (HB-HEA c/n V-1), built by FFA, made its maiden flight on 7th March 1969 followed by the SIAI prototype, I-SJAI c/n 01, on 7th May. The Swiss AS-202 was fitted with a 150hp Lycoming engine and the Italian prototype used a lower-rated 115hp Lycoming. As it turned out, SIAI did not continue with the venture and the Bravo was built in series by FFA (and is described under that company's entry).

SIAI-Marchetti entered the helicopter market by way of a 35% interest in Silvercraft SpA acquired in 1965 and this resulted in the two/three-seat Silvercraft SH-4 helicopter being developed as the SIAI SH-4. This little helicopter had first flown in March 1965 and was powered by a 160hp Franklin 6A-350-D piston engine. An agricultural version with spray bars was designated SH-4A. Production SH-4s were built at Sesto Calende and had reached c/n 21 when the line was terminated. SIAI also built a prototype of a developed SH-4, the SH-200 (I-SILD), which used a 205hp Lycoming IO-360-C1A engine and had a T-tail.

During 1964, Aviamilano of Milan had built the first example of the new F.250 all-metal design from Stelio Frati. In the F.250 the wings of Frati's F.8L Falco were married to the F.15 Picchio fuselage with the enclosed cabin cut back and replaced by a clearview sliding cockpit canopy. The first aircraft was followed by two prototypes of the F.260

SIAI-Marchetti FN.333 Riviera N95DR

SIAI-Marchetti SF.260C HB-EZZ

powered by the larger Lycoming O-540-E engine. However, Aviamilano decided not to build the F.260 and SIAI obtained a licence and started to build it as the SF.260 as an intermediate trainer for military and civil customers and took full ownership of the type certificate when Aviamilano subsequently abandoned aviation work.

Production got under way, following FAA certification on 1st April 1966, and initially, the SF.260 was built for civil sale with a few being exported to the United States where they appealed to owners who were attracted by the sleek Italian lines – even though the SF.260 was an expensive aircraft to buy. It was marketed as the Waco TS-250-3 Meteor and the American agents envisaged that a special American version with a Franklin 6AS-350A engine would be sold as the TS-250-3F Meteor 2. This did not happen and all the US imports were delivered with Lycoming engines. A batch of seven SF.260s went to the Belgian national airline, SABENA, for pilot training and Alitalia also bought some for its training school.

The cost of the SF.260 made it more marketable to military rather than private users, which resulted in SIAI developing the SF.260MX military variant. In its SF.260W Warrior guise it was given a hardened wing allowing ground-attack operations equipped with a variety of underwing stores and an equivalent maritime support version, the Sea Warrior, was also marketed. One major customer was the Philippines Air Force where a local derivative, the XT-001, was constructed – but it is believed that only the prototype was flown. Another large order came from the Libyan Air Force, reputed to have been for 240 aircraft. The SF.260W and SF.260M aircraft were tailored to the specific control and instrument layout favoured by each military user. The SF.260E was an upgraded model, entered unsuccessfully in the USAF's EFS (Enhanced Flight Screener) competition in 1991/92 but it is now the standard piston-engine variant on sale to new customers. SIAI went on to develop the SF.260TP which is a turboprop version of the basic aircraft powered by a 350shp Allison 250B-17C engine housed in a lengthened nose and around 60 have been completed including some upgrades of existing customer aircraft. On 1st January 1981, SIAI-Marchetti became a subsidiary of the Agusta SpA Group and became the division responsible for all fixed wing aircraft development and production. Among other projects, it developed the SF.600TP Canguro (detailed in the section on General Avia). The company later passed into the group structure of Finmeccanica and was then acquired by Aermacchi on 1st January 1997 at which time Aermacchi also acquired all rights to the Valmet Redigo turboprop trainer and liaison aircraft.

Because of the customising of interiors and systems, SIAI, in most cases, allocated a specific type designation to each customer. They adopted a dual method of normal c/ns (described later) together with separate batches of serial numbers for each customer. These had a numerical prefix for each customer followed by a sequential number starting at 001. Examples are the 36 SF.260MBs delivered to Belgium (numbered 10-01 to 10-36) and the nine SF.260MZs for Zambia (12-01 to 12-09). Owing to the high military content of SF.260 production, complete details are sometimes elusive, but, so far as can be ascertained, the principal prefixes and customers for the SF.260 series have been as follows:

Prefix	Customer	Model	No sold	Prefix	Customer	Model	No sold
10	Belgium	260MB	36	39	Singapore	260W	11
11	Congo/Zaire	260MC	21	40	Italy	260AM	22
12	Zambia	260MZ	9	41	Alitalia	260D	5
14	Thailand	260MT	13	42	Civil	260C	
15	Philippines	260WP	16	43	Burundi	260W	4
15	Philippines	260MP	30	44	Civil	260C/D	
16	Italy	260AM	45	45	Brunei	260W	2
17	Dubai	260WD	1	46	Martini Racing	260C	3
19	Tunisia	260CT	18	47	Alpi Eagles	260C	4
20	SIAI-Marchetti	260C	1	48	SIAI – USA team	260C	9
21	Myanmar	260MB	20	60	Sri Lanka	260TP	5
22	Zimbabwe	260W	16	61	Haiti	260TP	6
23	Zimbabwe	260C	17	62	Dubai	260TP	6
24	Eire	260WE	11	n/a	Turkey	260D	41
26	Civil (USA)			n/a	Ethiopia	260TP	12
27	Comores	3260W	3	n/a	Zimbabwe	260F	6
28	SIAI-Marchetti	260SW	1	n/a	Venezuela	260E	12
29	Libya	260WL	240	n/a	Uruguay	260E	13
31	Bolivia	260CB	6	n/a	Philippines	260TP	18
33	Thailand	260W	6	n/a	Uganda	260M	3
35	SIAI-Marchetti	260C	1	n/a	Mauretania	260E	4
36	Somalia	260C	6	n/a	Mexico	260E	30
38	SIAI-Marchetti	260C	1				

Details of the SF.260 variants are as follows:

Model	Notes
SF.250	Aviamilano-built all-metal low-wing three-seat trainer/tourer with 250hp Lycoming O-540-A1D5 engine, retractable tricycle u/c and tip tanks. 2,420 lb TOGW. Prototype I-RAIE/I-ZUAR (c/n 501) FF 15 Jul 1964
F.260	F.250 with 2,425 lb TOGW and 260hp Lycoming O-540-E4A5 engine. Two built by Aviamilano, I-ALLA c/n 502 and HB-ELP c/n 503

SF.260A	Production F.260 by SIAI-Marchetti. Fully aerobatic
SF.260B	Improved civil SF.260 with SF.260M airframe mods
SF.260C	SF.260B with 2,430 lb TOGW, increased fuel capacity, increased wingspan and further SF.260M structural improvements
SF.260D	Improved SF.260C with 260hp Lycoming IO-540-D4A5 or AEIO-540-D4A5 engine and strengthened airframe
SF.260E	SF.260D with 260hp IO-540-E4AF engine, enlarged cockpit canopy, semi-automatic fuel system, and instrumentation changes. 2,646 lb TOGW
SF.260MX	Military SF.260 with strengthened airframe and new cockpit layout. Prototype I-SJAV (c/n 3-79) FF May 1972
SF.260M	Production military SF.260
SF.260W	Warrior. SF.260M with strengthened airframe and underwing hardpoints for ground-attack stores. 2,866 lb TOGW
SF.260SW	Sea Warrior. SF.260W with specialised underwing and wingtip stores for maritime patrol and SAR
SF.260TP	SF.260M fitted with 350shp Allison 250B-17 turboprop. Prototype I-FAIR c/n 510 FF 8 Jul 1980

By mid-2004 around 850 aircraft had been built. The first three Aviamilano aircraft were c/n 501 to 503 and the first SIAI-Marchetti batch was c/n 101 to 125. Thereafter, SIAI introduced a production batch prefix with c/ns 2-61 to 2-75, 3-76 to 3-84, and then the military batches 10-01 to 10-36, 11-01 to 11-12, 12-01 to 12-09, 13-01 to 13-16, 14-01 to 14-12, 15-01 to 15-46, 16-01 to 16-20, 17-01 and 20-01. At this point a simple sequential numbering system returned with c/ns from 225 to 850 (but these aircraft also had a customer number such as '36-01' in addition to the basic c/n). With the takeover of SIAI-Marchetti by Aermacchi, SF.260s adopted the Aermacchi system of a number in the overall Aermacchi sequence followed by an SF.260 number starting at 2001. Thus, the first aircraft (for the Uruguayan Air Force) was c/n 6911/2001 and production had reached around c/n 6945/2025 by mid-2004. The company is currently engaged in production of a further batch of 30 SF.260EAs for the Italian Air Force.

SIAT   Germany

In 1950, the long established Siebel Flugzeugwerke GmbH merged with Algemeine-Transport-Anlagen GmbH to form Siebelwerke-ATG GmbH. This was subsequently known as SIAT and was eventually absorbed into Messerschmitt-Bölkow-Blohm (MBB). SIAT designed a low-wing four-seat all-metal training and sporting aircraft known as the SIAT-222 and the prototype (D-EKYT c/n 222-1) flew on 15th May 1961. It had a large blister canopy and a fixed tricycle undercarriage and was equipped with a 180hp Lycoming O-360 engine.

The SIAT-222 was the precursor of the SIAT-223, which had a shorter fuselage, redesigned wing and larger vertical tail surfaces – and was successfully entered in a WGL Competition for a new club aircraft. The first SIAT-223 (SIAT-223V-1, D-ECRO c/n 001) made its maiden flight on 1st March 1967. This was followed by three further prototypes (SIAT-223V-2 to V-4, c/n 002 to 004). Named Messerschmitt-Bölkow-Blohm Flamingo, the aircraft went into production fitted with a 200hp Lycoming IO-360-C1A engine but most of the orders came from military or governmental customers outside Germany. Two main types were produced – the SIAT-223A-1 aerobatic 2+2-seat trainer and the SIAT-223K-1 single-seat aerobatic version with an AIO-360-A1A engine.

Deliveries included 15 for the Turkish Air League and 10 for Swissair for use in their pilot training programme. SIAT serial numbers 005 to 101 were not used and production ran from c/n 011 to 017 (SIAT-223A-1) and c/n 018 to 035 (SIAT-223K-1). C/n 036 to 050 were not allocated. In addition, Farner at Grenchen in Switzerland built 17 examples of the SIAT-223K-1 for the Syrian Air Force (c/n 101 to 117).

In 1971, the company discontinued production of the SIAT-223 and handed over the whole programme to Hispano Aviacion in Spain (which shortly afterwards became part of the CASA Group). CASA built 50 aircraft (c/n 051 to 100), of which the first nine (-223A-1s) were used by the Spanish Air Force. 14 further -223A-1 aircraft (c/n 060 to 073) were converted to SIAT-223K-1 standard and delivered to the Syrian Air Force and the final 27 airframes (c/n 074 to 100) were delivered to Syria in kit form. Some SIAT-223s have seen service with private owners and rights to the design were passed back by CASA to Flugzeug-Union-Sud (an MBB subsidiary), which converted one CASA-built machine (D-EFWC c/n 051) as the MBB Flamingo Trainer T.1, which it intended to sell on the civil market. No production resulted from this. This particular aircraft was subsequently fitted with a Porsche PFM.3200 engine and designated SIAT-223M-4 with the new serial c/n 151. The total of all SIAT, Farner and CASA built -223 aircraft (including prototypes) was 96.

SIAT 223 Flamingo D-EHQI

Swearingen SJ30-2 N404SJ

Sino Swearingen — United States/Taiwan

In the mid-1980s, the ever-inventive Ed Swearingen designed a small six-seat business jet which was to be developed with Gulfstream Aerospace as the SA-30 Fanjet (later SA-30 Gulfjet). In 1989, Gulfstream left the programme and a new partnership with the Jaffe Group (Swearingen/Jaffe) was formed with the aircraft being re-designated SJ30. On 13th February 1991 the prototype (N30SJ c/n 0001) was flown and in the development process it was modified to become the SJ30-2 with a 58-inch fuselage stretch, a modified four-section windshield, anhedralled wing, new slats and 2,300 lbst Williams-Rolls-Royce FJ44A-2A turbofans. In this form it first flew on 8th November 1996. By this time, Jaffe had left the partnership and in 1996 a new organisation, Sino Swearingen Aircraft Company, was formed with Taiwanese backing. The US company was incorporated in 1999 with a main production plant at San Antonio, Texas. Work on the SJ30-2 became protracted but N30SJ was retired and a second prototype (N138BF c/n 0002) was flown on 30th November 2000. This crashed during high-speed testing on 26th April 2003 but by this time c/n 0003 (N30SJ) had flown (on 6th March 2003) and a further prototype (N404SJ c/n 0004) followed on 12th October 2003. Two static test airframes (c/n TF-2 and TF-3) have also been built and one further development aircraft (c/n 0005) is to be used in the programme. Testing continues toward certification and first deliveries in 2006.

SIPA — France

The Société Industrielle pour l'Aéronautique (SIPA) was formed in 1938 and was tasked by the Germans with production of the Arado Ar 396 during the years of the Occupation. Once France was liberated in 1944, the Ar 396 continued as the SIPA S-10 and several versions (S.11, S.111, S.12, S.121) were produced as trainers for the French Air Force. However, the company was turning its attention to types that could be sold in peacetime France. The first civil models were the S.20 low-wing trainer, S.50 club trainer and S.70 twin-engined light transport but none of these got past the stage of full-scale mockups for the 1946 Paris Salon. The SALS competition to design a new light two-seater for the French aero clubs prompted SIPA to build a prototype of the S.90 – a low-wing machine with a fixed tailwheel undercarriage and a 75hp Mathis engine. In the fly-off in July 1948, the S.90 emerged the winner and gained an order from the French government for 100 examples, which would be built at the SIPA factory at Suresnes. The designer of the S.90 was Yves Gardan (separately described). In the later stages of production of the S.90 series, the construction method changed from wood and fabric to a wooden frame with plywood cladding. The basic model was the S.901, but there were several variants with a variety of engines and a number of S.901s were converted to these other models. The main production batch of S.901s were serialled c/n 1 to 100 and the other aircraft had individual c/ns (01 etc).

Model	Built	Notes
S.90	4	Low-wing two-seat club trainer of wood/fabric construction with fixed tailwheel u/c, sliding clearview canopy and 75hp Mathis G4F engine. Prototype F-WDVA (c/n 01) FF 15 May 1947
S.901	100	S.90 fitted with 75hp Minié 4DC-32 engine. Prototype F-WDLV (c/n 1) FF 25 Jun 1948

SIPA 1000 Coccinelle LV-GFG

S.902		S.901 converted with 85hp Continental C85-12F engine
S.903		S.901 converted with 90hp Continental C90-14F engine
S.904		S.901 converted with 75hp Salmson 5AQ-01 radial engine
S.91	2	S.902 with plywood-covered fuselage and wings
S.92	1	S.91 fitted with 85hp Mathis 4GB-62 engine. F-WEYF (c/n 01)
S.93	1	S.91 fitted with 75hp Salmson 5AQ-01 radial engine. F-WEYC (c/n 01)
S.94	5	S.91 fitted with 90hp Continental C90-8F engine

SIPA's next project, conceived by Yves Gardan, was an all-metal light two-seat jet aircraft for military training and liaison. With side-by-side seating, a Turboméca Palas engine and a twin-boomed layout (similar to that of the DH.100 Vampire), the S.200 Minijet prototype (F-WCZK, c/n 01) first flew on 14th January 1952. A small production batch of six aircraft (c/n 02 to 07) was built – though no French military order was forthcoming. A subsequent project was the S.300R tandem-seat jet trainer (F-WGVR c/n 01), which was aimed at eliminating objections to the side-by-side seating layout of the S.200. This aircraft first flew on 4th October 1954 but it crashed on 26th September 1955 and the Armée de l'Air adopted the Fouga Magister instead.

Yves Gardan then designed a follow-on model to the S.901 in the shape of the all-metal S.1000 Coccinelle. The prototype (F-WHHL c/n 01) was flown on 11th June 1955. Intended as a very low-cost club trainer, the Coccinelle, which was powered by a 90hp Continental C90-8F, used various motor vehicle components and its tricycle undercarriage had three standard motor scooter wheels. Two further prototypes were built (c/n 02 and 03) but production was abandoned. The first and third prototypes still survive. SIPA also took over development of the Boisavia B.260 Anjou light twin whose prototype (F-WHHN c/n 01) had flown on 2nd June 1956 powered by two 170hp Regnier 4L-02 in-line engines. SIPA refitted it with a pair of 180hp Lycoming O-360-A1A

SIPA S.91 G-BDAO

engines and in this form, as the S-261 Anjou, it was re-flown on 24th July 1959. However, its tube-and-fabric construction was obsolete by comparison with the new American light twins and, even though there were plans for a stretched S.262 six-seater, SIPA abandoned the project.

SIPA then abandoned aviation to become a sub-contract manufacturer, mainly producing Renault car parts, but in the early-1960s they built the prototype S.251 Antilope, which had been designed by Procaer. Flown for the first time on 7th November 1962, it was a very streamlined all-metal four-seat low-wing cabin monoplane with retractable tricycle gear and powered by a 560shp Turboméca Astazou IIC turboprop. This aircraft (F-WJSS c/n 01) established a number of international class speed records and in 1964 was re-engined with a 665hp Astazou X that gave it a top speed of around 275mph, but the aircraft did not reach production.

Skyfox   Australia

The Denney Kitfox has been one of the most successful kit-built aircraft, the prototype being first flown by Denney Aircraft in the USA in May 1984. In Australia the design was adopted by Calair Corporation of Caloundra, Queensland who intended to produce a factory-com-

plete model (rather than a kit) and named the aircraft the CA-21 Skyfox. The prototype Skyfox (VH-CAL, c/n CA21001) first flew on 15th September 1989 powered by a 78hp Aeropower engine. Compared with the Kitfox it had greater wing dihedral, the wing struts positioned further out on the wings and a larger and taller rudder. Calair aimed to produce two models – the CA-21 (later CA-22 and CA-22A)

Skyfox CA-25N Gazelle VH-FFT

Calair Skyfox CA-21 55-752

which would be approved under the Australian AUF ultralight category (CAO 101:55) and the CA-25 as a fully certificated model under the JAR-VLA regulations.

Calair ran into some difficulties and was financially reconstituted as Hedaro International Pty (trading as Skyfox Aviation). The two models received their approvals on 20th March 1992 (CA-21, CA-22 and CA-22A) and 2nd June 1993 (CA-25). Both versions are in production with 39 examples of the CA-21 completed (c/n CA21001 to CA21039), 61 CA-22s (c/n CA22001 to CA22N061), comprising 53 CA-22s, 8 CA-22A Elans and one CA-22N, and 93 CA-25s (c/n CA25001 to CA25093) including nine CA-25 Impalas and 84 CA-25N Gazelles. The CA-25N Gazelle is the latest JAR-VLA certificated version with a Rotax 912 engine and a tricycle undercarriage.

Slepcev   Australia

The Slepcev Storch SS.4 is primarily sold as a kit aircraft but the Standard Storch is available factory-complete for certain markets. Designed by Nestor Slepcev and manufactured by Storch Aviation Australia Pty Ltd of Beechwood, NSW, it is a ¾-scale copy of the Fieseler Storch and has similar ultra-slow flying characteristics. The prototype (VH-ZOR) first flew in 1991 and Australian JAR-VLA certification was achieved in October 1999. Itt has a strut-braced high wing, enclosed side-by-side two-seat cabin and a fixed tailwheel undercarriage and standard powerplants are the Rotax 912 and 914 – although several other engines in the 80-100hp range have been fitted including the Rotec Fireball 7-cylinder radial engine (in the Storch Criquet). The versions available include the Standard Storch (also known as the Storch Muster), which is JAR-VLA approved, the 450kg Storch Microlight and the Super Storch and the Storch Moose (these three being kit-only models). The Super Storch, which has a strengthened airframe and a 1,900 lb gross weight, is powered by a 180hp Lycoming O-360 engine and the Storch Moose (1,500 lb gross weight) has a redesigned squared-off rudder and is fitted with a 360hp Vedeneyev radial engine. Over 120 aircraft have been flown to date and serial numbers are in the range SS4-0001 upwards.

Slepcev Storch G-BZOB

Slingsby T.67C Firefly G-BLRF

Slingsby   United Kingdom

Founded by Fred T Slingsby in the early 1930s, Slingsby Sailplanes was one of the most prolific and well respected of the British glider and sailplane constructors. From basic training gliders such as the T.21B Sedbergh and T.31B Tandem Tutor, which were used extensively by the Air Training Corps, up to the high-performance T.51 Dart and T.59D Kestrel, Slingsby established a reputation for high quality and technical innovation. The company only started to face major challenges when the German sailplanes from Grob, Schempp-Hirth and Rolladen-Schneider gained prominence in the late 1960s.

Brief details of the type numbers allocated to Slingsby gliders and powered aircraft are:

Type	Identity	Type	Identity	Type	Identity
T.1	Falcon I	T.24	Falcon IV	T.46	T.21C
T.2	Falcon II	T.25	Gull IV	T.47	20m T.43
T.3	Primary	T.26	Kite II	T.49	Capstan
T.4	Falcon III	T.27	Twin Cadet	T.50	Skylark 4
T.5	Grunau Baby	T.28	Sedbergh	T.51	Dart
T.6	Kite I	T.29	Motor Tutor	T.53	2-seat glider
T.8	Kirby Tutor	T.30	Kirby Prefect	T.54	Powered T.53
T.9	King Kite	T.31	Tandem Tutor	T.55	Regal (Eagle IV)
T.10	Kirby Kitten	T.32	Gull IVB	T.56	SE-5A replica
T.11	Kirby Twin	T.34	Sky	T.57	Sopwith Camel rep
T.13	Petrel I	T.35	Austral	T.58	Rumpler replica
T.14	Gull II	T.37	Skylark 1	T.59	Glasflugel Kestrel
T.15	Gull III	T.38	Grasshopper	T.61	Scheibe Falke
T.17	10/40 Troop carrier	T.39	Target glider	T.65	Sport Vega
T.18	Hengist	T.40	Hayhow racer	T.66	Tipsy Nipper
T.19	Target glider	T.41	Skylark 2	T.67	RF.6B derivatives
T.20	Tandem Trg.glider	T.42	Eagle	T.68	Phoenix RPV
T.21	Sedbergh (T.21B)	T.43	Skylark 3	T.69	Grob Viking tests
T.22	Petrel II	T.44	USAF project	T.70	CMC Leopard
T.23	Kite IA	T.45	Swallow		

In order to diversify, Slingsby had built a number of film replicas including the T.57 (Sopwith Camel) and a couple of Rumpler Taubes and had undertaken production of the Tipsy Nipper light aircraft for

Nipper Aircraft Ltd (as described in the section on Tipsy). This was disrupted by a fire at the company's Kirkbymoorside factory on 18th November 1968 – a tragedy from which the company did not fully recover. In the end Slingsby went into liquidation in July 1969 and its assets were bought by the offshore engineering group of Vickers Ltd They made it the Vickers-Slingsby Division and continued production of the T.61A, the Kestrel and the new 15-metre Vega sailplane.

In addition, Vickers took out a licence to build the Scheibe SF-25B Falke motor glider. Production of this started in 1970 and a total of 35 aircraft was completed together with a further 40 T.61E Venture Mk 2 variants which were delivered to the Air Training Corps from 1978. Some of these were later fitted with electric starters as T.61F and the T.61G was a variant powered by an SL.1700EA1 engine. The majority of the civil Falkes were the T.61A with a Stark Stamo MS.1500/1 engine (and some were retrofitted with a Rollason RS.1 engine as the T.61D), but one aircraft (G-AZHE c/n 1755) was fitted with a Franklin 2A-120-A engine and designated T.61B. A number of T.61Cs were built with an improved Stamo MS.1500/2 engine incorporating an electric starter. Serial numbers, in the general Slingsby integrated series, fell in the range c/n 1726 to 1778.

In addition to its aviation interests, Slingsby became increasingly involved in underwater exploration development for the parent Vickers Group and in 1980 it was reconstituted as Slingsby Engineering (later Slingsby Aviation Ltd) within the British Underwater Engineering group of companies. In February 1983 it was sold to Specialist Flight Training and subsequently became Slingsby Aviation plc. It then passed into the hands of ML Holdings Ltd and was sold to Cobham plc in 1997.

Slingsby took out a licence to build the Fournier RF-6B two-seat trainer/tourer and this resulted in an initial series of 10 T.67A aircraft being built at Kirkbymoorside from Fournier-supplied components. These were little different from the all-wood model with the single-piece canopy and fixed tricycle undercarriage built by Fournier in France. Using its experience in glassfibre technology, Slingsby then re-engineered the RF-6B in glass-reinforced plastic (GRP). the first all-GRP aircraft was designated T.67M (indicating its 'military' role) and first flew at the end of 1982 with a 160hp engine and constant-speed propeller. The civil equivalent was the T.67B, which had the same airframe but used the 116hp engine from the T.67A.

The next development was the fully aerobatic T.67M Mk II Firefly, which first flew at the end of 1982. Again, this was a military trainer, available with either a 160hp fuel-injected Lycoming engine or, as the T.67M-200, with a 200hp Lycoming. These models, and their civil equivalents, were fitted with a rear-hinged cockpit canopy and windshield in place of the rather complex single-piece canopy mounted on scissor-brackets which had gone before. Slingsby's largest order came in 1993 when it was awarded the contract for 113 T-3A Fireflys under the USAF EFS (Enhanced Flight Screener) programme in partnership with Northrop Aircraft Services. After the first two aircraft were completed at Kirkbymoorside, Slingsby provided the T-3A airframe in kit form with Northrop completing final assembly, engine installation and flight-testing at Hondo, Texas and deliveries were completed in February 1996. Subsequently, as a result of three accidents, the T-3A was withdrawn from use by the USAF. Details of all the T.67 variants are:

Model	Built	Notes
T.67A	16	All-wood low-wing side-by-side two-seat monoplane with fixed tricycle u/c and 116hp Lycoming O-235-L2A engine. Prototype G-BIOW (c/n 1988) FF 15 May 1981
T.67B Firefly	15	T.67A re-engineered in GRP with wider fuselage
T.67C Firefly	28	T.67B with 160hp Lycoming AEIO-320-D1B engine, fixed pitch 2-blade metal prop and two-piece windshield/canopy
T.67D Firefly		T.67C with wing mounted fuel tanks and constant-speed propeller
T.67M Firefly	32	T.67C with 160hp Lycoming AEIO-320-D1B engine32, 2-blade Hoffman constant-speed propeller and military equipment
T.67M-200	26	T.67M with 200hp Lycoming AEIO-360-A1E engine with 3-blade Hoffman constant-speed propeller
T.67M-260	165	T.67M with strengthened wingspar, 260hp Lyc AEIO-540-D4A5 flat-6 engine and 3-blade composite c/s prop. Prototype G-BPLK (c/n 2072) initially designated T.67G. T-3A for US Air Force

Slingsby serial numbers are all in a simple numerical series starting at c/n 1 (Slingsby Falcon 1) and this had reached c/n 1700 when Tipsy Nipper production started. A mixture of gliders and powered aircraft (T.59, T.61, T.65 etc) together with some airship gondolas for Airship Industries took the serial sequence to c/n 1988, which was the first T.67A. Certain serials (eg, c/n 2064 and 2065) have been allocated to spare fuselages and c/n 2088 to 2098 were a further batch of airship gondolas. Thereafter almost all serials have been T.67 and Firefly variants with the batch of T-3As for the USAF running from c/n 2123 to 2233 and the most recent deliveries being to the Jordanian and Bahrein air forces. The most recent production aircraft is c/n 2284 but the line was inactive in mid-2004.

SME   Malaysia

In September 1993, SME Aviation Sdn Bhd was formed to produce the Dätweiler MD3 Swiss Trainer. The MD3 had been developed by Max Dätweiler, who flew the prototype MD3-160 (HB-HOH c/n 001) on 12th August 1983. It was intended as a fully aerobatic trainer with simple modular construction incorporating a single design for all control surfaces, common fin and tailplane units and prefabricated wing panels. The MD3 had a fixed tricycle undercarriage and an enclosed side-by-side two-seat cabin with a forward-sliding canopy. A further four prototype and development aircraft were flown (c/n 002 to 005) and the aircraft received Swiss certification. Manufacturing rights were acquired by SME in Malaysia who commenced manufacture of the MD3-160 AeroTiga for civil and military customers with a batch of 20 aircraft for the Royal Malaysian Air Force (c/n 011 to 030) and 20 for Malaysian flying schools. The first Malaysian aircraft flew in May 1995 but it seems that only the military aircraft have been built and an Indonesian order has been suspended. SME have marketed the aircraft in the USA as the Aerotiga with a more powerful fuel-injected engine and a redesigned fuel system that would make the aircraft fully aerobatic. The MD3-116 is an alternative version with a 116hp Lycoming

SME MD3-160 Aero Tiga 9M-SME

O-235-N2A engine and SME Aviation have also carried out development work on a four-seat version. SME is also manufacturing the Eagle XTS two-seat trainer (see separate entry).

SNCAC (Aérocentre)   France

The Société Nationale de Constructions du Centre (SNCAC) was one of the companies formed under the pre-war French industry nationalisation plan. It combined the existing businesses of Farman and Hanriot at Bourges and Boulogne-Billancourt and started operations in this form in March 1937.

The end of the war found SNCAC building the NC.701 version of the German Siebel 204 Martinet for use by the Armée de l'Air. It was decided, however, to consider the postwar light aircraft requirement and the development department at Bourges produced the high-wing three-seat NC.832 and a derivative four-seater NC.840 Chardonneret. The great opportunity for light aircraft producers at this time was the design competition of the Service de l'Aviation Légère et Sportive (SALS) but the NC.832 had a larger powerplant than the 75 horsepower specified by the rules of the competition. Therefore, SNCAC produced the NC.850 with a shoulder-mounted wing and a two-seat cabin with a clear view bubble canopy. Three different versions were entered in the competition powered by the Mathis, Regnier and Minié engines, which were the three possible standards for the assessment. SNCAC also participated in the competition through the unusual AL.06 Frégate twin-boomed aircraft (F-WDVR) that they had built for M Larivierre.

The winner of the SALS competition was the Sipa S.90 but SNCAC built an initial series of ten NC.851s and then received orders from SALS for 100 modified NC.850s known as the NC.853. This was powered by a Minié engine but had the original single fin replaced by a twin tail unit. SNCAC got production under way at Bourges, but had only reached aircraft c/n 27 by June 1949 when the company was placed in liquidation and the assets taken over by SNCAN. In practice, this meant that SNCAC continued to build the NC.853S (the 'S' indicating the involvement of SNCAN) and eventually they completed 95 aircraft before the line was closed down in December 1951. While the NC.853 airframe was a good one the Minié engine left a lot to be desired and many NC.853s were subsequently re-engined with 65hp or 90hp Continental engines. In addition a small series of eight NC.859s were built, powered by the Walter Minor 4-IIIW engine.

In March 1949, SNCAC rolled out a light twin aircraft that was based on the NC.853 and was known as the NC.860 – but the crisis in the company's finances led to this project being abandoned. In the same month, SNCAC had flown the prototype NC.856 which was basically an NC.850 powered by a 105hp Walter Minor engine and an extended cabin similar to that of the NC.832, able to accommodate a third seat. SNCAN revived this project as a two-seat military observation aircraft and built a new prototype – the NC.856A (F-WFKF) – which was flown in March 1951. This had a rearward extension to the cockpit with additional glazed area beneath the wing and the production NC.856A Norvigie for the French Army (ALAT) featured much revised cabin transparencies and a 135hp Regnier 4LO-4 engine. In total, 112 Norvigies were built and most were ultimately replaced in the artillery-spotting role by the Nord 3400 or Cessna L-19. SNCAN did try to produce civil versions of the Norvigie, including the NC.856N four-seat model powered by a 160hp Regnier and the NC.856H three-seat floatplane, but neither type was attractive enough to be built for commercial sale.

The NC.851 aircraft built by SNCAC carried serial numbers from c/n 1 to 09 (plus the prototype, c/n 01). A completely new series of numbers was established for the production NC.853 and these ran from c/n 01 (prototype) and c/n 1 to 27 together with one NC.854 (c/n 41). When SNCAN took over, they started NC.853S production at c/n 51 and continued to c/n 145. The NC.858S batch was serialled from c/n 1 to 8 and NC.856A production ran from c/n 1 to 112. The following data table shows the individual models that were built:

Model	Built	Notes
NC.832	1	Strut-braced high-wing three-seat cabin monoplane with fixed tailwheel u/c, fully glazed cabin with clear vision cabin roof, single vertical tail and tailwheel u/c. Powered by one 100hp Regnier 4E0 in-line engine. Prototype F-WDVY (c/n 01) FF 1946
NC.840	1	Chardonneret. Four-seat high-wing cabin monoplane with fixed tricycle u/c and 140hp Renault 6Q.10 engine. Prototype F-WCDD (c/n 01) FF 3 Nov 1946
NC.841	1	Chardonneret with tailwheel u/c and 175hp Mathis radial engine
NC.850	2	NC.832 with two-seat cabin, bubble canopy and tailwheel u/c, single vertical tail and 75hp Mathis G4F. Prototype F-WCZM (c/n 01) plus F-BDZA (c/n 2)
NC.851	10	NC.850 with 75hp Minié 4-DA.28. Prototype F-WDVX (c/n 01). Three converted to NC.852/853
NC.852	1	NC.850 with 90hp Regnier 4E0. Prototype F-WDVY (c/n 01)
NC.853	28	NC.850 with twin fin/rudder assembly and 80hp Minié 4-DC.30 engine. Prototype F-WEPG (c/n 01). FF 15 Mar 1948. Most converted to NC.854
NC.853S	95	SNCAN-built NC.853 with 75hp Minié 4-DC.32 engine. Many converted to NC.854S or NC.858S
NC.853G		One NC.853 converted to 'aile flottante' system by M Gerard. F-WFSM (c/n 66)
NC.854	2	NC.853 with 65hp Continental A-65. Many conversions from NC.853. Prototype F-BDZI (c/n 01) plus F-BDZL (c/n 41)
NC.854SA		Two NC.854 converted for French Army use
NC.855	1	NC.853 with 75hp Praga engine. F-BFKO (c/n 01)
NC.856	1	SNCAN-built NC.853 with enlarged cabin glazing, repositioned bracing struts and u/c and third rear seat, 105hp Walter Minor engine. Prototype F-WFKF (c/n 01) FF 12 Mar 1949
NC.856A	112	Norvigie. Military NC.856 with fully glazed cabin, three seats and 160hp SNECMA Regnier 4LO-8 engine. Prototype F-WFKG (c/n 01)
NC.856B	1	NC.856 (F-WFKF) with four seats and Walter Minor 4-III engine
NC.856H	1	Floatplane NC.856A. Prototype F-WFAG (c/n 01) FF 21 Dec 1953
NC.856N		Two civil conversions of NC.856A with four seats
NC.858S		NC.853 conversions with 90hp Continental C.90-12F engine
NC.859S	7	Glider-towing NC.853 with 105hp Walter Minor 4-IIIW. Prototype F-BFOS (converted from NC.853 c/n 22)
NC.860	1	NC.853 built by Aérocentre with tricycle u/c, four-seat cabin, faired-in nose and two 105hp Walter Minor 4-III engines mounted on redesigned high wing of increased span. Prototype F-WFKJ (c/n 01) FF 28 Mar 1949

SNCAC NC.854 F-PMCB

SNCAN (Nord)   France

With the end of the war, the Société Nationale de Constructions Aéronautiques du Nord (known as SNCAN or just as 'Nord') was involved in building the Dornier Do 24T and the Messerschmitt Me 108 for the French military forces. The Me 108 was designated Nord 1000 and

Nord had already built around 170 for the German Luftwaffe during the war. When peace came in 1945, production continued with some 286 examples of the Renault 6Q-powered Nord 1001 and Nord 1002 Pingouin being completed. Nord did not build the Pingouin for civil sale, but the type did provide a basis for two models that were aimed at non-military customers.

SNCAN N.1203 Norecrin F-BBEG

The Nord 1101 Noralpha was derived from the Messerschmitt 208 (itself, an enlarged Me.108) which Messerschmitt had intended to build at the Nord factory at Les Mureaux. It was rather larger than the Nord 1000 with a full four-seat cabin, higher power and a retractable tricycle undercarriage and two prototypes were built in 1943 at Les Mureaux (one of which was destroyed in an allied bombing raid). Production only started after the war and, again, the majority of the 200 aircraft built went to the French Armée de l'Air as the Ramier but around 80 were sold to commercial customers and government agencies. Many examples of both the Ramier and the Pingouin appeared on the French civil register once they were retired from military service.

Nord entered the 1946 French Transport Ministry competition that called for a four-seat touring aircraft. The resultant N.1200 was based on the previous models and Nord emerged the winner of the competition with an order for the sponsored aero clubs. The N.1200 prototype first flew in December 1945 and was a two/three-seat cabin monoplane with pronounced dihedral to its wings, a tall retractable tricycle undercarriage and a 100hp Mathis engine. It soon became apparent that this low-powered engine seriously impaired the performance of the N.1200 with the result that a 140hp Renault was fitted and the aircraft became a full three-seater. Seating capacity was subsequently raised to four and several versions of the Norecrin were built

including some fairly large batches of machines sold to the Argentine and other South American countries.

Most of the postwar production of the Nord factory was for military service, and other designs included the NC.856 Norvigie that had been inherited from SNCAC. The company also flew the prototype of the N.1700 Norelic helicopter, which incorporated a highly unusual shrouded rear propeller and this was subsequently developed into the N.1750 Norelphe, which later became the Aerotecnica AC-13A. The Grunau Baby sailplane was built under licence as the N.1300 NorBaby and the DFS Olympia Meise was produced as the N.2000 with some 210 examples being completed.

Nord's largest single postwar light aircraft project was the Stampe SV.4 tandem two-seat open-cockpit biplane trainer. The SV.4 dated back to 1933 when the Belgian firm, Stampe & Vertongen, flew the original Gipsy III-engined prototype. Together with prototypes they finally built 33 aircraft including a batch of 24 SV.4Bs for the Belgian Air Force (c/n 2201 to 2224). The war halted Belgian production and also interrupted plans for the SV.4 to be built by Farman in France. After the Liberation, Nord established a production line at Sartrouville building aircraft for use by French aero clubs and for the Armée de l'Air with a total of 700 being completed during the period from 1945 to 1948. At the end of this time, Nord passed production responsibility to the Atelier Industriel de l'Aéronautique d'Alger which built a further 150 examples. Back in Belgium, the reconstituted Stampe & Renard company also built the SV.4, completing 65 SV.4Bs for the Belgian Air Force during the period from 1948 to 1955 and a single SV.4D. These aircraft carried serial numbers c/n 1143 to 1208.

Details of these postwar production Nord models and the Stampe variants are as follows:

Model	Notes
N.1000	French-built Me 108B four-seat low-wing cabin monoplane with retractable tailwheel u/c and Argus AS.10B engine
N.1001 Pingouin I	N.1000 with 220hp Renault 6Q.11 engine
N.1002 Pingouin II	N.1001 with Renault 6Q.10 engine
N.1100 Noralpha	N.1000 with larger fuselage, retractable tricycle u/c and 240hp Argus As.10C engine
N.1101 Ramier I	N.1100 with right-hand-turning Renault 6Q.10 engine

SNCAN N.1101 Noralpha F-BLQU

N.1102 Ramier II	N.1100 with left-hand-turning Renault 6Q.11 engine
N.1104 Noralpha	Experimental N.1101 (c/n 61) with 240hp Potez 6DO
N.1110	Two experimental N.1101s fitted with Turboméca Astazou turboprop. Prototype F-WJDQ FF 15 Oct 1959
N.1200 Norecrin	All-metal 2/3-seat tourer based on N.1000 with retractable tricycle u/c and 100hp Mathis G4R engine. Prototype F-WBBJ FF 15 Dec 1945
N.1201 Norecrin I	Production three-seat Norecrin with large rear windows and 140hp Renault 4PO1 engine. Prototype F-WBBO (c/n 01)
N.1202 Norecrin	N.1201 F-BBKA (c/n 02) fitted with 160hp Potez 4DO1
N.1203 Norecrin II	Four-seat Norecrin with 135hp Regnier 4L00 engine
N.1203 Norecrin III	Norecrin II with modified undercarriage
N.1203 Norecrin IV	Norecrin II with 170hp Regnier 4L02 engine and constant-speed propeller. F-BDHR (c/n 293)
N.1203 Norecrin V	Military two-seat Norecrin with 170hp Regnier 4L02 engine and machine guns and rockets
N.1203 Norecrin VI	Norecrin III with 145hp Regnier 4L.14 engine
N.1204 Norecrin	N.1203 with 125hp Continental engine
Stampe SV.4	Original wood and fabric biplane powered by one 120hp DH Gipsy III engine. Prototype OO-ANI FF 17 May 1933
Stampe SV.4A	SNCAN-built SV.4B re-fitted with Renault 4P-05 engine, inverted systems and strengthened airframe
Stampe SV.4B	SV.4 with rounded rudder and wingtips, swept wing and 130hp Gipsy Major engine. Some fitted with cockpit canopy. Production by Stampe & Renard and SNCAN
Stampe SV.4C	SV.4A powered by 140hp Renault 4P-01 engine
Stampe SV.4D	One SV.4C with 165hp Continental IO-340-A. OO-SRS (c/n 1208)

Stampe & Renard SV.4B D-EIHD

Serial numbers and production of Nord's production light aircraft were:

Model	Built	Serial batches	Model	Built	Serial batches
N.1002	286	1 to 286	Stampe SV4	700	1 to 700
N.1101	200	1 to 200	NC.856	112	1 to 112
N.1200 srs	378	1 to 378	AIAA SV.4	151	1100 to 1150

Sportavia   Germany

The Alfons Pützer KG started operations in 1953, building sailplanes – and in particular the side-by-side two-seat Doppelraab glider which had been designed by Fritz Raab. On 8th May 1955, following the ten-year limitation of the Treaty of Potsdam, powered flying was again permitted. The following day, Pützer made the first flight of the prototype of their Motorraab (D-EBAC c/n V.1). This was little more than a Doppelraab with a fixed tricycle undercarriage and a 32hp Volkswagen engine fitted in the nose. Three further Motorraabs were constructed, the third machine (D-EHOG c/n 03) having a 52hp Porsche engine. Using this powerplant, Pützer proceeded to develop the Motorraab into the Pützer Elster.

The first Elster (D-EJOB), which flew on 10th January 1959, was an all-wood aircraft with a strut-braced high wing and a fuselage which was really a deepened version of the Doppelraab's. The German Government ordered 25 examples for use by civil flying clubs and subsequently 21 of these were given Luftwaffe insignia and numbers. A total of 45 production Elsters (c/n 002 to 046) were constructed between 1957 and 1967; 32 of these were the standard Elster B model with a 95hp Continental C90-12F engine and the remaining

13 were Elster Cs with a 150hp Lycoming O-320 and equipment for glider towing.

Pützer built a number of experimental small aircraft during the 1960s including a pair of Horten Ho 33 flying wings (D-EJUS and D-EGOL), the Dohle (D-EGUB), the S5 (D-EAFA), the C1 (D-EBUT) and three examples of the C2. On 6th November 1961 they flew the prototype MS.60 single-seat training motor glider (D-KACO). This was powered by a 30hp JLO engine that was buried in the centre fuselage and drove two pusher propellers mounted on the inboard wing trailing edges. The propellers were designed to fold up when the engine was switched off for soaring flight. The company also flew the SR.57 Büsard (D-EHIV), which was a futuristic low-wing two-seat machine with a fixed tricycle undercarriage and a Y-shaped tail unit (later changed to a conventional fin/tailplane from a Bölkow Junior). Unusually, the SR.57 had its 95hp Continental C90-12F engine mounted in the nose driving a tail-mounted two-blade pusher propeller by means of a long flexible driveshaft that ran through the cabin. The sole prototype was built by Aachen Technical College students, being rebuilt later with a conventional nose-mounted engine.

During the mid-1960s, Pützer became increasingly involved in cooperation with the French company, Alpavia. Alpavia had been building the Fournier RF-3 motor glider and almost completely redesigned this

Putzer Elster B G-APVF

Sportavia RS-180 D-EFBS

as the RF-4. It was decided that RF-4 production should be undertaken by a new company – Sportavia-Pützer GmbH – that merged the existing Putzer organisation with that of Alpavia. Accordingly, Sportavia, based at Dahlemer Binz near Blankenheim, started to construct the RF-4D ('D' denoting 'Deutschland').

René Fournier subsequently established an independent design bureau that produced the design of the RF-5D, which was an enlarged tandem two-seat version of the RF-4. The Sportavia-built prototype (D-KOLT c/n 5001) first flew in January 1968 and 125 production aircraft were subsequently built at Dahlemer Binz. One RF-5 airframe became the Sportavia S.5 (D-EAFA c/n V-1) and was fitted with a Lycoming O-235-G2A engine with extensive sound suppression as a stealth reconnaissance aircraft for the German Defence Ministry. This led to a number of other prototype development machines (the S.5K, C.2 etc). The RF-5 was replaced in production in 1972 by the RF-5B Sperber which had a 10ft 9in increase in wingspan and a cut-down rear fuselage and larger cockpit canopy. Similarly, the RF-4D was replaced by the SFS-31 Milan which came from a cooperative manufacturing arrangement combining the fuselage of the RF-4D with the wings of the Scheibe SF-27 sailplane.

In 1969, Rhein Flugzeugbau GmbH bought a 50% interest in Sportavia-Pützer – and purchased the balance of the share capital in 1977. It was around this time that René Fournier became involved in the design of his new RF-6. This aircraft first flew as the RF-6B, which was a side-by-side two-seat low-wing monoplane of wood and composite construction with a fixed tricycle undercarriage and the familiar high-aspect ratio wing. The RF-6C was developed with a longer four-seat cabin and Sportavia built a prototype of this, D-EHYO c/n 6001, which first flew in April 1976. They also built a two-seater (D-EASK c/n 6002) that was similar to the RF-6B but had a larger canopy and a Grumman Traveler undercarriage. However, it was decided to concentrate on the four-seat model for series production.

Unfortunately, Sportavia ran into severe stability problems with the RF-6C and only two further examples (c/n 6003 and 6004) were built before a total redesign was initiated. The result was the RS-180 Sportsman (D-ENTY c/n 6005), which was still a wooden aircraft but had a cruciform tail unit with increased side area and a 180hp Lycoming O-360-A3A engine. This entered production in 1977 but its success was limited and eventually the last of the 18 production machines (D-EBFS c/n 6022) was delivered in 1979.

Starck   France

André Starck was an established pre-war light aircraft constructor. At the end of the war, he designed a new single-seat sporting aircraft that he named the AS.70 Jac. This achieved its first flight in May 1945 from Lognes and was the first aircraft to gain a restricted-category airworthiness certificate in France following the war. André Starck set up a small factory at Boulogne-Billancourt and his Avions Starck company built 23 examples of the AS.70 with assorted engines.

The AS.70 was produced as the standard model with a 45hp Salmson 9Adb radial but it also appeared as the AS.71 (60hp Walter Mikron), AS.72 (60hp Salmson), AS.73 (40hp Persy), AS.74 (65hp Continental) and the AS.75 (105hp Potez 5E). Obtaining engines was always the critical problem for postwar aircraft constructors and Starck was eventually forced to cease production after completing 23 machines (c/n 1 to 23)

Starck AS.70 F-AZGY

Starck AS.57 F-PCIM

due to these materials shortages. The low-wing AS.70 was always a popular aircraft, however, and a licence was granted to SCRA at Saint-Ange (Eure et Loire) who built a further four aircraft (c/n 24 to 26).

The second production design from Avions Starck was the side-by-side two-seat AS.57. In many respects it was a scaled-up AS.70 with a bubble canopy and lengthened fuselage and was delivered with a 75hp Mathis, 75hp Regnier, 95hp Walter Minor or 105hp Potez engine. The prototype AS.57 was F-WDVU (c/n 1) and ten production units were delivered (c/n 2 to 11) before the familiar engine supply problem halted further output.

André Starck did not return to full scale aircraft production, but he did build and fly F-WGGB, the prototype of the AS.90 'New Look', which was a small open-cockpit single-seater. He followed this with the AS.80 Lavadoux (F-WGGA), which was a Cub-like tandem two-seater for which plans were made available to amateur constructors. Starck also built a single example of the AS.27 (F-PURC) which featured biplane wings so closely separated as to create a strong slot effect and this was followed by a larger version, the AS.37, which was built by M Knoepfli and featured a single engine driving two pusher propellers by means of a belt drive.

Stark   Germany

The Stark Flugzeugbau of Minden was formed in the mid-1950s to build a specialised version of the low-wing, single-seat Druine D.31 Turbulent. Known as the Stark Turbulent D, the aircraft was fitted with a tailwheel instead of the normal skid, full brakes and a clearview bubble cockpit canopy. The powerplant was a 45hp Stark Stamo conversion of the Volkswagen engine and the prototype Stark Turbulent D was registered D-EJON (c/n 101). Stark built a production run of 35 further Turbulents with the serial numbers c/n 102 to 136.

Stark Turbulent D D-ENIN

Stemme   Germany

The Stemme S10, which was designed by Dr Reiner Stemme is a high-performance sailplane with a side-by-side two-seat cockpit and a retractable twin-wheel undercarriage which folds into a fully-enclosed under-fuselage well. The basic S10 Chrysalis was built in West Berlin but the prototype (D-KKST) was first flown at Peine on 6th July 1986 using wings based on the design of the Glaser-Dirks DG-500. It is powered by a 93hp Limbach L2400 engine which is buried in the centre fuselage and drives the propeller via a shaft running through the cockpit to a folding propeller which is freed for use by the aircraft nose sliding forward. The S10-v is a version with a variable-pitch propeller, the prototype (D-KGCX c/n 10-46) being converted to this form in 1993 with at least 20 S10s being converted subsequently. Production of the standard S10 gave way to the S10-v in 1994.

The S10-VT has a turbocharged 115hp Rotax 914 engine and the prototype was D-ESTE/D-KGCR, c/n 15-001 but later 11-001). This is now the current production version and at least one has been delivered to the USAF as the TG-11. Special applications have included atmospheric research, pollution sensing and infra-red mapping for which Stemme sells the S15 Utility (S15-8) which has a conventional non-retracting five-blade propeller and has four underwing pylons to mount equipment pods. The development aircraft for this model is the S10-VT prototype D-KGCR (now re-serialled 15-001). In addition, Stemme has announced the S2 two-seat 20-metre sailplane and the S6 and S8 two-seat touring motor gliders with fixed nose-mounted propellers – but none of these models has flown.

Stemme built 63 S10s (c/n 10-1 to 10-63) but ten of these were converted to S10-v standard and renumbered as c/n 14-001 to 14-010. This was later changed back to the original c/n with a 14- prefix and an M suffix (eg, c/n 10-46 initially became 14-001 but was later changed to 14-046M). Standard new-built S10-v aircraft were c/n 14-011 to 14-030 but S10 conversions continued to be given modified numbers, so, for example, c/n 14-018 and 14-018M both exist. The S10-VT has serials from c/n 11-001 to (currently) 11-091. Overall production to the end of 2004 has been 174 aircraft (63 S10, 20 S10-v and 91 S10-VT).

Stemme S10-VT D-KSIE

Stinson 108-2 Voyager G-BPTA

Stinson   United States

The Stinson Aircraft Corporation has one of the longest pedigrees in the aviation business. It goes back to 1926 when the company was formed by Eddie Stinson in Detroit for the purpose of building the SB-1 Detroiter four-seat cabin biplane. The Stinson line progressed with the SM-2 Junior, the eleven-seat SM-6000 and a succession of four-seat high-wing monoplanes culminating with the SR series of Reliants.

In the late 1930s, Stinson saw the need for an aircraft which was lighter and cheaper than the SR-10 Reliant. They designed the HW-75 (also designated Model 105), which was a side-by-side two-seater with a strut-braced high wing and fixed tailwheel undercarriage. The prototype HW-75 (NX21121 c/n 7000) was powered by a 50hp Lycoming engine, but the design was intended for greater things and the production Model 105 was built as a three-seat machine with a 75hp engine. The type certificate was issued on 20th May 1939 and a considerable number of 105s were delivered with both the Lycoming engine and also (as the HW-80) with an 80hp Continental A-80-6.

The Model 105 was followed by the Model 10 Voyager, which was generally similar but incorporated a wider cabin, modified engine cowling design and increased power. The advent of war called a halt to civil production of the Model 10 although a number of these aircraft were delivered to the Army Air Corps as the AT-19A (later L-9A). Stinson, as a division of Consolidated Vultee (Convair) then embarked on production of the Model 76 (the L-5 military cooperation aircraft) which was virtually a direct adaptation of the Model 10A with a 185hp Lycoming O-435-A engine and an extensively glazed cabin area.

In 1945, with L-5 production at an end, Stinson announced the postwar Voyager – the Model 108. This was, in fact, a rather larger aircraft than the Model 10 with seating for four people and a 150hp powerplant. The Voyager was built of steel tube and fabric with an all-metal tail unit and was offered in standard trim or as the 'Flying Station Wagon' with a utility interior. The final variant of this model featured an enlarged tail unit to compensate for the higher power of its 165hp Franklin engine.

In 1948, Convair decided that Stinson did not fit into its predominantly heavy commercial and military production organisation and, on 1st December, Stinson was sold to Piper Aircraft Corporation who were pleased to have a four-seater to market alongside the Cub, Supercruiser and Vagabond and also benefited from acquiring the rights to

Stinson 105 Voyager G-AFYO

Stinson 108-3 Flying Station Wagon NC6801M

the new Twin Stinson. Eventually, Piper phased out the design in favour of its own PA-20 Pacer. In due course, the Stinson 108 type certificate was acquired by Univair, who specialise in providing spare parts for the design. Stinson designs from the Model 105 onwards were as follows:

Model	Notes
105	Three-seat high-wing monoplane powered by one 75hp Cont A-75-3 engine. Also known as the HW-75. Prototype NX21121 (c/n 7000) FF Feb 1939
10	Model 105 with wider cabin and 80hp Continental A-80 engine. Named Voyager. Prototype N26200 (c/n 7501)
10A	Model 10 with 45 lb TOGW increase and 90hp Franklin 4AC-99 engine. Model 10B had 75hp Lycoming GO-145
108	Enlarged four-seat postwar Model 10. Powered by one 150hp Franklin 6A4-150-B3. Prototype NX87600 (c/n 108-1)

108-1 Model 108 with minor detailed improvements
108-2 Developed Model 108-1 with 250 lb TOGW increase and 165hp Franklin 6A4-165-B3 engine
108-3 Model 108-2 with larger vertical tail, increased fuel capacity and minor detail changes. Prototype N502C (c/n 3502)

Serial numbers for these models were:

Model	Built	Serial Batch	Model	Built	Serial Batch
105	277	7000 to 7276	108-1	686	108-1564 to 108-2249
10	260	7501 to 7760	108-2	1,252	108-2250 to 108-3501
10A	515	7761 to 8275	108-3	1,632	108-3503 to 108-5134
108	742	108-2 to 108-742	108-3*	126	108-5135 to 108-5260
108-1	821	108-1-743 to 108-1-1563			*Piper production
			Total	6,311	

Sukhoi   Russia

The pattern set by the Yakovlev Bureau with the Yak-55 was taken up by Sukhoi who, in 1984, broke from their traditional concentration on high-performance military aircraft to build the Su-26 single-seat competition aerobatic aircraft. The low-wing Su-26 (and its production Su-26M version) is a very sophisticated design constructed of steel tube and titanium with aluminium, fibreglass and carbon fibre cladding. Again, this design uses the M-14P engine. An upgraded version, designated Su-26M3, has a modified engine cowling, vertical tail and cockpit canopy and an SKS-94M ejector seat. Sukhoi exported a number of examples of the Su-26 before replacing it with the SU-31, first delivered in 1994. This is based on the Su-29 (qv) with a bubble canopy and cut-down rear fuselage, modified engine cowling, taller vertical tail and modified wings. Sukhoi's Su-29 is a tandem two-seat version of the Su-26M with a 17in-longer fuselage, a 16in increase in wingspan, heavier spars and skins and a modified aerofoil section. A special Su-29LL model with twin ejection seats has also been tested and a two-seat agricultural model, the Su-38 is under development. Serial numbers for each model consist of a batch number followed by (normally) a five or ten unit individual serial number. A typical Su-26

batch is c/n 05-01 to 05-10. The batches used to date are 01 to 07 and 52 to 54 for the Su-26, Batch 72 to 81, 90 and 100 for the Su-29 and Batch 01 to 05 for the Su-31. Details of the Sukhoi models are as follows:

Model	Built	Notes
Su-26	71	Advanced single-seat aerobatic aircraft with low wing, faired-in rear-hinged upward-opening bubble canopy, fixed tailwheel u/c and one 394hp Vedeneyev M-14PF radial engine. Prototype FF June 1984
Su-26M		Main production Su-26 with re-shaped rudder, reduced fuselage side glazing and minor refinements
Su-26M2		Su-26M with modified lightweight wings and larger fuel tank
Su-26MX		Su-26M for export sale
Su-29	64	Su-26M with 17-inch fuselage stretch, longer wings and tandem 2-seat cockpit with side-hinged canopy. Initial examples with M-14PF engine but M-9F engine from 1999. Prototype FF 1991
Su-29AR		Eight Su-29 for Argentine Air Force with new cockpit canopy and propeller
Su-29KS		Su-29 with test unit for lightweight Zvezda SKS-94 ejector seat system. One aircraft, RA-01485
Su-29LL		Initial designation for Su-29KS

Sukhoi Su-29 N229SU

Su-29T		Initial designation for single-seat Su-29. Became Su-31. Prototype FF June 1992
Su-31	22	Su-29 with rear cockpit only enclosed by side-opening canopy. Powered by M-14PF engine. Prototype FF June 1992. Also known as Su-31T
Su-31M		Su-31 with Zvezda SKS-94 ejector seat system and single-piece cockpit canopy
Su-32		Proposed military trainer version of Su-29 with retractable tricycle u/c. Not built
Su-38		Single-seat agricultural aircraft based on Su-29 with underwing spraybars and optional rear jumpseat. Not built
Su-38L	1	Completely redesigned Su-38. Low-wing single-seat agricultural aircraft with fixed tailwheel u/c and powered by one 207hp LOM M337 engine. Prototype (03 black) FF 2001
Su-49		Upgraded version of Su-32. Not built

Sukhoi Su-26 G-SIID

Taylorcraft   United States

When the famous C G Taylor left Piper in 1935, he set about designing a new two-seater that was superficially similar to the Cub – except for having side-by-side seating. The Taylor-Young Airplane Co was established at Butler, Pennsylvania and later at Alliance, Ohio. The Taylorcraft A, which was first delivered in mid-1937, with its 40hp Continental A-40 engine and a new price of $ 1,495, was a considerable success. It was followed by the 50-horsepower Taylorcraft B that, with its Continental engine, was known as the Taylorcraft BC and later, in 1939, became the BC-65 when fitted with a Continental A-65 engine. The company discontinued production of the BC-65 during the war while it was turning out the tandem-seat Model D, which was delivered as the L-2 to the US forces.

At the end of hostilities, Taylorcraft Aviation Corporation started to produce large quantities of the BC-65 (under the designation BC-12D) and the Lycoming-powered BL-12 for postwar civil purchasers. So successful were the Taylorcraft Bs that some 50 aircraft per day were leaving the Alliance factory in mid-1946. The company also flew a prototype of the Model 15 Foursome four-seater but its development

was pulled up short by a major fire in the Taylorcraft factory that put C G Taylor out of business – and into bankruptcy.

In 1949, C G Taylor bought back the assets of Taylorcraft at public auction and set up a new company – Taylorcraft Inc – at Conway, Pennsylvania. The company recommenced production of the BC-12D Traveller and the higher-powered BC-12D-85 Sportsman, which was later redesigned as the Model 19. The Model 15 went into production as the Model 15A Tourist.

Taylorcraft pursued improvements to the Model 15 through the Model 16 and the Model 18. The result of this was the Model 20, which appeared in 1955 and used the unusual (for that time) construction method of moulded fibreglass fitted to a tubular frame. Three models were marketed – the standard Ranch Wagon, the 20AG Topper with dusting equipment and the Seabird seaplane version. The line was modified in minor details in 1958 at which time the Ranch Wagon was re-modelled as the Zephyr 400.

Demand for the Taylorcraft line was hardly booming in the mid-1950s and, once again, production of new aircraft was brought to a halt with the type certificate passing into the hands of Univair. Eventually, in 1971, a new company – Taylorcraft Aviation Corporation,

Taylorcraft F-22 G-BVOX

Taylorcraft BL-65 N26653

owned by Charles Feris – brought the Model 19 back into production as the F-19, powered by a 100hp Continental engine. In 1980, this was phased out in favour of the 118hp Taylorcraft F-21.

Charles Feris died in 1976 and production trickled on until, in 1985, the company was sold to George Ruckle who moved the whole operation to the former Piper plant at Lock Haven, Pa – which was, ironically, the place where C G Taylor had started out. The new business only managed to build 16 aircraft before it was forced to cease production in August 1986 and declare Chapter 11 bankruptcy. The business was put up for sale and, in November 1989, was acquired by a partnership named Taylorcraft Aircraft Company owned by Aircraft Acquisition Corp of Morgantown, West Virginia and East Kent Capital Inc (the managing partner). Eventually, the remaining assets were acquired by Harry Ingram. He formed Taylorcraft Aviation Inc and moved operations to La Grange, Texas in 2003 where he has restarted production of the F22 Classic, F22A Tracker, F22B Trooper and F22C Ranger. In addition, the company is marketing the Taylor Sport, which is a version of the F19 engineered for the American light-sport aircraft category. A list of Taylorcraft models is as follows:

Model	Notes
A	Original side-by-side two-seat Taylorcraft with one 40hp Continental A-40-4. Prototype X-16393 (c/n 25)
BC	Model A with 50hp Continental A-50 and modified wing construction. Known as BC-50
BC-65	BC fitted with 65hp Continental A-65. Later known as BC-12-65
BC-12D Twosome	Postwar version of BC-12-65
BC-12D-85 Sportsman	Postwar BC-12D with 85hp Continental C-85 engine
BC-12D-4-85 Sportsman	BC-12D-85 with extra rear side windows
BF-60	BC with 60hp Franklin 4AC-171 engine
BF-65	BF fitted with 65hp Franklin 4AC-176 engine. Later designated BF-12-65
BL-50	BC with 50hp Lycoming O-145 engine
BL-65	BL with 65hp Lycoming O-145. Later BL-12-65
DC-65 Tandem Trainer	Tandem two-seat development of Model B with narrower fuselage and additional window area. 65hp Continental A-65-8. Also known as ST-100. Military deliveries as O-57 and L-2
DF-65 Tandem Trainer	DC-65 with 65hp Franklin 4AC-176 engine
DL-65 Tandem Trainer	DC-65 with 65hp Lycoming O-145-B2 engine
DCO-65	DC-65 with cut-down rear fuselage and extended plexiglass canopy for observation. L-2A/L-2M
15	Four-seat enlarged development of BC with 125hp Lycoming (later 150hp Franklin 6A4-150-B3). Prototype NX36320 FF 1 Nov 1944
15A Tourist	Production Model 15 with 145hp Continental C-145-2 engine
16	Experimental development of Model 15. Prototype NX40070 (c/n 15001)
18	Experimental military liaison aircraft with 135hp Lycoming O-290-D engine. Prototype N6678N (c/n 18-13099)
19 Sportsman	Revised BC-12D-4-85 with Continental C-85-12 engine and modified rear side windows
F19 Sportsman	Model 19 with Cont O-200 engine and increased gross weight
F19 Taylor Sport	Model 19 for LSA category certification with 1,320 lb TOGW and 100hp Continental O-200-A engine
20 Ranchwagon	Fibreglass-clad development of Model 18 with 225hp Continental O-470-J engine
20AG Topper	Agricultural version of Model 20
20 Seabird	Seaplane version of Ranchwagon
20 Zephyr 400	1958 version of Ranchwagon with detail changes
F21	F19 with 118hp Lycoming O-235-C engine. 1,500 lb TOGW
F21A	F21 with fuselage fuel tank deleted and 40 gal fuel capacity in two wing tanks
F21B	F21 with 42 gal total fuel capacity and 1,750 lb TOGW. New wing spars and aluminium under-fuselage skinning
F22 Classic	F21B with 118hp Lycoming O-235-L2C engine, new wing flaps, new adjustable seats, altered cabin cage structure with wider interior and hinged windows. Prototype N180GT (N44191, c/n 2201) fitted with tricycle u/c but production F22 has tailwheel u/c. 1,750 lb TOGW
F22A Tracker	F22 fitted with tricycle u/c. Formerly named Tri-Classic
F22B Trooper	F22 with 180hp Lycoming O-360-A4M engine. Formerly named STOL-180
F22C Ranger	F22B with tricycle u/c. Formerly named TriSTOL-180

Serial numbers for Taylorcrafts started at number 25 for the initial Taylor-Young Model A and continued to c/n 12501 as shown in the table below. Starting at c/n 13000, Taylorcraft used an integrated serial system with all models included. In the blocks marked *, each model was identified by a prefix number. Prefix 2- was the BC-12D-65 (eg, C/n 2-13009); 3- was the BC-12D-85 (eg, 3-13002); 4- was the BC-12D-4-85 and the Model 19 (eg, 4-13016); 5- was the Model 15A (eg, 5-13057).

C/n Batch	Built	Models/Notes	C/n Batch	Built	Models/Notes
25 to 630	606	A	12500 to 12501	2	BC-12D-85
631 to 999		Not used	13000 to 13059*	60	BC-12D, 19, 15A
1000 to 3400	2,401	BC, BL, BF	13099	1	18 c/n 18-13099
3401 to 3999		Not used	13100* to 13109*	10	15A and 19
4000 to 4199	200	DC, DF, DCO-65†	14101 to 14021*	21	15A and 19
4200 to 6318	2,119	O-57 & L-2 Prefixes O- (O-57) & L- (L-2)	15001	1	16
6319 to 6347	29	DC & experimental Civil aircraft	20-001 to 20-038	38	20
6348 to 6399		Not used	F-001 to F-153	153	F-19
6400 to 10590	4,191	BC-12D Postwar civil production	F-1001 to F-1022	22	F-21
10591 to 10778		Not used	F-1501 to F-1506	6	F-21A
10779 to 10800	22	BC-12D-1	F-1507 to F-1521	15	F-21B
10801 to 11999		Not used	2201 to 2221	21	F-22
12000 to 12038	39	BC-12D-85			
12039 to 12499		Not used	*Total*	*9,957*	

† C/n 4000 to 4199 contains mainly civil Model D but also O-57 c/n 4008 to 4011 and 4045 to 4066. Also XLNT c/n 4183.

Taylorcraft 15A Tourist N6653N

Technoavia   Russia

Technoavia was formed in 1991, operating from the Smolensk Aircraft Factory. Its first design was the SM-92 Finist which is a general-purpose six/eight-seat all-metal utility aircraft with a strut-braced high wing, fixed tailwheel undercarriage and an M-14P radial piston engine. Technoavia have also produced a prototype of the military SM-92P which has two rocket launchers and two machine guns fitted to the lower fuselage with a further machine gun mounted in the open door. It is believed that five development aircraft (c/n 00-001 to 00-005) and ten production units (c/n 01-001 to 01-010) were built but that output has been suspended following the closure of the Smolensk factory. The prototype Finist was converted to SM-92 Turbo Finist standard with a turboprop engine and this was followed by Aerotech Slovakia who converted HA-YDF as the SMG-92 Turbo Finist with a Walter M.601D2 turboprop. At least six aircraft were converted. The Finist was also intended for production in the Czech Republic by Moravan as the Zlin Z400 Rhino with a 485hp Orenda diesel engine and one airframe was converted as a prototype. However, the financial difficulties of Moravan resulted in this being suspended.

The Technoavia SP-91 high-performance aerobatic aircraft was designed by Vyacheslav Kondratyev, who also designed the Yakovlev Yak-55 and the Sukhoi Su-26 competition aerobatic aircraft. Initially known as the Interavia I-3 (of which 10 examples were built), it is an all-metal low-wing monoplane with a fixed tailwheel undercarriage and a Voronezh M-14P radial engine and first flew on 10th August 1993. It is constructed as a tandem two-seater but can be converted to single-seat configuration by replacement of the fuselage top decking and canopy with an alternative section. Five SP-91s were built at the Smolensk production factory from 1995 onwards, several being exported to the United States. The improved production SP-95 Slavia has longer wings and a deeper rudder but it is thought that just five examples have been built. Technoavia is believed to have had a further modified model, the SP-96, under development although production of the Slavia has now been suspended. Technoavia is now concentrating on the SP-55M, which is a much-modified development of the Yakovlev Yak-55M.

Technoavia took a licence to build the Yakovlev Yak-18T and made minor changes, producing it as the SM-94, which first flew on 22nd December 1994. From 1998 they built a small batch (said to be 15,

Technoavia SM-92 Finist RA-44512

using existing incomplete airframes) of a new version with a two-piece windscreen and other minor refinements. Kondratyev then embarked on a major redesign of the Yak-18T with a new tail unit and a new wing with a high-speed profile and new flaps. The aircraft, designated SM2000, was fitted with a 740shp Walter M601 turboprop and first flew in 2003. Technoavia also became involved in the Intracom Viper project. The Viper is a re-engined version of the Piper PA-31P airframe with the existing two engines replaced by a single nose-mounted 740shp Walter M601E turboprop and the prototype (RA-01559, c/n 31P-7530007) first flew on 6th December 2000. It is said that three further PA-31P airframes (including c/n 31P-7300141 and c/n 31P-7300167) have been converted. The aircraft is being marketed by the Swiss company, Intracom General Machinery.

Model	Built*	Notes
SP-55M	2	Technoavia version of Yak-55M with turtledeck rear fuselage and revised canopy, larger rudder, new wings with symmetrical section, 400hp M-14PF engine, tubular u/c legs, mod control surfaces. Prototype RA-44547
SP-91	5	Mid-wing two-seat aerobatic trainer with fixed tailwheel u/c and one 355hp Vedeneyev M-14P piston engine

Technoavia SP-91 RA-44496

SM-92 Finist	11	High-wing utility aircraft with fixed tailwheel u/c and one 355hp Vedeneyev M-14Kh radial engine. Prototype RA-44482 FF 28 Dec 1993
SMG-92	7	Turbo Finist converted by Aerotech Slovakia with 536shp Walter M601D-2 turboprop. Prototype HA-YDF (c/n 01-005) FF 7 Nov 2000
SM-92P	2	SM-92 for border guard use with external armament etc. Prototype RA-44493 (c/n 01-001)
SM-91		Original designation for military SM-92
SM-94	1	Yak-18T with two-piece windscreen, reshaped side windows, and minor improvements. Prototype RA-44486

| SP-95 | 5 | Improved version of SP-91 with deeper rudder with squared-off tip and increased wingspan |
| SM-2000 | 1 | Redesigned version of Yak-18T powered by one 740shp Walter M601 turboprop. Prototype |

* Estimated number of aircraft built.

Technoavia production totals are not confirmed but serial numbers follow the normal system of a batch number followed by the aircraft number in the batch. The first two Finist batches were c/n 00-001 to 00-005 and c/n 01-001 to 01-010.

Technoflug   Germany

Technoflug, based at Winzeln-Schramberg, is a German producer of motor gliders. The Piccolo started life as the Neukom AN-20B/AN-22, which was built in Switzerland in small series during the early 1980s. It is a single-seat powered sailplane of composite construction with a high strut-braced constant-chord wing, a fixed tricycle undercarriage and a T-tail. It is fitted with a pusher 23hp Solo engine mounted at the wing-fuselage intersection and has a foldable propeller to reduce drag when the engine is switched off for soaring flight. Technoflug's proto-

type was D-KHAI (c/n 001) and they commenced production in 1986. 125 Piccolos have been built to date (c/n 001 to 125). The Technoflug TFK-2 Carat is a completely new design and the prototype (D-KCTF c/n 001) first flew on 16th December 1997. It is a low-wing single-seat powered sailplane with a high-performance wing fitted with winglets, a T-tail and a retractable tailwheel undercarriage. The 54hp Sauer E1S engine is nose-mounted and fitted with a propeller which folds forwards when the engine is switched off for soaring flight. The Carat is built by AMS Flight in Slovenia and 14 examples (up to c/n 014) had been built by the end of 2004.

Technoflug Piccolo HB-2179

Tecnam   Italy

The SRL Costruzioni Aeronautiche Tecnam was formed in 1986 by Luigi Pascale, who was responsible for the design of the Partenavia aircraft types. It is based near Naples with a manufacturing plant and airstrip at Castelvolturno. The P92 Echo, which was designed by Pascale, first flew on 14th March 1993. It is a strut-braced high wing aircraft with an enclosed side-by-side two-seat cabin, a spring steel tricycle undercarriage and mainly metal, construction with composite parts. Over 500 P92s have been completed and the later P92S and Echo Super have a more streamlined rear fuselage and a faired-in fin. Several Rotax and Jabiru engines are available in the 80hp to 100hp range.

The P96 Golf, introduced in 1997, is, essentially, a low-wing version of the Echo. It has a side-by-side dual control cabin with a sliding canopy and is constructed of light alloy and composites with a steel tube fuselage structure. The cantilever undercarriage, vertical tail and fuselage top decking are the same as those of the Echo but the Golf has an all-moving tailplane and a wet wing. A retractable-gear version was introduced in early 2005. Total production of the Golf is approximately 250 aircraft. The Echo and Golf are available either in kit or factory-complete form depending on the country to which they are exported and both are produced as 450kg ultralights or as JAR-VLA certified aircraft at higher gross weights. Details of the various models are as follows:

Tecnam P96 Golf 100

Model	Notes
P92	All-metal side-by-side two-seat 450kg (992 lb) ultralight aircraft with enclosed cabin, strut-braced high wing, fixed tricycle u/c and 80hp Rotax 912UL engine. Prototype FF 14 Mar 1993. Also known as Echo 80
P92 Echo 100	P92 powered by 100hp Rotax 912ULS engine
P92J	P92 to JAR-VLA standards with 1,146 lb TOGW, extra rear windows etc. Powered by 81hp Rotax 912A2. Prototype I-TECN FF 1995
P92S Echo 80	P92 with redesigned wing, modified engine cowling, sloped windshield, new fuselage turtledeck fairing, rear vision window, tapered front wing roots, bulged doors, fin fairing. Either Ultralight or JAR-VLA versions available
P92S Echo 100	P92S powered by 100hp Rotax 912ULS engine
P92-JS	Improved P92J with 1,210 lb TOGW, 100hp Rotax 912S
P92 SeaSky	P92 fitted with Full Lotus amphibious floats
P92 Echo Super	P92S with shorter span wing, wider cabin, larger instrument panel etc
P92-2000RG	Echo Super with retractable u/c including small main gear sponsons
P2004 Bravo	P92S with new laminar-flow wing and modified flaps, wider cabin with deeper doors and enlarged rearview window. Prototype FF 9 Sep 2004
P96 Golf	All-metal side-by-side two-seater 450kg ultralight with low wing based on that of P92, fixed tricycle u/c, P92 tail. Powered by 80hp Rotax 912UL. Prototype FF Mar 1997

Tecnam P92S Echo 100

Model	Notes
P96 Golf 100	P96 powered by 100hp Rotax 912ULS
P2002 Sierra	Improved P96 with new tapered laminar-flow wing, slotted flaps, upturned wingtips and modified lower profile cabin
P2002-JF	P2002 certified to JAR-VLA standard
P2002-JR	P2002JF with retractable tricycle undercarriage

Ted Smith   United States

In 1966, Theodore R 'Ted' Smith left Aero Commander and set up Ted Smith Aircraft Co Inc It was his intention to create a new range of business aircraft based on one standard airframe with a variety of engines, offering very high performance. His design was a mid-wing six-seat cabin monoplane with a circular section fuselage and swept fin with a main cabin airstair door ahead of the wing. The aircraft which emerged was not unlike a mid-wing Aero Commander and the first model had two piston engines – although it was envisaged that there would be several single-engined models and, at the other end of the scale, a twinjet.

The prototype Aerostar 300/400 was first flown in November 1966. This aircraft was used for certification of the Model 360 initially and then the Model 400 and Model 600. In practice, however, the first production Aerostar was the Model 600 powered by two 290hp Lycoming IO-540 engines. As with the Aero Commander, Ted Smith gave designations based on the flat-rated horsepower of the engines (although

this system did vary during the life of the Aerostar line). The Model 360 (N540TS c/n 360001) had a more streamlined vertical tail than the original design and a slightly deeper fuselage, but, otherwise, the Aerostar underwent very little change during its development.

The first production Aerostar 600 (N588TS c/n 600-0001) was flown on 20th December 1967 and was soon followed by the Aerostar 601 (N587TS c/n 601-0001) with turbocharged IO-540 engines. Both models were built at Van Nuys, California, but, in June 1968, the company was bought by American Cement Co, who injected a considerable amount of working capital. The acquisition was not a great success, however, and in late 1969 after the company had undergone several crises it was again sold – this time to Butler Aviation who had also acquired Mooney.

The whole organisation was amalgamated under the name Aerostar Aircraft Corporation in July 1970 and it was intended to transfer Aerostar production to Mooney's Kerrville plant. Unfortunately, Butler's aviation manufacturing activities were short-lived and, in 1972,

Ted Smith bought back the design rights, setting up Ted R Smith & Associates to manufacture Aerostars. This company took over the line with effect from aircraft number 130 and soon introduced the pressurized Model 601P and then the Model 700 Superstar. The company name was changed to Ted Smith Aerostar Corporation in 1976.

Two years later, on 28th April 1978, Piper Aircraft acquired the Aerostar line. Production of the Models 600A, 601B and 600P continued in California with very minor changes. They subsequently introduced the Model 601P (known initially as the Sequoya) and then, after discontinuing the non-pressurized models, moved production to the main Piper plant at Vero Beach. The last Aerostar was completed in 1984. In early 1991, Idaho-based Aerostar Aircraft bought back the type certificate from Piper and proposed to build the Aerostar 3000 (known as the AAC Star Jet I) with the piston engines replaced by two Williams FJ.44 turbofans in underwing pods. This progressed into the Aerostar FJ-100 with rear-mounted FJ33-1 turbofans mounted on the rear fuselage, a 44-inch fuselage stretch and the tailplane raised to the middle of the fin. However this project, and a proposed turboprop conversion of the Aerostar 600 series, has been shelved pending funding being raised. Aerostar designs projected and actually built were as follows:

Model	Built	Notes
320		Six-seat cabin twin with mid-set wing, retractable tricycle undercarriage and two 160hp Lycoming IO-320 engines
360	1	Prototype Aerostar based on Model 320 but powered by two 180hp Lycoming IO-360 engines. Prototype N540TS c/n 320-1 FF Nov 1966
400	-	Certificated version with 200hp Lycoming IO-360. Not built
500		Projected version with two 250hp fuel-injected engines
500P		Model 500 with pressurized cabin
600	56	Initial production model with two 290hp Lycoming IO-540-K engines, deeper fuselage, enlarged fin etc. Prototype N588TS (c/n 600-001) FF Oct 1967. Production by TSAC, AAC, TSA, Piper
600A	204	Model 600 with minor detail changes
600		Designation of special European version. Also Models 601PE and 601E
601	117	600 with turbocharged TIO-540-S1A5 engines. Prototype N587TS (c/n 61-001)
601B	44	Model 601 with increased wingspan, 300 lb TOGW increase
601P	492	Pressurized Model 601 with increased gross weight
602P	124	Piper development of 601P with 290hp Lycoming TIO-540-AA1A5 engines. Initially named Sequoya
620	1	Pressurized Aerostar with 310hp Lycoming TIO-541 engines
700	1	Superstar prototype (N72TS c/n 60-0026-044) with 32-inch stretched fuselage and 350hp Lycoming IO-540M engines
700P	26	602P with 350hp counter-rotating Lycoming TIO-540-U2A engines. Designated PA-60. Prototype N68907 (c/n 60-8223001) FF Sep 1981
800	1	601P with stretched fuselage, enlarged tail and two 400hp Lycoming IO-720 engines. Prototype N72TS converted from Superstar prototype
Total	1,067	

Aerostar serial numbers combined an overall line number that included all models with an individual model serial number. For example, the 18th Aerostar 601P had c/n 61P-205-18 and this indicated it was the 205th Aerostar of all types to have been built (and the 18th Model 61P). Model 600s had serials prefixed 60-, Model 601s had a 61-prefix and the 601P had a 61P- prefix. When Piper took over, the 'all model' series had reached c/n 501 (ie, c/n 61P-0501-206) and they continued the Ted Smith c/n system for a while, starting at c/n 500 (ie, 60-500-162). Piper then moved to a hybrid system, combining the Ted Smith and Piper formats and incorporating the year of construction and a Piper type designator at the beginning of the individual model number together with the 'all model series number'. The first of these was c/n 60-0563-7961183 introduced at the start of the 1979 model year. When production was moved to Vero Beach from 1982, more standard Piper-style serials were used (eg, 60-8265001 to 60-8265057 and 60-8365001 to 60-8365021 for the Model 602P and c/n 60-8423001 to 60-8423025 for the small batch of Model 700Ps).

Piper Aerostar 602P N10FJ

IndUS Thorpedo N401SA

Thorp   United States

John W Thorp was involved in many designs including the Fletcher FU24, Lockheed Neptune, Wing Derringer and the Piper Cherokee. However, one of his earliest and least-known designs is the T-11 Sky Skooter – an all-metal side-by-side two-seat trainer with externally ribbed wing skins which first flew on 15th August 1946 powered by a 65hp Lycoming engine. This aircraft (NX91301 c/n 1) was followed by two further prototypes (c/n 3 and 4) and two production aircraft (c/n 5 and 6). Thorp proposed the T-11 as a basic trainer for the US Air Force – though without success.

The postwar general aviation slump forced Thorp to suspend development, but in 1964 the T-11 was taken over by Tubular Aircraft Products of Los Angeles. The T-11 had already been modified by Thorp to mount a 90hp Continental engine (and was redesignated T-111). Tubular Aircraft built a new prototype, the T-211 (N86650 c/n 007), which further increased the power to a 100hp Continental O-200A. Once again, however, the aircraft failed to reach production and, eventually, in 1975 the type certificate was acquired by John Adams of the Detroit-based Adams Industries Inc The T-211 went into production and one unit was completed in 1981 by Aircraft Engineering Associates (N29754 c/n 010). The type certificate passed to Thorp Aero Inc who purchased the parts inventory of Adams Industries. A new factory was set up at Sturgis, Kentucky for Thorp Aero to market a new version

named the T-211 Aerosport for sale to non-US customers and they produced c/n 11 and 100 to 102.

By 1992, the company was undergoing refinancing and a move to Mesa, Arizona where the aircraft was to be marketed by Phoenix Aircraft as the 'Phoenix Flyer' but this company was declared bankrupt in the summer of 1994. In 1998, DM Aerospace Ltd of Manchester, UK (later renamed AD Aerospace) acquired the type certificate and production rights, intending to put the T-211 into production either as a completed aircraft or as a kit and intending to offer the T-211 also with the 100hp Jabiru 3300 six-cylinder lightweight engine. Once again, this failed to progress and the T-211 was offered in the USA by Robert J Swanson's Venture Light Aircraft Resources LLC of Tucson, AZ who completed c/n 103 to 107 together with several kits. The Thorp designs then passed to IndUS Aviation of Dallas, Texas, which produces T-211 kits. They have also built two examples of the Thorpe 211SP-E Thorpedo (prototype N401SA c/n 0001) which is powered by a Jabiru 3300 engine. The aircraft is also being sold as the T-11 Sky Skooter with a Jabiru 2200 engine and IndUS have flown a development aircraft (N211TH c/n 003X). IndUS has contracted Taneja Aerospace & Aviation Ltd to build the T-211 in India where c/n 106 (N6524V) has been used as a pattern aircraft and first flew in this form on 2nd April 2004. Two further airframes were under construction in early 2005. In total, 17 commercial T.211s and at least eleven kit examples have been completed.

Tipsy   Belgium

The Tipsy light aircraft designs were the creation of Ernest O Tips – Managing Director of the Belgian Avions Fairey company – and these aircraft were always a secondary activity beside the main line military business of the Fairey company. Avions Fairey was established in 1931 by the British parent company and, while building the Fairey Fox and Firefly the company was able to produce the open single-seat Tipsy S-2 and two-seat Tipsy B (and enclosed cabin BC model). When the war was over, Fairey restarted aircraft production and the side-by-side Belfair started to be built. The Belfair was a low-wing monoplane con-

structed of wood and fabric with a fixed tailwheel undercarriage and powered by a 62hp Walter Mikron in-line engine. The prototype was a former Model BC that became OO-TIA (c/n 502) and it was followed by six production examples, of which half were completed in England.

Tips also built two prototypes of a new low-wing single-seater, the Tipsy Junior, which was, again, made of wood and fabric and first flew in 1948. The first aircraft, OO-TIT (c/n J.110), used a Walter Mikron engine, but the second machine (OO-ULA) had a JAP J-99. Unfortunately, Fairey decided to go no further with the Junior but they did not forget its original concept and, in the mid-1950s, they built the prototype Tipsy Nipper. Constructed of tube and fabric, the Nipper was a mid-wing machine with a fixed tricycle undercarriage and it was conceived as the smallest aircraft that could accommodate a single pilot. The first example, OO-NIP (c/n 1) was first flown on 2nd December 1957 powered by a 40hp Pollman Hepu conversion of the air-cooled Volkswagen car engine. It had an open cockpit.

Subsequent Nippers had a built-up rear fuselage faired into a large bubble canopy that served to protect the pilot. In this form it was known as the T.66 Nipper Mk 1 and Tipsy subsequently flew a further variant known as the Nipper Mk 2, which was powered by a 45hp Stark Stamo 1400A engine in place of the Hepu. The Nipper went into production at Gosselies in 1959 and continued until 1961 by which time aircraft c/n T66/59 had been completed. At this point, production was taken over by Compagnie Belge d'Aviation (Cobelavia) run by M Andre Delhamende and a further batch of 18 aircraft (c/n T66/60 to 77) was completed and designated Cobelavia D-158 Nipper.

In 1966, all rights to the Nipper were acquired by Nipper Aircraft of Castle Donington, England who produced 33 airframes before going into liquidation in May 1971. In fact, these aircraft were built for Nipper Aircraft by Slingsby Aircraft Ltd and four examples were destroyed on the production line in a fire at their Kirkbymoorside factory in November 1968. These Slingsby-built Nippers were given serial numbers c/n S.101 to S.133 together with a Slingsby number within their own serial system in the range c/n 1585 to 1676. English production aircraft were known as the Nipper Mk III and were pow-

Tipsy Nipper T.66 Srs 1 G-BYLO

ered by a 1,500 cc. Rollason Ardem conversion of the Volkswagen. Two units of the Nipper Mk IIIA were built (c/n S.104 and S.108) with the 55hp 1,600 cc. Ardem. One of these (G-AVKK c/n S.104) was also fitted with a conventional windscreen and sliding canopy together with wingtip fuel tanks.

TL Ultralight   Czech Republic

Based at Hradec Kralové, TL Ultralight was formed in 1990, initially to build trikes for weight-shift ultralights. They continue to build these as the TL.1 and TL.2 and in 1991 introduced the three-axis ultralight TL32 Typhoon. This was followed in 1993 by the TL132 Condor and in 1994 by the TL232 Condor Plus which are both kit-built and based on the design of the Rans S-6 Coyote. The Condor Plus is a 450kg strut-braced high wing ultralight with a tubular fuselage structure covered with light alloy and a metal wing with fabric covering. It has a fixed tricycle undercarriage and the all-round-vision cabin has side-by-side seating

for two. The standard powerplant is an 80hp Rotax 912 although the Rotax 582 can be installed as a lower-powered option and the 100hp Rotax 912S can also be fitted.

The next design was the TL96 Star (again a 450kg ultralight), which first flew in November 1997 and is sold as a factory-complete aircraft or kit. The very streamlined TL96 is built entirely with glassfibre shells for fuselage, wings and tail and has side-by-side seating for two with dual controls. The cabin has a large clearview canopy which hinges forward for entry. The Star is fitted with flaps and has a fixed tricycle undercarriage and the standard powerplant is an 80hp Rotax 912 but Rotax 912S or Rotax 914 options are available. In 2002, the Star was

TL Ultralight TL-2000 Sting Carbon 59-CFD

TL Ultralight TL232 Condor Plus 57-QM

joined by the TL2000 Sting Carbon which uses carbon fibre composite construction and, while outwardly similar to the TL96, is a higher-performance model, having a shorter-span modified wing with a forward-swept trailing edge. Both aircraft are sold in the USA as the Star Sport and Sting Sport under the Light Sport Aircraft rules. The Sting Carbon RG is a retractable undercarriage version of the TL2000. Also introduced in late 2004 was the TL96 Sting, which is a Star with carbon fibre construction. Serial numbers for the Star consist of two digits for the year (e.g. 98 or 00), the letter S and an individual serial number commencing 01. Current production has reached around c/n 04S140. The Sting TL-2000 has a similar system with ST as identifying letters and has reached approximately c/n 05ST111. Sting Sports for the United States are prefixed TLUSA1 followed by an individual serial number from 01 to (currently) 20 and, on the first batch, the Rotax engine type. Typical serial numbers were c/n TLUSA104914 and TLUSA118. Overall production is around 270 aircraft.

Transavia   Australia

Transfield NSW Pty Ltd is a major Australian heavy engineering company based at Seven Hills on the outskirts of Sydney. In 1965, it established a division named Transavia which embarked on development and production of the PL-12 Airtruk agricultural aircraft. The PL-12 had its origins in the Kingsford Smith PL-7 Tanker, which was designed by Luigi Pellarini and first flew on 21st September 1956. The PL-7 was a biplane with twin booms attached to the upper wing, which carried the tail section and a pod fuselage built around a large chemical hopper with the pilot's cockpit to the rear and a Cheetah engine in front. Pellarini's concept was to create 'an agricultural machine that flies' rather than 'an aircraft which can spray crops'.

The Tanker concept developed into the rather more refined PL-11 Airtruck, two of which were built by Bennett Aviation (later Waitomo Aircraft Ltd) in New Zealand. The PL-11 was a monoplane with a vesti-

gial sesquiplane lower wing which carried the main wing bracing struts, and the cockpit, with a canopy taken from a T-6 Harvard, was mounted high above the chemical hopper with a loading aperture just behind the pilot. It had a fixed tricycle undercarriage, a Pratt & Whitney Wasp radial engine – and the same twin-boom layout as the PL-7 with two separate tailplanes on top of the fin/rudder units.

For production by Transavia, Pellarini produced the revised PL-12, which was smaller and lighter than the PL-11 thanks to a considerable amount of glassfibre construction in the fuselage, and was known as the Airtruk. It was a more elegant aircraft and was powered by a 285hp Continental flat-six engine. This powerplant was only just adequate for the Airtruk's needs and the aircraft was quickly upgraded to 300 horsepower.

The agricultural version was the main model and it incorporated a glassfibre rear cabin with a bench seat for transport of two ground operators. Transavia also built nine examples of the PL-12U, which had

Transavia T300A Skyfarmer VH-UJA

a freight compartment in place of the hopper/passenger compartment. The PL-12 was subsequently re-engined with a 320hp Continental Tiara engine, which proved to be very reliable, but discontinuation of the Tiara meant a further engine change in 1978.

The Airtruk name was changed to Skyfarmer for the 1981 Paris Air Show. Transavia subsequently studied a turboprop version (the T-550) and built a mock-up of the M.300 military support model but neither was built. 118 examples, including the prototype, were eventually completed at the Seven Hills factory near Sydney. Transavia's serial number system consists of a basic series number which started at c/n 01 and has now reached 117 – but this is prefixed by a number indicating the year built. The first production aircraft was c/n 601, built in 1966 and serials continued to the 1972-built c/n 1247. To identify the decade change, Transavia then prefixed the serial numbers 'G' for the 1970s (serial batch c/n G248 to G9102) and 'H' for the 1980s (c/n H0103 to H5117 being built between 1980 and 1985). Details of these models are as follows:

Model	Notes
PL-11	Bennett Airtruck mid-wing all-metal sesquiplane, powered by one P&W R-1340-S3H1 Wasp radial engine. Prototype ZK-BPV (c/n BA-001) FF 28 Apr 1960
PL-12	Airtruk. Re-engineered version of PL-11 with 285hp Cont IO-520-A engine, 3,800 lb TOGW, new cockpit, rear passenger compartment and enlarged lower plane. Prototype VH-TRN (c/n 1) FF 22 Apr 1965. Production aircraft fitted with 300hp Continental IO-520-D engine
PL-12U	Utility version of PL-12 with cargo area instead of hopper
PL-12-T320	Airtruk fitted with 320hp Continental Tiara 6-320B engine
PL-12-T300	T-320 with 300hp Lycoming IO-540-K1A5 engine and minor detail modifications
PL-12-T300A	Skyfarmer. T-300 with new oleo-damped u/c, strengthened upper fuselage, larger cockpit with new rollover truss, electric flaps, new nose u/c design and 300hp Lycoming IO-540-K1A5 engine
PL-12-T400	T-300A with 400hp Lycoming IO-720 engine, 30-inch longer tailbooms with larger dorsal fins and 40% larger lower sesquiplane wings

Uetz   Switzerland

During the mid-1950s, the Walter Uetz Flugzeugbau was actively building the CAB Minicab and Jodel D.11 for sale in Austria and Switzerland. In July 1962, they flew the prototype U2V, which was essentially a Jodel D.119 with a straight wing rather than the cranked Jodel wing, a single-piece clear windshield that hinged upwards for entry to the cockpit and a 100hp Continental O-200-A engine. A new dorsal fin was also fitted. Only a few U2Vs (probably three) were built, together with one U2-MFGZ (HB-SOV c/n 1131/17) that retained the standard Jodel wing. All the Uetz Jodels have a two-part serial which uses the Jodel plan number followed by a consecutive Uetz number.

Following the basic design of the U2V, Uetz designed the U3M Pelikan, which had a four-seat cabin with a long transparent canopy, a swept vertical tail and fixed tailwheel undercarriage. It was powered by a 135hp Lycoming O-290 engine and the prototype (HB-TBV c/n 25) was flown on 21st May 1963 followed by one further U3M (c/n 26). The production model was the U4M, which had flaps and a 150hp Lycoming O-320-A2B engine. Two of these were manufactured by the company (c/n 27 and 29) and two other examples (HB-TBX c/n 5 and HB-TBU c/n 7303) were built by amateurs. Uetz was also responsible

Uetz U4M Pelikan HB-TBY. M J Hooks

for the initial construction of the prototype of the 1-01-140 Marabu three-seater under contract from Albert Markwalder. Walter Uetz Flugzeugbau finally abandoned aircraft construction in 1965 having built 29 aircraft.

Urban Air   Czech Republic

Urban Air has created a small family of all-composite factory-complete JAR-VLA light aircraft based on its UFM-11 Lambada. The Lambada has a high aspect ratio shoulder wing, a side-by-side two-seat cockpit with a blister canopy, a T-tail and fixed tricycle undercarriage. The prototype made its first flight on 23rd May 1996. The aircraft is sold in two versions – the UFM-11/14, which has a standard 39ft 1in wingspan, and the UFM-13/15, which is identical but has wing extensions increasing the span to 49ft 3in and allowing soaring unpowered flight. The Lambada can be supplied with a tailwheel undercarriage and Urban Air is developing the UFM-13W pure glider version.

In standard form the Lambada is powered by an 80hp Jabiru but the 80hp Rotax 912ULS can be fitted. The second Urban Air model is the UFM-10 Samba which is of similar construction but has a redesigned low-set wing of shorter (32ft 9in) span and a conventional tail unit. The prototype (OK-EUU 38) was first flown in the summer of 1999. A modified version of the Samba, the Samba XXL (prototype OK-IUA 54), has a modified fuselage with a larger and repositioned cockpit canopy, modified engine cowling and a more streamlined tail unit. By the end of 2004, Urban Air is understood to have built 42 UFM-13 Lambadas (c/n 01/13 to 42/13) and 16 UFM-11s (c/n 01/11 to 16/11). In addition, 40 Sambas had been completed (c/n 01/10 to 40/10).

Above: **Urban Lambada UFM-11 D-MPUE**
Right: **Urban UFM-10 Samba OK-GUA 28**

UTVA-66 N10734

UTVA-65 Privrednik YU-BIM

UTVA   Yugoslavia

This company was a part of the Yugoslav Government aircraft factories group but by the mid-1960s it had been reconstituted as the Fabrika Aviona UTVA with a factory at Pancevo. Its earliest activities involved series production of the Cijan Trojka light aircraft for the Yugoslav flying clubs. It was a low-wing monoplane with a fixed tailwheel undercarriage and side-by-side seating under a framed bubble canopy and it made its first flight in October 1947. The Trojka was designed by Boris Cijan and Dragoslav Petkovic in response to a requirement from the Yugoslav Aeronautical Union and the Trojka was prototyped by the Ikarus factory. UTVA production commenced in 1947, the main version having a 65hp Walter Mikron III engine, and the first aircraft were delivered in 1949. A later version used the105hp Walter Minor 4-III engine. 80 examples of the Trojka were built. Once production had

been completed, Petkovic and Branislav Nikolic, moved on to a completely new four-seat utility aircraft to meet the needs of flying clubs and for military liaison and artillery spotting, for ambulance and general duties and as a crop sprayer.

The result was the UTVA-56, a strut-braced all-metal high-wing aircraft with a fixed tailwheel undercarriage and a 260hp Lycoming GO-435-C2B2 flat-six engine. The prototype (YU-BAF c/n 00672) made its first flight on 22nd April 1959. The production version was known as the UTVA-60 (prototype YU-BAK c/n 00673) and, among other changes, it had modified flaps and a 270hp Lycoming GO-430-B1A6 engine. It is believed that around 35 examples were completed together with 80 of the improved UTVA-66. Construction numbers are not confirmed but the UTVA-66 is thought to be in the range c/n 0801 to 0880. Deliveries were mainly for the Yugoslav military forces, although many have been civil registered including ex-military aircraft

UTVA-75 9A-DHF

sold in western markets. Several versions were manufactured from 1962 onwards including:

Model	Notes
UTVA-60-AT1	Utility four-seat version for liaison, club use, freight and air taxi work
UTVA-60-AT2	Model AT1 with dual controls
UTVA-60-AG	Agricultural model with rear cabin hopper and under-fuselage duster or underwing spraybars
UTVA-60-AM	Ambulance version with hinged rear window and two stretcher stations to starboard
UTVA-60H	Seaplane version fitted with twin BIN-1600 floats, strengthened fuselage, ventral fin. Prototype FF 29 Oct 1961
UTVA-66	UTVA-60 with wing slats, larger tail, improved u/c and 340hp Lycoming GSO-480-B1A6 engine
UTVA-66AM	Ambulance version of UTVA-66 with upward-hinged rear window
UTVA-66H	Seaplane version of UTVA-66 with BIN.1600 floats. FF Sep 1968
UTVA-70	Proposed twin-engined six-seat UTVA-66 with two 295hp Lycoming GO-480-G1J6 engines on stub wings. Not built

Much of the design and many components of the UTVA-60 were used on the UTVA-65 Privrednik agricultural aircraft. The Privrednik was a classic low-wing single-seat crop sprayer, similar to a Cessna Agwagon, powered by a 295hp Lycoming GO-480-G1A6 flat six engine and having a hopper between the cabin and the firewall and a fixed tailwheel undercarriage. UTVA flew the first prototype (YU-BBZ c/n 0691) in 1965 and followed this with a small series of production aircraft – believed to total 45 (c/n 0692 to 0736). A further version, the UTVA-67 Privrednik II was also proposed with a redesigned fuselage, larger capacity hopper and a 400hp Lycoming IO-720-A1A engine, but this does not appear to have reached prototype stage.

In 1974, following completion of UTVA-66 production, UTVA moved on to a new light two-seat trainer and club aircraft – the

UTVA-75 (UTVA-75A21). It was a modern low-wing all-metal aircraft similar to a Piper Cherokee with side-by-side seating, a fixed tricycle undercarriage and upward-opening gull-wing cabin doors. The powerplant was a 180hp Lycoming IO-360-B with a two-blade Hartzell variable-pitch propeller. For military use, each wing was provided with an underwing hardpoint to carry armament or supplementary fuel tanks. The first prototype UTVA-75 (JRV53001) was flown at Pancevo on 19th May 1976 and production for the air force (as the V-53) and flying schools totalled 138 examples. An improved version, the UTVA-75R had numerous cabin and instrument improvements but the prototype was destroyed in 1999 when the UTVA factory was bombed.

UTVA also built prototypes of two developments of the Model 75. The UTVA-78 was a variant with a GA-W supercritical wing and a deeper fuselage and one prototype was built. This was destroyed in an accident and its fuselage was used as the basis for the first of two prototype UTVA-75A41s. This was a four-seat version with a higher gross weight and the cabin extended rearwards with the entry doors enlarged to allow access to front and rear seats. The prototype (YU-XAC JRV 53263) was first flown in 1986 and in the mid-1990s this was revived as the UTVA-96 and two prototypes were under construction in 2004. The second project was an agricultural version of the UTVA-75 designated UTVA-75AG11. In this model, the fuselage was redesigned to provide a single-seat cockpit over the wing centre section with a chemical hopper between the cockpit and the engine firewall and the undercarriage was strengthened. The powerplant was changed to a 300hp Lycoming IO-540-L1A5D. A prototype was flown on 3rd March 1989, (YU-XAF/JRV53265), but development ceased as a result of the destruction of the prototype at the factory in 1999 and the political crisis of the former Yugoslavia. The company, now named LOLA-UTVA Fabrika Aviona, currently concentrates on military contracts for overhaul of the Galeb, Orao and An-2 but it is working on a new version of the UTVA Lasta-95 military trainer for the Air Force of Serbia and Montenegro.

Vajic   Yugoslavia

The Vajic V.55, which was designed and built by Aero Technicki Zavod in Zagreb, was built in small series during the 1960s for aero clubs in Yugoslavia. The first V.55 was flown in April 1959 and five examples are known to have been completed. In its basic form, the V.55 was a tube-and-fabric tandem two-seater with a strut-braced high wing, fixed tailwheel undercarriage and an 85hp Walter Minor II engine. An alternative three-seat model was also available with a 105hp Walter Minor 4-III.

Vajic V.55 YU-CMR

Valentin   Germany

The Valentin Taifun 17E is a sophisticated two-seat motor glider which was built by Valentin Flugzeugbau GmbH of Hassfurt. It is of all glass-fibre construction with a T-tail, side-by-side seating, wings which fold back alongside the fuselage for storage and transport, and a manually-operated retractable tricycle undercarriage. The wingspan of the 17E is 17.0 metres but Valentin also built two examples of the Taifun 12E with a new 12.0 metre wing which were registered in Germany as standard light aircraft rather than motor gliders. Valentin also flew the Taifun 11S prototype (D-EVFB), which was powered by a 115hp Lycoming O-235 engine and had four seats with a forward-hinged cockpit canopy and a fixed undercarriage. However, this was abandoned in late 1987.

The Taifun JR.1 prototype (D-KONO c/n 01) was first flown on 28th February 1981 powered by an 80hp Limbach L.2000EB (Volkswagen) engine. After a substantial production run (c/n 1002 to 1107) this was upgraded to a 90hp Limbach L.2400EB powerplant and the aircraft designated Taifun 17E-II. The Taifun went into production in 1982 and 135 production examples (c/n 1002 to 1136) were completed. The

Valentin Taifun 17E F-CGAF

company also built 19 examples of the Kiwi motor-assisted single-seat sailplane (c/n 001 and 3002 to 3019) Valentin production was taken over by FFT based at Mengen.

Rockwell Commander Darter LV-WDT

Volaircraft   United States

Volaircraft Inc was formed at Aliquippa, Pennsylvania to develop the Volaire 10. This aircraft was an all-metal high-wing machine with an 'omni-vision' cabin somewhat similar to that of later Cessna 150 models. It had a distinctive vertical tail that appeared to be swept forward and the prototype (N6661D c/n 10) was powered by a 135hp Lycoming O-290-D2C engine. The basic Model 10 was a three-place aircraft with a gross weight of 1,900 lb, but the definitive version was intended to be a full four-seater with a 350 lb increase in gross weight. It is believed that only six Volaire 10s (c/n 10 to 15) were completed and the four-seat Model 10A replaced it on the production line. Also known as the Volaircraft 1050, this model was fitted with a 150hp Lycoming O-320-A2B powerplant.

On 12th July 1965, Rockwell Standard Corporation bought Volaircraft Inc and the Model 1050 was built by the Aero Commander Division at Albany, Georgia. Initially, this aircraft became known as the Aero Commander 100 (and the few remaining Volair 10s became the Aero Commander 100A) but, in 1968, a number of improvements were made. The front and rear windshields were altered and this version was titled Aero Commander Darter Commander. Production continued until 1969, at which point the model was terminated with 335 units completed (c/n 26 to 360).

In September 1967, Rockwell obtained certification for a redesigned version following engineering testing on two modified Darters (c/n 043 and 068). This was the Model 100-180 Lark that was of generally similar construction but had a 180hp Lycoming O-360-A2F engine and a gross weight of 2,450 lb. The angular tail of the Darter was replaced by a swept fin and rudder and the engine cowling was larger and more streamlined. The Lark Commander also had new wheel fairings and a much higher quality interior. The first production aircraft was N3700X (c/n 5001) and deliveries started in 1968. Lark production ceased in 1971 after 213 aircraft had been built (c/n 5001 to 5213). Rockwell later sold the type certificate for all the Volaire designs to S L Industries of Oklahoma City and the Lark then passed into the hands of DYNAC International Corporation who made a brief attempt to relaunch production in association with Christen Industries.

Rockwell Commander Lark N4033X

Wassmer   France

Benjamin Wassmer formed the Société Wassmer in 1905 as a specialised woodworking organisation – but the company's entry into aircraft manufacture did not come until 1955 when it embarked on production of a batch of basic Jodel D.112 two-seaters at its factory in Issoire (Puy de Dôme). These carried Avions Jodel serial numbers within the batches – c/n 224 to 266, 1013 to 1021, 1063 to 1082, 1112 to 1130, 1162 to 1181, 1204 to 1223, 1253 to 1272, 1293 to 1322 and 1343 to 1352. The D.112s were followed by the improved Jodel D.120 Paris-Nice which was a refined version of the Jodel D.119 and these carried Wassmer serial numbers from c/n 1 to 337. Wassmer also built large numbers of the single-seat Wa-20 Javelot glider and its two-seat counterpart, the Wa-30 Bijave.

A new powered aircraft appeared in 1959 from the Wassmer factory. The Wassmer Wa-40 Super IV was a smart low-wing tube-and-fabric

Wassmer Wa-40 Super IV D-EHSF

Wassmer Wa-41 Baladou G-ATZS

design with a retractable tricycle undercarriage and four seats under a clear sliding canopy. It was offered with varying standards of equipment as the Sancy, President, Pariou and Commandant de Bord. The initial production Wa-40 was followed, in due course, by the Wa-40A with a swept tail and by the fixed undercarriage Baladou. It was clear, however, that the Wa-40 would benefit from higher power than the 180hp engine which had been fitted thus far and Wassmer produced the Super 4/21 prototype which used a 235hp Lycoming and featured a revised engine cowling, modified undercarriage and streamlined cockpit canopy. The production Super 4/21 (otherwise known as the Wa 41-250) had a 250hp engine. Serial numbers for the basic Wa-40 models ran from c/n 1 to 168 and the Super 4/21 from c/n 401 to 430.

Over a number of years, Wassmer had developed a working relationship with Société Siren of Argenton-sur-Creuse. In 1972, the two companies combined to form the CERVA partnership (the Consortium Européen de Réalisation et de Ventes d'Avions) which redesigned the Super 4/21 as an all-metal aircraft with an integral cabin and a 250hp Lycoming engine, in which form it was titled the CE-43 Guepard. They also built one example of the higher-powered CE-44 Cougar. The basic

construction of the Guepard was carried out by Siren, while final assembly and testing was Wassmer's responsibility. A French military order for 18 Guepards was received and this provided CERVA with the basis for a respectable production run with serials in a batch from c/n 431 to 473.

Wassmer continued in the design and construction of sailplanes, eventually producing the glassfibre Wa.28 and the CE-75 Silene and H-230 which were built in cooperation with Siren. The move away from traditional materials led Wassmer into the use of full plastic/composite construction for light aircraft and the company gained a decisive technological lead. They built the Wa-50 prototype – a four-seat low-wing touring model with a retractable undercarriage – and went into exhaustive testing of its plastic airframe with certification being achieved in 1970. The range of production Wa-50 derivatives, with fixed undercarriages, gull-wing cabin doors and a variety of engine options, incorporated considerable design changes from the prototype and did not use the proposed metal-to-plastic bonding which had been intended. A new serial sequence was used for the Wa-50 series running from c/n 1 to 154.

Wassmer Wa-54 Atlantic D-EFVS

Wassmer's final design was the Wa-80 two-seat trainer, which used the same construction as the Wa-50 series. Named Piranha, the Wa-80 was really a scaled-down version of the four-seater but it had unusual main undercarriage legs made of composites and a 100hp Rolls-Royce Continental engine. The Piranha serial batch ran from c/n 801 to 824. With both the Wa-80 and the various Wa-50 models in production, Wassmer was running into severe working capital problems and it was forced into liquidation on 16th September 1977 at which time all production was suspended. In February 1978 a new company, Issoire Aviation, was established to acquire the assets of Wassmer. Its activities are described separately. Details of the Wassmer powered aircraft line are as follows:

Wassmer Wa-80 Piranha F-GAIF

Model	Built	Notes
Wa-40 Super IV	52	Four-seat low-wing tourer with retractable tricycle u/c and one 180hp Lycoming O-360-A1A engine. 2,645 lb TOGW. Prototype F-BIXX FF 8 Jun 1959
Wa-40A Super IV	57	Wa-40 with swept tail and lengthened nose. Named Sancy
Wa-41 Baladou	58	Economy version of Wa-40A with fixed undercarriage. Prototype F-BNAZ (c/n 89)
Wa-4/21 Prestige	30	Wa-40A with 250hp Lycoming IO-540-C4B5 engine, electric flaps and u/c, streamlined cockpit canopy, lengthened nose, 3,108 lb TOGW. Prototype F-BOBZ (c/n 401) FF Mar 1967
CE-43 Guepard	44	All-metal development of Wa-4/21 with integral cabin, revised tail, 3,219 lb TOGW. Prototype F-WSNJ FF 18 May 1971
CE-44 Cougar	1	CE-43 with 285hp Continental Tiara 6-285P engine. Prototype F-WXCE
CE-45 Leopard	-	CE-43 with 310hp Lycoming TIO-540. Not built
Wa-50	1	All-plastic four-seat low-wing cabin monoplane with retractable tricycle u/c and one 150hp Lycoming O-320-E engine. Prototype F-WNZZ FF 18 Mar 1966
Wa-51 Pacific	39	Production Wa-50 with fixed u/c, modified tail, Lycoming O-320-E2C engine, 2,425 lb TOGW. Prototype F-BPTT (c/n 01) FF 17 May 1969
Wa-52 Europa	59	Wa-51 with 160hp Lycoming O-320-D1F engine
Wa-53	-	Wa-51 with 125hp Lycoming. Not built
Wa-54 Atlantic	55	Wa-51 with 180hp Lycoming O-360-A1LD engine and 2,491 lb TOGW
Wa-80 Piranha	6	All-plastic side-by-side two-seat low-wing cabin monoplane with one 100hp RR Continental O-200-A engine. Prototype F-WVKR (c/n 801) FF Nov 1975
Wa-81 Piranha	18	Wa-80 with additional third rear seat

CERVA CE-43 Guepard OH-WAA

Weatherly United States

The Weatherly agricultural aircraft manufacturing business has its origins in John C Weatherly's fixed base operation at Dallas, Texas where the first designs were conceived in 1960. In fact, the Weatherly Aviation Company was not established in Texas – but started instead in 1961 at Hollister, California where the prototype of the WM-62C (N3775G c/n W-1) was built. This was a conversion of a Fairchild M-62

Cornell for agricultural tasks and it gave the company valuable experience over the five years in which the Cornell conversion programme lasted. When some 19 WM-62Cs had been built and the supply of Cornell airframes was drying up, Weatherly was able to build its own version from scratch.

The Weatherly 201 was a low-wing, tailwheel-undercarriage design with an enclosed cockpit and the wing design was particularly efficient because of a system of boundary layer control through vortex genera-

Weatherly 620A N4627G

tors and a wing booster fairing. Two prototype Weatherly 201s were built (N86686 c/n 101 and N86687 c/n 102) and production of the Model 201A, powered by a 450hp Pratt & Whitney R-985 radial engine, started in 1968.

The Model 201A (c/n 110 to 114) was followed by the 201B (c/n 601 to 645) and then the Model 201C (c/n 1001 to 1038) – each of which differed in minor respects but used the same engine. The 201C and subsequent versions could be fitted with small vanes attached to the wingtips to improve the swathe width of sprayed liquid chemicals. The prototype of the current Weatherly model, the 620, (N9256W c/n 1501) first flew in 1979 and was externally similar to the 201 but with the gross weight increased to 5,800 lb which provided a hopper capacity of 310-US gal and, in the production 620-A, a 65-US gal fuel capacity. In 1991, the company moved to Lincoln, California and the 620-A was replaced by the Weatherly 620-B which has a 4-inch fuselage stretch to provide 88 gallons of fuel, improved pilot protection and a 355-US gal hopper.

Weatherly Aviation fitted the second prototype 620 (N9259W c/n 1502) with a Pratt & Whitney PT6A-11AG turboprop and marketed two turboprop models, the 620-A-TP and 620-B-TP both with an enlarged rudder, but only delivered one (N4607C, c/n 1508TP). The turboprop aircraft are serialled in the main sequence, but with the suffix 'TP'. By 1997, Weatherly Aviation was under financial pressure and declared bankruptcy in 1999 by which time production had reached aircraft c/n 1655. Eventually, in 2000, Weatherly's assets were acquired by Gary E Beck who formed Weatherly Aircraft Company and moved the business to a new plant at McLellan Park Industrial Complex in Sacramento, California. The first new-build Weatherly 620-B (V3-HGM, c/n 1656) was delivered in January 2003 and production had reached c/n 1658 by mid-2004. The company has also flown the prototype Weatherly 620-BTG (LV-ZHB, c/n 3000) which is powered by a Honeywell TPE331-1 turboprop.

Windecker United States

Doctor Leo Windecker formed Windecker Research in March 1967 to develop aircraft constructed of glass reinforced plastic (GRP). He had been investigating the use of this material for aircraft structures over a number of years and had fitted wings made from Dow Chemicals' 'Fibaloy' material to two Monocoupes. The first product of his venture was the X-7 (N801WR c/n 1) which first flew on 7th October 1967 and was a low-wing four-seat light aircraft with a fixed tricycle undercarriage and a 290hp Lycoming IO-540 engine. The X-7 proved that Windecker's concept of a structure using large GRP shells with some fibreglass-covered polystyrene section was valid and it flew in tests until it was retired in 1968.

The production prototype of the AC-7 Eagle I was N802WR (c/n 001) which flew in early 1969. This differed from the X-7 in having a retractable undercarriage, redesigned wing and a 285hp Lycoming IO-520-C engine. It was destroyed in a spinning accident on 19th April 1969, but the second AC-7 (N803WR c/n 002), which was lighter and

had a ventral fin, received its type certificate in December 1969 and the aircraft went into production. By late 1970, however, the company was in financial difficulty and ceased operations. The last completed airframe was c/n 008 and this was delivered to the US Air Force for stealth test evaluation as the YE-5 (73-1653). One Eagle was converted to turboprop power with an Allison 250 engine.

In 1976 the tooling and stocks of Windecker were bought by Gerald P Dietrick, who formed Composite Aircraft Corporation in April 1979. Composite designed various improvements to the Eagle but did not build any aircraft. The type certificate was acquired in early 1991 by Richard Lehmann of National Aircraft Rental Systems, who proposed to build Eagles at Georgetown, Delaware. These new aircraft would be only for rental to customers and would be destroyed after seven years in order to limit product liability exposure. This scheme, again, did not progress and the design was acquired by the Canadian Aerospace Group (CAG) of Hamilton, Ontario who announced plans in mid-1996 to produce a new version named Windeagle. The two models contemplated were the Windeagle E-285 with a 285hp Continental IO-520

Windecker AC-7 Eagle N4196G

and the Windeagle E-750T with a Pratt & Whitney PT6A turboprop. CAG announced that the Windeagle would be built in China by Jiangxi Hongdu Aviation Industry Group and a new company, Windeagle Aircraft Corporation, was formed to also build the aircraft at St Hubert in Canada. Windeagle collapsed after defaulting on loans and in the wake of a financial crisis at CAG, and no Windeagles were built.

Wing   United States

The Hi-Shear Rivet Tool Company of Torrance, California had a background in conversion of war-surplus aircraft for crop spraying but came into full aircraft manufacturing in the mid-1950s when it established the Transland Aircraft company under the management of George S Wing. This company adopted the AG-2 agricultural aircraft designed by Fred Weick (who had designed the AG-1 and later went on to produce the Piper Pawnee). The prototype AG-2 (N8330H) first flew on 11th October 1956 powered by a 450hp Pratt & Whitney R-985 radial engine (later upgraded to a 600hp R-1340). It appears that this was exported to Uruguay (CX-AYC) and that two further AG-2s were built (N8231H c/n 2 and N8232H c/n 3) before Hi-Shear decided to abandon production. However, George Wing did adopt the D-1 Derringer light twin which was originally designed in 1958 by John Thorp as the T-17 – a twin-engined version of the Sky Skooter. A new Hi-Shear subsidiary, Wing Aircraft Co, was formed to build the aircraft. The first prototype Derringer (N3621G c/n 01) was initially named Transland D.1 and made its maiden flight at Torrance on 1st May 1962. It was fitted with two uprated 115hp Continental O-200 engines, had a very streamlined fuselage and was designed to carry just two people – on the premise that the average business aircraft seldom uses the four- or six-passenger capacity that is normally offered. The Derringer had a retractable tricycle undercarriage and an unusual cockpit canopy that opened upwards and backwards. The second aircraft (N88941 c/n 1) was flown in November 1964 but was lost in an accident less than a month later. Wing proceeded to build a static test airframe and two further aircraft to production standard (c/n 2 and 3). These enabled the company to obtain a type certificate on 20th December 1966 for the aircraft powered by two 160hp Lycoming IO-320B1C engines.

Unfortunately, an internal dispute blew up at Hi-Shear and production plans for the Derringer did not materialise. In 1978, George Wing resigned from Hi-Shear and set up Wing Aircraft Co. The Derringer went into production at Torrance and the company built one pre-production example (N821T c/n 24) and six production machines (c/n 005 to 011) before it ran out of money and filed bankruptcy papers in July 1982. The assets of the company, including seven unfinished airframes, were sold to George and Ike Athans of Chicago but they did not progress with the project and all rights were acquired by Derringer Aircraft Company LLC, based at Mojave, California. Derringer intended producing the GT-320 two-seater and the T-320 trainer version together with the four-seat GT-400. They claim to have flown a new production aircraft in November 1998 (which may have merely been the development aircraft, N8602J smartened up for the occasion) and to have had five aircraft under construction but this is unconfirmed and no further production appears to have taken place to date.

Wing Derringer N8602J

Yakovlev Yak-18 D-EYAK

Yakovlev   Russia

The Yakovlev design bureau was well known for its range of trainers and light aircraft. One of its best-known utility types was the high-wing Yak-12, which was first produced during the late 1940s. Responsibility for the Yak-12 was transferred to Poland in 1955 and its development is covered in the chapter on PZL-Okecie.

The standard primary trainer in the USSR during the 1930s and early 1940s was Yakovlev's AIR-10/AIR-20, better known as the UT-2. It was a conventional low-wing monoplane, derived from Yakovlev's UT-1 single-seat sporting aircraft of which over 1,200 had been built, with a fixed tailwheel undercarriage, tandem seating, either open or enclosed cockpits and a partially cowled 100hp 5-cylinder M-11 radial engine. More than 7,200 were built during World War Two. At the end of the war, Yakovlev's design bureau set about an update of the UT-2, which resulted in the UT-2MV, produced in 1943. It had an all-metal framework with part-metal and part-fabric covering. The tandem seating was covered by a long multi-section canopy and the 160hp M-11FR radial engine was enclosed in a 'helmeted' cowling (ie, incorporating bumps to cover the cylinder heads). The fuselage was over one metre longer than that of the UT-2 and the gross weight had risen from 2,075 lb to 2,360 lb. The second prototype was fitted with a pneumatically-operated rearward-retracting main undercarriage and in this form it went into production in 1947 as the Yak-18.

The Yak-18 became the standard basic trainer both for the Soviet Air Force and its state flying organisations and in other Warsaw Pact countries with production totalling 3,752 (and 379 also built in China). In 1955, Yakovlev introduced the Yak-18U with a tricycle undercarriage, incorporating forward (rather than rearward) retracting main legs and a lengthened forward fuselage. 960 were built between 1954 and 1957 at Arseniyev. Because it was very underpowered, this led to the Yak-18A with the new Ivchenko AI-14R engine in a smooth cowling and a series of specialised aerobatic versions of the basic design were also produced for international competition.

The Yak-18 series was succeeded by the Yak-50 and its derivatives. The Yak-50, which had a tailwheel undercarriage, was based on the design of the Yak-18P but adopted modern all-metal monocoque construction. The initial model was designed as a single-seat competition aerobatic aircraft but the later Yak-52 returned to the tandem two-seat layout of the Yak-18U. Production of the Yak-52 (also referred to as the IAK-52) was undertaken by the Romanian company I Av Bacau, which later became Aerostar (see separate entry). Details of the Yak-18 and its derivatives are as follows:

Model	Built*	Notes
Yak-18	3,752	Basic version, developed from UT-2, of steel tube-and-fabric construction with retractable tailwheel undercarriage incorporating rearward-retracting main legs, tandem two-seat cockpit with multi-section sliding canopy and one M-11FR radial engine in a 'helmeted' cowling
Yak-18	379	Chinese production
Yak-18U	960	Yak-18 with retractable tricycle u/c incorporating forward-retracting main legs and rearward-retracting nosewheel, 18-inch longer fuselage, cleaned-up helmeted engine cowling and M-11-FR-1 engine
Yak-18A	927	Initially designated Yak-20W. Yak-18U with improved nosegear, smooth engine cowling, fin leading edge fairing, 12-inch wingspan increase, 18-inch rear fuselage stretch, and a 260hp Ivchenko AI-14R radial engine in a smooth cowling
Yak-18A	1,796	Chinese production

Yakovlev Yak-12M SP-FKD

Yakovlev Yak-18PM '28'

Yakovlev Yak-18T RA-44480

Yakovlev Yak-55M N55YA

Yak-18P	25	Fully aerobatic single-seat Yak-18A with forward cockpit deleted, single cockpit canopy, extended ailerons
Yak-18P		Later version of Yak-18P with cockpit in forward seating position, enlarged rudder and modified u/c including inward-retracting main gear legs
Yak-18PM		Yak-18P with cockpit moved further back, reduced wing dihedral and 300hp Ivchenko AI-14RF radial engine
Yak-18PS	6	Yak-18PM with rearward-retracting tailwheel u/c
Yak-20		Initial designation for Yak-18A
Yak-50	321	Low-wing aerobatic aircraft based on Yak-18PM with all-metal monocoque construction, a reduced span constant taper wing without the Yak-18 centre section, retractable tailwheel u/c and 360hp Vedeneyev M-14P radial engine
Yak-52	1,807	Yak-50 with tandem two-seat cockpit, retractable tricycle u/c similar to Yak-18U and M-14P engine
Yak-52M		Improved Yak-52 with large blister canopy, modified engine cowling and Zvezda SKS-94 ejection seats
Yak-52W		Yak-52 with detail changes for US sale
Yak-52TW	20	Yak-52 with tailwheel u/c incorporating inward-retracting main legs
Yak-53		Fully aerobatic Yak-52 with single-seat cockpit in rear pilot position. Built in Arsen'yev, USSR

* Approximate number of aircraft built.

The Yak-18 designation was also applied to the Yak-18T, which was Yakovlev's answer to the needs of Aeroflot for a light air taxi aircraft to replace the long-serving Yak-12 and first flew in 1967. Essentially, the Yak-18T was a completely new tube and stressed-skin design with a large fully-enclosed four/five-seat cabin, two-spar wings broadly based on the Yak-18 design with a parallel-chord centre section and tapered outer panels, a retractable tricycle undercarriage with inward-retracting main units and a Vedeneyev (OKBM/Voronezh) M-14P engine. Around 600 were built by the Smolensk Aircraft Plant between 1968 and 1982. In 1993 new production of the Yak-18T was set up at Smolensk but the production plant declared insolvency in 1996 after 54 had been completed. The Yak-18T then became the responsibility of Technoavia who revived it as the SM-94, which first flew on 22nd December 1994 and from 1998 built a small batch (said to be 15, using existing incomplete airframes) of a new version with a two-piece windscreen and other minor refinements.

In 1982, Yakovlev announced a completely new aerobatic aircraft – the Yak-55. Designed by Vacheslav Kondratyev (who was later responsible for the Su-26 and Technoavia SP-91), the Yak-55 is a light competition aerobatic aircraft produced for the 1982 world aerobatic championships at Spitzberg in Austria. It was an all-metal mid-wing single-seater with a bubble canopy and a fixed spring-steel tailwheel undercarriage. It was of smaller dimensions than the weighty Yak-18 – but was still powered by the 360hp M-14P radial. This gave it an exceptional power to weight ratio. The basic Yak-55 was followed in 1989 by the Yak-55M which has ailerons interconnected with the elevators (so-called 'flaperons') and a modified wing with a new symmetrical wing

section. Production ceased in 1992 but a new variant has been built by Technoavia at Arsenyiev as the SP-55M and it features many detailed improvements including, more power, an enlarged rudder, tubular undercarriage legs (similar to those on the SP-91 Slava) a new cockpit canopy faired into a fuselage spine and modified control surfaces. The Yak-54 is a tandem two-seat derivative of the Yak-55. The Bureau's other light aircraft developments have included the Yak-112, which is a high-wing four-seat aircraft with a large bulbous cabin section that has been mooted for production at the Irkutsk Aviation Plant. They also designed the Yak-58 4/6-seat twin-boomed executive and utility aircraft, which was to have been produced by the Tbilisi Aviation State Association. Neither has advanced beyond prototype stage. In summary, details of these models are as follows.

Model	Built	Notes
Yak-18T	536	5-seat light transport based on Yak-18 but with new fuselage, rudder and main u/c. Powered by one 355hp Vedeneyev M-14P radial. Prototype FF 1967
Yak-55	110	Single-seat mid-wing aerobatic monoplane with fixed tailwheel u/c and 360hp M-14P engine
Yak-55M	106	Yak-55 with interconnected ailerons, redesigned u/c and modified wings with more taper
SP-55M	10	Technoavia version of Yak-55M with turtledeck rear fuselage and revised canopy, larger rudder, new wings with symmetrical section, 400hp M-14PF engine, tubular u/c legs, mod control surfaces. Prototype RA-44547
Yak-54	15	Tandem 2-seat aerobatic aircraft derived from Yak-55, powered by M-14P engine with large clamshell canopy faired into rear fuselage, tubular undercarriage legs and enlarged rudder. Prot FF 24 Dec 1993
Yak-54M	0	Proposed military trainer version of Yak-54 with retractable tricycle u/c. Not built
Yak-58	4	General-purpose 6-seat transport with twin booms, high aspect ratio wing and retractable tricycle undercarriage. Powered by one M-14PT shrouded pusher engine fitted behind the cabin. Prototype FF 17 Apr 1994
Yak-112	7	4-seat strut-braced high-wing light aircraft with large main cabin section and extensive glazing and slim tailboom with conventional tail unit. Powered by one 260hp Continental IO-550-M or alternative 210hp Continental IO-360-ES or 260hp Continental IO-540E. Prototype FF 20 October 1992

* Estimated number of aircraft built.

Construction numbers for these types vary, depending on which production plant built them. The Yak-18T has three known c/n systems, the earliest (used for original Smolensk production) consisted of 7 digits ranging from approximately 4200305 to 8201016. The second system, probably used in the 1980s, ran from approximately 22202021950 to 22203044761. The method of allocation of all these c/ns is not clear. The revived 1993-1996 production used a four-digit hyphenated number from approximately 01-31 to 19-33, the second

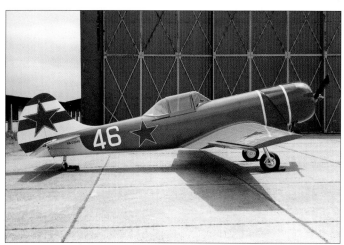

Yakovlev Yak-50 RA-02246

Yakovlev Yak-54 RF-00944

pair of digits being the batch number and the first being the aircraft within the batch. Yak-55s and Yak-55Ms have a six-digit c/n of which the first two digits are the year built (eg, c/n 890701 was built in 1989). The next two digits are a batch number and the last two digits are the aircraft within the batch (with 10 aircraft per batch). Some batch numbers have been re-used. The Yak-54 uses batches of two or three serials. Those known to date are c/n 01001 to 01002 (prototypes), c/n 02001 to 02003, 03001 to 03003, 04001 to 04003 and 05001 to 05002.

It is also important to mention the series of new-build Yakovlev Yak-3U/As and Yak-9UMs that have been produced from a limited production line in Russia. Identical to the wartime Yakovlev fighters, the Yak-9UMs have a second rear seat and are powered by an Allison V-1710 engine. Production started at the STRELA facility at Orenburg in 1992. Eleven have been built as Yak-3U/As (c/n 0470101 to 0470111) and eleven as Yak-9UMs (c/n 0470401 to 0470411), mostly for American customers.

Yakovlev Yak-112 RA-00001

Yugoslav Government Factories   Yugoslavia

During World War Two, the Yugoslav aircraft industry, particularly the Ikarus factory at Zemun, was destroyed by German action. In the immediate postwar period, what remained of the Ikarus, Zmaj and Rogojarsky companies were reconstituted as the nationalised Yugoslav aircraft industry and took over repair and maintenance of Russian-built military aircraft for the Yugoslav Air Force. Thereafter, under the Ikarus name, several new military aircraft were developed including the Ikarus 212 and 522 advanced trainers and the Ikarus 214 light transport.

In 1947, the Yugoslav government had put out a specification for a new two-seat basic trainer – primarily for military use but also with an eye to the flying clubs. Ikarus built a prototype of the Type 211, which was a conventional wooden low-wing aircraft with a fixed tailwheel undercarriage and open tandem cockpits. It first flew in 1947 from the Zemun factory near Belgrade, powered by a 160hp Walter Minor 6-III engine but, as a result of the Aero 2 being selected for large-scale pro-

duction, only a handful were built (primarily for the Yugoslav Air Force). A development of the Type 211 was the Type 212 with enclosed cockpits and a retractable undercarriage but this also failed to get beyond prototype stage.

Ikarus was also responsible for the construction of the prototype Cijan Trojka (referred to under UTVA). Another design of Boris Cijan was the two-seat DM-6R Kurir which was designed as an observation aircraft for the Yugoslav Army. The Kurir was an all-metal cantilever high-wing design with large electrically operated flaps and a fixed tailwheel undercarriage. The Kurir prototype, which flew in 1955, was fitted with a 140hp Walter Minor 6-III in-line engine but the 145 production aircraft used a Yugoslav-built version (the JW-6-IIIR) uprated to 155hp As an observation aircraft the prototype was remarkable for the very limited forward view available as a result of the relatively low positioning of the foldable wings. In the production Kurir the wing position was raised and the aft port window was hinged to allow a stretcher to be loaded when the aircraft had to be used for ambulance duties. The Kurir could also be operated on floats.

Aero 3 F-AZEC

At the same time Cijan and Petkovic produced the very similar Aero 2, which was available with either open cockpits (the Aero 2B, 2C and 2F) or an enclosed cabin (the Aero 2BE, 2D and 2E). There were two alternative engine options – for most variants the 160hp Walter Minor 6-III was fitted but a 145hp Gipsy Major 10 engine was used on the Aero 2B and Aero 2BE. The Aero 2, which first flew on 19th October 1946, was selected for production in competition with the Ikarus Type 211 and the Bulgarian LAZ-7 and 280 were delivered to the Yugoslav Air Force and government flying clubs. A few examples of the Aero 2D were converted with twin floats and designated Aero 2H.

By the mid-1950s, the Aero 2 was showing its age and an upgraded version – the Aero 3 – was developed. This was a slightly larger aircraft with a bubble canopy over its two tandem seats and a 190hp Lycoming O-435-A flat-six engine. Commencing in 1957, 110 were constructed for military and civil use.

Cijan Kurir YU-CWX. J Blake

Zenair   Canada/United States

In 1973, Christophe Heintz left Avions Robin in France and emigrated to Canada, establishing Zenair Ltd just outside Toronto. The company refined the Heintz Zenith CH200, which had flown as a prototype in France on 22nd March 1970 (F-WPZY, later C-FEYC), and offered plans and kits to amateur builders. The CH200 led to a range of homebuilts including the CH100 Mono-Z, CH300 Tri-Z and the current CH601 Zodiac. In 1992, Zenair established the Zenith Aircraft Company at Mexico, Missouri to produce aircraft for the United States market and to develop a certificated two-seater based on the other Zenair low-wing designs. The prototype CH2000 (C-FQCU c/n 200001) flew on 26th June 1993 and first deliveries were made following US certification in August 1995. The aircraft is of all-metal construction and, compared with the CH601, it has a new parallel-chord wing and a wider fuselage with a fully-integrated cabin. It has a fixed tricycle undercarriage with cantilever spring steel legs and powered by a 116hp

Lycoming O-235-N2C engine. A basic two-seat trainer variant is designated CH2T. In 1999, a new company, AMD (Aircraft Manufacturing and Development Inc) was set up at Eastman, Georgia and the aircraft was renamed the AMD.2000 Alarus. In Jordan, the Alarus is being built as the Sama-CH2000 and the first example flew on 14th December 2003. 114 production aircraft had been completed by Zenair/AMD by the end of 2004 comprising 68 Zenair CH2000s (c/n 200002 to 200069) and 46 of the Alarus (c/n 20-1001 to 20-1046).

Zenair's other major amateur kit-built aircraft is the CH701, which first flew in 1986. It is a simply constructed side-by-side two-seater with fixed leading edge slats and full-span flaperons on its strut-braced high wing to give STOL performance. The all-metal CH701 has a slab-sided fuselage, fixed tricycle undercarriage and a 65hp Rotax 582 engine. While Zenair only sells the CH701 as a kit, there are several derivatives produced in Europe that can be obtained factory-complete. Many of these have extensive redesign, although they all use the principles of the Zenair wing, but Zenair does not support these changes and cau-

Aerotrophy TT2000

tions buyers as to the engineering that has taken place. ICP in Italy developed the MXP-740 Savannah and the lower-powered Bingo which are, essentially, lighter versions of the CH701. The Italian-produced Yuma originated in 1994 with DEA Aircraft of Cremella/Lecco (now taken over by Alisport SRL) and this aircraft, which features a wider cabin and enlarged tail, is offered with the 80hp Rotax 912, 100hp 912S or 115hp Turbo 914T. The Yuma is apparently marketed as the Guérin G.1 in France by Espace Liberté of Rouen (which is related to Luxembourg-based DKL Air Light SARL). Another French marketer of the design is Aerotrophy who offer a factory-assembled version as the STOL Trophy TT2000. This was formerly sold by Air Domi and is manufactured at Wroclaw in Poland by ZUT. Further afield, Aero Bravo in Brazil sell a version with a modified cabin and tail as the Aero Bravo 700. Finally, the Romanian company, Griffon-Aero (see Interplane) offer the Griffon 100, which is a fairly unmodified version of the CH701.

Alarus CH2000 N649AM

Zivco Aeronautics United States

The Zivco Edge 540 competition aerobatic aircraft is manufactured by Zivco Aeronautics of Guthrie, Oklahoma. It was designed by Bill Zivco using the basic fuselage design of Leo Loudenschlager's Stephens Akro Laser 200 with a new wing of symmetrical aerofoil section designed by John Roncz. The initial model was the Edge 360, and a handful of these were built by amateur constructors. The single-seat Edge 540 prototype, which first flew in 1993, is a mid-wing aircraft with a fixed tailwheel undercarriage and a 340hp Lycoming IO-540 engine. The Edge 540-T is a tandem two-seat version with a longer fuselage, wingspan and gross weight. Both models are sold as kits but can be supplied in complete form by Zivco. To date, 25 Edge 540s (c/n 010 to 034) and nine Edge 540-Ts (c/n 2010 to 2018) have been built.

Zivco Edge 540-T N540ZA

Zlin Aviation Czech Republic

Not to be confused with Moravan (builders of the Zlin Trener and other light aircraft), Zlin Aviation sro is the manufacturer of the two-seat Savage 450kg ultralight. This is a high-wing strut-braced tandem two-seater with a fixed tailwheel undercarriage, easily mistaken for a Piper Cub. It is powered by a 68hp Rotax 912S engine and is built of tube and fabric. It can be supplied in factory-complete or kit form. It was originally designed by a group of Aeritalia engineers but the prototype was built and flown by Pasquale Russo, who formed a company known as MZAS (Morava Zlin Aero Service). Early examples were built in Italy in 1997/98 but production was taken over by Zlin in 1999 and 60 had been delivered by mid-2005. The Savage is also built in France by ALMS at La Ferté Alais both as the standard Savage and as the ALMS Calao utility version, aimed at aerial photography and crop spraying work.

Zlin Savage 91-VG

US Aircraft Delivery Table

Commercial Aircraft Deliveries by the Principal American General Aviation Manufacturers

Manufacturer	1946	1947	1948	1949	1950	1951	1952	1953	1954	1955	1956	1957
Aero Commander							39	69	67	72	154	139
Aeronca/Champion	7,555	1,218	599	314	171	34					162	217
Beech	299	1,288	746	341	489	429	414	375	474	654	694	749
Bellanca	288	214	49	27	75	8						
Callair					6	3	1	2	4	11	20	33
Cessna	3,959	2,390	1,631	857	1,134	551	1,373	1,434	1,200	1,746	3,235	2,399
Emigh				44	14							
Erco	4,126	805	152	53	21	10	1				10	19
Funk	174	41	6									
Globe/Temco	1,617	225	252	52	23	14						
Helio										24	15	33
Luscombe	2,490	1,401	716	157	22	28						
Mooney				74	51	26	49	37	14	41	79	107
N American/Ryan	146	871	483	215	250	104						
Piper	7,817	3,464	1,479	1,278	1,108	1,081	1,161	1,839	1,191	1,870	2,329	2,300
Republic	196	818	24									
Stinson	1,436	2,662	801									
Taylorcraft	3,151	196	105	37	22	14	20	32	16	14	35	12
Total	33,254	15,593	7,043	3,449	3,386	2,302	3,058	3,788	2,966	4,432	6,733	6,008

Manufacturer	1958	1959	1960	1961	1962	1963	1964	1965	1966	1967	1968	1969
Aero Commander	97	148	155	139	121	114	109	110	239	297	to NA/Rockwell	
Aeronca/Champion	296	274	248	112	91	99	60	271	331	267	255	293
Alon									138	50	25	2
American											33	270
Beech	669	802	962	818	830	1,061	1,103	1,192	1,535	1,260	1,347	1,061
Bellanca									65	86	94	107
Callair	43	45	13	22					89	65	to NA/Rockwell	
Cessna	2,926	3,564	3,720	2,746	3,124	3,456	4,188	5,629	7,909	6,233	6,578	5,887
Grumman									70	52	N/A	36
Helio	21	12	9	41	6	11	1	29	25	63	17	19
Lake	6	17	5	9	5	16	27	19	24	15	30	39
Learjet							3	80	51	34	41	61
Lockheed									24	19	16	14
Maule									51	43	25	18
Mooney	160	182	172	286	387	502	650	775	779	642	554	374
NA/Rockwell									36	24	471	344
Piper	2,162	2,530	2,313	2,646	2,139	2,321	3,196	3,776	4,437	4,490	4,228	3,951
Taylorcraft	9											
Total	6,389	7,574	7,597	6,829	6,703	7,580	9,337	11,881	15,803	13,640	13,715	12,476

Manufacturer	1970	1971	1972	1973	1974	1975	1976	1977	1978	1979	1980	1981
Aerostar	223	53										
American	202	319	463	469	428	512	487	640				
Beech	793	519	787	1,102	1,286	1,210	1,220	1,203	1,367	1,508	1,394	1,242
Bellanca	96	208	493	683	636	444	315	252	370	440	102	
Cessna	3,730	3,859	4,964	7,262	7,187	7,564	7,888	8,838	8,770	8,380	6,405	4,680
Champion	205	to Bellanca										
Fairchild/Swearingen									51	70	94	85
Grumman/Gulfstream	15	N/A	157	194	200	246	275	226	946	404	167	295
Helio	14	12		20	35							
Lake	43	54	60	66	71	81	88	99	98	96	79	53
Learjet	35	23	39	66	66	79	84	105	102	107	120	138
Lockheed	N/A	N/A	10	6	1				7	8	4	
Maule	26	40	71	85	114	114	96	108	88	66	60	44
Mooney	to Aerostar				130	210	227	362	379	439	332	343
NA/Rockwell	211	202	242	418	544	434	595	435	243	164	146	37
Piper	1,675	2,055	2,461	3,233	3,415	3,069	4,042	4,499	5,264	5,253	2,954	2,495
Taylorcraft			1	8	15	22	15	10				
Ted Smith	to Aerostar			18	49	81	100	101				
Swearingen	23	14	12	36	24	26	30	38				
Total	7,291	7,358	9,760	13,666	14,201	14,092	15,462	16,916	17,685	16,935	11,857	9,412

Manufacturer	1982	1983	1984	1985	1986	1987	1988	1989	1990	1991	1992	1993
American General									10	82	51	30
Aviat/Christen								75	68	71	50	56
Beech	526	402	401	288	304	314	372	371	432	402	348	305
Bellanca								2	3	4	3	4	1
Cessna	2,140	1,216	978	859	546	187	161	183	171	176	140	173
Fairchild/Swearingen	49	39	29	35	37	39	29	13	14	10	14	20
Gulfstream	88	68	50	53	24	30	51	40	34	29	25	26
Helio		12	6									
Learjet	99	45	33	33	20	16	23	25	25	25	23	38
Lake	20	28	29	23	26	23	28	23	17	11	9	3
Maule	39	35	64	88	65	54	55	35	28	66	33	70
Mooney	188	151	151	89	142	143	142	143	147	88	69	64
Piper	1,043	660	664	540	326	282	282	621	178	41	85	99
Rockwell	2	1										
Taylorcraft	12	13	12	15	4				10	11		
Total	4,206	2,670	2,417	2,203	1,494	1,088	1,145	1,532	1,138	1,015	851	885

Manufacturer	1994	1995	1996	1997	1998	1999	2000	2001	2002	2003	2004
American Champion	n/a	46	n/a	46	74	91	96	56	53	63	94
Aviat/Christen	47	42	56	61	85	83	91	57	38	47	42
Beech/Raytheon	317	363	382	370	395	421	476	364	259	263	310
Bellanca	n/a	1	n/a	2	1	1	1	1			
Cessna	172	200	229	612	1,072	1,202	1,256	1,202	944	841	899
Cirrus						9	95	183	397	469	553
Classic Waco	n/a	7	n/a	6	6	6	6	6	6	5	5
Commander	22	25	15	14	13	13	20	11	7		
Fairchild	16	7	7	10							
Gulfstream	22	26	27	51	61	70	71	101	85	74	78
Learjet	36	43	36	45	61	99	133	109	60	31	48
Lancair							5	27	24	51	78
Maule	65	68	63	54	63	69	57	57	46	32	27
Micco							6	10			
Mooney	71	84	73	86	93	97	100	29	10	36	37
Piper	132	165	183	222	295	341	395	441	290	229	189
Tiger Aircraft									14	18	19
Total	900	1,077	1,071	1,579	2,219	2,502	2,808	2,654	2,233	2,159	2,379

Index

LONDON UNDERGROU
ROLLING STOCK
in Colour
for the Modeller and Historian

John Glover

Ian Allan PUBLISHING

CONTENTS

Captions: all photographs as credited

Title page: Those wishing to see 1938 tube stock in normal service and in London Transport red have to proceed to the Isle of Wight where all 12 traffic vehicles are now so painted. This is Ryde Pier, with a train from the Pier Head to Shanklin made up of two, two-car units with set No 483009 leading, on 21 August 2004. The intervening disused structure was once occupied by the Pier Tramway. *Author*

First published 2009

ISBN 978 0 7110 3348 1

© Ian Allan Publishing Ltd 2009

Published by Ian Allan Publishing

An imprint of Ian Allan Publishing Ltd, Riverdene Business Park, Hersham, Surrey KT12 4RG

Printed by Ian Allan Printing Ltd, Riverdene Business Park, Hersham, Surrey KT12 4RG

Code: 0909/B1

Visit the Ian Allan Publing web site at
www.ianallanpublishing.com

1. INTRODUCTION

Today's Underground system is derived from two distinct origins. The first section of the Metropolitan Railway of 1863 was built largely as a conventional local railway, distinguished from the others in that it was mostly underground. As the whole purpose was to provide for short-distance passenger movements, the line was constructed by cut-and-cover work. In this, a trench was dug for the railway down the middle of the roadway; it was then lined with bricks, the trackbed prepared and the track laid, with the whole then covered over to allow the restoration of the road above.

This same pattern was followed for network extensions, and by the Metropolitan District Railway (later the District). Together, these companies built up an extensive network. Route extensions beyond the heavily built-up areas did not need to be underground, and use was made of viaducts in these areas as well as construction at grade.

As befitted their origins, traction was exclusively by steam locomotives, but attempts were made to use condensing gear to limit the filth which permeated everywhere in the necessarily confined spaces, although ventilation was provided. By all accounts, though, the situation remained grim. Collectively, these are known as the sub-surface lines.

THE TUBE RAILWAYS

Building tunnels deeper created many practical problems. Steam traction was clearly impossible, and cable haulage in the early days was the only real alternative. Access for passengers was going to be a problem too, with huge numbers of stairs to climb, while the problem of providing sufficient fresh air to breathe also needed attention.

The first tube railway to be built was the City & South London, which opened from King William Street in the City of London to Stockwell in 1890. Construction was by use of the Greathead shield, forced through the earth using hydraulic rams, while miners inside the shield excavated the spoil at the workface. The newly formed tunnel was lined with cast-iron segments as the shield advanced. Traction problems were solved by using newly developed electric power systems, passenger access by the invention of a safe lift system, and ventilation by the construction of shafts and pumps – although the passage of the trains through the tunnels, which they fitted tightly, did at least move the air around.

Below: This is Praed Street underground junction, where the broad gauge Great Western train is taking the original route to Paddington main line platforms (and now on to Hammersmith), as opposed to what subsequently became the Circle Line with the route to High Street Kensington in the foreground. There was however, a great deal of artistic licence taken, since the junction itself did not come into existence until long after the Great Western had withdrawn from this service. *Author's collection*

The two types of underground railway thus had considerable differences. One of the most important was that of tunnel diameters and hence the types of rolling stock that could be used. The original City & South London Railway running tunnels were 10ft 2in (3.1 metres) in diameter. Later lines saw the internal tunnel diameters rise to 3.6 metres, and 3.8 metres with the Victoria Line in 1967. The structure gauge of the sub-surface lines was much nearer that of the main-line railways, although not to the extent that they could be used freely by main-line stock.

SUB-SURFACE AND TUBE

Should the tube railways have been built to larger dimensions, say 16ft diameter tunnels (4.9 metres)? This was later adopted for the Great Northern & City Line from Finsbury Park to Moorgate to allow the through running of trains. The subject was considered by the Joint Select Committee (House of Commons and House of Lords) on Electric and Cable Railways (Metropolis) in 1892, but they decided that 11ft 6in (3.5 metres) was an adequate minimum size to be imposed.

Thus was instigated one of the main determinants of the future development of London's underground railways, and the two types of line have ever since had to pursue the separate development of rolling stock to meet their own particular needs. Besides tunnel diameter, other physical features such as line curvature, platform length, and in recent times the signalling system installed, all mean that rolling stock is now increasingly only able to be used on one specific line.

The useful asset-life of rolling stock is generally considered to be 40 years. Major refurbishment can perhaps prolong that life by another 10–15 years and costs around one-sixth that of a new train.

Successively, this book discusses and illustrates the sub-surface and the tube lines. It then considers the service stock, much of which is common to both, and the use of Underground rolling stock on the Isle of Wight. A conclusion then looks at the present situation and the rolling stock replacement schemes presently under way.

*Below:*The first City & South London Railway locomotive, and indeed those which followed, were diminutive machines. They were a mere 14ft long over the centre buffers, weighed about 10 tons and were carried on four wheels with a 50hp motor on each axle. Doors for the crew were at the ends only. No 13 is seen here at the Science Museum, when believed to be No 1, but it is now on display at the London Transport Museum, Covent Garden correctly identified. *Author's collection*

Right: The tube loading gauge is very different from that for sub-surface stock. For engineering vehicles which may be required to operate anywhere on the system, it is important that mistakes are not made. This is the pair of loading gauges at Lillie Bridge permanent way depot, which can be swung into use as needed. Behind is rail wagon No R826. The photograph was taken on 18 May 2004. *Author*

The Great Western Railway had agreed to work the Metropolitan Railway from its opening on 10 January 1863, and for this Daniel Gooch of the GWR designed some 2-4-0 broad gauge tank engines with condensing apparatus. A total of 22 were built.

Rolling stock comprised 45 eight-wheeled compartment coaches, each 42ft long. These included first, second and third class carriages, but until 1874, smoking was not allowed, either in the carriages or anywhere else on the company's premises. The trains were lit by coal gas carried in long flexible bags arranged along the centres of the roofs.

This arrangement did not last long, since a dispute with the Metropolitan led to the prompt withdrawal of Great Western services on 10 August, to be replaced by whatever the London & North Western and the Great Northern between them could rustle up at short notice.

Following this debacle, the Metropolitan determined to buy its own locomotives and rolling stock, with the result that Beyer Peacock & Co of Manchester gained an initial order for 18 of the 4-4-0 side tank locomotives, known as the 'A' class. Subsequently, the District Railway made similar purchases, and these locomotives formed the backbone of all such operations until electrification.

The first trains of the District Railway were composed of eight four-wheeled carriages – two first class, two second class and four third class compartment stock – lit by coal gas supplied from the mains at Mansion House and High Street Kensington stations. Like the Metropolitan, the gas was carried on the roofs. The first class coaches had four compartments, the others five, and each seated ten passengers. The class of travel was also reflected in the varying quality and comfort of the upholstery.

ELECTRIFICATION

By 1900, electrification was the name of the game. Both the now greatly expanded companies standardised on 600v dc, third and fourth rail, with the positive rail 16 inches outside the running rails and 3 inches higher, and the negative rail in the centre but 1½ inches higher.

The Metropolitan's new electric rolling stock was of the open-saloon type, but compartment stock was still used on the main line out to Aylesbury. Following construction of Neasden power station in 1904 and the building of a fleet of electric locomotives, electric haulage was extended successively to Wembley Park (1906), Harrow (1908) and Rickmansworth (1925). These became the changeover points where steam locomotives were substituted for electric. Electrification to Amersham and Chesham in 1961 and curtailment of London Transport operations beyond Amersham saw the end of all such changeovers.

The first electric locomotives were constructed between 1904 and 1906. None lasted long, all being replaced by 20 very capable Metropolitan-Vickers machines built at Barrow-in-Furness in 1922.

Both the Metropolitan and the District companies constructed their own designs of multiple units, with varying degrees of success, but these were still relatively early days. Traffic was growing fast, and the following is adapted from an account of 1919. Some of the problems and indeed the remedies are equally applicable today.

F-STOCK

By 1920, the central London part of the District was the busiest railway in Britain. Given that it was not practicable to increase the number of trains other than marginally, the best alternative was to increase the length of each to 400ft – the maximum length permitted by the station platforms.

The F stock trains consisted of eight cars. The width was extended from 8ft 8in to 9ft 7in, or about the limit of the step boards in earlier stock. The length was 50ft as against 49ft, and the trains were capable of 45mph when working 'non-stop' services.

The trailer cars were fitted with three double sliding doors, each wide enough for two passengers to enter or leave the car simultaneously. On motor cars and control trailers, single doors were fitted at the ends of the cars, which were available for use by passengers when not occupied by train staff. On each side of an eight-car train, this gave the equivalent of 52 external single doors for passenger use, materially reducing the time taken at stations for loading and unloading. In turn, this enabled more trains to pass over the congested section of line in the rush hours. The car doors were spaced equally along the side of the coach, making them that much more accessible.

The F stock had slightly curved instead of straight sides, with improved springing. The cars had larger bogies and wheels, and were higher powered. This materially improved the running speed and passenger comfort. The improved acceleration was brought about by additional traction motors.

Improved braking equipment secured more rapid stopping. The problem of getting more trains through the tunnels depended not only on the time taken between stations, or absorbed

Left: This vehicle was built as a Metropolitan Railway carriage for steam haulage, served also as an electric control trailer car, but later again in steam mode on the Chesham push-pull set. The interior shows that Metropolitan feature of the rounded top to the door, provided so that should it be opened accidentally in a tunnel, damage to the door would be minimised. It is now at the London Transport Museum. *Author*

Right; The F stock trains had a good reputation, and like many other long-lived stock found themselves eking out their last days on the East London Line. This is a rear view of a southbound train leaving Surrey Docks station (later Surrey Quays), showing its distinctive elliptical windows.
Harry Luff Collection/
Online Transport Archive

by station stops, but in the period taken by starting and stopping.

Internally, greater gangway room was provided. Seats in non-smoking accommodation were upholstered in moquette velvet, and washable leather or similar in smoking compartments. At each end of the car were large elliptical plate glass windows, designed to give an artistic appearance and finish. Ventilation was designed to meet the difficult conditions of a train running both in tunnels and the open air. Handrails and vertical pillars were provided next to doorways and in otherwise open sections of the cars. Construction was of steel throughout except for a small amount of woodwork which was chemically treated to make it fireproof.

Transverse seats, each seating two people, were confined to the ends of the cars as facing pairs, or with an extra row where there was no vestibule or driving cab. Most of the seating was in longitudinal rows of six, fully occupying the space between each adjacent pair of double doors.

The double door openings were 3ft 6in, contrasting with 2ft 7in on their predecessors. Overall, the seating capacity of a set of three vehicles was reduced from 144 to 132, but the number of first-class seats within those totals rose from 24 to 32. First class was finally abolished on all Underground services in 1941.

The F stock had an enviable reputation as efficient crowd shifters, and lasted in service until 1963.

AIR DOORS

Subsequently, a substantial variety of new cars was built, although hand-operated sliding doors (as opposed to air-operated doors) continued until 1935. This did not preclude

later conversion to power operation. They were followed by the O stock (Hammersmith & City services, with the guard in cabs) and P stock (Uxbridge services with the guard in the saloon). The Os and Ps were known as the Metadyne stock (control and regeneration equipment). Conversion to PCM (resistance) control took place from 1955 onwards, since the advantages which were gained by regeneration in practice were less than the costs of achieving it. The trains then became CO/CP.

The whole programme was hamstrung for a number of reasons. These included differing electrical equipments, the abandonment of uncoupling in service, the extension of electric working from Barking to Upminster in 1932, longer platforms, and different crewing practices. The result was often a mixture of stock, and the somewhat ragged appearance of trains put together from many sources.

The situation was eased and regularised by the introduction of the R stock and some associated conversions, with the R stock trains built in batches until as late as 1959. Eventually, these took over all the main District services, while the Metropolitan became monopolised by the A60 and A62 stocks. The Circle, Hammersmith & City and eventually the Edgware Road–Wimbledon services became the preserve of the CO/CP stock.

The scene was now set for the final changes to date, in which C69/C77 urban stocks assumed the duties previously performed by the CO/CP trains, and new D78 stock took up all District services. The following gives some more detail of the stock types presently in operation.

A-STOCK

A stock trains are made up to eight cars with two four-car sets of two driving motors

sandwiching two trailers (DM-T-T-DM +DM-T-T-DM). In general, the intermediate cabs can no longer be used as such. A limited number of A stock sets remain truly double-ended in the sense that they can work alone as four-car units. The Chesham branch train is now the sole use for these.

There were two batches, built by Cravens of Sheffield. The A60s were for Amersham, and the A62s for Uxbridge. (The '60' indicates the nominal year of introduction). The vehicles are unusual for Underground cars in that they have high-backed transverse seating only for their longer distance work, with two or three seats either side of a central gangway. Overhead luggage racks were also provided. They were refurbished by Adtranz Ltd at Derby between 1994 and 1997.

Driving motors have two pairs of double doors per side and one single-leaf door at the end; trailers have three pairs of double-leaf doors.

Length per car	53ft 0½in (16.17m)
Height	12ft 1in (3.89m)
Width	9ft 8in (2.95m)
Seating capacity (eight cars)	448
Standing capacity (eight cars)	976
Total capacity (eight cars)	1,424

C-STOCK

C stock trains are made up to six-car trains of three two-car sets, each with one driving motor car and one trailer and are always used in this formation (DM-T+DM-T+T-DM).

There were two interchangeable batches, both built by Metro-Cammell. The C69s were for the Circle and Hammersmith & City Lines, the C77s for the Edgware Road–Wimbledon service.

These trains were designed specifically for busy short-distance urban operation, with plenty of doors and standing space. In both vehicle types, there are four sets of double doors per side.

All trains were refurbished by RFS Industries in Doncaster between 1991 and 1994. The seating was originally transverse except at the outer ends of the cars where it was longitudinal, but all seating is now longitudinal throughout. This kept the amount of seating the same, but provided additional standing room in the gangways. Windows were introduced in the car ends that do not include driving cabs to enhance personal security.

Length per car	DM 52ft 7in (16.03m), T 49ft (14.94m)
Height	12ft 1in (3.68m)
Width	9ft 7in (2.92m)
Seating per car	32
Seating capacity per train	192
Standing capacity per train	1,080
Total capacity, six cars	1,272

D-STOCK

The fleet of six-car all-aluminium D78 stock was introduced in 1980 for the District main line. They were manufactured by Metro-Cammell of Birmingham. The trains comprise two three-car units formed of a driving motor, a trailer and an uncoupling non-driving motor car. These last are fitted with traction/control equipment, operated from a small cabinet to allow uncoupling and shunting moves.

They are similar in total length to the seven-car trains they replaced, each car being longer than usual. This had the advantage of lessening the total number of wheel-sets, thereby reducing maintenance costs and by being lighter, lessening train noise and vibration. Seating is mostly longitudinal with a double pair of transverse seats in the centre of each car.

Uniquely for sub-surface stock, these trains have tube-sized wheels. Traditionally, surface stock has always had 1,067mm diameter wheels, whereas tube stock has 790mm wheels. This allowed more headroom in the cars, and was also an attempt to reduce maintenance costs by reducing the different types of wheels and bogies in use.

They were refurbished by Bombardier Transportation UK, Derby from 2006 to 2008.

Doors consist of four sets of single leaves per side of each vehicle.

Length per car	DM 60ft 3¼in (18.37m), T/UNDM 59ft 5½in (18.12m)
Height	11ft 10.5in (3.62m)
Width	9ft 4¼in (2.85m)
Seating	DM 44. T/UNDM 48
Seating capacity per train	280
Standing capacity per train	1,092
Total capacity, six cars	1,372

Above: West Kensington station on the District Line lies in an open-air cutting and has a suburban feel to it, although in reality this is shattered by the proximity of the A4 road, above and to the right. Here, a D stock train arrives with an eastbound service to Barking in the spring of 1985. *Author*

CAR LIVERIES

It was announced in 1952 that aluminium rolling stock was to be left unpainted as a trial, with a car from the R stock order going into service on the District Line in June. Traditional red appeared only in a 3in band below the windows and in the name transfers.

This was on the grounds of savings in initial cost and maintenance. Thus was begun a move to 'silver' trains, which was completed in the 1980s. However, the later rise of the graffiti artist saw many trains severely disfigured, and a return to painted finishes began, with a new livery of an off-white body with red ends and doors, coupled with a low-level blue band. Excluding engineering vehicles and those not in regular passenger service, the completion of the D stock refurbishment saw this livery being applied universally on London Underground.

3. THE TUBE RAILWAYS ROLLING STOCK

As already recorded, the tunnels of the pioneering City & South London Railway were decidedly tight in diameter, and the trains correspondingly small. Trains were hauled by electric locomotives and were composed of three long cars, each seating 32 passengers, with doors at each end, electric lights (four in each car), and no windows.

Ventilation was by narrow slits just below roof level and one car was reserved for smokers. There was only one class of travel and originally 30 cars were built. The upholstery was heavily padded and was carried high up the sides of the vehicles, hence their commonly used nickname of 'Padded cells'. This meant that passengers could not tell where they were other than by counting the stations since they boarded, and it was up to the conductor to shout out the name of the station at each stop.

The Central London Railway followed in 1900 with its route from Shepherd's Bush to Bank, and then the Yerkes tubes, which formed the nucleus of today's Bakerloo, Northern and Piccadilly lines.

The early days of tube stock relied on comprehensive staffing and gates, which remained a problem until power doors were introduced under the direct control of the guard. The lines were not uniform, either; thus the CLR (today's Central Line) used a centre third rail, and the platform lengths were not built with future expansion in mind. This required major remedial work in the late 1930s, with general track replacement, extension of all platform and station tunnels by 102ft, and tunnel enlargement throughout to take an outside current rail. Thus was the Central Line equipped to take eight-car trains of pre-1938 stock. These trains, which had a number of minor design differences, were generally of a length between 49ft and 52ft. They seated only 30 in the driving motor cars due to a large equipment compartment behind the driver, although other vehicles seated around 40.

Similar work in the 1920s, but on a rather bigger scale, was needed to bring the extended City & South London up to standard and link it in with the enlarged Northern Line.

Tube stocks are usually identified by the year in which first delivery of the type is scheduled.

1938 STOCK

The design of this extensive fleet of cars was a breakthrough in the provision of increased passenger accommodation and improved performance. As originally built for the Northern Line, a seven-car train could be divided into two permanently coupled units, one of three cars and the other of four cars, both with a driving cab at each end. A four-car unit consisted of two driving motor cars, a non-driving motor car and a trailer car; a three-car unit of two driving motor cars and a trailer car. All vehicles were 52ft 2½in long.

All the electrical equipment was placed below the car floor, and by this means the carrying capacity of a seven-car train matched that of an eight-car train of pre-1938 rolling stock.

Two other important features were the increased acceleration and braking rates, which by permitting a reduced headway, gave increased line capacity. This was achieved by driving a larger proportion of the axles. Every motor car was equipped with two 168hp nose-suspended motors, one in each bogie.

Right: Passenger access to tube cars was generally by lattice gates controlled by a gateman, which led to a saloon door and the vehicle interior. This is part of one of the original Hungarian-built vehicles for the Piccadilly Line, on show at the London Transport Museum and dating from 1906. *Author*

Above: A southbound train of 1959 stock leaves the wayside West Finchley Northern Line station on 24 April 1997. Unpainted aluminium alloy replaced steel panels, while rubber suspension and fluorescent lighting marked other developments from their 1938 tube stock predecessors. These seven-car trains came from the Piccadilly Line, where they were displaced by the new 1973 stock built for the Heathrow extension. *Author*

A seven-car train therefore had 10 motors totalling 1,680hp compared with 1,440hp on the pre-1938 stock.

The driving motor cars had seats for 42 passengers, and other vehicles 40. Deep-cushioned seats with bucket-type backs were provided, and the finishes were selected to give the interior a light and roomy appearance. All the doors on the cars were worked by compressed air and controlled as a whole by the guard, or by the passengers using individual push buttons subject to the guard's ultimate control.

A four-car train of 1938 stock has been restored to operational standard in London, but in two-car formations, they still provide passenger services on the Isle of Wight.

The tube stock in use today is described here briefly, the oldest first.

1967 STOCK

Victoria Line. The 1967 tube stock was designed and built by Metro-Cammell for the then new Victoria Line, the world's first fully automatic railway. The aluminium-alloy car bodies on a steel underframe have wrap-round windscreens without corner pillars. The secondary suspension incorporates hydraulic suspension-control units. The trains underwent mid-life refurbishment by Tickford Rail at Rosyth Dockyard between 1991 and 1995.

Length of cars	DM 52ft 9½in (16.08m),
	T 52ft 5½in (15.98m)
Height	9ft 5in (2.87m)
Width	8ft 8in (2.64m)
Seating per car	40
Seating capacity per train	304
Standing capacity per train	1,144
Total capacity, eight cars	1,448

1972 MkI STOCK

Selected vehicles only of this fleet, which were similar to 1967 stock but with technical differences for crew operation, are still in use. Modified as necessary, they are incorporated in trains on the Bakerloo and Victoria lines.

1972 Mk11 STOCK

Bakerloo Line. Slightly modified from the MkI versions, these too are similar to 1967 stock. They are made up as seven-car trains and have been refurbished by Tickford Rail.

Seating capacity per train	264
Standing capacity per train	1,014
Total capacity, eight cars	1,278

1973 STOCK

Piccadilly Line. These trains were built by Metro-Cammell in connection with the increased stock required for the original Heathrow extension of 1977. Extra floor space was provided by setting back the glass screens at door openings to provide larger vestibules. This also helped speed up discharging and embarking passengers. The cars are longer than normal tube stock: a six-car train is 350ft (107.6m) long, which is only 17ft (5.23m) shorter than the seven-car trains they replaced. The stock was refurbished by Bombardier Prorail from 1995.

Length of cars	DM 57ft 3¾in (17.68m),
	others 57ft 1½in (17.47m)
Height	9ft 5in (2.88m)
Width	8ft 7¾in. (2.63m)
Seating	44
Seating capacity	228, plus 44 perch seats
Standing capacity	966
Total capacity, six cars	1,238

1992 STOCK

Central and Waterloo & City lines. The 1992 tube stock was built by Adtranz and was the outcome of trials of three prototype four-car trains of 1986 tube stock, two of which were built by Metro-Cammell and one by BREL Ltd (later Adtranz). These trains trialled features such as electronic traction control and a fully integrated train control and management system.

The 1992 stock order was for 85 eight-car trains for the Central Line, later expanded for 10 additional two-car units for the Waterloo & City Line. At that time, the W&C was under the control of British Rail. Both sets are identical, except that those trains on the Waterloo & City Line are not fitted with automatic train operation (ATO) equipment.

Trains were delivered from 1992 onwards, entering service from Spring 1993. The body shells are made from welded extruded aluminium sections. The twin sliding doors, plus one single door at each end of each car, are wider than any used previously on tube stock. Each door leaf is 832mm wide, and the doors are externally hung. In-cab closed circuit television is provided for platform observation, this stock being designed for one-person operation and ATO.

In common with all subsequent builds, the car interiors have longitudinal seating only. Perch seats are also provided at the car ends.

Length per car	16.25m
Width	2.62m
Height	2.87m
Seating capacity	272
Standing capacity	1,380
Total capacity, eight cars	1,652

1995 STOCK

Northern Line. These trains are generally similar to the 1996 stock which preceded them into service (on the Jubilee Line). The main differences are in the bogies and equipment. They were built by GEC-Alstom, who had by then acquired Metro-Cammell of Birmingham.

The trains are fully equipped for one-person operation, their introduction seeing the withdrawal of guards on the Northern Line. The cars have longitudinal seating only and have six automated LED scrolling-visual-display units in each, along with automated audio station-announcements and a driver-operable public address system. The passenger alarm offers talkback facility with the driver.

Length per car	17.77m
Width	2.63m
Height	2.875m
Seating capacity, six cars	200,
	plus 20 perch seats,
	48 tip-up seats and
	24 wheelchair spaces.
Total capacity, six cars	914

1996 STOCK

Jubilee Line. As built by GEC-Alstom there were initially six cars per train, each comprising two three-car units. Of these, four cars are powered. At the end of 2005, an additional trailer car was added to each train and the fleet was increased by a further four trains, making it up to 63 seven-car units.

The trains are equipped for conventional one-person operation with tripcock train protection, but also equipped for automatic train operation or manual train operation with transmission-based automatic train protection (ATP).

Internally, the trains are similar to the 1995 stock on the Northern Line, but additional perch seats replace the tip-up seats. They are

built to a slightly more generous loading gauge than their 1995 counterparts.

Length per car	17.77m
Width	2.63m
Height	2.88m
Seating capacity	
	234, plus 24 wheelchair spaces
Standing capacity	730
Total capacity, seven cars	964

It is perhaps unnecessary to add that the various types of train on the Tube are not fully interchangeable between lines, although there have been many instances where stock has been cascaded from one line to another. For instance, when the 1983 stock (now withdrawn) was introduced to the Jubilee Line, it displaced the 1972 stock to the Northern Line, which in turn meant that 1959 stock from there was able to be transferred to the Bakerloo Line to replace the 1938 stock which was being withdrawn.

Other variations are that the Central and Victoria line platforms are 400ft long and have ATO signalling systems specific to each train type. Most other tube platforms are only 350ft. The western part of the Circle Line has platforms too short to accommodate District Line D78 Stock, and the Metropolitan A stock is too wide to use most of the District Line.

Below: A completely new fleet of trains was delivered to the Northern Line as 1995 stock and one is seen here entering the Edgware terminus on 7 May 2008. Part of an order for 106 trains, they took over the services completely in January 2000. They consist of two, three-car sets, which are completely reversible to cope with the terminal loop at Kennington and any reformations which might be needed. *Author*

4. TRAIN EXAMINATION AND MAINTENANCE

The need for periodic overhaul, when the whole vehicle is stripped down for major attention and minor or perhaps major modifications, is well known. Nowadays, this is carried out in the line depots. What, though, needs to be achieved on a more frequent and regular basis?

Most immediate is the daily train preparation at the depot. The aim here is to check that a train is in a safe and proper condition when offered for service, and to ensure that any defects reported by drivers or others have been acknowledged and corrected.

PERIODIC EXAMINATION

Periodic examinations are undertaken to ensure that trains remain in a wholly serviceable condition. This involves examining elements of the train which are not accessible in normal usage, for damage and degradation, checking and adjustment of wearing parts and consumable items to ensure that they remain serviceable within defined limits, and to check secondary protective structural devices.

This can be divided into a number of specific tasks such as:

- to ensure that all rapidly wearing parts remain serviceable until the next examination
- to check items which will not last 36 weeks without attention
- to adjust tripcock and shoegear.
- to examine undersides for structural problems such as loose equipment or dirt build-up
- to check that systems are working correctly, noting and rectifying any defects if possible
- to give the passenger saloon and cab a thorough examination, highlighting and replacing or repairing any defects such as excessively soiled seats, missing handgrips, and safe but loose heater panel coverings.

The intervals between successive car examinations are determined by the rate at which consumables wear out, and the time it is

considered prudent to run trains before having a good look underneath. In short, the aim is to make sure that nothing falls off.

With consumables the time between replacements can be increased, but it must be recognised that the rate of wear depends upon the use made of the train. Thus, if a brake block is not fully worn when it is replaced some wastage will result, but this is unavoidable on a time-interval-based system rather than usage.

There is thus a long list of items for examination, and the minimum testing and inspection requirements need to be defined. This ensures that the train is fit for service.

Right: Modern Underground tube stock has to incorporate virtually all equipment beneath the floor, which makes for an intensive use of not very much space. This is the view of the underside of a 1996 stock driving motor, No 96009, which was at Ruislip depot on 17 March 1997. *Author*

5. SERVICE FLEET AND PRESERVED STOCK

The service stock which has been used on London Underground from time to time consists of a number of groups. These include locomotives of various types, special purpose vehicles such as cranes or the tunnel cleaning train, pilot cars for moving otherwise disabled cars around the system, and permanent way vehicles generally including wagons.

Such railborne vehicles are an essential part of the engineering efforts to keep a large system such as London Underground properly maintained and to carry out major projects as necessary. They may also be needed to help deal with mishaps.

The preserved sector includes London Underground's 'official' heritage department, the London Transport Museum. Besides the main Covent Garden premises, the LT Museum also has The Depot near Acton Town station, which houses the reserve collection as well as some of the larger rolling stock items. Other former London Underground items of rolling stock are widely scattered, but some may be found operational on preserved railways from time to time.

Below: The maroon-liveried Acton Works shunter, No L10, had its origins in 1907 as two of the original Hampstead motor cars, split in half and with the two cab-ends (and their motors) joined together. This conversion was completed 1930, and the new locomotive was given adjustable couplers to match either tube or sub-surface rolling stock. This picture is undated, but the locomotive was cut up on site in 1978. *Harry Luff Collection/ Online Transport Archive*

Above left: Lifting is underway at Ruislip depot with a car of 1962 stock in green 'engineering' livery on the jacks, on 15 March 1997. The whole of the Central Line had been worked by their replacements, the 1992 stock, since 1995, so individual vehicles were only being retained for special purposes. *Author*

Right: Battery locomotive No L47 was built at BREL Doncaster in 1974. In this picture of August of that year it is apparently brand new and in the maroon livery used by London Transport for service stock at that time. These were not lightweight machines, and the tare weight of this one is 57ton 7cwt. The legend above the door reads: 'No smoking or naked lights allowed in this cab'. Presumably, either was acceptable everywhere else in those days. *Harry Luff Collection/ Online Transport Archive*

6. THE ISLE OF WIGHT

London Underground rolling stock has made its way to a number of locations outside the capital over the years, mostly for preservation purposes, but the one that stands out is the Isle of Wight. Here, electrification of the one remaining line was completed in 1967, and two types of ex-LT rolling stock have been used. Successively, these have been 43 vehicles of pre-1938 stock, which lasted for over 20 years, and then 18 cars of 1938 stock.

In their heyday, the Isle of Wight railways totalled 55½ route miles, but the network was considerably thinned during the 1950s until all that remained were the Ryde–Ventnor and Ryde–Newport–Cowes lines. Both were included in the closure list published by Dr Beeching in his 1963 'Reshaping' Report.

To the surprise of many, the then Minister agreed closure of the Cowes line, and that beyond Shanklin to Ventnor, but reprieved the 8½ miles from Ryde Pier Head to Shanklin with its then four, but now six intermediate stations.

For some time, the Southern Region of BR had been concerned about the age of the existing rolling stock; a major problem being the tunnel outside Ryde that had very restricted clearances. Consideration was given to the use of:

- withdrawn British Railways' 1953-built 84000 series Class 2MT 2-6-2T steam locomotives
- London Underground pre-1938 stock in conjunction with dc third-rail electrification
- London Underground pre-1938 stock, converted to diesel-electric or diesel mechanical operation, or as trailers in a push-pull format using separate diesel locomotives

The steam option was abandoned, since this involved the expense of locomotive modification and still left the question of replacement coaching stock unresolved, while the Minister said in his decision that the one remaining line should be modernised.

PRE-1938 STOCK

Electrification was the chosen means, although the various uncertainties meant that the types of cars needed had to be selected on the basis of both availability and condition. London Transport was then phasing out all the pre-1938 stock, but the types and quantities of each available were not necessarily what British Railways was seeking.

All of course needed to be converted to third-rail operation, with rewiring and the installation of luggage shelves, and overhaul as required. This work was shared between Acton Works for London Transport and Stewarts Lane for British Railways.

The net result was that the new Island fleet consisted of 43 cars, formed into six four-car units, Nos 041–046, with a driving motor, two trailers and a driving motor ('4-VEC', but later Class 485) and six, three-car units, Nos 031–036, made up of a control trailer, trailer and driving motor ('3-TIS', subsequently Class 486). There were thus the equivalent of six seven-car trains, which could be run as four cars only if required. The other vehicle was a spare driving motor car. Electric services commenced on 20 March 1967.

Unsurprisingly, with a fleet of this age and also a number of mishaps, matters changed considerably over the years. The numbers of vehicles and the service that they provided dwindled, and by 1987 the remaining 27 cars had been reformed into five, five-car trains and one, two-car train.

Liveries were initially Rail blue with large yellow ends, later Rail blue and grey. Cab end embellishments subsequently took the form of black window surrounds and an Isle of Wight outline. They were later painted in Network SouthEast colours.

1938 STOCK

The availability of 1938 stock being withdrawn from London Transport service led to a replacement of the pre-1938 vehicles, which were by then roundly 60 years old. The 1938 stock as used on the Island consisted entirely of driving motor cars in pairs, placed back to back. Guard's control panels were retained in one vehicle only, and the whole underwent extensive overhaul, refurbishment and conversion to fluorescent lighting. Passenger-operated open-and-close door buttons were reinstalled.

A total of 18 cars were thus treated, forming nine, two-car sets, Nos 483001–483009. They entered service in NSE livery from 1989 onwards. Subsequent withdrawals mean that the entire passenger-carrying capacity of this railway now consists of six, two-car sets, or 12 vehicles in total.

With the franchising of the national network from 1995, Island Lines was initially a separate franchise, but is now part of South West Trains and operated by Stagecoach. Today, all trains are painted externally in a close approximation of London Transport rail red livery, with small yellow panels.

Right: The blue and grey livery of British Rail was once reserved for InterCity, but by 2 October 1988 it had spread to the lowly Island Line. The front cab windows have been given black surrounds and the end doorways have been plated over. Car No S2 is at the leading end of set No 485041, part of which is now in Network SouthEast livery. The location is Brading and the train is bound for Ryde Pier Head. The left-hand side of the island platform once served the branch to Bembridge. *Author*

7. CONCLUSION

That, then, is a brief overview of the rolling stock of London Underground, past and present. It is a huge and growing operation, with passenger numbers averaging around three million a day. That has substantial implications for the system itself, its upkeep, the investment profile – and the quality of its operation.

Table 1 *(right)* shows the number of Underground trains needed for service, by line and by day of the week, in 2008.

Thus, as might be expected, the greatest number of trains is needed during the Monday to Friday peak periods, and this is virtually identical in both the morning and the afternoon. More surprising perhaps is the midday profile, which requires slightly more than 80% of those trains, and the Saturday profile which is much the same. Even Sunday, traditionally the lightest day of the week in traffic terms, shows only a marginal further decrease, although the operating hours are also slightly reduced.

This all adds up to a continuously busy railway, and there are 4,070 Underground cars to provide the service. Trains do vary in length, layout and capacity, while the signalling is a major determinant of what can be provided by

Above: The 1996 stock was built for the Jubilee Line extension to Stratford, and this train had only just been taken out it its box on 18 October 1999. Built by Alstom as six-car trains, a seventh car was added over the Christmas/New Year holiday period in 2005/06. This solved the somewhat odd situation of there being more platform doors than there were train doors on the Jubilee Line extension. *Author*

way of service frequency. But so too are the passengers, and luggage-encumbered tourists finding their way from a Eurostar service on to the train they want at King's Cross St Pancras will move much more slowly than the average daily commuter with only a newspaper to carry.

Station stop times can be critical in determining the maximum number of trains per hour that can be operated, while congestion on platforms, escalators and in passages also affects the rate at which people can join or leave trains.

Table 1: Maximum number of Underground trains needed for service, 2009

Line	Monday to Friday peak	midday	Saturday	Sunday
Bakerloo	33	29	29	27
Central	79	67	67	58
Circle/H&City	31	29	29	26
District	77	61	61	58
Jubilee	51	35	41	41
Metropolitan	47	34	34	34
Northern	91	72	72	72
Piccadilly	79	68	69	68
Victoria	38	29	29	29
Waterloo & City	5	3	3	0
Totals	531	427	434	413
As %	100	80.4	81.7	77.8

INVESTMENT PLANS

The whole thus has to be operated as a system, although this book is concerned only with the rolling stock. Give or take a few vehicles, while the trains on the Central, Jubilee, Northern and Waterloo & City are of 1990s build, all the others date back to the 1970s or even the 1960s. There are no passenger trains from the 1980s in the present fleet.

Railway vehicles are assets with long lives, and 30 years is about average. Thus a large fleet replacement programme is looming, and it was indeed built into the Private & Public Partnership (PPP) schemes let before London Underground became a subsidiary of Transport for London (TfL) in 2003. Under these 30-year contracts, the infrastructure companies of tube Lines and Metronet Rail were made responsible for the maintenance and renewal of London Underground's assets, and that included the rolling stock.

While tube lines (Jubilee, Northern and Piccadilly) continues unchanged, the 2007 collapse of Metronet Rail, which covered all the other lines in two separate contracts, and which was subsequently acquired by TfL in 2008, was at best very unfortunate.

Nevertheless, new rolling stock is going to be provided. The new trains are not covered in detail here, as at the time of writing much is still to be determined. The expectations are:

- 2009   The first of 47 new trains (the 2009 stock) enters service on the Victoria Line.
- 2010   The first new air-conditioned trains, the S stock, are provided for all sub-surface lines, starting with the Metropolitan.
- 2011   First S stock trains for the Edgware Road–Wimbledon, Circle and Hammersmith & City lines will enter service.
- 2013   First S stock train for the District main line will enter service.
- 2014   First new trains for the Piccadilly Line will enter service.
- 2017   Half-life refurbishment of Central, Northern, Jubilee and Waterloo & City line fleets will occur.
- 2020   New trains for the Bakerloo Line will enter service.

The expected outcomes, according to Transport for London, are improved reliability owing to reduced rolling stock failures, reduced scheduled journey times from increased stock availability, with ambience and accessibility improvements and increased capacity as fleets are refurbished or replaced.

Finally, in official sound-bite mode: 'London was the first world city to boast a metro system. At the dawn of the 21st century, London deserves a world-class transport system to meet the expectations of Londoners.'

REFERENCES

London Underground Investment Programme 2008. Transport for London.
London Underground Rolling Stock. Brian Hardy. Capital Transport, various editions.
London's Underground. John Glover, Ian Allan Publishing, various editions.
Motive Power Recognition: 4 London Transport Railways and PTE Systems. John Glover & Colin J. Marsden, Ian Allan Ltd, 1985.
Principles of London Underground Operations. John Glover, Ian Allan Publishing, 2000.
Railway Track Diagrams No 5, Southern and TFL. Trackmaps, 3rd edition 2008.
Steam to Silver. J. Graeme Bruce. Capital Transport, 1983.
Tube Trains on the Isle of Wight. Brian Hardy, Capital Transport, 2003.
Workhorses of the London Underground. J. Graeme Bruce, Capital Transport 1987.
Modern Railways, The Railway Magazine, Railway World and *Underground News*, various issues, also Transport for London website.

Left: The London Transport Museum at Covent Garden displays Metropolitan No 23 and second-class coach No 400 together. The latter was built in 1900 as steam stock, although it was converted in 1921 to electric working and subsequently back for use with steam in 1940. It ended its days on the Chesham shuttle in 1960. From a distance across the gallery, the pair give a passable impression of a train in a large station with an overall roof. *Author*

Centre left: The Isle of Wight is home to some remnants of Metropolitan Railway coaching stock. Seen here at St Helens on 1 April 1994 is a row of beach huts, albeit a little worse for wear. The arched tops of the doors however indicate conclusively their Metropolitan origins. Preservation is perhaps not quite the word to describe them. *Author*

Below: That extraordinary appendage of the Metropolitan Railway, known as the Brill tramway, was operated between Quainton Road and Brill, This is one of the two Aveling & Porter four-wheeled geared steam locomotives which were purchased in 1872 to run the modest service of mixed trains over the 6½-mile branch. It lasted there until 1894, after which it was used in a Northamptonshire brickworks until 1940. It was acquired for preservation by the Industrial Locomotive Society and is now on display at the Buckinghamshire Railway Centre, Quainton Road. It is seen here at Covent Garden. *Author*

Left: Metropolitan No 23, the Beyer Peacock Class A 4-4-0T which has survived from its construction in 1866, was withdrawn in 1948, and is seen on display at the Museum of British Transport, Clapham in September 1970. Then, it was a mere 104 years old. It is now part of the London Transport Museum and can be seen at Covent Garden. *Author*

Right: The locomotives supplied by Peckett & Sons of Bristol were of a very distinctive design, which changed little over the years. The Metropolitan purchased two of these for yard work at Finchley Road and Harrow. This is 0-6-0 saddle tank No 101, dating from 1897, which became No L53 under London Transport. Seen here in red-brown livery at Neasden in 1938, it was withdrawn from service in 1960. *Colour-Rail (LT4)*

Left: The seven 'E' class 0-4-4Ts were built at Neasden Works and Hawthorn Leslie between 1896 and 1901. They were designed by the Metropolitan's own T. F. Clark. The class was very successful, and while all were withdrawn by 1963, No L44 reacquired its early Metropolitan number 1, which survives today in preservation. It can be found at the Buckinghamshire Railway Centre, where it was photographed on 26 July 1987. *Author*

Right: This is 'F' class 0-6-2T No L52, seen here at Neasden in nice clean condition. Built as Metropolitan Railway No 93 by the Yorkshire Engine Co in 1901, the four locomotives in this class were used mainly for freight operations. There was no facility for steam heating of coaching stock. No L52 was the last survivor, and was withdrawn in 1962. *Harry Luff Collection/ Online Transport Archive*

Right: The Chesham push-pull set used in pre-electrification days is seen in the bay at Chalfont & Latimer. The conductor rail has clearly been laid recently. On the left are some mineral wagons for the still-extant local wagon load services operated by British Railways. On the right is a train of 'Dreadnought' hauled stock with its distinctive red outer ends forming a train to Baker Street, making a cross-platform connection. *Harry Luff Collection/ Online Transport Archive*

Left: On leaving Chalfont & Latimer, the Chesham branch runs along the north side of the main line to Aylesbury for nearly a mile, gradually diverging until it sets off on its own. Here, Ivatt Class 2 2-6-2T No 41284 is seen with the set of three Chesham coaches at the beginning of the branch proper in April 1960. This was the oldest stock on London Transport at the time, dating from between 1898 and 1900. They were withdrawn upon electrification, the following September. *The late J. P. Mullett/Colour-Rail (BRM438)*

Right: The earliest electric locomotives on the Metropolitan are represented here by this fine model on display in the London Transport Museum. This is one of the 10 'camel-backed' locomotives ordered from Westinghouse. These entered traffic in 1906. These were double-bogie vehicles with a central cab and bonnets at each end. Originally, and somewhat oddly, only one control position was provided. This was hastily doubled up, since driving trains one way while facing the other (as might happen unavoidably with a steam locomotive) was found not to be a good idea. *Author*

Right: Fast and fleet of foot is how the 4-4-4T locomotives, a decidedly un-British wheel arrangement, might be described. This is Metropolitan No 109, one of the eight 'H' class tanks designed by Charles Jones and built by Kerr, Stuart in 1920-21 and seen here in 1938. As with the 'G' and 'K' classes, these locomotives passed to the LNER, when that railway took over all steam passenger working formerly carried out by the Metropolitan and its successor, London Transport. *Colour-Rail (LT3)*

Left: The year 1922 saw the first of 20 new electric locomotives for the Metropolitan Railway emerge from Metropolitan Vickers works at Barrow-in-Furness. These were powerful and capable machines, and this somewhat eulogistic description by W. J. Passingham dates from around 1930: '*A journey beside the driver is a remarkable experience. Underground from Aldgate, the locomotive gives the impression of a high-spirited horse held in check and ready to leap forward at any slackening of control. The long tunnels stretch away into darkness and automatic signal lights gleam like green and red stars in a black firmament ...*' Seen here at Ruislip on 17 March 1997 is the operational survivor, No 12 *Sarah Siddons*. *Author*

Right: A Metro-Vick locomotive for the Metropolitan, No 10 *W. E. Gladstone,* sported a Wembley Park destination board when it was photographed at Neasden depot. Some locomotive-hauled coaching stock may be seen behind it.
Harry Luff Collection/
Online Transport Archive

Below: Moor Park today is hardly recognisable from the modest station seen here in March 1961. Here, Metro-Vick Bo-Bo No 11 *George Romney* is in charge of a southbound service for Baker Street. The coaching stock is one of the 'Dreadnought' sets, which needed vacuum brakes for steam haulage north of Rickmansworth.
Frank Hornby/Colour-Rail (LT12)

Right: The former Metropolitan Railway's electric locomotive, No 12 *Sarah Siddons,* responds magnificently to careful external attention, and is seen here at Acton depot on 9 March 2008 in bright sunshine following earlier rain. The withdrawal of the class which she represents was the end of locomotive haulage of passenger trains on the Underground. Perhaps surprisingly, half a century later, a similar situation is now approaching for passenger trains on National Rail. *Author*

Left: On 14 September 2008, No 12 *Sarah Siddons* was coupled to a set of former British Rail unpowered multiple unit trailers with cabs, a '4-TC' set, which was used from 1967 to 1989 on Weymouth services. Power at the other end was available from a Class 20 diesel, No 20189. She is seen here heading north through the sharply curved platform at Rickmansworth, on a Harrow-on-the-Hill to Amersham train. The headboard reads 'Metropolitan Heritage Train' and is surrounded by an Underground roundel, the Metropolitan Railway shield, and the Metronet logo. *Author*

Below: The Metropolitan's No 12 *Sarah Siddons* made one out-and-back trip from Amersham to Watford on 14 September 2008, and is seen here on the return journey crossing the Grand Union Canal. She is hauling the ex-BR '4-TC' set which has rather unconvincingly been covered in vinyls which suggest that its steel sides are really wood. Should the Croxley link to Watford Junction ever be built, a new bridge would be needed to replace this one across the Grand Union on a different alignment. *Author*

Right: The locomotive providing a helping paw to No 12 *Sarah Siddons* on 14 September 2008 should it be needed, was green-liveried Class 20 No 20189. It is seen here approaching Chalfont & Latimer with the TC set (and *Sarah*) following, en route to Harrow-on-the-Hill. *Author*

Centre right: These are 1927 Q stock driving motor cars seen at Ealing Common depot in a photograph probably from the 1960s. These trains were made up of converted cars of various stocks and some new build, which gave them an untidy appearance. The panelled doors also gave an impression of old age. The oil tail-lamps seen here were a curious hangover for an electric railway, but they lasted many years. *Harry Luff Collection/ Online Transport Archive*

Below: The mixed nature of Q stock trains can be seen in this view of April 1959 of a westbound District Line train leaving Plaistow on a service to Wimbledon. From left to right, are a Q23 motor car (leading), followed by a Q38 (with flared sides), Q35, Q27, Q31, and a K (1927) motor car bringing up the rear. *Trevor Owen/Colour-Rail (LT31)*

Above: Unusually, this train of District Line Q stock is on the north side of the Circle. It was working a Bank Holiday special westbound train, photographed here arriving at Farringdon and bound for Putney (Bridge). On the right are sidings for the Underground and beyond them the tracks of the Widened Lines. These are now closed permanently east of Farringdon. *Harry Luff Collection/ Online Transport Archive*

Centre left: Q23 driving motor car No 4248 now resides permanently in the London Transport Museum. It was built by the Gloucester RC&W Co in 1923 as a G class vehicle with hand-operated sliding doors. These were later converted to air operation. It was photographed in 1998. *Author*

Left: The interior of the Q23 car in the London Transport Museum is typical of sub-surface stock in the inter-war period. In those days, strap-hanging meant what it said and the lighting intensity would nowadays seem very inadequate. The seating moquette used reds and greens, with paintwork in cream and green. The opening windows were of the hopper style. This vehicle was photographed in January 2003. *Author*

Right: Q35 stock District Line trailer No 08063 was built as a member of the N class with hand-operated sliding doors, the last to be so fitted. It was converted to air-operated doors in 1950. Withdrawn in 1972, this car has been restored to 1950s condition by the London Underground Railway Society, although ownership is now with London Transport Museum. *Author*

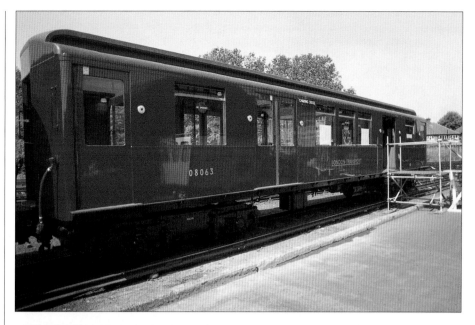

Centre right: This is an eight-wheeled steam breakdown crane, No C604, built by Cowan Sheldon in 1925 for the Metropolitan Railway with a jib length of 28ft 6in. The lifting capacity was 30 tons. It is seen here in Neasden yard with its jib carrier No J683 nearest the camera. Behind it to the left is four-wheeled tool van No BD702 converted from a ballast wagon in 1946, and another four-wheeled vehicle, No BD700, converted from a milk van. Apart from the milk van, all the vehicles were scrapped in 1965, this being restored for the centenary celebrations of the Metropolitan, and was subsequently found a home at the London Transport Museum. *Harry Luff Collection/ Online Transport Archive*

Below: A six-car train of the brown electric T (originally MW) stock is pictured here between Northwick Park and Harrow-on-the-Hill in August 1961. These trains were built from 1925 onwards, and unusually, consisted of compartment stock. This was partly because the passengers preferred it, but also because it was quick to unload at key stations such as Baker Street. These trains, in various formations, maintained the services to Watford and Rickmansworth until the last were displaced by the A stock in 1962. *John Baker/ Colour-Rail (LT206)*

Left: As tank engines go, this really is large. The Metropolitan's No 114 was one of the six powerful 2-6-4 'K' class tank locomotives, which originated from kits of parts for 2-6-0 tender locomotives manufactured at Woolwich Arsenal. These had been ordered by the government using designs based on those of the South Eastern & Chatham Railway, but many remained unsold. The Metropolitan saw them as a way of obtaining some freight locomotives with a shorter coupled wheelbase. Armstrong Whitworth supplied new cabs, side tanks and bunkers, and erected all the locomotives in 1925. No 114 is seen here in 1938. *Colour-Rail (LT2)*

Below left: A Piccadilly Line train of 1932 stock approaches Turnham Green, heading towards Acton Town in October 1957. Then, as now, the District Line trains used the outer pair of rails, and the stopping of Piccadilly trains at Turnham Green was a rarity. *Colour-Rail (LT227)*

Above: This is Ruislip, and an eastbound service of Piccadilly Line stock of 1934 vintage has arrived with an Uxbridge–Wood Green service in July 1960. The shortage of passenger doors in the nearest vehicle is accounted for by most of this area not being passenger accommodation, something easily forgotten today. *John Baker/ Colour-Rail (LT151)*

Centre left: Ickenham station lies on the Uxbridge branch in a rural setting, and a train of pre-1938 stock is leaving on an eastbound working to Arnos Grove in 1956. Quite how the Piccadilly service west of Rayners Lane is best split with the Metropolitan has always been a problem. The Metropolitan is the choice for the City but only serves the north side of the Circle directly. The Piccadilly penetrates the West End rather better, but takes an age to get there. Service provision also has to match the rolling stock available. *P. H. Grace/Colour-Rail (LT301)*

Left: In 1931, the District Railway purchased two shunting locomotives from the Hunslet Engine Co. These 0-6-0Ts were the first to be given 'L' prefixes to their numbers from new; they were neither intended for, nor used on passenger work. Both were withdrawn in 1963. This is No L30, seen here in steam at Lillie Bridge. *Harry Luff Collection/ Online Transport Archive*

Left: The predecessors of the 1938 stock were 24 cars of 1935 experimental stock. The first 18 sported a streamlined front and the later ones a flat front, something very close to that adopted for the production vehicles. Some of the survivors spent their last days on the Woodford–Hainault shuttle service. A pair is seen here in red livery, with pre-1938 stock as intermediate trailers, entering Chigwell station with a train from Hainault in 1963. *Richard Hill/Colour-Rail (LT280)*

Below left: The Mill Hill East branch starts off as double track (that in the middle is a siding), becoming single only when the Dollis Viaduct is reached. A train of 1938 stock leaves Finchley Central behind as it heads north on 5 August 1976. The straightness of the alignment towards Edgware contrasts with the sharp curve towards High Barnet, leaving little doubt that the former was the first to be constructed. *Author*

KEEP CLEAR OF THE DOORS
DO NOT ALIGHT FROM MOVING TRAIN

Above: A southbound train of 1938 stock arrives at West Finchley on 21 August 1967. On the Northern Line branches, it is very important for many passengers to know whether the train will run via Charing Cross or via Bank. This information appears on the yellow board in the destination indicator as well as the final destination. In this case the train is for Morden via Charing Cross. *Author*

Centre left: The buttons inviting passenger to 'press to open' were a feature of the 1938 stock which was discontinued in the 1950s. This example is to be found in the London Transport Museum. Likewise, the warning wording on the door panel has been updated, although the message has not really changed. *Author*

Left: One of the 15 sets of 1938 tube stock which were allocated to the Piccadilly Line is seen here passing through Turnham Green in the westbound direction. This was the result of changing plans and circumstances brought about by World War Two and its aftermath. Only the Bakerloo and the Northern were equipped 100% with 1938 stock, and the Bakerloo had to include 58 trailers from 1927 stock to make up its trains to seven cars. *Harry Luff Collection/ Online Transport Archive*

Left: Bakerloo Line services were restored as far as Harrow & Wealdstone (only) on 4 June 1984. This put further pressure on resources and a train of 1938 stock in the latterly used bus-red is seen here shortly afterwards. It would be another four years, however, before the stock was withdrawn from ordinary LU passenger service. *Author*

Below: Morden to High Barnet is about 21 miles and there are 30 intermediate stations. Seen here passing northbound at Woodside Park on 29 June 2008 is the 1938 stock heritage train, nearing the end of a non-stop journey. Missing out all the intermediate stations does not result in a super-fast journey time, as the train path has to be fitted in between all the other ordinary services. *Author*

Right: Chorleywood was opened in 1889 and is a typical Metropolitan Railway wayside station. It does not usually find itself served by 1938 tube stock, and indeed, the southbound four-car train of such stock owned by London Transport Museum was not stopping. This was a special run on 14 September 2008 from Amersham to Watford. *Author*

Below: The 1938 tube stock dated from before the era of strip lighting, and the 'shovel' type shades were a distinctive feature. The interiors were as depicted here at Amersham in the London Underground heritage set, on 14 September 2008. *Author*

Above: Here, a CO/CP stock train arrives at Kew Gardens in May 1978; the concrete lamp post is a real Southern Railway period piece. The sub-surface trains of 1935–59 stock all have flared-out lower body panels, disguising the lack of footboards. *Author*

Left: The CO/CP stock was the last of the sub-surface train sets to bear red livery, and apart from the precise shade this never changed during its lifetime. In May 1978, a train approaches Ealing Common station. Over time, this rolling stock operated in anything from five to eight-car sets. *Author*

Centre right: Sleet locomotive No ESL 107 was the last of its kind and was acquired by the London Transport Museum. It is now painted in brown, as seen here at Ruislip on 15 March 1997. The sleet locomotives had a driving position at each end and a tank for the de-icing fluid in the centre. There were large access doors adjacent to the tank on either side. *Author*

Right: Twelve motor cars and 16 trailers were built in 1940 for the Waterloo & City, then owned by the Southern Railway. Operated either as single motor cars, or in pairs with three trailers, these were the complete passenger stock for London's shortest railway. It is 1 mile 46 chains in length and has two stations only. This is motor car No S55 which had been lifted to the surface in March 1987, in the area later filled by Waterloo International station. *Author*

Right: No ESL 107 was constructed originally in 1903 as a pair of Central London Railway cars, Nos 3944 and 3981. They were reconstructed in 1939 to provide a single tube-sized electric vehicle, to keep electrified lines clear of ice and snow. The de-icing equipment was carried on two central, unpowered bogies, with the outer bogies retaining the traction equipment. In a somewhat overpowering yellow livery, it is seen at Acton Works on 3 July 1983. *Author*

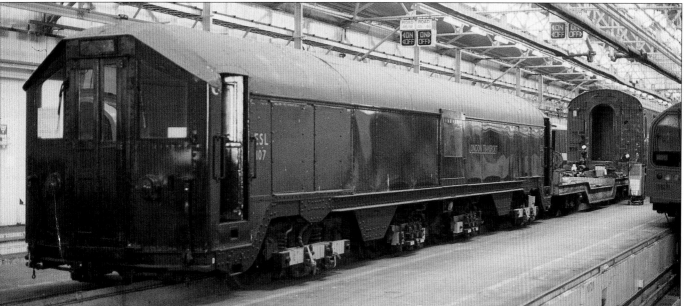

Left: An early attempt to extend the areas of glazing in tube cars was that afforded to driving motor No 10306 of the 1938 stock, which was thus modified in 1949. The aim was to enable standing passengers to see out better. Thus the upper portions of all the doors were glazed, and a similar treatment was applied to six other windows per side. The remainder were given smaller round apertures, which resulted in the ensemble becoming known as 'porthole' stock. This vehicle is seen at Mill Hill East in 1976. However, as most of the Northern is underground there was not much to be seen, and most passengers would have a seat by the time the open-air sections were reached. The result in the tunnel sections or after dark might best be described as cheerless.
Harry Luff Collection/
Online Transport Archive

Below left: The first part of this train is in London Transport bus red with white roundels and the remainder in train red. It is seen arriving at Acton Town in May 1978. The constant reformation of trains owing to regular coupling and uncoupling frequently mixed 'silver' portions and 'red' portions, which was one of the reasons for standardising on silver, or unpainted aluminium finish, for the R stock fleet.
Author

Above: Earl's Court District Line station has a splendid overall roof covering the pair of island platforms. This is a major interchange point across the platforms, but also to and from the Piccadilly Line in deep tube below. This view, in May 1978, is from inside the main entrance looking to the eastern end of the station, but there is another such view from the opposite end, which is used in particular by visitors to the Earl's Court Exhibition Centre. An R stock train arrives in Platform 1 on a service to Dagenham East. *Author*

Left: Kew Gardens station, seen in May 1978, still has a very 'Southern' look about it, emphasised in this view by the concrete footbridge. (This is a public bridge; the route between the platforms is by subway.) A train of R stock arrives bound for Richmond; Dagenham East must have been the destination for the last, or perhaps the next, journey. *Author*

Left: This District Line R stock driving motor, No 22624, was originally a Q38 trailer car, No 014178, but was one of those built with the idea that it might be converted at some stage. Thus cab doors were provided, but locked out of use. So it came to pass, and the work was carried out in 1950 by Gloucester RC&W as part of an order for 125 such conversions. Together with new construction, this enabled trains to be made up of four and two-car units that might run as six or eight cars. This vehicle is now at Mangapps Railway Museum, Essex and was photographed there on 25 May 2008. *Author*

Below left: A train of District Line R stock, which once all but monopolised that line's operations, approaches Acton Town station with an eastbound service from Ealing Broadway in May 1978. The rolling stock just visible above is in Ealing Common depot. That portion is now where the London Transport Museum's reserve collection is housed. *Author*

Above right: At the beginning of the 1950s, 125 Q38 driving trailers were converted by Gloucester RC&W Co to become R38 driving motors cars. This was part of the overall plan to create the R stock, which was to form the District's main fleet for the next quarter-century. No 22635 was a 'D' end car, photographed in smart red livery at Ealing Common. *Harry Luff Collection/ Online Transport Archive*

Centre right: This four-wheeled vehicle, No FB 578, was created from a flat wagon in 1950. Together with the similar No FB 579, they were needed to form brake vans on long welded-rail trains. It is coupled here to a rail wagon, No RW 494. The notice reads 'Prohibited for use on tube gauge lines' – or, one assumes, the guard might otherwise get a bit of a headache! *Harry Luff Collection/ Online Transport Archive*

Right: The acquisition of pannier tanks from BR for use on the London Underground began as early as 1956. No L94 was built by the North British Locomotive Co for the Great Western Railway as No 7752 in 1930. This '5700' class 0-6-0PT was owned by London Transport between 1958 and 1971 and is seen here on a permanent way train being loaded at Lillie Bridge depot in August 1970. *Harry Luff Collection/ Online Transport Archive*

Right: Ex-Great Western/BR pannier tank No L99, (No 7715), was built by Kerr, Stuart & Co for the GWR in 1930. It passed into London Transport ownership in 1963 and was retired in 1970. It is now resident at the Buckinghamshire Railway Centre at Quainton Road, where it was seen on 13 April 1998. On the right is the four-wheeled, vertical-boilered Sentinel shunter *Susan*, dating from 1952. *Author*

Below: Ex-GWR pannier tank No L99 at Quainton Road is very smartly turned out for the type. This is the rear view on 13 April 1998, with the fireman's shovel securely attached. *Author*

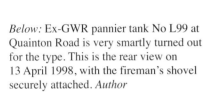

Right: London Transport maroon livery is shown off to good effect as a splendidly clean No L97, formerly No 7749, is seen at Acton on a bright, cold winter's day in December 1962. This locomotive was acquired by London Transport that year, and stayed until withdrawal in 1968. That steam traction on the London Underground, of all places, should survive longer than on the national system always seemed mildly bizarre. *A. C. Ferndale/Colour-Rail (LT248)*

Right: There were three prototypes for the 1959 stock, built by Metro-Cammell, Birmingham Railway Carriage & Wagon, and Gloucester RC&W. Their bodies were of unpainted aluminium alloy, fluorescent lighting was fitted, there was a roller blind above the central cab door, tell-tale 'fried eggs' were fitted to draw attention to any door which did not shut, and rubber suspension took over. Here, the Metro-Cammell unit arrives at Colindale, Northern Line, on a service to Edgware via Bank in July 1989. *Author*

Above: This is Finchley Central, Northern Line, with a 1959 stock train arriving on a High Barnet service on 24 April 1997. Headcodes were being abolished, so marker lights were provided instead. The area to the left of the running tracks was once a railway goods yard, but has now been turned over to other uses. The station itself would have been rebuilt to have two islands, but the permanent truncation of the Edgware line at Mill Hill East meant that no work of any consequence was ever done. *Author*

Left: The 1959 stock was built in quantity for the Piccadilly Line, with a total of 76 seven-car trains. With the addition of the three 1956 prototypes and the 15 1938 stock trains which remained on the line, this resulted in a fleet total of 94 sets. This is the interior of the driver's cab of DM No 1030 on 25 May 2008, which is now resident at Mangapps Railway Museum. *Author*

Right: Internally, the 1959 stock matched that of its 1938 predecessors in all but minor details. By the time it was ordered, passenger door opening was out of favour and was not provided. There were minor alterations to the seating layout, but the numbers of seats did not change. Uncovered centrally placed strip lights did however give a rather harsh light. This one was photographed at Mill Hill East on 24 April 1997. *Author*

Right: The 1959 stock acquitted itself well over a 30-year life. On 31 May 1990, this train is south of Brent Cross, heading for Morden. Much of the line north from Golders Green is on viaduct as the housing in the area had already been built by the time the railway was constructed in 1923. In the vicinity of this picture a road had to be cut in half and some houses demolished to enable the railway to proceed. The footbridge from which this photograph was taken forms part of the otherwise severed Pelier Rise. *Author*

Left: A train of 1959 stock at the long tunnel entrance at Morden in November 1990. Apart from the tube lines which are wholly underground, such as the Victoria and the Waterloo & City, the Northern Line train crew too cover large distances where the only illumination is artificial light. *Author*

Below: In 1990, this train of 1959 stock was repainted in the 1923 livery to celebrate 100 years of the Northern Line, or more particularly that of its City & South London Railway predecessor. Units Nos 1031 and 1044 retained this for the rest of their working existence, as indeed do those parts which survive in preservation. In this 1995 view, the train appears to have migrated to the Piccadilly Line, with the 1973 'United Airlines' stock alongside. *Harry Luff Collection/Online Transport Archive*

Above: The guard's controls, here painted green on 'heritage' DM No 1030, allow the guard to open the doors (bottom right, but only when pressed in conjunction with the button third along), close doors (second button), signal to the driver that the train was ready to start (fourth button). Other buttons allowed him to open and close his own door (right), speak to the driver (top), turn the heating on and cut out the end doors for short platforms (both left). There was a mirror image panel on the other side, minus the driver communication. *Author*

Above right: The cab end of 1959 stock DM No 1030 painted in the heritage livery applied in 1990, is seen here at Mangapps Railway Museum on 25 May 2008 with the unusual destination of Hampstead shown on the blind. As can be seen, these Metro-Cammell units had very simple lines. *Author*

Right: The use of guards came to an end on London Underground on 27 January 2000, when the last of the 1959 stock was withdrawn from the Northern Line. This was the scene at Borough on the last day; passengers always found guards a helpful source of information. That being dispensed here was a well-timed 'Mind the doors'. *Author*

Above: The centenary of the Metropolitan Railway was celebrated at Neasden in 1963. Here, Beyer Peacock No 23 is at the head of the two wagons cosmetically treated to appear like those of contractors Smith & Knight, who built the original section between Euston Square and Paddington. They are not yet occupied with suitably attired guests. The ensemble is to be propelled by a battery locomotive. *Harry Luff Collection/Online Transport Archive*

Below: The shuttle service from Hainault on arrival at Woodford had to vacate the main westbound platform and proceed to the sidings beyond, to reverse. This shows the surviving 1960 stock train after it had arrived in the siding on 3 May 1990 and the 1962 stock train into which it made a connection, passing it on its way to West Ruislip. Both look a little the worse for wear owing to the scrubbed-off graffiti. *Author*

Above: The 1960 Cravens stock worked the Woodford–Hainault shuttle and a three-car train is seen here arriving at Hainault in July 1985 with a 1938 stock centre car and is passing the depot in the background. Had this line been part of the national system, one wonders if it would have successfully avoided the attention of Dr Beeching. *Author*

Below: The 'heritage' 1960 Cravens set is seen here at North Weald in 1990, heading for Ongar although the destination blind suggests, unhelpfully, that the destination is Epping. By this time the trailers were sourced from 1938 stock, which was of a more sympathetic profile to the driving motors than the angular pre-1938 trailers. *Harry Luff/Collection/Online Transport Archive*

Left: By 1997, the 1960 Cravens unit, with 1938 intermediate trailer, was owned by Cravens Heritage Trains and was in need of a repaint. This was being undertaken on 17 March in Ruislip LUL depot. The vehicles concerned are Nos 3906, 4927 and 3907. Given that only 12 driving motors of this stock were built in the first place, they have lasted amazingly well. *Author*

Below left: The Widened Lines were created to ease line capacity problems east of King's Cross, for freight traffic to the wholesale markets. There were connections from the Great Western, the Midland and Great Northern, and offered passenger services to Moorgate. On the Metropolitan proper, an Aldgate train of A stock arrives at Farringdon with a service to Aldgate on 5 August 1976. *Author*

Above: Four-car trains of the A stock were used on the East London Line for several years, and coming off the New Cross branch at Surrey Canal Junction with a train for Whitechapel is the blue doors train on 3 May 1990. *Author*

Left: At 9ft 8in wide, the A stock exceeds all others on the Underground, and its bulk can readily be seen in this view of a train departing Chalfont & Latimer for Amersham in April 1998. This has allowed the 3+2 seating to be reasonably spacious and they are 12ft 1in high, too. The writing is now on the wall for these veterans; the new S stock is said to cope with anything from relatively long-distance commuting to quick on-and-off workings on the Circle Line. It remains to be seen how many variations are built in for different types of operation. *Author*

Left: Continued delays in executing the Amersham electrification and associated work meant that the A stock of 1960 and 1962 was conceived many years before it was actually built. The results were outstanding, and later resulted in what became the oldest stock in use on any Metro system, anywhere. This is a view of the interior, showing the 3+2 high-backed transverse seating and the luggage racks, both aimed at giving their users the nearest possible to compartment stock comfort. This view was taken at Watford on 14 September 2008. *Author*

Left: This is what might be termed a classic view of sub-surface stock with typical London Transport architecture. Apart from the paint scheme of the train, little else has changed over the past 45 years. This is Eastcote station, with an A stock train arriving with an Uxbridge-to-Aldgate working on 26 April 2008. Such scenes are not destined to last for much longer however. *Author*

Right: The traditional air-operated sliding doors on Underground stock are seen here, fully retracted into the open position between the bodywork panels, when they all but disappear from sight, on an A stock train. This is forming the Chesham branch working at Chalfont & Latimer in March 1997. *Author*

Left: This is North Acton Junction on 1 May 1990. The approaching train of 1962 stock is from the original Ealing Broadway line; the other is the West Ruislip route. On the right is the Birmingham main line of the Great Western, from which the Central Line extension was designed to remove the local traffic. Today, the GW route is very little used. *Author*

Left: One of the quietest stations on the Underground network in terms of passenger usage is Roding Valley, Central Line. In reality, most of the local population can just as easily walk to Buckhurst Hill or Woodford, where rather better services are provided. Here, an eight-car train of 1962 stock is pictured from the station footbridge, returning from the Woodford direction as a special to Hainault depot in 1985. *Author*

Right: The unadorned nature of the aluminium-bodied trains of 1959/62 stock saw little variation, although this driving motor of the latter did acquire a red front-end in a similar style to that associated with the 1973 stock of the Piccadilly and the D stock of the District before corporate colour schemes took over. It is seen here arriving at Woodford with a train for Epping. *Author*

Left: After the culling of the Verney Junction and Brill outposts of the Metropolitan in the late 1930s, Underground services did not come any more remote than Blake Hall in deepest Essex, until it too succumbed in 1981. The station is seen here in March 1977 with a four-car train of 1962 stock on the Epping–Ongar shuttle. The lack of traffic potential is only too apparent. *Author*

Above: The junctions at Leytonstone are seen in this view of 1962 stock departing for Epping and arriving from Hainault on 3 May 1990. The use of grade-separated junctions avoids conflicting movements and is a very positive help in making the best use of line capacity. *Author*

Left: Here, 1962 stock emerges from the tunnel beneath Eastern Avenue to run up to the surface at Newbury Park, beside the link from the Great Eastern main line. By 3 May 1990, it was only a headshunt and it has now been completely removed. The arrangement is similar to that adopted at East Finchley for the connection to the Great Northern, although that visible from the station is still in place for depot access. *Author*

Right: The availability of withdrawn T stock following the Amersham electrification allowed a pair of driving motor cars (originally Nos 2758 and 2749) to be converted to a self-contained unit for de-icing and latterly leaf-clearing. The cars were subsequently numbered ESL118A and ESL118B. The intermediate wagon for leaf clearing is No F311, which carried additional equipment. From the 'A' end, the ensemble is seen at Acton Works on 3 July 1983. A withdrawn CO/CP stock unit is seen on the right. *Author*

Right: A few of the 1962 stock trains, shortened to seven cars, were latterly employed on the Northern Line such as this northbound service for High Barnet seen arriving at West Finchley on 24 April 1997. It is only the position of the tail light, to the left rather than the right of the marker lights, which enables the 1959 and 1962 stocks to be readily distinguished. *Author*

Left: No L11 was the Acton Works shunter, and is seen here on 3 July 1983. It was converted in 1964 from a pair of 1931 tube stock cars, Nos 3080 and 3109, the locomotive having powered bogies at both ends. It always operated facing the same way and different coupling facilities were provided at each end. This view of the 'A' end, facing Acton Town, is fitted with tube-type couplers and nose-end air pipes. *Author*

Left: This almost monochrome shot is of a rubbish train at Earl's Court Piccadilly Line westbound platform in May 1970. The train is formed of two pre-1938 pilot cars with two intermediate flat wagons.
Harry Luff Collection/
Online Transport Archive

Right: Battery locomotive No L25 was one of the batch of 13 built by Metropolitan Cammell in 1965. It is seen here in yellow livery at an open day held at Old Oak Common on 6 February 2000. All buffers on battery locos are hinged, enabling them to be raised clear for coupling to Underground passenger stock, although here they are seen in their horizontal position. *Author*

Left: This is battery locomotive No L21 at Acton Works on 3 July 1983. It is fitted with buck-eye couplings at one end only. Other bufferbeam equipment consists of main reservoir/brake pipes, control jumper receptacles and trip cock, and driver's safety device isolating cock. *Author*

Above: One of the Metro-Cammell batch of battery locomotives, No L31, hurries north through Ealing Common towards Ruislip during traffic hours on 9 March 2008. The 'top-and-tail' provision of power as seen here (the locomotive at the rear is No L50) avoids the need to run round trains if they are to be reversed which, given the distances between crossovers, could be a lengthy process. On the other hand, it uses two locomotives where one would otherwise suffice. *Author*

Right: Battery locomotive No L20 is hoisted off its bogies in Ruislip depot on 15 March 1997 for underside inspection and attention. This was one of the Metro-Cammell-built machines, and dates from 1964. *Author*

Above: The debut of ex-London Underground pre-1938 stock on the Isle of Wight in 1967 was perhaps an unprecedented event. Trains, between 30 and 40 years old, were reconditioned to see another 20 or so years service (as it turned out) on a commercial railway. In this 1980 view of Ryde Pier Head, the shuttle formed with '3-TIS' unit No 032 is leading to Ryde Esplanade and stands on the right, the Shanklin train with '4-VEC' unit No 045 at the front is on the left. The Rail Blue livery had been lightened by painting the train doors grey. *Author*

Centre left: North of Brading on 9 August 1980, a seven-car formation is seen as it was meant to be used, heading towards Ryde. Today, with a total of only 12 cars left in service for the whole of the Island Line, this train on its own would have represented over half the entire fleet. *Author*

Below left: Network SouthEast came to the Isle of Wight too; this five-car train with unit No 045 is leaving Ryde St John's Road for Pier Head on 2 October 1988. The island logo has appeared between the cab windows and the whole looks commendably smart. The siding on the right, once a loop, is the end of the station's third platform track, although no longer used as such. *Author*

Right: Victoria Line 1967 stock was used from time to time on the Woodford–Hainault shuttle, since the ATO equipment on one was in many ways a test bed for the other. Any upsets on this lightly used part of the network, most of which lay outside Greater London anyway, would not be crucial as far as the general operation of the Central Line was concerned. A four-car unit is seen here from Grange Hill station overbridge in 1985, emerging from the tunnel of the same name. *Author*

Left: In the days when Sandown was the end of the double-track section from Brading, this large signalbox on the up platform dwarfed the station premises. From here, the signalman would also have been able to see the branch trains on the former line from Newport, which approached from the west. This view looks north towards Ryde; the NSE-liveried train for Shanklin, with unit No 044 leading, carries 'Ryde Rail' branding. *Author*

Above: The Victoria Line has one depot at Northumberland Park, reached by a spur from Seven Sisters and is the only part of the line in open air. Here, a 1967 stock train on 4 September 1985 (long before the days of graffiti ruined the unpainted aluminium finishes) makes towards the tunnel mouth. It is the beginning of the evening peak, and several more trains can be seen in the distance. The control tower is on the left and beyond it, out of sight, is the Lea Valley line of National Rail. *Author*

Above: This is the interior of the 1967 stock in as-built condition, the greys on the station platforms being matched by the grey train interiors — although with the introduction of some reds to brighten it up a bit. The seating layout remained unchanged from that of the 1959/62 stocks, giving 40 seats in total, although one trailer in each four-car set had longitudinal seats throughout. This reduced the seating in those vehicles to 36. *Author*

Left: The simple controls on the driver's desk of a 1967 stock Victoria Line train, seen when new in 1968. When trains are driven automatically, drivers would have little to do other than opening and closing doors, and this could become excessively boring. Were drivers really needed at all? It was decided that the public were not ready for driverless trains, so they were given some additional tasks.
Harry Luff Collection/
Online Transport Archive

Above: A train of refurbished Victoria Line 1967 stock in corporate livery makes its way around the depot at Northumberland Park on 24 April 1997. These trains were the update on the 1959/62 stocks for the Piccadilly and Central lines respectively, but with automatic train operation. There have never been guards on the Victoria Line. *Author*

Below: The beginning of the descent from Northumberland Park depot to the line itself at Seven Sisters can be seen from the inclination at the far right of the trains on 24 April 1997. These are both 1967 stock trains, the one on the far side arriving, and the other departing and going into service. *Author*

for the Modeller and Historian

Above: Articulated stock has had several supporters over the years, Eurostar trains being a present major fleet-wide example. Experiments by London Transport were carried out on a couple of cars of the 1935 experimental stock in the late 1960s for possible application on Bakerloo Line replacement stock. The two cars involved, seen here at Northfields on 10 March 1971, were DMs Nos 11011 (left) and 10011. Both car bodies were shortened in a rough and ready fashion, with the corners of the vehicle ends rounded. Circumstances changed with the rolling stock cascades following new stock orders for the Piccadilly Line, and no more was heard of this project. *Harry Luff Collection/Online Transport Archive*

Below: To replace the pannier tanks, London Transport purchased three Rolls-Royce 'Sentinel' 0-6-0 diesel-hydraulic locomotives second-hand from Thos Hill of Rotherham. No DL81 was built in Shrewsbury in 1968 for the Park Gate Iron & Steel Co, and was acquired by LT in April 1971. All the locomotives ran with a runner wagon (No DT81 in this case), which was required to operate the track circuits. The locomotive thus went everywhere with it. Sleet brushes were also attached to the runners for snow clearance duties. The locomotives retained their original green livery. *Harry Luff Collection/ Online Transport Archive*

Above: One of the three 'Sentinel' shunters owned for a time by London Transport, No DL83, but without its runner wagon, can now be seen on the Nene Valley Railway. On 29 April 2001 it was keeping company with a variety of steam locomotives outside the shed at Wansford. *Author*

Right: The 1972 MkI stock was a crew-operated version of the 1967 stock and the fleet shared Northern Line duties with ex-Piccadilly Line 1959 stock. This is the High Barnet terminus, opened originally by the Great Northern Railway in 1872. It was transferred to London Transport with the extension of the Northern Line over LNER tracks in 1940. *Author*

Left: East Finchley is renowned for Eric Aumonier's *Archer*, firing his rapid-transit arrow towards the heart of London. This was the only station on the Northern Line extensions to High Barnet and Mill Hill East of 1940/41 to be completely rebuilt, although the two centre platforms thus created have never really been used due to the abandonment of service provision from Finsbury Park. Here, a 1972 MkI train is about to perform that duty, running to Kennington via Charing Cross. *Author*

Below left: For a time, the Northern Line was worked by a combination of the remains of the 1938 stock, 1959 stock from the Piccadilly, and the 1972 MkI stock, which was built for the role. Supplied by Metro-Cammell, these too were of seven cars and crew-worked, although they otherwise closely resembled the 1967 stock. This unit, seen here entering Morden depot on 31 May 1990, has been given an experimental livery, which led eventually to the corporate livery applied universally today. *Author*

Right: Later on, the 30 trains of 1972 MkI stock became largely surplus, and although many vehicles were adapted for use in trains of 1967 stock and 1972 MkII stock, thus strengthening these fleets, others fell by the wayside. Seen here are units dumped at Hainault depot awaiting their fate in May 2001; most were subsequently cut up. That on the right is part of a 1992 stock train. *Author*

Left: The subsequent build of 1972 MkII trains, a total of 33 seven-car units, saw them turned out with red doors and red roundels replacing the Underground transfers. At the time, this was a positively daring livery! The first allocations were to the long-suffering Northern Line, which was thus enabled to dispose of all 1938 stock. A train of the new stock is seen here at Woodside Park on a southbound working to Kennington via Charing Cross, on 6 June 1977. It matched the then station colour scheme admirably. *Author*

Right: Before the Jubilee Line was separated from the Bakerloo, the 1972 MkII stock was widely used. On 13 June 1985, a train of the red-door stock is seen arriving at Canons Park station from Stanmore, seemingly before graffiti was invented. *Author*

Left: The 1972 MkII stock found its way to the Bakerloo Line, where the intention was that it would be used on what became the Jubilee Line. Here, a train approaches Willesden Green on a northbound working in May 1988. The outer tracks are used by the Metropolitan, and a train of A stock can just be seen disappearing in the distance. Far right are the tracks used by what is now Chiltern Railways. *Author*

Below left: The remarkable arrangement at Queen's Park, Bakerloo Line, involves all trains arriving from Elephant & Castle running into this shed after completing station duties. The two outer tracks are part of the running lines and trains continue with passengers to Harrow & Wealdstone (left), or in the reverse direction, out of sight to the right. The centre two tracks from which this 1972 MkII train is emerging on 28 June 2008 (Track 23) are dead ends, used solely for reversal purposes. It is not done like this any more elsewhere, but no one seems unduly worried since the practice here carries long-established grandfather rights. *Author*

Above right: Internally, the Bakerloo's trains closely resemble the 1967 stock, but the line's brown colour has been used for the handrails in this refurbished car. Since this photograph was taken on 28 December 1996, the armrests have disappeared, to be replaced with curious pouches which protrude a few centimetres from the areas between the seat backs. *Author*

Centre right: The Bakerloo Line is operated entirely by the 1972 MkII trains, one of which is seen arriving at Stonebridge Park on a northbound working, with Network SouthEast's No 313021 on a Watford Junction to Euston working alongside. Just about everything which can differ between the trains does so, including (from the passenger viewpoint) floor height. Mixed operation, as here, is never entirely straightforward or satisfactory. *Author*

Right: Corporate livery days see the 1972 MkII stock still on the Bakerloo, where their numbers have been judicially strengthened by an importation of some of their MkI counterparts. This is Queen's Park, where the Underground comes to the surface and track and stations give way to those of National Rail. A southbound train for Elephant & Castle is leaving as a northbound service enters the platform at speed, on 28 June 2008. *Author*

Left: Underground trains on the Bakerloo terminate at Harrow & Wealdstone, and have done so since 1982, when operation to Watford Junction was abandoned and left to British Rail. For a short time, all Bakerloo Line operation north of Stonebridge Park was suspended, although services resumed to Harrow & Wealdstone in 1984. Here, a 1972 MkII stock train comes out of the turnback siding between the running lines, ready to take up a working to Elephant & Castle, on 28 June 2008. *Author*

Below left: A new supply of battery locomotives was required in the 1970s and Nos L44–L54 were the result. They were built at what was then BREL Doncaster Works and delivered in 1975. No L50, seen here in blue livery, brings up the rear of a permanent way train heading north through Ealing Common station on 9 March 2008. *Author*

Above right: The four-tracking of the Piccadilly and District Line extends from the east of Barons Court, where the Piccadilly comes to the surface, and Northfields, although the District Line no longer runs beyond Acton Town in this direction. Here, an eastbound 1973 stock Piccadilly Line train approaches Barons Court in 1985. *Author*

Below: Arnos Grove station consists of two island platforms with a total of three tracks. This is the view facing north with a train of 1973 stock arriving from Cockfosters. The wide separation of the tracks and the resulting spare space may be noted, which is one of the inevitable down sides of such a layout. *Author*

Left: This overhead view of a 1973 stock train shows it arriving at Arnos Grove, where it will terminate. It has just emerged from the long tunnelled section, on 24 April 1997. These six-car trains, with each vehicle longer than the seven-car trains they replaced, were over five metres shorter overall. This enabled them to fit completely into all line platforms. *Author*

Below left: Boston Manor is an interesting mix of the 1930s at street level, and that at platform level which dates from several decades earlier. The whole has a quite stylish appearance, and could still accommodate sub-surface trains if so required. Approaching is a westbound train of unrefurbished Piccadilly Line 1973 stock in August 1990. *Author*

Above right: A train of the refurbished version of the 1973 tube stock is seen here entering Hounslow East station on the Piccadilly Line with a westbound working on 22 March 2003. The Piccadilly always had two western branches, but the addition of Terminal 5 in 2008 adds further variations, plus the puzzle of why you should not get on the first train if you want T1, T2 or T3 and that one is going via T4. Luck means that it will be followed by an Uxbridge train, then an extended interval *Author*

Right: The 1973 stock consists of three-car units joined together in pairs. Most of these have a cab at one end only, although with basic driving controls in the other end for use in depot areas when uncoupled (UNDMs). Others have full cabs so that they can be used on their own, but the reason for this, the Aldwych branch, was closed in 1994. A pair, featuring one of each with UNDM D end No 384 coupled to DM A end No 870, was photographed at Cockfosters on 10 August 2008. The inter-car barriers are intended to prevent falls onto the line by passengers. *Author*

384 870

Right: Refurbished 1973 stock saw all cars being converted to longitudinal seating only, albeit with some perch seating in lieu. Seats as such were reduced from 44 to 38 per car. The use of the end positions in the centre of each car was used for the perches, as seen here at Arnos Grove on 24 April 1997. *Author*

Below: The old Hillingdon station had to be moved to allow the A40(M) road to be constructed, and the new premises were opened on 6 December 1992. A 1973 stock Piccadilly Line train crosses the bridge, bound for Cockfosters, with the road below, on 28 June 2008. Access to the platforms is via the station footbridge, reached either from the main road via the walkway, or by steps from the car park below. *Author*

Left: The tunnel on the Piccadilly Line which includes Southgate station, is being entered by a southbound train of refurbished 1973 stock in June 2003. The tracks are already beginning to separate to allow the escalators to descend in the middle of the island platform. The front of this train will just be becoming visible from the platform itself, one of the very few instances on tube lines where the tunnel exit can be seen by passenger waiting for a train. *Author*

Above: Piccadilly Line 1973 stock at South Ealing, where there are nominally four platforms, but in reality only three. The track serving the fourth platform (the other side of the island and out of the picture to the left) is used for test purposes only, following the demise of District services to Hounslow in 1964. The second westbound track is needed for Piccadilly trains which have been routed via Platform 1 (nominally for District use), at Acton Town. This photograph is dated 18 May 2004. *Author*

Right: West Brompton is a well-kept station on the sub-surface lines, as seen here with a C stock train arriving on an Edgware Road–Wimbledon service in 1985. Only a small part of the total platform length is covered by the roof, through which stairs lead to the street. Unfortunately, the lack of other platform shelter leads passengers to congregate under the roof when it is raining, which can cause quite an obstruction. *Author*

Above: The fine overall roof at Paddington (District and Circle platforms) sees a C stock train arriving with an inner-rail train in July 1989. Four pairs of double doors on the side of each vehicle makes for quick station times, but the number of seats has to be reduced as a result. The leading two cars are from the C77 batch. *Author*

Left: The Hammersmith & City Line dives under the Great Western main line between Royal Oak and Westbourne Park. The nearer train is providing a Hammersmith to Barking service, while a Hammersmith-bound train can just be seen approaching. Both are made up of C69 and C76 units, which could then be told apart by their roof colours (C69 was black, C77 unpainted). As originally built, this was a flat crossing; the complications which this would cause nowadays hardly bear thinking about! *Author*

Above: Hammersmith & City services have not always been extended east of Whitechapel, at least outside peak hours. Here, a C stock train for the usual terminus of Barking arrives at Bromley-by-Bow in June 2003. From here, the District parallels the London, Tilbury & Southend line through to the Upminster terminus. *Author*

Below: A refurbished C stock train for Wimbledon arrives at Fulham Broadway in July 1997, bound for Wimbledon. The impression given here is much more that of an ordinary suburban railway, but with Underground paraphernalia. *Author*

Left: The interiors of the C stock when refurbished saw all seating changed to longitudinal layout, but with no alteration to the total number of seats provided. This, however resulted in a greater amount of standing space, and accidentally kicking the passenger seated opposite is not very likely. A converted set is seen here in May 2001. *Author*

Right: A pair of refurbished C stock trains is seen here at Fulham Broadway from the now effectively redundant footbridge, looking towards Earl's Court on 28 June 2008. This part of the station retains its overall roof, but the entrance/exit is now in the new construction halfway along the platform. *Author*

Left: The C stock and the D stock always appeared considerably different when viewed from the front, although to some extent this was due to the red band on the D stock compared with the aluminium all-over finish on the C. Now that both are in corporate livery, the differences can be seen to be minimal, these being the position of the lights, the curvature of the body sides, and not much more. At Wimbledon on 24 June 2008 are a D stock train left, and a C stock train, right. *Author*

Right: The tunnel cleaning train was constructed between 1972 and 1977 by Acton Works. This is a five-car formation, numbered TCC1– TCC5. The end vehicles, Nos TCC1 and TCC5 (nearest camera) are driving motors from 1938 tube stock. These cars contain the traction equipment for moving the train to site and in addition No TCC1 has a hydraulic drive unit used when the train is tunnel cleaning. Behind the driver's position there is an operator's cabin from which the train is controlled when in use. Coupled to the driving cars are filter vehicles Nos TCC2 and TCC4, which unload dust drawn in from the middle nozzle car, No TCC3. When in operation, the train travels at between ½mph and 6mph. Above the cab roof may be seen the three high-powered headlights which are used when cleaning is in progress. It was photographed at Acton Works on 3 July 1983. *Author*

Right: A smartly turned-out pair of 1938 stock driving motor cars were specially converted for weedkilling duties, entering the engineering fleet in 1978. In yellow livery at Ruislip, cars Nos L151 (leading) and L150 were photographed on 15 March 1997. *Author*

Below: A pair of ballast motor cars sourced from 1938 stock are seen at Ealing Common with No L140 (formerly DM No 10088) leading. Ballast cars are used for topping and tailing ballast trains to move them round the system to where they are needed. This view is from July 1975, when the cars were in dark-maroon livery. *Harry Luff Collection/ Online Transport Archive*

Right: These Q38 driving motors, latterly part of the R stock fleet, found new life as pilot cars for the sub-surface fleet. In this guise, they were used to ferry odd bits of rolling stock which were not proceeding under their own power between depots, as required. Renumbered L126 and L127 in the engineering fleet, they were photographed at Acton Works on 3 July 1983. They have since reverted to red livery and their original numbers of 4416 and 4417. Both now belong to the London Transport Museum. *Author*

Centre right: Some of the pre-1938 cars, or Standard stock, were also used by London Transport after withdrawal from passenger operation. One such became No L131 in the engineering fleet. Seen here together with its partner, No L130, these were pilot cars used to transfer tube cars around the system. Originally built in 1934 by Metro-Cammell as No 3693 for the Piccadilly Line, it was from the last batch of Standard stock to be constructed. It is seen at Acton Works on 3 July 1983, by which time both vehicles were painted yellow. *Author*

Below: The first Unimog tractor/trailer unit was delivered to LT at the end of 1982. Basically, it is a road vehicle with a Mercedes-Benz engine hauling a trailer, with two sets of wheels which enable it to run on both road and rail. This was part of a leaf-clearing programme, in which the leaves would be sucked up by nozzles on the tractor unit and deposited in a 16cu m tank in the trailer. Seen here at Acton on 3 July 1983, the transfer-to-road mode takes around 20 minutes. Rail fleet numbers were TMM774 (motor) and TMM775 (trailer). It also carried the registration number A723 LNW. *Author*

Above right: A warm day sees an open offside cab-door on this train of eastbound D stock surmounting the steep gradient from Aldgate East, as it arrives at Whitechapel in June 2003. The two island platforms at this level are no more than adequate in width and in access terms. The forthcoming extended East London Line and later, Crossrail, will make some major changes necessary here. *Author*

Right: This view of West Ham station in May 2001 shows the rear of one of the now-defunct Class 312 EMUs on an outer-suburban service to Shoeburyness, and a westbound service of District Line D stock bound for Richmond. This picture, too, demonstrates that the sub-surface Underground stock is considerably more tightly dimensioned than its main line counterparts. *Author*

Above: The District Line east of Hammersmith, and the Piccadilly tracks too, have to circumvent the former London & South Western Railway route to Hammersmith Grove Road and beyond, of which the remains in the centre of this 1990 picture are all that is left. The D stock trains pictured are on the outermost tracks; both Piccadilly Line tracks are between the westbound train on the left and the disused embankment. *Author*

Left: The D stock upholstery was turned out in the orange and black moquette, which was very popular when they were new at the beginning of the 1980s. As can be seen, the use of a pair of facing transverse seats does cause slight layout problems with the cramped appearance of the single longitudinal seats, one on each side. The single doors on this stock date from when Underground traffic was falling, and are less suitable than double doors for coping with the volume growth of recent years. *Author*

Above: Parsons Green on the Wimbledon branch of the District Line sees a westbound train of D stock approaching on 28 April 1997. Of note is the 'joggle' in the platform edge, necessary because of the overhang of rolling stock using the crossover between the tracks. Longer but fewer vehicles can mean a more productive use of passenger space and a reduced capital cost, but greater problems on curved platforms, as seen here. *Author*

Centre right: Between Putney Bridge and Parsons Green there are a number of sidings on the viaduct, and this is all that remains of an abortive attempt at four-tracking. The District Line train of D stock on the left has terminated at Parsons Green and will shortly return, while the approaching C stock train in the foreground is forming a Putney Bridge–Edgware Road service. This is one of the few instances where one line runs two types of stock on a regular basis. This situation has been dictated by the short platforms to be found on the west side of the Circle Line. *Author*

Right: East of Barons Court station, just out of sight in the distance, the Piccadilly Line dives underground, to emerge again at Arnos Grove. In the foreground, a train of D stock is approaching West Kensington station, on 11 March 2008. *Author*

Right: This view shows the interior of the D stock after refurbishment, giving a much cooler finish. The curious curves in the handrail system are designed to give clearance where it is most needed, although the first reaction is to wonder if the vehicle has been at the centre of a major fight! However, they are all the same. *Author*

Right: D stock refurbishment has meant the replacement of some fixed seats with the tip-up variety, as seen here. As indicated, this can provide space for wheelchairs, but also for children's buggies, shopping trolleys and so on. Quite how some of this fits in with the basic objective of a mass-transit system to carry large numbers of people, who need to be packed in reasonably tightly to move them at all, perhaps needs further consideration. *Author*

Left: Terminal working as here at Upminster, where the Underground has exclusive use of three platforms, involves some movements which will cross with others. An eastbound train of D stock is making here for Platform 3 on 29 March 2008. The track on the extreme right is that of the shuttle service from Romford, serving Platform 1; to the left (out of picture) are the c2c lines which use Platforms 5 and 6. There is no rail inter-connection between the three groups of services. *Author*

Left: The 1983 stock was designed and built for the Jubilee Line, but its tenure was relatively short, being replaced by the 1996 stock. In general terms, this small fleet of trains was built at a time when Underground traffic was shrinking, and the single-leaf doors employed would later have had difficulty in coping with the traffic boom at Canary Wharf. They were thus scrapped, although this was after they had reached the average lifespan of a service bus. Here, a train is entering Wembley Park from the north in May 1988. *Author*

Below: A northbound 1983 stock train of six cars approaches Willesden Green in December 1996. These trains were built in two similar but not identical batches of 15 trains (Batch 1) and 16½ trains (Batch 2). It may be noted that the Jubilee Line as operating today uses a fleet of 63 seven-car trains, thus giving well over twice the carrying capacity of these two small builds together. *Author*

Above: At Finchley Road, the Jubilee Line enters the tunnel section, to emerge again nowadays just short of Canning Town. Seen arriving is one of the Batch 2 1983 stock trains. Cross-platform interchange with the Metropolitan is much used, although there is a fine line for the staff between keeping as close to the timetable as they can and waiting for passengers to make the quick hop across. Few passengers realise just how disruptive the actions of a 'kind' driver can be. *Author*

Left: The interior view is of a Batch 2 vehicle of 1983 stock in January 1997, with standard fluorescent strip lighting. The generous width of the gangway in the transverse seating section is noticeable, although this was presumably made possible through savings in seat width. Slightly longer cars and single-leaf doors made it possible to accommodate 48 seats in all types of vehicle. *Author*

Above: This is the driver's cab of a 1983 tube stock train, seen here in 1988, and now consigned to history. The comparison with, for instance, 1959 stock shows just how far matters progressed in a quarter of a century. *Author*

Above: Scrapping was not the fate of all 1983 stock cars, such as the four (two only visible from ground level) on top of what was once the viaduct taking North London Line trains into Broad Street. They are however without bogies and are described as 'recycled'. These car bodies are used as studios by Village Underground Workspace, a charitable organisation which styles itself as a centre for creativity. This photograph was taken from Great Eastern Street in Shoreditch, on 15 December 2007. *Author*

Below left: A fleet of 41 30-tonne general purpose wagons was constructed by Procor in 1985. This is No GP928, seen at Ruislip depot on 18 May 2004. Others include 'Turbots' (for ballast), hopper wagons and rail wagons. *Author*

Right: The 1986 Prototype Tube Stock was an attempt to find out what the rolling stock industry had to offer for the forthcoming Central Line procurement, given a performance specification. What came about consisted of three different types from three different manufacturing groups. All were four-car formations or, more accurately, two, two-car units, one of which had a cab. Train A was painted red and is seen here at Northfields. This was the joint product of Metro-Cammell in association with GEC. *Harry Luff Collection/ Online Transport Archive*

Left: The blue train is also seen at Northfields in 1987. It was built that year by British Rail Engineering Ltd at Derby, with electrical equipment by Brush. This was Train B. It was BREL (now part of Bombardier) who finally won the contract for the supply of the 1992 stock. *Harry Luff Collection/ Online Transport Archive*

Below left: The green train of 1986 stock, Train C, was also built by Metro-Cammell, with electrical equipment by Brown Boveri of Switzerland. The four cars are pictured here in the sidings at Stanmore, the buildings behind looking more like those of a school than an Underground station. One car only, of this stock, is all that remains of the 1986 prototypes. *Harry Luff Collection/ Online Transport Archive*

Above right: The recording of track condition for future remedial action is important. This is the track-recording train assembled for the process, and which may be found anywhere on the Underground system. It consists of a former 1973 stock trailer, now *Track Recording Car 666*, top-and-tailed by a pair of Cravens driving motors (now Nos L132 and L133). It is seen here at Neasden in October 1987 when almost new, but with a modest level of external graffiti, which was by then becoming a major menace. *Harry Luff Collection/Online Transport Archive*

Below: The scale of the cutbacks in service provision on the Isle of Wight is emphasised by the comparison of this picture with the earlier one of the pre-1938 stock train from the same viewpoint. Seven-car capacity is reduced to two, in this view north of Brading. No 483005 in NSE livery, is heading for Ryde Pier in June 1992. *Author*

Right: Railtrack was created on Good Friday, 1 April 1994. On that day, 1938 stock No 483006 in Network SouthEast livery, then the oldest class of train on the national system, headed a four-car Ryde Pier Head to Shanklin service. It is seen here at Lake, which was at that time one of the newest stations to have been opened, dating only from 11 May 1987. Few would then have guessed that Railtrack would be the first of these three to bite the proverbial dust! *Author*

Right: In May 1992, the shuttle service between Ryde Pier Head and Ryde Esplanade was still being operated. This is the view from the latter, and although these appear to be double lines, they are in reality two unconnected single tracks. NSE-liveried No 483005 is in anonymous mode as far as the destination is concerned. *Author*

Below: The pier at Ryde is 750 yards long; far enough to seem quite a long walk when carrying luggage and perhaps battling against inclement weather, but very quickly covered in a train. No 483004 sets off from Ryde Esplanade for Pier Head on 21 August 2004. *Author*

Above right: It is still somewhat mildly un-nerving to be standing on the station platform at Ryde Pier Head on the Isle of Wight and see a train of LT1938 stock in red livery approaching. Set No 007 is leading in this view of 21 August 2004. The considerable technical achievement of getting all the electrical equipment below the car floors does not seem quite such a good idea when the sea is really rough. *Author*

Right: Unit No 483004 arrives at Ryde St John's Road station with a train from Shanklin on 21 August 2004. This is the only signalbox on the Island Line, its semaphores controlling the local area, while the loop points at Sandown are self-acting. The view here from the footbridge suggesting a double-track railway and several points leading off left (to the depot) is not in keeping with the simplicity of the whole operation. *Author*

Left: The 1938 stock on the Isle of Wight appeared in dinosaur livery from 2000, and unit No 483006 is seen here at Brading on a train for Ryde Pier Head. This view shows where the second track once was, its removal being somewhat detrimental to the provision of regular services. *Author*

Below left: This interior view of Isle of Wight car No 127, formerly London Transport No 10291, shows that many original features have been retained, although strip lights have replaced tungsten and the floor is no longer slatted wood. Set No 483007, seen here in June 1992, can hardly hide its origins. *Author*

Right: North Acton station on the Central Line lies in a deep cutting; this view is looking towards central London on 28 June 2008. Both trains are of 1992 stock. Normally, trains for West Ruislip and Ealing Broadway leave from Platform 1, right, as is happening here, and eastbound trains use Platform 3 of the island platform. Platform 2 is mainly used for reversals, but it is part of a complete loop to and from both lines in both directions. On the far left is the single-track remnant of the Great Western's main line to Birmingham. *Author*

Below: At Leytonstone, the original line continues on the surface to Epping, while the branch to Newbury Park and Hainault dives underground on both sides. In this busy view of 10 June 2003, 1992 stock trains are seen heading for Hainault (left), arriving from Epping (centre) and arriving from Hainault (right). Leytonstone, it might be added, has two platforms in the westbound direction (only). *Author*

Above: Great Eastern Railway platforms were not in general short of capacity. This is Chigwell in March 2001 with a 1992 stock train heading towards Hainault. The height of the canopies does not exactly dwarf a modestly sized tube train, but one is left with the impression that greater things were expected. *Author*

Right: An eastbound train of 1992 stock arrives at Leytonstone on 10 June 2003. This is from a fleet of 85 eight-car trains, the Central Line being unusual in that it can cope with trains of that length. Thus each train is made up of two, four-car units, avoiding the conundrums provided on other lines in the past with a mix of three and four-car sets. They do however have to cope with reversing via the Hainault loop during normal operation. *Author*

Left: White City station is one of those rare situations where trains run on the right. This is due to the terminating loop used formerly by the Central London Railway, now long departed. A flyover further west restores normal left-hand running before reaching the next station of East Acton. Here, a 1992 stock eastbound train leaves on 11 July 2007. *Author*

Right: Few Underground lines have to cope with very tight platform curves as here on the eastbound line at Bank, as seen on 29 March 2008. At the very best, the platform-to-train gap slows people when boarding or alighting, which is not good news at a busy station where it is important to keep dwell times as short as practicable. *Author*

Below: The westbound Central Line track at Stratford is having another platform built on the south side as part of the preparations for the Olympic Games in 2012. The aim is to separate passenger flows as far as possible; one of the busiest times will be when all the spectators try to depart. This 1992 stock train is seen rising up to the station from the deep level tubes from Leyton as it arrives at Stratford's Platform 3 in July 2002. *Author*

Right: This is Leytonstone, with a Hainault loop service formed of 1992 stock leaving the station in June 2003. The Woodford–Hainault operation is now part of the whole and not treated separately. Passenger door-control buttons were fitted to this stock from new, and also all other modern stocks but there seems to be a marked reluctance by management to make use of them. *Author*

Left: The interiors of the 1992 stock trains feature windows extending high up the sides of the vehicles, but a relatively spartan interior. Notably, the manufacturers did not seem able to make armrests which withstood the vigour of the local inhabitants; this view from 1997 shows how long they have now been missing. Curiously, the same stock on the Waterloo & City Line retains them to this day. *Author*

Right: The 1992 look-alike versions for the Waterloo & City supplied to Network SouthEast later passed to London Underground together with the line itself. This workshop view was taken on the centenary of the line on 8 August 1998. *Author*

Right: On London Underground the gap formed between vehicles has now largely been filled by flexible barriers between the cars to prevent any access from platforms. This is a depot view of what the area contains on the Waterloo & City line 1992 stock vehicles, photographed on 8 August 1998. The windows in the car ends may be noted. *Author*

Below: The 1992 tube stock in four-car trains provides a frequent service between Bank, seen here in September 1998, and Waterloo. An enduring problem at the latter is the need to run via the depot tracks before making the next trip to Bank. *Author*

Above: Woodside Park sees northbound (left) and southbound (right) trains of 1995 stock crossing on 29 June 2008, from the viewpoint of the public footbridge here. The area behind the bushes was once a railway goods yard, but now serves for car parking. The use of redundant railway land for parking is only likely to be possible at stations which were once owned by the main line companies, the Great Northern Railway in this case. *Author*

Above left: A Northern Line train of 1995 stock arrives at Platform 3 of the Edgware terminus under the overall roof – except that it is not actually overall as Platform 1, at which the train on the far right is standing, is completely open to the elements. This is an indirect result of the abandonment of the Northern Line extensions in the post-war period, which would have required further expansion of the present station. This view is dated 7 May 2008. *Author*

Below: This is the driver's cab of No 51501, showing the steps which were provided to allow passengers to be detrained away from a platform if necessary. The Ruislip depot location allows reasonably easy access to the test track at South Ealing, for rolling stock commissioning purposes. *Author*

Left: Newly delivered 1995 stock is shown off at Ruislip depot on 15 March 1997, with DM No 51501 leading a train being put cautiously through its paces. With a total of 106 trains, the Northern Line has one of the biggest Underground fleets. *Author*

Right: The 1995 Northern Line stock has tip-up seats provided on each side of three fixed seats on both sides in the centre section of each car. The tip-up seats are noticeably less comfortable, in the way that standard class seats on National Rail are usually outshone by their first-class counterparts. The arrangement is all part of the scheme to provide for wheelchair occupants, without denying seats to passengers when the space is not so required. *Author*

Centre right: Recent years have seen much more openness applied to Underground vehicles, in a literal sense. Whether by work during half-life refurbishment or, as here, with new construction, windows in the car ends to provide through-views have generally been included. Like everybody else, the Underground has to move with the times, but what would those who fought (unsuccessfully) to keep their compartment stock on the Amersham service in the late 1950s have made of it? This is DM No 51501 of the Northern Line 1995 stock on 15 March 1997. *Author*

Below: Schöma four-wheel diesel-hydraulic No 3 *Claire* is one of a fleet of 14 such machines built in Germany in 1996 and used for the construction of the Jubilee Line extension, photographed here when new. They were constructed to tube loading gauge (although with full-height buffing gear), necessary to operate in a situation with very limited headroom. The others are named: 1 *Britta Lotta*, 2 *Nikki*, 4 *Pam*, 5 *Sophie*, 6 *Denise*, 7 *Annemarie*, 8 *Emma*, 9 *Debora*, 10 *Clementine*, 11 *Joan*, 12 *Melanie*, 13 *Michele*, and 14 *Carol*.
Harry Luff Collection/
Online Transport Archive

Above right: Freight operators have purchased large numbers of locomotives from General Motors/EMD, with delivery from 1985 onwards. Here, English, Welsh & Scottish Railways No 59202 *Vale of White Horse* is seen in Ruislip LUL sidings, with a battery locomotive alongside, on 18 May 2004. This is one of the few places where rail access between National Rail and London Underground remains, via a connection at West Ruislip. *Author*

Right: The Stanmore branch of what is now the Jubilee Line was opened by the Metropolitan Railway in 1932, shortly before the coming of the London Passenger Transport Board. Here, a train of 1996 stock in original six-car formation is on a southbound service at Queensbury in April 1998. It was bound for Charing Cross, the then southern terminal. *Author*

Left: Between Stratford and Canning Town, the Jubilee Line runs alongside what was in 2001, when this picture was taken, the North London line of National Rail. The fence is provided to separate the two and the latter is presently being converted to operation by the Docklands Light Railway. This picture was taken to the north of West Ham; the line to the left leads to Stratford Market depot. The 2006 stock train is heading for Stratford. *Author*

Below left: Cable bridges over the tracks are not made to more generous dimensions than is necessary. This example, with a 1996 stock train below it, was photographed near West Ham in October 2001. *Author*

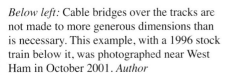

Above: This internal view of a 1996 stock Jubilee Line train was photographed at Stanmore on 9 April 2008, showing the bright and cheerful environment. In contrast with the 1995 Northern Line stock, the central part of the vehicle has only three fixed seats on each side, the remainder being perch seats for standing passengers, or for use by those in wheelchairs. *Author*

Centre left and left: The advantage of external train doors is that they do not require space for a pocket in which to slide within the body of the car, which takes up a small part of the car width and slightly weakens the bodyshell. It is also a dirt trap. They are seen here in March 2003 on the 1996 Jubilee Line stock in an open position and, below, closed. *Author*

Above: Platform doors as installed on the Jubilee Line extension underground platforms require the train of 1996 stock to be lined up very accurately with them. This is Waterloo on 28 May 2008 where, as can be seen, arrows have been painted on the platform to indicate to waiting passengers where not to stand. Unless, of course, they are more interested in getting the last empty seat. *Author*

Below: The amount of what one might rather unkindly call 'railway junk' in this picture of the country end of Finchley Road station is quite remarkable. Through it all, a 1996 stock Jubilee Line train threads its way to Stratford in March 2003. The Jubilee is underground continuously, from the far end of these platforms, until it emerges again at Canning Town — a rather different type of area. *Author*